PENGUIN BOOKS

MAKING PEOPLES

James Belich is Professor of History at the University of Auckland. A former Rhodes Scholar and James Cook Fellow, he has held visiting positions at the Universities of Cambridge and Georgetown. He wrote and presented the award-winning television series 'The New Zealand Wars'. His other books include *The New Zealand Wars*, *'I Shall Not Die'*, and *Paradise Reforged*, the sequel to this volume.

MAKING PEOPLES

A History of the New Zealanders

From Polynesian Settlement to the End of the Nineteenth Century

JAMES BELICH

James Belich

PENGUIN BOOKS

For
Margaret, Maria and Tessa

PENGUIN BOOKS
Penguin Books (NZ) Ltd, cnr Airborne and Rosedale Roads, Albany,
Auckland 1310, New Zealand
Penguin Books Ltd, 27 Wrights Lane, London W8 5TZ, England
Penguin Putnam Inc, 375 Hudson Street, New York, NY 10014, United States
Penguin Books Australia Ltd, 487 Maroondah Highway,
Ringwood, Australia 3134
Penguin Books Canada Ltd, 10 Alcorn Avenue, Toronto,
Ontario, Canada M4V 3B2
Penguin Books (South Africa) Pty Ltd, 5 Watkins Street,
Denver Ext 4, 2094, South Africa
Penguin Books India (P) Ltd, 11, Community Centre, Panchsheel Park,
New Delhi 110 017, India
Penguin Books Ltd, Registered Offices: Harmondsworth, Middlesex, England

First published in Allen Lane for The Penguin Press by Penguin Books (NZ) Ltd, 1996
This Penguin paperback edition published 2001

1 3 5 7 9 10 8 6 4 2

Editing and book design by Richard King
Maps by Jan Kelly
Typeset by Egan-Reid Ltd
Printed in Australia by McPherson's Printing Group, Maryborough

ISBN 0 14 100639 0

www.penguin.com

CONTENTS

PREFACE

New Zealand is a group of islands in the South Pacific. Historically, human settlement probably dates back no further than a thousand years, when the ancestors of the Maori people arrived from tropical Polynesia. Geographically, New Zealand has no near neighbours. The least distant country, Australia, is almost 2,000 kilometres away. At 270,000 square kilometres of land mass, New Zealand is small compared to Australia; in international relativities it is medium-sized. Many other Pacific Islands, and some European countries, would disappear in it as it would disappear in Australia. But, at less than four million people, mainly of British, Polynesian, and Irish descent, its population is undeniably small in international terms.

These characteristics of small population size, great isolation, and short history, combined with various cultural cringes, have sometimes given New Zealand history a mundane reputation – educative to the dutiful, exemplary to the patriotic, but a good place for those in search of inspiration or insight to slit their wrists. This work sets out to show that, on the contrary, New Zealand is an historian's paradise: a laboratory whose isolation, size, and recency is an advantage, in which grand themes of world history are often played out more rapidly, more separately, and therefore more discernibly, than elsewhere.

Inward-looking parochialism is too easily mistaken for cultural decolonisation, and engagement with global history is one aim of this book. But I have not always approached my work like some scientist dissecting a fascinating creature. As the twentieth century closes, and the twenty-first opens, New Zealand stands at a cusp in its development, and the future requires that we confront the past. If we do so, we may find that dynamic and exciting history, as well as tragic history, has happened here, and that it has happened to non-Maori as well as Maori. Although I have tried to write this book without fear or favour, I confess that my aspirations for it are cultural as well as scholarly, local as well as global. I am a New Zealander. It is my past on the slab.

Making Peoples covers Polynesian settlement and its development into the Maori tribes between the eleventh and eighteenth centuries; the great encounter between independent Maoridom and expanding Europe, 1642–1916; and the foundation of the Pakeha, the neo-European people of New Zealand, between the 1830s and the 1880s. It is intended as a stand-alone work, describing the making of a neo-Polynesia and a neo-Britain, and the traumatic interaction between them. That such things also happened elsewhere makes them more interesting, not less. The book is also intended as the first of two volumes that between them embrace, if not comprehensively include, the whole history of the New Zealanders. The second, *The Bridge of History*, covers the period from the 1880s to the present, but the division is not wholly chronological. History seldom compartmentalises neatly, and within each book, as well as between them, thematic sections reach forward and back as appropriate, while remaining very broadly in sequence.

This book is a general history, and it accepts a responsibility to generalise. Because I believe that historical debate in New Zealand needs some crash-starting, I also accept a responsibility to try to challenge and reinterpret. The reader needs to be aware of the risks this involves. General historians cannot hope to test their hypotheses to the same level as specialists. Improving historical understanding is often a matter of better educating our guesses. My guesses may be wrong, but their assumptions are set out. They are not random but the products of a type of historical analysis that draws on a range of methods, theories and tools. Bad workers blame their tools; worse workers believe they are allowed only one; and perhaps the worst workers of all do not have any. The methodological scaffolding used to construct this book has largely been removed from the final text. Sufficient remains for those interested to deduce its nature. It is perhaps enough to note here that the approach involves respecting, but not accepting, the various demi-gods of the historian's trade, and recognising that some traditional dichotomies are only notionally opposite. Theory and empiricism, 'scholarly' and 'popular', narrative and analysis, text and context, determinism and particularism, myth and history – all are sometimes best seen as rubber gloves for handling each other.

In New Zealand as elsewhere, recent times have seen a vast broadening in historical inquiry: old subgenres have been stretched; new ones have proliferated. This explosion in scope has led some to conclude that single-author general histories such as this one are no longer possible. They are very nearly correct. Writing this book without research assistance would indeed have been impossible if I had not had other kinds of help and support. Foremost of these is the work of my colleagues – amateur and professional, student and tenured – in New Zealand history and its associated disciplines. I have accepted, rejected, redeployed, converted and even subverted their work to produce this book, and I could not have done without them. Specific debts are acknowledged in the references.

The book and its successor volume took six years in the making. Three years of this was full time, free of teaching responsibilities, thanks to the James Cook Fellowship. This fellowship, administered by the Royal Society of New

Zealand, was vital to the project. I thank all concerned, notably Ross Moore and his staff at the Royal Society; Jim Traue, then Alexander Turnbull Librarian, who arranged accommodation during my tenure of the fellowship; and the staff of the Document Supply Services of the National Library, whose patience with me must have broken all records.

I owe my best thanks to the following for reading and commenting on the draft of the book: Angela Belich, Jim Belich, Janet Davidson, Colin Feslier, Gary Hawke, Richard Hill, Peter Munz and, especially, Melanie Nolan. Some of these individuals, notably Richard Hill, also provided constant help and support throughout. I am grateful for numerous less formal inputs from students and colleagues at Victoria University of Wellington, in particular to Kim Sterelny, Bob Tristram, Miles Fairburn, John Morrow and other members of the Old Bailey interdisciplinary seminar. The advice of these and other friends and colleagues was very gratefully received, but it was not always followed, and naturally I remain responsible for the views expressed in this book.

May I also gratefully acknowledge various kinds of help and support from Valerie Belich, Evana Belich, Colin Davis, David Fieldhouse, Dolores Janiewski, Paul Johnson, Sonia Mazey, Peter Moon, Michael and Tric Kyrke-Smith, Jock Phillips, Rei Rakatau, Huw Richards, Jane Tucker and the late Keith Sinclair. Brian Sweeney and Jane Vesty have played a special role in the initiation and completion of this project.

While the father remains unknown, the chief midwives during this book's long and tortuous gestation have undoubtedly been my publisher, Geoff Walker, and my wife, Margaret Scott Belich. Both have shown patience, kindness and acumen above and beyond the call of duty. I must also thank Geoff's colleagues at Penguin Books for sharing his faith in me; Richard King for his enlightened editing and book design; and Nik Andrew for his cover design. My debt to Margaret and our other offspring is further acknowledged in the dedication.

LIST OF MAPS IN PAPERBACK EDITION

Making Maori

CHAPTER ONE

The Prehistory of New Zealand

Hawaiki

Four centuries after the death of Jesus Christ, two migrant ships pushed through dangerous seas. Strong men and women tended oars and sails; children crouched amidst livestock and household goods. Each crew valued kin above all, walked with live gods – Tu and Thor, Woden and Tane – and lived and died for weregild and utu. Each crew headed for a place of which little was known and a great deal hoped. Too much can be made of their similarities, but they did have one thing in common: both were forebears of the New Zealanders.

The ultimate origins of both crews are shrouded in myth and mystery, but we know that the immediate origin of one ship was the north coast of central Europe, probably Germany or Denmark, and that its destination was the teetering Roman province of Britannia. This ship was crewed by people who later became known as 'English'. According to their canoe legends, they were invited into South Britain, about AD 450, by the Romano-Celtic ruler Vortigern, to save it from the Picts and Scots, whose raids had intensified with the withdrawal of the Roman legions in 410. They came initially in three longships. Their leaders, Hengist and Horsa, who were Jutes, soon turned against the treacherous Vortigern, called in their Germanic kin, the Angles and Saxons, and quickly displaced the natives of South Britain. Later Anglo-Saxon kings traced their whakapapa, or genealogy, back through Hengist and other canoe captains to Caesar, Noah and Woden. As 'Anglo-Saxonism', the myth came to include the belief that the invaders, though fierce and rude, were indelibly stamped with intelligence, courage, patriotism and the love of law and liberty.

Mean-minded scholars now suggest that Hengist and Horsa were horse-gods. Two canoes, the Franks and Frisians, were summarily dropped from this 'Great Fleet' because of unseemly French and Dutch connections. The first Anglo-Saxon settlers, it seems, were Roman legionaries, who may have mounted a kind of military coup when the decline of the Roman Empire stopped their pay. They may have served in Britain since the fourth century –

the fifth-century date, 410, may arise from a confusion between Britain and Bruttium, southern Italy, in the single Roman document on which it is based. The second, larger wave of Anglo-Saxon immigrants came in the 430s, pushed by floods rather than pulled by visions of empire, and some scholars now describe them as refugees or 'boat people' rather than invaders.[1] If so, they set a most unfortunate precedent for boat people.

The Anglo-Saxons 'colonised' Britannia in two senses. First, they formed a new people from an old through a process of migration and settlement. Until the twentieth century, this was the main meaning of 'colonisation', a method of reproducing peoples, and it is a key meaning used in this book. Second, the Anglo-Saxons subordinated the natives, a process for which this book prefers the label 'imperialism' or 'empire'.

The native Britons were not completely displaced – some Celtic place-names and kings' names survived. In the fifth and sixth centuries, they put up a good fight, despite their superior civilisation. But in South Britain they were quite quickly killed, subjugated or pushed out – to Brittany in France, and to maroon-lands or King Countries in North and West Britain: Strathclyde, Wales and South Wales, or Cornwall. 'Welsh' was apparently an Anglo-Saxon term for serf or slave,[2] but in the western mountains the name turned, like 'Slav' and 'Black', to one of pride. Political conquest was not achieved until the ninth century in Cornwall, the tenth century in Strathclyde, and the thirteenth or even the sixteenth century in Wales. Cornish explorers in New Zealand were still using words of their native tongue in the eighteenth century, and in Wales cultural conquest still has some way to go.[3]

Poor Britain was also assailed in the north by another set of invaders, the Scots of Ireland, or Hibernia. Raiding and migrating from the first century, they established themselves in the western islands of Caledonia, or North Britain, fought and mixed with the native Picts, and eventually, in the ninth century, succeeded in imposing their name on the country. Indeed, the Scots colonists in Caledonia entirely took over the name of their source people, who became known as Irish. So the Britons were partly overlaid by colonists from English Germany and Scottish Ireland. The tribes of Anglo-Saxon England, if the goods in an East Anglian king's grave at Sutton Hoo are anything to go by, developed a rich material culture. They were taught to read, write and worship Christ by French and Irish missionaries. From the late eighth century, their wealth became the target of Norwegian, Danish and French raiders and colonisers. All were eventually absorbed, leaving legacies of genes, names and culture traits, but not before England had spent a couple of centuries, from the 'Norman Conquest' of 1066, as a French colony.

Before, after and even during these 'Dark Ages' of the fifth to fourteenth centuries, the peoples of Britain interacted with 'Western civilisation': a remarkable floating bank of beliefs and techniques that financed many great enterprises but was occasionally threatened by bankruptcy and often charged heavy fees. It originated in Africa and Asia, Egypt and Sumer, and was influenced by its links with India and China. It was adapted and transmitted to Europe by Greek and Phoenician middlemen, and preserved after the fall of Rome more by Islamic and Byzantine Empires than European monasteries. From the fifteenth century, Western Europeans increasingly took guardianship of it, developed it greatly, and came to see it and themselves as synonymous. In fact, many peoples have always made withdrawals and deposits. But Western Europe's donations were indeed enormous, capable of generating a rate of change like an avalanche.

Western civilisation bequeathed various approaches to the past. Among the most brilliant was that of the Arab historian Ibn Khaldun, but others can be associated with three Asian and European Greeks: Thucydides, Herodotus and the group, man or woman known as Homer. One could say that Homer shaped and transmitted traditions that had functions more important than mere accuracy; that Thucydides was seen as the father of empirical history in which accuracy was all important; and that Herodotus was somewhere between the two. But fact invaded Homer, and myth invaded Thucydides. In the 1870s, archaeologists found Homer's Troy, hitherto thought by some to be mythical, in Asia Minor. In the 1900s, one historian argued quite convincingly that Thucydides' work was structured by myth-drama, also derived from Asia Minor.[4] Herodotus took myth and history seriously, and emphasised inquiry, questioning, which was the original meaning of the term 'historia'. This book stumbles more in his direction than that of Homer or Thucydides. But it must be admitted that Herodotus was sometimes prone to invention. He helped invent Europe, for example, by contrasting it to invading Persian hordes from Asia.

The English found history useful for similar purposes. Their Venerable Sinclair was a monk named Bede, who in the eighth century described the rival Anglo-Saxon kingdoms collectively as 'the English'.[5] The concept was given some substance in the next century by Alfred of Wessex, a bad cook but a clever king. Like Herodotus, Alfred forged a new collective identity from the contrast with enemies, in his case Danes. The name 'English' actually derived from his Anglish rivals in Mercia. He let them have the name while he took the country. A similar sleight was later employed in subordinating the Welsh and Scots under the rubric 'Great Britain'. The process extended from names to kings. Taking Welsh and Scots monarchs when England's own royalty was infertile or unsatisfactory proved to be a good method of subordinating those countries. Even the legendary Welsh resistance leader Arthur was co-opted in retrospect. History was useful in decolonisation as well as colonisation. Forget the long line of Angevin French monarchs who succeeded the Normans, forget the French cultural dominance of Normandy in 1066 and the largely French composition of William's army. Emphasise the Viking influence on Normandy and – hey presto! – the Conquest was not French at all but a fraternal Teutonic tiff.

These were no mere semantic games but brilliant forms of cultural co-option, a key characteristic of English imperialism in New Zealand as in Old Britain. During the thirteenth century, the English swamped their French masters by outbreeding them, the technique now known in Quebec as the revenge of the cradle. From the fourteenth to the seventeenth centuries, the English economy generally expanded; the country developed its collective identity and some progress was made in the political subordination of Scotland and Ireland.

New Zealand has long seen British history as its own prehistory. Glowing accounts in school texts were more Anglocentric than in England itself, where the great historical propagandist T. B. Macaulay gave history a low starting point to maximise its rise.[6] Englishness is no longer so fashionable, and it is true that, until the fifteenth century, England was seldom hugely important to anyone except itself. When William the Conqueror's domains were divided among his heirs, the eldest got Normandy and the next got England as second prize. But, from the fifteenth century, England grew like Topsy. Through such individuals as Shakespeare and Newton, through such creeds as Protestantism and mercantile capitalism, and through such industries as commercial farming and textile milling, it developed a material and non-material culture that would have been impressive at any time, anywhere. New Zealanders share ownership of this legacy. It is our history too, and we should respect and question it, as long as we stop pretending it is the only one.

All was not onward and upward in Mother England – or Father Polynesia for that matter. There were some nasty plagues and wars. Empire, even within the British Isles, still lay in the future. Indeed, in the mid-seventeenth century the Irish and Scots, and even the Welsh and Cornish, repeatedly invaded England, taking advantage of the English Civil War, or 'Great Rebellion' or 'Revolution'. These armies roamed the Green and Pleasant Land, Catholic Irish privateers swept Albion's seas, and the King of England eventually lost his head completely. French, Dutch and Spanish fed arms to the conflict, and for a while England seemed the sick man of Europe. Here, in temporary chaos, we leave Old Britain, about 1642, when Tasman sailed the ocean blue.

The second migrant ship sailed the Pacific Ocean. Its crew were 'Polynesian', the people of many islands. When Europeans first discovered just how many islands, they were stunned. How could stone-age folk have spread themselves from Hawai'i in the north, on the Tropic of Cancer, to Stewart Island in the south, just short of the subantarctic; from Tonga in the west to Easter Island in the east, traversing the great Pacific like a garden pond many centuries before Europeans made it across the petty Atlantic? Some scholars felt forced to posit a giant sunken Pacific continent, of which the Polynesian Islands were remnants left high and dry, but most confronted the facts: here were the greatest voyagers the world had ever seen. They were called 'the Vikings of the sunrise', and it is true that both Vikings and Polynesians appear to have discovered then forgotten America. But the Polynesians voyaged further and earlier than the Vikings, and it is fairer to call the latter the Polynesians of the sunset. Some time ago – current scholarship suggests between AD 250 and 1150, if that's any help – a group of Polynesians became the first people to settle New Zealand. With the peoples of Britain, they are the main ancestors of the New Zealanders, and New Zealand is now their main country – more live here than in any other place. Their history, like that of Britain, is part of New Zealand prehistory. Who were they? Where did they come from?

Guesses about the origin of Polynesian genes and culture have ranged far and wide. Early European observers, in the eighteenth century, tended to favour South-east Asia. The nineteenth century argued variously that Polynesians were Asian or American Indians, the Lost Tribe of Israel or proto-European Aryans. The twentieth century has suggested Bolivian, British Columbian, Spanish, Portuguese or Basque influence.[7] On 24 May 1847, a Maori elder, Tumu Wakaire, added to the confusion by asserting that his people had come direct from Britain. Had they 'not left the other side of the sea they would all have been pakehas'.[8] Most modern scholarship comes full circle and accepts the eighteenth-century view. Proto-Polynesian genes and language came from somewhere between Taiwan and New Guinea. It rejects the belief that Polynesians conquered the Melanesians, the island peoples of the western Pacific, who were long believed to be 'inferior', or less like Europeans. Debate continues, however, on the point of origin of Polynesian culture and the degree to which it should be distinguished from Melanesian. Did Polynesian cultural characteristics migrate more or less fully formed, somehow leapfrogging Melanesia, or did they develop on the spot in Polynesia?

Both sides of this migrationist/anti-migrationist debate, of course, are partly right. It seems Melanesians and Polynesians both stem from a varying mix of 'Mongoloid' and 'Australoid' genes, with another mix of Austronesian and non-Austronesian languages cutting across this. The mixing may have taken place in and around New Guinea about five thousand years ago. Melanesians were genetically and culturally diverse Pacific Islanders more influenced by nearby Asia; Polynesians were homogenous Pacific Islanders more influenced by the wide and isolating ocean. Melanesian diversity and interaction with Asia, together with Polynesian isolation, rapid adaptation and descent from a small original group subsequently accentuated the differences. Research on Lapita pottery, long considered the visiting card of proto-Polynesians, supports this view. This research 'allows us to say with some confidence that the basic human adaptation to the Pacific island world occurred in the Bismarck Archipelago', off the coast of New Guinea.[9] 'Melanesian' and 'Polynesian' can still be used to mean the peoples of the two great island zones, as long as they do not indicate any rigid cultural typology, still less hierarchy. The Maori of New Zealand share ancestors with both.

In the Bismarck Archipelago, then, ocean voyaging was developed, and through this, perhaps, Lapita pottery and a range of domesticated plants and animals were acquired from South-east Asia – not brought by technologically superior invaders. People with this culture spread through the Pacific Islands, arriving in Tonga and Samoa from Fiji perhaps about 1000 BC. Here, sufficient adaptations, discards and innovations occurred to make the culture recognisably 'West Polynesian'. Migration then renewed, reaching the Society Islands (which include Tahiti) and the Marquesas Islands either around 200 BC or AD 300 – the authorities differ.[10] 'East Polynesian' culture developed in these island groups, and it was from them, directly or indirectly, that the boldest voyagers of all made their way to Hawai'i, Easter Island and New Zealand. It is even possible that some went to South America, and returned, for the South American sweet potato, or kumara, was available in time for it to be taken to New Zealand.

Kumara joined an impressive inventory of cultivated plants, including breadfruit, hue gourd, coconuts, aute (paper mulberry), the tropical cabbage tree, bananas, plantain, pandanus, sugar cane, turmeric and arrowroot, as well as yams and taro.[11] Because most plants were tended individually, their cultivation is described as horticulture, or gardening, rather than as agriculture. Pigs, chickens and dogs were domesticated and eaten, and rats were sometimes consumed. Fishing was also important, and the Polynesians hunted when they could. Little is known for certain of their early culture and social system, but we can guess that the latter was organised around kinship, or at least the language of kinship. Institutions were strong but fluid, and three leading ideas – mana, utu and tapu – were probably central even a thousand years ago, although their manifestations changed over time. Mana was a kind of spiritual capital, often translated as prestige or authority, inherited, acquired and lost by both individuals and groups. Utu was not simply revenge, but reciprocity, obliging one to return a gift as well as a blow. It was particularly important in relations between groups: the exchange of gifts and hospitality were positive utu; vengeance and warfare were negative utu. Tapu, a system of sanctity, social constraint and sacred laws, was complemented by its opposite – noa, which can be translated as normal, ordinary or unrestricted.

For Polynesians, as for many peoples, social, natural and supernatural dimensions were not rigidly divided. Their tohunga, or experts, were not just priests, but mediators between the three dimensions in particular areas of expertise. Magic, prayer and technical skill packaged each other. Ocean voyaging and colonisation over staggering distances are often seen as the Polynesians' most impressive technological achievement: their great double-hulled canoes could carry two hundred people a short distance, and half that number, with their supplies, over a long distance. Migration was not necessarily the obvious solution to overpopulation on small islands. Warfare, abortion, infanticide, abstinence, contraception, coitus interruptus and even bouts of compulsory homosexuality were all available alternatives.[12] Very long-range journeys seem to have ceased by the sixteenth century. The rise and fall of long-range voyaging and colonisation remains a major mystery of Polynesian history.

We may never pin the Maori Hawaiki, or place of origin, down to a single island. Rarotonga, in the Cook Islands, has long been a favoured candidate, but there were political motives for this, and the evidence is not entirely convincing. Rapa and Mangareva Islands, south of the Austral and Tuamotu Archipelagoes, are dark-horse possibilities, as is Pitcairn. Prehistorian Janet Davidson writes that Pitcairn contains artefacts 'which reveal close similarities to New Zealand examples – almost to the point of suggesting direct contact between the two'.[13] These are strong words from so careful a scholar. It is possible that the inhabitants of Pitcairn all packed up and went to New Zealand, leaving no-one to turn out the light. But experts now prefer to emphasise groups of interacting islands as the sources of migration. On this basis, the Society Islands were probably an (but perhaps not *the*) immediate Maori Hawaiki; an intermediate Hawaiki was probably Tonga/Samoa; and the ultimate Hawaiki in any meaningful sense looks likely to have been the Bismarcks. As fate and Tumu Wakaire would have it, the largest island of the Bismarck Archipelago is New Britain. In this purely nominal sense, the Maori may have come from Britain too.

Lenses on Prehistory

When, how, in what numbers and at what particular place did the Polynesians settle New Zealand? How, ultimately, did they transform themselves into the dynamic kaleidoscope of Maori tribes encountered by Europeans from 1769? It is customary for general histories to avoid these questions or pass over them lightly – for some good reasons. Most general historians, including this one, have not had the skills to fully engage with Maori history. But this leaves us with a choice between evils: do we plunge in, underequipped as we are, or do we pretend that Maori history before contact is somehow a disconnected preface to real history, a ghostly prologue? This book prefers to risk the former evil. But we have first to consider the lenses through which we look at pre-contact history, and their angles of refraction.

Historians often prefer evidence that has been snap-frozen (by being recorded) as close as possible to the time of the things it recounts. Hitherto, most such evidence happens to have been written on paper, and the preference for it is sometimes assumed to be inherently Eurocentric. But it is the freezing, not the writing, that counts. Snap-frozen evidence from a known source is affected by only one set of refractors: the biases of a particular person, time and place. It does not matter whether it has been recorded on paper, clay tablets or audio tape, as long as one can put a specific name, date and context to it. Because the Polynesians (and the early Anglo-Saxons) were paperless, tabletless and tapeless, snap-frozen evidence is not available for them. Three main types of evidence are available: post-contact accounts by outside observers, loosely known as ethnography; tradition; and archaeology. Each comes to us through several sets of refractors.

Until the nineteenth century, the outside ethnographer who knew most about the Maori was the Tahitian priest Tupaia, who accompanied James Cook's expedition to New Zealand in 1769. Maori and Tahitian languages were mutually comprehensible, and only Tupaia could conduct conversations of any substance with Maori. From the Maori viewpoint, Tupaia, not Cook or the gentleman-scientist Joseph Banks, was the most important visitor, and they knew the *Endeavour* as 'Tupia's Ship'.[14] Most of the information in the Cook and Banks journals that goes beyond material, easily observable things comes via Tupaia. Regrettably, neither Tupaia's English nor Banks's and Cook's Tahitian were yet very good, and one sometimes wonders about Cook's English as well. Strained through all this, the Maori account of Creation became a divine act of 'Copolation'.[15] This referred to the original warm embrace of Ranginui and Papa-tu-a-nuku, Sky Father and Earth Mother, and was accurate as far as it went. But it did not go very far. Tupaia was a good linguist and would soon have mastered English. Tragically, he died on the return voyage, and his unique knowledge of pre-contact Maoridom went with him.

Tupaia had his biases. He was inclined to see Maori as failed Tahitians, and was more disgusted by their practice of cannibalism than was Cook. Tahitians had abandoned cannibalism centuries before, and converts are often the worst fanatics. European visitors, who provided the great bulk of ethnographic evidence, also had their biases, which is often said to make their record unreliable. Ethnocentrism (the tendency to measure others using yourself as the yardstick), the perceived precedent of previous encounters, and a growing body of racial theories and myths of expansion did lead European observers to stereotype Maori and other 'savage' peoples. The stereotyping distorted 'Us' as well as 'Them', through racial 'archetyping' and 'antityping'. An archetype positively idealised Us, teaching you what to be; an antitype negatively idealised Them, teaching you what not to be. The worst of non-European societies was compared to the best of European. Observers compared temporary Maori shelters to the houses of London merchants rather than to the tenements of Hogarth's Gin Lane. Such stereotyping varied quite predictably, more according to the needs of the observers than the actual character of the observed. Settlers had to live in new worlds, felt more threatened by Them, and tended to archetype and antitype more intensively to shore up their own self-image and collective identity. Early explorers, visiting briefly, felt less threatened. In the nineteenth century, Europeans in general felt increasingly threatened by the new, and stereotypes tended to harden accordingly over time. While most stereotypes played up or invented Maori vices, others played up or invented virtues.

The relevant European lenses on 'savages' in general, and Maori in particular, can usefully be simplified into seven, a septifocal set of distorting spectacles through which new worlds were perceived. The seven colours of this race-bow were clear, grey, white, black, red, brown and green.

The clear lens was not really a stereotype at all, but a relatively unbiased view of Maori. It was never perfectly clear but always smudged by the deeper kinds of ethnocentric measurement, from which it is very hard to detach oneself. But some lenses were clearly clearer than others. In 1772, after the *Endeavour* had returned, one of its scientists, Daniel Solander, breakfasted with racial theorist Lord Monboddo. Monboddo tried to impose his harsh lens, through which savages appeared as brutish missing links, on Solander's clearer lens. 'Have they tails, Dr Solander?' 'No, my Lord, they have no tails.'[16] There was always a struggle between the intensity of the need to maintain preconceptions and the stubborn obviousness of fact. This is important because it means that European evidence remains usable. If sifted with care, the effects of the clear lens can be sorted from those of the coloured.

The grey lens saw Maori as a shadowy, declining or dying race. Mild eighteenth-century versions attributed decline to corruption by European vice and disease, regretted it and hoped it was reversible. Nineteenth-century versions, including the ideas of fatal impact and Social Darwinism, were much harsher: 'inferior' Maori were dying out, and a good thing too. The white lens portrayed Maori as quite European-like, with great potential for conversion, civilisation and Europeanisation – the best of savages, so good that they were potentially almost white. The black lens, harshest of the seven, saw them as unsalvageably savage and bestial. Although never dominant, it was more common in some phases of New Zealand ethnography than is generally acknowledged, as were its relatives, the red and brown stereotypes.

Red Savages were inherently ferocious, chronically warlike among themselves, ruthless in their dealings with nature, and formidable if not admirable. Brown Savages were natural subordinates: potentially faithful, sometimes comic, but almost as unimprovable as the red and the black. The Green Savage, nature's gentry, at one with their environment, was a comparatively generous stereotype but was invented to highlight, by contrast, perceived weaknesses in European society. A composite lens, it began with the barbaric but freedom-loving Germans and Caledonians of the Roman historian Tacitus; developed with the

Noble Savages of Dryden, Diderot, Rousseau and Commerson; became the Romantic Maori of one long strand of New Zealand scholarship; and continues in the present as the Environmentalist Maori, whose very rats were vegetarians. Like the white, the green stereotype was used by Europeans to reshape and co-opt Maori culture and history for their own purposes, as the English did with the Celtic Britons.

These stereotypes permeate the European evidence. Sometimes they bequeathed an impenetrable tangle of myth and fact, but they were quite predictable and consistent, and sometimes their effects can be subtracted out. European ethnography is not unreliable; it is reliably biased and, appropriately sifted, it is quite good evidence of Maori society in the eighteenth and nineteenth centuries. But can this be read back into pre-contact history? I think that to some extent it can, and that assumptions that non-European peoples were instantly transformed by Europe are deceptive. They may overestimate European impact, and underestimate native resilience. Specific changes did occur, of course; some very major. But it is hard to believe that all Maori social and cultural institutions were immediately revolutionised by European contact to the point where ethnographic accounts of them are useless.

Maori social practices in the early nineteenth century may well indicate the practices of the previous century or so. The problem is not that Maori changed instantly on European contact, but that they changed before it. A reliable bias of European ethnography was that peoples like the Maori did not change, except through European agency, and that this was a defining difference between Us and Them. Their present was like Our distant past, because They had not progressed. This myth of the Frozen Maori persists in some European and Maori minds, downplaying self-directed change in Maori society both before and after contact, fossilising 'traditional Maori' at circa 1769. It also meant that early ethnography was interested in the Maori present but not very interested in the Maori past.

Maori, on the other hand, were very interested in their past and preserved it carefully in oral tradition. They also preserved myth, religion, custom, geography, lore and law, explanations of nature, guidance about the future, and many other types of knowledge in the same medium. These strands are not easily separated, and they were not intended to be. They were integrated so that each assisted the remembering of the other; a tapestry that could be wholly unravelled or revealed by continuous tugging on one of its threads. Myth and history, in particular, packaged each other, mutually facilitating remembering. Integration was coupled with selection. Emphases changed over time and context to the point where some things virtually disappeared. The experts who preserved and developed tradition were capable of staggering feats of memory, but memory is less infinite than paper. Because knowledge grew constantly, selection was required, and it was made on the basis of utility, broadly defined. Knowledge of failed acclimatisations of plants and animals, of extinct creatures and of redundant techniques tended to be discarded.

The various strands of tradition adapted at different speeds. Ritual, waiata (songs and poems) and karakia (prayers and incantations) changed rarely and slowly. They were the hard parts of tradition, like bones in a body; embedded in, yet helping to structure and preserve, the rest. They were helped in turn by origin legends, whakapapa (genealogy) and by the naming journeys of founding ancestors – oral maps recorded in place-names. Whakapapa and naming journeys were sequences across time and space that had hard symbols in their endpoints: living people and places. They could be very accurate about recent centuries and nearby regions. But their functions sometimes required them to be flexible. Obviously, they had to expand to accommodate new people and places. There was naturally a preference for naming journeys that trumped those of competitors, for genealogies that bonded a group together, usefully linked it to some neighbouring groups and distinguished it from others, and for both genealogies and naming journeys that legitimated claims to status and resources. This is not so different from nationalist European history, but the limits of memory were an added incentive to adapt and select. Why spend precious memory for the benefit of rivals? For the far past and distant places, whakapapa, naming journeys and settlement traditions had to converge with myth and legend simply to survive.

This distinction between hard, recent, more accurate, though still partisan traditions, and ancient, soft and less accurate ones is not a Eurocentric imposition, but something long accepted by a range of Maori scholars. In 1849, the Northland tohunga Aperahama Taonui gave a long whakapapa but noted that the 'real men' started with Rahiri, the founding ancestor of the Nga Puhi tribe. He described earlier names as 'tapu removers'.[17] A later Nga Puhi historian, Wiremu Wi Hongi, has confirmed that whakapapa before Rahiri are variable and suspect.[18] At a meeting late in the nineteenth century, the Ngai Tahu scholar Teone Taare Tikao teased his Nga Puhi hosts about their recent origins.

> I told the Nga-Puhi they did not bring their name from Hawaiki but clapped it on in New Zealand, tacking it on to various ancestors picked at random . . . I jokingly told them they were dunces at reciting whakapapa, and I added, 'There is no doubt that you people are descended from boulders.'

Ngai Tahu's firm whakapapa were not much longer, though Tikao claimed to have owned but mislaid a genealogy of 200 generations.[19] Maori anthropologist Te Rangi Hiroa (Peter Buck) wrote in 1936 that 'genealogies are important in showing common ancestors and a common descent but beyond a certain distance back, they cannot be relied upon to give accurate historical dating'.[20]

The famous authority Apirana Ngata affirmed the reliability of recent whakapapa; 'in the case of more remote ancestors, however, it was quite correct to use what Ngata called a tatai hikohiko, or a random selection of ancestors'.[21] Remote whakapapa were selective, flexible and variable, but not random or purposeless. They were used to link phases of tradition across an intervening generation gap; to give continuity and completion to tribal history, claim appropriate bonds and distinctions, and assert prior right.

Between 1840 and 1930, the origin legends of many Maori tribes were collected by European scribes such as S. Percy Smith. Smith and others sifted out their perception of historical gold from mythical dross, and (in both senses) forged these disparate histories into an attractive and coherent account of Maori settlement: the heroic explorer Kupe discovered New Zealand about 925; Toi settled it about 1150; and a Great Fleet of seven canoes arrived via Rarotonga about 1350, assimilated or subordinated the descendants of Toi and gave birth to the modern Maori tribes.[22] The canoes make a well-known list: *Te Arawa, Tainui, Mataatua, Tokomaru, Kurahaupo, Takitimu* and *Aotea*.

'Smithing' seems the appropriate name for this process of constructing Maori history. One Smithian, John White, paid Maori £5 per exercise book full of legends in the late nineteenth century. This expanded, repeated and distorted tradition, but New Zealand history has seldom been so highly valued.[23] Another important Smithian, the indefatigable Elsdon Best, emitted a stream of monographs on 'The Maori As He Was'. His Maori were biased towards inland economics and forest lore, partly because Best's favourite subjects were the untypical people of the Urewera Mountains, and partly because a propensity to seasickness in later life made him avoid sea voyages.[24] He pretended respect for tradition to the elders he interviewed, and disrespect for it to his European readers – 'with serious mien' the ethnographer 'listens to puerile tales and wild myths'.[25] He outsmarted himself on both counts, and his work is both suspect and vital. Raymond Firth relied heavily on Best's research, married to the theories of Bronislaw Malinowski, to produce his classic, *The Primitive Economics of the New Zealand Maori*.[26] We must 'anthropologise colonial interlocutors',[27] but we cannot afford to do without them. Nor were Maori, as is often assumed, naive victims of the Smithing process. Their participation was selective and sometimes designed to further their own purposes. But it does add another layer of refraction to tradition. So, too, do other contexts in which traditions were recorded: the exceptional violence of the 1820s, in which White's informants were educated; the late nineteenth-century proceedings of the Native Land Court; and the late twentieth-century proceedings of the Waitangi Tribunal.

In 1976, D. R. Simmons attacked the Smithed version of Maori settlement, which he called the Great New Zealand Myth. Simmons sought to strip Smith's added layers back to the good wood of genuine tribal tradition.[28] He effectively debunked the notion that Maori tradition postulated a Great Fleet, confirming the suspicions of Ngata, who had written in 1933: 'I think a lot of mischief has been done by Percy Smith in giving the impression of a great fleet, that bore down on New Zealand in the fourteenth century. I do not think that the traditions establish more than that Te Arawa and Tainui arrived together at Whangaparoa.'[29] Simmons rightly noted that origin legends were never intended to help historians grope for facts, but he sometimes took them very literally anyway – for example, by accepting Kupe and Toi as historical figures, combining two possible versions of the former into one, splitting the latter into two, and adjusting the dates of both. In 1985, Margaret Orbell criticised Simmons for this, arguing, like the German scholar Schirren in 1856, that the origin legends were religious myths that could be used to study Maori ideology but not history.[30] Orbell argued that Kupe and many other legendary figures were semi-divine archetypes, some shared with tropical Polynesian islands, and suggested that Hawaiki was a mythical land. Simmons and Orbell made important contributions but seem also to fall into two equal but opposite traps: an excessive tendency to see myth as history, and an excessive tendency to see myth as mystery. Kupe probably did become a legendary archetype, the Original Explorer, finding several island groups over hundreds of years. Hawaiki was shrouded in myth. But Maori must have come from somewhere.

Myths, broadly defined, might be seen as a culture's legitimating explanations for natural, supernatural and social phenomena, for the relationship between them and for the culture's place in the world. They can have kernels of truth, sometimes so large that they are actual historical forces as well as myths. The mythical dimension works in tandem with an actual historical dynamic, which pushes history along, or an actual historical imperative, which holds history in place. But the cultural function of myth, which goes beyond mere accuracy, can put pressure on its truth, leading it to exaggerate or distort its partner dynamics and imperatives. Literacy, print, secularisation and specialisation have freed Western civilisation from the traditional need to interlock all knowledge to preserve it. For this and other, less forgivable reasons it has tended to see its own myth as history, and other peoples' history as myth. The two are not easily separated in any society; their relationship is close but indirect. Myths should not be read as either straight history or arcane mystery. But myth and history help determine each other, and they should conform to changes in each other. Change in myth can be evidence of change in history. This is generally best investigated by looking less at specifics and more at patterns and purposes, divisions and convergences. An attempt at such an analysis of Maori myth-history is made in Chapter Two, and of Pakeha myth-history in Part Three.

Tradition may seem a minefield better avoided by the inexpert; regrettably this is also true of the alternative – archaeology and its associated disciplines, whose practitioners are known as prehistorians. It is often said that archaeological remains cannot lie, but they cannot speak either, and they are inevitably refracted, not reflected, by those who speak for them. Two pitfalls for prehistorians and historians alike are romanticism (the fallacy that the most interesting explanation is automatically the most likely) and minimalism (the fallacy that the least interesting explanation is automatically the most likely, or that no explanation at all is required). Prehistorians' accounts of the Maori settlement of New Zealand seem to me to have bounced between these pitfalls, in three loose schools of thought.

The first school, which held sway until the 1950s, was influenced by romanticism and associated with the Smithian interpretation of Maori tradition. A central component in its thinking, the 'Great Fleet' thesis, has been outlined above. This implied at least two settlements between 1150 and 1350 – the second large in scale – and the fairly rapid coverage of the country thereafter. It was often linked to the belief in a pre-Maori New Zealand people, called the Moriori or Maruiwi, sometimes said to be Melanesian, shorter, darker and inferior to the Maori newcomers, who exterminated or assimilated them.[31] Pan-Pacific prototypes of this legend emerged in the late eighteenth century and were quickly applied to New Zealand.[32]

In addition to Smithed Maori tradition, the Moriori myth received support from nineteenth-century ethnography and archaeology. Ethnography brought the idea of a rigid Polynesian-Melanesian distinction and hierarchy to New Zealand, and was capable of seeing physiological evidence of an inferior race in two short, dark Maori brothers. Early archaeology was convinced that artefacts found in association with the bones of moa, the extinct giant birds of New Zealand, indicated a distinct race. The Moriori myth was rejected as early as 1859 by the able historian and ethnographer Arthur Thomson, and, as anthropologist H. D. Skinner pointed out in 1923, there has never been very solid evidence for it.[33] But the Smithian Great Fleet/Moriori view still persists in some quarters. It survived partly because it was confused with a real (probably Maori-derived) culture called Moriori that developed in the Chatham Islands, east of the mainland, and with a 'moa-hunter period' of Maori culture postulated by archaeologist Roger Duff in 1950,[34] but mainly because it served cultural functions discussed elsewhere.

From the 1950s, in scholarly circles at least, romanticism was progressively replaced by a second, more minimalist school of thought, beginning with Andrew Sharp's 1956 sinking of the Great Fleet in favour of settlement by the accidental drift of a fishing canoe, or by desperate flight into the unknown from war or famine.[35]

The drift-voyage idea was never very reasonable – fishing canoes are not normally packed with domestic plants and animals – and it hardly required an expensive computer simulation in 1972 to disprove it. 'Desperate flight' is more credible, and the notion of a tiny and solitary initial settlement seems to underlie much of the professional archaeological work of the 1960s and 1970s. Such a settlement was theoretically possible – as few as six first settlers had a 48 per cent chance of establishing a viable population.[36] But at the slow rates of growth usually attributed to neolithic peoples, it would have taken them a long time to get to the Maori population of 1769, which was usually guessed to be between 125,000 and 175,000, or even more. Radiocarbon dating, available from the 1950s, placed most early New Zealand archaeological sites in the thirteenth century, with some in the twelfth and tenth centuries. But the sites were quite widespread, and archaeologists were inclined to allow two or three centuries for the first tiny settlement to diffuse to them. About AD 750 or 800 increasingly became the orthodox guess for the date of first settlement, and some felt that Northland was the place.[37] There, in a sort of cultural reservoir, Polynesians adapted to New Zealand conditions for some time before bursting out and settling the rest of the country. This interesting thesis is the point where the minimalist label is least fair.

The crowning achievement of the minimalist school, and to some extent going beyond it, was Janet Davidson's 1984 *Prehistory of New Zealand*, an impressive and thorough but hyper-cautious synthesis. Davidson stayed uncommitted on single or multiple settlement, but accepted first settlement around 800. It is not clear that the evidence for this date was ever strong, and the popular preference for it may suggest an antiquity bias, as though longer histories are somehow more creditable.

In the late 1980s and early 1990s, new views began to emerge. This third 'school' in fact diverged more than it converged, but shared a partial reaction against minimalism. It split dramatically on the date of first settlement – arguing that it was either much earlier or much later than the minimalist 800. Various scholars suggested multiple founding settlements, return voyaging between New Zealand and tropical Polynesia, earliest settlement in the South Island. They drew on three important developments in wider Pacific (and North American) scholarship. By considering their local applications, we can form a position on the when, where and how questions of New Zealand prehistory.

First Settlement

The first outside hypothesis was Patrick Kirch's 1986 argument that the date of Marquesan first settlement should be pushed back from AD 300 to about 200 BC, and that the dates of some other East Polynesian first settlements should also be pushed back.[38] Douglas Sutton was quick to apply Kirch's 'paradigmatic shift in Polynesian prehistory' to New Zealand.[39] Largely by pointing to certain environmental changes he associated with human settlement, Sutton suggested that the ancestors of the Maori arrived at some time between 1 and 500 – say, AD 250. This was a bold and exciting thesis, marred only by the absence of acceptable evidence. Expert critics swiftly pointed out that Sutton's reasoning also proved human settlement between 5,000 and 10,000 years ago.[40] But by taking antiquity bias to such extremes, Sutton cracked it.

Radiocarbon dating is a good technique for dating millennia but not centuries. Since the 1970s, archaeologists have been expressing doubts about its New Zealand applications but were reluctant to throw out the chronology based on it. There are many potential sources of error in the technique; one is that it is the raw material of samples that is dated, not the time humans used them. Charcoal is the most common sample, which can come from very old wood – a totara doorsill has been dated to 1950 BC.[41] It appears that charcoal dates, unscreened for old wood, often overestimate age by up to 300 years. Young wood, such as twigs, is more reliable but is not always easy to identify. Other common samples, bone and shell, can absorb modern carbon and so underestimate age by up to 150 years – hence some exciting false finds of recent moa. Some errors are consistent and predictable, and can be corrected. Others are not. For all its merits, archaeology often does not know when it is talking about. About the best radiocarbon techniques can do is divide prehistory into early (to the fourteenth century), middle (fourteenth to sixteenth centuries), and late (sixteenth to eighteenth centuries). But how early is 'early'?

In 1991, provoked by Sutton, Atholl Anderson cut a swathe through the accepted dates on these grounds and others.[42] He rejected all tenth-century dates, most twelfth-century dates, and some others to boot. There are some signs that he has culled too enthusiastically. But basically Anderson's important revision seems sound: while earlier visits are possible, archaeology does not prove ongoing human settlement of New Zealand before the thirteenth century. Anderson seems inclined to allow a century beyond this – say, to about 1150 – for the spread of settlement, and for some less unreliable twelfth-century dates in the South Island. First settlement in the South Island was earlier suggested, by Graeme Caughley in 1988.[43] Previously, those scholars who nominated a specific area of first settlement tended to prefer Northland, at the opposite end of the country. They assumed that generations would have been required to adapt the cultivation of tropical plants, most notably kumara, to the new temperate environment. The settlers succeeded in acclimatising kumara, which became the most important food plant, hue gourd (for containers and food), aute, or paper mulberry (for bark cloth), taro, yam and ti pore, the tropical cabbage tree. Notable adaptations included the artificial improvement of soil through the addition of sand, gravel and ash, and the development of underground stores, in which the whole of the kumara crop would be kept over winter, and so saved from the frost that would have killed it if it had overwintered in the ground, as in tropical Polynesia. Prosaically called 'pits' in minimum-speak, these cellars eventually ranged widely in type; some had raised rims, thatched roofs, drainage systems and little cupboards in the corners.[44]

Clearly, the full range of these developments was made over time, to meet changing requirements, but some scholars went further and assumed that it would have required many frost-free Northland seasons to evolve even basic versions – a 'Northland reservoir' of Maori horticulture, which subsequently spread from there. Advocates of first settlement in the South Island, on the other hand, could argue that mounding and made soils had precedents in tropical Polynesia, and that yams, though not kumara, were sometimes wintered in pits there too. The first settlers were perfectly capable of instantly applying these techniques, and could therefore have settled first at Wairau, Kaikoura or even Banks Peninsula, which archaeology suggests was the southern limit of kumara growing, and perhaps also of the relatively hardy hue gourd. Some go further and suggest that gardening was not very important in the early period anyway.[45]

The hitch with this is that taro and yam might not have been able to survive in the South Island, and that aute and tropical ti certainly could not. One could get around this by postulating a first settlement in the South and subsequent plant-bearing settlements in the North. Multiple settlement, however, is discounted below. Climatic changes are another possibility, a favourite archaeological explanation for the otherwise inexplicable, but no-one has suggested that these were extreme or consistent enough to turn the South Island into another 'winterless' Far North. Moreover, the first settlers are likely to have brought other plants with them, which eventually failed to acclimatise.[46] These might have included some of the most valued crops of tropical Polynesia, such as breadfruit, coconut and sugarcane (which was successfully grown on Easter Island), and common sense seems to suggest that every effort would have been made to preserve them.

Whatever the initial landfall of the first settlers, this meant going as far north as possible, as quickly as possible, to escape frost. Wind and currents make any point on the east coast between the East Cape and North Cape of the North Island equally likely for first landfall. But my guess is that, after recovering from the rigours of the voyage, some or all of the first settlers pushed north to save their plants. Bear in mind that they could not know how far north New Zealand went. They may have sailed on north, hoping New Zealand was a northern continent, just as Joseph Banks sailed on south in 1769, hoping it was a southern. The top of the Aupouri Peninsula is as far north as they could go. Other parts of the country are also almost frost-free, but 'almost' was not good enough for some tropical plants. 'All parts of the country, except the extreme tip of Northland, experience frosts.'[47]

Surveys show that the extreme tip of Northland contains numerous archaeological sites, which suggests long settlement. Few of these have been excavated, and radiocarbon dates for them earlier than the thirteenth century are unreliable. But research published in 1989 does suggest that first settlement in the region was earlier than this, and there is some evidence of early gardening. This research 'attributes the sudden decline in bird population after about AD 1000 primarily to human destruction of the habitat by fire'. Houhora, or Mount Camel, at the base of the Aupouri Peninsula, is a very early site, and Twilight Beach, at the top of the peninsula, now replaces it as 'the earliest dated site in Northland'.[48]

Anderson argues that the first sites of settlement have been found, and that they are mainly in the South Island, notably the famous Wairau Bar in Marlborough,[49] and it is true that even Twilight Beach does not pre-date the twelfth century. But it may be that none of these early sites, north or south, are the very earliest, because no tropical Polynesian stone or shell has been found in them. The Far North is subject to coastal erosion and shifting dunes that can hide coastal sites. Such factors are unlikely to hide the hundreds of sites generated by centuries of settlement, but they could hide the dozens created by two or three generations.

These considerations should not be mistaken for endorsement of the 'Northland reservoir' hypothesis. Simmons marshals quite substantial support from Maori tradition for first settlement in Northland, but it is not entirely convincing – as Orbell points out, it tends towards 'myth as history' for one thing.[50] I do not suggest that the Far North was the *only* home of the first settlers, or deny that they spread rapidly. But I do feel that their first homes were restricted to the northern third of the North Island, that the Far North was one of them, and that their spread to the South Island was rapid but not instant. Accepting that they reached the South in the twelfth century, this suggests the later eleventh century as the period of first settlement.

The second important outside development behind the new views of New Zealand prehistory was an argument for the planned, multiple settlement of Polynesia by two-way or return voyaging. Experimental voyages in the 1970s and 1980s, in Thor Heyerdahl's *Kon-Tiki* tradition, were one stimulus to this.[51] These showed that traditional Polynesian navigation, by stars and seamarks, was sophisticated, and that return voyaging to New Zealand was possible. It was sometimes romantically assumed that such voyaging had therefore taken place, as though a one-person row across the Atlantic proves the discovery of America by Irish monks in coracles. But, as developed by Geoffrey Irwin in 1989, the 'case for systematic exploration' is impressive.[52]

The early Polynesians had large, seaworthy double canoes, more like a big modern sailing catamaran than a modern Maori single-hulled war canoe, though they had a limited capacity to tack into the wind. Irwin argues that the

Polynesians explored eastward against the prevailing winds, using brief periods of westerlies in the knowledge that the normal easterlies would get them home swiftly and safely, when they reached the limits of their supplies. They sailed west–east along latitudes, which star sign determines more easily than longitude, and they 'expanded' their target islands through seamarks such as currents, driftwood, bird sign and cloud formations. They found new lands, returned to tell the tale, and so prompted planned migrations, return visits, and more migrations. This is convincing for tropical Polynesia and for medium-range voyages of up to, say, a thousand kilometres. Regrettably, it seems unconvincing for New Zealand.

For one thing, wind patterns in New Zealand seas differed from those of tropical Polynesia, and were less reliable for the return voyage to possible Hawaikis. For another, Irwin's explorers were committed to getting home, whether or not they found land where they could replenish their food and water. If New Zealand, almost 3,000 kilometres away from any possible immediate Hawaiki, was within their threshold of no-return, then this implies a capacity to travel 6,000 kilometres non-stop. The Vikings never made it more than a thousand or so kilometres in one hop, and modern Europeans did not discover the Azores, 1,200 kilometres off Portugal, until the fifteenth century. Polynesian navigators are in danger of becoming deified rather than merely superhuman.

The eighteenth-century Tahitians had traditions of most of tropical Polynesia but not New Zealand,[53] and if voyagers did travel between the two, they forgot to bring much with them. No New Zealand products, including immensely valuable ones such as greenstone, have been found in tropical Polynesia. Only one tropical Polynesian artefact, the Tairua pearl-shell fishing lure, has been found in New Zealand. It was found in a site dated to the fourteenth century but could have been an heirloom even then, and may be the sole direct vestige of the first settlers.[54] The absence of pigs in New Zealand also counts against return voyaging, a point first made by Tupaia in 1769 when a tradition of return voyaging was recounted to him by the Maori of Doubtless Bay.

> And have you no hoggs among you? said Tupia. – No. – And did your ancestors bring none back with them? – No. – You must be a parcel of Liars then, said he, and your story a great lye for your ancestors would never have been such fools as to come back without them.[55]

Banks recorded this exchange patronisingly, as 'a specimen of Indian reasoning'. It was also a specimen of good reasoning. Polynesians possessed and valued four domesticated food animals: the pig, chicken, dog and rat – the last probably a delicacy rather than a stowaway. Only dogs and rats survived in New Zealand. The pigs and chickens may have been eaten or died of cold or hunger en route, or the initial tiny numbers may have succumbed to accident in New Zealand. One can imagine the beginnings of corporal punishment in such an accident: 'Bad news, Mum, I've lost the pig.' The idea that voyagers may not have bothered to bring pigs with them is contradicted by both Tupaia and rational probability: pigs were the most highly valued of animals in the Pacific – 'pigs are our hearts'.[56]

Pigs and chickens might have been more vulnerable to cold during the voyage than were rats or dogs, but even in the tropics ocean temperatures can be low at night, and pigs and chickens survived to reach Hawai'i. A Bermuda Triangle fatal only to them and not to dogs and rats seems unlikely. The risks in transporting animals were always high, but do not seem to have selected species. Chickens but not pigs or dogs made it to Easter Island; dogs and rats but not pigs and chickens made it to New Zealand; and rats but not dogs made it from New Zealand to the Chatham Islands. The repeated attempts at acclimatisation implied by return voyaging and multiple settlement should probably have overcome the risks and difficulties.

Another argument in favour of multiple settlement – that the kumara did not arrive in the Pacific in time to be brought on to New Zealand by the first settlers – has recently been disproved by a rare find of kumara remains in the Cook Islands, dated to the tenth century.[57] A further consideration is that the physiological evidence of Maori skeletons suggests a genetically homogenous population, with quite recent descent from a single group.[58] Finally, the next chapter argues that unSmithed tradition also provides some support for the notion of a single major founding settlement.

Repeated intercourse between New Zealand and tropical Polynesia should probably be dismissed on present evidence. A second, coincidental migration is a little more credible – if it could happen once, it could happen twice – and is sometimes used to explain regional differences in Maori linguistics and material culture, especially when they seem similar to those in other parts of the Pacific. But this smacks of the 'invasion hypotheses' now discredited in European prehistory, and of 'lost caravel' theories that attribute the 'best' bits of Polynesian culture to outside influence. The second-migration idea may underestimate the capacity of both language and culture for self-generated change, and for convergent adaptation where purposes are similar and the basic source is shared. There are other possible explanations for regional variation, as we shall see in the next chapter. Anyway, it seems that the second migration most commonly posited by recent writers is deduced from a peculiarity shared by Marquesan and Maori bone reel necklaces, which have since been discovered elsewhere.[59]

A second settlement remains possible, as does reverse migration from New Zealand to tropical Polynesia by descendants of the original voyagers. But neither is likely to have been significant. Such migrants would have been less numerous than the locals, and less well armed – there was a limit to what one could carry, even on a great voyaging canoe. With no opportunity to adapt to local raw materials, they are also unlikely to have been technologically superior. Rather than imposing their culture on the locals, they are more likely to have been absorbed or wiped out, as happened to an unfortunate canoe-load of Marquesan migrants to the Tuamotu Islands in historic times.[60]

Return voyaging is not very credible for New Zealand, but the idea remains valuable in two respects. First, it has shattered the implicit but common assumption that, after voyaging 3,000 kilometres to New Zealand, the first settlers suddenly abandoned their ocean-going technology on the beach and crept cautiously along the coasts for the rest of their history. On the contrary, they were willing and able to range widely in New Zealand and adjacent waters. Second, the new knowledge of Polynesian seafaring suggests a capacity for canoes to keep in company. They might follow an agreed route, though to an unknown destination, and make rendezvous at known seamarks a few hundred kilometres from home, and perhaps at agreed types of seamarks thereafter. If separation occurred a few hundred kilometres off New Zealand, the seamarks associated with such a large land mass might still bring all in. An unknown destination need not mean an unorganised migration, and a single migration need not mean a single canoe. European exploratory ships preferred to travel in pairs or small groups for mutual supply and support, and experienced Polynesian seafarers thought likewise. Even when unSmithed, Maori canoe traditions speak of tenders, or supply vessels, accompanying a main canoe, and of major canoes travelling in pairs, as Polynesian canoes often did in historic times.[61] It may be that the Great Fleet, or at least a Little Fleet, will strike back. We cannot, of course, do more than guess at this, but it does seem to me that the probable pattern of settlement, discussed in the next chapter, better fits a founding group of one or two hundred than the minimal six or fourteen.

The third important development in prehistoric scholarship derives from North America. There, as early as the 1960s, some scholars had begun to doubt the notion of the Green Savage, at one with nature, exterminating nothing. Instead, it was suggested, some prehistoric peoples cut through the available big-game animals like a knife through butter, causing a 'rolling wave' of extinctions as they went. Subsequently, archaeologists tentatively began to apply this idea to tropical Polynesia and New Zealand, especially to the disappearance of the moa, which some scholars had previously been a little reluctant to attribute to the obvious culprits: the Maori. It is now claimed that, apart from a dozen species of moa, the Maori wiped out another twenty species of birds, and burned off a third of the native forest for good measure. The (real) Moriori of the Chatham Islands, often seen as the ultimate environmentalists, did away with several species, the Cook Islanders nine, and the Hawaiians 40 or more.[62] One Hawaiian chief had a cloak containing the feathers of 80,000 birds.[63] Even the Maori rat (kiore), long considered the consort of the Maori in oneness with nature, and once described as 'a kind of small rabbit',[64] has recently been attacked as a part-time carnivore. Is nothing sacred?

The list of extinctions is probably roughly accurate, but there is something disturbing about too eager a displacement of 'Green Savages' with bloody-handed 'Red' ones. Of course, rats ate anything they could get – the kiore was caught killing albatrosses as early as 1867.[65] The early Maori settlers *did* impact adversely on the New Zealand environment. But the implications of this should not be exaggerated. To the early settlers, the resources of their new world must have seemed infinite, and were treated as such. When it became clear that they were not infinite, some efforts were made to conserve, and to create a sustainable economy – a somewhat green-tinged phase following after a red-tinged one. The key point about the early extinctions is that they may have created a 'protein boom'.

Long isolated from the rest of the primeval Gondwanaland supercontinent, New Zealand had no land mammals except for two species of bat so small as to be hardly a snack for the hungry hunter-gatherer. What it did have was large numbers of flightless birds. The largest of these were called 'moa', after the domestic chicken of tropical Polynesia. 'It must have tickled the old fellows to apply the spare term of moa to such a hypertrophied fowl,' wrote Apirana Ngata. 'They certainly were one up on Hawaiki.'[66] The height of the biggest species, *Dinornis giganteus*, is disputed because no-one knows how it held its head, but estimates go as high as 3.67 metres, and as heavy as 242 kilograms. Even the 'little bush moa' could have been 1.3 metres high and weighed 60 kilograms. The average weight of moa slain by Polynesian hunters is usually taken to be 75 kilograms, providing 37.5 kilograms of boned meat, enough to feed 50 people for a day. The spiky speargrass in many New Zealand gardens today may well be the moa's sole living legacy. 'One can only assume it originally evolved to rebuff the attentions of hungry moa.'[67]

Moa are the glamour birds of New Zealand prehistory, but there were also other ground-bound giants: large rails, swans, ducks and geese, which were flightless or poor fliers, and weighed up to fifteen kilograms.[68] Sea mammals – dolphins, fur seals, sea lions and elephant seals – were perhaps even more important than giant birds. Elephant seals, at up to three tonnes the ultimate flesh-mine, were rare, and dolphins and sea lions were hard to catch. But at first settlement, fur seals were common, vulnerable and their rookeries were then quite widespread.[69] Fur seals weighed up to 200 kilograms and had a higher percentage of edible meat and fat than did moa. The stupidity and defencelessness of moa can be overestimated – they could outrun humans and swim short distances.[70] But the only indigenous predator of adult moa was the giant New Zealand eagle, which seems always to have been quite scarce, and thus moa were not used to being hunted. Seals likewise have everywhere proved vulnerable to human predation. A seal or a moa was many times more 'profitable' – yielding a better ratio of calories of food for calories of effort – than the gathering of shellfish, small birds or even sea fish. Big, easy game was numerous and was clearly hunted on a large scale, eventually to extinction in the case of moa, other large birds and most seal-breeding rookeries. For the first settlers, therefore, virgin New Zealand offered a sustained protein boom.

Apart from boosting the health of mothers and children, ample protein lowers the age at which a woman can first give birth, and reduces the interval between births. Thus the availability of protein has a major effect on population growth. Ironically, this case is made very effectively in another essay by Douglas Sutton.[71] He is concerned to show that the Maori birth rate in late prehistory was low because of a shortage of protein, and he does so convincingly. But, redeployed to early prehistory, his material suggests very high population growth, and so undercuts his contention that the high Maori population of 1769, or the widespread settlements of the thirteenth century, required a long lead time to achieve.

Let us pursue the question of lead time by a highly speculative exercise of counting back birth rates instead of generations. In Chapter Seven it is argued that the Maori population in 1769 was far lower than conventional figures – say, 85,000. The demographer Ian Pool, conducting a similar kind of exercise, takes 0.5 per cent as his annual growth rate throughout Maori prehistory, with no allowance for protein booms.[72] Counting back even from 85,000 in 1769, one would have to reach a first settlement date of well before 500 to give a founding population of a hundred people time for the necessary expansion. This, of course, supports Sutton's dating of first settlement. But if we allow for an early protein boom, the picture is very different.

The notion of a protein boom leading to high population growth contradicts certain preconceptions about 'hunter-gatherer' societies, which derive from those surviving to the present in difficult environments, such as the San, or Bushmen, of the Kalahari Desert. The fertility of such societies, notes Pool, is limited by 'restricted diet', the need to carry children and 'continuous walking to seek food'; hence his preference for 0.5 per cent.[73] New Zealand game was not only big but also easy and abundant, and Maori boated to it more than they walked. Nantucket may be a better source of analogies than the Kalahari. Caughley suggests that the early flesh-fuelled growth rate may have been as high as 3.7 per cent, using the analogy of the *Bounty* mutineers and their Polynesian wives on Pitcairn, of all places.[74]

The 1960s have shown us that Maori are physiologically capable of such growth rates, but the figure is unacceptably high for neolithic people with short life spans and high infant mortality. On the other hand, skeletal evidence shows that very few Maori women were ever infertile. A conservative (for protein booms) figure of 1.5 per cent increase per year seems a reasonable guess. Let us take Pool's 0.5 per cent back for three centuries from 1769, allow a century of even slower growth of say 0.2 per cent for what is generally agreed to have been a period of transition and conflict, and continue back from 1369 at protein-boom rates. We should also allow for even higher growth in the first generation, because original canoe crews were largely adults of breeding age, selected for health by their voyaging hardships. On these bases, we get back to a founding population of a hundred in the year 1066. Isn't science wonderful?

History is often a matter of improving best guesses. To sum up mine on the beginning of human settlement in New Zealand, the ideas of multiple settlement, in the South Island first, are rejected for a single but quite substantial settlement including, but not necessarily restricted to, the Far North. A single, one-way settlement does not imply drift voyage or unplanned migration. The first settlers never returned home, nor perhaps expected to return home, but such things as the number of their plants suggest that their migration was planned. It was only the particular destination that was unknown. Anderson's late date for first settlement is preferred to Sutton's early date, but is shifted back a little from the twelfth century to the later eleventh.

The ideas of a highly mobile population in a protein-powered phase of high growth are used, in the next chapter, to help construct an hypothesis about the dynamics of New Zealand's first society, and perhaps of early Polynesian societies in general. The suggestions that the ancestors of the Maori came from the Bismarck Archipelago, and that they arrived in New Zealand in the later eleventh century are seriously intended, although new evidence can, of course, overturn such hypotheses at any time. It is probably unnecessary to say that pinning down the precise place and time to New Britain and 1066 is not quite so serious. Both are perfectly possible, but such coincidences are not important in themselves. What they highlight, however, is the role of history in history, retrospectively linking and distinguishing peoples in the past for the purposes of the present. Old Britain, New Britain and New Zealand are all artificial labels. It is myth and history that shape and reshape their contents.

CHAPTER TWO

Hunters and Gardeners

After an unknown number of millennia, people at last worked out how they procreate as individuals. In 1859, Charles Darwin theorised effectively about the procreation of species. But we are still not too sure about the procreation of *peoples*, also known as nations, races, societies and cultures. One option is spawning through the formation of colonies, which then grow up. Colonising has come to imply the dominance of one group over another; we are interested here in its older meaning: the planting of whole communities of migrants in new lands, whether or not these contain indigenous inhabitants, and their growth into new peoples. New Zealand is the most recent product of two of the world's great colonisers: the British and the Polynesians. Although not quite a human Galapagos, it is a good place to study an origin of peoples: the process by which a new society forms from an old.

Discussion of such issues tends to polarise: were new societies dominated by their old source society or by their new environment; is their culture best explained by spread or local development? Migrationist/anti-migrationist debate, touched on in the previous chapter, is one example of this. Another is the historians' argument about whether the 'fragment' (the time and place from which most early migrants came) or the 'frontier' (the new environment, rich in opportunity) determines the leading features of new societies. Both are dubious dichotomies, though fragment and frontier are useful shorthand. They stress the dominance of old source or new environment rather than the interaction between them; and they neglect what this book will argue is a third factor in the equation: the 'ethos of expansion'.

The ethos of expansion is primarily a system of ideas – the assumptions, hopes and fears of colonists – but it also has important social, technological and economic elements and implications. It helps to trigger colonisation, to determine its direction and form, and influences its development in the new land. It is 'cultural baggage' taken by colonists from their source society, but it is not merely a fragment of the home culture. It is not necessarily used at Home, and is influenced as much by the experience and mythology of previous colonisations. Because the British colonised already-occupied lands, their perceptions of other peoples, and of themselves in relation to other peoples, were key elements of their ethos. The Polynesians colonised empty lands, and were not strictly comparable in this respect. But both Polynesian and British colonisations were influenced by imperatives and dynamics drawn from their ethos of expansion. It is suggested that the ethos of expansion is the missing link in the study of the formation of new societies. It did not dominate fragment and frontier, but interacted with them.

A little before AD 1100, we guess, an East Polynesian 'fragment' arrived in New Zealand. It consisted, let us say, of a hundred people, and the ideas, artefacts, plants and animals they brought with them. This fragment was affected from the first by 'ethos' and 'frontier'. Even before the fragment set out, the ethos of expansion, transmitted by canoe legends, determined the selection of its components, provided the voyaging skills necessary to transport it and shaped the way in which the migrants conceived themselves and their migration. Once discovered, the character of the new frontier helped determine which aspects of fragment and ethos were emphasised, and when. Ethos and fragment in turn helped determine the way in which the frontier was perceived, exploited and changed.

This chapter suggests that the earliest settlers approached New Zealand as a constellation of 'resource islands'. They ranged widely and rapidly among these by sea, but their spread was neither unpatterned nor 'sequential' – gradual outward growth from the point of first settlement into neighbouring areas.[1] It was patterned by a 'gardener imperative' and a 'hunter dynamic' drawn from the Polynesian ethos of expansion and adapted to the conditions of this particular frontier. This thesis is tentative, but I think it accommodates variations and changes, explains similarities and continuities, and solves some key problems a little better than the alternatives. Something was said about the nature of the East Polynesian fragment in the last chapter. Here we look first at the physical character of the frontier, then at the ethos of expansion and the relationship between the two. We then briefly test the 'hunter-gardener thesis' against the evidence of bone, stone, style and story.

The Thickening Archipelago

From the inside looking out, New Zealand is dominated by mountains: a long, irregular massif of ranges and foothills and uplands, sprawling almost the whole length of both islands. Backbone is the obvious metaphor. Physically at least, no-one can accuse New Zealand of being spineless. The mountains blow hot and cold. There are live or dormant volcanoes and their associated thermal regions in the central North Island. There are glaciers in the south-west, marching towards the sea with all the speed of an economic recovery. The mountains are sociable: they tend to group. The Southern Alps contain 223 named peaks over 2,600 metres. Taranaki, the Lone Mountain, is the exception, a social outcast in Maori mythology.

Three-quarters of New Zealand is more than 200 metres high, but from the outside looking in, the country is dominated by the sea. It has nearly 6,000 kilometres of coast, and nowhere, not even Samuel Butler's Erewhon, is more than 120 kilometres from the sea. Auckland, the narrowest place, is an afternoon stroll from two oceans. New Zealand is a compromise between sea and mountain. The two are linked by numerous rivers, fast and slow; by peninsulas that probe out to sea; and by fiords, harbours and inlets that probe in. Plains and lowlands, mostly small and coastal, mediate.

New Zealand today is warmer than Old Britain, colder than tropical Polynesia, and wetter and windier than either. Some scholars suggest that climatic change had dramatic historical effects, but one learns to suspect climatic determinism in prehistory, along with inevitability in modern history and sea monsters in medieval geography. It was once argued that the Roman Empire had been rained off, and some nineteenth-century Pakeha explained their difference from Australians in climatic terms: in New Zealand you had a chance of remaining white. Between the eleventh and the nineteenth centuries, changes in average temperature do not seem to have exceeded 0.5°C,[2] even during the 'Little Ice Age' of the seventeenth and eighteenth centuries, which ethnography also suggests was not that cold. Compared with tropical Polynesia, however, the regional and seasonal range of climate was great – from almost subantarctic in the Deep South, to almost subtropical in the Far North; from wet and relatively cool in the west, to warm and relatively dry in the east, with peculiar micro-climates in between. Central Otago can be hotter than Auckland in summer, colder than Stewart Island in winter. It has one-thirtieth the rainfall of some parts of nearby Westland.

Vegetation has changed far more than climate. In the eleventh century, only fifteen per cent of the country was unforested – peaks above the timberline, swamp, seashore and small patches of scrub and grasslike tussock. The predominant forest was of three types: a broad belt of beech forest in and around the huge mountain spine; dense broadleaved and coniferous forest mainly in the wetter west; and similar trees in the drier east, except that the forest they formed was more open and pocked with lighter vegetation. By the eleventh century, Maori had burned off a good deal of the last two types, and Pakeha have now almost finished the job. From the eleventh century, then, a growing human-induced category emerged: cultivations (eventually including introduced grasses), open tussock land (especially in the south-east) and transitional scrub in the process of reversion to forest.[3]

New Zealand has always had a self-effacing streak. None of its three main myths of origin suggests a voluntary emergence into the world. Science says that New Zealand was expelled from the Gondwanaland supercontinent by

Continental Drift about 80 million years ago, and thrust unwillingly into prominence by the buckling of tectonic plates. European mythology is less helpful. Through some strange conspiracy, the Bible says nothing at all about New Zealand. In Polynesian mythology, New Zealand was fished up by the great demi-god Maui, like many other Pacific islands. The earliest recorded versions imply Maui's fishing spot was to the north of New Zealand, but in the authorised version the North Island is Maui's fish (Te Ika), the South Island his canoe (Te Waka) and Stewart Island its anchor (Te Punga).[4] Europeans were surprised at how well this accorded with the actual size and shape of the three islands. Like other evidence, it suggests that Maori had a good understanding of the topography of their country at an early stage. Another name, 'Aotearoa', is variously translated as 'The Land of the Long White Cloud', 'The Land of the Long Bright Day', 'The Land of the Long Lingering Day', and, best of all, 'The Long Bright World'. The name probably applied only to the North Island before European contact but is now used as the Maori name for the whole country.

Maui's lumping of the country into two main islands remains the most basic division to this day. In a sense, this is deceptive. Until the advent of rail in the late nineteenth century, the most important forms of transport, especially for load carrying, were by water. Boats were the trucks and trains of both Maori and European colonisation; lakes, rivers and especially coasts were the major highways. Both peoples came to New Zealand in ocean-going vessels, and continued to use them once here. Fragment (the actual availability of ships brought from Hawaiki), frontier (the great distances to be covered and the abundance of water) and ethos (voyaging skills and traditions) combined to make them the natural form of transport. Water was more bridge than barrier, and the distinction between North and South Islands is partly artificial. The Southern Alps were much more of a barrier than Cook Strait. New Plymouth is twice as far from Nelson as from Taupo as the crow flies, but twice as close in terms of travelling time. The ocean funnel leading into Cook Strait can be seen as an inland sea, if a rough one, largely landbound on three sides. It linked the top of the South Island and the bottom of the North, making central New Zealand a natural macro-region. The role of the Hauraki Gulf and Foveaux Strait in the North and South Islands was not entirely dissimilar. For the long seaborne part of history, north, centre and south are useful divisions to add to that between North and South Islands. They accord roughly with ecological macro-regions.[5]

The intermixing of land and sea, the mountain ranges, the numerous rivers, together with variations in climate and vegetation, split New Zealand into numerous distinct subenvironments, some of which are very much more useful and accessible to humans than others. This fragmented yet water-linked environment showed a different face to the first settlers than it does to us. It was almost inconceivably vast and varied in their experience: larger than the whole land mass of tropical Polynesia put together. Far from being small, Aotearoa must have seemed to them as America seemed to Europeans. No tradition could stretch back over 4,000 years to provide a continental precedent for this.

Like the first Europeans in America, Aotearoa's first settlers would have adapted old concepts to cope with the new world. It is useful to suppose that they approached the country as a huge archipelago of 'islands' – patches of useful land separated by patches of less useful land, and best accessed by sea.[6] At first, they might have focused only on the very richest islands, over quite a wide area. There was no need to accept second best in an empty country, and a sea-voyage of a few days between islands was nothing to people who had just crossed an ocean.

As the abundant resources of the premium islands declined through use, and as population grew, new islands beyond the boundary of knowledge were sought and second-class islands behind the boundary were brought into use. As the process continued, the chain of coastal resource islands became almost continuous, and economic penetration of the interior began, initially by river. The key concept in all this is that of a *thickening* archipelago. The archipelago was extended by discovery and thickened by progressive exploitation of resource islands that had previously been found but not used while better options existed.

These resource islands can be classed in two trios by type of main economic activity. Aotearoa offered many small items of wild food; areas in which they were especially plentiful were the best 'gathering islands'. These contained a range of edible plants, notably aruhe (bracken fern), whose roots were an important food. 'Gathering' can be stretched for convenience to include the catching of small birds and, soon, the trapping of introduced Polynesian rats. We will call the second category 'wood islands' – areas containing the types of timber and other flora used as raw materials. Wood, by bulk, was the main raw material, used for canoes, houses, tools, weapons and carving. Maori preferred particular trees for particular purposes – totara, for canoes and for carving, was probably the most prized.[7] Some implements were made and decorated with great care; others were made crudely from materials at hand and readily discarded. With wood, we can associate other raw materials such as flax, whose fibre was woven into clothing, baskets, mats, rope and fishing nets. 'Fishing islands' were the third type, including not only marine fish, shellfish and crustaceans, but also freshwater fish, notably eels.

The use of gathering, fishing and wood islands was always vital to the Maori economy, providing much of the total diet from the outset. Resources such as wood and fish were obviously familiar, and the first settlers rapidly adjusted to their local forms, and to some unfamiliar resources as well. Wild plants, for example, were used in tropical Polynesia after natural disasters like hurricane had destroyed the gardens. This may have provided instant precedents for the processing of the many New Zealand plants that were poisonous or unpalatable in their raw state.[8] But the full range of exploitation of these resources can only have developed over time, as population increased and alternatives diminished. While abundance varied, and was not huge anywhere the whole year round, these three island types were quite widespread. Most places in the country were close to a full set, and they could be taken for granted to some extent. We can therefore focus, like the first settlers themselves, on the second trio: stone, gardening and game islands.

Polynesians made many kinds of tools, weapon, utensils and ornaments from stone, but the most important can be grouped into two: adzes, and related chisels and gouges, used especially for woodworking; and knives, with related scrapers and choppers, used especially for food processing. Stone tools were more effective for such purposes than is sometimes assumed, but they did have one great disadvantage: they broke and lost their edge easily. Maori communities therefore required regular access to stone.

New Zealand contained many varieties of adze stone and knife stone, and some less prized varieties such as greywacke and the lesser cherts were quite widespread. But the premium stones were basalt, 'baked' argillite, greenstone and perhaps gabbro for adzes; and obsidian, silcrete and perhaps the best cherts for knives. These were only available in accessible form at restricted locations: the leading 'stone islands'. As far as adze stone was concerned, these included the basalt of Tahanga (on the Coromandel Peninsula) and perhaps Northland gabbro, in the north; the argillite of the great Nelson–D'Urville Island mineral belt in the centre; and Southland argillite in the south. Greenstone, or New Zealand jade, occurs in the west of the South Island; its deposits were quite isolated and obscure; it was not easy to work, and it appears infrequently in the earliest sites. Early finds may come from a small source in Nelson, only recently rediscovered.[9] Greenstone can therefore be left out of the argument for the moment.

The most important source of knife stone was obsidian, or volcanic glass, and the most important early source of this was Tuhua, or Mayor Island, in the Bay of Plenty and close to Coromandel. Obsidian was also available in Northland (at Kaeo and Whangarei) and at various places in the interior of the northern zone. The central zone had no obsidian and had to make do for knife stone with flint-like chert, especially from the Wairarapa, but the southern zone had silcrete, especially in Central Otago.

Garden islands were the second key type. New Zealand's climate is good for temperate-zone plants but not so kind to tropical ones. Many died out, as we have seen, and the whole surviving range could grow only in the north.

Kumara, gourd and perhaps taro could be grown in the central zone, and none at all could be grown in the south. Moreover, only restricted patches of soil in the north and centre were optimal for gardening. The unassisted fertility of New Zealand soils is something of a myth. 'Apart from the small areas of fertile alluvial terraces and flood plains the soils of New Zealand have only moderate to low chemical fertility.'[10] Developing techniques and the discovery of volcanic loams and river plains in the interior eventually extended and multiplied the gardening islands. But, initially, these were restricted to points where river soils intersected with well-drained flats and gently sloped hills on the eastern coast. The coast was warmer, had the sandy soil preferred by kumara and offered access to marine resources and the main highway – the sea. An irregular chain of first-choice garden islands stretched south down a thin east-coastal strip from the top of the Aupouri Peninsula to the southern limit of the central zone, Banks Peninsula.

Aotearoa was richer in the third key category of resource island: those that provided big game, most notably moa and fur seals. The eleven or twelve species of moa had differing habits, and their distribution is not easy to deduce. It was long assumed that they preferred open grassland. We now know there was very little of this 900 years ago, but it does seem that the most numerous species of moa were most abundant in the drier, easterly, more open type of coniferous-broadleaved forest, especially in the eastern South Island.[11] Within these limits, the rivers, mountains and so on that cut up the country subdivided moa populations into 'islands', as they did every other natural resource. The best islands were those where moa abundance intersected with sea and river access, as in eastern Otago and Canterbury and a few scattered parts of the North Island.

Temporary rookeries of fur seals were scattered widely around the coasts, but breeding rookeries, where seals were most numerous and where some stayed all year round, were their best islands. Permanent breeding rookeries existed in the Far North and Coromandel, in the northern zone; on both shores of Cook Strait in the centre (and just possibly in South Taranaki); and in a band round the bottom of the southern zone, from the Otago Peninsula through Foveaux Strait to Fiordland.[12] Seal islands were the best of all in terms of regularity of supply and return on effort. It may be that 'seal hunter' is more appropriate than 'moa hunter' for the first inhabitants of Aotearoa. It seems best to treat both as representing basically the same type of activity: the hunting of big, easy game, 'island' by 'island'.

This idea of a thickening archipelago with its three key types of resource island may help us understand the organisation, pattern and dynamics of early settlement. In later prehistory, claims were staked to all major resource areas, and those who lacked one valuable acquired it through gift exchange, often through intermediaries. In earliest prehistory, there were no claims and no intermediaries, and the first economic communities – we will call them 'colonies' – got everything for themselves. A colony therefore consisted not of one settlement but of a family of settlement sites and campsites, permanent or semi-permanent, seasonal and temporary, covering the full set of resource islands. Because the first settlers possessed ocean-going skills and technology, and because there was as yet little need to congregate for security, these sites did not have to be close together. A single colony could conceivably be a constellation of sites, scattered over hundreds of kilometres and linked by sea routes.

The forces that held such a colony together were associated with gardeners and gardening islands: the 'gardener imperative'. The forces that kept the colony spread, expanded it rapidly and eventually caused it to split were associated with hunting and hunting islands: the 'hunter dynamic'. Some caution is needed here. The thesis is speculative. Preconceptions about the relative sophistication of hunters and gardeners may prove false. Although there was some tendency to specialisation over time, hunters and gardeners were often the same people doing different things at different times. But let us develop this hunter-gardener thesis a little.

The Hunter-Gardener Thesis

The parts of resource islands in use expanded and multiplied at different rates according to the type of island. Outcrops of premium stone were few but large, and they were exhausted slowly. Stone islands therefore expanded slowly and multiplied slowly, though access to at least one pair, for adzes and knives, was vital. Polynesian gardening, in which the use of manure was looked upon with disgust, required soil regeneration through long fallow periods. Population growth, or an increased dependence on gardening, required that more gardens be burned out of the adjacent forest. This growth was steady but not exponential, because fallow areas could eventually be reused. It may therefore be that garden islands also expanded and multiplied relatively slowly.

Hunting islands, on the other hand, multiplied fast. Maori probably sliced through the most vulnerable game, such as the flightless goose, quite quickly. The northern seal-breeding colonies may not have survived very long either, and it has been suggested that man and moa co-existed for no more than a century in any given region.[13] But it does not seem likely that Maori hunters were propelled from game island to game island by the absolute extinction of their prey. Abundance plus access to sea and river transport, crucial for extracting heavy kills, was the equation that determined the best game islands and the pattern of exploitation within each island. Seals and moa were taken from the most accessible points until a threshold was reached where it was more economic to find another island than to foray further into this one. European sealers in the early nineteenth century were sometimes drowned or injured in falls when pushing into the rockiest and least accessible parts of rookeries, and they had only to carry out the skins, not the whole carcass. Why lug 200-kilogram seals to a processing site over kilometres of rocks when you knew that they waited right beside such sites a few days' sail away? Similar considerations applied to 200-kilogram moa. It was more sensible to cream off the accessible game and move on, leaving descendants with fewer options to mop up in the future. Hence the survival of moa populations for several centuries in some relatively inaccessible northern regions. So conceived, hunting can be seen as the dynamic behind the early spread of settlement.

Gardening may have contributed less to the early settlers' diet than did hunting, and perhaps less than fishing and gathering as well. This may seem to support the view that gardening was initially not very important. But the immense effort invested in the storage pits, stone walls, forest clearance and made soils of early gardening, the care that must have gone into importing plants from the tropics and the importance of kumara in traditions seem to contradict this. Crops needed more effort to obtain than wild plants, but they were more easily processed for eating and storage, and their production was more controllable. The simple survival of six tropical plants in difficult conditions, through periods when alternative foods were easily available, itself indicates that a high value was placed on them, and suggests that the maintenance of gardening was a strong cultural imperative. The ethos of expansion may even have had previous experience of the demise of hunting when game islands were worked out. Perhaps it insisted, through tradition, that gardening be maintained as insurance.

For some time there was also a strong economic factor behind the gardener imperative. Where the food obtained by hunters had to be taken to consumers, rather than vice versa, it had to be preserved and transported. A major Maori method of preserving meat was to pot it in fat in taha, airtight containers made from hue gourds. One tends to think of gourds as small vessels, and some were harvested young to provide food and small 'bottles' for such things as precious cosmetics. But others were large, able to fit up to 180 small birds – twenty or more kilograms of boned meat – or several gallons of water.[14] 'Casks' may be a better translation for this type of container, and they were vital for food preservation. Hunters needed the gourds that gardeners provided, not only to supply distant kin but also to feed themselves outside the peak hunting season. The discovery that bull kelp could be made into large airtight bags eventually freed hunters from this dependence. But it was only available in the southern zone. In other areas, and before the discovery of bull kelp's utility as a container, economics as well as culture demanded that hunters have strong links with gardeners. When forming a new colony, hunters had to pull gardeners after them.

Voyaging skills must have been important to both hunters and gardeners, especially to the former, who travelled regularly back and forth from old hunting islands and explored to find new ones. Canoe building, maintenance and repair demanded plenty of stone tools, as did the processing of large game. Hunters had the motivation and the opportunity to find and use new stone sources, and therefore had a special link to stone islands and stoneworking, as well as to voyaging skills. They also discovered new garden islands. A full set of premium islands in close proximity may have been worked by the whole population, shifting from site to site, taking mouths to food. As game islands were creamed off and the colony spread, small parties might have ventured out from a gardening or stoneworking base to hunt for a few days or weeks, bringing back food to mouths. Their camps on rich and distant game islands might have been repeatedly reused, and for increasing periods, requiring only one long voyage to and fro per season. When stone and garden islands were discovered close to such a hunting station, there must have been a temptation to dispense with the annual voyage home altogether, encouraged perhaps by population growth and rivalry between leaders. A final voyage might be made to collect plant seedlings, plus spouses and children if they had not already shifted to the hunting station, and a new colony would form. Irregular visits and links of kinship, intermarriage and gift exchange might continue, but economic dependence would not.

Can this model tentatively map New Zealand's first colonies? The last chapter argued that the Far North, which had garden, seal and moa islands, contained some of the first sites, but others must have existed in the Coromandel and Tuhua. Tuhua obsidian and Tahanga basalt dominate the stone artefacts and fragments found in the Far North's earliest sites, despite the fact that other sources of adze and knife stone were closer. With no intermediaries available – archaeologists see the east coast of Northland south of Houhora, or Mount Camel, as an 'archaic gap' – only direct contact can explain this. 'The people at Mount Camel,' writes Davidson, 'were clearly dependent on the Coromandel for their raw material.'[15] The Far North and Coromandel were the only regions in the northern macro-region with seal-breeding rookeries, the best resource of all. The Far North, as we have seen, offered the best chance of survival to tropical plants. The Far North/Coromandel/Tuhua seems a likely first colony. That it was spread over more than 300 kilometres was perhaps not ideal, but it was no great problem to people who had just crossed 3,000. Coromandel had stone, seal, moa and garden islands of its own. Once the unviable tropical plants succumbed, it did not need the Far North. The Far North did need Coromandel, until it found its own obsidian at Kaeo and adze stone in the form of Northland gabbro. Both parts of the colony had acquired a full set of resources, and the two could then have split.

Even before this, hunting expeditions would have ranged south along the more benign east coast. Rookeries of non-breeding seals and small numbers of moa may have delayed them for a few seasons, and tempted them on, but successive expeditions found no breeding rookeries or rich moa or stone islands for hundreds of kilometres. At Cook Strait, they finally struck the jackpot: seals breeding near present-day Nelson and Wellington, together with moderate numbers of moa; adequate garden islands nearby, at Wairau and Palliser Bay, for example; and a vast source of premium stone in the form of Nelson–D'Urville argillite. New colonies formed.

The process then repeated itself, with hunting expeditions exploiting the exceptionally rich moa islands of the eastern South Island from bases around Cook Strait. This led hunters into finding the vast seal and stone resources of the southern zone. Once bull kelp replaced gourds for meat storage, a third set of colonies may have formed, this time without gardens and perhaps based on the seal rookeries and stone sources of Southland, but with hunting extending up the Otago coast.

These three early colonies or sets of colonies had things in common that could be fully provided nowhere else: breeding seals, proximity to both adze and knife stone, moderate-to-good moa islands, and strategic locations on the nearest New Zealand had to inland seas – the Hauraki Gulf, Cook Strait and Foveaux Strait.

Mapping the precise direction, time and place of this first colonisation is obviously highly speculative, and mapping subsequent colonisations is even more so. Exploration, exploitation and settlement may have spread south–north and east–west after the putative first three colonies were established. We should make other qualifications too. Hunting or gardening were defining but not exclusive economic activities. Everyone everywhere gathered and fished when they could. Hunters and gardeners were initially the very same people. Over time, individuals and groups might tend to one activity or the other, as hunting required longer and longer periods away from home. The split may have run along age lines, with very young and very old remaining at garden settlements while the others voyaged out for stone and game. It could have run along gender lines – this issue is discussed in Chapter Four. It could have been a split between the families of those particularly skilled at one activity or the other. Some gardening settlements were pulled into marginal locations by the demands of their hunters. Gardeners who had prime sites and innovative methods, on the other hand, might gradually become less dependent on hunting expeditions, and rich enough to exchange gifts with all and sundry for stone. Colonies might therefore have different balances between hunting and gardening. Hunters might even abandon gardener links altogether, with the aid of bull kelp, as they did in the south. Gardeners who most successfully made the change from an exploitative to a sustainable economy might abandon hunting. One could add four categories to the abstract co-equal balance: hunters, hunter-gardeners, gardener-hunters and gardeners.

In sum, my best guess is that first settlement was in the Far North and Coromandel, beginning as one far-flung colony in the eleventh century and perhaps splitting into two or more in the twelfth. In the twelfth and thirteenth centuries, while the population still numbered in mere hundreds, exploitation followed by colonisation spread to the far south, focusing on Cook and Foveaux Straits, and driven by the 'creaming off' rather than the extirpation of big game. Early gardening settlements, linked to hunters operating further south, may have formed outside these areas, on the east coast of the North Island and the north-east coast of the South. Colonisation continued in the thirteenth and fourteenth centuries, when the population numbered in thousands, with increasing acceptance of less than a full hand of resources, the deficiency made up by gift exchange and access to the resources of related colonies. Hunting, and the associated exploitation of stone islands, shifted to 'back filling' the lesser islands of the east coast, to the west coast and eventually to the interior.

In the fourteenth and fifteenth centuries, with the population now numbering tens of thousands, big game diminished towards extinction. People mopped up its vestiges in the major game islands, searched with increasing desperation for more isolated islands in the interior, and began making the adjustment to a non-hunting economy. Population growth slowed overall, famine occurred in some areas, and marginal gardening sites were abandoned, their function as adjuncts to hunting having ceased. A last frenetic round of colonisation took place, now motivated more by push than pull, as people scrabbled for resources. This crisis of mid-prehistory occurred at different times in different places, perhaps stretching from about 1350 to 1550, or even 1600. In this period, the highly mobile, far-flung colonies concentrated and became more sedentary, and split and lumped into a new form of socio-economic organisation: the tribe.

Early prehistory is therefore a 'colonial era' – eleventh to fourteenth centuries – and late prehistory a 'tribal era' – sixteenth to eighteenth – with a painful transition period in between. This seems to make more sense in the abstract than the alternatives: early unpatterned, 'chaotic' expansion, or sequential spread, from a South Island first settlement; change caused by fresh settlements from tropical Polynesia; a Northland cultural reservoir suddenly bursting its bounds; or no explanation at all.

The period 1350–1600 is widely agreed to have been a period of transition, and the time when moa died out – legends of late survival have now been dismissed.[16] Using artistic and traditional evidence, Maori scholars date a great social and cultural reshuffling to the period.[17] It is the time when most firm tribal whakapapa, and presumably the modern tribes themselves, begin. There is quite solid evidence of early settlement in the Far North/Coromandel, and Cook and Foveaux Straits, and of the three regions being linked, despite large unpeopled tracts between them. Whatever the disputes about actual dating, most of the agreed earliest sites are in these regions. Coromandel produced the Tairua lure and the earliest evidence of pits for storing kumara over winter.[18] There are some similarities in artefacts such as ornaments and fishing gear. They are very close between Coromandel and the Far North, close between that region and Cook Strait, and quite close between both and Foveaux Strait.[19] The three regions shared the artefact styles most closely related to those of tropical Polynesia. They also shared a genetic peculiarity in their dogs.[20] If New Zealand was settled as late as the eleventh or twelfth centuries by only one or two hundred people, then the rapid spread of settlement to these regions and not others is difficult to explain except by something like the hunter dynamic. Why else should they spread so early to these particular far-flung places, neglecting the areas in between?

The establishment of early gardening settlements in marginal areas, at a time when many superior and unoccupied locations were available, is also difficult to explain without something like the gardener imperative. A particular case is Palliser Bay, at the bottom of the North Island, which thanks to a team study in the 1970s is among the best known of early communities.[21] Its first settlement is dated to the twelfth century, while most evidence of the later phases of occupation comes from the fifteenth. There are few moa bones in its middens, and its people invested immense effort in gardening in marginal conditions. This has been taken to mean that they lived a harsh life from the outset, scraping a living from an adverse environment. Yet the early occupants suffered no famine and were relatively long-lived. They received stone from distant regions. The few moa bones found were leg bones and were not obtained locally.[22] The early Palliser people placed surprising emphasis on growing gourds, lower in food value than kumara. Although less rich than those of the Wairau Bar, their grave goods were not contemptible. The later occupants, on the other hand, did suffer famine, depleting the local shellfish beds in an increasingly desperate search for food,[23] and eventually abandoned the settlement.

The assumption that the early occupants were poor could be a case of minimalist error. They might have been supplied with boned meat and stone by hunting kin, and gave gourds in return. They might have been part of a colony, a branch of an economic community, not the whole of it. It might have been colonial dynamics and imperatives that pulled them into a marginal gardening environment in the first place, when better alternatives were available. Once its hunters ceased to find game, Palliser Bay was thrown back on its own resources and did not survive. Its people went elsewhere – this time pushed, not pulled. Several other marginal gardening sites, notably on the north-east coast of the South Island, were also abandoned.

The fit between the hunter-gardener thesis and the archaeology of Palliser Bay is by no means perfect, but the thesis also explains several general shifts and contradictions in the countrywide archaeological evidence. 'Paddling grooves', indentations in human bone resulting from a great deal of canoe paddling, hint that canoeing was more common in early prehistory than in late.[24] It has been suggested that early adzes were oriented to canoe building, whereas later types were more suitable for general woodwork.[25] This supports the notion of a shift from a mobile colonial society to a more sedentary tribal society in mid-prehistory. Human tooth wear strongly suggests a shift, at about the same time, from a diet in which meat featured large to greater dependence on fibrous vegetable foods and gritty seafood.[26] The change does not seem to be restricted to the areas where seals and moa were once abundant. This, and the bias of protein to the south yet population to the north, is hard to explain unless the one was regularly transported to the other. Changes in tradition, non-hunting economics, warfare and social organisation, posited below, also fit the thesis.

Minimalists might feel that this ties loose ends into too neat a knot. But the various dimensions of human history normally interact, with changes in one reflected in others. To deny a connection between the demise of big game and economic and social transition seems an unnecessary fear of the obvious. Yet it is true that we should not be too ready to embrace the obvious, and that we need to subject the hunter-gardener thesis to the tests of bone, stone, style and story.

Bone, Stone, Style

Hunting during the protein boom tells its tale in the bones of the victims. These show that groups of Maori killed large numbers of large animals in a restricted area and in a short time. Large flightless or semi-flightless birds other than moa seem to have been the very easiest prey, and they were wiped out first. A wide range of their bones therefore indicates a very early site in a particular district, and sites in our putative areas of early colonisation fit this criterion. Seals, as we have seen, were probably the most attractive early prey, but in the Far North/Coromandel and Cook Strait they often intersected with moderate numbers of moa. Seals were not only large, they were also good eating, as the scientist-explorer J. R. Forster discovered at Dusky Sound in 1773. Seal steaks were 'by far more tender & juicy than beefstakes . . . their good taste soon got the better of my prejudice'.[27]

In the Far North, seals seem to have been exploited first at the topmost bays, close to the presumed original garden island. At least 67 fur seals were killed in a brief occupation of the early site at Twilight Beach. At Houhora, a little further south, at least 59 fur seals, sea lions and elephant seals were killed in about twelve successive seasonal visits by up to 50 people, providing four times as much meat as the 50 moa killed at the same time.[28] These figures represent bones of clearly different individual creatures found; they could be only a fraction of the number killed. Seasonal occupation, an expedition of about 50 people (one large canoe-load) and something like twelve years to 'cream-off' a small game island might be a common pattern. Certainly, bursts of seal hunting supplemented by moa hunting was a pattern replicated in a score of early sites in Coromandel, Cook Strait and Foveaux Strait.

As we might expect, hunting seems to have wiped out the seal-breeding rookeries in the Far North first, in Coromandel next, then at Cook Strait, and on the Foveaux Strait coast last. The phase of intensive exploitation in all three areas was the twelfth to fourteenth centuries. Breeding rookeries on the Otago Peninsula survived until, or revived by, the seventeenth or eighteenth centuries, and in Fiordland and the offshore islands until European contact.[29]

The most striking archaeological evidence of early hunting is a number of vast moa-butchering sites, up to 120 hectares in extent, mainly in the South Island. Generally, these were not permanent settlements but base camps, meatworks or hunting stations, where moa were processed, located at the mouth of a major river. Coastal moa may have diminished within a few seasons, and hunters travelled into the interior from base, killed moa and did some preliminary processing. Small moa might be carried whole; medium ones had the head and feet discarded; and only the thigh and middle leg of large birds were carried off – a greatly disproportionate number of these bones appears in the archaeological record. These huge leg joints made up 35 per cent of the body weight but 70–80 per cent of the meat weight,[30] and the best part of even a large moa could therefore be carried by two people. It is tempting to imagine a line of successful hunters with giant drumsticks over their shoulders.

Their immediate destination might not be the base camp but the river that led to it. Here reed boats were rapidly constructed, each capable of carrying up to a tonne.[31] The trip to the sea could be made fast, using the current, bringing fresh meat to base, where it was cooked in earth ovens. Such ovens might be used more than once, but their number permits rough estimates of the number of moa cooked. Estimates of the number killed at the largest site, at the mouth of the Waitaki River in the south, range from 29,000 to 90,000. Here concentrations of ovens are still apparent from aerial photographs.[32] There was a moa-hunting station at the mouth of almost every substantial river on the east coast of the South Island, some with estimated takes of between 5,000 and 10,000 moa. Stations in southern Taranaki may have approached the same size, but North Island moa-hunting sites were generally smaller and more scattered. This may reflect a shortage of suitable rivers as much as moa, but it does help explain a rapid expansion southwards – abundance *plus* access was the key equation. The total number of known moa-hunting sites is over 300.

Much of this is drawn from Atholl Anderson's magisterial 1989 study of moa and moa hunting, *Prodigious Birds*. But Anderson seems less convincing on several important points. He concludes that hunting was carried out by individuals or very small parties, and that most moa were consumed on site.[33] Elsewhere he doubts the notion of 'hunting stations' run by people from other places, first posited in the 1930s by amateur archaeologist David Teviotdale, and suggests that humans and moa could co-exist in a given region for several centuries.[34] While he himself is cautious about going further, it is easy to assume from this that big sites were the main settlement of a whole community, which continuously hunted out moa over a number of years and then moved on. This would imply that moa hunting was a socio-economy in itself, and would not fit well with the hunter-gardener model.

It is indeed very difficult to guess how moa were actually caught. When scholars first confronted the sheer mass of bones at the great hunting stations, they thought in terms of massive drives, perhaps using fire. Such moa ranching is now rightly seen as unlikely. But the alternative of hunting by individuals is not much better. Maori did not use the bow and arrow, and moa could outrun humans. Anderson suggests that Polynesian dogs, which developed powerful jaws in New Zealand, might have been used to physically catch moa. But the notion of these gallant fox-sized canines clinging to the ankle of a 200-kilogram bird is not very credible.[35] Dogs were no doubt used to find and drive moa – they could not bark but could cry – but they are much more likely to have developed their Hapsburg chins from eating tough moa scraps than from catching them.[36] Snaring and trapping is possible. Driving moa with dogs or fire towards hunters behind a natural obstacle and firebreak such as a river, where they could be despatched with clubs and lances, seems a likely hunting strategy. But it would have required two parties of hunters. There is also reason to believe that moa were often brought to the base camps in groups of around half a dozen. Bones often cluster (sometimes by species) in this number, and so do ovens.[37] These factors suggest one or more parties of a dozen or so hunters operating out of the station.

The moa breeding season – possibly late winter to early spring – may also have been the preferred hunting season.[38] If similar birds such as emu are anything to go by, male moa hatched the eggs and became torpid while doing so. Chicks stuck with their fathers.[39] The type of ground preferred for breeding was predictable, and torpid birds were easy prey. Even more important were the eggs. Eggshell is seldom very common at the stations; even moa eggs could break, and they could not be stored. But eggs were a natural food for hunting parties, as other birds' eggs served Maori travellers in the nineteenth century. They could not run away, they were high in energy value, and they required little, if any, preparation. Moa eggs could weigh up to seven kilograms – equivalent to a hundred hen eggs.[40] Thus moa hunting in the breeding season was virtually self-funding, and the moa population was attacked at both ends, eggs and fathers, hastening their decline.

All this also suggests that the best time for hunting was seasonally restricted, and that the best base camps for hunting moa were not the best places to live all year round. Anderson concedes that hunting stations were occupied temporarily and for a limited number of years. There is little evidence of permanent housing or of the full range of domestic artefacts. The huge kills at Waitaki were made by a series of temporary sojourners. The fact that they cached adzes suggests they were the same people, expecting to return successively. Recent dating exercises indicate that the Shag River mouth in Otago, long thought to be the likeliest example of a southern moa-hunting village, was only briefly occupied during the fourteenth century. At least 6,000 moa were killed there. Papatowai was visited only a few times during a 50-year period, but at least 7,000 moa were killed there.[41] A few hunting stations, such as the Wairau Bar, where about 9,000 moa met their doom, did become permanent villages, and it is perfectly possible that a hunting expedition might stay over several years, perhaps as a transition phase leading to the formation of a new colony. But seasonal work at the major meatworks appears to have been the norm, and this creamed off moa islands quite quickly.

Dogs also increased the yield from hunting, but even more importantly they were a means of storing moa protein. Dogs were more numerous in early prehistory than in late,[42] and it seems fair to assume that they multiplied while fed on the scraps of moa and seal hunts. One site in the Coromandel seems to have been a specialised dog abattoir. Little attention seems to have been paid to this or other forms of preserving moa and seal meat. An emphasis on storage does not fit well with the notion that most moa were consumed at the processing site. Yet Maori preserved every other type of food possible; voyaging required storage; potted birds were the most esteemed kind of food at contact. Smoking and drying meat in strips is possible and, with the emphasis on thigh meat, introduces the interesting concept of moa ham, but preservation in fat in taha and kelp bags was probably the major method. Such containers leave little trace, but there is a some indirect evidence of their use: beaked wooden vessels, perhaps for pouring fat, and a large pair of lined pits linked by a runnel, perhaps vats for rendering it.[43] Bones, of course, would seldom find their way into the storage containers. The absence of bone at non-hunting sites does not mean the absence of meat.

Some hunting stations show clear signs of considerable waste, and one expert writes of 'an orgy of hunting and eating'.[44] It is very difficult to believe, however, that hunters would go to the effort of catching moa *and* taking them back to the station, only to waste them. Waste seems more likely to have resulted from large kills – say two or three hunting parties returning simultaneously – and a desperate flurry of cooking and preservation before the meat went bad. The grouping of ovens, sometimes in double rows, back to back, also suggests mass cooking. Either the people at the station were feeding an army or they were cooking meat for storage as it came in. This meat could have been kept on the spot for lean times, or exported or taken home by canoe. Adzes at hunting stations were very often used for woodworking, and Anderson finds this something of a mystery.[45] But the repair and maintenance of canoes and their associated equipment might explain this. The likely organisation of hunting, its tendency to seasonal stations rather than once-only camps or permanent settlements, and its emphasis on storage and transport seem to fit the hunter-gardener model better than the alternatives.

It is sometimes said that moa hunting did not necessarily contribute a huge amount to the early Maori diet. Assuming that moa had a similar food value to turkey meat, on Anderson's calculations, one person living exclusively on moa would have required ten birds a year – about a kilogram of boned meat a day.[46] On this basis, it is true that the 50 moa consumed at Houhora, for example, would not have gone far to feed a group of 50 people over twelve years. But several other considerations support the importance of hunting. Our hypothesis assumes that gardening, gathering and fishing always contributed to overall diet, and archaeology confirms that, even while on hunting expeditions, hunters fished and gathered on the side. Meat, of course, can be an important staple without implying a totally carnivorous diet – 200 grams daily would meet protein requirements, even for growth, hard work and pregnancy. Dogs and eggs must have boosted the yield from moa hunting, perhaps very substantially. Above all, moa were not the sole targets of hunting. Other large birds were also hunted to extinction. Sealing very probably contributed more meat. Seals made up 60 per cent or more of the meat weights suggested by bones at many early prehistoric sites.[47] The moa kill at Houhora and other small sites was not huge but could have been much greater than 50, which represents the minimum number of distinct individuals whose bones were actually found, whereas the southern station bags are extrapolated total figures. Shag River's 6,000 or more moa, taken in a short occupation, must surely have been important to the diet of their hunters.

Stone survives even better than bone. Stone tools were constantly sharpened, frequently broken and discarded, or reworked into smaller tools, all of which produces stone fragments. Many of these can be attributed to a particular source, from which one can form an idea of the contacts of a particular site. The nature of the contact depends on the way the stone was used. Archaeologists have long agreed that Tuhua (Mayor Island) obsidian is very common in archaeological excavations spread around the whole country, especially in early sites. New sourcing technology has confirmed and re-emphasised this.[48] Five-sixths of the obsidian fragments at the Wairau Bar on Cook Strait, and two-thirds of those at Houhora in the Far North, for example, are from Tuhua.[49]

'Tuhua' is a Maori word for obsidian. This does not prove that Tuhua was the capital of early New Zealand, in constant contact with most other sites. Obsidian was taken in blocks and knives were flaked off as needed. A 48-kilogram Tuhua block was found at the Hurunui River in North Canterbury, almost 1,000 kilometres from its source.[50] Such a block might last a group for many years and does not necessarily indicate regular contact with Tuhua, or that Hurunui was a far-flung part of the first colony. But it does suggest that the occupants of Hurunui, and other early hunting sites where Tuhua obsidian is very common, had some contact with Tuhua or the colony of which it was part. The block must have been taken by canoe, probably directly – so large a block is unlikely to have been gifted from hand to hand by intermediaries. Either way, clearly Tuhua must have been discovered first.

Anderson, an advocate of rapid but unpatterned spread from a first settlement in the South Island, has to argue that early hunters had been *to* Tuhua rather than come *from* it. He accommodates the presence of Tuhua obsidian in so many southern and central sites by suggesting that 'all the main sources [of stone] were found within the first generation'.[51] If the South Island was settled first, only this can explain why North Island stone is found in the earliest southern sites, while the reverse is not the case. Anderson claims that Pakeha found the country's gold sources as quickly. In fact they took about a century, and then only with considerable Maori help. The first settlers were intrepid explorers, but they were not Joseph Banks, conducting expensive expeditions for fun and science. Exploration was funded by exploitation. The hunter dynamic driving settlement from first colonies in Northland and Coromandel, including Tuhua, better explains the early distribution of obsidian.

Because a large block of obsidian might last a group for years, fragments do not necessarily tell us much about regular interaction, or therefore the shape of colonies. Adzes, on the other hand, were very often made at or near the source of stone in early prehistory. A regular supply of adzes suggests regular contact. When the source is distant, intermediaries are lacking and closer sources of stone exist, close relations between site and source seem probable. We have seen that Coromandel and Northland had such links, and Tahanga adzes as well as Tuhua obsidian are widely distributed in early northern and central zone sites. In the central zone, the key adzes were made at or near the quarries from Nelson–D'Urville argillite, and are even more widespread. Fragments of this stone are common at many early sites – for example, in the earliest layers of the Waitaki Mouth moa-hunting site in North Otago, in Hawke's Bay and in sites in Westland.[52] It is particularly closely associated with moa hunting in the central region. Southland adze stone, from quarries near Bluff, is widespread in the southern zone, from Stewart Island to Waitaki – and in Fiordland and Westland, though these may reflect later contacts.[53]

The distribution of silcrete may also indicate hunting, even colonisation, from the southern zone – against the direction of our preconceptions. Silcrete was a unique southern knife stone around which an unusual technology developed, manufacturing large blades up to 30 centimetres long – probably for big-game butchering.[54] Because both the stone and the technology were restricted to the south, silcrete finds outside the area may indicate gift exchange, kin supply or expeditions by southern colonies. Finds at Wairau Bar and Palliser Bay may be explained by gift exchange, but blocks of silcrete found at the major hunting site of Kaupokonui in southern Taranaki suggest a direct voyage from the south.[55]

All this is not intended to suggest that the distribution of Coromandel, Nelson and Southland stone proves the size or centres of colonies. Stone islands were stable parts of colonies, but not necessarily their epicentres, because like game islands they could be exploited by seasonal expeditions. But it does seem to support the idea of three early sets of colonies, or at least indicate the exploitation of one district by people from another. Why else should people virtually sitting on local stone sources use Coromandel, Nelson and Southland stone instead?

Later in prehistory, there was an increasing tendency to rely on local stone for basic requirements. The most valued types of adze stone, with greenstone now prominent, continue to move but in a somewhat different way – as small blocks of raw material or adze-sized 'blanks' rather than finished products. Obsidian also kept moving, with Tuhua still prominent but with an increasing number of minor sources as well.[56] The switch from few to many sources may well reflect a shift from kin supply and direct visits to gift exchange through intermediaries. Multiple sources reduced dependence on a single supplier, and so weakened the links between stone producer and consumer.

There is also an incomplete but marked shift in the organisation of production. In the colonial era, adze manufacture was quite large in scale, even to the point of 'assembly line' production in huge quarries, especially in the Nelson–D'Urville mineral belt. This implies that stoneworkers specialised to some degree, perhaps relying on others for their food at certain times, and that consumers in turn relied on them for finished or near-finished adzes. This in turn may imply a close relationship, more kin supply than gift exchange. In late prehistory, less stone was imported and this came in raw blocks, not finished products. 'By the 15th–16th centuries,' writes Helen Leach, 'the era of the great quarry-workshop complex was over.'[57] Changes in the production and distribution of stone were coupled with changes in styles and methods, not only in stonework but in material culture in general.

Several schemes for periodising prehistory, often according to material culture, have been suggested. Most are binary: Moriori and Maori, Moa-hunter and Maori, East Polynesian and Maori, Archaic and Classical. We have already dismissed the first. The second and third are quite reasonable but forget about seals and, on the chronology we are using, delay the transformation of East

Polynesians into Maori unacceptably long. The problem with the fourth, apart from an increasing tendency for 'Archaic' to hint at 'hidebound' in common usage, is that 'Classical' implies a period by which Maori should be classed. But they were not necessarily any less Maori before or after the 'Classical' era. Davidson offers a three-part scheme: Settlement (about 800–1200), Rapid Expansion and Change (1200–1500) and Traditional (1500–1800).[58] It is argued here that her 'Settlement' period scarcely exists, and to the extent that it does is hardly distinguishable from 'Rapid Expansion'. 'Traditional' seems dangerously similar to 'Classical'.

None of these schemes is entirely satisfactory, and, more importantly, none explains much in themselves. Yet they do have some substance. Most archaeological speculations about big shifts from 'Archaic' to 'Classical' are based on real changes in artefact styles, and they tend to centre on a turning point around the fifteenth century. But these shifts vary according to different kinds of tools and ornaments, mostly of stone and bone. They are not consistent across the whole country but occur at different times in different regions. The shifts are also very incomplete: examples of 'Classical' styles and techniques are found in 'Archaic' sites, and vice versa.

Perhaps the hunter-gardener distinction can help explain both these broad shifts and their diverse and partial nature. Hunters had ready access to large quantities of stone, and a heavy and specialised demand for it. They had the means and the motives to use expensive but speedy and effective production techniques. Their artefacts might correlate with those known as 'Archaic', in some respects technically superior to 'Classical', in other respects less rich and sophisticated. As hunting declined, so did the associated material culture, with a corresponding rise of 'Classical' styles and techniques that might be correlated with gardening. Because most early colonies carried out both activities in varying proportions, the two trends in material culture were often a matter of emphasis rather than exclusive use of one or the other – hence the incomplete and varied nature of the change.

Hunting and gardening could also help explain specific regional variations. The most hunting-oriented region of all was the southern zone, rich in stone and game, but bereft of gardens. The earliest gardening-oriented area may have been around East Cape in the northern zone, which was poor in game and stone but rich in gardening islands and marine resources. These are in fact the two areas most often cited as being especially different in material culture. This is sometimes explained in terms of multiple settlement. But their early emergence as single-activity colonies could also explain it. There is an obvious danger of oversimplification here, and it needs to be noted that 'hunter-Archaic' and 'gardener-Classical' material cultures were not two frozen sets of artefact styles but trajectories of development that were diverse within themselves. Yet the hunter-gardener model may be a better way of understanding some differences and changes in style, as well as the patterns of bone and stone, than existing hypotheses. Let us turn now from style to story: the way Maori themselves perceived the early period of their history.

Story

As noted in the last chapter, the application of 'soft' and early Maori traditions to empirical history is a dangerous game – for experts, let alone general historians. The Smithians made some monumental gaffes. Yet a general history of New Zealand should not ignore the Maori conception of their own far past, nor banish it to a romantic, wholly mythical prologue – both customary approaches. The following analysis accepts the risk of error and asks how well the patterns of Maori legend fit both the hunter-gardener thesis and the case for a single foundation made in the previous chapter.

UnSmithed, the origin legends of the various Maori tribes at first present a bewildering diversity.[59] The first seaborne explorations were made by the famous Kupe, by Ngahue, by Tamatea, by none of these or by all three. Some Maori traditions – not just Smith – were adamant that Kupe predated all, making islands as well as finding them in his canoe, *Matahourua.*[60] Others put Kupe in a later canoe, diminish his role or neglect him altogether. Many deified ancestors explored overland, naming places as they went – mapping and claiming regions that sometimes intersected. Like Kupe, the great Arawa tohunga Ngatoroirangi and others sometimes made as well as mapped. Paoa urinated several rivers into being.[61]

The canoes most often referred to were Smith's seven. But at least twenty others are mentioned in various traditions, and Maori historians in the mid-nineteenth century referred to 'many others' whose names had been forgotten even then. Many canoes turned into stone or other landmarks, physical reminders of origins and assertions of ownership. Canoes were not the only form of transport. Some founding ancestors scorned mundane vehicles and came from Hawaiki on taniwha (water monsters), giant birds, whales, rainbows or floats of wood, gourds or pumice propelled by magic. Others had no need to make voyages at all but emerged from the New Zealand soil. If these were simply tribal variations, doing justice to more than one tribe would be difficult enough, but some single tribes claim multiple origins. Ngati Porou originated in all three ways – canoe voyage, magic voyage and local emergence – while one early list puts Ngati Ruanui on ten canoes.[62] We can neither dismiss all this nor easily accept specific versions as accurate, or as more authentic than others. We must look for patterns.

A basic core of these traditions is shared with tropical Polynesia. Toi and Whatonga are known in the Cook Islands, where the word 'toi' is associated with 'original inhabitant', and a very similar figure appears in Hawaiian legend.

Kupe has somewhat less certain echoes in the Marquesas and Tuamotus. Tamatea appears in Tahitian legend.[63] The same is true of other captains, and may be true of their canoes.

About 1897, S. Percy Smith himself visited Rarotonga, whence the elder Taramua Oremetua listed six canoes as having departed for New Zealand. His list conformed to Smith's 'Great Fleet', leaving out only the *Aotea*.[64] There are various possible explanations, and we should concede that Smith being right after all is one – although in his excitement at Taramua's revelations Smith forgot to ask where this fleet came from. A single reverse migration to the Cook Islands from New Zealand during the last phase of hunter expansion, perhaps by people with *Takitimu* associations, is a little more likely. Taramua maintained, in contrast to Maori traditions, that the *Takitimu* had returned to the Cooks. A later reunion of New Zealand and tropical Polynesian tradition is more likely still. Cooks and New Zealand Maori were in contact, through European ships, from the early nineteenth century; they recognised their kinship and exchanged historical notes. Taramua's account includes some information that was almost certainly obtained in this way. But it is also true that *Mataatua*, one of the seven founding canoes, was the ancient name of a Cook Island kin group, and that the sharing of core traditions extended far beyond the Cooks. Perhaps the most likely explanation of all is that both canoes like *Takitimu* and captains like Tamatea were ancient archetypal legends drawn from tropical Polynesia – old names of orally transmitted books into which the new was bound.

As Roger Duff has suggested, the core canoes may have come to New Zealand as 'concepts not convoys'.[65] The ancient names may have been regularly applied to new canoes, or more probably to descent groups of people. This is made explicit in some stories of one canoe, *Kurahaupo*, whose 'name' was brought in another canoe.[66] Canoes were not just the vehicle but also a natural social unit for expanding Polynesians – the ship is conceptually as well as physically important in the ethos of expansion, across cultures. Polynesian social organisation, of course, was centred around kinship. But even when migrants were drawn from a single broad kin group, some went and some stayed, and the migration must have reshuffled families. Migration might also have interrupted the memory of whakapapa, which, as we have seen, had their limits anyway. Canoe crews could act as packages of ancestors, actual or potential collective identities. This is common enough even in recent Maori usage; the canoe and the group tracing descent from it are used as synonyms, waka tangata, as in Tainui and Te Arawa.

The existence of a half-dozen group identities in the cultural baggage brought from Hawaiki does not indicate against a single founding settlement. One or two hundred Maori could easily accommodate this many subdivisions, which might have been more potential than actual. Maori kin groups could retrospectively align themselves to different elements of a shared past as they split up – and sometimes rejoin their pasts if reunification was required in the present. One simply emphasised a different ancestor or a different ancestral canoe if a separate group identity was required. Moreover, there are strong signs of a period of shared experience in the traditions of the core canoes. Different canoe legends are separate in Hawaiki and separate in Aotearoa, but funnel through a phase of strong similarity at the cusp between the two: the founding migration and the very first settlement.

The grouping of the core canoes is not purely Smithian invention – some are associated together in clearly pre-Smithian Maori tradition.[67] This does not mean they were seen as a fleet – the canoes are usually said to have been built together in Hawaiki rather than to have sailed or landed together – but it does imply some sort of packaging. Virtually all are said to have made initial landfall at Whangaparaoa, named for a beached sperm whale encountered there. It does not matter whether the whale was real, well-remembered manna from heaven for starving voyagers, or a 'symbol of abundance' as Orbell suggests.[68] It was a *shared* whale or symbol. Most crews saw pohutukawa or rata flowers in bloom, mistook them for valued red feathers and cast away the real thing before discovering their mistake. Each canoe contained a wise woman who preserved her kumara tubers with great care, while others ate or neglected theirs – she was Rongorongo in the *Aotea*, Whakaotirangi in no fewer than five others. Some notable crew members are shared by more than one canoe, and there are other strong convergences – regarding the circumstances of departure from Hawaiki, for example. Most core canoes visit the Far North; one legend speaks of all but one being built there, and of all Maori being descended from its crew. But it is unwise to push this type of analysis too far into specifics. The main point is that the convergence of canoe legends supports a single foundation, while their divergence hints that this consisted of several actual or potential groups.

One could posit three phases in myth that conform to phases in history: Hawaikian, colonial and tribal. In the first, 'Hawaikian' phase of departure, voyage out and initial settlement, canoe names/group identities are brought, packed tight, from a single Hawaiki by a single expedition. After a period as one founding community, identities are unpacked as colonial splits occur. The third phase, which dominates the traditions that have come down to us, is largely determined by the needs of particular tribes for identity, for links with and distinctions from other tribes, and for claims to land and mana. Genealogy dates the beginning of this phase of myth to middle prehistory, the fifteenth and sixteenth centuries. Our hunter-gardener thesis, the archaeological record and students of art and tradition all agree that this was a period of change. During it, perhaps, pre-existing group identities were reshuffled into the modern tribes or their immediate predecessors. Whakapapa from this period, as we have seen, are among the harder parts of Maori tradition, resistant though not immune to change. Most tribal genealogies go back between twelve and 22 generations – say, three to five centuries – from about 1900 to one or two key founding ancestors. Tribal tradition then reaches back to the Hawaikian phase, linking the tribe to acts of foundation but leaving out, telescoping or very selectively remembering the period in between: the 'colonial' era of the hunter-gardeners.

Links with ancient canoes and captains gave continuity and completion to tribal history, claimed appropriate bonds and distinctions, and asserted prior right. But they were not necessarily ideal for this last purpose. An ancestor who came from Hawaiki by magic could pre-empt a canoe, and be in turn pre-empted by one who sprang from the local soil, just as naming could be pre-empted by adjusting or even making the landscape. There were many canoes that were not Hawaikian, and many elements of the core canoe traditions that were not either. Mythical origins, and real colonisations from within New Zealand during the hunter-gardener era, may have been selectively remembered in the tribal phase for tribal purposes and fused with Hawaikian origin legends. Tribal tradition incorporated and transformed colonial, just as colonial had presumably done with Hawaikian. Each telescoped its predecessor in time, a well-known characteristic of orally transmitted tradition. Less relevant time was compressed to help join two more relevant times. Tribal history subsumes colonial history, but like the stones, bones and styles of the hunters, some vestiges of the latter may survive.

The stories of Tamatea, Ngahue and Kupe, for example, could tentatively be associated with explorations of the central and southern zones. Tamatea explores the Deep South along with the rest of the country, and is associated with great fires in that region. Ngahue is closely linked with greenstone, and is said to have preserved moa flesh in a taha, then taken it home, together with news of an abundant southern land. Kupe's greatest importance is in the traditions and place-names of Raukawa, the Cook Strait area,[69] perhaps reflecting actual early naming journeys from northern New Zealand, linked back to the tropical Polynesian Kupe archetype and, later, forward to the tribes of central Aotearoa. Toi is aligned with early settlers in a number of regions, especially on the east coast of the North Island.[70] Toi and his peoples, Te Tini o Toi, survived for a period on gathered foods and made voyages to 'Hawaiki' for kumara, rather like hunters running out of game and making an early adjustment to gardening.

Most canoe traditions contain this contradiction: settlement is made by original canoes from Hawaiki, whose crews nevertheless find settlers already in place. The general impression is of secondary colonisation, from within New Zealand, but fused in memory with older, Hawaikian migration legends. As Ranginui Walker has observed, there is seldom said to be fighting between first-comers and late-comers for the first few generations of secondary colonisation.[71] This accords with a contraction or reunification of early colonies –

hunter expeditions and hunter-oriented semi-independent colonies rejoining gardener-oriented kin. As population grew, friction developed and new tribal identities formed in opposition to each other, sometimes separating their pasts as well as their presents. Apirana Ngata noted the 'scant whakapapa' on the East Coast relating to the early settlement period. 'I suspect that the . . . experts expurgated them . . . The lines are laid right back to Hawaiki. Women that I supposed from other evidence were bred in Aotearoa appear on [tropical Polynesian] island groups and marry men who later take part in a migration.'[72]

Another possible legacy of the colonial phase is the broad distinction between single and multiple tribal origins. In the former case, many tribes with contiguous territories spring from a single canoe and its single main settlement. Tainui and Te Arawa are the most obvious examples. Each first touches at various places, presented as a single initial voyage in tradition, but perhaps reflecting the compression of a remote past, which it is tempting to associate with hunting. Each then establishes a single coastal settlement, at Maketu in the east for Te Arawa, and Kawhia in the west for Tainui. This may represent a successful adjustment to gardening, fishing and gathering. Each finds good garden land and other resources inland, then expands overland, splitting into tribes as it does so but retaining a strong sense of shared canoe origins.

Other tribes affiliate more loosely to their canoes, emphasise more than one, and often even couple these with non-canoe origins. This may reflect a different sort of adjustment to the decline of hunting, emphasising the merging or reintegration of groups rather than expansion into unpeopled inland areas. Expansion featured largest in the west and the interior; reintegration on the East Coast. To quote Ngata, himself from the East Coast: 'Our people here never set much store by Horouta or Takitimu or any of the historical migrators. Our land titles go back to Toi – our history [is] the gradual absorption of later arrivals . . . these were clearly related to the older stock, so the whakapapas say, and rejuvenated the old blood.'[73]

These reflections on the Kupe class of early explorers, secondary colonisation and the distinction between single and multiple origins are merely illustrative speculations. The analysis of myth structure is one context where the general is safer than the particular. Colonial Maori, like all other peoples in all other times, adjusted their past for the purposes of their present. This was in turn adjusted to serve the new purposes of a new tribal present. The guess is that colonial Maori collective identities centred around actual or archetypal Hawaikian canoes or canoe groups. These diverged in Hawaiki, converged in the founding settlement, then diverged again as the hunter-gardeners spread and split. As hunting ended, tradition was redeployed, compressed, adapted and discarded to match the social reshuffling of tribe formation.

We have still to consider the forgotten dimension of myth: the future. In tribal tradition, the canoe legends were used to emphasise claims to land, courage in war, living enmities and the bonds between kin. By showing how ancestors had acted, they taught descendants how to act. Martial renditions of Anglo-Saxon mythology taught raw English and Pakeha recruits precisely the same lesson as they trembled on their first battlefield. Such were the future uses of myths of origin. But in the colonial Maori era, it is suggested, the canoe legends were part of a somewhat different ethos – that of expansion. They told people when and how to expand, and encouraged them to do so. They functioned as myths of *settlement* as well as myths of origin.

Hawaiki may have been goal as well as source, Promised Land as well as Paradise Lost. Savai'i in Samoa, Havai'i (Raiatea) in the Society Islands, and Hawai'i were all named for it. Parts, perhaps even the whole, of New Zealand were also originally named Hawaiki. Tikao claimed that new lands were usually named Hawaiki.[74] The stories of departure from Hawaiki could be interpreted as cultural signals for migration as well as records of it. They stress pressure on garden land and the horrors of warfare between kin, notably the 'great crime': eating one's relatives.[75]

This warfare is an intermittent background pressure; actual migration is usually preceded by temporary peace. One cannot mount an expensive, fully equipped migration in the actual midst of war or famine. The trick, tradition instructs, is to predict these things and leave before them. Tales of the archetypal shipwrights Rata and Toto tell how the great canoes have been/are to be built. The heavy emphasis on the need for able tohunga-experts, whose mana often equals or exceeds the canoe captains, makes it clear that physical and metaphysical skills are crucial in so great an enterprise. So much is Hawaikian; but even in their vestigial form it is clear that canoe myths of departure were adapted to the new frontier, to colonising within or from New Zealand.

The stress on the need to preserve kumara is one example. Kumara was the most important crop in New Zealand, not tropical Polynesia. An Aotea chant combined reference to the Hawaikian origin of kumara with instructions on mound cultivation.[76] Voyage traditions also gave karakia and instructions for the preparation of cabbage tree and fernroot.[77] Tropical plants that failed to acclimatise are seldom mentioned, and pigs and chickens almost never. The prominence of New Zealand plants and animals in the canoe inventories, noted by Simmons and others, is also important evidence of colonial pages bound into Hawaikian books. Many are mentioned, with karaka among the most regular and prominent. Karaka kernels were a poor replacement for the great tree crops of tropical Polynesia, but they were quite important. One early French explorer compared their niche to that of olives in the Mediterranean.[78] Bay of Plenty tradition held that hue gourds were introduced long before any other plants, as we might expect if hunters' requirements initially dominated new gardening settlements.[79] Normally, hue are listed along with kumara, but not as prominently. This could reflect the tribal overlay, as could a tendency to emphasise single-hulled canoes. But where double canoes had some specific function, such as providing the deckhouse on which Ngatoroirangi sat to quell a storm, they were remembered. Similar indirect survival occurred with tropical plants and animals that failed to acclimatise but are remembered in names given to somewhat similar New Zealand ones.[80]

Greenstone is another New Zealand product emphasised in most traditions. Many canoes are said to have been built with tools made of it, implying the binding of Aotearoa pages into Hawaikian books. Greenstone, harder than iron, was the best of all adze stones. As mentioned above with regard to Ngahue, this may indicate exploration and exploitation of the South Island from the North. It also suggests that even the vestiges of the myths of settlement date from the later part of the colonial period, when greenstone was coming into wider use. These myths of settlement, perhaps, were the centrepiece of the ethos of expansion, steering Maori colonisation within New Zealand just as hunting powered it and gardening anchored it.

Agriculture is often seen as a prerequisite of social and cultural complexity, providing the controllable surplus that breeds hierarchy and specialisation, and thereby political and technological development. The prehistory of the southern Californian seaboard, for example, suggests this is not true, and on our hunter-gardener scenario the early history of New Zealand supports this.[81] Wild foods, if sufficiently abundant and harvested, stored and transported efficiently, can also produce a surplus and a complex and impressive culture, more volatile and less cumulative than sedentary gardeners, but perhaps also more dynamic. New Zealand's earliest culture was exceptionally mobile. Discovery was not instant, but it was awesomely rapid – the first settlers pursued their preferred prey and their most valued raw materials from Far North to Deep South within a century or so. Colonisation became an increasingly frenetic game of musical chairs, played to the tune of the ethos of expansion.

The first round saw colonies formed in the full sets of premium resource islands. In the next, 'back filling' occupied game and garden islands around the whole coast. The exhaustion of moa and breeding seals then removed many chairs, but not before their protein had greatly expanded the population. Colonisation now pushed inland and squeezed up in garden islands, generating further traumatic transformations discussed in the next chapter, as well as the tribalising of colonial myth. Some made the adjustment from hunting and colonising less readily than others. They were not necessarily the losers in the game of musical chairs but perhaps those most addicted to winning. These diehard hunters, perhaps from the southern zone, searched hardest for the last game islands, ricocheting around Aotearoa until they shot off into the unknown. Behind them, in and around the fifteenth century, the colonising hunter-gardener era ended and the tribal gardener-gatherer era began.

Might we see in this a general explanation for the beginning and end of Polynesian long-range voyaging and colonisation? Many Pacific islands originally contained quite large and vulnerable birds, turtles and sea mammals.[82] Hunters could have spread fast through one island group, or through several contiguous ones, rejoining their gardeners when the game declined or founding new colonies by back filling or striking out into the ocean. They were taught how to do so by their ethos of expansion and myths of settlement – in particular, to pack their canoes with plants and gardening technology as insurance against the demise of game. The ethos stated that new lands had always been found in the past, and therefore would be in the future. Failed migrations told no tales. Hunting, voyaging skills and expansion fed on each other. In the old island group, voyaging declined with the demise of hunting, to the relatively modest level encountered by the first European explorers, and colonisation ended. In the new group, if canoe timber permitted, the cycle repeated itself while the game lasted.

Colonisation *from* New Zealand did indeed take place. One possibility is Norfolk Island, about a thousand kilometres to the north-west, later annexed by mistake to Australia. There is some archaeological evidence of a Polynesian settlement of Norfolk, such as the remains of kiore, and Irwin suggests it may have been from New Zealand.[83] Furthermore, in the 1790s fragments of two old Maori canoes were also found there, together with 'a wooden figure (very rudely carved)'.[84] Maori colonists may also have settled the Kermadec Islands, a thousand kilometres to the north-east, where karaka trees are found. The archaeological remains here were thought to represent long settlement, possibly direct from tropical Polynesia. But subsequent work suggests that settlement was quite brief, dated to about the fourteenth century and derived from New Zealand – Tuhua obsidian again.[85] The Kermadec artefacts are stylistically very similar to those of southern New Zealand. These islands were small; their game could not have lasted long, and a gardening economy may not have seemed viable. Their inhabitants remigrated and were lost at sea or found their way somewhere else. Direct reverse migration to New Zealand, and indirect reverse migration to tropical Polynesia, are immensely intriguing but not immensely important possibilities.

New Zealand's third Pacific colony was the Chatham Islands, 860 kilometres to the east. Sutton dates their settlement to AD 800–1000, but other experts are adamant about the fifteenth century or even later, and existing evidence seems to support them.[86] Moriori legend, recorded by Maori not Pakeha, tells of a departure from the South Island in mid-prehistory, in one migration of several canoes. 'Their atua [god] told them that there was land to the east and they went and peopled it.'[87] The Chathams were rich in seabirds, fish and seals. These settlers rapidly expanded to a population of about 2,000. Some species of groundbirds were exterminated, but the absence of canoe timber eliminated the possibility of hunter-driven expansion. The settlers made the transition from extractive to sustainable economics, uncontrolled to controlled hunting, despite the absence of gardens. Even in their reed rafts, they made voyages of up to 70 kilometres over hostile seas to harvest fifteen-kilogram albatross fledglings from the outlying islets.[88] As in early New Zealand, their main settlements closely followed the distribution of seal rookeries, which were the main source of food,[89] and, as in New Zealand, the original colonial collective identity was unpacked into seven groups. Far from the little dark people of Pakeha myth, they were physically 'the most Polynesian of Polynesians'.[90] There they sat, the Moriori of the Chatham Islands, trapped by the lack of canoe timber, but the vanguard, not the rearguard, of Polynesian expansion.

CHAPTER THREE

The Rise of the Tribes

In Chapter One, we noted the tendency of European ethnography to assume that non-European peoples were static, unchanging. The myth of the frozen Maori is still with us, swallowed and used in different ways, by both Maori and Pakeha. Maori traditional practices, for example, are often considered fixed. Something is either traditional or it is not – such as the custom among some tribes that women are not allowed to speak on the marae, the tapu assembly place of the Maori village. The Pakeha fallacy is that this custom can be changed from the outside. The Maori fallacy is that it cannot be changed from the inside. The delusion that traditional practices cannot be changed without reducing 'Maoriness', like the term 'Classical', buys into the European ethnographic myth that freezes Maori culture and society around 1769.

Chapter Two sought, however inexpertly, to put change back into early Maori pre-contact history. This chapter carries the task to late pre-contact history. Early New Zealand prehistory and late were linked yet separated by the crisis in the middle, centred around the fifteenth century. The crisis stemmed from a simple physical fact: the progressive extinction of big game in region after region. To surmount this crisis, Maori transformed their economy, their politics, including warfare, and their social organisation. These three transformations are the foci of this chapter.

The Sophisticated Economics of the New Zealand Maori

The demise of big game left Maori communities with more mouths than they could feed in the customary way. The crisis hit different colonies at different times, between the fourteenth and sixteenth centuries, and they responded in varying ways and with varying success. Some starved. 'Harris lines' in skeletons, indicating seasonal famine during bone growth, appeared in people such as the fifteenth-century inhabitants of Palliser Bay. Some migrated, expanding into unpeopled or thinly peopled inland and western areas, or rejoining kin in the east and north. Others sought a larger share of existing fishing, gathering and gardening resources through warfare, discussed below. But perhaps the most common and successful response was to extend and intensify the remaining types of production.

Some writers give the impression that Aotearoa was a slimmer's nightmare: teeming fish and flocks of fat birds flinging themselves into the oven, while nature's crops of fruits and roots sat up for the plucking to the point where they impeded bush travel. This 'myth of natural abundance' also features large in Pakeha history, and that of other new societies. Dropping its advocates, foodless, into the bush in winter for a week would soon cure any survivors. Early European explorers sometimes made the opposite error of assuming parts of New Zealand were a slimmer's paradise, yielding only fish, if that. The truth was that times and places of abundance did exist, but that they were limited. An all-year-round living could be wrested from New Zealand nature, even in the absence of game or gardens, but it took immense effort and organisation, aimed at a wide range of targets.[1]

In the 'gathering islands', at least 40 wild plant species were used for food, including a dozen types of drupes, fruits and berries, such as hinau, tawa and miro, various greens such as puha or sowthistle, the hearts of nikau palms, the roots of perei, the shoots of speargrass, the stems of katote, and the bracts of kiekie. Honey was taken from flax, cakes were made from raupo pollen, and a drink was made from tutu berries – the sealer John Boultbee enjoyed it by the litre in the 1820s.[2] Other major plant foods were karaka, mentioned above; mamaku or tree fern, whose pith early explorers variously compared to mashed potato, turnip and sago; four species of cabbage tree; and, of course, fernroot.

Apart from the 30 species killed off by late prehistory, birds ranging from tiny native quails to fifteen-kilogram albatross fledglings were eaten. Targets included forest birds such as pigeon, parakeet, tui, kaka and many others; groundbirds such as kiwi, weka and kakapo; waterbirds such as duck; and various seabirds. Maori also ate rats and huhu grubs. They ate tuatara, the famous 'living fossil', but seldom the smaller true lizards – 40 species of gecko and skink, which were believed to have demonic qualities. They ate some fungi and a type of seaweed known as karengo, which was valued, preserved and gifted far inland.[3]

'Fishing islands' were also important. Inland waters provided eels and freshwater crayfish and mussels, and a dozen species of freshwater fish such as kokopu or 'native trout', grayling, whitebait and lamprey – like the English king, some Taranaki Maori are said to have feasted themselves to death on the last-named delicacy. Marine fishing specialised in snapper in the north and barracouta in the south, but shark, kahawai, tarakahi, cod and various flatfish were also important. The range extended from great groper to strange hagfish, plus small wrasses such as parrotfish when times were tough. Seals and their relatives were still taken – rarely except in the Deep South. Dolphins and perhaps blackfish (pilot whales) were sometimes harpooned at sea or driven ashore;

and larger whales were eaten if they beached themselves. A score of species of shellfish, crustaceans, and marine creatures such as kina, or sea-eggs, completes the inventory. Aboriginal foods are undergoing something of a renaissance in avant-garde Australian restaurants. If the same thing happens in New Zealand, the full menu might include two or three hundred different species of plants and animals. Almost nothing edible was neglected.

This vast range demonstrates a comprehensive exploitation of nature, which can only have developed fully over time. But range is not abundance or profitability, and range was not in itself a solution to overpopulation and the demise of big game. Some plant foods were regionally restricted or widely but sparsely distributed; others were poisonous in their raw state, and in many cases only small parts were edible, even after complicated processing. Even fernroot, sometimes said to be ubiquitous, was unavailable in good quality and quantity in some regions. Forest birds were often difficult to catch because Maori had no really effective projectile weapons; they were much easier prey for people armed with fowling guns. Birds were not always very abundant anyway – New Zealand beech forest supports only 40 per cent of the bird population of Danish forest.[4] Food values and the return for effort expended were often low – an adult surviving on cabbage-tree pith alone would have to eat 18.8 kilograms daily, a daunting prospect.[5] Shellfish were an important item of diet, but their role as a staple can be exaggerated, because by definition they yielded far more archaeological evidence than they did food.

One way of maximising production from gathering was to use human knowledge and technique to make nature more bountiful. Forest birds were taken when fat and flightless, when their favourite berries were in fullest flower and when numbed with cold on frosty nights. Rats, creatures of habit, were trapped at night on their customary trails. Toxic and almost inedible plant foods were made to yield something: poisonous tutu berries were washed and rewashed, then carefully strained through special finely woven bags; fernroot was dried for two weeks, then baked and pounded; mamaku pith, cabbage-tree roots and karaka kernels had to be cooked continuously for a day or two. Fowling often required quite specialised and sophisticated equipment, as indicated in the saying 'You cannot make yourself a bird spear as you go'.[6]

The picture of gathering as an ad hoc, hand-to-mouth activity is false, for New Zealand at least. One could rarely pluck and eat in the New Zealand bush; exploiting 'nature's bounty' was a matter of foreknowledge, planning and complex processing. Few groups ever survived on gathering alone – even Best's Tuhoe had garden lands until the nineteenth century,[7] and the wide interior of the southern zone was mainly exploited by visits from the coast. Another way of intensifying and extending production can perhaps be understood as the application of hunter-like organisation and techniques.

Although the archaeological evidence is seldom conclusive, one gets the impression that the mass collection of certain smaller creatures came to partially replace big game, and that it had some hunter-like characteristics. Large-scale marine fishing was most important, but there were also colony-breeding seabirds such as muttonbirds, small groundbirds such as weka, plus eels and, to a lesser extent, freshwater mussels. Most or all had always been taken by Maori, big-game hunters included. But the emphasis on, and valuation of, these foods seems to have increased over time, and the organisation of production came to echo hunting methods.

Fishing seems to have increased in importance from mid-prehistory, and became more hunter-like in method and scale. In the south, something akin to 'fishing stations' emerged. At Purakanui, a fourteenth-century site on the Otago coast, 230,000 fish were caught in three visits within a few years. These represent 89 per cent of the total food obtained there – 400 tonnes on one estimate[8] – and fishing at this and other southern sites specialised heavily in barracouta, caught by trolling from squadrons of canoes.[9] In the north, which tended to specialise in snapper and shark, many eighteenth- and nineteenth-century examples of fishing using traditional methods indicate huge scale and yield. In one famous case at Rangaunu Harbour in the Far North in 1855, 50 canoes containing 1,000 workers caught 7,000 small sharks in two days. The canoes co-operated, fishing the place at the same time under joint leadership and making joint preparations for preservation on shore. But they also competed – for the first fish and the largest catch. Fishing with vast seine nets up to two kilometres in length was at least equally significant. At Maketu in 1886, such a net obtained about 40,000 fish in one day. The net took a whole community an entire winter to make, and was carried out on a platform lashed between two canoes crewed by 30 people, under the direction of a tohunga.[10]

The mass capture of eels, weka and muttonbirds shows up rarely in the middens, early or late. This could be a matter of the poor survival of fragile bones, or of processing away from settlements. All three creatures were important for food in the nineteenth century, when each was taken by the tonne, and there is good reason to believe this was no sudden development – the existence of numerous Maori words for eel, for example, suggests established importance. Tradition hints that snake-like eels may once have had demonic associations,[11] like lizards, and it could be that these were overcome when the demise of big game demanded it. Weka and muttonbirds no doubt seemed paltry targets when compared with moa or seal; by contact, however, gourd casks and kelp bags of them, preserved in their own fat, were the most esteemed foods of all.[12] In one traditional story, freshwater mussels were considered a mean gift, yet by contact they were highly valued, preserved and gifted over considerable distances.[13]

Eeling was often a substantial operation, sometimes involving large weirs, dams and canals, with annual mass collection by considerable groups of workers at prime times and places. Catches in the southern Wairarapa were said to total up to 30 tonnes.[14] Even the collection of mussels could be quite large in scale, with several canoes, using big dredge rakes, combing the prime part of a lake in the prime season, both co-operating and competing.[15] In the south, weka were taken in large numbers in the interior, with the help of dogs, by substantial seasonal hunting parties. Muttonbirds were also taken seasonally, on the offshore islands of Foveaux Strait, by even larger, canoe-borne expeditions involving hundreds of people. Packed in kelp bags, they were supplied to kin as far north as Banks Peninsula, and gifted as far north as Taranaki.[16]

These activities were all major seasonal enterprises involving large groups and complex collective work. Some required substantial expeditions and the use and reuse of base camps on the appropriate 'islands'. Huge catches were made in short periods, leading to an organised frenzy of processing and preservation for which preparations had been made beforehand. Europeans at contact were struck by storage techniques. 'No people can be more provident or industrious than the New Zealanders in supplying themselves with stores of provisions.'[17] They also noted the high valuation Maori placed on rarely available whale and seal meat and fat.[18]

All this echoed hunting. Other features may throw some light on hunting in retrospect. Competition between individual workers and teams was important, but was contained within a wider co-operation, often under a single expert leader. There was a balance between food taken to mouths and mouths taken to food – most of a community might spend the appropriate season at a fishing or muttonbirding village. One could therefore have a single base settlement, from which gathering and fishing forays were made, or several co-equal settlements, each for a particular part of the year and a particular set of economic activities. Both options fell well short of true nomadism, and the preservation of food remained crucial. Except in the thinly populated south, where seals may have remained significant and gardening was not possible, communities shrank in territorial breadth and big-game hunting disappeared. Its methods, perhaps, did not.

A continued emphasis on travel and culturally transmitted expertise was also reminiscent of hunting but shifted emphasis towards the interior. Ocean voyaging and double canoes did not entirely disappear – there were voyages between Taranaki and Westland, for example, in late prehistory. But coast-bound and river travel by single-hulled canoes over shorter distances became much more common. So, too, did overland travel – a complex equation because bush foods were only reliable at very specific places and times, and many required long processing. There was no point in a foraging expedition that used up more calories than it brought back. These problems were minimised by preparation and foreknowledge. Routes were a series of localities a short march apart, where quickly caught and processed food such as freshwater crayfish or birds' eggs could be obtained. They were remembered as travellers' tales or oral maps, whose place-names described resource localities. They were sometimes prepared in advance by leaving crude canoes or rafts at riverbanks, by making steps or ladders on cliffs, by planting karaka groves at camp sites, and even by burning off dense obstructing bush. If suitable stakes for shelters were rare en route, you took a couple with you. If the trip was made by a group large enough to reduce the route's food supply, the return trip was made by a different route.[19]

This network of resource localities linked by routes was only available to those who knew its secrets; the people of the land could always obtain more from it than outsiders, and this may have reinforced the bonds of particular groups with particular areas. The network linked and expanded gathering and other islands, and gave access to inland goods valuable enough to be worth transporting overland, such as esteemed foods and premium stone. The archipelago thickened inland, to the point where many of its islands joined up. There was a matching, though incomplete, shift from supplying kin, and from distant expeditions to get things for yourself, to gift exchange and the acquisition of distant goods through intermediaries. Tribes had narrower ranges than colonies, though gift exchange and other networks meant their zones of interaction were still quite substantial.

Gardening also extended and intensified in mid-prehistory. Some marginal garden settlements in the central region may have collapsed as kin supply from hunters faded away, but coastal gardening colonies expanded in the east, formed in the west and moved inland from both as they lumped and split into tribes. Such movements combined with developing technique to broaden the definition of gardening islands: coastal hillside and alluvial gardens were now joined by gardens in inland river valleys and terraces, even flood plains, sometimes drained by ditches. Substantial areas of made soils have been found in many parts of the country – 400 hectares at Tasman Bay, Nelson, for example.[20] The largest concentration – 4,000 hectares – is around the Waikato River.

Volcanic loams also became important. A dozen patches of such soils, totalling 900 hectares, exist inland of the Bay of Islands in Northland. In early prehistory, this was part of the 'Archaic Gap', but people had moved in and begun cultivating around the fifteenth century.[21] Sometimes large volcanic cones were artificially terraced, as at present-day Auckland. It was once thought that these engineering feats indicated giant fortifications, but archaeologists now believe that most terraces were for living, storage and gardening, with fortified citadels restricted to the topmost levels.[22] Gardens were sometimes sheltered from the wind by manuka screens or stone walls, which also served as boundaries to mark off family plots. Pests were warded off by the burning of acrid smoke, and even by tame seagulls.[23] Gardening and storage techniques must have developed further. Ways of enriching soil were transmitted by migrants to new regions – one such transfer south to north is recorded in a Northland tradition and place-name.[24] New types of pits emerged. The raised-rim pit appeared on the East Coast in the fifteenth century, probably to combat hard subsoil.[25] Helen Leach argues that storage accidentally selected tubers for hardiness and fertility, though not size, so improving crops over time.[26]

Questions have been raised about the productivity of Maori gardening, but recent research suggests that it could produce about half the total food requirement in favoured regions.[27] Without manure, production of kumara per hectare was not huge – around four to six tonnes – and even this required hard and efficient work, an average of about six hours a day from the whole community for half the year. Gardening production was more controllable and reliable than gathering, but still had to be supplemented by it. It may be that we can detect a movement of gardening as well as hunting techniques into gathering and even fishing. The most obvious element of this was the semi-cultivation of wild plants.

Fernroot grew well in newly cleared land, and good fernland was regularly burned off to promote its regrowth. Fire was sometimes also used to facilitate harvesting, by clearing away upper vegetation and leaving the roots more accessible. Harvesting tended to be a team rather than an individual activity, with two or three diggers lifting the roots and other people gathering them into baskets. Its importance, especially in relation to kumara, may be somewhat exaggerated by the time spent eating it. Sitting around for hours in groups chewing fernroot may have been equivalent to drinking tea socially – chewing the fibres rather than the fat. But it was clearly an important food – a staple at some times and places. Its collection was more like gardening than gathering.

Cabbage trees were also important in some areas, especially the southern zone, a staple source of carbohydrate, though not protein. The tropical Polynesian variety, ti pore, was restricted to the north, but indigenous species, especially ti kouka, were widespread and were deliberately planted, like ti pore, in suitable areas. Even where this was not the case, clumps of ti were marked down on oral maps as permanent resources, like good fernroot grounds. Harvesting was done in such a way that new plants sprouted from the old. Tikao claimed that ti was harvested in January, when its food value was highest, and that its sugar content was augmented by cutting the tops off the plants well before harvesting. Scientific tests have confirmed his claim.[28] This was somewhere between gathering and gardening, and arguably more like the latter. Karaka groves are well known to have been deliberately planted. Plants were also cultivated for raw materials. Flax was deliberately planted. Twigs and even whole trunks were trained or pruned to promote desired shapes, then cut months or years later when they had grown to plan.[29]

It may be that gardener-like systems of ownership and tapu were also increasingly applied to gathering and fishing. The stone-walled plots at Palliser Bay are designed to divide varying qualities of soils equally, presumably between families.[30] The traditional 'ownership' system is the subject of some debate, but 1980s research stimulated by the Treaty of Waitangi claims process suggest that fishing and gathering resources were allocated in a similar way, as 'mahinga kai', or resource localities.[31] A family might inherit or be allocated the sole or shared right to use a bundle of resource localities, covering the full range of their needs – some clumps of ti and mamaku, a few birding trees, crayfishing rights to a particular stream, and one or two prime shore-fishing spots. Such resources were best used by individuals or single families, and were owned or controlled by them; other resources were best exploited by groups, and were controlled by them. Individualism and collectivism, rivalry and co-operation were harnessed to maximum production as appropriate. But the whole community exerted an increasing overall control of the new economy, through tapu and chiefly rahui – restrictions or proscriptions enforced by the mana and tapu of the proscriber.

Several prehistorians allude to signs of increasing tapu from mid-prehistory. It is in this period that we first find caches of objects, such as combs, made tapu by their contact with the sacred heads of chiefs and hidden away to avoid their use in magic. There is a more marked separation of noa cooking places and tapu sleeping places in housing. It is tempting to correlate the increase of tapu to increasingly controlled economic exploitation of nature. Because nature and supernature pervaded each other, tapu was the obvious mechanism for such control, and controls clearly did come into being. The great Mangaunu shark-fishing enterprises were annually restricted to two days, and the same was true of Arawa dogfishing in the 1850s. Taking dogfish outside this time broke tapu and was punished by muru – the legal plundering of offenders, in which blood was rarely shed.[32] Other resources also had restricted-use seasons, enforced by tapu and rahui, and converging precisely with prime productivity. Such controls even invaded the last of the game islands. Seals in the Chathams were clearly harvested, in numbers limited to what their population could sustain, not creamed off or extirpated as in the past. Here, perhaps, we have a shift from the ethos of expansion to an ideology that emphasised the restricted and therefore sustainable exploitation of the environment, the point where the Green Maori stereotype converged most closely with the truth. This ideological shift underwrote the change from an extractive to a sustainable economy.

By extending, expanding, intensifying and controlling production by the innovative adaptation of economic practices and ideology, Maori overcame the crisis brought about by the decline of big game and the increase of population. Most practices may have had roots in early prehistory but were developed, adapted and intensified over time. This was more a matter of human endeavour and systemic flexibility than natural abundance, and it did not succeed in making life easy, long or frequent. Birth rates were not restored to the presumed levels of the protein boom. Reserves or 'surpluses', here defined simply as the excess of production over the most basic requirements, were achieved, but they were small, often unreliable, and there were many demands on them. One of the most important was war.

Children of Tu

'Ka mate, Ka mate' – It is death, It is death. So opens New Zealand's most famous poem, the haka said to have been composed by the great nineteenth-century warleader Te Rauparaha. War haka present the frightening paradox of frenzied discipline. The tongue gyrates and the eyes protrude, each individual seems berserk, yet every slap and stamp is uniform and precise. Uninhibited examples by a thousand armed warriors could freeze the blood, just as they were intended to, and some missionaries seem never to have recovered from the experience. Such haka symbolise an enduring stereotype, the Red Maori, with a special propensity for war – 'once were warriors'. This is no more wrong than its opposite – the Green Maori, living in harmony with each other as well as with nature. Both are partly true, partly self-fulfilling and partly deceptive, and both were created by Maori as well as Pakeha.

The Pakeha contribution to this myth peaked in the half-century around 1900, and is mainly discussed elsewhere. Briefly, Maori gradually ceased to be feared; their frequent courage and occasional chivalry in earlier Anglo-Maori conflicts was emphasised to divert attention from their success; Pakeha collective identity was helped by comparing their tigerish natives to other colonists' pussycats. The Smithians were influenced by Social Darwinism, for which militarism could indicate fitness to survive, and it is important to remember that the warlike label was originally intended as a compliment, though a loaded one. The alleged Maori extermination of their 'Moriori' predecessors was considered highly commendable.

Smithed tradition was often derived from Maori who had been educated in the 1820s, a time of unprecedented tribal warfare. Maori in this period naturally emphasised useful traditions, and stories that taught tactics and fired up young warriors were useful. In at least one large area, the term 'whare purakau', schools that taught warfare, originally only one of several types of whare wananga, or houses of learning, came to be used for all.[33] Tradition, like most history, was in any case biased towards great and terrible events such as battle. To the dismay of conscientious social historians, people sometimes seem to find hearing about sitting, sleeping and excreting almost as boring as doing it. Conflicts with particular enemies, which might actually have occurred sporadically over centuries, were telescoped in the telling into cohesive wars.

The peaceful times between were squeezed out. Some traditions became a succession of battles, and history tended to be told by the victors, just as it was written by them. War haka themselves do not necessarily indicate that Maori society was peculiarly warlike. Europeans also have militaristic encounter rituals, greeting VIPs with displays of armed soldiers and artillery barrages. One does not judge the Pope by his Swiss Guard. Such ceremonies originate in the desire to show visitors that you are not defenceless, and created misunderstandings on both sides during early contact. But they are designed more to prevent conflict than to provoke it.

All this makes some exaggeration of warfare in Aotearoa predictable, and there is evidence to support this. 'Parrying fractures', other signs of actual combat, and weapons themselves are quite rare in the archaeological record.[34] When spread out again over the appropriate number of centuries, conflicts between neighbouring tribes are not so common in some traditions. Warfare is the most expensive of social activities, and Maori reserves were limited. Sustained and intensive conflict, however desirable, was a luxury they could rarely afford. Such considerations can lead to the view that war was virtually non-existent in early prehistory. This may have come quite close to the truth in the Chatham Islands, where the remarkable treaty known as Nunuku's Law, and perhaps the close relationship of the local tribes, minimised violent conflict.[35] But there is some archaeological evidence of early violence on the mainland, small scale yet merciless, and European explorers leave us in little doubt that warfare was important by the seventeenth and eighteenth centuries. The most obvious and overwhelming sign of this was the vast number of pa (forts or fortified villages), one of which the explorers stormed in 1772. Let us see what this historical Franco–Maori War can tell us about group violence in prehistory.[36]

It is sometimes said that New Zealand prehistory was 'caught alive' by the earliest European explorers. On 9 June 1772, it was certainly caught dead. On the afternoon of that day, a young French officer, Ensign Jean Roux, was hunting quail on the hills above the Bay of Islands. He came upon two Maori men, fighting desperately. For 'about six minutes' they exchanged blows with great two-handed wooden weapons (taiaha), 'demonstrating the greatest skill and at the same time an astonishing agility'. Then, as if by common consent, they threw these aside, drew small one-handed weapons (patu) from their belts and fell upon each other afresh. One of the duellists was probably of the kin group later known as Nga Puhi; the other was a member of Ngati Pou or its affiliates, but we do not know which was which. Roux, who had hitherto imagined this might be some type of fencing exercise, realised his error and humanely ran forward to intervene. 'But I was too late because at that very moment one of them had his skull split open by a blow from his opponent's war club and he fell down dead.' The victor ran off and Roux inspected the victim: 'his head was cut open at the level of his eyes as if by a blow from a cutlass.'

Although Roux denied it, one suspects that his intervention may have lethally distracted the victim – a case in which Europe actually did have a Fatal Impact in New Zealand. Roux was impressed by the swordlike effectiveness of stone 'clubs', by Maori skill with them and by the use of deadly duels or single combats to settle affairs of honour. For a few days, these impressions fed into a French view of Maori as 'Noble Savages', illustrating the tomes of Rousseau and Commerson that lay in their cabins. Then, on 12 or 13 June, their beloved leader Marion du Fresne and 25 others, after five weeks of peaceful interaction with the Bay Maori, were set upon by surprise and killed. Their flesh was eaten, their bones made into forks and flutes, and their Maori suddenly became ignoble if not bestial, illustrating a different book. Rousseau himself could scarcely believe it. 'Is it possible that the good Children of Nature can really be so wicked?'[37]

The Maori attack is usually said to have been motivated by French breaches of tapu, but such breaches from ignorance were often forgiven in the history of contact, and it seems that local politics was also a factor. Nga Puhi, under the chief Te Kauri, seem to have been expanding into coastal areas at this time, by intermarriage as well as war. Some Ngati Pou sought to conciliate them; others to resist. Two groups had been seen shaping up to each other as if for battle on open ground on 6 May, and one side induced the French to frighten off the other with gunfire. The French were therefore a new factor in a delicate local balance involving at least three parties, at least one of which saw the newcomers as potential allies, not enemies. Some Maori traditions, now defunct, remembered Marion favourably.[38]

The month until the French departure on 13 July saw a series of skirmishes, during which various Maori leaders attempted to negotiate. Some of these attempts were ploys to induce the French to break formation and come within range of Maori weapons; others were genuine. But again, neither the French nor historians knew which was which. The French also failed to grasp that more than one Maori group was involved, and took their vengeance wherever they could. On 14 June, a picked and heavily armed party of 26 Frenchmen attacked Paeroa pa on Moturua Island. The pa was surrounded by cliffs on three sides and was difficult to approach even without the ditches, earth banks and multiple lines of palisades, topped by fighting stages accommodating up to twenty men. But the Maori warriors, and the women who handed them weapons, were shot on the palisades and stages by French gunfire before they had much opportunity to use their own projectile weapons – throwing spears and stones. Two Frenchmen were slightly wounded by thrown spears, and Chevalier de Lorimer received a nasty blow on the nose from a long spear thrust through gaps in the palisading, but the pa was taken and 46 Maori were killed inside it, some futilely trying to ward off the bullets with their flax cloaks. Inside, the French found large, well-filled storehouses and, allegedly, no living wounded. They claimed to have killed a couple of hundred more Maori as they fled, which would have made their two dozen musketeers the best marksmen in history. But there can be no question that the French attack was cheap and successful.

Eked out with archaeology and tradition, ethnographic accounts shed light on war in prehistory, undercutting some existing assumptions and supporting others.[39] One view is that the causes of war were normally 'traditional' – insults and breaches of tapu, with the iron law of utu leading to an escalating and inescapable cycle of retaliation. But I suspect such factors tended to converge with more pragmatic ones, as in the Franco–Maori War. A formal 'take', or 'just cause', often clothes economic motives in European warfare too. We will see below that there were forms of competition other than war, and there were also well-established procedures for peacemaking. Individuals and groups with links to both sides acted as mediators, and in the nineteenth century we find something close to professional peacemakers. Negative utu debts did not necessarily result in war. The weaker party might bide its time or seek to avenge itself in other ways; stronger parties could place offenders in their debt by forbearance. The wounds of conflict could be healed by reciprocal gift visits, feasts and the great binding institution of intermarriage. They could also be healed by the return of prisoners taken as slaves – a phenomenon usually associated with the advent of Christianity in the 1830s, but which in fact pre-dates it.

Slavery is one area where Red Maori mythology blatantly trips over itself – Maori could not both take prisoners and be merciless. But Maori warfare did sometimes plumb the depths. Even in early prehistory, children were sometimes killed, and beaten arch-enemies could find themselves decapitated, their heads preserved to be mocked, their flesh eaten, their bones made, like Marion's, into cutlery. Cannibalism was the ultimate revenge, not an item of diet, desecrating the victims beyond the grave by turning them into cooked food. Groups, rather than individuals, tended to be the targets of vengeance, which therefore extended to young and old, living and dead. But the direst forms of vengeance, such as cannibalism, were reserved for some and not for others. Tradition taught that eating one's kin was the ultimate sin, and there are numerous nineteenth-century examples of limited, almost ritual conflicts between close kin. Confrontations between groups that did not result in battle, and duels between individuals, were both witnessed by the French in 1772. Thus it may be that warfare ranged across a spectrum of ruthlessness, scale and intensity: from frequent semi-ritualised encounters, in which little blood was shed, through sporadic raiding, to infrequent wars to the death. The technology of combat supports this view.

As Ensign Roux discovered, Maori hand weapons were surprisingly effective, though made of wood, stone and bone. Like 'canoe', the term 'club' is deceptive. Short one-handed weapons, for which patu was a general name, were usually sharp-edged and made of quality stone such as greenstone. They functioned as hatchets or tomahawks – the word the French sometimes used for them and the steel weapons with which Maori eventually chose to replace them. Large two-handed weapons, such as taiaha, were made of hardwood or bone, and functioned as much as fighting staffs and axes as clubs and spears. George Grey translated taiaha as 'two-handed wooden swords'.[40] Their use was a well-developed fighting art, and a dubious sign of cultural maturity in the future may be the displacement of imported kung fu by local taiaha movies. Both types of hand weapon were formidable, and carefully made and decorated. Maori projectile weapons, in contrast, were relatively ineffective and crudely made because they were expendable. Fending off thrown spears was a common sport – in living memory, one old man gathered firewood by challenging boys to throw sticks at him[41] – and even a heavy flax cloak provided some protection against such missiles.

This basic dichotomy between good hand weapons and poor projectiles has important implications. It must have curtailed guerilla tactics – harrying an enemy from a distance and the most deadly types of ambush require effective projectiles. Hand weapons, and a warrior ethos based on them as exemplified in the haka, suit open battle better, and such battles clearly did occur. But their prominence in tradition, markers between eras, could indicate infrequency as much as frequency. As elsewhere, open battles probably only took place when both sides thought they could win. Both probability and tradition suggest that surprise raids and counter-raids were more common, a staple of Maori warfare. Confrontations that stopped just short of open battle, in exchanges of haka, fairly harmless volleys of missiles, and perhaps duels between champions, may have been another staple.

There must, however, have been one context in which projectiles were potentially decisive – the defence of pa. A key principle of prehistoric military architecture was to give defenders a height advantage over attackers. Ditches, banks, terraces, palisades and fighting stages all performed this service. At some point in their advance, storming parties would face defenders as much as ten metres directly above them. This suddenly changed the efficacy of crude projectiles – but only for the defenders. A large stone was not a very formidable weapon on flat ground, but hurled down in these circumstances, it was deadly. Unlike the French, prehistoric attackers had no missiles effective enough to clear the fighting stages from which stones and spears were thrown. Pa were thus carefully designed to compensate for the deficiencies of projectiles. They were lethal, vertical skittle alleys. Without some compensating advantage such as fire or massively overwhelming numbers, storming a pa must have verged on the impossible. It therefore comes as no surprise that Maori appear to have seldom bothered trying it.

Few pa show archaeological evidence of sack, and fire features in most of those. Pa were hard to storm and equally difficult to take by siege. Storage pits usually dominated their interiors. Fortified food stores are sometimes seen as a specific category of pa, but it seems likely all pa were basically such stores, with or without permanent dwellings as well. Siege rations were only one of the functions of the stored food, and not necessarily the most important. It also represented the accumulated reserves of the owners – a sort of bank – and the denial of these resources to enemies. Outside the kumara season, when the tubers were growing in the ground, the stores contained the whole crop, seed tubers as well as usable reserves. One source suggests that, during the growing season, any forewarning of an attack would be used to pull the crops from the ground and pile them in the stores, whatever their state of growth.[42] Attackers' supplies were constrained by limited reserves and carrying capacity. Foraging around the pa while besieging it would have so reduced their numbers as to render them vulnerable to counter-attack, because gathering wild foods required so much labour and time. They must normally have hoped to co-opt the crops of their enemies, but could not do so if these were safe in store. This may explain why pa often have large facilities for storing food but few for storing water. One did not need much water to survive the few days before the besiegers began to starve. If surprise failed, the attackers might as well go home, and such failed forays against pa do feature in tradition. Long sieges also feature, but they cannot have been very common. With due allowance for exceptions, it seems reasonable to conclude that, with the weapons and supplies available in prehistory, pa made successful offensive warfare very difficult.

A total of 6,000 pa sites have been discovered, mostly prehistoric. They appear to have mushroomed in regional spasms from the fifteenth and sixteenth centuries.[43] The assumptions that this indicates a massive and permanent upsurge in warfare, and that it was a direct response to food shortages, are questionable. Pa were so difficult to take that there was often little point in trying. They were designed to protect food reserves, and they were themselves costly to build. They are evidence of the presence of reserves, not their absence. They must post-date, or emerge in tandem with, the successful shift by some groups from an extractive to a sustainable economy. They must have absorbed resources that might otherwise have been used for active warfare. Calculating the amount of warfare from the amount of pa is rather like deducing the number of modern house fires from the number of insurance policies. Long-term states of feud, flaring spasmodically into war, were probably common in Maoridom, and bloody conquests did occur. But it seems doubtful that seventeenth- and eighteenth-century Aotearoa was more violent than Europe at the same time.

There is an obvious temptation to link the proliferation of pa from the fifteenth century to the other great shifts of mid-prehistory. Might gardening-oriented groups have built them for protection against the raids of hunter-oriented groups trying to survive without game? We need not fear the obvious, but we should not be too eager to embrace it either. Let us put this problem aside for the moment and consider the people who actually built the pa. Individuals, of course, never built them. They were always the product of groups.

Regrouping and Rivalry

Human societies sometimes have powerful engines that drive their social history – the formation, re-formation and interaction of groups and their relations with individuals. Competitive capitalism is usually seen as the engine, or dynamic, of modern Europe. A key element of the myth that non-industrial peoples like the Maori were sentenced to stasis is the assumption that they lacked such engines. This was not true of the colonial era of Maori history. We thought to find, in hunting, an economic dynamic with technological and cultural ramifications. But we could not guess much about its social dimension. Here, for the tribal era, we focus on social organisation, with an argument in three parts. The first sees a social engine in the rivalry for mana between individuals and between groups. The second joins an increasing number of scholars in questioning the conventional understanding of Maori social units, such as tribes, and suggests different ways of seeing them. It argues that they were more fluid than is sometimes believed, but that they did cluster into 'zones' in which the rivalry for mana, a deadly serious game, was played out at differing intensity. Third, it is suggested that the game involved successive forms, or currencies, of rivalry, one of which was the building of pa. I should confess that this argument derives in part from the study of nineteenth-century Maori society, when European technology and settlers became currencies of rivalry, and is read back into tribal prehistory, itself a dangerous but fruitful game.

Descent was the language of Maori social organisation, though not always the thing itself, and mana as well as kin was derived from one's forebears.[44] The senior chiefs and the senior subgroups were those descended most directly from key ancestors. The key ancestors were those who defined the group, and often named it. The senior chiefs therefore symbolised and encapsulated the group; their mana was its mana. These living icons were wheeled out, displayed and honoured, like modern monarchs of England, when the identity, unity and prestige of the group needed to be affirmed. Firm whakapapa linked them back to the founding ancestor of the group. As with Anglo-Saxon kings, loose whakapapa linked them further back to the gods themselves. An anti-aristocratic age needs to understand this when considering the élitism of Maori chieftainship. The modern tribe does not have pyramids, palaces or temples to focus collective identity, but they do have sacred chiefs. There are signs that hereditary chiefs increasingly came to be clothed in tapu, reinforcing it just as it reinforced them. As in other Polynesian societies, this may have had a cause/effect relationship with the increasing control, through tapu, of the economic exploitation of nature. 'Rangatira' was the general term for chief or person of chiefly descent; 'ariki' was usually reserved for the most tapu of hereditary chiefs, living monuments to collective identity.

By the time of contact, the dignities accorded to some sacred chiefs had reached considerable heights. They did not handle food but were fed by attendants, and certain religious rituals could only be performed by them. In some areas, their treatment even echoed that of the priest-kings of some parts of tropical Polynesia. Te Kani-a-Takirau of Ngati Porou, for example, was widely revered, had chiefs as his attendants and was normally accompanied by a guard of honour.[45] A missionary recorded encountering a great Northland chief choking from a fishbone stuck in his throat, his people lamenting around him but not daring to help because his head was too tapu to touch.[46] But generally the priest-king echoes were quite faint. Many tribes placed little emphasis on individual ariki. Most chiefs worked like other people and were not always distinguishable by richer dress or moko (tattooing).

Sacred chieftainship was not leadership. Te Kani was not much use as a warleader because he was too valuable to be risked, and there are examples of ariki retaining ritual but not political leadership because they were not good enough at the latter.[47] As this suggests, mana could be achieved and lost, as well as inherited. Mana achieved through demonstrated competence was essential for leadership, whereas inherited mana was only useful. Mana was not simply the stuff of leadership, it was also the medium through which individuals and groups gained status and advanced themselves. Inheritance consolidated the gains and losses made by each generation, but achievement determined whether it be gain or loss, and by how much.

Achieved mana involved rivalry with one's peers, against whom achievement was measured. The competitive pursuit of mana in Maori society has been discussed by several scholars and needs no extensive demonstration.[48] But it does need some redefinition, emphasising *rivalry* over competition. Competition between closely related individuals and groups could be ruthless and even violent. But mana was actually achieved mainly in the minds of one's kin. Taking competitiveness to the point where it damaged the public good, or exploiting status too far for personal ends, was therefore inherently counterproductive. One lost respect where it mattered most – among one's own community. Mana could also be gained by superior beneficence or self-sacrifice, or by showing more commitment to some collective enterprise – rivalry through co-operation. 'These are the ways by which men gain influence in the world,' said Maui's brothers, 'by labouring for abundance of food to feed others – by collecting property to give others, and by similar means by which you promote the good of others.'[49] Other traditions confirm that the ability to obtain food, generous distribution and hospitality were among the talents expected of a chief.[50] The noble communalism of this was somewhat spoiled by Maui himself, who bested his brothers on all possible occasions, turned his brother-in-law into a dog, then made it eat his excrement. Both co-operation and competition were components of rivalry. Collectivism did not displace individual and group competition, but it did contain them.

The collectivities that contained the rivalry for mana included various categories of kin group, the second focus of our argument. Practice conspires with theory to make analysis of these groups a complicated business. Until recently, Maori social organisation was discussed in terms of a neat four-part taxonomy: whanau (extended families), which combine into hapu (clans), which combine into iwi (tribes), which combine into waka (canoe groups). Kinship determined membership of these groups, the trunk, main branches, small branches and twigs of the tree of descent. All four categories existed, and all had some importance. We have suggested that waka, the top category, may have been the collective identities of the colonial era, and in the tribal era they were still invoked occasionally. Whanau, the bottom category, had several meanings that could change over time, like the English word 'family'.[51] Best found whanau of up to 92 people,[52] and an extended family of a dozen or so people is the conventional definition. But as Raymond Firth noted in 1929, nuclear families – Mum, Dad and the kids – also played some role.[53] Garden-plot boundaries at Anauru Bay cater for nuclear families.[54] Families, nuclear or extended, were the basic domestic unit. Some kinds of economic activity were best handled by families, which could therefore be an economic unit as well. Where such small-scale economics predominated, families could live by themselves as mini-communities. Both ethnography and archaeology provide some evidence of whanau-based settlement patterns, and one archaeologist has come intriguingly close to the concept of 'family farms' in describing some pre-contact settlement sites in Hawke's Bay.[55] Some types of gardening and gathering may have tended to split groups into their smallest components. But such diffusion can seldom have been the whole story. Other types of activity required larger groups, and whanau can hardly have been social units in themselves. Incest between very close kin was proscribed in Maori society as in most others. People found spouses outside the whanau but normally within a wider group.[56]

The two middle categories, hapu and iwi, are no less problematic.[57] Both were used to mean medium or large lines of descent, but also medium or large groups acting or living together. People could have more than one hapu affiliation in the former sense. Tikao had 24: 21 Maori, two English and an American.[58] An individual might invoke different affiliations at different times to assert a right to various places or resources, or to membership of varying groups.[59] Iwi or tribes could be defined as neighbouring clusters of related hapu whose clustering had some internal and external recognition. They were eventually frozen and formalised into their modern shape partly for the convenience of the European state and European scholars.

These modern 'official' tribes were not wholly artificial. It has been suggested that there was a trend to 'state-like' larger tribes even before contact.[60] After it, some Maori certainly used the official tribe concept for their own purposes; the people involved *were* generally linked in some way; and it was the type of artificial grouping that had some tendency to make itself real over time. But in the nineteenth century, one rarely finds official tribes acting as cohesive units. Maori and well-informed Pakeha then tended to use 'tribe' flexibly: for a large hapu, a group of two or three hapu, or a larger network of hapu, as the case might be. Dividing all Maori into about 30 official tribes neatened, romanticised and Europeanised a more fluid reality, although Maori were not above exploiting the trend.

But recent scholarship seems to me to tend towards the opposite, minimalist, error. It sees small hapu, of around 30 people, as the main unit of social organisation, and we are advised to 'think small'.[61] It is true that this, along with even smaller groups, was quite a common pattern of settlement at contact. But contact ethnography makes it clear that such groups could coalesce into much larger ones, of up to several hundred people. The speed of assembly and efficiency of co-operation in greeting, fighting, or trading with the early explorers indicates that such large groups were not ad hoc but were accustomed to acting together. Added to this, a hapu of only 30 people would find it hard to make and maintain a great war canoe, a giant net or a large pa. Yet nineteenth-century practice shows that the groups larger than hapu were seldom whole official tribes, but groupings of hapu within them. Neither the small hapu nor the large official tribe was the common unit of joint action. A term intermediate between hapu and tribe is needed, such as 'hapu group'. This might be one large hapu or several, a large part of one or several such parts. Hapu groups could be short term or long, centred around the mana of particular chiefs or around the need to oppose a particular enemy.

Where diffuse settlement predominated, hapu groups would be loose and latent – the set of kin with whom one normally intermarried and occasionally co-operated in large-scale enterprises and emergencies. If such enterprises and emergencies became more frequent, even to the point where the hapu group sometimes lived together in a large pa or kainga (village), the group identity would become more entrenched. This identity would be expressed in terms of kinship. Unity in the present might go hand in hand with a retrospective emphasis on unity in the past – on shared or compatible traditions and ancestors. One could not play fast and loose with hard whakapapa, but since the hapu being grouped were usually related anyway, it was more a matter of reunification. Furthermore, the key institution of intermarriage, especially among chiefly pairs, could literally link the past through the present, marrying groups as well as individuals.[62] This process, in reverse, could apply to splitting as well as lumping. Motivated by economic necessity, the ambition and rivalry of leaders, or some other factor, part of a group could split off and live and act in isolation from the rest, becoming a separate 'hapu group' as it developed its own subdivisions. Over time, it might reconstruct its myth and history to legitimate its separateness, just as combining groups did to legitimate their unity. In these ways, perhaps, hapu groups became iwi.

This process of tribe formation may have happened on a large scale in mid-prehistory, but it did not suddenly stop when that great reshuffle was over. Some modern tribes may have formed as recently as the nineteenth century, and perhaps some are forming still. But contact did tend to snap-freeze the process with the juggler's balls in the air. It could be that in the hapu group we have the embryo of the tribe in prehistory, with European contact making the normal birth process more difficult in history.

One way of understanding all this may be to distinguish between actual and 'imagined' groups,[63] both of which might be described in the language of kinship as hapu or iwi. Actual groups lived together permanently, or assembled regularly for major enterprises or operated together occasionally but reliably in emergencies. Imagined groups, on the other hand, might be no more than a vague collective identity, based on descent, with no corporate functions at all. Yet even this created a sense of insiders, among whom actual groups could more easily form, and a sense of outsiders. An imagined group such as a race or nation often defines itself in relation to other groups of the same order of size. The Other groups are sometimes artificial projections, imagined by Us not by Them, and need not themselves have a collective identity. But if neighbours grouped them long and consistently enough, the external name and identity might catch on from the inside as well, creating an internally imagined group with enhanced potential for operating together. Te Rangi Hiroa believed that such a process had succeeded in grouping and naming at least three clusters of hapu into tribes – two after contact and one before.[64]

From the perspective of a single individual, humanity can seem a spectrum of groups graduated from innermost Us to outermost Them. For a pre-contact Maori individual, such a spectrum might have three concentric circles, or zones, looking from the inside out.

Innermost was the kin zone, one's own and closely related hapu, an imagined group. It was within this zone that actual hapu groups could most easily form. Kin zones in the nineteenth century sometimes converged with a single large official tribe, but often to closely associated groups of them. Next came a neighbour zone: groups that had long lived in close proximity to you or with whom you had an established relationship of friendship, enmity or something between the two. Some intermarriage may have occurred, and often linked hapu, affiliated equally to both you and them, might form a sort of hinge. 'Neighbours' in this sense need not live in close proximity but might be distant kin or people with whom regular gift-exchange networks had been established. Finally came a 'stranger zone', which included everybody else and did not matter very much to you. It could be that various maps drawn or told by Maori for inquiring Europeans in the earliest phase of contact reflect a real sense of such zones. They show thorough knowledge of the local area and a good knowledge of a wider zone of interaction, sometimes strangely shaped because it reflected interaction rather than mere proximity. Outside this, in the stranger zone, geographical knowledge was telescoped and sketchy.[65]

Kin, neighbour and stranger zones, perhaps, were the arenas in which the rivalry for mana was played out, and they helped determine its nature and intensity. Reputation among kin mattered most, among neighbours next, and among strangers least. Mana in the inner zone could be enhanced by actions in zones further out. But what your kin thought of some successful feat of violence or generosity towards strangers mattered much more than what the recipients thought of it. It was this, perhaps, that helped calibrate warfare along its spectrum of intensity. Violence in the kin zone was most important and least bloody; and least important and most bloody in the stranger zone. In Maniapoto tradition, two brothers quarrelling over an eel weir decided to make war on another tribe and allocate the weir to the brother who did best.[66] The 'Musket Wars' of the 1820s, discussed in Chapter Seven, abound in similar examples.

The third part of this argument involves the types, or currencies, of rivalry. Positive utu – feasting and gift giving – may have been the most basic, often more important than negative utu, including muru and war. Between groups, a munificent feast or gift beyond the recipients' ability to reciprocate could humiliate them, place them in your debt or even subtly subordinate them. Ngata wrote of a forgotten motive of Maori hospitality, 'that of beating the other man or tribe', citing the example of a chief who made a habit of visiting rivals when the season or the weather made munificent reception impossible.[67] Great feasts were named and remembered as marker events, the peaceful equivalent of a battle. Within groups, as Maui's brothers suggested, the generous distribution of goods, obtained by your own efforts, to your kin was a major means of augmenting mana. Even the great hero Kahungunu owed some of his repute to skill at finding fernroot and seafood, as well as to his impressive sexual capacities. Obtaining and distributing resources through collective enterprises was the point where rivalry, leadership and regrouping intersected.

When hapu grouped for some great enterprise such as large-scale shark fishing, leading chiefs timed and controlled the enterprise and allocated its profits to hapu and whanau, taking into account both need and the fishing performance of individuals and canoe crews. But their power seems to have been strictly limited.[68] Chiefs' kin were their judges as well as their followers; if they broke accepted rules of fairness and generosity, they would eventually cease to be leading chiefs. For leaders, though not sacred chiefs, the rivalry for mana was a continuous election. Within these limits, their power to control and distribute must have been greatest when some large *indivisible* asset was involved. In some collective enterprises, the people brought their own means of production – tools, weapons and small canoes. In others, the means of production were too large and costly for individuals or whanau. Large capital assets were therefore especially important as currencies of rivalry between chiefs and groups, and for the entrenching of group identity.

In the colonial era, we may guess, the key asset of this type was the large double-hulled voyaging canoe. Groups built and owned these ships, and perhaps were defined by and named for them. Groups built new canoes when they split, and shared canoes when they lumped. New leaders may have obtained some mana through skill at hunting or voyaging, and then initiated the building of new canoes to gain parity in mana with more established leaders. Tapu and sacred chieftainship may have been less important in this era. Rivalry of this kind helps explain the rapid expansion of colonisation posited in the last chapter.

Voyaging canoes declined in importance along with game. In the abstract, the simple shift of emphasis to gardening, fishing and gathering might have split groups and reduced the importance of chiefs. But these activities also intensified, often through collective enterprise and sometimes with collective assets, such as great fishing nets. Groups had to lump in order to make and use such nets, which Joseph Banks noted were 'the joint work of a whole town'.[69] A chief who controlled a net scored over one who did not – and gained more followers. But, while the net itself was indivisible, the profits from it could be distributed in a single act. The chief allocated piles of fish to each subgroup, which could then go home.[70] It required living and acting together under the authority of the chief only occasionally. Pa were another matter. They were even more costly than large nets or canoes, and their output – security – was long term, vital and could not be divided up and taken home. They were not always occupied permanently, but they did require a lot of joint action and dwelling. This helped entrench collective identity, making whanau and hapu into hapu groups. Groups made pa, but pa also helped make groups.

Once one group had a pa, others needed them too, for perfectly pragmatic reasons. People with pa could raid people without, and then protect themselves from the retaliatory raid that would otherwise have made them hesitate. Having pa when others did not thus gave an advantage in offensive as well as defensive warfare, which others would have little choice but to try to match. Such an 'arms race' helps explain the sudden appearance and rapid proliferation of pa. The function of pa as fortified food stores was also a factor. Pa normally had to be close enough to areas producing a surplus of food to make its transport to them viable. If a group had several such areas, it had to have several pa. But pa also proliferated because of the rivalry for mana.

A chief or group that had a pa could offer more protection, gain more mana and attract more supporters than kindred chiefs and groups that did not. Whether or not they were under immediate attack from outsiders, chiefs and groups had to build pa to maintain their mana and support. This, rather than spasms of civil war, could explain spurts of pa building in particular times at particular places. In the Okato district of Taranaki and the Kaipara district of Northland, for example, the same kin zone contained dozens of pa, built at similar times – many more than were needed to protect any conceivable population from attack.[71] When, in the nineteenth century, flour mills, churches and the sponsorship of Europeans displaced pa as major currencies of rivalry, Maori acquired more of these, too, than they strictly needed. This process of competitive emulation, driven by the rivalry for mana within the imagined zones, explains more than the proliferation of pa. It is a general explanation for the spread of innovation in Maori society, and for its particularly rapid spread in particularly competitive times, places and currencies.

The various techniques for extending and intensifying economic production spread even further and faster than pa themselves and, like pa, required new and more permanent groups. These groups reconstructed myth and history and used intermarriage, legitimating and entrenching themselves to the point where they became 'tribes'. With or without pa, a small group was vulnerable to being outfought or outfeasted by a large group, so that tribe formation itself could become a currency of rivalry. Competition between groups to impose their name and mana on the wider group was a variant of this, as we shall see in the next chapter. Rivalry could take off into non-pragmatic competition. Rivalry in such things as pa was a means to a pragmatic end, but could also become an end in itself. 'A carved house standing in a palisaded pa is the sign of a chief,' ran one proverb. 'A carved house standing in an open place is food for the fire.'[72] Mana and Realpolitik were not wholly explicable by each other, but they did converge so closely that the seam is often imperceptible. Far from being frozen, Maori society was good at change – at its own pace, in its own way and for its own purposes.

The 'tribal era' is still with us. Tribes are still a major form of New Zealand social organisation, and may soon become important economically as well. In this sense, this chapter is not just about middle and late prehistory, but about the origins of modern New Zealand. Interaction with the European state froze and formalised tribal identity to some extent in the century around 1900. Internal tribal politics sometimes exploited and sometimes ignored this. As the twentieth century closes, lumping and splitting continue. Old/new groups claim tribal status and seek to split themselves off from prevailing units. This is happening in the context of a new currency of rivalry – claims for recompense and the acknowledgement of wrongs from the state. This currency, too, has spread like wildfire through Maoridom, and it, too, has a competitive, even counter-productive side. As one set of Maori negotiators seem to verge on success, like determined dentists drawing impacted teeth from a reluctant patient, rivals emerge and inform the relieved state that it has been talking to the wrong people. But the claim leaders co-operate too, and they are at last having some success. Like capitalism, the rivalry for mana can get things done. Prehistory, history and the present are all 'caught alive' in each other. Since each helps produce the other, this should come as no great surprise.

CHAPTER FOUR

Life Before History

In the mid-seventeenth century, the Ngati Mamoe chieftainess Te Maiairea Te Riri Wairua Puru, also known as Te Amaru, with a party of her people visited Lake Hauroko in Fiordland, perhaps on a fowling expedition. They came originally from a village near Christchurch and had moved to the south-west, either because of pressure from invading Ngai Tahu or as part of the normal economic round. Te Maiairea's husband, Nekeneke Puauau, a chief of the Waitaha people, had died in this area sometime earlier, leaving her with two children. 'Nekeneke is said to have deliberately struck his head on a rock and died so that his blood would forever flow in the lake', an ultimate sacrifice to affirm his people's title. Now his wife also died beside Lake Hauroko, from unknown causes. She was buried with great care and ceremony: wrapped in a fine cloak trimmed with kaka feathers, placed in a sitting position on a decorated bier and hidden at the mouth of a cave on an islet in the lake. There, for three centuries, sat Te Maiairea, looking out, until she was encountered by archaeologists in 1967.[1] Her story is one of the few points where tradition and archaeology converge in an individual life.

Archaeology can produce unknown soldiers unaided. One was found buried in a rock cleft at Palliser Bay, with four small children. He was about 50 years old, regarded highly enough to have food specially prepared for him over the ten years since he lost his teeth – molars first. Harris lines in his bones show that he suffered famine for thirteen successive years in his childhood, but he survived to become a strong and active adult – a worker and a warrior. His arm bones were fractured three times, presumably by enemy weapons. The fact that he survived these fights may suggest that the enemies suffered even more. But one day, in or around the fifteenth century, the old warrior's foes caught up with him. They seem to have raided his village while the fit adults were out fishing or foraging, and he was at home taking care of his grandchildren. A nine-month-old baby buried with him shows no evidence of illness; a two-year-old shows marks of violence; and we can guess that the four- and five-year-olds in the graves complete the list of victims. Their kin may have returned just too late to attempt a rescue. The two-year-old was mortally wounded, not killed outright, and might have survived long enough to die in its parents' arms. The burials were hidden, perhaps from fear that the enemy might return and desecrate them. This tale is no less human or tragic for being told in bones.[2]

In the preceding chapters, we have seldom put names, places and sexes to particular groups or individuals. There are practical reasons for this. Archaeological remains have no name-tags; tribal traditions are not designed to be fair to more than one tribe, or to recount daily life; and ethnography can only tell us who was who after 1769, and often gets it wrong even then. But must we be content with a grey, nameless, faceless picture of pre-contact history, patterns and processes with the lives left out? The present writer has neither the skills nor the space for a full-colour history of pre-contact Aotearoa. We cannot do a lot about individuals either. But what we can try to do is put names and places to the groups in which they lived, then look at the way the divisions within these groups affected life. Finally, we make some guesses about such things as games and gods, the intangible life of the mind. We begin with a cursory political geography, centred on the eighteenth century. It arbitrarily divides the country into seven regions, converging very roughly with the 'neighbour zone' of their most central tribes.[3]

A Political Geography of Eighteenth-Century Aotearoa

Northland, our first region, is today sometimes seen as an appendage of Auckland; in prehistory the reverse was closer to the truth. The traditional origins of the Northland tribes are a complex mix, with migrations in and out, and old groups reshuffled into new. But one could say that eighteenth-century Northland fell into four kin zones. North of the Bay of Islands were the five tribes of Muriwhenua, the Land's End: Ngati Kahu, Ngati Kuri, Ngai Takoto, Aupouri and Rarawa.[4] All shared old ancestors and new marriages as well as the rich marine resources and the fertile but small gardening islands of the region, said to be capable of two kumara crops a year in the extreme north. Some of the tribal names may have been adopted and reshuffled before and after contact.[5] In the nineteenth century, the names of Aupouri and Te Rarawa were often used to package the rest. Muriwhenua's neighbours to the south were the tribes of central Northland. In the nineteenth century this came to form one kin zone, dominated by Nga Puhi. It was two in the eighteenth: Nga Puhi and other groups, some linked to Ngati Kahu. Non-Nga Puhi included Ngati Pou (and associated groups), Ngati Rehia and Ngare Raumati. The Nga Puhi and non-Nga Puhi zones were based respectively on the marine resources of Hokianga and the Bay of Islands, and competed for the garden lands between, notably the Taiamai Plain. Nga Puhi were probably already expanding in the eighteenth century at the expense of Ngati Pou and Ngare Raumati. But it is possible that some Nga Puhi's post-contact successes were read back into prehistory. Nga Puhi were quite cohesive genealogically and had up to 150 hapu, but by the early nineteenth century they fell into three competing and co-operating hapu groups: western, or Hokianga, and northern and southern Bay of Islands.[6]

South of Nga Puhi, and linked to their western section, were Ngati Whatua. They are said to have come from the Far North, and their carving styles share more features with Aupouri than with Nga Puhi, but they also had some links with Tainui. Perhaps as late as the eighteenth century, Ngati Whatua displaced the previous inhabitants of southern Northland and the Auckland isthmus, including the Kawerau and Waiohua peoples. The latter are traditionally associated with the volcanic-cone settlements of Auckland from about the fourteenth century.[7] Ngati Whatua absorbed these groups as much by intermarriage as violence, and possibly acquired their own tribal identity in the process. They were a powerful tribe at the end of the eighteenth century, a match for Nga Puhi, though they shared modern-day Auckland with another tribe from further south: Ngati Paoa.

All these Northland kin zones had associations outside the region, especially with Coromandel and, through it, with the East Coast. Perhaps these were a vestige of older links. There are also signs of positive and negative utu relations with Taranaki. It may be that these regions were the intermediary sources of greenstone, of which Northland had a surprising quantity in 1769, though the locals did not know how or where the cherished stone was found.[8]

Tainui territory is our second region. Tainui settled at Kawhia around the fifteenth century and began expanding into the unpeopled or lightly peopled interior around the sixteenth, exploiting its exceptionally extensive garden lands.[9] By the eighteenth century, Tainui expansion and tribal splitting had gone so far that that it might be seen as three kin zones. In the south, Ngati Raukawa, the oldest tribe, retained links with Ngati Toa, of Kawhia in the west, and its associates. This kin zone feuded with another – three large 'Waikato' tribal groups, who were quite closely allied: Ngati Maniapoto, Ngati Haua and the several tribes, such as Ngati Mahuta, that are conveniently packaged as 'Waikato proper'. Anthropologist Peter Cleave uses this powerful alliance as his major example of a trend towards 'state-like' Maori organisations beginning before contact and continuing after it.[10] Again, there is some danger of 'reading back'. But the Waikato tribes did unite to overcome an exceptionally broad alliance of invaders at the Battle of Hingakaka, famous in tradition, in about 1807.[11] The third Tainui kin zone was centred around, and sometimes packaged under, Ngati Paoa of Hauraki. In the eighteenth century, this tribe and the associated Ngati Maru, Ngati Tamatera and Ngati Whaunanga were expanding into Coromandel and the Auckland isthmus.

Ngati Paoa expanded at the expense of another kin zone, the Coromandel-

Hauraki tribes Ngati Hei, Ngati Huaere and Ngati Hoko, whom they eventually subsumed. These tribes were linked to Ngati Pou in the north but were also affiliated to Arawa. As such, they formed part of our third region, centred on the Bay of Plenty and tribes linked to the *Arawa* canoe. In the eighteenth century, Coromandel was raided from the Far North and the Bay of Plenty, as well as by Ngati Paoa. The two northern Bay of Plenty tribes, Ngai Te Rangi and Ngati Ranginui, had some Arawa links but claimed multiple origins and to have driven Arawa from Tauranga.

Arawa settlement from Maketu had spread inland in much the same way and time as Tainui, though their great historian Te Rangikaheke claimed nationwide precedence for them.[12] The half-dozen core Arawa tribes of the central Bay of Plenty, such as Ngati Rangiwewehi and Ngati Whakaue, traced descent from Rangitihi and his sons.[13] Later packaged as one under the name 'Arawa', they were a kin zone but may have had little political unity until as late as 1865. The use of 'Te Arawa' for all six tribes, according to Te Rangi Hiroa, 'developed in recent times through political reasons. I have heard that it was inaugurated by the N' Rangiwewehi and others because the N' Whakaue name was beginning to include the others.'[14] In the nineteenth and twentieth centuries, Arawa's active culture, military alliance with the government and engagement with tourism gave them an enormous influence on the European conception of Maoridom.

The farthest Arawa penetration inland was to Lake Taupo, where the various hapu groups of Ngati Tuwharetoa formed their own kin zone.[15] Tuwharetoa show that fission and fusion could be simultaneous, competing processes. There are signs of splitting into eastern and western factions in the eighteenth century, and northern and southern in the nineteenth. At the same time, the whole tribe usually recognised a paramount chief – drawn from the eighteenth century onward from the Heuheu dynasty. Ngati Tuwharetoa cultivations and their vast lake replaced direct use of marine resources, but they had local obsidian sources and were well placed for overland gift exchange. They had strong links, ratified by chiefly intermarriage, with the Waikato on the one hand and the Bay of Plenty on the other.

Our fourth region is the East Coast, including for this purpose the southern Bay of Plenty and northern Hawke's Bay. One is not sure whether its three main constellations of tribes were kin zones or neighbour zones in themselves. The first included Tuhoe, Ngati Awa and Whakatohea. The Tuhoe, or Urewera, actually incorporated several hapu groups/tribes, such as Te Whakatane, and shared one of its origins, the *Mataatua* canoe, with Ngati Awa and Whakatohea.[16] The three distinguish themselves partly by disputing the particulars of this shared origin, such as precisely which female crewmember of *Mataatua* – Wairaka or Muriwai – gave Whakatane its name by paddling the drifting canoe to shore, so 'acting like a man'. The lively writer Ngahuia Te Awekotuku has recently trumped this debate by seeing the origins of Maori lesbianism in the incident.[17] In the nineteenth century, Whakatohea were frozen into six large hapu, or hapu groups. They were the hinge between this kin zone and the next, which centred around Ngati Porou of East Cape.

Ngati Porou had an especially wide range of origins, even for the East Coast, including Northland and Coromandel connections and descent from Maui and Toi. A key ancestor was Hingangaroa, whose three sons founded Te Aitanga a Hauiti, a section of Ngati Porou, and the associated tribes of Whanau Apanui and Te Aitanga a Mahaki. Like Whakatohea and many other hapu and tribes, Te Aitanga a Mahaki linked one kin zone with the next, being also closely associated with the important Rongowhakaata people of Poverty Bay. Cook found the two allied in a feud against Te Aitanga a Hauiti in 1769. For several centuries up to and including the eighteenth, Poverty Bay and the surrounding region was the source of a series of migrations. Some of Rongowhakaata's Ngati Kahungunu and Ngai Tahu kin still lived in northern Hawke's Bay, while others had migrated much further south. There is considerable evidence – Tahitian as well as European – that the East Coast was unusually wealthy and was a leading centre of artistic activity.[18] If one had to name an eighteenth-century cultural capital of Aotearoa, the East Coast might be it.

Moving west to our fifth region, Taranaki-Whanganui, we find that this, too, was a land of mixed origins and three kin zones.[19] The *Aotea*, or *Aotearoa*, under Turi or other captains, was quite prominent in their origin legends, though many other canoes featured as well. In the north were Te Ati Awa, divided in the nineteenth century into two hapu groups and associated with three other North Taranaki tribes: Ngati Mutunga, Ngati Tama and Ngati Maru (distinct from the eastern Ngati Maru). South Taranaki was held by the Taranaki tribe, and by Ngati Ruanui and Nga Rauru. All three were sometimes grouped together in the nineteenth century, and were lumped and split through debates about descent that continue in the present. A Nga Rauru scholar has argued that the Turi origin legend and associated place-names were imposed on his people by Ngati Ruanui as an act of cultural colonialism, to obscure Nga Rauru's prior right.[20] The chief hapu groups of Ngati Ruanui itself, Nga Ruahine, Pakakohe and Tangahoe, also assert tribal status.

The southern element of this region was the large Whanganui kin zone, extending almost the whole 290-kilometre length of the river of that name until it abutted Maniapoto and Tuwharetoa. Whanganui (also known as Te Ati Hau, Ngati Hau or Ngati Haua) were sometimes treated as a single tribe, but their hundred or more hapu were more often lumped into two or three great groups: upper, lower and, sometimes, middle.[21] Ngati Apa, to the south, was an associated tribe, said, with their migratory kin Ngati Kuia, to have distant and distinct origins at Mahia on the East Coast. The river valleys of Taranaki were rich in fertile garden land, fish and flax – Taranaki was famous for fine cloaks. Like the East Coast, Taranaki-Whanganui had links north and south, and may similarly have acted as a redistribution centre for goods and an exporter of migrants and invaders. These two regions can be seen as giant hinges between the northern part of New Zealand on the one hand and the centre and south on the other.

The lands around Cook Strait can be treated as one, our sixth region.[22] As we have seen, the strait was more bridge than barrier, and the people around it intermarried and constantly interacted – and shared at least an element of their origins in the *Kurahaupo* canoe. The Whanganui tribes, especially Ngati Apa, influenced the western flank of the region, the Manawatu, Wellington and Nelson-Marlborough. A kin zone centred around the Rangitane people had originally been based in the Wairarapa and Hawke's Bay, where the Ngai Tara tribe was associated with them. Rangitane and Ngai Tara spread across the ranges to Wellington and the Manawatu, sometimes in conflict with Ngati Apa, and also to the top of the South Island. Successive streams of newcomers from the East Coast fought, intermarried and passed through Rangitane: Ngati Mamoe, Ngati Ira, Ngai Tahu and Ngati Kahungunu, their names but not necessarily their genes overlaying those of their predecessors.

At contact, Ngati Kahungunu were pre-eminent, a kin zone in themselves, with 600 hapu and about 30 hapu groups stretching from northern Hawke's Bay to the southern Wairarapa, blurring though not eliminating other tribal identities.[23] A new tribe, Muaupoko, is said to have formed in the eighteenth century from a combination of Rangitane, Ngati Ira and Ngati Apa elements, though whether they themselves would have accepted this is another matter.[24] As in European nationalist history, the general rule was that one's own group was ancient and eminent; most others were Hone-come-lately.

The tribes of Nelson and Marlborough were mostly the southern flanks of North Island groups, or perhaps vice versa.[25] Ngai Tara, under pressure from Ngati Ira, moved south as early as the fifteenth century, and were followed by other Rangitane-linked groups. The Whanganui-linked tribes Ngati Kuia and Ngati Apa did likewise soon afterwards. Another tribe, Ngati Tumata Kokiri, also had links with Whanganui. These groups and their traditions suffered more than most from the Musket Wars of the 1820s. One sometimes gets the impression that their nineteenth-century misfortunes have been read back, and there are signs that this is misleading. One is a scrap of ethnographic evidence from the Dutch explorer Abel Tasman's brief visit in 1642, which suggests that the Ngati Tumata he encountered in Nelson were a powerful and self-confident tribe, able to muster up to 300 warriors in two days.[26] Ngati Kuia and Ngati Apa traditions maintain that they drove Ngati Tumata from Marlborough to Nelson, which suggests that they were quite powerful too, and Ngai Tara are also said to have been able to muster large numbers of warriors.

When Ngati Mamoe and Ngai Tahu moved through this area in the sixteenth and seventeenth centuries, they appear to have done so in fairly small groups. Ngai Tahu traditions refer to defeats inflicted on the Nelson-Marlborough groups, but alternative traditions put things the other way around, though Ngai Tahu were sometimes defeated by dirty tactics. Their chief Puraho was said to have been killed on the latrine by Ngai Tara warriors 'secreted in the hole'.[27] Ngati Mamoe and Ngai Tahu may have moved around the Nelson-Marlborough tribes rather than through them, or even bounced off them. After all, they did not occupy the top of the South Island, which they would presumably have done if they had defeated the previous incumbents.

The rest of the South Island constitutes our seventh and final region. The collective identities of its people before the advent of Ngati Mamoe and Ngai Tahu are something of a mystery, intriguing Europeans with tales of lost tribes.[28] As Tikao frankly put it, tradition 'did not preserve much information about the people who were here before the main lots came'.[29] A number of groups are named: Hawea, Ngati Matamata, Te Rapuwai, Waitaha. 'Waitaha', a name also associated with some early groups in the North Island, is sometimes used to package the rest. Variants of the name 'Mamoe' are also quite widespread. The generally accepted tradition, supported to some degree by archaeology, associates them with the ancestress Hotu-Mamoe and the pa of Otarata in northern Hawke's Bay.[30] In the sixteenth century, Ngati Mamoe are said to have migrated from there, passed through Nelson-Marlborough and spread south, merging by conquest and intermarriage with the locals. Ngati Mamoe had links with and knowledge of the South Island before their migration. They pushed far south rapidly to Foveaux Strait, with its stone and seals, which may have become their base. Two of their best-known chiefs were buried at Bluff, though they sometimes lived and fought much further north.[31] It is tempting, but perhaps too convenient, to see a postscript to hunter colonisation in them.

In the seventeenth and eighteenth centuries, Ngai Tahu did much the same thing, starting from much the same place. Like Ngati Mamoe before them, they split into several hapu groups that sometimes fought among themselves, centred on Kaikoura, Kaiapoi, Banks Peninsula, Lake Ellesmere (together 'northern Ngai Tahu'); the Otago Peninsula and Foveaux Strait ('southern Ngai Tahu'); with a particularly distinct section, Poutini Ngai Tahu, in Westland. The precise nature of Ngati Mamoe and Ngai Tahu colonisation is a matter of current debate. It is probably broadly true to say that Waitaha, Ngati Mamoe and Ngai Tahu successively merged with and overlaid each other. But there are signs of complete displacement in some areas, such as the loss of knowledge of important resources like the greenstone of Lake Wakatipu and a sealing island in Foveaux Strait.[32] There is also some evidence of the late survival of old identities in other areas. Waitaha and Te Rapuwai could apparently still muster their own war parties in the eighteenth century, and some fairly distinct Ngati Mamoe groups survived into the nineteenth century in Southland and South Westland. European visitors found Fiordland Maori much more fearful of strangers in the 1790s than the 1770s; sealers reported battles at Foveaux Strait about 1810 and South Westland before 1820.[33] This may indicate a last round, 1790–1820, of a Ngai Tahu assertion of dominance over older groups.

This survey illustrates themes from the preceding chapter, such as the fluidity of tribal grouping and naming. Rangitane, Ngati Ira and Ngati Kahungunu were names that competed as package labels for the mixed peoples of Hawke's Bay and the Wairarapa, just as Waitaha, Ngati Mamoe and Ngai Tahu did in the South Island. Who subsumes whom was – and is – almost a currency of rivalry in itself. This again is not so different from nationalist European and neo-European history. Much subsumption appears to have consisted less in full displacement than the imposition of new names on much the same group or groups. It corresponds less with invasion and immediate conquest by newcomers, than with long-term efforts by both old and new groups to impose their pre-eminence. Some groups adjusted to sustainable economics better than others. Population growth and a degree of colonisation continued or renewed in some regions. All of the late prehistoric expansions and migrations we have managed to identify stemmed directly or indirectly from Northland, Waikato, Taranaki and the East Coast – areas particularly rich in gardening and/or marine resources. Although compressed summary may give a contrary impression, these movements were not very frequent. Most groups encountered by Europeans around 1800 had lived on the spot, or a regular rotation of spots, for centuries, though their names and relative eminence might have changed.

The major movement in late prehistory seems to have been from the southern North Island to the South Island: groups of Ngai Tara, Rangitane, Ngati Ira, Ngati Apa, Ngati Kuia and Ngati Tumata all made this journey between the fifteenth and eighteenth centuries, as well as Ngati Mamoe and Ngai Tahu. Overpopulation in the Taranaki-Whanganui and East Coast source areas may have been the push, and traditions claim that greenstone was the pull. Some scholars tend to discount this, but they may not take full account of two factors. First, the assumption that northern Westland was the only source of greenstone has been shown to be false. Fields also existed in South Westland, the great lakes of western Otago, and Nelson. Fiordland bowenite could also be fire-treated to a hardness approaching true greenstone, or nephrite, making a total of five sources.[34] Nelson-Marlborough, the most popular target for migrants to the South Island, was not only a source in itself but also gave land and sea access to other sources, and to the Otago coast, where greenstone appears to have been processed into tools and weapons. Second, some research suggests that the population of Westland was much larger and more permanent than has been thought, and that these people worked a lot of greenstone.[35]

Greenstone literally had an edge over other adze stones. It was a rather metal-like stone, rating 6.5 on a scale of lithic hardness (with diamonds at 10), and it may have given a small but significant economic and military advantage – in the speed with which canoes and pa could be built, for example. It also made the best chisels for prestigious carving – as good as steel, though slower – and was a munificent gift.[36] It may therefore have become an important currency of rivalry. Early migration may have upset existing networks for the gift exchange of greenstone, pulling rivals in after it. Ngai Tahu's acquisition of independent control over the northern Westland greenstone source may have been a cause as well as a consequence of their rise to ascendancy in the South Island in the late eighteenth and early nineteenth centuries. Prior to this, having bounced off the tribes of Nelson-Marlborough, they appear to have co-existed with 'Waitaha' and Ngati Mamoe on the basis of rough parity, with hapu groups intermarrying, feuding and allying across tribal lines. This history was subsequently reshaped, with Pakeha help, into a 'Norman Conquest' and pushed back and compressed in time. The ultimate prize in the rivalry for mana was imposing one's name on a kin zone.

The politics of greenstone, and its impact on tribe formation and its myths, makes an interesting precedent for life after contact, when some groups succeeded in imposing their names on kin zones, partly through superior access to the new greenstone – iron and its works. The rivalries for access to greenstone and iron may even have merged. Migration, conflict and displacement or subsumption was continuing between 1769 and 1820 at Queen Charlotte Sound, a distribution centre for both iron and greenstone.[37] If Ngai Tahu conquest of Westland was not completed until about 1820, then it was soon challenged by a fresh incursion from the north – one that pursued both iron and greenstone.

The vast array of Maori groups, nuclear and extended families, hapu and hapu groups, tribes and kin zones, were the stuff of social prehistory, calibrating relationships from stranger to close kin, and constituting the babushka doll of social environments within which individuals lived out their lives. There were also divisions within groups. We have already touched on those related to status and leadership. Sacred chiefs and leaders were a hereditary and meritocratic élite, but status differences were not great compared with those of eighteenth-century Europe. Some early European visitors tried to invent a rigid hierarchy; others saw beyond this and remarked with surprise, and sometimes disapproval, on the egalitarian chaos of Maori society.

All free tribespeople, by definition, were related to their chiefs and could withhold obedience and compete for higher status, or at least help judge the rivalries of others. It was said that commoners did exist in Maori society, but that it was difficult to find one.[38] Slaves were not a hereditary caste and, as prisoners of war, were not numerous in normal times. The treatment of slaves could be extremely cruel, as one hostile missionary witness observed. But he also noted that 'in no instance, nor under any circumstances, have I known a case where a slave has been afraid freely to enter into conversation with a chief, or to treat him with the utmost freedom and unconcern'.[39] Slaves oscillated between the status of enemies, subject to sudden execution if further utu against their old tribe was required, and of adopted members of the new tribe, whose children were always free. But it remains true that being a Maori slave was no fun.

Chiefs sometimes enforced laws compounded from tapu and custom, but other forces were at least as important. In small, tight, kin-based communities, moral or peer pressure is especially powerful, and in Maori society it was backed up by divine sanctions associated with breaching tapu, by the threat of human-initiated magical retaliation and by more mundane sanctions such as muru and utu. This range of social and cultural constraints was generally effective, but no legal system is perfect. There appear to have been a few cases of something like outlawry, non-tribal bandits or hermits who may have transgressed norms and refused to accept the consequences. Ethnography records a southern outlaw, Tuai Te Kura, who killed an old woman and committed 'other outrages', and was eventually hunted down and killed. Te Kura was Ngati Mamoe and might be seen as a resistance fighter against Ngai Tahu, except that his own tribe appear to have participated in hunting him.[40] Archaeology contributes a mysterious case of a woman living alone, in a cave shelter at Teviotdale in North Canterbury. She had borne several children, but for some reason opted or was pushed out of society. She suffocated at about the age of 30, with her dog, during a bush fire.[41]

Gendering Prehistory

Within groups, gender is in some respects the great divide, and is an important theme of this book. We focus on three questions: the difference gender made to one's life experience, the interaction of this distinction with other dimensions of history, and change and continuity in these things through time. But New Zealand historiography is still quite weak on these issues – prehistory weaker still – and often we must speculate in a virtual vacuum of evidence. Let us look first at the gender situation at contact, then try to work back.

On 23 November 1773, at a Maori village in Queen Charlotte Sound, Marlborough, 'a child desired his mother to give him a piece of broiled Pinguin & as she did not immediately comply & refused to do it, it threw a large stone at her, whereupon she beat the Child, but her husband beat her unmercifully for it'. Six months earlier, the same diarist, the seal epicure Johann Forster, had observed another incident of Maori domestic violence at Dusky Sound, Fiordland, where his ship, Cook's *Resolution*, had also touched. 'The old Man beat his two wives, & the young girl beat her father, then fell a crying.'[42] The

Dusky man, a pioneer of contact, took his daughter aboard the *Resolution* on several visits, sending his two wives off fishing. She went armed, and her friendliness to the European sailors did not extend to sexual favours, price or no price, whereas prostitution was rife at Queen Charlotte.

Both the Dusky and Queen Charlotte men favoured their children, male or female, over their wives, against whom they were prepared to use violence. Forster concluded disapprovingly that the women were 'perfect slaves' to the men. Several other ethnographers also used the treatment of women as an 'index of civilisation', archetyping towards European queens on pedestals and away from brothels and sculleries, and rated the Maori low. Tupaia, of course, maintained that Maori women fared less well than Tahitian.[43]

But other outside observers were adamant that women were well treated and that violence was rarely directed towards them. In Northland in 1814, after founding the first Christian mission, Samuel Marsden wrote:

> I saw no quarrelling or domestic broils while I was on the island. They are kind to their women and children. I never observed a mark of violence on any of them, nor did I see a woman struck, and the missionary settlers informed me that they had never seen any difference among the native people of [Rangihoua village] during the period they had resided there.

John Nicholas, who accompanied Marsden, emphasised that males, including chiefs, participated in the childcare of both girls and boys, though he ungenerously attributed this to a desire to free their wives for housework.[44] Richard Cruise, visiting the same region in 1820, combined both the Forster and Marsden views. 'Husbands,' he wrote, 'considering women as beings infinitely inferior to themselves, often treat them with great brutality.' But he also noted that men were very tender towards children, both boys and girls, 'no partiality on account of sex was in any instance observed'.[45]

The Forster view began a long strand of assumption that Maori women lived in utter subjection to their men, which needs correction. The contradictions between the treatment of women between north and south and between wives and daughters may have stemmed from status, not gender. Women were favoured as prisoners in warfare – men were more likely to be killed – and became the slaves or low-status wives of their captors. Dusky and Queen Charlotte Sounds are both good candidates for such a situation, as is Northland in 1820 – but not 1814. The offspring of these unions carried no stigma. Where their fathers rated their own genes highly, as was often the case, they had corresponding status. Slave-wives were at the extreme end of a gender-relations spectrum, and even here girl children were valued – something that traditions such as the legend of Tawhaki tend to confirm. The hoary notion of frequent Maori infanticide of females has recently been discounted by Ian Pool.[46]

Although male lines were sometimes held to be senior, there are many traditional examples of women like Te Maiairea counting among the highest sacred chiefs. There are also cases of women heroes and, occasionally, leaders. One chiefly Northland woman carried a gun and participated in war haka soon after contact – even doing so naked, a privilege normally reserved strictly for males.[47] There was the custom of 'puhi' maidens: 'a young woman of chiefly rank, celebrated for her good looks and social skills, who was set up by the community as a focus of social esteem'.[48] Women had vital formal roles in encounter rituals, such as calling visitors on to the marae. Modern examples of the informal communal power of Maori women, even on marae on which they were not allowed to speak, could hold good for prehistory. Pretentious male outsiders could be deflated by means ranging from verbal interjection to such earthy insults as the whakapohane – baring the buttocks in the direction of the victim, a cross-cultural gesture of contempt also practised by Australian convict women. Research on Maori women after contact indicates that they had their own well-established kinds of tapu, influence and status.[49]

However, the temptation to reverse the pendulum too far should be resisted. Women's history can share the pitfalls of retrospective Utopianism, and one should not make too much of such things as the Maori 'Man on the Moon' being a woman. International prehistorians now point out that the worship of Earth Mothers does not necessarily indicate high female status any more than the veneration of the Virgin Mary. Women chiefs and leaders could be seen as having 'honorary male' status, augmented by manlike deeds such as that of Wairaka (or Muriwai) at Whakatane. Even if this was not the case, chiefly women might have been honoured less as such than for the fact that their bloodlines enshrined the mana and collective identity of the group, like the revered queens of sexist England. Even non-chiefly women did not lack tapu in some contexts, but Maori tradition and modern custom emphasises, sometimes quite strongly, that they were normally less tapu than men.

The European legend that Maori lords and masters sat back and watched women work is false, but there appears to have been a fairly rigid division of labour at contact. Although some women's work was highly respected, men's work usually outranked it and tended towards more valuable and prestigious items: paua but not pipi, crayfish but not crab. Best wrote that women were the best at catching crayfish, but ethnography suggests it was the men who ate the best ones.[50] A tendency for men to try to appropriate women's work after contact is identified in Chapter Seven. Research based on traditional Maori evidence suggests that 'young women were often treated as chattels, their relative value tied to their rank'.[51] Some Maori and Pakeha scholarship may romanticise Maori gender relations. Maori society at contact was male-dominated, 'sexist' in today's usage, though not completely so. One could say it was somewhat more sexist than Europe believed itself to be, and somewhat less sexist than Europe actually was.

Male ascendancy, if not dominance, appears to cross most times and cultures. Differences between men and women obviously do exist, though they can be exaggerated, and some can be socially constructed – more products of nurture than nature. The problem is not difference but the ranking of it, which men have consistently managed in their favour. Male ascendancy, however, is often contested. Women's resistance stems fundamentally from the contradiction between myths of male superiority and the reality of rough parity, though not sameness. It is limited by very close links with the opposition – 'sleeping with the enemy' – and by the existence of forces other than gender of which both men and women can be victims and beneficiaries. It therefore takes subtle forms. One, tending towards continuity, is the maintenance of a semi-independent women's domain, or subculture. In Maori society, this was associated with such things as midwifery and weaving. At Queen Charlotte Sound, there was continuity in women's crafts around the time of contact, but change in men's crafts – the men were displaced by invaders; the women were not.[52] This suggests an autonomous women's element of culture. Such domains were not wholly independent, nor incompatible with male ascendancy, but, like the importance of women in greeting rituals, they did give some autonomy and leverage.

Another form of resistance, tending towards change, is the exploitation of contextual transformation to loosen constraints and increase centrality. Women take these opportunities to improve their lot. A powerful male defensive reflex then tightens things up again. Because it is good politics to maintain that subjection is unchangeable, and because men tend to have greater influence on the dominant interpretation of the past, history itself can be a tool of the tightening. The loosening is largely written out, and the wound in male ascendancy is less often apparent than the scab: an intensification of rhetoric about female subordinacy and maleness. But women are reluctant to give up their gains, and they maintain memories and residues of them. I suggest that the rhythm in this story, in both history and prehistory, is one of three steps forward and two steps back.

First settlement itself may have provided Maori women with an opportunity to improve their lot. Women's status is said to have been quite high in forager societies. The yield from women's gathering often exceeded that from men's hunting of small game, and women sometimes hunted anyway. International prehistory suggests that women's status was also high in the earliest phase of cultivation – gardening or horticulture – which may have been practised mainly by them. Male status is believed to have increased with the rise of agriculture, and more individualised ownership of the equipment and domestic animals associated with it.[53] Maori did not practise agriculture in its narrow sense: the mass cultivation of grains. They had little in the way of productive domestic animals. Women are strongly linked to the early use of kumara in the traditions, as we saw in Chapter Two. Skeletons suggest that women paddled canoes more in early New Zealand prehistory than in late.[54] One can imagine that the first hunters, eager for game and with limited labour, were unconcerned about the gender of that labour. In short, there are hints that the circumstances of migration and early Maori economics may have enhanced women's economic centrality. Two other factors support this: weaving and grave goods.

Tropical Polynesia clearly required far less clothing than Aotearoa. Ocean voyaging could be cold, but tapa cloth may have met some of its needs, and this was so rare in Aotearoa because of the shortage of aute that it was used only for small ornaments. The colonisation of Aotearoa must therefore have suddenly increased the importance of making clothes, and demanded new raw materials and technologies. Seal, dog and even moa hide may sometimes have been used, but the Polynesians never appear to have been great tanners, and indigenous flax was the main solution. As Europeans discovered, processing this was no easy matter, and weaving (strictly, plaiting) it into the large Maori range of kilts and cloaks was a skilled art, whether or not it was adapted from tropical Polynesian basketmaking.[55] This art was developed and dominated by women, whose work should therefore have suddenly become more valuable.

Where possible, archaeologists try to deduce something about the status of prehistoric women from the value of the grave goods buried with them.[56] This is a tricky business. It is sometimes said that female grave goods solely indicate high hereditary status, but if this were the case, well-born children would be buried with similar goods, which is often not so. There is also some tendency for male-associated valuables to be made from stone, which do survive, and for female ones to be made from organic raw materials, which do not survive. Valuables woven from flax are obvious candidates. Given this, several women buried early in New Zealand prehistory, notably at the Wairau Bar, are quite well endowed with grave goods.[57] They have fewer fine adzes and moa-egg containers than men, but they do have some, and they may have had fine cloaks as well. One cannot read much into this, because burying grave goods with anyone is a custom that declined over time. But it just might indicate a less differentiated society, where able women achieved mana as well as inheriting it.

From the outset, however, there were countervailing forces, which prevailed after a time. The hunting of large or distant game probably tended to be male-oriented activities. Originally, this was simply because males were more expendable. Motherhood was, on average, the most dangerous of all human activities, but groups have no choice about risking their women in it. Where they do have a choice, as with war and dangerous hunting, they tend to risk their men, because they need fewer of them to reproduce. Men also have advantages in upper-body strength, though women are physically tougher in some other respects, such as surviving infancy. Through hunting, men acquire weapons and the skills to make and use them, and it is tempting to see the origins of male dominance in a primeval military coup. Hunting enhanced male mana directly through the distribution of large game – the occasional distribution of large items gives more prestige than the constant supply of small items – and control of the associated technologies, notably stoneworking and canoes. Childbirth and childrearing must have restricted women's involvement in hunting. Maori women appear to have had an average of between three and five children each. In late prehistory, when less protein was available, it was closer to three. In early prehistory, we guess, it was higher – it has been suggested that the skeletal evidence could actually reflect an average of four or five.[58]

In recent times, outside the cities, Maori tended to see birth parents as mere apprentices at childcare; grandparents were the real experts. This may have been true of prehistory too. Some use of classificatory relationships, whereby all women of the right generation within the hapu were your 'mothers', and frequent adoption by kin increased the pool of carers, as did male involvement. Motherhood may therefore have restricted women's activities less than we might expect. But pregnancy, birth and breastfeeding were not very easily compatible with chasing moa. Perhaps an initial period of lower sexual differentiation of labour, when women often crewed canoes and perhaps participated in hunting and even stoneworking, was progressively replaced by a male focus on hunting and stonework, and a female focus on gardening and gathering. Hunting was more mobile, involved more valuable, larger equipment, and single expeditions provided big yields for mana-enhancing distribution. Its crews and teams provided opportunities for the development of male subculture. It may therefore have enabled men to counteract an initial improvement in women's status.

As the big game disappeared, women's work in gardening and gathering was again suddenly revalued in relation to men's by the demise of the alternatives – a second opportunity for a loosening of male ascendancy. It was again reined in ways at which we can only guess. Hunter techniques and organisation invaded gardening and gathering. Women no longer crewed canoes as a matter of course, as the exceptional nature of the 'Whakatane' incident indicates, and were sometimes not even allowed to accompany offshore fishing expeditions.[59] Gardening was masculinised to the point where women, at contact, of some tribes were barred from aspects of kumara cultivation. Firth noted that this was especially so where gardening was most important. Gardening became more significant and, therefore, more male – a shift echoed in European dairy farming in the late nineteenth century.

The sexual division of labour was also quite marked in other economic activities, with men getting the most dangerous but also the most interesting and prestigious jobs.[60] Increases in warfare, pa building, tapu and the sanctity of chieftainship presumably benefited men's status more than women's.

Polygamy and the taking of slave-wives may have increased. Male influence on the early indoctrination of children may conceivably have increased as well, rigidly defining male and female roles even in baptismal prayers.[61] By whatever means, male dominance increased to the situation found at contact. But the two temporary improvements in the woman's lot did not erode entirely. Weaving, for example, remained a bastion of women's subculture, a female source of mana, taught by women to women.

It must be stressed that all this is guesswork. It is superior only to the assumption that nothing ever happened in the prehistory of gender. The guess is that changes associated with the two great transformations of Maori prehistory, first settlement itself and the decline of big-game hunting, revalued women's work and enabled women to loosen restrictions placed on them. A reflexive male 'backlash' then tightened things up again, but not completely. Later chapters will argue that this pattern of three steps forward and two back features in post-contact history as well, when Maori women's work was again suddenly revalued, and that it is also a theme of Pakeha history. Male ascendancy crosses cultures; its patterns may do so too.

Gods and Games

Like gender, age divides people. Prehistoric New Zealanders did not have a lot of it. One ethnographer claimed Maori normally lived to 80 or 90 years old,[62] and tradition, as with the Old Testament, features geriatric procreators by the score. But the news from skeletal remains is not so good. Maori were relatively big, powerful, healthy people, whose voyaging forebears had outpaced most contagious diseases, but infection, bronchial complaints and the loss of teeth appear to have killed most by the age of 40. The early inhabitants of the Wairau Bar died, on average, at about 29. The countrywide average age at death is usually pushed a little higher, to 31 or 32. There could be an element of minimalist over-reaction to the ancient patriarchs of traditional and ethnographic evidence here. The average age at death of 33 women was 35, despite their bearing at least 101 children, and other intersecting samples averaged 37 and 38.[63] The skeletal evidence on which all this is based is much less reliable for ages above the thirties. Traditional and ethnographic evidence does suggest that at least a few people had long lives. For those who survived infancy, the late thirties may have ended the normal innings, rather than the early thirties – an important difference to some of us. This compared quite favourably to the rest of the world. But it remains true that old age began at 40, and that the value of elders must have been enhanced by their rarity.

Childhood was dangerous, though not as much as in some other countries. Recent analyses suggest an infant mortality rate of between a fifth and a third.[64] Virtually all sources agree that children were well treated and seldom struck.

Education took place in daily life and in various types of whare wananga (school; literally, house of knowledge), whose high tapu usually excluded women, except for the type devoted to weaving. Marsden saw boys as young as four being schooled.[65] Whare wananga seem to represent a surprisingly formal education system. These schools ran during the economic off-season, sometimes literally in special houses. Tradition suggests that some were inter-regionally famous before contact. Ngai Tahu of Otago are said to have sent chiefly sons to a famous East Coast Eton, 'Te Rawheoro University'.[66] There are said to have been various categories of whare wananga: for the heirs of priestly ariki; for the teaching of ritual and genealogy to chiefly boys; for carving, moko (tattooing), everyday crafts such as housebuilding; and for makutu, or witchcraft. There were also women's schools, where weaving was taught, and even some provision for adult education.

There could be some Smithing in this formidable list of university faculties,[67] and the reality may have been less formal. Tikao specified only three types of school: whare maire, whare pu-rakau and wharekura – for general, military and sacred knowledge respectively. But there can be little doubt that schooling was wide-ranging and highly organised, at least for boys of rank. Adopting the examination practices of the whare makutu would certainly open up the academic job market. 'The highest evidence of the skill of the pupil was to will the death of his teacher . . . if your incantations did not kill your instructor you were not firm in the lessons given.'[68]

Picturing Maori education as organised around Eton and university-faculty equivalents is a symptom of a propensity to place the components of prehistory into the modern European box that seems least inappropriate. It has elements of romantic Green and White stereotypes, and of Smithing, and is reminiscent of the Flintstone television cartoons, which endow prehistory with all the machines and household utensils of modern America, dressed as adapted dinosaurs. Talk of Maori 'priests', 'prophets', 'generals', 'land sale' and 'law' takes something of this risk. But it is often worth it because the opposite myth is at least as deceptive. This portrays pre-contact Maori in solemn, sombre, lifeless terms, bent under a vast load of tapu and custom, and so integrated with nature that they almost disappear in it like the birds of the air and the fish of the sea. Their spiritualism is emphasised above all, sometimes for modern Maori and Pakeha purposes. This, too, would rank as a caricature if it were more amusing. Fun and games, laughter and irreverence did exist, even if they are hard to recover in full colour.

Not everything Maori gathered served a pragmatic purpose. They used a range of cosmetics: hair and body oils, paints and scents. Red and white bird feathers were highly valued – the name of the beautifully carved little feather boxes, wakahuia, derives from a favourite decorative bird. Soon after contact, a Nga Puhi purveyor of white feathers persuaded a Hauraki woman to trade her hapu's winter food stocks for them. Stone, bone and shell were used for ornament by men and women – one enthusiast wore an enemy's arm bone as an earring, another a live bird.[69] At least outside its source areas, greenstone appears to have been used mainly for mere, adzes and carving chisels until iron freed more of it to be used for ornaments.

Personal decoration, of course, had its social and cultural functions, but some things appear to have been collected from curiosity. Europeans were not the first to fossick for fossils in New Zealand. Groups of regularly shaped stones found in excavations may have been used for the draughts-like game known as mu. Pumice was used for toys, for carvers' experiments and perhaps for models to convey innovations from one part of the country to another.[70] Scholars have not yet managed to find evidence of the use of alcohol or other drugs, but there was chewing gum in the form of kauri resin, and there were various games, sports and entertainments. Some, like spear throwing and playing with model pa and canoes, had educational functions; others, like many waiata (songs), had spiritual and cultural functions. Some had neither. In tradition, women seeking revenge on the sorcerer Kae used a whole gamut of comic acts to make him laugh in order to identify him by his uneven teeth. 'A droll comic song', combined with 'making curious faces', eventually succeeded. The sealer John Boultbee referred to a 'song used on comic occasions . . . and when it is sung I have generally seen the singers standing on their heads'.[71] For some reason, modern Maori culture troupes seem to avoid these traditions.

Solemnity is more appropriate in considering Maori decorative art. Rock paintings, most common in the South Island, may have been the work of camping hunters. A difference between two contemporary rock-painting styles in North Otago and South Canterbury may reflect a division between two groups.[72] The Moriori of the Chathams inscribed somewhat similar drawings on living trees. Moko was an important form of conspicuous personal consumption. It required both the leisure to be tattooed, a long and painful operation, and the wealth to reward the tattooers, who are said to have been travelling professionals.[73] Weaving was highly developed, but woodcarving, which Joseph Banks rightly described as being 'like nothing but itself', was arguably the crowning achievement of Maori art, and it defies brief description.[74] Chests and boxes, weapons and tools, canoe prows and the main timbers of pa were all carved, as were the lintels of storehouses and chiefs' houses. At one level, the shapes and motifs of Maori carving had a fairly consistent range of styles. Shapes are sometimes divided into serpentine and square, and motifs into curvilinear and rectilinear. Within very broad limits such as these, there was great diversity. There were almost as many styles as there were tribes; these changed over time as well, and whenever you think you have the art neatly categorised, you see something incongruous and unique.[75]

It is probably true that carving was redolent with symbolism, some of it systematic; and that, with myths, legend, songs and whakapapa, it formed an important part of the matrix by which tradition was preserved. But there are dangers in seeing it as some sort of hieroglyphic spiritual language. Maori carvers not only performed religious ceremonies in wood, and developed an inherited tradition, but also expressed and amused themselves. Neither systematic symbolism nor individualism should be denied or exaggerated. Two sources claim the spiral motif in both moko and carving originated as copies of fingerprints.[76] Around 1820, some Northland chiefs invented the practice of copying their moko on paper as signatures. Such designs might therefore symbolise both descent – the fingerprints of one's ancestors carved on one's skin – and individualism – a unique stamp. Sexual organs literally featured large in some carvings, until castrated by Christianity – as symbols of descent and the great powers associated with virility, rather than as the self-portraits of egomaniacs.

Marae may also have had prosaic origins. It has been argued that they began simply as the porches or forecourts of large houses, places to meet and work in fine weather, and to greet visitors.[77] One can also out-spiritualise oneself with regard to the ideology of housing. Immediately to the right of the door was the place of honour, not necessarily because of its orientation towards Hawaiki or some other Mecca, but because this was where you got stepped on least. The modern meeting house, or wharepuni, is believed to have developed fully after contact from the chief's house, perhaps combined with houses especially built for important visitors, but a very large house was seen on the East Coast in 1769.[78] They were tapu places, but not shrines or temples; their sanctity could be lifted or limited, and they could host an evening's chat and children's games as well as formal meetings. Raymond Firth was allowed to dine in one but was fined threepence for failing to remove his shoes.[79]

Most excavated houses, early and late, small and large, tend to follow the shape and internal organisation of the wharepuni. Two other substantial and permanent types may have existed. Anderson argues that, in the south at least, round houses were more than mere temporary shelters, and one might add that a large round house appears in the legend of Kae.[80] The excavations at Pouerua in Northland seem to have resurrected partly sunken houses, once dismissed as storage pits.[81] Interestingly, there appears to have been a tendency for stoneworkers to occupy these houses, perhaps because these rich and respected old men liked to insulate themselves from the cold.

We move now to still more dangerous ground: religion. Io, the alleged supreme god, was probably but not certainly adapted or even invented after contact, and the versions of Maori cosmology that have come down to us may be rather homogenised.[82] In some accounts, there were many phases of Te Kore and

Te Po, pre-existence, and many stages of heaven, culminating in the emergence into Te Ao Marama, the world of light. Creation of the human world took place when Rangi, the Sky Father, and Papa, the Earth Mother, hitherto clasped together in eternal embrace, were forced apart by their rebellious sons. Tikao listed many sons, but Te Rangikaheke – the core source of most published accounts, via Governor George Grey – gives six, each the god of a sphere of nature.[83] The short versions of their names and attributes are: Tane (forests and birds), Tu (man and warfare), Tawhirimatea (winds), Haumia (wild plants), Rongomatane (cultivated plants) and Tangaroa (fish and the sea). Tane and Tu receive most emphasis. Tane played the leading role in separating his parents, then went on to create the first woman, producing the rest of humanity by cohabiting with their daughter, Hine-ti-tama. Learning of this incest, she fled in shame and became Hine-nui-te-po, the Great Woman of the Night and goddess of death. Meanwhile, Tu became dissatisfied with the performance of his brothers in the conflict with Rangi and Tawhirimatea, who sided with his father. Tu therefore turned against his brothers, vanquished them, including Tane, and reduced them to food and tools for himself and humanity.

Apart from these great 'departmental' gods, there were at least three other types of deity: major gods of unknown but ancient origin such as Uenuku and Maru, who might or might not represent elemental forces; great natural features endowed with divinity such as the mountain god Taranaki; and a whole spectrum of deified or heroic ancestors. Since loose genealogies might be traced back as far as Rangi himself, the distinction between elemental gods and deified ancestors was by no means rigid. As in European folklore, the Maori also populated their world with numerous fairies, monsters, demons and spirits. Tohunga, chiefs, seers and sorcerers invoked, propitiated and manipulated these forces through prayer, ritual and magic. There was, of course, no unnatural divide between magic and religion. We can only speculate about how this rich cosmology changed over time.

The worship of elemental forces is said to be characteristic of the early stages of human prehistory, with personalised gods emerging later. Maori cosmology features both, so this is no great help. The story of Hine-ti-tama clearly legitimates proscriptions against incest, but the wars of children against parents, and brother against brother, are hardly morality parables. Tane and Tu seem almost to compete for precedence, and it is not inconceivable that the stress on Tu and war in general partially overlaid an earlier emphasis on Tane, and that this change correlated with the transformations of mid-prehistory. But we cannot know, or even guess very meaningfully, and the great prominence of Tu and his works could even be as recent as the Musket Wars of the 1820s.

What is clear is that Maori religion did change over time. As Te Rangi Hiroa noted, the gods were 'by no means as immutable as some are inclined to think'.[84] The pantheon regularly incorporated newly deified ancestors and newly significant natural features, and it exhibited regional variation in selection and emphasis. Religion was not solely the domain of priestly tohunga, but also of other experts. The exploitation of new resources required appropriate handling of their supernatural dimension. Complex rituals developed around the gathering and processing of greenstone, for example. If social, natural and supernatural worlds were interlocked, then surely changes in one required corresponding changes in the others. What might the mechanism of change have been? We reserve our attempt to answer this question for Part Two, when we examine the Maori religious change we know most about: the incorporation of Christianity.

The close integration of the supernatural and daily life, the sheer mass of gods, and a commendable but somewhat gullible reaction to old Eurocentric dismissals of it can combine to give a false impression of Maori religion. People in prehistory, as noted above, can seem flies caught in a web of sacred forces, groaning under the weight of their own spirituality, lives dictated by the divine. Maui is the appropriate antidote to this. He is usually categorised as a demigod, between hero and deity, yet several early European inquirers were given the impression that Maui dominated the Maori pantheon, and perhaps in a sense he did.[85]

There was little fatalism, conformism or solemn reverence about Maui. When reprimanded by his parents, he replied: 'Oh, what do I care for that: do you think my perverse proceedings are put a stop to by this? Certainly not; I intend to go on in the same way for ever, ever, ever.'[86] Maui ultimately met his death between the thighs of Hine-nui-te-po while trying to conquer the human mortality embodied in her. But this defeat was preceded by many victories. Apart from turning his brother-in-law into a dog, Maui wrested the North Island and perhaps the rest of the world from the deep, and performed numerous other great feats such as vanquishing the sun, so lengthening the day for human enjoyment. His adventures, 'the seven fights of Maui', are a series of conquests of nature and supernature. Maui, though divine, was also human, an ambiguity that should not give Christians too much difficulty. He has been compared to trickster figures such as Loki and Odysseus, but these two did not create their Scandinavian and Greek worlds. Maui was a trickster figure, but he was also more – embodying, perhaps, a struggle against fate in which humanity was not entirely helpless.

Something other than fatalism and utter reverence for the divine is also found elsewhere in Maori tradition. Tikao told a story of first contact in which an early European explorer, said to be James Cook himself, was suspected of divinity because he smoked a pipe. A Maori chief tested this hypothesis by dowsing the explorer with a bucket of water to see if the sacred fire would be put out. Tikao suggested that a similar reaction might explain the death of

Cook in Hawai'i: the Hawaiians may have killed him simply to test his divinity.[87] It is often said that Maori believed the first Europeans, and their death-dealing ships, to be gods. If so, they did not flinch or flee, but fought and traded with gods. After all, Maui had conquered the sun.

PART

2

Contact and Empire

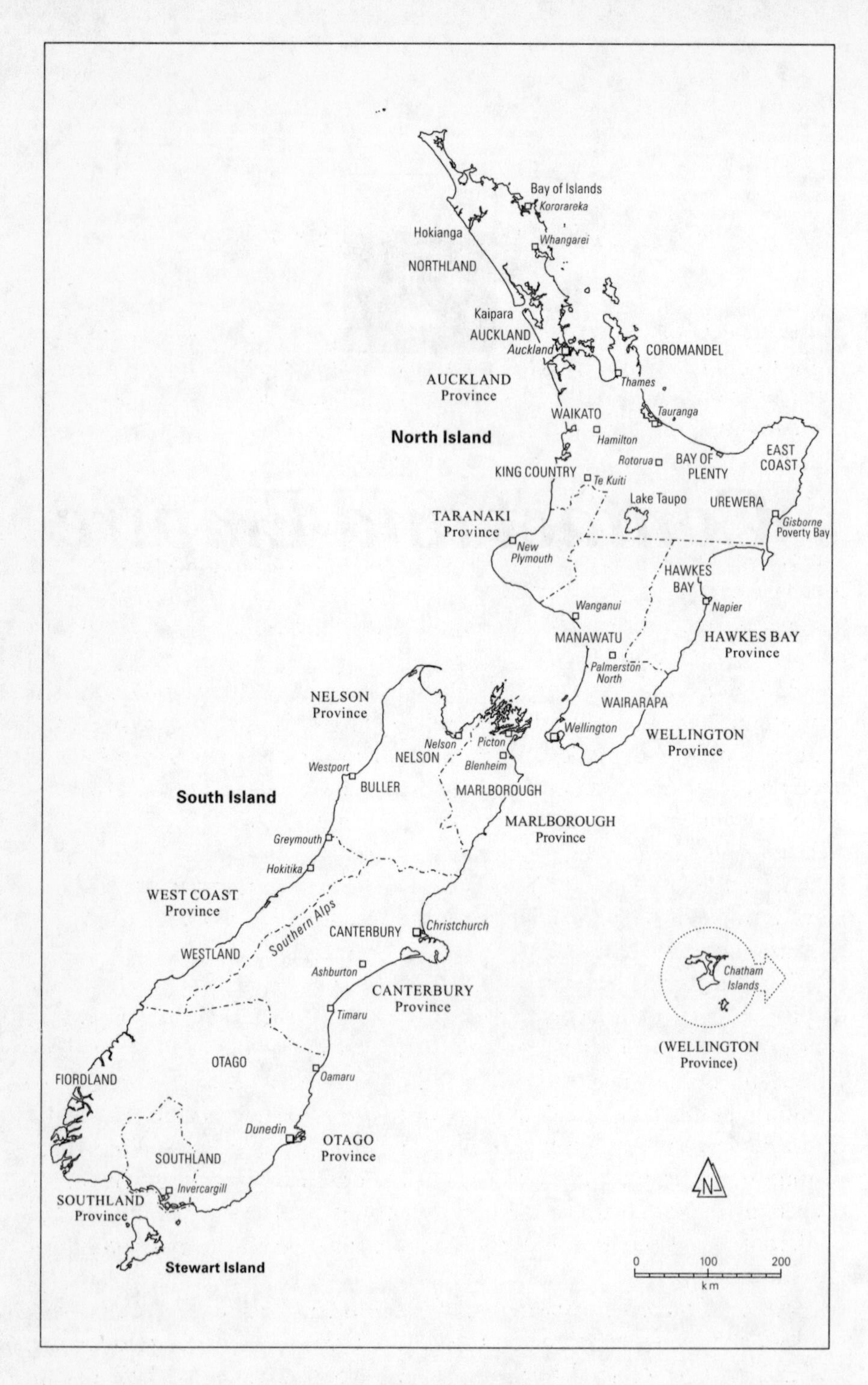

Colonial New Zealand

In the eighteenth and nineteenth centuries, Europe exploded outward in one of the most phenomenal expansions in human history. This explosion impelled three tides of people on to New Zealand's shores. The first tide, from 1769, came in hundreds; the second, from 1840, in thousands; the third, from 1860, in tens of thousands. The actual and mythical dynamics of these migrations, and the way in which they congealed into a society, are discussed in Part Three. The explosion also impelled European and non-European worlds into each other; the peoples of the latter often found this the biggest challenge they had ever faced. Many are said to have crumpled under the weight of expanding Europe, and some did. But on the whole their responses are the great survival story of modern times.

Europeans found that exploding was not entirely pleasant either. Massive outward expansion was entwined with the massive domestic expansion of an age of revolutions from 1750: in science, industry and religion, and in America and France. New ideas stemming from both expansions corroded old certainties; the old fought back, and the two left great wounds in each other. An ideology of expansion hardened like a scab over these wounds, determined in part by what Europe found in the outside world. The ideology in turn helped determine what Europeans saw and did in the outside world, an ongoing ricochet. Expansion created myths that helped shape the history of expansion.

Expansion and its myths took three main forms: contact, settlement and empire. Settlement, the reproduction of peoples through colonisation, was the subject of Part One, for Polynesians, and will be the subject of Part Three, for Europeans. Contact is intended to mean not just the initial encounter but the continuing process of interaction between Europeans and non-Europeans. It could be very substantial but did not necessarily subordinate. Empire, by definition, did involve the subordination of non-Europeans, though it did not necessarily deprive them of cultural autonomy or identity. Part Two of this book looks at the relationship of contact, empire and their myths with New Zealand history.

Stories of Maori–European relations are usually balanced on the fulcrum of 1840, and there are some good reasons for this. In 1840, Edward Gibbon Wakefield's New Zealand Company began planting its remarkable instant townships, the British colony of New Zealand was set up, and representatives of the British Crown and many Maori tribes signed the Treaty of Waitangi. But important processes began before 1840, and continued after it, and the year is in some respects an artificial watershed.

Apart from real and mythical prologues, European ships began visiting New Zealand in 1769. In that year, there were two ship visits; in the 1830s there were something like a thousand. Long-term settlers began arriving about 1800: at first they came as isolated individuals, living with Maori as Maori; then in camps killing seals and cutting timber; then, from 1814, in stations of missionaries, shore whalers, timber workers, and traders. About 1830, some settlers began clustering into towns or town-like entities, and from that year the settler population at least doubled each decade until the 1870s, reaching half a million in the early 1880s. Generally, Maori welcomed Europe and its things and thoughts until the 1860s, when co-operation collapsed into conflict. The settlers, by now self-governing, squeaked home to victory in these wars, with the help of Maori allies, Australian recruits and the British Empire. The level of Maori success, however, dictated caution, and British or neo-British rule was not finally imposed on Maori until the end of the century. The following chapters try to understand contact and empire, and to understand how and why the former became the latter.

CHAPTER FIVE

The European Discovery of New Zealand

During the late Middle Ages, while Maori began their painful transition from hunters to gardeners in complete isolation, Europe and Asia were loosely linked by trade, the exchange of occasional visitors, and the existence of intermediary empires: Byzantine, Mongol and Islamic. Eurasia was, for its inhabitants, the Old World. In the fifteenth and sixteenth centuries, searching for quicker routes between the extremities of this world, Europeans learned of a new one: the Americas. In the eighteenth century, now motivated by science as well as short cuts, Europeans found an even newer world, the Pacific, which Spanish galleons had hitherto seen as a mere vacuum to be crossed. These European explorers were not, of course, the first people to see these places, but they did 'discover', uncover or reveal them to Europe. At the same time, Europe was revealed to, or discovered by, the inhabitants of the Pacific. Europeans were obviously crucial catalysts of this process, and understandably assumed themselves to be its sole active agents. Historians have traditionally accepted the basic paradigm: the ship arrives, the shore sits and waits. Yet, metaphorically and sometimes literally, non-European Marco Polos went and got the things and thoughts of Europe as much as they were brought to them. Discovery was mutual.

Discoveries and Inventions

European New Zealand, or at least something that incorporated it, was invented in Africa during the second century after Christ. In the great Hellenic cultural centre of Alexandria, the geographer Ptolemy asserted that a Southern Continent, or Great South Land, must exist to balance the world. The earliest-known European discoverers were looking for this when they bumped into New Zealand, testing a 1,500-year-old Greek hypothesis based on a wrong premise. It was not always clear that Ptolemy *was* wrong. One of his intellectual heirs, Alexander Dalrymple, calculated that the Southern Continent had 50 million fair-skinned people and spanned the whole Pacific, which is exactly what some nineteenth-century settlers thought New Zealand would become.[1]

The first Europeans to visit New Zealand just might have been French captain Binot de Gonneville and his crew, on 5 January 1504. Gonneville claimed to have been driven by storms to a land two months away from his last-known position, south of the Cape of Good Hope. Well treated by the natives during their six-month stay, the Frenchmen managed to repair their ship and return to Europe. When almost home, they were taken by pirates and lost everything, including their charts and logbooks. The survivors made it back to France, where Gonneville made a sworn statement of his adventures, confirmed by his officers. Gonneville did exist, and he was stranded somewhere, but regrettably it is more likely to have been South America or Madagascar than New Zealand.[2]

There are even more persistent stories of Portuguese or Spanish discoveries before Tasman. In 1893, the *New Zealand Official Yearbook* thought it widely assumed that the Spanish sailor Juan Fernandez had found New Zealand in 1576. There are still legends and theories of lost caravels.[3] As with Maori voyaging, minimalist scholarship, convinced that the most mundane possibility somehow becomes the most likely, exaggerates the improbability of such visits. Scores of ships did cross the Pacific between the Spanish possessions in South America and the Philippines, and some were driven far off course. One may indeed have ended up in New Zealand. But it is unlikely to have returned to tell the tale, and its crew would probably have been wiped out or absorbed by the Maori without influencing them much, as the far larger Scandinavian settlement in Greenland was absorbed by the Inuit. The really interesting question is why many New Zealanders thought that this mattered enough to accept or reject beyond the evidence.

One answer is simple romance: people like lost tribes and lost caravels. Another answer, perhaps, is that New Zealanders were a little embarrassed about the shortness of their European history and liked to lengthen it, forgetting that it is not the length that counts. There was a comparable tendency to compare landforms to ruined castles and abbeys, and Maori carvings to hieroglyphics, populating a ruinless and runeless land with history.[4] Another factor is the European penchant for 'co-option', for somehow attributing to themselves that which they found good in non-European peoples. Archbishop Richard Whately credited Inca civilisation to a European washed ashore.[5] Lost caravels similarly explained the sophistication of Maori culture through European influence. Searchers have unearthed a Tamil bell, as well as Spanish helmet, but no-one seems very interested in positing a Sri Lankan caravel. Spanish discovery Europeanised Maori, but it did not Teutonise, which was preferred, or Anglicise, which was ideal. One solution was to simply forget about the lost caravel or to underplay its possibility. Children's novelist Ronald Syme addressed the problem directly in *The Spaniards Came at Dawn*.[6] His lost caravel fetched up in New Zealand with some English prisoners aboard. The arrogant Dons mistreated the local Maori, but the English were nice to them. Together, English and Maori attacked the Spaniards, seized the ship and sailed it back to both Hawaikis. The pirates who seized Gonneville's ship were English too. Myths of the White Maori and the Britain of the South, processes of Europeanising Maori and Anglicising New Zealand, got ahead of history – and helped determine it.

Between 1567 and 1648, the rebel Dutch republic performed the remarkable feat of fending off the Spanish superpower with one hand and grasping the world's trade with the other. The farthest outstretched finger of the grasping hand touched New Zealand in 1642, was pricked and recoiled. We can say more about this next discovery. In August 1642, Antonio Van Diemen, Governor-General of the Dutch East Indies, ordered two officers to sail south and test Ptolemy's hypothesis. As is often the case, the less well known of the two, Pilot-Major Francoijs Visscher, had actually conceived the expedition, but it was Abel Janszoon Tasman, an experienced and capable seaman, who led it. The expedition aimed not at discovery for its own sake but at wealth, power and fame for its authors and their fledgling nation. All three men were convinced they would find the opulent 'Great South Land'. Van Diemen cited the example of 'the highly renowned naval hero Christopher Columbus', noted that the new America they would find was bound to contain 'many excellent and fertile regions' and gave detailed instructions. Each of the two ships, the *Heemskerck* and *Zeehaen*, were to carry two hogsheads of strong arrack 'for the sake of the men's health', and the crews were to pretend to any natives they met 'that you are by no means eager for precious metals, so as to leave them ignorant of the value of the same'.[7]

By 18 December 1642, the expedition seemed to have met with quick success. *Heemskerck* and *Zeehaen* lay at anchor at what is now called Golden Bay, first sighted five days before. Two canoes came out and the natives in them addressed the Dutch, 'but we could not understand a word they said'. The natives then blew a trumpet-like instrument, and a Dutch trumpeter responded, but musical communication proved no more effective than words. Ngati Tumata Kokiri, the people in the canoes, were equally bewildered. But they were used to invasions from the north and concluded that the strangers in the weird fat canoes had defied their ritual challenge. Next day they put out again. This time the lead canoe had a high and pointed prow – a war canoe. The officers of both Dutch ships were in council aboard the *Heemskerck*, discussing how best to find and exploit the local riches. They were called on deck as the war canoe approached to within 50 metres. The Dutch held up trade goods, 'white linen and some knives', but the natives did not seem interested. Tasman despatched a boat to the *Zeehaen* to warn the crew to be cautious. Ngati Tumata now had an accessible target. They raced towards the boat, surprising the Dutch with their speed, and rammed it. The officers watched in horror as 'short thick clubs' rose and fell.

Ngati Tumata killed three Dutchmen and mortally wounded another. They took one body ashore, and very probably ate it to show their contempt for the invaders. The first of many European imports consumed in New Zealand was a dead Dutchman. The surviving Dutch held another council, named the bay 'Murderers', and concluded they had no choice but 'to consider the inhabitants of this country as enemies'. The Dutch had enough enemies, so they sailed up the coast and away, and did not come back for 300 years, when 30,000 of them settled in New Zealand after the Second World War. Indeed, no known Europeans at all came back for 127 years, which may make Ngati Tumata's the cheapest and most effective resistance to European expansion in all history.[8]

Neither contemporaries nor historians were pleased with Tasman's efforts. Both felt that he had 'left everything to be more closely inquired into by more industrious successors', and were unimpressed by his cartography as well as his diffidence.[9] He was demoted into a disconnected prologue to European contact, of little more actual significance than Gonneville and Fernandez. To some extent this is justified. Tasman found, but he did not look very hard nor tell very well, and in discovery the telling is as important as the finding. He opened a fleeting window between the world and New Zealand, then, with the help of Ngati Tumata, promptly closed it.

Tasman himself may have had some sense of being hard done by fate. He marred his subsequent career with a drunken attempt to personally hang one of his own sailors, and has been described as 'rather a nasty piece of humanity'. Yet modern research has also suggested that his charts were not so bad.[10] He guessed that there was limited wealth in his new land, and that what there was would not be easy to trick or take from the natives. He guessed right. And he did bequeath, indirectly, something quite important: a name. Tasman called his discovery Staten Land, thinking Ptolemaically that it might be linked to the Staten Land previously discovered south of Cape Horn.

Unimpressed by this logic, a Dutch mapmaker, probably Johan Blaeu, renamed it Nieuw Zeeland, Zeelandia Nova, to match New Holland, as Australia was then known.[11] Some would now prefer 'Aotearoa' to 'New Zealand', just as some nineteenth-century British settlers would have preferred 'The Britain of the South' or its variants. The neutral Dutch name, 'New Sea-land', is not a bad compromise. Old Zeeland was Holland's junior partner; the two provinces led the Dutch struggle against Spain and the sea, eventually mastering both. Its motto is 'I struggle and emerge'. Today, Old Zeeland gets few root-seeking tourists from New Zealand. It and Tasman extend New Zealand's European history, and so they are remembered. They do not extend New Zealand's British history, and so are not remembered very hard.

From 1769, contact between New Zealand and the world was reopened by a series of European exploratory expeditions. Motives varied. Jean de Surville's privately financed French expedition in 1769 sought a new El Dorado. In the first English expedition, the same year, Joseph Banks, the wealthy man of science who at first threatened to overshadow his shipmaster James Cook, sought the old Southern Continent. As their *Endeavour* nosed its way down New Zealand's south-east coast, Banks's journal records how hopes rose, only to be dashed by the open sea south of Stewart Island – 'the total demolition of our aerial fabrick calld continent'.[12] It is tempting to associate this founding disappointment with New Zealand's enduring sense of guilt at being small.

National rivalry stimulated or justified expensive exploration in a way that has been compared to the American–Soviet space race of the 1960s. Dumont d'Urville, a nineteenth-century French explorer, sent an officer to the museums of Holland and Britain before setting out for the Pacific, to check out what specimens France needed to keep up. More personal competition was also a factor. Dumont d'Urville confessed himself 'haunted by the example of Cook', and lost no opportunity to criticise his charts and his place-names.[13] But a major motivation was science, or at least the romance of science. Great scientists accompanied the expeditions. Exploration was the field research branch of the scientific revolution. The early explorers were the eyes of the Enlightenment, on very long stalks.

The scientific exploration phase of New Zealand's contact with Europe actually lasted for 90 years after 1769, *Endeavour* to *Novara*, fusing with the subsequent phases of trade and settlement. In comparison with the preceding 127 years, these expeditions came thick and fast. Cook visited New Zealand five times on three voyages, 1769–70, 1773–74 and 1777. Other English expeditions were led by Vancouver (1791); Robert FitzRoy (1835), who later became governor; Ross (1840–42); and Stokes (1848–51). French eighteenth-century visits included those of de Surville (1769) and the unfortunate Marion du Fresne (1772). Marion was followed by d'Entrecasteaux (1793), and succeeded in the next century by Duperrey (1824), Dumont d'Urville (1827 and 1840), Laplace (1831) and Dupetit-Thouars (1838). Arguably, one could add the voyages of Cécille (1838), Lavaud (1840–43), and Bérard (1843–46), all three of which carried out scientific research as well as other business. In 1793, a definite Spanish caravel arrived at last in the form of Malaspina's expedition, one of whose boats entered Dusky Sound. There were also Russian, American and Austrian expeditions: Bellingshausen in 1820, Wilkes in 1840 and von Wüllerstorf-Urbair in the *Novara* in 1858–59.[14]

That Britain monopolised early New Zealand contact with Europe is clearly a myth. If the early explorers were engaged in a cross-country teams race, the Dutch would have crossed the line first by a country mile and France would have won on points. But the Anglicising of New Zealand is the larger shadow of a large reality – it needs pruning, not uprooting. A significant part of the kernel of truth is James Cook, a Yorkshireman of humble birth.[15] By sheer professionalism, he rose to high rank: to post-captain in the Royal Navy, to greatest scientific explorer in history and to Pakeha Kupe in myth. Cook's deification began soon after his death in Hawai'i in 1779. He was compared to Ulysses, and even Christ.[16] A New Zealand folk-tale alleged that an *Endeavour* wrecked in Dusky Sound in 1795 was Cook's *Endeavour*, come home to die.[17] In 1822, one D. Erskine petitioned the British Government that New Zealand be colonised, that 'grants of land and seniority of rank' be given to Cook's descendants, and that both islands and their capitals be named after him, which would have been rather confusing.[18] Cook's humble birth, his quiet pragmatism, his trumping of a bunch of intellectuals made him the prototype of an archetype. One might even see his imprimatur in the popular American television series *Star Trek*. Captains Kirk/Cook and the *Enterprise/Endeavour* both boldly went where no (White or Earth) man had gone before.

Cook was the first of a Pakeha pantheon of deified ancestors. Others, like the great coloniser Wakefield, the great missionary Samuel Marsden and the great governor George Grey, had feet of clay. Cynics can find feet of clay on Cook's ankles too. In later life he developed the nasty habit of cutting the ears off petty thieves.[19] In contrast to Anglicising legend, his early treatment of Maori compares unfavourably to de Surville's – in practice as against principle. De Surville killed no Maori and kidnapped one. Cook killed several Maori and tried to kidnap a few. There is little doubt that Cook has been emphasised to the unfair exclusion of the massive French contribution to European knowledge of New Zealand.[20] But on the whole Cook still ranks first on merit, as well as Englishness. His central virtue was stubbornness: a determination to complete. He insisted on completing the outline of Australia, the outline of New Zealand and the search for the Southern Continent. Some of his largeness of spirit is not the invention of eulogists. On his second voyage, ten of the crew of his subordinate captain, Tobias Furneaux, were killed by Maori at Queen Charlotte Sound. On the third voyage, Cook found that the chief Kahura was the leading instigator. Disdaining vengeance, and suspecting that his own men may have provoked the incident, Cook entertained Kahura to dinner, pleased that the chief trusted him enough to expect to be anything other than the main course.[21]

Cook found better than his predecessors and contemporaries, investigated more thoroughly and carefully, and he and his associates told better. Their publications dominated the European idea of New Zealand for half a century. Thousands of New Zealanders now live in Cook's place-names as contentedly as they live in Kupe's. But it may be going a little far to assert that 'Cook's metaphorical mode of naming . . . represents an authentic mode of knowing, a travelling epistemology', and to find arcane meaning in place-names as resonant as 'Sandy Bay'.[22] We cannot know, wrote Cook, 'what use future ages may make of the discoveries made in the present'.[23]

The Myths of Empire

Maori and explorers massacred each other on several occasions. Both had militaristic encounter rituals, salutes of cannon and haka, and it was a while before each learned the other intended to warn enemies rather than make them. The bourgeois Cook took an especially hard line on theft. But few of the twenty expeditions encountered much violence, and the explorers were able to distribute seeds, animals, glass beads, bottles, cloth, nails, small iron tools and venereal disease quite generously. Most of the seeds and animals failed to acclimatise, and the effect of VD was not great. The nails, adapted by Maori into wood chisels, may have led to a flowering of carving, and the explorers may have revolutionised Maori entertainment. Maori made a holiday of European visits, coming from far and near to visit the *Endeavour*, that novel seaborne circus complete with strange beasts, unusual foods, magic tricks and even clowns. Horeta Te Taniwha remembered his visit as a young boy: 'as we could not understand them we laughed, and they laughed also . . . we gave our mats for their mats, to which some of our warriors said "ka pai" [good], which words were repeated by the goblins, at which we laughed and were joined in the laugh by the goblins'.[24] Maori were delighted by the drills of marines and soldiers. In 1820, some from a visiting ship were paid to give drill performances in several villages – inverted tourist haka.[25] But on the whole the direct effect of the explorers on Maori was not vast.

What the scientific explorers did do, however, was reopen the sea links between New Zealand and the world, and the traffic was not one way. They took back the notes, pictures and objects that helped create Europe's image of New Zealand, and new worlds like it. Each expedition published findings, spread information and misinformation, and encouraged speculation and romance. Alexander Dalrymple and Benjamin Franklin published a scheme for the civilisation of Maori in 1771. A 400-page fantasy set in Cook's New Zealand, *The Travels of Hildebrand Bowman, Esquire, into Carnovirria, Taupiniera, Olfactaria, and Auditante, in New-Zealand*, appeared by 1778.[26] Each exploring expedition assembled collections of samples and artefacts. Richard Owen, the British scientist who deduced the moa from bone fragments without ever visiting New Zealand, appealed for more bones 'for the honour of our country'. Charles Meryon, 'the most important European artist to have worked in New Zealand', included Maori war canoes in his etching of the French Navy Ministry in Paris; French writer Antoine Foley, a friend of Auguste Comte, wrote a fanciful history of southern Maori.[27] Glass cases of New Zealandiana built up in Vienna and Moscow, as well as London and Paris. The collections included shrunken Maori heads, sold by their enemies to carry vengeance beyond the grave. They sat, and sometimes still sit, in European museums. There, they took their own vengeance by contributing to evidence of great human diversity, a fact subversive of comfortable old certainties.

Scientific exploration spanned the age of European revolutions and technological development, and contributed to the ideological ferment these caused. One of the first French explorers of New Zealand, Marion du Fresne, escaped the British Navy after rescuing the Young Pretender, 'Bonnie Prince Charlie', from Scotland in 1745, only to be killed by a Maori who had never known metal. One of the last French explorers, Dumont d'Urville, was killed by a railway train. Cook's ship was not so different from Tasman's; John Lort Stokes's *Acheron* was a paddle-steamer. Technological progress fed Europe's high opinion of itself, yet at the same time produced change trauma. Europe's knowledge of, and relations with, the outside world did the same. Ricochets took place between things and thoughts and Us and Them. To help salve these wounds and provide fresh certainties, Europe's ethos of expansion hardened into a mythology of empire.

Before the rise of science, most Europeans believed literally in the Bible. The acceptance of the orthodox Christian world view was beyond proof, evidence was unnecessary, as with the Maori belief system. But the eighteenth and nineteenth centuries saw a great rise in the demand for proof, and the evidence gained by explorers and classifiers did not always fit well with Christian mythology and other cherished beliefs. Australian rock, redolent of age, made it hard to believe, with a seventeenth-century Chancellor of Cambridge University, that 'mankind was created at 9 a.m. on 12 September 3928 BC'.[28] It was difficult to visualise New Zealand's tuatara and kiwi skipping off the Ark, two by two. The European belief system was flexible and resilient, and it did not break – indeed, Evangelism was Christianity's powerful reassertion of faith – but it did stretch and crack, notably around views of Us and Them. To simplify a complicated story, the cracks and stretchmarks were papered over by intensifying racial and race-related beliefs in European superiority and destiny. These did not always denigrate non-Europeans; those who liked Europe or seemed European-like could do rather well. But rising racialisms did lead to a shift away from the green and clear lenses on tribal peoples, and towards the black, white and grey. And they did contribute to a tendency to write the history of contact and empire in advance.

Once started, contact, or ongoing interaction between European and non-Europe, was increasingly thought to be unstoppable. Sailing away again for 127 years as Tasman had done was no longer an option; there would always be some trader willing to try his luck, some explorer wishing to make his name. There were solid reasons for European interest in New Zealand from the 1790s, as we will see in the next section. But contact was also driven by dreams of El Dorado. Explorers' published accounts were pored over for hints of exotic riches that could be plucked from the wild. Dreams and solid reasons were not always easy to distinguish, for contemporaries or historians. Another belief that burgeoned in the nineteenth century was that contact would inevitably lead to empire. It was never universal. Some humanitarians and free traders maintained that empire was immoral or unnecessary. But many expected empire to arise naturally from contact, or from the need to control contact, and so render it more humane. Empire was expected to come in one of three ways: conversion, conquest or fatal impact.

'Conversion' is used here to mean not only religious conversion but the whole package of agencies by which non-Europeans were to be transformed into something European-like and peacefully subordinated to Europe. In principle, Europeanisation and subordination were not the same thing; in practice, there was a strong tendency to blur them. In principle, non-Europeans could be converted all the way to equality; in practice, equality was usually a step ahead of even the most eager converts, dangling ever in front of them like the hare in front of a racing greyhound.

The classic agencies of conversion were commerce, civilisation and Christianity. But such things as European technology, governments, treaties, laws and settler-neighbours were also thought to convert. Conversion could be intended, as with missionaries, or unintended, a side-effect of trade; it could be unofficial – the work of private organisations; or official – the work of governments. It could be soft – the gentle persuasions of idealised evangelism; or hard – the coercions of economic pressure. Associated with the relatively benign White Savage lens, and with 'monogenist' beliefs in the original unity of humanity, there was something almost generous about the European desire to convert, and something wonderfully naive about their confidence in their capacity to do so. Europeans had something marvellous to share – themselves, and their things and thoughts. Surely conversion would be the heart's desire of the whiter and brighter kinds of native?

Few tribal peoples were seen as brighter or whiter than the Maori, but a harsher view of them lurked in the wings, prophesying empire by conquest. This was linked to the irreparably ferocious Red Savage, who had to be spoken to in the only language he understood; to the ultimately unsalvageable Brown Savage, whose limited virtues had to be brought out with a touch of the 'beneficent whip'; and to the indelibly inferior Black Savage, who needed to be swept from the path of progress. Such ideas were in turn linked to 'polygenist' racial theories that stressed the fixity of racial characteristics throughout time, and even argued that the different races were actually different species, descended from separate Adams and Eves. Moderate versions of this thinking were more common in New Zealand than some scholars concede, and they flowered during conflict, causing and being caused by it. The rhetoric of conquest and indelible Maori difference was couched in terms of realism: you could not make a silk purse out of a sow's ear, whatever wishy-washy humanitarians and philanthropists might say. In the end, the savage reflexively resisted progress and civilisation, and would have to be crushed. There could be absolutely no question of the European capacity to crush. It was unEuropean to be beaten by savages.

Fatal impact was the belief that peoples like the Maori would crumble, collapse and ultimately die out as a result of European contact. The fit with the Grey Savage lens was obviously close, but it was not perfect: Grey Savage societies could simply die of old age, with or without European contact. Fatal impact was carried by bacilli who were themselves immune to it – European agents of contact, especially ruthless ones. Fatal impact was thought to work through the corrosive effect of European things and thoughts, through moral degradation and loss of confidence in the face of mighty Europe's vices and virtues, through the greater destructiveness European weapons gave to warfare, and through European disease. But it was usually seen as more than the sum of its parts, a product of 'more mysterious causes' – immutable laws of Nature or Providence. Fatal impact led to empire by ploughing the field for it, sweeping away previous inhabitants to clear the field for Europe. In pure versions, it left no natives to rule. In moderate versions, which might be called 'crippling impact', it weakened them and either left them vulnerable to evil empire or obliged agents of virtue to step in and save them from the agents of vice by imposing benign empire. As early as the 1820s, well before it was reinforced, from 1859, by Social Darwinism, fatal impact pervaded the thinking of many European visitors to New Zealand. They were predisposed to see an empty Maori village as evidence of it, rather than of the inhabitants having gone to the beach for the summer. Sometimes they were right.

There is a sense in which myths of European superiority and empire were understandable enough. From the quarrelling backwater of the fifteenth century, a pimple on the backside of Asia, to the multi-dimensional expansion of the eighteenth and nineteenth centuries was a journey few cultures have matched. Europe's diversity, specialisation and speed of change *were* extraordinary. Some of its technologies *were* superior, if we are to believe the Maori, who went to great lengths to acquire them. Is it surprising that Europeans constructed theories more flattering than mere accident to explain their remarkable rise? Perceived precedent piled on precedent. America, the first new world, was always an important model for subsequent European expansion. Tasman sought to emulate Columbus, missionaries followed Bartolome de Las Casas in converting the heathen. Rousseau's Noble Savage shifted from Huron to Tahitian, and to some extent to Maori. When Caribs turned to dust instead of Christians at Europe's fatal touch, it was natural to expect this to happen elsewhere, as it was to expect the frequent collapse of contact into empire, of peaceful interaction into violence. Tahiti was also an important precedent for New Zealand, with its Whitened and dying savages. Case followed case, and Europeans sought general rules to accommodate many examples. These rules naturally took account of prevailing ideas of Us and Them, which in turn took account of what appeared to be the rules.

Empire, conversion, conquest and fatal (or, at least, crippling) impact did happen, at particular times and places in New Zealand history. They were actual historical forces. But they were also myths. Their kernels of truth might be large, but there was a built-in tendency to exaggerate them. All implied favourable roles for Europeans: rulers of subjects, teachers of converts, masters of the conquered, heirs to the dying. The general sense of superiority they supplied gave confidence to those washed up on alien shores, instructed them on how to behave to native peoples and on how natives should behave to them. For these and other reasons they were cherished beliefs, not to be questioned lightly. Because it was important to the European self-image that contact should have such outcomes, there was an over-readiness to assume that they had happened, were happening or would happen.

Agents of Vice and Virtue

The 'Industrial Revolution' is now seen as older, slower and less industrial than was once thought. Even so, it was the ultimate push behind settlement of New Zealand by British people and capital. Its factories generated increased demand for lubricating oils, such as those provided by whales. It increased both the wealth and the fear of crime in the dark in England's great cities, which therefore wanted whale oil for street lamps – £300,000 worth a year for London alone in the 1780s.[29] Its newly affluent bourgeoisie aspired to gentility and its status symbols, which included whalebone corsets and sealskin hats.

Whaling had two main branches: deep-sea or ocean whaling, which pursued sperm whales in any part of the ocean, and shore whaling, which pursued right whales (also known as black whales) from boats based at shore stations. As the Greenland fishery diminished and demand grew, a deep-sea whale rush spread to the Pacific. The constant search for new grounds, the founding of Sydney in 1788 and the hostility of Spanish warships off South America brought ocean whaleships to New Zealand waters by the 1790s, and, by 1815, drunken Russian soldiers celebrating the defeat of Napoleon were drinking New Zealand whale oil from London street lamps.[30] The first shore-whaling station was established in 1827.

The American Revolution created a new nation, the United States, with strong Pacific interests, though it had no Pacific seaboard until 1848. Many thousands of New England ocean whalemen visited New Zealand from the 1790s. Defeat in America also increased Britain's concern about its naval and economic strength, and created a need for a new penal settlement in which to dump those criminals it was too humane to hang. Adequate stocks of gold were considered necessary for national well-being, and increasingly adequate stocks of tea were considered necessary for individual well-being. China provided the latter but would take nothing in exchange but the former – it would accept nothing but bullion, for all the tea in China. This was seen as a drain on English fiscal strength, and English governments and merchants of the late eighteenth century cast anxiously about for things the Chinese might want. They eventually settled on opium, but in the interim they used furs, including seal furs. Tens of thousands of New Zealand sealskins sold in Canton and Macao in the 1790s and early 1800s, before many had sold in London. New Zealand's first imperial market was Ch'ing.

During the American Revolutionary War, the French admirals Suffren and de Grasse, helped by the Dutch and Spanish, came quite close to toppling England from its mastery of the seas. A league of other nations blocked English access to Baltic spars and Riga hemp. England could still build ships from Indian teak and its own oak, but without hemp or flax for cordage, and long, clean spars for masts and yards, it would have to row them. After the French Revolution, a new Baltic League and Napoleon's continental blockade pounded this lesson home. Mast timber and flax were not marginal products but essential military supplies, basic components of the wind-engines that drove the fleets on which Britain depended. Whaling was also believed to fall into the category of vital national interest. It was seen as a 'nursery for seamen', available to the Royal Navy in a crisis. Interest was expressed in New Zealand flax as early as 1783, several ships visited for spars in the 1790s, and New Zealand featured in British thinking as a source of military supplies.[31]

A case can be made for seeing proximity to New Zealand flax and timber as a key factor in the founding of European Australia in 1788. The settlement, variously known as Botany Bay, Port Jackson, New South Wales and Sydney, was a replacement penal colony, and a strategic base for whaling and sealing in the South Pacific, giving Britain an advantage over the French and Americans. Sydney Town had 5,000 inhabitants by 1813; 12,000 by 1826. It was also a base for missionary activity in the Pacific, a product of the evangelical revival commenced in England by John Wesley in the 1740s. Initially working within the Church of England, evangelical Protestantism split in 1795 into Methodism, or Wesleyanism, and 'Low Church' Anglicanism – so called to distinguish it from 'High Church', which placed more stress on the Catholic heritage and less on mission work. The evangelicals emphasised simplicity of worship, a personal relationship with God, and the ever-present threat of sin. Echoing seventeenth-century Puritanism, it was especially attractive to the rising middle classes, reinforcing the 'Protestant work ethic'. It was closely interwoven with that patronising but ultimately commendable moral movement known as humanitarianism, which preached 'the white man's burden' and played the leading role in the abolition of the slave trade in Britain's dominions between 1807 and 1833. The need to convert the heathen – to capitalism as well as Christianity

– was central to the evangelicals, who therefore saw discoveries of unusually convertible heathens in the Pacific as a special opportunity. Missionary organisations, of which the (Anglican) Church Missionary Society and (Methodist) Wesleyan Missionary Society are most relevant here, were founded from 1795, began operations in the Pacific in 1797 and reached New Zealand in 1814.[32]

So it was that Europeans came to New Zealand for flax, timber and whales; seals, sex and souls. They came in numbers that dwarfed those of the exploring expeditions, and they were much more important direct agents of contact with Maori. The hybrid world this interaction created, 'Old New Zealand' in Frederick Maning's nicely ambiguous phrase,[33] began in the 1790s and survived for many years after 1840, until it was eventually swamped by new tides of settlement. The missionaries were fewest but had the busiest pens, and they divided this wave of Europeans into two: themselves, the agents of virtue; and almost everyone else, the agents of vice, who very often came from Australia.

New Zealand itself was considered as a site for the penal settlement planned by England in the 1780s, but its natives were thought to be too dangerous and bloodthirsty. Thus the Maori killers of Tasman's, Marion's and Furneaux's men prevented New Zealand from becoming Australia. Arthur Phillip, the first Governor of New South Wales, did envisage an auxiliary role for New Zealand. He suggested that convicts guilty of murder and sodomy should receive the one punishment even worse than being sent to Australia: being sent to New Zealand. 'For either of these crimes I would wish to confine the criminal until an opportunity offered of delivering him to the natives of New Zealand, and let them eat him.'[34] New Zealand would serve as the still more fatal shore when the fatal shore proved not fatal enough. No convicts were in fact sent in this way, but many did come – more than some New Zealand historians have cared to admit. The convict settlements of Sydney, Norfolk Island (founded 1789) and Hobart (1803) were the bloody triangle from which early Australian influence on New Zealand flowed.

Convict society had fascinating dynamics, some of which crossed the Tasman. Initially, conditions for some convicts were almost indescribably harsh, though Robert Hughes has come close. Freshly imported convict women on Norfolk Island danced naked, numbers on backs, for their gaolers to choose a carcass in order of rank. Children boiled and burned to death in accidents while unattended in their parents' shacks. Convict men were simply hanged for stealing pigs because they were starving, despite the humanitarian protests of a Maori visitor, flogged to death for being cheeky or died of starvation while trying to walk to China to get away from it all.[35] We must take our hats off to Australian mythology for constructing a paradise out of this.

But it is an ill wind that blows nobody any good, and some Australian historians feel Hughes and others paint too grim a picture. They see in the convict system the origins of democratic attitudes, of expanded socio-economic opportunity and of the acceptance of state intervention. Some also see the origins of 'male mateship' in the convict era, bonding bondsmen, and they may be right about the legend. But, treated like dogs, dog often ate dog. The most impressive thing about these early Australians is not their loyalty to each other but their selfish energy against the odds, lives that built something out of worse than nothing, hope as well as hate in the eyes lowered respectfully as the officer passed. The Sydney experience suggests that prison is a good training ground for capitalism. Simeon Lord, a twenty-year-old convicted thief in 1790, had an eighteen-room mansion in Sydney by 1803, and did £102,000 worth of business with his London agent between 1804 and 1810. An incredible willingness to take risks, to scrabble a profit from unpromising opportunities, and to bounce back from bankruptcy like cast-off rubber, characterised the convict capitalists – the 'pedlars, dealers and extortioners' who emerged against all odds in the 1790s. Once they had received one of the various kinds of parole, such as a 'ticket of leave', or worked off their sentences, they began trading. At first they retailed Sydney imports, notably illicit rum, for officers and officials who wanted profits but not dirty hands. The problem was always paying for imports from England, China, India, the Cape of Good Hope, and the newly free Sydney merchants were soon trading sandalwood and sea-cucumbers in the Pacific Islands, and hunting seals – or rather, hunting for sealing grounds in which to slaughter seals.[36]

A couple of English ships pioneered sealing in New Zealand as a sideline to whaling as early as 1792, and a few American ships were involved later. But it was the early Australians who dominated sealing. Leading captains were John Grono, William Stewart and J. R. Kent, and leading companies included Lord, Kable and Underwood, Cooper and Levy, all ex-convicts. John MacArthur, ex-officer and pioneer New South Wales pastoralist, was also involved. From 1803, the focus of activity, using the same ships, the same men and the same money, shifted from the coasts and islands of Bass Strait to those of Foveaux Strait. Around 1810 it shifted again, to New Zealand's subantarctic islands – Auckland, Campbell, Bounty and Antipodes – and Australia's Macquarie, and then back to Foveaux about 1813. Like Maori before them, the sealers went through the defenceless animals like a knife through butter, and their knives were even sharper and greedier. Simeon Lord alone exported 200,000 sealskins to London between 1806 and 1810; one shipment sold for £10,000. The grounds were soon depleted, then picked over for leavings, and huge bags were a thing of the past by 1820.[37]

Sealing ships were much smaller and less specialised than ocean-whaling ships, and the industry therefore had a much lower entry cost. But this could still amount to £2,600 for a ship, and the fledgling Sydney merchants had to scrabble for capital. The Napoleonic Wars helped here. English warships and privateers sold their prizes cheap in Sydney to save the trouble of sailing them home. New Zealand's extractive industry began partly with capital, in the form of ships, plundered from the Spanish and French. London agents also supplied capital, in the form of credit, an indirect linkage that was to become traditional. Another traditional source of capital, pioneered locally by sealing, was underpaying the workers. Around 1810 one sealer earned £38 in seventeen months, less than a Sydney day labourer, and his working conditions could hardly have been poorer.[38] Sealers stuck to their trade for its illusion of self-employment – wages came as a share in profits – and this must have been a powerful myth. No novelist has yet imagined a worse voluntary existence than sealing on a subantarctic island, freezing works in which the workers froze and the dead meat rotted. Ships left three or four gangs of half a dozen men at what it was hoped were seal rookeries, then returned some months later to pick up the gang and its hundreds or thousands of dried or salted skins. The ships did not always return. One gang was marooned on the Snares Islands, off Stewart Island, for seven years.[39]

Sealing was smaller in scale than whaling and has generated less interest among historians. But it was important as the major medium of early contact for southern Maori – Ngai Tahu and Ngati Mamoe. Outbreaks of violence between sealers and these tribes were initially quite frequent. But as early as 1803, one sealing captain found Maori 'very friendly, and ready to render every assistance he could possibly require', and this was always the majority experience.[40] From about 1820, the relationship settled down and changed the pattern of both sealing and Maori economics. Sealers now lived semi-permanently in European-Maori communities, acquired sealskins and other trade goods with Maori help, and sold them to the Sydney ships, which visited regularly – about ten in 1824, for example.[41] While the absolute quantity of Maori–European contact generated by sealing around Foveaux Strait was much less than by whaling at the Bay of Islands, the quantity relative to the number of local inhabitants may have been comparable. Between 1816 and 1826, about a hundred sealers lived semi-permanently in and around Foveaux Strait, and hundreds had visited before that.[42] Hybrid communities formed on Codfish, Ruapuke and Stewart Islands, and at a few points on the mainland coast. Theories of culture contact applied in New Zealand have to accommodate what happened at both ends of the country.

Sealing also pioneered a Tasman world. Along with whalers, sailors and other wandering workers, sealers were part of a strange social and cultural entity that did not see Australia and New Zealand as markedly separate places. It was predominantly male, crossed the Tasman very readily and might be called 'Tasmen' for short. Strange forms of 'egalitarianism' and 'mateship', and a certain fear of women and intellectualism, were among its legacies. Tasmen sealers disliked their colleague John Boultbee for being a 'Swell's son run out' and a 'regular scholard', and one told him that 'if I had my way there should be no gentlemen'.[43] Product of the space between fragment and frontier, Tasmen and the Tasman world were important to nineteenth-century New Zealand, and sealers were their forerunners. Sealing was the first of a series of trans-Tasman industries, staffed by the same wandering pool of Tasmen workers, in which the distinction between Australia and New Zealand was artificial. The general name of Bass and Foveaux Straits and the subantarctic islands, 'the Sealing Islands', was one of several to incorporate both Australia and New Zealand, part of a joint past historians in both countries seem reluctant to recognise.

New Zealand hesitation may stem from the fact that 'the majority of sealing gangs were composed of ex-convicts'.[44] 'Ex-convicts' in this context includes those who escaped or broke their conditions of probationary release, as well as those who had served out their time or obtained tickets of leave. Sealing ships left Sydney under-manned, and completed their crews from the outlaw camps of Bass Strait. Convicts also stowed away on other ships, in such surprising numbers as to imply an organised racket or organised resistance involving the ships' legitimate crews. One ship 'discovered' no fewer than 46 convict stowaways after clearing Sydney in 1795 on its way to being wrecked in New Zealand.[45] Some ten per cent of the 30,000 convicts shipped to east Australia before 1820 escaped, and New Zealand was one of their destinations, before and after 1840.[46]

Escaped convicts, like the numerous deserters from whaling ships, did not advertise their existence and may be missing from accepted statistics, which suggest that there were only about 300 permanent or semi-permanent European residents in New Zealand in 1830, rising to about 2,000 by 1839.[47] One of the first Europeans to actually settle in New Zealand, at the Bay of Islands around 1800, shunned European contact and was very probably an escaped convict. Four men deserted from a timber ship at Hauraki in 1799.[48] A band of ex-convicts and deserting seamen had built up at the Bay of Islands by 1830, and others settled individually with Maori tribes as middlemen and court jesters. These became known as 'Pakeha Maori'. Some converted in reverse, quite wholeheartedly, and were accepted quite wholeheartedly by Maori. Examples include the white Ngai Tahu James Caddell, said to have forgotten most of his English; the tattooed white Ngati Kahungunu showman Barnet Burns, whose subsequent stage name in London was 'Pahe-a-Range'; and the cannibal white Nga Puhi Jacky Marmon.[49]

One remarkable story among many was that of Charlotte Badger, a London pickpocket transported to Sydney in 1801. In 1806, she and her friend Kitty Hagerty were sent to Hobart in the brig *Venus*. The first mate Benjamin Kelly fell in love with Hagerty and fell under the strong-willed Badger's influence. Together they mounted a mutiny and seized the ship. Badger is said to have flogged the captain before forcing him ashore. The *Venus* then sailed for New

Zealand, raiding several ships for supplies along the way – piracy in the Tasman. The crew continued their depredations on the New Zealand coast, kidnapping several isolated Maori women, until they picked the wrong tribe and met the fate recommended by Governor Phillip: killed and eaten. Kelly and the two women had previously left the ship and settled at the Bay of Islands. Hagerty soon died, Kelly was captured and hanged, but Badger lived for some years with a Maori chief before allegedly sailing off with a New England whaling captain.[50] Australia's only female pirate leader, and one of New Zealand's first resident white women, she must have been quite a personality, clawing her way from so many frying pans and fires, their few frail escape ropes marked 'men only'. That she was said to be extremely fat may further endear her to some of us.

Sealing did not suddenly cease as the seals diminished, but turned in the 1820s to other trades to supplement reduced catches. Sealing diversified and merged into a broadening range of New Zealand trades. Foodstuffs, especially pigs and potatoes, were bought from the Maori and sold in Sydney. 'Curios' – greenstone weapons and ornaments, carvings, fine cloaks, preserved heads – eventually found a market in Europe. Timber and flax, the most valuable New Zealand products apart from whales, had a market in both places. Virtually all European visitors to New Zealand – explorers, whalers, missionaries, as well as sealers – engaged in this general trade, but by the late 1820s specialist traders were beginning to emerge. They ranged from Pakeha Maori and other individuals who set themselves up as middlemen for a particular hapu; through the flax agents of Sydney merchants, of whom there were dozens during a flax boom in 1829–32; to Northland merchant chiefs like Thomas McDonnell, James Clendon and Gilbert Mair. By 1830, there were several trading stations, each containing half a dozen or a dozen Europeans. Timber stations, which cut their own timber as well as traded for it, and sometimes built boats and ships as well, appeared at Hokianga in the 1820s and spread to Coromandel and elsewhere in the 1830s.[51]

As well as sealers and convict settlers, Australia contributed nearly all the shore whalers whose stations began to dot New Zealand's coast from 1827. Each station employed a dozen or two dozen Europeans, who divided their year into drinking and whaling seasons. Each developed strong links with its Maori neighbours, on whom it depended for food and protection as well as supplementary labour and wives. Whaling magnates emerged, like Johnny Jones, who had eight whaling stations and 200 cats, and the Rhodes and Weller brothers. Whaling stations took about £2,000 to establish, and £1,200 a year to maintain. Yields might reach £5,000 a year but were usually far less. More than 80 whaling stations were established in New Zealand between 1827 and 1850, though never more than 50 were in operation at the same time.[52]

Philip King, Governor first of Norfolk Island then of New South Wales, was the British official to have most early influence on New Zealand. In 1792, he arranged for the kidnapping of two Maori men, Tuki and Ngahuruhuru, hoping they would teach his Norfolk Island convicts how to process flax into rope. This proved to be women's work, and King was disappointed.[53] But he treated his prisoners kindly, took them home himself in 1793, loaded with gifts, and his subsequent interactions with New Zealand were benign. He sought to foster whaling in New Zealand, to acclimatise useful plants and animals, and to establish good relations with Maori. King and his successor governors of New South Wales were the leading European chiefs known to most Maori. In 1833, a New South Wales winemaker and public servant, James Busby, became the first British official to be stationed in New Zealand. As British Resident, Busby was expected to control contact through sheer force of character and moral superiority. He failed. But he was not without influence as British ambassador to the Bay of Islands, 1833–40, chief reporter on New Zealand to Britain, and promoter of declarations of independence – one for Northland Maori in 1835, and one for Auckland Europeans in 1865.

Most whaling, timber and trading stations were funded and staffed from Sydney. Sydney has long been one of New Zealand's most important cities, and for a century New Zealand was one of Sydney's most important hinterlands. Much European influence on New Zealand was strained through Sydney first. Most Europeans living in New Zealand before 1840 had done time in New South Wales; it was also the most popular overseas destination for Maori. Sydney's nominal imports from New Zealand fluctuated from £30,000 in 1826 to £72,000 in 1839, peaking at £135,000 in 1829.[54] These figures did not include most seal and whale products, which in 1830 were worth £58,000, 42 per cent of Sydney's own total exports. Most probably came from New Zealand waters, and flax and timber from the same source, some landed at Thomas Raine's 'New Zealand Timber Wharf' in George Street, was a significant fraction of remaining exports. At this stage, New Zealand products were more important to Sydney than wool. By 1840, the value of whale and seal products exported had quadrupled to £224,000, though its relative importance was now less than wool.[55] Throughout the nineteenth century, the Tasman Sea was more bridge than barrier.

God also came to New Zealand through Australia. By 1808, missions founded in Tonga, Tahiti and the Marquesas had all collapsed. Pacific evangelism was revived by the Anglican Chaplain of New South Wales, Samuel Marsden, 'the Saint Augustine of New Zealand'.[56] Frustrated by the Pacific failures and by his efforts among Australian convicts and Aboriginals, he turned with hope and relief to the Maori. Marsden and allies such as John Nicholas, author in 1817 of the first major book on New Zealand, tirelessly argued that Maori were the perfect prospects for conversion – despite their reputation for aggressiveness and cannibalism, and the almost total absence of converts until 1830.[57] Confidence in Maori convertibility was not restricted to rhetoric. The Church Missionary Society (CMS) gave prospective missionaries to New Zealand two years' training, as against three for India. Trainee missionaries practised on Catholic Irish in London, only to be threatened with red-hot pokers and bricks through church windows.[58]

Marsden set up the first mission station at Rangihoua, in the Bay of Islands in 1814, and supervised operations from his base at Parramatta, near Sydney, until his death in 1838. The CMS had established three stations at the Bay of Islands by 1823, when Henry Williams, an able and energetic ex-naval officer, if somewhat narrower in outlook than Marsden, took up the local leadership.[59] The same year, the CMS was joined by the Wesleyan Missionary Society, whose Reverend Samuel Leigh established a station at Whangaroa. This station was abandoned in 1827, but the Wesleyans were re-established at Hokianga the following year, and between 1830 and 1836 were led by the choleric and colourful William White.[60] The CMS and the WMS formed an uneasy cartel, with the former as senior partner, and the latter allocated the western coast. Neither mission broke out of Northland until 1833, but the number of stations exploded in the mid-1830s. In 1839, CMS missionaries and their families numbered 169; WMS 37.[61] By 1845, the WMS had a dozen small stations, and the CMS two dozen, some large, unevenly spread across the country.[62] The Anglican–Methodist alliance was seldom comfortable, but both were united in their dislike of Catholics – they would rather the Maori stayed pagan than become Papist. The first Roman Catholic mission station was established in 1838, by Bishop Jean Baptiste Pompallier. Catholicism came late but fast, backed by the new Marist organisation in France and, at first, by substantial funds. By 1844, it had brought 41 French missionaries to New Zealand and established a dozen mission stations.[63]

It is often as difficult to empathise across times as it is across cultures. From some modern perspectives, the evangelicals are hard to like. They dressed like crows; seemed joyless, humourless and sometimes hypocritical; they embalmed the evidence poor historians need to read in tedious preaching, in which the love of God was often dwarfed by the fear of sin. Marsden forbade his daughter to read novels, and showed a certain lack of human sympathy. 'Mrs. Hill is very low spirited and a few days ago she cut her throat – and has not been able to swallow anything since.'[64] He provided a curious reference for a New South Wales boy named William Evans: 'I do not know him – if he had been bad I should have known him.'[65] In Australia, he was known as the 'Flogging Parson', for good reason. He faced repeated accusations of corruption – of using his official position, the moral high ground of evangelism and his privileged access to the New Zealand trade to feather Parramatta. He did make a lot of money – £30,000 to be precise – and despite the indignant denials of subsequent biographers, it is tempting to see fire in the smoke. But he also spent a great deal of his own money on the New Zealand mission, as well as two years of his own time, and seven voyages at great personal cost – he was always extremely seasick. It is difficult not to admire him and his fellows. The New Zealand missionaries, men and women, spent their lives on the psychological equivalent of a fearsomely alien planet for something else's sake. They buried their children, braced their shoulders and served their God. Perhaps it was years in purgatory in this world exchanged for years off purgatory in the next, but the mean-spirited can find self-interest in every altruism.

Satan surrounded the early missionaries in the form of naked Maori bodies. Marianne Williams spent her first night in New Zealand thinking of them. 'The tall muscular forms of the New Zealanders flitted before my mind's eye, whenever I endeavoured to sleep.'[66] Missionary women are not known to have succumbed to temptation, but some of their menfolk did. They included William White, William Colenso, Charles Creed and Thomas Kendall, and in at least the last case sex was not the only temptation. As on other islands and beaches of the Pacific, fear of sin competed with the seductions of sinlessness, and it was not always clear which would convert which. The 'apparent sublimity' of Maori religious ideas, wrote Kendall in 1822, has 'almost completely turned me from a Christian to a Heathen'.[67] This battle also raged in the soul of the CMS missionary William Yate. His influential book on New Zealand, published in 1835, portrayed Maori as 'neither too ignorant nor too savage to be made the subjects of the saving and sanctifying influence of the gospel', but as pretty ignorant and savage all the same. Maori mothers fed their infants pebbles to harden their hearts, though 'it is not true that Maori mothers eat their own children. This is too horrible even for them.'[68] 'Poor Mr Yate' was subsequently sacked for alleged sexual relations with between 50 and 100 young Maori males.[69] The Catholics maintained their chastity or their secrets, but the British missions always struggled against reverse conversion. Children and single men were considered especially vulnerable to Maoriness. Marsden reproved Kendall for leaving his eight children to visit England 'at an Age when they in a very special manner require the Eye of the Parent, to prevent them from mingling amongst the Heathens and learning their ways'. As early as 1811, he wrote: 'Never upon any Account send a single man out.'[70] But some went.

We should not deride the missionaries' efforts, or sneer too hard at their self-defined failures, but we should equally avoid accepting their account of their own impact, which claimed the wholesale religious conversion and partial 'civilisation' of Maori by the 1840s. Even when their interpretation of results is not accepted, they are still often portrayed as the main agents of contact, largely because they dominated the written record. In 1990, an academic biographer claimed that Marsden 'transformed the Maori economy and laid the foundations of New Zealand agriculture', that he at least greatly hastened a Maori religious conversion, and that the British intervention that saved New Zealand from 'anarchy' was 'in large measure due to the apostolic labours of Samuel Marsden'.[71] Marsden was important, but this overstates the case. Missiology and hagiography are still too closely related.

The largest group of European agents of contact, ocean whalemen, is also the most elusive. They did not settle, they scarcely even sojourned, but merely visited New Zealand for a few weeks. Ocean whaling 'was the eighteenth-century equivalent of today's petroleum industry'[72] – Moby Dallas. Initially, the only New Zealand content of the whaling industry was the vast, intelligent, gentle animals themselves: fixed to a boat by harpoons, pursued to exhaustion, lanced to death, then left to rot in rough weather, and tried or fried into oil in calm. But whaleships, years from home, regularly needed water, to soak salt meat into edible form, as well as to drink; fresh food to keep the crew from rotting with scurvy; firewood and charcoal to cook and start the fires under the trypots until scrap whale blubber could take over; and time ashore to maintain and repair the ships. The crews also believed they desperately needed sex with women. Self-restraint, self-abuse and the Yate solution in the crowded stinking holds of whaling ships were not seen as adequate alternatives. There was also social pressure. 'If they see you reading or writing,' wrote an unusually scholarly whaler, 'or know that you have not got a girl aboard, you must then be a missionary man . . . a most opprobrious name.'[73] From 1800, ocean whaleships began to call at New Zealand harbours to obtain all these things.

From the first, the various harbours of the Bay of Islands in Northland were the favoured ports of call. We shall see in the next chapter that Maori combined with nature, Governor King and the whalers to make this choice. About 50 ships visited the Bay between 1806 and 1810.[74] The Anglo–American War of 1812–15, lower prices for oil, and two Maori attacks on ships stemmed the flow somewhat, but between 1815 and 1822 some 92 ships called at the Bay, mostly whalers. At one point in 1827, a dozen lay at anchor there at the same time. These numbers were dwarfed in the 1830s, when several hundred whaleships visited, each with a crew of about 30 men.[75] Visits were seasonal, mostly between November and April. Ocean whaleships stayed only two to five weeks. But the Bay was often their first well-serviced port of call after many months at sea. Each visit was an intensive burst of contact with Maori, many months of purchasing and recreation crammed in to one.

Portuguese, Dutch, Canadian, German and Danish ocean whaleships visited New Zealand, but the main players were the British, French and Americans. Helped by a government subsidy, duties on competitors' products and the expertise of American captains who were more interested in whaling than independence, Britain held the early lead. But in the 1830s it was overtaken by the Americans, and possibly by the French as well. France featured large from 1836 to 1845. Virtually the whole French whaling fleet of about 60 ships called at New Zealand in the late 1830s, preferring Banks Peninsula to the Bay of Islands. About a hundred of their crews deserted during the 1840s, some intermarrying with Maori and forming little Franco-Maori communities at Banks Peninsula and the Bay of Plenty.[76] The first American whaler to visit New Zealand waters came in 1797, and no fewer than 271 New England whaleships called at the Bay of Islands alone between 1833 and 1839, as against 126 British visits.[77]

The decline of the British industry has been attributed to its over-regulation and to an American competitive edge similar to that of Japanese over American industry today.[78] Whatever its causes, the decline of British and the rise of French and, especially, American whaling in the 1830s has intriguing implications. It seems that the most numerous national category of European visitors to New Zealand before 1840 may have been American whalers, and that whalers were particularly prone to engage in sexual relations with Maori women. Maori descended from early European–Maori liaisons are quite likely to have the Stars and Stripes in their whakapapa. Certainly, the intensity and sheer numbers of ocean whaler visits compensated for their brevity, and their role in bringing Europe to Maori remains to be fully explored. The importance of French and American whalers as agents of contact has been underestimated, partly because they were ships passing in the night, but also because of the tendency to Anglicise New Zealand history.

Another shadowy but possibly important set of agents of contact were non-Europeans. They were important less for their numbers than for what they suggested to Maori about the diversity of the world and about Europe's usual relations with it. In some cases, they were also better able than Europeans to communicate with Maori. We have seen that, from the Maori perspective, 'Cook's expedition' was more like 'Tupaia's expedition'. Tupaia was succeeded by other Pacific Islanders who sojourned and even settled among Maori, as a few Maori sailors did in their home islands, reopening pan-Polynesian links that had been closed for centuries.[79] De Surville's and Marion's expeditions contained African and Asian slaves and sailors, as did many subsequent ships, and like their white crewmates some deserted in New Zealand. Maori sometimes spared black sailors in attacks on European parties, intriguing indications of their perceptions of graduated difference.[80] There were Australian Aboriginal men – and at least one woman – among the sealers.[81] A brilliant Tahitian known as Jem, after a sojourn in Sydney during which he worked for Macarthur and learned how to read and write in English, set himself up as a chief at North Cape. Jem, a classic 'transculturite', was managing European–Maori contact in the region in 1814. Like his predecessor Tupaia, he believed the Maori people were 'inferior to his own'.[82] Europe has no monopoly of ethnocentrism. A Bengali 'lascar' settled in Northland about 1810, and remained there for at least ten years – the first known Indian settler. He advised Europeans in 1820 'not to appear alarmed' at anything Maori did. Like the missionaries, he believed that 'the firm and undaunted demeanour of a white man will keep many natives at bay'.[83] Whether he defined Bengalis as white is not clear.

Whalers, sealers, escaped convicts and deserting seamen, as distinct from the small but growing minority of 'respectable' settlers such as missionaries, were consistently portrayed as agents of vice and fatal impact. They themselves mixed pragmatic acceptance of the Maori terms of economic and cultural trade with spasmodic racial contempt. Some expected recognition of superiority; to be Lord Jim among the savages. They were generally disappointed, but looked for opportunities to make their personal myths of empire true. They were not wholly pragmatic. The capitalist push behind empire pursued dreams of profit as much as profit itself. For a hundred years after 1783, Europeans dreamed of spinning New Zealand flax into gold, and risked their money and even lives on various projects for doing so. 'The subject of New Zealand flax could generate great excitement . . . Hard-headed men like Simeon Lord found themselves plunging into schemes surrounded by dangers and pitfalls and spending money wildly; the language of their documents, their business agreements, and their memorials becoming more exotic as they became less realistic.'[84] There was a certain romanticism, dreams of an oily El Dorado, about investment in whaling too – most shore-whaling stations failed to turn long-term profits. 'People,' wrote George Weller in 1837, 'are Black Whaling mad.'[85] Even sealing was viewed as a potential 'mine of wealth'.[86] George Bass, the Australian explorer, proposed in 1803 to make his fortune from a 21-year monopoly of the export of South Island fish to Australia.[87] Such hopes helped generate large-scale contact, which in turn generated expectations of fatal impact and empire. The pre-1840 settlers and sojourners were significant in actual history too, bringing the things, thoughts and genes of Europe to Maori in considerable bulk. Non-Europeans, missionaries, Tasmen, Australian governors and entrepreneurs, British, American and French ocean whalemen – all were important agents of contact. But none was the most important.

CHAPTER SIX

The Maori Discovery of Europe

In 1805, Official Surgeon John Savage of Sydney was suspended for refusing to attend a woman in childbirth. He made his way to England for court-martial, via the Bay of Islands. His stay was brief, his grasp of the language limited, and his published account of Maori was generous but ill informed. Still, hoping to mitigate his fault, he dedicated his book to his influential acquaintance Earl FitzWilliam, and also presented another New Zealand product to the Earl – Moehanga, a young warrior from the Bay of Islands. Moehanga's response to England was not so dissimilar to English responses to New Zealand. He mistook the European haka, a salute by cannon, for a prelude to aggression and was frightened by it. He spent his money (given him in ignorance by Countess FitzWilliam) on a London prostitute.[1] He liked to meet chiefs and was prone to exaggerate his own impact. His subsequent accounts of his experience expanded his friendships with the nobility from the FitzWilliams to the King, the Queen and the Duke of York. He also overestimated his mastery of local custom, trying to shake hands with everyone he encountered in the street, saying, 'How do you do, my boy?' 'His appearance,' noted Savage, 'intimidated many, and they withdrew from his proffered kind shake by the hand.' Savage took Moehanga around London to see what he would like. Moehanga disapproved of the agricultural poverty of London – 'plenty of men, plenty of houses, but very little fish and very few potatoes' – and of the large number of decrepit, lame, and infirm: 'good for nothing man or woman'. He approved of drapers, ironmongers and coaches: 'Very good house, it walks very fast.' And he found wooden legs absolutely hilarious. Even more than St Paul's Cathedral, the highlight of his visit was meeting a man with two of them.[2]

Both Savage and Moehanga himself believed European knowledge and gifts of tools would make the latter great on his return to New Zealand. But Moehanga, though brave and intelligent, did not have the status, determination and vision to make this happen. His chiefs appropriated his goods, his stories were disbelieved, and, while he did some service as a go-between (whaling captains used him as a kind of postmaster), he soon forgot most of his English, though he would not admit it. In frustration, he stole an axe from a visiting ship and was exiled by his hapu. In 1815, John Nicholas found him, verbose and importunate, getting the locals to link arms with European visitors, forming a long chain, in what he claimed was a European custom.[3]

Poor Moehanga was the Tasman of a Maori discovery of Europe. He was followed by a Marion (Te Pahi) and a Cook (Ruatara). He may have been preceded by a Maori 'lost caravel'. When Binot de Gonneville left his South Land in 1504, he took with him two natives, one of whom survived to settle in France. He was known as 'Essomeric', a challenge to transliterators. Essomeric married and had many descendants – perhaps including Rousseau, who knows? One great-grandson became a Catholic priest, who in 1663 published an appeal for the establishment of Christian missions in the Southern Continent.[4] But ultimately, lost caravels, true or false, are not very important.

Moehanga and Savage were a linked pair of agents of contact, operating through each other. Governor King also had a Maori alter ego – Te Pahi, leading chief of Rangihoua in the northern Bay of Islands. In 1805, Te Pahi and a group of fellow tribesmen visited Sydney, stayed several months and exchanged gifts and ideas with King. Te Pahi greatly impressed King and the *Sydney Gazette*, and for several years his reputation for co-operation with Europeans was a key factor in attracting whalers to the Bay of Islands.[5] Historians still credit this, the first reciprocal relationship ever established between New Zealand and the outside world, to King, who 'spared no effort to convince Te Pahi of the benefits of an association with Europeans'.[6] King does deserve credit for his foresight, but he may as well have saved his breath. Te Pahi had long nurtured a plan to respond to King's gift visit of 1793. He went first to Norfolk Island, going on to Sydney only when he found that King had shifted there. King had been trying to create a secure whaling base in New Zealand since 1793 by establishing relations with Maori and introducing crops and livestock among them to trade with the whalers. He succeeded in 1805 only because of Te Pahi. But late in 1809, the ship *Boyd* put into Whangaroa, north of the Bay, and was attacked by Ngati Pou as utu for the mistreatment of a tribesman in its crew, Te Ara, or George. The ship was burned, the cargo plundered – Simeon Lord lost £12,000 – and perhaps 70 Europeans were killed. 'That old rascal Tippahee, who has been so much and so undeservedly caressed at Port Jackson', was blamed, though even his Ngati Pou rivals subsequently exonerated him. The crews of six whalers destroyed his pa and wounded him in retaliation the following year.[7] In the final irony, he was mortally wounded in battle by Ngati Pou soon after. So died the Maori Marion.

The Legacy of Ruatara

Like Moehanga and Te Pahi, Ruatara came from the Bay of Islands, the northern nexus of Maori–European mutual discovery. In 1805, when only in his late teens, he set out on the ultimate gift visit, to King George III of Britain. Trials and tribulations on whaling and sealing ships took him twice to Sydney, and to Bounty Island, but it was not until 1809 that he made it to London, only to find that his ship master would neither pay him nor allow him to spend a single night ashore. Thwarted in his great ambition, he managed to get passage on another ship back to New Zealand. Among his fellow passengers was an old friend, Samuel Marsden, whom he had met in 1805. On reaching Sydney in 1810, Ruatara stayed with Marsden at Parramatta for eight months, taking an intensive course in European agriculture. He had more difficulties with unscrupulous shipmasters on his voyage home, and it was not until 1812 that he finally returned to the Bay, having been absent for all but six months of the past seven years. Although only about 25 years old, he succeeded the recently dead Te Pahi, presumably by judiciously distributing the goods and knowledge he had brought back with him. His mana suffered a blow when, lacking a mill, he was unable to grind the wheat he and other chiefs had grown from seed he had brought from Sydney. 'The chiefs ridiculed Duaterra much about the wheat', and now doubted the 'fine stories' of the 'great traveller'.[8] In early 1814, they were literally forced to eat their words when Ruatara ground some into flour with a hand-mill sent at his request by his ally Marsden. By this time, he had fine fields of wheat, as well as cabbages, turnips, carrots and onions, to add to the potatoes and pigs bequeathed by Te Pahi. He also possessed rum, tea, sugar, flour, cheese and chests of European clothing.[9]

In Sydney in 1805, Te Pahi, Ruatara and others had helped shape Marsden's view that New Zealand was a promising field for missionary activity. The *Boyd* massacre and the difficulty of finding ordained missionaries willing to risk the oven caused Marsden to postpone his plans, but in 1810 he discussed them with Ruatara, one of the few Maori who could then speak good English. Ruatara

> not only readily acquiesced in the proposal . . . but expressed an anxious solicitude to have it commenced as soon as possible; and guaranteed to all persons engaged in it, hospitality and kindness from his own tribe, and safe protection from the attacks of any other. Availing himself of this favourable circumstance, Mr. Marsden, in the year 1810, proposed to the Church Missionary Society . . . that they should send out to New Zealand, certain proper persons to form a Mission. To this they readily assented.[10]

In 1814, Marsden purchased the brig *Active* as a mission ship and sent it to New Zealand to bring over Ruatara to bring over the missionaries. Although Ruatara described his village of Rangihoua as something near paradise, it was not in fact a favourable site. 'Had Marsden and his catechists searched the whole coastline, a more dismal location for their settlement could scarcely have been found.'[11] Perhaps there was some talk of this on the return voyage, on which Marsden and John Nicholas accompanied Ruatara and his missionaries Thomas

Kendall, John King, William Hall and their families. Just out of Sydney, Nicholas noticed that Ruatara had suddenly lapsed into 'morose melancholy', which the good but simple fellow was unable to conceal. Marsden enquired the reasons for his change of mood, and, 'after some hesitation', Ruatara explained that he had been informed that the missionaries' real intention was to enslave or exterminate the Maori. The distraught Marsden managed to reassure him, offering to instantly abort the voyage and 'never more think of holding any intercourse with his country' if Ruatara wished it. Apparently mollified, Ruatara gave Christianity permission to proceed – on one condition, seemingly added as an afterthought. His own people would welcome the missionaries, but his ignorant countrymen 'might be prompted to acts of violence', and the mission station really must be sited at Rangihoua, 'where he and his tribe could easily protect it'. 'Mr. Marsden, highly gratified at having undeceived him, readily promised to comply with his wishes, and Duaterra immediately resumed all his usual good humour.'[12] Well he might. Ruatara had just secured a monopoly over the first permanent European settlement in New Zealand, a goose that would reliably lay eggs of iron, if not gold. He had also introduced Christianity into the country as a side-effect.

Ruatara's Maori neighbours were left in no doubt about who ran the new mission station or about who was the rising star of the Bay of Islands. He had not forgotten to procure eight muskets in Sydney, and had borrowed a brace of pistols from the missionaries, which he omitted to return. In 1815, this probably made him the best-armed chief in the country, as well as the wealthiest in terms of European plants, tools and settlers. He controlled the mission's stores, withholding access to its whole stock of iron on one occasion to remind them who was boss, exacted regular tribute, prevented an attempt to move the station to a better site and planned a European-style town at Rangihoua. He translated Marsden's sermons as he chose, shortening them considerably for one thing. He accompanied the *Active* when it cruised the Northland coast and the Hauraki Gulf, with his musketeers. When rival chiefs came out to the ship to trade, Ruatara and his men hid, springing out as the visitors climbed on deck, firing off their guns, dancing a ferocious haka and nearly causing several heart attacks. A few weeks later, aged about 28, Ruatara himself was dead, probably victim of a disease from the same source as his new-found power.

Ruatara exemplified four features of the Maori engagement with Europe. First, he was a Maori agent of contact, distributing European goods and knowledge more effectively and selectively than Europeans could. Second, he adapted what he distributed, packaging it in Maori terms and turning it to a Maori purpose. It was his words, not Marsden's, that Maori understood at the first sermon. Third, Ruatara was the first of many successful Maori sponsors of European settlement. Marsden's own account makes it quite clear that there would have been no mission in 1814 if Ruatara had not wanted it, and it was

Ruatara who determined its location and function. Fourth, he was an early mediator or middleman between Maori and Pakeha, what one might call a tohunga Pakeha, an expert in managing Europeans. Pakeha were to have their equivalents – called 'Maori doctors' by the envious. A characteristic of both Pakeha and Maori mediators was the use of influence in one world to lever up their status in the other. Europeans described Te Pahi as 'King of New Zealand', and it was Ruatara, a young man in his mid-twenties, who succeeded him. Neither was in fact anything like a king, but their mediation of Europe clearly boosted their power and their mana.

A steady trickle of Maori followed Moehanga, Te Pahi and Ruatara. A few names are known. Maui, or Tommy Drummond, after living with Marsden for several years, taught Sunday school near Edgeware Road, London, in 1816.[13] Tuai and Titeri visited London in 1818, also through the good offices of the CMS. Titeri saw 'plenty guns, thousands', and struggled with reading and writing. 'Cannot yet understand to read the Book some words easy, some very hard.'[14] Two Ngati Maru were displaying their tattoos to admiring English crowds in 1829.[15] Establishing relations with European high chiefs remained a motive for visits. Nahiti of Ngati Toa went to France in the mid-1830s to meet Louis-Philippe. Like Ruatara, he was balked of his king. In 1837, Wakefield brought Nahiti to England, where he helped form the New Zealand Company image of the Maori.[16] The trickle of Maori tourists continued throughout the age of scientific exploration. Tumohe and Paraone of Waikato returned with the *Novara* in 1859 to Austria, met their king (or, rather, emperor), studied printing and returned home with what they had learned. In 1863, there were dozens of Maori in London, most members of two entertainment troupes: one 'rowdy', performing risqué dances; and one respectable, preaching as well as dancing. 'At 12 o'clock we arrived at London. Our mouths just gaped in wonder at the many ships and at the big houses. Looking everywhere one got tired of looking all the time.'[17] Many more Maori visited Europe's outliers. From 1793, hundreds of Maori followed Tuki and Ngahuruhuru to the Australian settlements, especially Sydney. One-third of the oarsmen at a regatta in Hobart in 1838 were Maori, as were all of the Sydney harbourmaster's boat crew in 1840. As many as a hundred may have stayed with Marsden at Parramatta, that great Maori college of European studies.[18]

Dozens of Maori chiefs visited Sydney and further afield on what amounted to state visits. They sought, with varying success, to emulate Ruatara in acquiring guns and settlers.[19] Most Maori going overseas worked their passage. Beset by desertion, European sea captains were seldom fussy about the ethnicity of their crews. Maori quickly became part of a cosmopolitan pool of sailors, joining whaling and other vessels in their hundreds. American whaling ships left New Zealand with an average of two more men than they had when they arrived, and most of the fresh recruits were probably Maori.[20] Six Maori joined an

American vessel in 1829, five joined a Danish whaler in 1839, and there were enough aboard a ship that touched at Tahiti in 1826 to frighten the locals with a haka. One whaler had a Maori mate; another a Maori ghost.[21] By the 1820s, an increasing number of young Maori had seen something of the outside world with their own eyes, often quite a lot. They gained mana for it; they brought back European goods and knowledge, ranging from sea shanties to the use of artillery; and they were often paid in muskets.

Once European enclaves formed in New Zealand, Maori agents of contact no longer had to leave the country. Close relations with at least one Maori chief were a virtual necessity for ships and stations; they required Maori suppliers and workers, and their crews took short- or long-term Maori wives. These Maori all became stationary discoverers of Europe, adjusting and distributing it to other Maori. While such figures are mere guesses, it may be that a thousand Maori travelled overseas before 1840. Another thousand may have become informal wives of European sojourners and settlers in New Zealand. Yet another thousand or so worked closely with shore whalers and sealers in the south and missionaries and traders in the north. There must have been thousands of sex contracts at the Bay of Islands alone, each a crash course in European language and customs. In London in 1818, Titeri had seen an elephant. 'I see Elephant quite astonished my countrymen no believe it when I tell them.'[22] Moehanga and Ruatara also encountered this problem of disbelief at first. Very soon, however, Maori tales of Europe became a major source of amusement and information, much more effective, if not accurate, than stumbling direct communication with Europeans, with whom little language was shared. Until the 1830s, few Europeans were really fluent in the Maori language. Most Maori learned most of what they knew about Europe from other Maori.

Cook, Marion, King and other early European agents of contact tried to stock New Zealand with European nature. Since plants and animals are poor autobiographers, it is difficult to deduce who introduced what, when, where. Cabbage allegedly ran wild from the gardens of Marion's expeditions; some weeds and pests such as dock and rats introduced themselves and fended for themselves; and Cook may have succeeded in introducing potatoes and possibly pigs at his main haunt, Queen Charlotte Sound, after several attempts. But most very early efforts to acclimatise plants and animals appear to have failed, because Maori lacked knowledge of, and interest in, them. 'Thus all our endeavours for stocking this Country with usefull animals,' wrote Cook, 'are likely to be frusterated by the very people whom we meant to serve.'[23]

The two most important eventual successes were potatoes, to which Maori could apply the techniques and values of kumara cultivation, and pigs, fast-breeding, fast-growing, omnivorous lodes of rare protein. King's first attempt to introduce pigs in 1793 failed, like Cook's – two years later, Tuki had only one left of the twelve he had been given. Norfolk Island had 10,000 pigs by 1795, and

King tried again once he had established gift relations with Te Pahi. He sent over a total of 56 pigs in three ships in 1804–05. By 1808, a surplus was available for trade, and it is probably from this Northland stock that pigs spread throughout the North Island by the 1820s. Potatoes were being traded at the Bay of Islands and Hauraki by 1801, and became a staple crop in these and neighbouring areas within about fifteen years. It has been suggested that pigs and potatoes might have come to Southland, the other focus of contact, through the Maori of Queen Charlotte Sound, but sealer introduction is more likely. By 1815, there were large acreages of potatoes under cultivation on the shores of Foveaux Strait and at Otakou, and pigs became available for trade a little later. Some European observers thought that pigs were allowed to run wild, then hunted as necessary, but Maori pig husbandry really fell in the traditional middle ground between farming and hunter-gathering. They were taken to suitable feeding grounds well away from unfenced crops, and then checked and culled periodically.[24]

King's early attempts to introduce pigs failed; his later attempts succeeded. The difference was Te Pahi. Marsden could have sent wheat seed and hand mills without effect indefinitely but for Ruatara. From the initial hatcheries of Northland, Southland and Queen Charlotte Sound, and from new introductions by the agents of vice, the new moa and kumara spread throughout the country. The need for products to trade with Europeans was one factor behind the eager reception of pigs and potatoes; their fit with existing Maori economic practices was another. Attempts were made to introduce goats, geese and garlic. They failed because Maori were not interested, although the garlic apparently ran wild for a time. European buyers would have been just as happy, or happier, with beef and cabbage, but pork and potatoes is what they got. 'Potatoes and Pork, Pork and potatoes wherever we went,' wrote one European traveller. 'I began to get tired of Pork and Potatoes.'[25]

Like discovery, misunderstanding was mutual at the cultural interface. Explorers were wholly male floating communities, which on investigation appeared not to be war parties or hunting parties. This seems to have led to some early Maori confusion about European gender and sexual proclivities. On Cook's first voyage,

> One of our gentlemen came home to day abusing the natives most heartily whoom he said he had found to be given to the detestable Vice of Sodomy. He, he said, had been with a family of Indians and paid a price for leave to make his adresses to any one young woman they should pitch upon for him; one was chose as he thought who willingly retird with him but on examination provd to be a boy; that on his returning and complaining of this another was sent who turnd out to be a boy likewise; that on his second complaint he could get no redress but was laught at by the Indians.[26]

There are other instances of Maori feeling European men's chests to establish gender and offering homosexual hospitality.[27] On first contact, it may well have seemed to Maori that all Europeans were gay. They soon learned that this was not so; and mastered the art of managing Europeans without giving too much offence, even at some cost to their own rules – of tapu, for example. Europeans went through the same learning curve in reverse, but with a greater reluctance to abandon their preconceptions. Whereas ditching the idea that all European men were homosexual was no great sacrifice to Maori, ditching myths of empire and racial superiority was more difficult for Europeans – because they were interlocked with collective identity, individual self-images and dreams, and because they were shored up by a vast cumulation of perceived precedent, of which Maori were relatively free. But Maori themselves made some contribution to the persistence of the myths of empire in European minds.

Maori themselves were among the people who told Charles Darwin and others that they were dying out. 'As the clover killed the fern, and the European dog the Maori dog; as the Maori rat was destroyed by the Pakeha rat, so our people also will be gradually supplanted and exterminated by the Europeans.'[28] There were Maori believers in fatal impact, and Maori also contributed something to the myths of conquest and conversion. Ruatara helped construct a dual image of Maori in the minds of European humanitarians. By blackening the names of his rivals, he helped create the image of the dangerous, unpredictable, degraded Maori, vulnerable to fatal impact and urgently requiring both Christian salvation and the protection of missions by the likes of Ruatara. Blackening the names of tribal rivals was quite common Maori practice from the time of Cook. 'Their jealousy lest the ship should go into any other district than their own was extreme: and they took every opportunity of representing their neighbours to be murderers whom we should avoid.'[29] Once it was clear to them that cannibalism horrified genteel Europeans, Maori tended to allege that it was something that happened down the road.

Ruatara contributed even more to the whitening, convertible Maori, perhaps not wholly by accident. 'His deportment,' wrote Nicholas, was 'dignified and noble . . . not disfigured with the disgusting marks of the tattoo . . . His complexion was not darker than the natives of Spain and Portugal, and in general the lineaments of his countenance assumed the European character.'[30] His English was fluent, and unlike other Maori, thought Nicholas, he did not look uncomfortable or out of place in European clothes. So much was physical accident and acquired habit, but Ruatara may also have consciously manipulated the Marsden/Nicholas conception of Maori. His account prepared them to see even Rangihoua as a natural paradise – 'the country in the interior, he said, abounded with everything, as the land was both fertile and excellent'.[31] His defence of Te Pahi's reputation led them to turn the *Boyd* affair into a European offence against Maori; his interpretation of Maori metaphysics induced them to conclude that Maori were descended from a people 'familiar with the Mosaic account of creation', at least dimly aware of a Supreme Being. Above all, it was Ruatara's enthusiasm for things European that led them to conclude that Maori were the perfect prospects for conversion. Marsden and Nicholas saw his premature death as a near-martyrdom. It put a sudden stop to growing doubts about his motives. A fourteen-page poem on his death won a prize at Cambridge University in 1823.[32] Behind the admirably convertible Maori of the missionary and humanitarian literature lies the ghost of Ruatara.

The Iron Patu

After leaving New Zealand in 1770, Cook's first expedition visited New South Wales and encountered Australian Aboriginals. Expecting to be greeted as munificent demigods, the Europeans were ignored and their gifts left untouched. The Aboriginals were never forgiven for their disinterest in Europe. Maori, on the other hand, embraced European trade and technology with fervour. Most tribes had iron tools, imported blankets and garments, pigs, potatoes and guns by 1830. Many had much more extensive inventories of alien goods. By 1850, there would have been few if any Maori in whose lives European things did not play an important role, and large-scale trade with permanent European settlements, often through the medium of cash, had replaced bartering with ships and stations at the heart of economic interaction. There is no doubting the length and breadth of Maori economic engagement with Europe, nor that it substantially changed traditional society. How far it facilitated fatal impact, conversion or empire is more debatable.

Maori did use European technology, in the form of guns, to kill each other in considerable numbers, as we shall see in the next chapter. Technology could also have had more subtle corrosive effects. By adopting it on its own terms, Maori could convert to European wants and values. As they became increasingly addicted to European tools and consumer goods, as novelties became luxuries and luxuries became necessities, they could be forced to abandon traditional activities to produce trade goods such as potatoes and processed flax. They could be forced to pay high prices, and even alienate capital, such as land and independence. Europe's things, like its thoughts, could undermine the traditional ways in which individuals and groups obtained mana, creating a social ferment. Still worse, as Maori turned to profit, they might do so as individuals, using their money to make more, and doing so for themselves, not their groups – tribespeople turned into entrepreneurs, peasants and proletarians by the bubonic dollar. All these things did happen, but not very much.

In 1815, John Nicholas met a Maori chief, Te Puhi, who possessed a very unusual weapon, a patu, or club, beaten with infinite patience from bar iron. 'I could not have thought it possible for it to have been effected by the simple processes of a New Zealander,' wrote Nicholas, 'had I not many other proofs of their astonishing ingenuity.'[33] If museums were to choose one object to symbolise the Maori response to contact, Te Puhi's iron patu might be it. From the outset, Maori adapted, even converted, European objects. The early explorers saw perfect earrings ground from bits of glass, large nails made into chisels, small nails made into fish-hooks. Physical transformation was only the obvious tip of an iceberg. Europeans offered Maori a range of things. Maori selected those they valued most highly, ensured that adjustments were subsequently made to the range offered, and adapted the function as well as the form of those they selected. They distributed the Maorified desire for these things and the knowledge of how to use them, as well as the things themselves.

It was obviously European visitors who initially determined the range of goods offered to Maori. They tried to keep them cheap – trinkets, cloth, glass and small tools of iron – and exploited their rarity value as much as possible to obtain high prices. But they quickly discovered that Maori were ornery consumers. Cook found that the price of fish increased very rapidly in New Zealand, that Maori were sometimes able to impose their concepts of value on his crew, and that enterprising chiefs were quick to establish themselves as middlemen.

> Their greatest branch of trade is for the green-talk or stone (called by them Poenammoo) a thing of no sort of Value, nevertheless it is so much sought after by our people that there is hardly any thing they would not give for a piece of it . . . At first the exchanges were very much in our favour till an old man, who was no stranger to us, came and assisted his countrymen with his advice, and in a moment turned the exchanges above a thousand per cent in their favour.[34]

Maori determined that large nails should be the most prized trade item in the 1770s, iron tools in the 1790s and 1800s, and guns thereafter. As competition among European traders increased, Maori preferences began to help determine the goods on offer. Sydney traders imported heavy blankets and dogskins from England especially for New Zealand.[35] Maori also changed the types of iron artefacts most commonly traded, from small nails to large nails, to use as chisels in woodcarving, and from large axes to small axes, which were more easily carried by a musket-armed warrior. 'Nor can we dictate to them,' wrote Thomas Kendall, '[what] they must receive for their property and services. They dictate to us!'[36] Muskets themselves, the main import, are the outstanding example of this.

The end of the Napoleonic and Anglo–American Wars in 1815 meant that muskets were available in quantity, but they were not cheap compared with nails, beads and bits of glass. No Europeans particularly wanted guns to become the staple item of the New Zealand trade. Some disliked them on grounds of policy or principle; others on grounds of cost. Yet guns did become the staple, because Maori insisted on it. The missionaries and naval ships, who had a policy of not trading in muskets, found it difficult to obtain supplies, came under immense pressure to trade in guns, and sometimes succumbed to it.[37] Other ships, the great majority, put up much less resistance. At first, old and corroded guns were traded in small numbers for high prices, but Maori quickly developed the technical expertise and market leverage to insist on more and better weapons. They used axes not only for cutting wood, as they were intended, but also to kill each other. They used guns not only for killing each other, as they were intended, but also for other purposes. 'Indeed, so prodigal were they of their powder [in the firing of salutes],' wrote an observer in 1820, 'that one might presume little of it would remain . . . for the destructive purposes for which they had gone so far to procure it.'[38] Muskets were also stockpiled as a display of tribal wealth, and used as gifts to augment mana or make peace with erstwhile enemies. Goods 'which they have been at much pains to acquire, they will freely give away'.[39]

Maori used muskets in their own way, but the transfer of such technology could create dependence on the donors, and to some extent it did. Guns were not only one-off purchases, but also consumer goods that demanded an ongoing supply of ammunition and replacements. Using guns did addict Maori to Europe. 'As they are in constant want of fresh supplies of ammunition, I feel it will always be their wish to be on friendly terms with us, for the purpose of procuring these desirable stores.'[40] Other dependencies built up: first to iron tools, then to clothing and blankets, then to a broadening range of things including patent medicines, Epsom salts and calomel, sugar, which is quite addictive, and tobacco, which is very addictive.[41] Wiremu Tamihana, later the 'Kingmaker' and most Christian of chiefs, 'withdrew his application to attend the theological department of St Johns [College] on learning that he would not be permitted to smoke his pipe'.[42] The European prophets of conversion believed Maori were becoming 'irrevocably enslaved by wants which were unfelt by their ancestors'.[43] But a number of things qualified these dependencies.

There is considerable evidence of Maori making ammunition themselves, especially after 1840, but with some attempts in the 1830s. Quality varied – Papi Ropata, a Ngati Ruanui ammunition manufacturer, blew himself up in 1856 – and home-made gunpowder was seldom a major source of supply, although one source listed four Maori gunpowder 'stations' in 1860.[44] Yet Maori did produce their own bullets, from imported lead and pewter spoons; their own firing caps, from match heads; and their own cartridges – in one 1830s case from the pages of Voltaire.[45] They also repaired their own guns and did not need to replace them very often. There were no major changes in small-arms technology in the first half of the nineteenth century, and armouries could be accumulated over a long period without becoming obsolete. Dependency was also qualified by the existence of Maori suppliers, who went to Sydney for their guns, and by the multiplicity of competitive European suppliers, who were remarkably unconcerned about the uses to which their guns were put. Economic dependency can transmute into political control only when the suppliers can co-ordinate, select and ultimately withhold supply. Maori pressure to buy guns, and the eagerness of Europeans to sell them, meant that supply was not controlled even in the 1860s, let alone before 1840. The colonial government was unable to stop arms sales by its own subjects, still less by American whalers. In the 1830s, muskets were the basic currency of New Zealand commerce, the forebear of pounds and dollars. Even small trans-Tasman vessels carried a few dozen muskets for trade; one New England whaling ship carried 757.[46]

Maori dependence on the things of Europe tended to increase in step with European settlement, notably in the form of trading and whaling stations, which were economically dependent on Maori. The stations were also militarily dependent. If a trader refused to sell powder, buyers might shoot him with the last round from their previous purchase. Even if Europeans could stop the supply, they could not do so quickly enough to prevent their stations becoming hostages to fortune. That dependency was mutual reduced its bite, as did the fact that European suppliers competed rather than co-ordinated. In the abstract, Maori did become technologically dependent on Europe, but in practical politics there was no such thing as a Europe united enough to exploit that dependence. If one trader did not supply the required goods on the required terms, another one would. The delusion that technological dependence necessarily leads to corrosion or control is an important and enduring part of the myths of both fatal impact and conversion.

Guns and other tools and goods did subvert aspects of traditional Maori society and culture. Individuals and groups whose mana, wealth and power had depended on privileged access to resources, such as prized foods, dyes or stone, or special skills in processing them, suddenly found they had competition, and some no doubt lost out altogether. Cultural leadership, to the extent that it existed, shifted from the East Coast to Northland. But new goods sometimes joined and perhaps adapted the old inventories rather than displaced them. Greenstone, for example, continued to be highly valued, though the use of it shifted from tools to ornaments. Traditional foods continued to be valued for gift giving and hospitality. Pork, blankets and iron were not necessarily better or more valued than potted birds, flax mats and greenstone, but they did become cheaper. Opting for a whaleboat instead of a canoe was arguably more like opting for a Japanese instead of a British car in the 1970s than a culturally subversive acknowledgement of European superiority. Nails were selected from the trinkets offered by the explorers, converted into carving chisels and used to underwrite a flowering of artistry in wood. Was this change malign? Was it greatly different in kind from the discovery of greenstone? Was it a symptom of insidious corruption by Europe, an example of Europe-led progress and Conversion, or just another change? Some chiefs and some groups lost mana through the changes triggered by European technology and contact in general. But other chiefs and tribes gained it. *Nett* damage to the mana of chiefs and groups did not occur. Currencies of rivalry had changed before. The same game played on.

Price was the area in which Maori remained at most real disadvantage. They were quick to realise that prices fell as the number of Europeans increased – this was a major and enduring factor behind their desire for more settlers and sojourners. Prices fell from around eight large pigs *and* 150 baskets of potatoes per gun in 1812, to ten pigs *or* 120 baskets of potatoes in the 1820s, and to as little as six pigs in the 1830s. Prices in dressed flax fell from a ton per gun to eight hundredweight. But this was still quite high. A Maori woman could process five to nine pounds of flax per day.[47] Eight hundredweight therefore amounted to at least a hundred days' solid work, leaving aside gathering the flax and other duties, and six months was probably more common. The guns traded in New Zealand, on the other hand, were valued at about 27 shillings each in 1831[48] – perhaps two weeks' wages for a woman worker in Sydney. Even allowing for the cost of transport, a substantial profit and the market principle that value is the price people are prepared to pay at a particular time and place, there was still an imbalance in Europe's favour in the exchange of goods. The imbalance was corrected by services, especially sex.

Early European chroniclers, many of them missionaries or their associates, often mentioned the New Zealand sex industry but, with the exception of the French, gave few details. Edward Markham, a loose-living young gentleman who visited in 1834, was another exception. Markham invented a unique form of cross-cultural greeting: shaking breasts. His account was considered unpublishable for 130 years, though it now seems tame enough.

> Thirty to five and Thirty Sail of Whalers come in for three weeks to the Bay and 400 and 500 Sailors require as many Women, and they have been out one year. I saw some who had been out Thirty-Two months and of course the ladies are in great request . . . These young ladies go off to the Ships, and three weeks on board are spent much to their satisfaction, as they get from the Sailors a Fowling piece [shotgun] for the Father or Brother, Blankets, Gowns and c.[49]

The sex industry began at first contact in 1769, and from the 1810s it became large and important – very probably preceding wool, gold and dairy products as New Zealand's leading earner of overseas exchange. Northland in particular received many thousands of sailor visits, normally involving a sexual contract with a Maori woman for the duration. Sometimes the sailors would live ashore with the women; sometimes women would live aboard ship in their dozens for the whole of its stay in New Zealand waters.[50] Unsurprisingly, the missionaries portrayed the massive sex industry as a terrible degradation for Maori women, the moral dimension of fatal impact. This was far from the whole story.

The normal price for sex contracts is said to have been a gun for the tribe plus something such as a dress for the woman. This represented a tenfold improvement on the yield for women's work compared with flax processing, and it was far more than any man could make. Dire consequences in the form of venereal disease did exist, but we will see in the next chapter that they have probably been exaggerated. Sex before marriage carried no stigma for most women; temporary marriage was quite an easy shift from a tradition of sexual hospitality; and the capacity to earn guns for the tribe could well have increased women's status. Ex-shipgirls were said to be much in demand as wives for Maori men. Most contracts were for the whole duration of the European's visit – more temporary marriage than brothel-like supermarket sex. The double price, dress as well as gun, and the fact that women normally had one partner per ship visit rather than several, suggests that they gained an element of control of the industry, and a few other signs support this. A Bay of Islands woman known as Mary, in 1815 already a veteran of the sex industry, harangued Marsden for forbidding, with mixed success, intercourse with the crew of the *Active.*[51] Henry Williams preached unavailingly to a 'company' of shipgirls, 'congregated together on the beach, rolling about in the sun', who appear to have had their own camp or settlement. A kind and jovial chiefly procuress known as 'Mrs Goshore' was highly respected by Maori.[52] One observer denied that the shipgirls were ever unwilling, even when their work was managed by Maori men. 'They were eager to get on board . . . the whole unmarried female population appeared to be at the service of the ship.'[53]

But there was also a grimmer form of the sex industry, which could involve greater male control, multiple partners rather than temporary marriage, a single price (which went to Maori men), 'very little girls' and, increasingly, slavery. Slavery is obviously bad for the slaves, and it also tends to devalue the labour of free workers in the same industry. 'Enslaved women were given to the Europeans that came . . . in the whaleships in exchange for guns,' remembered Te Kaahui of Taranaki, 'but it was not the slave women alone who were thus treated for the free women . . . were also sold to the Europeans.'[54] In one horrifying case, the entire crew of a French ship tried to penetrate a virgin 'without any of them being able to capture the prize they all felt honour bound to conquer'.[55] It has been suggested that the vagina of this girl was blocked as a consequence of syphilis, but she may simply have been very young, and it is impossible to believe that she was willing.

This more male-led form of the sex industry does not neatly succeed the woman-led; both are apparent from earliest contact. Cook's second expedition found that some Maori women had sex very willingly, and negotiated an extra price for themselves. Others, presumably married or of high rank, refused, and were not forced by their menfolk. Still others refused and were forced, allegedly by their own families but possibly by their slavemasters. 'Two I believe served with reluctancy to the pleasures of the young [European] Men & cried bitterly, who were hard-hearted enough to use them in Spite of their tears.'[56] But the male-led variant rested partly on female slavery, and this increased greatly with burgeoning intertribal warfare in the 1820s. There appears to have been an increasing tendency for chiefly male procurers to control the industry, whether the workers were slave or free. 'The chiefs come and offer their sisters and daughters for prostitution and expect a present in return.'[57] It therefore seems reasonable to see the sex industry as containing its own loosening and tightening processes, unleashing and backlash. It revalued women's work and status, but also gave men an opportunity to co-opt the value and reduce the status. The sex industry, then, had mixed implications for women within Maori society. But economically it helped balance the contact equation.

European sailors were no strangers to mass prostitution. It was a fact of life at their home seaports. But for them its value in New Zealand or Tahiti was increased tangibly by their being islands of sex in a vast sexless ocean and, less tangibly, by the local absence of a sense of sin or immorality – a recurring theme in lower-deck romanticism. The wide sexless ocean, the romance of sinless South Sea sirens and a tendency to believe that they were somehow duping their partners in non-marital sex led the whalers to overvalue it. One gets a sense of Europeans sniggering behind their hands at duping naive savages in the New Zealand trade – at acquiring a pig or a poke for a few trinkets. Sex was one industry where Maori men at least could snigger back. The act was cheap, many women were clearly willing, and those who were not were being exploited as much by their menfolk or masters as by Europeans. Valuable guns flowed in return for sexual hospitality that Maori communities might have provided anyway.

Maori did not passively receive Europe but actively engaged with it. They chose, adjusted and repackaged the new, in many respects into a less culturally damaging form. They did so with courage and perceptiveness, exploiting a technologically formidable Europe that thought it was exploiting them, separating Europe and its things like a fool and his money. But Maori did not perform this feat as an act of collective wisdom, with an eye on the future and the common good. Instead their goal was the immediate subtribal good, or apparent good. Each group sought to bilk its rivals by exploiting the new resources more effectively, the age-old dynamic. Each new currency of rivalry gave way to the next, in different times in different places, but in a similar sequence: nails, iron tools, potatoes, pigs, muskets; whaleboats, ships, chapels, mills; individual Pakeha, shiploads of Pakeha, stations of Pakeha, towns of Pakeha. All these were sources of mana in themselves, wholly new arenas of rivalry, and they also augmented the traditional arenas – hospitality, gift giving and war. This was the dynamic behind the energetic exploitation of contact, and it was a multiplier in the contact equation. Rivalry helped spread Europe faster, developing a life of its own. The equation was not European agency *plus* Maori agency equals the outcome of contact, but Europe *multiplied by* Maori agency. In some respects, this made fatal impact and conversion more likely, not less. It certainly helped spread Christian ideas and two new forms of death – by imported disease and by the bullet.

CHAPTER SEVEN

Fatal Impact?

Conversion, conquest and fatal impact were alternative hypotheses about the way in which contact became empire. Maori were either to be transformed, subordinated by force or unintentionally swept from the path of Europe. But there was room for intersection. The missionaries saw conversion as a solution – the only solution – to fatal impact. But some thought a touch of the latter could serve the former by ploughing the field for it, breaking down traditional Maori society and culture. 'I agreeably hope,' wrote Henry Williams, anything but agreeably, 'that this universal illness may tend to their spiritual good.'[1] Theoretically, fatal impact rendered conquest redundant, but the two were often thought to work in tandem in practice, making each other still more certain. Conquest could also help conversion when converts proved recalcitrant, by supplying a touch of that 'great civiliser, the sword'. 'We must,' wrote Frederick Maning, 'conquer them and thereby save them.'[2] Conversion could return the favour, by reducing the number of enemies conquest had to face, even converting some into allies.

During the first half of the nineteenth century, the three dynamics, led by fatal impact but often working together, attacked Maori society on four fronts: intertribal conflict, which European guns greatly intensified in the 1820s and 1830s; the advent of Christianity, with which most Maori engaged between 1830 and 1850; interracial conflict, of which there were quite a number of cases even before official British annexation in 1840; and depopulation through European disease, which reduced Maori throughout the nineteenth century.

The Musket Wars

When Ruatara died in 1815, the missionaries were left bereft of their protector and naturally considered leaving New Zealand. But they were soon comforted by other local chiefs, notably one named Hongi Hika – 'Shungee' to the missionaries. Thomas Kendall wrote: 'Shungee told me and my colleagues not to be afraid: Duaterra was dead, but they would be our friends.'[3] Hongi was as good as his word. Until his death in 1828, the Christian mission in New Zealand was essentially his vassal. If Marsden was the St Augustine of New Zealand, then Hongi was the Emperor Constantine. Christianity was only one of Hongi's business interests. He also inherited from Ruatara a leading role in the development of Maori agriculture, and for a long time his northern Nga Puhi subtribe had more acres of potatoes and other crops than any other group. Hongi was something of a Leonardo – a good craftsman, artist and surgeon, who learned to write the English alphabet in a few days.[4] But his speciality was guns. He can be used, in the same way as Ruatara, as both the leading example and a symbol of another complex process in contact history: the extraordinary explosion of tribal conflict beginning in 1818 and known as the Musket Wars. In 1815, Governor Lachlan Macquarie of New South Wales had appointed Hongi, along with Ruatara and Korokoro, as 'constables' policing contact, at a salary of one cow.[5] Australian policemen have been accused of many sins over the past two centuries, but Constable Hongi Hika surely takes the cake.

The Musket Wars were the largest conflict ever fought on New Zealand soil. They killed more New Zealanders than World War One – perhaps about 20,000. They involved most tribes and caused substantial social and economic dislocation, and are therefore key evidence in favour of fatal impact. The wars changed the political map of Aotearoa and helped determine the location of the first European mass settlements in the early 1840s. Given this importance, it is staggering to consider how little historians know about them. We do not know when they ended, for example – at which point in the 1830s did tribal warfare resume normal levels? This is partly because we have not tried to find out, but also because what we do know depends mainly on the interpretations as well as the evidence of two unreliable groups: missionaries and Maori victors. The former saw few battles themselves; they were not used to counting armies, and they were so influenced by fatal impact that they used the Musket Wars to explain the depopulation of communities that had been at peace. They bequeathed estimates of up to 80,000 killed, which would have left few Maori alive. Like most victors, successful Maori combatants exaggerated their triumphs. Land claims, important contexts for the recording of traditional history, were an added incentive to assert that rival claimants had been completely subjugated or displaced. For these and other reasons, the following attempt at an explanation of the Musket Wars must be speculative.

Around 1818, Nga Puhi appear to have been divided into three groups, as noted in Chapter Four: northern, led by Hongi; southern, whose leading chiefs included Te Morenga and Pomare I; and western, led by Moetara, Te Taonui and the brothers Patuone and Waka Nene. The three Nga Puhi hapu groups were all close kin, and they were also connected by intermarriage and long proximity to two associated groups: the people of Whangaroa, including Ngati Pou, led by Te Puhi, owner of the Iron Patu, and Te Ara of *Boyd* fame; and the people of the eastern Bay of Islands, including Ngare Raumati, led by Korokoro among others. These two groups had links with non-Nga Puhi tribes, Ngati Kahu of Muriwhenua and Ngati Wai respectively, but they had long been part of Nga Puhi's neighbour zone. A sixth group, less closely connected but still related to western Nga Puhi by intermarriage, was Ngati Whatua of Kaipara. Led by the talented and formidable Muripaenga, hero of a novel by Dumont d'Urville, they had heavily defeated Nga Puhi in 1807–08.[6]

The three Nga Puhi hapu groups formed the Nga Puhi kin zone; all six groups together (leaving aside northern Muriwhenua neighbours for the sake of clarity) formed the Nga Puhi neighbour zone. The intense rivalry for mana between the chiefs and groups of this neighbour zone was an important dynamic in New Zealand history. At one level, rivalry was expressed in perfectly traditional ways: war within kin and neighbour zones, of which there were at least half a dozen outbreaks between 1818 and 1837; separate and competitive operations against outside enemies; competitive co-operation against outside enemies; competitive peacemaking, hospitality and gift giving; and competition in the exploitation of resources, both to fund all these activities and as a source of mana in itself. The difference was that resources now included Europeans, and their things and thoughts.

Ruatara's and Hongi's monopoly of Europeans generated resentment among their rivals. When they went to Sydney to fetch the first missionaries in 1814, Korokoro went along to keep an eye on them, and was intensely frustrated by his failure to establish a comparable relationship, even to the point of engaging in a physical fight with John Nicholas.[7] Hongi's success in 1819 in obtaining the second, Kerikeri, station as well was very nearly the last straw. Southern Nga Puhi confronted Marsden with the issue. 'All that they wished was that Shungee should not monopolize the whole of the trade by having all the Europeans living under his authority, as this made him and his people assume more consequence than they were entitled to.'[8] Marsden failed to satisfy them, and shortly afterwards, led by Te Morenga, they went to war against Hongi, plundering his new missionary vassals at Kerikeri along the way. A semi-ritual battle was fought – Hongi forbade his men to use their muskets – and eleven men were killed. Peace was made immediately, with Te Morenga giving Hongi a war canoe, but the rivalry continued in other ways.[9]

Although Hongi dominated the missionaries, they did not trade as readily in muskets as did whalers, who were increasingly preferring the better anchorages of the southern and eastern Bay of Islands, notably the village of Kororareka. By 1820, southern Nga Puhi and Ngare Raumati were therefore able to acquire guns in numbers that probably equalled those of their northern Nga Puhi kin – Te Morenga was said to have had 35, and Korokoro 50.[10] Western Nga Puhi and Ngati Whatua also acquired a few guns, probably from the Bay people, who gained mana through such munificent gifts. Between 1818 and 1821, these groups launched the expeditions that began the Musket Wars.

Hongi, Te Morenga and Korokoro led competing and separate expeditions to Thames and the Bay of Plenty. In the same years, Ngati Whatua and western Nga Puhi embarked on two astonishingly long-range raids, making both allies and enemies along the way. Both were known as Te Amiowhenua (Encircling of the Land). One reached Cook Strait; the other traversed a thousand miles. It was these two expeditions, rather than those of the Bay Nga Puhi, that broke all distance records in Maori warfare and raised these conflicts above the norm. They were actually undertaken by the Northland groups with fewest muskets, as though to compensate for that fact by acquiring mana in other ways.[11]

Some of these expeditions were justified in terms of utu for events that had occurred between ten and 25 years before, but this does not explain their timing, and there could scarcely be utu justification for the people of Kaipara attacking Wellington. The acquisition of muskets does not wholly explain the timing either. Northland Maori had had muskets since about 1805 – few, but enough to give a morale advantage over tribes with no experience of them. It could be argued that they waited to acquire really substantial quantities of guns, but this did not occur until 1821, and it was the groups with fewest muskets that launched the longest expeditions. Muskets, even in small numbers, helped make all these expeditions successful in killing or enslaving several hundred people of various tribes. But it was not guns in themselves that made the new intensive, long-range warfare possible.

The key constraint on the range, duration and frequency of Maori campaigns had always been economic. It was loosened around 1818 by a Maori agricultural revolution, pioneered by Te Pahi and Ruatara, the key element of which was the mass production of pigs and potatoes. Potatoes were hardier than kumara and had a better ratio of output to labour. Maori were good cultivators of root crops. Their potato gardens allegedly compared favourably with those of New South Wales, and they achieved much higher tonnages per hectare than kumara. Maori agriculture at last had a reliable surplus. Potatoes helped feed long-range expeditions, to an extent limited by carrying capacity, and more importantly helped replace absent warriors in the home economy. It may well have been in 1818 that acreages of potatoes and other crops became really substantial and reliable among all the Northland groups. 'Potato Wars' might therefore be more accurate than 'Musket Wars'.[12]

Hongi Hika held the early lead in possession of the new resources: potatoes and guns. But by 1820, his kin and neighbour rivals had caught up. They had also caught up in the new currency of rivalry these resources made possible: long-range raiding. Indeed, in this field, the achievements of Ngati Whatua and western Nga Puhi exceeded his own. So, in 1820, Hongi embarked on the ultimate gift visit. Like Te Pahi and Ruatara, and in a sense as their heir, he made full use of mediator status to increase his standing in both worlds. He, too, was considered a king of New Zealand, though only when outside it. He succeeded where Ruatara had failed, in meeting King George. He made something of a splash in high society, where he 'conducted himself with an air of conscious superiority, and that scrupulous regard to etiquette by which he was generally distinguished'. He studied for a time at Cambridge, attending soirées, assisting Professor Samuel Lee with a Maori-language grammar, and gathering gifts. Thomas Kendall accompanied him on the visit, against the wishes of Marsden but in accordance with the wishes of Hongi. Hongi spent four months in Sydney on the way home, selling the gifts he had received in England and buying guns with the proceeds. In 1821, he arrived home with as many as 400 or 500 muskets, perhaps the largest single shipment Maori ever acquired. This was a remarkable feat of procurement, and it seems impossible to see Hongi as a passive victim of Europe. Kendall may have helped, but in a sense he was Hongi's creature.[13] The rivals as well as the enemies of northern Nga Puhi trembled, as well they might.

In 1821–23, Hongi mounted three campaigns, each as unusual in scale as Te Amiowhenua had been in range. The victims, Ngati Paoa of Tamaki, Ngati Maru of Thames, Arawa of the Bay of Plenty, and the powerful Waikato tribes, had few muskets and were all heavily defeated. This could be the only series of campaigns in which the number of killed and captured, and of the armies involved, may actually have numbered in thousands. For probably the first time in Nga Puhi history, Hongi was able to form an alliance of most factions and most warriors, and keep them away from home for several months on end. He was able to cobble together this alliance by distributing his new muskets – it was not so much that he gave guns to his warriors, but that men became his warriors when he gave them guns. Even so, rivalry persisted within the combined army. In 1823, for example, Pomare I and southern Nga Puhi attacked the Arawa pa of Mokoia themselves to pre-empt Hongi. They were repulsed, and the pa fell to Hongi.

Hongi was able to use his success in this round of the Northland rivalry for mana to gain him victory in the next. By 1825, he felt his power and mana were sufficient for him to take on Muripaenga and Ngati Whatua, who during the previous round had been more allies than enemies. They had participated in several Nga Puhi expeditions, and taken a leading role in the two Amiowhenua forays, with some Nga Puhi as their junior allies. Muripaenga had peacefully visited the Bay of Islands in 1823. These links meant that the army Hongi was able to bring against Ngati Whatua was much smaller than that he could muster for operations outside the neighbour zone – perhaps as few as 300 men. But it was better armed with guns and had developed better methods of using them. Hongi was therefore able to decisively defeat Muripaenga at the Battle of Te Ika-a-Ranginui in 1825. In 1826, Nga Puhi invaded and subordinated Ngare Raumati in a low-intensity campaign. In 1827, they did the same to the people of Whangaroa, though Hongi received his death wound in the process. He died in 1828, after entertaining visitors in his last months by making air whistle through the bullet hole in his chest.[14]

The endgame was played out without Hongi. In the year of his death, northern and western Nga Puhi fought a brief feud in the Hokianga – twelve were killed. The western group had slightly the better of it, and their chiefs went to Sydney and fetched back the Wesleyan mission station displaced by the fighting at Whangaroa the previous year. They also successfully sponsored several European trading and timber stations. This, together with their successes further afield, made them co-winners in the Nga Puhi kin rivalry. In 1830, a lesser chief of northern Nga Puhi clashed with southern Nga Puhi in a brief conflict known as the 'Girls' War', which consisted of one quite fierce battle at Kororareka. The southern subtribe apparently won the day, but the senior northern chiefs – Rewa and Titore, heirs of Hongi – used their greater power and mana to exact Kororareka itself as the price of peace. Although Pomare II, now leader of southern Nga Puhi, compensated to some extent by sponsoring the traders James Clendon and Gilbert Mair in his remaining territory, and by promoting his pa of Otuihu as an alternative trade and prostitution centre to Kororareka, the northerners had become first among equals.[15] Thereafter, chiefs who felt they still had something to prove made some spin-off forays to the south, and there was a large though half-hearted expedition to Tauranga in 1831–32, but broadly speaking Nga Puhi had finished with the Musket Wars.

Kin, neighbour and stranger zones were three arenas in which the same game was played in different ways. Rivalry with kin, whose respect mattered most, was most important and least bloody; rivalry with neighbours was quite important and quite bloody; rivalry with strangers was most bloody but least important – it was a means to the end of success in the other zones. This helps explain why Hongi, to the mystification of Europeans, did not build a territorial empire as he might have done. He could easily have occupied Auckland, for example, but chose not to. The process also helps explain otherwise bewildering shifts in alliances. A related or neighbouring group might be allies in one year or one context, and enemies in another, but they were always rivals. A key dynamic behind the wars was rivalry for mana *within* a single zone.

Guns, potatoes and Europeans were new currencies of rivalry, ends in themselves. Their uneven distribution gave new advantages in traditional currencies, such as feuding with kin and neighbours, and therefore intensified rivalry in them. They also encouraged raids on strangers, for slaves and mana. The use of guns and food surpluses in this way moved through three phases. In the first, tribes acquired a few muskets, enough for a shock effect against those who had never faced them. They also acquired a sufficient economic surplus to use their new weapons more often and further from home than had previously been possible. In the second phase, the tribal armoury contained hundreds of muskets, and food and goods were sufficient to cobble together and maintain unusually large armies. Hongi's return from Europe with his guns instantly projected him into this phase. In the third phase, Maori acquired more than one gun for every warrior – 'saturation'. Henry Williams wrote that Ngai Te Rangi of the Bay of Plenty had a surfeit of guns by 1831. 'Each boy had two or three and men ten.'[16] Tribes moved through the phases by improving their access to Europeans and guns, by developing agriculture – flax was important outside Northland – for trade and war supplies, and by capturing prisoners who could be used to grow more food and work in the sex industry to obtain more guns. In the third phase, agricultural production and trade with Europeans reached levels where neither slaves nor guns were so urgently needed. Since neighbour and stranger tribes were by this time likely to have reached at least the second phase, slaves were not so easy to acquire either. Spin-off expeditions by groups with something to prove occurred, but conflict gradually returned to normal levels.

Technical military developments paralleled economic, also moving through three phases. European observers sometimes wrote disparagingly about poor Maori selection and maintenance of guns, and poor marksmanship – they were allegedly only able to shoot pigeons at a range of one foot, which cannot have left much of a meal.[17] But this was true only of a first phase when Maori were inexperienced musketeers. Once they had the guns and ammunition to practise, they naturally became better marksmen. By 1819, Nga Puhi were said to have acquired 'much skill in the use of gunpowder and firearms'. In 1821, a ship's officer noted 'the meeting of two or three hundred people for firing at marks'.[18] Hongi led the way here too, shooting ducks on the wing as early as 1815, when John Nicholas could not.[19] In the third phase, he and others developed musket tactics, such as firing in controlled volleys, and antidotes to them, such as rifle trenches and bullet-proof flax matting on pa stockades. *Musket* pa emerged – a transitional stage between the *traditional* pa that had preceded them and the *modern* pa that succeeded them from 1845. In this third phase, Maori took good care of their guns and insisted that they be of reasonable quality, avoiding cheap 'sham dam iron' weapons. In 1833, a whaler wrote: 'Muskets are now used altogether as war instruments by the Natives . . . they are now as good judges and keep them in as good order as the Europeans.'[20] This was already true of Northland and some other regions by 1827.

Bloody routs, the main cause of casualties in most warfare, occurred when a tribe encountered another much lower on the scale of technical adaptation. Casualties decreased as the balance became more equal. Even before this, kinship restricted the lethality of local feuds, and slave taking was a key objective among strangers. European accounts sometimes imply that the armies of the Musket Wars massacred whole populations and took thousands of slaves. They should never have been allowed to have it both ways. Some population statistics from 1840s Wellington, where musket warfare was quite heavy in the 1820s and 1830s, support the belief that lethality, though sometimes great, was often exaggerated. They show an excess of males over females, twice as great among adults as among children, and cannot therefore be explained by possible female infanticide or the general but slight tendency for male births to outnumber female. Although neither sex was by any means immune to either fate, slavery in the Musket Wars tended to select for women, while death selected for men. Childbirth, the killer of women, outpaced war, the killer of men.[21]

Hongi's war aims were to outdo his rivals, not conquer strangers according to European rules. Once his northern subtribe succeeded in this, by 1830, it fought against strangers less often. Because the stranger tribes had by this time entered the third phase, Nga Puhi also won less often. Winning less often was an additional reason for fighting less often. Outside Northland, the same processes occurred in varying but intersecting shapes and times. Hongi's descent on the powerful Waikato tribes in the early 1820s did not stop their long-standing rivalries with their kin and neighbours Ngati Toa, Ngati Raukawa and Ngati Maru. Waikato entered the second and third phases from the mid-1820s, acquiring guns in great numbers through the flax trade. Led by their great generals Te Wherowhero and Te Waharoa, they were able to match Nga Puhi, complete their expulsion of Ngati Toa and their partial expulsion of Ngati Raukawa, and repel Ngati Maru. All four groups also embarked on long-range expeditions into their stranger zones against less well-armed tribes, on the Nga Puhi model. Those strangers who had not embraced European contact and entered the arms race were now forced to do so. Waikato launched a series of large-scale invasions of Taranaki in the 1820s and 1830s, devastating but not occupying. In the late 1820s, Ngati Maru made numerous raids on the East Coast, and Ngati Raukawa invaded Hawke's Bay. Ngati Toa, under Te Rauparaha, migrated south from 1822, gathered a wide range of allies, subordinated the Wellington, Manawatu, Nelson and Marlborough tribes, and established an unusual territorial hegemony around Cook Strait.[22]

Ngati Toa and company began raiding the South Island in 1827, and had some successes before encountering the new war complex in reverse. In the 1820s, northern and southern sections of Ngai Tahu fought a civil war of unusual intensity, known as Kai Huanga (Eat Relations). The southerners, with more muskets and potatoes, had the better of it. Peace was made in 1828. The weakened northern Ngai Tahu fell victim to Ngati Toa, notably in a horrific attack on Akaroa in 1830 in which a European ship, the *Elizabeth*, was used by Te Rauparaha as a Trojan horse. But Ngati Toa bounced off the weapon-rich southern Ngai Tahu, under Tuhawaiki, Taiaroa and other chiefs, polar equivalents of Nga Puhi as veterans of guns and contact. Allies of Ngati Toa, especially those pressured out of Taranaki by Waikato, feeling they had yet to obtain their share of mana, slaves or land, launched spin-off campaigns. In 1828, one group attacked Poutini Ngai Tahu in Westland. In 1836, wishing to score points over his Ngati Toa allies and rivals, Te Puoho of Ngati Tama, originally of north Taranaki, launched the longest-range raid of all – to Southland, where he met his death. Yet another group, Ngati Mutunga, from north Taranaki, bribed a European ship into taking them to the Chatham Islands in 1835. Here they killed or enslaved the peaceful Moriori inhabitants and took over their land. Like hunter-gardener expansion, and perhaps for similar reasons, the Musket Wars ended in the Chatham Islands.[23]

It will be clear that another reason for historians' avoidance of the Musket Wars is their sheer complexity, a bloody kaleidoscope, a Maori Mfecane, whose shapes are not easy to discern. At one level, however, they moved in three great spasms: Northland impacting on Waikato, Waikato impacting on its neighbours, and these neighbours impacting on the rest of the country. But the deeper pattern cannot so easily be divided up by space or time. The new military resources flowing from European contact were differentially distributed and exploited, by a mix of European and Maori agency. Those who had them used their advantage against traditional kin and neighbour rivals, and, less traditionally, against strangers. The cycle ceased when the advantage ceased – when the new crops and weapons were universally distributed – and the wars speeded up the distribution. They were undeniably brutal and immensely damaging in some places and at some times. A few of the least fortunate groups almost disappeared. But the wars diminished in lethality as differentials declined in each region, and they had a built-in endpoint – one well short of fatal impact for Maori as a whole. They began when and because some Maori had muskets and potatoes, and stopped when and because everyone had them.

Guns and Bibles

It has often been suggested, not least by the missionaries themselves, that the Maori conversion to Christianity and the peacemaking efforts of the missionaries brought an end to the Musket Wars. Mass conversion, or, rather, a massive upsurge of Maori interest in Christianity, did begin around 1830, just as the wars began to wind down. Christianity is a strong and cohesive religion, which promises much and does bless the peacemakers rather more than the Maori belief system. The acquisition of missionaries, of Christian knowledge and of the literacy that often went with it provided a new and non-violent arena of rivalry. Without relatives among the contending parties, missionaries did sometimes make good neutral mediators. But most missionary peacemaking feats, on close examination, have Maori peacemakers behind them.[24] We have seen that Musket War rivalry had a built-in endpoint independent of Christianity, and the notion that peace was a missionary gift should probably be dismissed. Yet it seems unlikely that two such major and simultaneous shifts as peace and Christianity could be entirely unrelated, and there *was* something strange about the end of the wars.

In 1829–31, the number of firearms in New Zealand suddenly doubled. Six thousand guns were imported from Sydney alone in 1831, traded for flax.[25] A disproportionate number went through Kawhia, Raglan and Tauranga to Waikato, who suddenly became as well armed as Nga Puhi. In Te Waharoa and Te Wherowhero, Waikato had leaders to match the Nga Puhi generals, and there were potential allies in plenty with a grudge against the latter. Now was the time for revenge. But the showdown never came. It was not that the thought never occurred to Te Wherowhero – in 1827 he counter-raided as far as Whangarei. It was not military exhaustion – Waikato embarked in this very period on five years of campaigns against Taranaki, some very large in scale. There was no problem with precedent, no reputation as a grave for invading armies akin to that of the Urewera Mountains. Ngati Whatua and Ngati Maru had both successfully invaded the Bay of Islands within living memory, though before the gun. Why then was utu suspended, and why did the Bay of Islands remain inviolate?

Let us temporarily exchange this question for another: the reasons for the Maori conversion. Explanations include the grace of God, favoured by the missionaries and the faithful; the shock of fatal impact (or at least crippling impact), undermining Maori faith in traditional religion;[26] an improvement in missionary methods and resources, associated with the leadership of Henry Williams and involving the inversion of Marsden's 'civilise first, Christianise later' policy;[27] and superficial conversion, as a means to the end of literacy.[28] The first explanation is unarguable, for or against. The second depends on whether or not fatal, or crippling, impact occurred. The third has some merit but fails to explain why Methodists and Catholics 'converted' roughly as many per mission station as the Anglicans, despite inferior resources and the absence of a Henry Williams. The fourth has considerable merit. There is some evidence that Maori initially saw reading and writing, or even books themselves, as magical keys to European knowledge – which in a sense, they were. Maori were interested in learning to read and write, and missionaries had a much tighter monopoly of books in Maori than traders had of muskets. No Hongi brought back hundreds of books from overseas. But Maori literacy in the 1830s has been exaggerated somewhat by writers overeager to praise the Maori for being like 'Us'.[29] And the Christianity-literacy thesis implies that Maori conversion was false, a pretence intended to trick the missionaries into handing out literacy. The Maori interest in Christianity was rather deeper than this.

Another possibility is that belief systems like the Maori were inherently likely to accept, not reject, any coherent and convincing new religion if they had sufficient access to it. We have seen that pre-contact Maori religious beliefs must have changed over time to incorporate new deities. Changes must have varied from region to region, to incorporate different natural/supernatural phenomena and different newly deified ancestors. When strangers entered the territory of a new tribe, they entered a new variant of the Maori religious system, and their first reaction is unlikely to have been disbelief. Naturally, different people had some different gods, and of course they were real. It is Eurocentric – and Islamocentric – to assume that because closed religious systems automatically disbelieved all others, open systems should do likewise. The exploitation of new resources also required appropriate handling of their supernatural dimension, as with the rituals developed around greenstone. Maori kept some religious teachings secret, guarding their magical powers from strangers and rivals. Europeans did not.

The strangers who entered the Maori world in increasing numbers from 1769 were intriguingly novel and possessed useful things that obviously required their own rituals. Their gods were bound to be interesting and useful too, if Maori could learn about them. Maori in 1769 had listened eagerly to the sermons of Tupaia, the only person on the *Endeavour* who could speak to them. Two black sailors performed some kind of Afro-American religious ceremony in 1836 at the Bay of Islands before an admiring Maori audience, a case of voodoo evangelism.[30] From the 1830s, Maori were intensely interested in Judaism, the Bible's other religion, and interest increased as more of the Old Testament became available in the Maori language in later years.[31] If Arabic missionaries had arrived and learned the language, Maori might have engaged with Islam. This changes our problem from explaining the Maori 'conversion' of the 1830s to explaining why it took so long. If the incorporation of new religions was the natural thing for Maori to do, why did the missionaries have to wait sixteen years for their first converts?

There is evidence of Maori interest in European religious practices well before 1830. Apart from the Parramatta students, hundreds of Maori spasmodically attended the Northland mission schools from 1814. Chiefs eager for good relations with Europeans respected their tapu – by avoiding work on Sunday, for example – at least within sight of the missionaries. Ruatara respected the Sabbath from 1811; another chief is said to have suggested that, if not working on Sunday was good, then not working on all seven days would be even better.[32] But the spread and depth of Maori interest in Christianity was hampered by the absence, in most areas, of people to tell them about it; and by the fact that, where such people existed, they could not speak Maori very well. Many missionaries understandably took years to acquire a really fluent command of Maori. Henry Williams, for example, began to preach substantially in Maori only in 1828, five years after his arrival.[33]

Improved Maori language grammars and translations of the New Testament became available to the Northland missions from 1827. This not only enabled missionaries to teach Christianity much more readily, but also consolidated its link with literacy and gave them textbooks with which to improve their own grasp of the language. Maori interest in both Christianity and literacy had both long been there; the books had not. Added to this, the missions' lack of success had been frustrating their controlling authorities in London, and a feeling that they might have to close down had become known in New Zealand by 1830.[34] In this context, it was tempting for the missionaries to ease the theological qualifications required before baptism, and so increase their scores in souls for the consumption of home authorities. With books, and teachers fluent in the language, Maori interest moved closer to the point missionaries were prepared to define as conversion. The missionaries' definition moved closer to the state of Maori interest at the same time.

A complementary explanation of the delay in Maori 'conversion' was Hongi's monopoly of the missions. Other groups had less access and may also have resented the missionaries as his creatures. A missionary asserted in 1827 that other Maori groups dared not show their interest in Christianity for fear of Hongi's jealousy.[35] Hongi himself valued but did not greatly respect his missionaries. He teased Marsden for going to sleep at his colleagues' sermons. A missionary was subjected to muru when his daughter asserted he was the equal of Hongi. Hongi had little need to propitiate the missionaries by offering them slaves and children as regular pupils, and by facilitating their work. The missionaries were virtually ineffective by being so firmly under Hongi's thumb, but they believed that he alone protected them from the hostility of his rivals. When Hongi was mortally wounded in 1827, the missionaries began preparations to leave New Zealand before their stations were destroyed. Henry Williams buried £50 in his garden, a sure sign that the situation was perceived as serious.[36] Instead, they found that Hongi's removal reopened the patronage of mission stations as an arena of rivalry, in which there was no longer one clear leader among the Northland chiefs. These chiefs had to compete more vigorously to attract mission stations, and had to share their successes.

Three new mission stations were established in Northland between 1828 and 1834, doubling the number existing in 1827 after the Wesleyan evacuation of Whangaroa; five more were set up by 1840. Stations now sometimes had more than one master. More slaves and young people were allowed freer access to the mission schools and services, to keep the missionaries happy as well as to gain new knowledge for their hapu. It is an exaggeration to say that missionaries became economically or politically independent of their Maori sponsors, but they did become less dependent, benefiting from the competitive multiplicity of suppliers of potential converts, just as Maori did with the suppliers of guns.

Hongi's death released Christianity in Northland. It also began the process that released it from Northland to the rest of the country. After Hongi's death, there was widespread fear among Nga Puhi that their erstwhile victims, now well armed, would retaliate.[37] Various efforts were made to cement a peace, through marriages, visits and gifts. A European saw Nga Puhi make one gift of a thousand muskets to a southern tribe in the early 1830s.[38] But the main way of ending war was to return its living evidence – slaves. During the 1830s, thousands of prisoners were released to return to their homes – first by Nga Puhi, then by Waikato. They included the leading Maori Christian theologians of the day. Christianity took credit for the release of these slaves, but it is really they who should have credit for Christianity. There are known instances of slaves being released as part of a peacemaking process, well before Christianity had any influence, and releasing prisoners of war to cement peace seems an obvious enough thing to do.[39] So the Maori religious conversion – better defined as the Maori incorporation of Christianity – *was* related to the end of the Musket Wars. But it was peace that made Christianity more than Christianity that made peace. By 'peace' is meant the end of the exceptional levels of violence characteristic of the Musket Wars. Moderate levels of warfare continued throughout the 1830s and beyond – indeed until as late as 1888. When Henry Williams died in 1867, a tribal war was stopped in honour of the great missionary peacemaker who had ended tribal war.[40]

Each of the three Christian missions to New Zealand owed its arrival and survival partly to Northland Maori sponsors. Ruatara did the job for the CMS. In 1828, Hokianga chiefs relocated the Wesleyan mission expelled from Whangaroa the previous year.[41] In 1835, several Maori, again from Hokianga, went to Sydney for a denomination of their own and converted to Catholicism, which encouraged the advent of Pompallier.[42] When the missionaries finally broke out of Northland, from 1833, we find that they followed Christianity, carried by released prisoners, not the other way around. These prisoners had worked as slaves for their captors, but they were allowed to attend mission schools, and they learned reading, writing and the gospel from each other as well. Around 1830, Nga Puhi began releasing them, and they returned home with their new knowledge. It was they, not the European missionaries, who generated the first mass Maori engagement with Christianity.

Before 1835, missionaries preaching in new areas were told by their audience: 'We know all that!'[43] Piripi Taumata-a-kura of Ngati Porou returned home to Waiapu about 1834, after his release by Nga Puhi. He taught reading and writing on wooden slates, together with his own version of Christianity. Maori missionaries gathered around him, and he used his new mana from one sphere to gain more in another, by leading Ngati Porou to victory in a feud with their neighbours in 1836. Mission stations established at Waiapu and Hicks Bay in 1842 and 1843 inherited his work. When William Williams, Henry's brother, went to Turanga in 1839, he found that the returned slave Putoko had already 'converted' 3,000 locals.[44] The same year, Octavius Hadfield at Waikanae began reaping the harvest of souls previously sewn by Hohepa Matahau, and two more released captives took Wesleyanism to Wellington. Catholic missionaries functioned 'to follow up the earlier dissemination of the Catholic message by Maori catechists and travellers'.[45]

The Maori Henry Williams, Wiremu Nera Ngatai of Ngati Ruanui, returned home to South Taranaki from Northland in 1837. So great was his 'influence and preaching that nearly all the tribes for more than 200 miles along this coast had renounced idolatry before a single European missionary had been near them'.[46] He built churches, sent acolytes to evangelise Nga Rauru, Whanganui and Ngati Tuwharetoa, and like Piripi proved himself a muscular Christian in warfare. 'Thus had instruction,' wrote Henry Williams, 'been conveyed from Tribe to Tribe, and many had been taught to read in the remotest parts of the Island and had the word of God conveyed to them who had never seen a European.' These developments, he went on to claim, 'are the fruits of the instruction given in the schools of the CMS', but he did not always approve of the novel dishes into which the fruit was made.[47] These are discussed in Chapter Nine.

Harriet and the *Alligator*

Early in 1834, the trader, whaler and ex-convict Captain John Guard, who had set up a whaling station at Te Awaiti in Marlborough in 1827, took his family for a visit to Sydney aboard the ship *Harriet*. Guard has a reputation in New Zealand legend as a tough but worthy pioneer. Contemporaries were less kind, seeing him as a classic agent of vice. He had 'such a name for rascality and ill-dealing that few of the chiefs would deal with him.' 'Mrs Guard was one of the regular "trades" in which her husband engaged.'[48] Betty Guard had sailed with her husband since she was thirteen. In 1834, she was nineteen, with two small children. On the way back from Sydney, the *Harriet* was wrecked on the Taranaki coast. Guard and company made it to the beach and set up camp. Maori from the Taranaki tribe plundered the wreck but left the castaways alone. A second tribe, Ngati Ruanui, missed out on the plunder and attacked the castaways. Official Maori tradition says they were provoked by the theft of some potatoes. Unofficial tradition says that they were incensed that Taranaki had got gunpowder and they had not. After a fierce gunfight – both parties were quite well armed with muskets – the Maori defeated the Australians. Twelve of the crew were killed. Betty Guard and her children were captured. John Guard and fourteen others escaped.

John Guard made his way to Sydney to arrange his family's ransom, but changed his mind and persuaded Governor Richard Bourke to mount a punitive expedition. In September 1834, Guard again landed on the Taranaki beach, this time backed by a powerful warship, HMS *Alligator*, and a detachment of the Sydney garrison. An unarmed Maori envoy named Whiti came to arrange Betty's release. Guard and his men took him prisoner, stabbing him ten times with bayonets. With the help of cannon, the troops attacked and burned a Maori pa, Te Namu, but Betty and one of her children were released in exchange for the injured Whiti. The other child was then released without ransom. Betty complained of her captivity, naturally enough, but it seems all three were fairly well treated after the first few days – perhaps too well. Edward Markham alleged that Betty Guard had had an affair with Whiti. She had twins in Sydney soon after her release, he wrote, 'and they are rather dark'.[49] So instead of losing two children, John Guard allegedly gained two, but he did not seem pleased. 'How would I civilise them?' he said of the Maori. 'Shoot them to be sure! A musket ball for every New Zealander is the only way of civilising their country.'[50]

Fatal impact thinking has it that John Guard's policy was pursued with some success. Missionaries castigated the brutalities perpetrated by the agents of vice upon the helpless Maori. British Resident James Busby's voluminous reports created a picture of extreme 'frontier chaos'. Arthur Thomson wrote of an undeclared 'war of races' to which 2,000 Maori had fallen victim.[51] And it is quite true that violent clashes dot the history of contact before 1840. Those involving Tasman's, Cook's and Marion's expeditions first gave New Zealand its reputation as a dangerous place. There was a violent incident involving the timber ship *Fancy* at Thames in 1795, in which three Maori were killed. In 1806 came Charlotte Badger's *Venus*, whose piratical depredations are sometimes said to have kept the coasts in an uproar, and in 1808 the crew of the schooner *Parramatta* was wiped out after shipwreck. Te Pahi and King between them succeeded in improving New Zealand's image, only to have their work undone by the attack on the *Boyd* in 1809. There were two attacks on whaling ships at Coromandel in 1815, and there were several violent clashes between southern Maori and sealing gangs and ships in 1817–26. One six-man American gang was captured in 1821 and obliged to eat each other. In the words of survivor Joseph Price of Wilmington, Delaware, Americans 'tasted very much like roasted pork'.[52] The *Alligator* incident in 1834 was the last major clash, and the only one to involve regular troops. Europeans actually killed no Maori in the most famous of these 'frontier chaos' incidents. In 1830, Te Rauparaha hired Captain William Stewart and his ship *Elizabeth* to transport his warriors to attack northern Ngai Tahu at Banks Peninsula.[53]

There are specific explanations for some groups of clashes. Most of the incidents involving sealers seem to have been part of a feud between local Maori and two particular captains, James Kelly of the *Sophia* and Abimelech Riggs of the *General Gates*. Maori took seals for food and were therefore in competition with the sealers for resources. This was not true of whaling, flax or timber, which generally speaking did not interfere with normal Maori resource use. Compatible resource use reduced conflict – a very important general point in contact history. Increases in the number of southern chiefs visiting Sydney and establishing gift-exchange relations with particular captains may correlate with a decline in violent clashes with sealers. The people of Whangaroa made three attacks on Europeans, cutting right against the grain of Northland Maori policy. They attacked the *Boyd* in 1809, they plundered the brig *Mercury* in 1825, and they sacked their local mission station in 1827. This enraged their neighbours, and it could be that this is why they did it. Their Bay rivals had superior access to Europeans. Ruining the area's reputation for being Europe-friendly damaged the Whangaroa tribes less than it did their rivals. This was a dangerous game, as the Whangaroa people found out when Hongi invaded their territory.

Many of these incidents have been exaggerated or misinterpreted. The depredations of the *Venus* were carried out by fewer than a dozen crew, who in fact seem to have restricted themselves to kidnapping isolated women when no-one else was looking. The 'dozens' of Maori alleged killed in an attack on John Boultbee's sealing gang in 1826 amounted to one wounded according to a Maori account.[54] Busby's accounts of violent chaos were mostly confined to the plundering of property – he mistook the law of muru for the apotheosis of lawlessness. Captain Stewart, who single-handedly gave a huge boost to the notion of violent European ravages, was really no more than Te Rauparaha's taxi driver. Above all, the level of Pakeha–Maori violence is dwarfed by the sum total of contact. There were perhaps one or two score of violent clashes, as against one or two thousand ship visits, and one or two hundred whaling, trading and mission stations. Among all the interaction at the Bay of Islands from 1800, the only fatal violence against Europeans seems to have been the attack on the *Parramatta*. While the ruthless armies of the Musket Wars ranged the land, very few European stations were plundered, and virtually no Europeans seem to have been killed. As with Maori religious conversion, we have to invert our question. We have less to explain why there was so much Maori–European violence than wonder why there was so little.

Many of the European agents of contact were hard men who believed natives to be inferior, and were well armed. But they were not stupid. Before Maori had guns, Europeans had the whip hand, and the ratio of violent incidents to total contact was massively higher before about 1820. Even in this period, however, it was cheaper and less risky to trade than to take. As prices increased to the point where buccaneering became worthwhile, potential buccaneers found that Maori were too well armed. The violent European agents of fatal impact had brought their own antidote: guns. Maori scruples about attacking strangers were not great either, but Maori wanted European contact. They valued their reputations for being Europe-friendly even to the point of attacking neighbouring hapu who threatened it, and of tolerating insults to chiefly mana. Ngai Tahu leader Te Whakataupuka, described by the *Sydney Herald* as 'one of the worst disposed chiefs' towards Europeans, once played a game with some sealers consisting of shying potatoes at each other. A potato struck the chief's tapu head, and he verged on killing the offender but managed to swallow his rage.[55] Europeans were valued not only for the trade goods they provided but as possessions in themselves – they were 'our Pakeha'. The sponsorship of Europeans was a new arena of rivalry – one gained more mana and resources by cherishing them than by shooting them. But as contact increased and permanent stations formed, this did present Maori chiefs with a problem of control.

The problem was solved largely through the traditional mechanism of marriage alliances. Virtually every non-missionary station – trading, timber and whaling – and every individual trader and Pakeha–Maori was quickly linked to Maori sponsors by marriages. They were usually informal on the European definition, and sometimes temporary, but they were the cement of Old New Zealand. Important traders, station managers and sometimes ship captains married chiefly women; their followers married women of lower rank. The sealers of the south, the timber workers of Hokianga and the shore whalers in between – almost all had Maori wives.[56] Literally scores of cases could be cited. José Manuel, Ngati Porou's Pakeha from the 1830s, made five successive marriage alliances. Poverty Bay trader Thomas Halbert, known as Henry VIII, made six. The marriages changed when the alliance changed, but long-term partnerships, political and conjugal, were more common, and Pakeha did not have much choice about making them. John Howell, manager of a Southland whaling station and later a wealthy pastoralist, at first refused to marry into his Ngati Mamoe sponsors but eventually conceded defeat. Edward Markham noted that 'it is not safe to live in the country without a chief's daughter as protection'.[57]

The missionaries were a problem here. Marsden laughed off an offer of marriage alliance from Hongi, and to say that miscegenation was frowned on by the evangelicals is to understate the case. The mission authorities feared reverse conversion, and sought European wives for their male agents in New Zealand. But to some extent the practice of supplying pupils for the mission schools, who usually lived at the station, substituted for marriage alliance, and, with some exceptions such as the 'piratical parson' William White, the missionaries were not prone to violence or disorder anyway. Ships' crews were prone to violence and disorder, and here the sex industry intersected with marriage alliance. Not only were such captains as William Brind tied into the system by chiefly marriages, but the sailors ashore and the women aboard insured against violent clashes. Like the more benign variant of the sex industry, marriage alliance may have boosted the status of Maori women – not so much because association with Pakeha was inherently prestigious, but because mediators normally used their influence with one group to lever up influence with the other. Marriage alliance dominated Maori–European relations before 1840, and was quite important after it. It was an alternative model of ethnic relations to the dynamics of empire, and initially it worked rather better than they did.

Disease and Depopulation

Fatal impact through disease is an immensely powerful fact in culture-contact history, and an equally powerful fiction. Between 1200 and 1500, the growth of insanitary cities, hothouses of infection, and increasing contact with the rest of the Old World, notably through successful Mongol and Turkish invasions, had exposed Europe to major outbreaks of disease. In the five years after 1346, bubonic plague – the Black Death – killed off perhaps a third of Europe's population, and there were other pandemics. Immunity, the specialists tell us, cannot be directly inherited – for that you have to catch and survive the disease yourself. But the survival of pandemics must surely select for genes less prone to 'clinical' disease – as against the milder 'subclinical' versions, which confer immunity without killing you. For this and other reasons, such as immunity passed to infants through mothers' milk and the tendency of endemic disease to confer immunity as well as death, relatively disease-hardened European populations did emerge. From 1500, though local epidemics occurred and endemic disease regularly killed people, there were no more Black Deaths in Europe. The peoples of long-isolated regions like the Americas, on the other hand, were virgins in terms of most of the diseases bouncing around the Old World. As expanding Europe encountered them, therefore, they sometimes died like flies while the newcomers bred like rabbits. This is the kernel of truth in the myth of fatal impact.

Ironically, the one area where Europeans *were* biologically superior – adjustment to pox and pestilence – was a complete mystery to them. Through folklore as much as science, they gathered that some ills were contagious, but they did not know how. Little was known of bacteria until the work of Louis Pasteur in the later nineteenth century, and viruses were a mystery for even longer. Prior to this, Europeans sought to explain the high death rates of virgin populations, and their own relative immunity, in a vacuum of knowledge. They listed specific causes, some reasonable, some ludicrous, but in the end tended to resort to irrevocable laws of Nature or Providence. Beginning as a false but not unreasonable explanation of a real phenomenon – the differential effect of epidemic diseases on seasoned and unseasoned populations – fatal impact thinking became a force in itself, exaggerating the inevitability, implications, spread and sometimes the size of the phenomenon. This is the kernel of myth in the truth of fatal impact.

Imported diseases did indeed afflict many Maori from the 1790s: viral dysentery, influenza, whooping cough, measles, typhoid, venereal diseases, and the various forms of tuberculosis and similar diseases then known as phthisis, scrofula and consumption. Many (but not all) missionaries and other observers reported massive Maori death rates and plummeting birth rates. They were right to some extent, in some places and at some times, and the general pattern from the 1790s to the 1890s does appear to have been one of disease-induced population decline. The question is: how great was it? There are reasons for believing that it has been, and still is, exaggerated.

For one thing, the powerful myth of fatal impact made European observers see what they expected to see. Fatal impact thinking both pre- and post-dated its evidence. In 1805, John Savage wrote:

> Neither the appearance or accounts of the natives indicate the prevalence of disease [yet] . . . in a few years how great will be the change – children of diseased parents, they will grow up a stunted race . . . both miserable and disgusting; in no respect resembling the hardy inhabitants previous to their contact with civilised man.[58]

The view that Maori were a dying race persisted to 1930, a generation after census evidence showed conclusively that Maori were on the increase.[59] The notion that Maori were subjected to 'crippling impact' – devastated and demoralised, if not destroyed – is still widespread. In the nineteenth century, the suggested causes of Maori demise ranged from the sublime to the ridiculous. Missionaries suggested the will of God, the work of the Devil, the sins of William Yate. Secular explanations included the disuse of traditional foods, clothing and customs; the misuse of new foods, clothing and customs; living in cold draughty houses; living in hot airless houses; working too hard, and not working hard enough. While disease predominated, other alleged causes of death and low birth rates included mass suicide, deaths from sulking, colds, excessive excitement, fatness, too much sex, horse riding and the ravening katipo spider.

What such commentators did not see was that New Zealand's vast girdle of ocean was a partially effective natural quarantine. The voyage from Europe took four months or more; many whalers had been at sea for a year or more before arriving in New Zealand. On voyages of such length, the sick either died or recovered, usually ceasing to be infectious in both cases. The most virulent European diseases – malaria, bubonic plague, smallpox, yellow fever, typhus and cholera – did not manage the jump to New Zealand. Diseases such as measles, consumption and what was then diagnosed as scrofula did kill many Maori, especially the very young and very old, but the lethality of some diseases was exaggerated. Drawn themselves from classes experiencing increasing life expectancy and high fertility, missionaries mistook high but not grossly abnormal Maori death rates and low birth rates for something catastrophic.[60] Missionary families had up to fifteen children – the fourteen couples who came out before 1833 had 114 children between them – and few Maori could match this.[61]

Moderate lethality from epidemics seemed high. When nineteen died of 800 sick with influenza and tuberculosis, mission doctor Samuel Ford considered this toll 'very great' and evidence that the Maori would soon be extinct.[62]

Augustus Earle claimed that while many Maori suffered from the new diseases, they seldom died.[63] There are also signs that Maori were becoming immune to some diseases by the late 1830s. Venereal disease might not kill, but it could lower fertility. Influenced by moral factors – 'we want to see sorrow for sin' – as well as by the myths of fatal impact, missionaries exaggerated the prevalence of venereal disease. One even asserted that 49 out of 50 Maori women were sufferers.[64] Medical observers in the 1820s, 1850s and 1880s convincingly denied that syphilis and gonorrhoea were widespread among Maori, and modern research gives some support to this view. Dr Fairfowl maintained in 1821 that 'it has not spread much among them, as they strictly tabboo the infected persons'.[65] The incidence of VD was no doubt quite substantial, especially in centres of the sex industry – ironically, whalers blamed Maori women for it, calling it the 'New Zealand fever'.[66] It may well have had a significant adverse effect on Maori women's fertility in some areas. But it was not a plague or a pandemic, and we shall see that there were compensating factors in birth rates. We need to cut through the mythology on contact disease and tentatively suggest a general pattern in the hope that experts will improve upon it.

Contagious diseases kill pandemically, epidemically and endemically.[67] Pandemics ravage whole virgin populations on a broad front, then 'burn out' quickly. Pandemics of the same disease cannot devastate the same population twice in quick succession, because the first attack should have conferred immunity on the survivors. Epidemics similarly attack fast and fiercely, and depart quickly, but are more restricted in space and less comprehensive. Both types of pestilence tend to come from outside a population – in this context, a large, regularly interacting network of people. Endemic disease becomes a permanent unwanted guest, entrenched in a population, but kills fewer people more slowly and seasonally, and distributes immunity as well as death. Epidemiologists argue that some endemic diseases, which kill infants disproportionately, require a base population of 200,000 to 500,000.

There may have been outbreaks of influenza, measles and dysentery of pandemic proportions in the early contact period, but it seems unlikely. A merging of neighbour zones was taking place in the early nineteenth century, with longer-range warfare and gift exchange, and European networks reinforcing and extending traditional networks of interaction. It was more likely than ever before for a Nga Puhi to be found at Foveaux Strait, and a Ngai Tahu in Northland. But my guess is that this process did not merge Maori neighbour zones into a single interactive network until the 1850s. Prior to this, with one partial exception, Maori were not part of a single interactive 'population' in epidemiological terms, and were quite thinly and widely spread across the country. Both factors limit infection. Until about 1850, we therefore tend to find disease striking in fierce but localised epidemics, introduced into one neighbour zone but not others. Some diseases such as measles are infectious only for a restricted period, during which the sick person would find it difficult to travel. This did not limit the spread of sickness within a village, but it did limit its spread from village to village. From 1850, however, neighbour zones began to merge and span the whole country, and we see the first well-documented pandemics taking place.[68] In the 1870s, the combined Maori and Pakeha populations reached the size where they could support endemic disease. This scenario suggests that mortality from disease was moderate during the epidemic phase, before 1850; peaked during the pandemic phase 1850s–70s; and dropped during the endemic phase thereafter, though with continuing high infant mortality.

There was a significant exception to these tentative rules: the Tasman world. Sydney was close enough to New Zealand to evade the natural quarantine of distance. By about 1830, New Zealand and Australia between them may have formed a single epidemiological population to some extent, large enough to sustain some endemic diseases such as influenza. Epidemic and endemic disease in the north and south of New Zealand, the areas of most intensive contact, does appear to have come from Australia. A measles epidemic that struck Foveaux Strait in 1835 was brought by the *Sydney Packet*.[69] Trans-Tasman unity in terms of disease was thin and partial. Smallpox, for example, was introduced to the New South Wales Aboriginals possibly as early as 1788, but did not make the jump to New Zealand.[70] Endemic influenza seems to have appeared in Northland in the 1830s, when it struck both Maori and Pakeha seasonally – twice a year. 'However, the Maoris were beginning to develop resistance to influenza by the end of the decade and after the middle of 1839 the missionaries began reporting better health among them. The bi-annual pattern was broken.'[71]

The new diseases must have had an adverse impact on Maori infant-mortality rates, but there were also countervailing factors. Research into European medical history suggests that improved nutrition is as important in population growth as dramatic public health schemes or heroic developments in medical science, and we have seen that high protein diets can boost birth rates. Late in pre-contact history, Maori had limited food sources, which could only be rendered adequate through hard work and good organisation, and which resulted in low birth rates even so. Not everything Europe brought was bad, and iron tools, pigs and potatoes eventually gave Maori better nutrition and a larger and more reliable economic surplus. Pigs in particular created a second protein boom. The need to reserve pigs and other foodstuffs for the musket trade may have reduced the effects of this in the 1820s and 1830s, but there was another new protein source as well – whalemeat. This was traditionally a rare but desirable food, and between 1827 and 1850 it was available in bulk at the numerous shore-whaling stations, a side product of oil production. There is some hard evidence that Maori consumed it.[72]

The need to reserve protein for the gun trade, and the moderate adverse effects of venereal disease on fertility during the heyday of the sex industry, appear to have neutralised such factors for a time. But, in striking contrast to the legend, Douglas Sutton has argued that they did lead to an increase in Maori birth rates by the 1850s at the latest. 'It is possible that the proportion of children present in the Maori population in 1858 was higher than ever before,' writes Sutton. 'It is certain that the proportion was increasing.'[73] If this is true, more children died as a result of European contact, but more were born as well. By the 1890s, this had combined with increasing immunity to push births ahead of deaths, as it was always likely to do eventually.

An important link between fatal impact and conversion was the belief that the ravages of disease turned Maori towards the missionaries as physical as well as spiritual saviours. Missionaries claimed that 'a great part of their existing influence among the natives' stemmed from the medical help they provided.[74] It is true that Maori could not help but observe that the new diseases killed them more than Europeans. It was this that led Maori themselves to make statements prophesying fatal impact – they were as ignorant of immunology as Europeans. It is also true that most missionaries acted, with greatly varying skill and resources, as amateur doctors, and that on the whole European medicine was more effective against European diseases than Maori medicine. But not by much. Maori herbal treatments of sores and abrasions were effective enough to attract European patients.[75] Maori sought to treat fever by dousing the patient with cold water, but a glance at a book on the nineteenth- and early twentieth-century European treatment of tuberculosis will reveal equally misguided remedies. A whalers' cure for scurvy was to bury the sufferer up to his neck in earth when land was at last reached. This treatment allegedly resulted in some patients at Banks Peninsula having their heads eaten by wild pigs, a cure surely worse than the disease. As late as 1865, a Pakeha patient was killed by emetic treatment for his hernia.[76] The assumption that Maori treatment of imported contagious diseases was ineffective is largely correct. The assumption that nineteenth-century European treatment was necessarily much better is not. It is a classic case of racial archetyping.

In short, a case can be made for suggesting that the decline in Maori population caused by contact was not huge. It depends partly on reconsideration of the degree of mortality and infertility caused by disease, attempted above, and partly on the baseline used – the Maori population at contact. The first estimate with any claim to reliability, F. D. Fenton's census of 1857–58, was 56,000. It has been shown that this was a slight underestimate and should be rounded up to about 60,000.[77] Most estimates of the population in 1769 are wild guesses, or uncritical regurgitations of wild guesses. At one extreme, archaeological science provides us with an estimated pre-contact birth rate of up to 37 per thousand per year, and a death rate of up to 39, which leaves a population of negative several thousand Maori in 1769.[78] At the other extreme, more common but no less ludicrous estimates have ranged up to Dumont d'Urville's one million for the North Island alone. A modern geographer has even suggested two million.[79] There are similar tendencies in historical demography elsewhere: the Aztecs were a wonderful people, therefore there must have been thirty million of them. If one accepts anything like the high figures for Maori, then the decline to 60,000 in 90 years proves crippling impact without further ado. Even the more reasonable figure of 125,000 to 175,000, still widely accepted, suggests massive depopulation by 1858.[80] But scholars have at last begun to do the obvious and calculate back from Fenton's census, the earliest firm figure.

The most moderate calculation, and in my view the likeliest guess, gives 86,000 as the population in 1769, and 70,000 in 1840, an average decline of 0.3 per cent per year between 1769 and 1858.[81] There was then a steeper fall to perhaps 48,000 in 1874. Taking account of probable underestimation, and including all half-castes, the decline in Maori population was quite small between 1874 and 1896. It rose slightly in two censuses and dropped in three to reach a nadir of about 42,000 in 1896.[82] Although Maori–Pakeha conflict was also a factor, these figures seem to support the notion of a pandemic phase of high mortality in the 1850s–70s, with somewhat lower rates of decline before and after. The decline was unevenly spread across space and time, and it may have 'crippled' particular Maori communities in particular periods. But overall it was not crippling impact, still less fatal impact.

There is a danger of reversing the pendulum here, leaving the impression that European impact flowed off Maori like water off a duck's back. This is not so. Some groups were devastated by war, disease and the other traumas of contact, and most suffered to some extent. But in the end, to 1840 at least, Maori society bent but did not break under the weight of Europe, even though they had multiplied this weight through their own agency. The overall connection between population decline and social and cultural disintegration is almost as suspect as high population estimates. Maori suffered nothing comparable to the decline by one-third within a decade experienced by England in the mid-fourteenth century, Ireland in the mid-nineteenth, and Russia in the mid-twentieth. Why should Maori be thought to have undergone socio-cultural collapse, to have been a dying or crippled race, when European peoples who suffered even more traumatic demographic disasters were not? The enduring myth of fatal impact is my answer to this question. The myth was strong enough not only to overshoot the evidence on Maori depopulation and to have an enduring effect on historians' interpretations, but also to help project the British Empire into New Zealand in 1840.

CHAPTER EIGHT

Empire?

In the year of 1839, in the official and unofficial power centres of a great European nation, a plan was devised for the acquisition of New Zealand. Powerful private interests established a 'New Zealand Company', found allies in government and painted a picture of a great future colony in an abundant and temperate environment, ideally suited for Europeans. There was considerable interest in emigrating to this new El Dorado, which it was hoped would reduce disorder among the poor. The plan envisaged a 'wonderful peaceful conquest' of the Maori. The five great agencies of this conversion were to be missionaries, of whom some were already in place; civilisation by land sale and proximity to European settlers; the detribalising and commercialising effect of engagement with European economics; the judicious application of European laws and government; and a treaty that was to transfer sovereignty by consent as well as facilitate the purchase of Maori land. Preparations were made in secrecy, for it was hoped to steal a march on a rival power. Difficulties were overcome – one emigrant changed her mind and drowned herself rather than proceed to New Zealand. In 1840, the company's first ship and a government warship, sailing separately, left to plant the colony. They did, and for several years the French colony of New Zealand existed in a strange limbo at Akaroa on Banks Peninsula, a history that almost happened.[1]

French New Zealand was not entirely farcical. For at least five years, some 300 French settlers and naval personnel, together with a fluctuating number of whalers, lived as a little French semi-state, under French law and French custom. It was the French who established New Zealand's first public health service, and its first state farm. The colony was ruled by a royal commissioner; it was the headquarters of the 'French Naval Station in New Zealand', and the warship permanently stationed there gave it a modicum of real power. At various stages, both the colonists and their public and private backers in France hoped to expand French control over the whole of the South Island, if not the whole of New Zealand. The city of Wellington could quite easily have been the city of Soult – the Iron Duke's great rival in the Napoleonic Wars, Prime Minister of

France at the time of the Akaroa settlement and an enthusiastic backer of it. But the hopes that both caused and were caused by the French colony of New Zealand were illusory. Poor, tiny and weak, spasmodically pretending to govern the Maori in its immediate neighbourhood, and struggling to convert them on the cheap – 'If they become Catholic, they will become French' – it was rather like the British colony of New Zealand formed the same year.

The French Empire in New Zealand died in infancy. The power of the British Empire in New Zealand did grow. Between 1853 and 1867, elements of it were handed over to settler legislatures, but whether empire was British or neo-British, 'imperialist' or 'subimperialist', did not make a huge amount of difference to its targets: the Maori. The contest between Maori independence and both forms of British Empire in the half-century after 1840 is the subject of the next four chapters. Empire over Maori desperately chased the shadow of itself until it finally caught up.

British Intervention

Why did New Zealand become part of the British Empire? The question is even more complicated than it seems, because the event to be explained did not happen when many people still believe it did, in 1840. Projects for colonising New Zealand and civilising Maori originated around 1771, in the fertile mind of Benjamin Franklin; Sydney merchants proposed a chartered commercial New Zealand Company in 1814.[2] Pressure on the British government to add New Zealand to its empire began to build in the 1820s, when British colonising projectors and entrepreneurs with New Zealand interests began advocating annexation.[3] It mounted greatly in the 1830s, and the British government succumbed to it late in 1837. For a year it dithered about what form its intervention should take, then decided to try to acquire sovereignty over existing Pakeha settlements and to attempt a benign indirect influence over the rest. William Hobson, who had reported on the New Zealand situation as captain of HMS *Rattlesnake* in 1837, accepted appointment as Lieutenant-Governor and Consul in February 1839, and left for New Zealand in August. At the last moment, he was given discretion to extend the claim of sovereignty from small parts of New Zealand to the whole of it, which is exactly what he did.

A proclamation by Governor George Gipps on 14 January 1840, extending New South Wales to include New Zealand; various proclamations by Hobson through 1840; official gazetting in London in October 1840; and the treaty signed at Waitangi on 6 February 1840, and at other places thereafter, were all part of the British sovereignty claim.[4] The significance of the treaty and the nature of the Maori consent it symbolised will be discussed later. But, from the official British perspective, full sovereignty over the whole of New Zealand was acquired in 1840.

Most accounts of British expansion into New Zealand focus on this act, the moment when official cartographers inked New Zealand British pink. But maps can be myths. Nominal sovereignty is not actual control. English monarchs claimed sovereignty over France for centuries after the claim lost all substance. If a European power asserting sovereignty to its own satisfaction under some smidgen of international law is what matters, then New Zealand became part of the Spanish Empire under the Treaty of Tordesillas in 1494, when the Pope allocated Spain the latitudes in which New Zealand was eventually discovered. Nominal sovereignty did not necessarily have much immediate practical impact, though its ideological importance was considerable. The reasons why pressure was placed on the British government to intervene and assume sovereignty, and why it eventually succumbed, are part of a wider question: why, how and when was British rule imposed on the Maori? We have to explain movement along three scales: intervention, or the application of resources; ostensible authority; and actual control.

The intervention scale measures the power exerted to obtain empire, through conversion and conquest. In 1833, with the appointment of James Busby as Resident, Britain made a token intervention in New Zealand. In terms of state resources, increased intervention in 1840 was still very limited. Hobson estimated that establishing the colony would cost a mere £4,005, and his armed forces consisted of a dozen drunken police constables and a small warship.[5] It was not until 1846 that his successors' military and financial resources became significant, and not until 1860 that they became really substantial. By 1864, there were more imperial combat troops in New Zealand than in Britain, and New Zealand was costing London £500,000 a year.

Between 1833 and 1840, Britain found itself moving much faster up the ostensible authority scale, which measures the nominal or imagined situation. In 1835, it disclaimed sovereignty by recognising the Maori as an independent people in response to a 'Declaration of Independence' by the 'United Tribes of New Zealand'. The declaration was inspired by Busby, who intended it to warn off the French and bilk his rival, the merchant Thomas McDonnell, though northern Maori may have had their own motives in adhering to it.[6] Britain hoped to exercise informal but substantial influence through Busby, the missionaries and respectable traders and occasional gunboat diplomacy – the system too readily described as 'informal empire' by theorists of imperialism. Between 1837 and 1839, it toyed with other forms of indirect rule, such as a protectorate, and with partial sovereignty, over the European settlements alone. But in 1840 it found itself going the whole hog and claiming complete authority. In short, intervention moved in spasms from 1833 to 1864: token in the beginning, minor in 1840, significant in 1846, substantial in 1860, massive in 1864. Nominal authority moved much faster up its scale, from an expression of interest in 1833 to ostensibly full sovereignty in 1840. The control scale measures the success of intervention and the substance of authority, and it is a more complicated story.

British governments around 1840 were, overtly at least, reluctant imperialists. Britain had the lion's share of world shipping and industrial trade goods; they got most of the profits from trade with far-flung regions anyway. As long as trade could flow freely with distant regions, why go to the bother of governing them? Whalers got their whales, pork, sex and potatoes, and merchants got their flax and timber in New Zealand, empire or not. This view was influential at the Colonial Office, the cramped and understaffed house in Downing Street, London, where questions of expansion were processed. It was reinforced by humanitarian beliefs that empire, despite the best intentions, was often a bad thing for indigenous peoples, and by the Colonial Office's most consistent principle: parsimony, an extreme reluctance to incur new costs. The progressive ratcheting-up of intervention in New Zealand, from cheap to extremely expensive, was completely contrary to this principle, and arguably contrary to humanitarian principles as well. Yet, despite all this, Britain acquired quite a number of new colonies in the mid-nineteenth century, New Zealand among them. How is this to be explained?

Many explanations have focused on the 'push' behind state expansion – the domestic factors that may or may not have pushed the chanceries of Europe into becoming chanceries of the world. It is useful to shift emphasis towards the 'pull' behind European expansion, ways in which 'the metropolitan dog' was 'wagged by its colonial tail'.[7] To adapt this metaphor, the tip of the tail was the agents of contact who established themselves in potential colonies and somehow managed to pull their states in after them, thereby becoming agents of empire. The base of the tail was the metropolitan backers of these agents, who exerted leverage on the imperial government to make it (the metropolitan dog) wag. The key to leveraging, and the key to the wag reflex in the tail, was neither push nor pull but something in between: the myths of empire, existing in the space between metropolis and periphery. In New Zealand, Britain was a dog with three tails. One was the missionaries, virtuous agents of the 'Civilizing Mission', who came to both justify and encourage expansion as a shouldering of the 'White Man's Burden'.

The tip of this tail was the missionaries actually in New Zealand; the base was their metropolitan parent organisations, especially the influential Church Missionary Society, led by Lay Secretary Dandeson Coates. In the early 1830s, the alliance between evangelical humanitarianism and imperial expansion was not yet firm. Most evangelicals opposed the mass settlement of Europeans in New Zealand, and some in Britain opposed its acquisition, full stop. By the late 1830s, however, many New Zealand missionaries were advocating a Protestant colony or protectorate that would keep out the papist French, control the agents of vice and facilitate mission work.

Advocates and agents of 'Organised Immigration' or 'Systematic Colonisation' made up the second tail. Foreshadowing the theories of J. A. Hobson and V. I. Lenin, they maintained that the Industrial Revolution had led Britain to overproduce both labour and capital. Profits were declining, and disorder, arising from poverty and unemployment, was increasing. The solution was to export labour and capital to new colonies, at once improving the lot of the emigrants, strengthening imperial power and relieving the domestic situation. Edward Gibbon Wakefield was among the leading advocates of this view. He and his allies backed the organised settlement of South Australia in 1836, but they considered that their plan had been poorly implemented there and thought New Zealand the perfect place for a second go. Their New Zealand Association, formed in 1837, was transformed into the New Zealand Company in 1838.

Wakefield's plan required that land be bought cheap from the Maori and sold dear to immigrants and absentee investors, to finance the whole project. This created a somewhat ambiguous attitude to government intervention. The New Zealand Company wanted state backing, to reassure potential investors, but it did not want state interference in land buying, with government instead of company pocketing the difference between purchase and resale prices. Ideally, it wanted private intervention in New Zealand, monopolised by itself and backed by a government charter and government help, like the East India Company's corporate empire in India. But Wakefield was a master of apparent compromise, and he was prepared to shift this position if need be. On paper, the company also tried to accommodate humanitarian concerns. It promised to convert the Maori through interaction with its virtuous organised immigrants. Maori chiefs would become brown gentlemen, sipping port and reading the Bible and the *Wealth of Nations* on estates reserved for them by the company; other lands would be set aside for the education and welfare of lesser Maori. This was not very convincing and it did not convince the CMS. The tip of the company's tail was its planned land-buying expedition, in the ship *Tory*, poised high above New Zealand like that of a scorpion, ready to plunge in when the time was ripe.[8]

These two pressure groups each had considerable influence in government circles. But this was not enough of itself to move the cautious Colonial Office. Moreover, the CMS's opposition to the New Zealand Company tended to neutralise the influence of both, and both wanted just enough intervention to facilitate their goals, but not so much as to impede them. It is therefore tempting to speculate that a shadowy third pressure group – merchants and capitalists – was decisive. The tip of this tail was the traders established in New Zealand; the middle was the Sydney merchants; the base was the London capitalists, like the Enderby family, with New Zealand interests. The New Zealand trade, especially whaling, was larger than is generally acknowledged, and capitalist imperialism should not be too readily dismissed as Marxist conspiracy theory.

Historians have gone to a great deal of trouble to establish that empire for Britain very often did not pay.[9] This misses the point that some people hoped and dreamed that it would pay, and that they were sometimes able to wag dogs. In 1849, the Enderbys risked their own money on a dream empire in the desolate Auckland Islands. Charles Enderby was 'Lieutenant-Governor', announcing to Maori colonisers, who had preceded him by seven years, that 'I am the Lord of the island. I claim all the land which you are using and all the pigs you possess.' The Enderby colony was intended to grow rich on farming and whaling, but was abandoned in 1852, having killed one whale.[10]

On the practical side, though New Zealand whaling in 1840 was more important to France and the United States than it was to the declining English industry, it remains possible that English whaling magnates hoped to revive a dying trade. Empire was quite often triggered by the desire to shore up falling profits, rather than boost rising ones, on the assumption that imperial rule would reduce costs, with the state meeting what would otherwise be private overheads. Both illusory and pragmatic hopes could explain London merchants' support for colonisation, but there is as yet little evidence that they exerted much influence on the imperial government, except through their alliance with the New Zealand Company. This is still more true of the Sydney merchants. Ex-convicts did not rank high with Downing Street. Moreover, it was not clear that British sovereignty was in the best interests of the Sydney merchants and the New Zealand traders closely allied to them. It would bring customs dues and other imposts – free traders were not supposed to want state intervention or more taxes – and might lead to the bypassing of Sydney as a conduit for New Zealand imports and exports. In the event, this is exactly what happened: whale-oil exports through Sydney declined by 43 per cent in 1841, largely as a consequence of competition from the New Zealand Company settlement of Wellington.[11] The support of all three groups for British sovereignty is something of a mystery. Protectorate, effective informal empire or no empire at all may have suited their interests better.

The three tails, alone or in concert, could not exert enough direct leverage to wag the British Empire into New Zealand, and it is not clear why they should have wanted to. We have to explain both how and why they managed to pull Britain into New Zealand. They had to operate through a nerve centre, or ganglion, digging their fingers into pressure points to which official minds were sensitive. One was Anglo–French rivalry, and from 1831 the three pressure groups repeatedly asserted that France had designs on New Zealand. The interesting but ineffective French adventurer Baron Charles de Thierry, who settled on 800 acres in Northland in 1837 as 'Sovereign Chief of New Zealand' but was later obliged to become an Auckland piano tuner, was portrayed by Protestant missionaries as the architect of an evil empire.[12] The advocates of British intervention did not look on Bishop Pompallier much more kindly either. There was potential sensitivity to these claims in Britain. 'Were we tamely to allow that beautiful island to become the dunghill of France?' asked a public meeting of Glasgow merchants on hearing of plans for the Akaroa colony.[13] But practical French plans post-dated the British decision to intervene in New Zealand, and earlier outcries about French designs had little effect on the British government.[14] As a ganglion, the French threat did not work. What did work, what finally did enable the tails to wag their stubborn dog, were the myths of empire.

From 1830, the British government was increasingly inundated by reports from New Zealand, and by petitions based on them from the metropolitan pressure groups, that argued along fatal impact lines. The flow reached a crescendo in 1837–38. It indicated that unorganised immigration from Australia was inevitably increasing at a great rate, featuring the agents of vice; that these immigrants were inevitably subordinating the Maori for their own evil purposes in the short term, and destroying them through fatal impact in the long. The 'frontier chaos' this created was also impeding mission work and legitimate commerce. The authors of these reports, the agents of empire ensconced in New Zealand, usually believed what they said. Yet, without conscious deceit, they often stretched even contemporary imperialist credulity, claiming, for example, that intertribal warfare and interracial violence were endemic or even increasing at the very time both were declining. Many of the fears about the ill doings of the agents of vice actually referred to the threat they presented to respectable Europeans, not to Maori. In a strange sense, the agents of empire were victims of their own propaganda, influenced by a feeling that fatal impact and unofficial conversion were not happening fast enough. Both myths required that European moral superiority gain them ascendancy and great influence over the natives with whom they dealt, for good or ill. But actual European–Maori relations tended to be too equal, or worse. 'They suppose we are dependent on them, this makes them impertinent.'[15] The missionaries, noted an observer in 1835, 'looked up to the Chiefs as their Protectors, and, in fact, their Masters'.[16]

Some missionaries were not happy with their client status. By the late 1830s, Henry Williams, George Clark, Robert Maunsell and others were advocating British intervention, with a 'substantial sanctioning force'.[17] Merchant princes like Mair, Clendon and McDonnell could not feel fully princely while beholden to their patron chiefs. They therefore advocated colonisation, though it put them out of business.[18] Mair was contemptuous of a colleague, Hans Tapsell, who accepted his conversion by Maori. He 'put himself on a footing with the Chiefs, allowing his hair and beard to grow long, having himself occasionally tapued and calling himself king'.[19] The most famous trader, author Frederick Maning, wrote of beating Maori in wrestling matches; Edward Markham saw him being beaten by them, and an underlying resentment of Maori dominance pervades Maning's writings.[20] The same can be said of Joel Polack and William Yate, whose publications were influential. Polack's four volumes on New Zealand were not uninfluenced by his having once received a severe beating from Benjamin Turner's Maori wife.[21] In 1834, Otago whalers noted resentfully that their Maori patrons 'take from us whatever suits their fancy'.[22] The Maori did not seem to understand who was supposed to wear the trousers in the great marriage alliance, and despite their own best material interests, the denizens of Old New Zealand hoped that British sovereignty would teach them.

Establishing superiority over peoples such as the Maori was one of the ways in which Europeans defined themselves. Myths of empire, fatal impact and conversion dictated that they should succeed. The New Zealand frontier was in disjuncture with the prophecies of the ethos of expansion, and I suggest that this explains missionary and trader attitudes. Resentment at the failure of prophecy had special importance in the case of James Busby, author of the most numerous and influential series of fatal impact reports, whose officially objective voice was heard in London, if not New Zealand. Wounded in one incident by the Maori he was supposed cheaply and effortlessly to dominate, humiliated and plundered in others, his backyard a site for the feuds he was supposed to stop, his busy pen scratched far into the night at his Waitangi Residency at the Bay of Islands, writing myth into reality, Britain into New Zealand, and himself out of a job.[23]

The official minds at the Colonial Office were cautious and sceptical. It is easy to conclude from their shrewd marginalia that they were a match for tales or tails of empire. But the Colonial Office was ultimately a blind giant. It had few other sources of information and enquiries to New Zealand might take a year to be answered. Its officials saw through specific misinformation but tended to be overwhelmed by sheer mass. And, for all their scepticism, they too were subject in some degree to the myths of empire. They were predisposed to believe that what myth taught would happen was happening. They accepted fatal impact. They accepted that the low-key feud between Pomare and Titore in 1837 was evidence of it, though it killed fewer people than a riot at Newport in 1839. They accepted that Kororareka was a hellhole of vice, though one witness admitted it was no worse than the average English seaport. They accepted that the agents of vice were subordinating and oppressing the Maori, without asking how a few hundred traders, whalers and grog sellers had acquired the whip hand over thousands of musket-armed and battle-hardened warriors. They passed over statements that 'the White Man possesses no Power at all, for if the New Zealanders chose they could annihilate the whole of the Europeans in one day', and that the agents of empire 'exaggerated the Condition of the Country in consequence of their Wish to have a stronger Support than has hitherto been afforded them'.[24] And they accepted that empire had its own momentum – that colonisation, once commenced, was a slippery slope; that order on one side of a frontier would be forced to control disorder on the other, even if the frontier was a thousand miles of sea. 'If we really are in that situation that we must do something,' wrote the British Prime Minister, Lord Melbourne, 'it is only another proof of the fatal necessity by which a nation that once begins to colonize is led step by step over the whole globe.'[25]

It was a big 'if'. There was no 'fatal necessity', but the imperial government came to believe that there was. Learning of the government decision to intervene, the New Zealand Company sought to jump the gun to get land cheap and lowered its tail, complete with sting, into New Zealand in the form of its land-buying expedition in the *Tory* and its first immigrant ship, despatched in May and September 1839. Hobson hastened to proclaim sovereignty over the whole country on 21 May 1840, to assert authority over the company and to pre-empt the French in the South Island. It was therefore the company and the new, real, French threat that triggered the shift from partial to full sovereignty. But Hobson had always seen partial sovereignty as an interim solution; he was himself subject to the myths of empire, as were his masters in London, despite their humanitarian and financial hesitations. 'A striking feature of the discussions of early 1839 is the assumption by most politicians and officials that intervention, however slight, would evolve into colonisation.'[26] And it was the myths that induced Britain to step up intervention in 1840 and to acquire sovereignty, full or partial. Empire in New Zealand, and perhaps elsewhere, was caused mainly by its myths.

The imperial government was predisposed by the myths of empire in general to accept a particular illusion constructed by the agents of Empire in New Zealand – that empire already existed. If Britain did not acquire New Zealand, wrote Busby, it abandoned the country to 'the evil ascendancy of its own unprincipled subjects'.[27] New Zealand, wrote John Ward, one of several propagandists commissioned by Wakefield, 'is, in fact, already a considerable, though an irregular, British Colony'.[28] In the end, James Stephen, the influential Permanent Under-Secretary at the Colonial Office, concurred. 'In fact the Colony does exist altho' by the mere usurpation of the rights of the New Zealanders.'[29] In this light, the acquisition of sovereignty in 1840 merely nationalised a pre-existing, evil and private empire, and rendered it good, or at least better. One could say that this false empire of the 1830s caused the real empire of 1840, if it were not for the fact that the empire of 1840 was not real either.

States and Treaties

Old New Zealand, the Maori-Pakeha shore of the Tasman world, continued after 1840, empire or no empire. Its oldest, deepest roots were in the Deep South and the Far North, where it had existed in the 1800s and where it left an enduring legacy. Northland was still recognisably different from the rest of the country in the early twentieth century: divided within itself into distinct subregions, closely linked but not fully integrated with autonomous and strong Maori partner communities, dependent on sea communications and extractive industries. Old Southland was swamped by pastoralism and progress from the 1850s, but survived offshore in Stewart Island for some years. The local advent of the state was perhaps marked by the seizure of the biggest illicit still in Australasia in 1868. The island remained 'a refuge for Europeans reluctant to submit to official norms of behaviour' in the late 1860s, and, with all due respect, was still a bit strange a hundred years later.[30]

Between Far North and Deep South were clusters, stretches and sprinklings of stations, shanty ports, Pakeha-Maori hamlets and Pakeha individuals – at Otago and Banks Peninsula, the Marlborough Sounds, Hawke's Bay, the East Cape, Bay of Plenty and Waikato. This old Maori–European interface changed in its parts but persisted as a whole until the 1860s, and in some cases the 1880s. Desertion from American whalers was still a problem at Kororareka in 1886, though the problem was now handled as much by Auckland lawyers as Nga Puhi chiefs.[31] Old New Zealand did not finally fade away until the early twentieth century, but in the half-century before this it was largely transformed into what a later chapter will call 'crew culture'. This culture differed sharply from mainstream Pakeha society, shared many of the characteristics of the Old New Zealand Tasmen, and was their heir. But it tended more to miners and navvies than whalers and sealers; was much larger; worked more in tandem with mainstream Pakeha; and from the 1860s was increasingly disconnected from its old Maori partner.

It can be argued that 'New' New Zealand, the mainstream of settler society, also bridged the great divide of 1840, originating in the previous decade, when substantial clusters of Europeans, including women as well as men, first emerged. But it remains true that 1840 marked a sharp upturn, bringing a remarkable demographic entity to New Zealand's shores: the instant township. Auckland was established in 1840–41 through a joint venture between Hobson's new government, Sydney merchants and local Maori. It originated as a purpose-built capital, like Washington and Canberra, though plans soon went awry. Five other instant townships were founded by the New Zealand Company and its affiliates, including the Otago and Canterbury Associations: Wellington, Nelson and New Plymouth (1840–42), and Dunedin and Christchurch (1848 and 1850). The new towns each had between 1,000 and 4,000 people within two years of first settlement. They were known as the 'main settlements', or even the 'six colonies of New Zealand', with significantly separate histories to which this book cannot do full justice. Nominally, they split the whole of New Zealand between them when they became the six provinces in 1853. But they grew their own immediate hinterlands only slowly. In the interim, they survived by competing with Sydney and the Old New Zealand ports for the old extractive trades; through the process of immigration itself – the addictive system of growth through growth discussed as 'progressive colonisation' in Chapter Fourteen; and through Maori co-operation.

The main settlements became bases of secondary colonisation, establishing outsettlements at first by sea because there were no roads. Their success in expanding varied according to geography, economic opportunities and Maori consent. These factors quickly reduced New Plymouth from relatively big to medium, and condemned it to stasis until the 1870s. Nelson expanded into Marlborough after 1847 and Buller in the 1860s; Christchurch into coastal and inland Canterbury by the 1860s; Dunedin into North and Central Otago and Southland. Hemmed in by its hills, overpopulated and overcapitalised in relation to immediate local opportunities, Wellington in particular expanded by sea from the outset to such places as Maori would let it. In the 1840s, it colonised Wanganui, the Wairarapa and Marlborough – the last jointly with Nelson and Old New Zealand. Its attempt to colonise the Christchurch area in the same decade was swamped in 1850 by the Canterbury Association. Wellington colonised Hawke's Bay (with help from Old New Zealand) and the Rangitikei in the 1850s, and the Manawatu from the mid-1860s. By the 1850s, two offshoots, Wanganui and Napier, were closing on New Plymouth in size. Dunedin and Christchurch took longer to breed, forming Invercargill, Oamaru, Timaru and other towns by the 1860s. Auckland also expanded by sea. Overland expansion outside the immediate environs of the town was not great until after 1864.

All the main settlements sought to plug into Old New Zealand and the Maori trade, with varying success. Auckland did best. Wool, roads and Pakeha food exports were unimportant to it. Commerce, sea transport and extractive industries – gold, kauri gum and especially timber – were central. The Maori trade was crucial to the early 1860s, and important to the 1870s. Few roads led to Auckland town, but most sea lanes within the province did. Auckland ruled by sea and credit over an archipelago of islands of Pakeha settlement and extraction, in Northland, Thames, Coromandel and the Bay of Plenty, like the early Maori colonies. Seaborne mercantilism and extraction were also quite important for Wellington, but for it and the other main towns the chief shape of the early spread of settlement was sheep.

There were recessions and fluctuations in the rate of growth, but by 1860 there were Pakeha settlers in most parts of the country, and Pakeha sheep runs in much of it, south of and including Hawke's Bay. By 1844, there were 12,000 Pakeha; by 1851, 26,000 and 223,000 sheep; by 1858, 59,000 and 1,523,000 sheep. In 1861, the census counted 99,000 Pakeha and 2,761,000 sheep. The six main towns ranged between 2,000 and 8,000 each. Wanganui, Napier and Invercargill approached or exceeded 1,000, and there were a dozen other settler concentrations of a few hundred, notably in Northland and Marlborough, and the outsettlements of Dunedin and Christchurch.

Each major Pakeha settlement was politically and economically led, though not wholly dominated, by small élites, and formally ruled and run by what became quite a complex machinery of state.[32] The governors, with their advisers and officials, dominated to 1853 and remained key figures in relations with Maori to 1867. Hobson found New Zealand too much for him and died in 1842, after a series of strokes caused by 'violent mental excitement'.[33] *He* did not find New Zealand history boring. After an inter-regnum under Administrator or Acting Governor Willoughby Shortland, he was succeeded by the scrupulous but not brilliant Robert FitzRoy (1843–45) and the brilliant but not scrupulous George Grey (1845–53). After another inter-regnum under Robert Wynyard, Grey was succeeded by Thomas Gore Browne (1855–61), before returning for a second term, 1861–67.

All these governors and administrators were military and naval officers. Their power over European New Zealand varied but was always substantial, and they were only loosely controlled from London. Grey looms by far the largest in both history and myth, some of which he wrote himself. The other governors feature as something of a supporting cast, played down to elevate Grey by contrast. Revisionist historians have argued quite convincingly that Hobson, FitzRoy and Browne were not as grey as they were painted, and in the fullness of time Wynyard will no doubt be retrospectively refurbished too – he was the life and soul of most parties, social and political. But in the end, Grey's precedence is warranted.[34]

George Grey was born in 1812 and trained as a soldier, but he made his name exploring the western Australian outback in the 1830s. Apart from his two long governorships of New Zealand, he ruled South Australia, 1840–45, and South Africa, 1854–61, and made a dramatic return to New Zealand politics in the 1870s, becoming premier in 1877. A disciple of Archbishop Richard Whately, Grey believed that savages were incapable of invention, and that neither nature nor natives could raise themselves to civilisation without the outside help of a European 'wizard wand'.[35] Grey was to be Wizard of Aotearoa, and the savages were expected to be grateful. A strange, complicated man, whose real charisma and genius almost matched his flaws, Grey was a perfect candidate for psycho-history, the archetype of a Noah complex. He built himself a paradise and game park on Kawau Island from 1862, where one of his 'chief amusements . . . was to provoke a wild bull to charge him and shoot it with a rifle when it was a few yards off'.[36] His wallabies throve, his zebras died, and he tired of his troops of monkeys and shot the lot.[37]

An autocratic demagogue and philo-Maori hammer of the Maori, this living paradox both served and mastered the imperial government. Rueful official recognition of his manipulations, pencilled in the margins of his reports to

London, should not be mistaken for control. Grey is rumoured to have had numerous sexual liaisons, yet did not speak to his wife Eliza for 36 years after finding her flirting with a naval officer – a trifle harsh even for the days of the double standard.[38] He had one eye on his place in history, occasionally reflecting on what historians would think of his actions in a hundred years, and carefully placing his own gloss on them to ensure that they thought right. Yet Grey was widely and correctly seen as one of the most able proconsuls of Britain's imperial history. He and his Scots lieutenants Donald McLean for conversion and General Duncan Cameron for conquest were the most dangerous enemies Maori independence had ever met.

Between 1848 and 1853, the colony was nominally split into two provinces on the line of the Patea River, New Ulster to the north and New Munster to the south, with a lieutenant-governor under Grey. This early Pakeha subdivision failed to take, and in 1853 the six more enduring provinces were established, each with an elected legislature and superintendent: Auckland, New Plymouth or Taranaki, Wellington, Nelson, Canterbury and Otago. Four more provinces arose – and in the case of Southland, fell – before all were abolished in 1876. Hawke's Bay split from Wellington in 1858; Marlborough from Nelson in 1859; Southland split from Otago in 1861 and reunited in 1870; and Westland split from Canterbury, first as an experimental 'county' in 1868, and then as a full province in 1873. A colonial parliament staggered to its feet between 1854 and 1856, and survived uneasily in the space between governors, provinces and Maori before eventually inheriting the power of all three. Superintendents such as Isaac Featherston of Wellington and McLean, during his reign as uncrowned king of Hawke's Bay, had partially deserved reputations as 'Maori doctors' – master native handlers. Long-serving premiers such as Edward Stafford and William Fox had considerable influence on native policy, but it was usually the governors who took the lead in relations with Maori until the end of Grey's second term of office in 1867.

Hobson's civil service consisted of 39 genteel officials and their assistants, and his army of eleven alcoholic New South Wales police troopers.[39] At one point in 1843, FitzRoy had £3 1s 5d in the Treasury.[40] It is a little hard to understand how anyone could ever have thought that such resources could have much impact on Pakeha, let alone Maori. But organs for state interaction with Maori did grow up, notably in the areas of war, law and land buying. From April 1840, as noted above, the governors' military resources increased in four steps: a hundred or two imperial infantry (to 1845); a thousand or two (1845–60); over 3,000 (1860–63); and over 10,000 (1864–66).

Legal machinery expanded more incrementally. English-style higher courts, magistrates, justices of the peace and small police forces appeared quickly in the main settlements, and increasingly claimed some jurisdiction over Maori visitors and neighbours. Other officials sporadically ventured further afield.

The first agency of state–Maori relations, the Protectorate Department, was replaced by a Native Department and resident magistrates system in 1846–47. Both systems were intended to take law to the Maori – the latter less gently than the former.[41] The shift from protectors to magistrates was coupled with the emergence of a substantial Armed Police Force, whose Maori members were intended by Grey to act as moral exemplars for, as well as coercers of, their brethren.[42] The provinces took over most policing in 1853, and Maori policemen disappeared from the provincial forces by 1861. Many historians have noted the unhealthy administrative intersection between 'native policy' and land buying – often one and the same thing. But Grey did create or support Maori hospitals (in New Plymouth, Wellington, Auckland and Wanganui between 1847 and 1852) and schools, and both he and his successors distributed gifts, subsidies and official positions to chosen chiefs.[43] It was Grey who employed New Zealand's first professional historian, Te Rangikaheke, publishing the results under his own name in *Polynesian Mythology.*[44] Often derided by the settler press as a 'flour and sugar policy', the scale of all this munificence was in fact never lavish. But Grey did hope to convert Maori by addicting them to the benefits of individualism, civilisation and subordinacy.

In the twenty years after 1840, then, there were three New Zealands: Aotearoa, or independent Maoridom; the persisting Old New Zealand interface; and the New New Zealand of mass European settlement. No historian would now accept the ancient delusion that the first two disappeared in a flash into the third in 1840, but the new did seek to dominate the old, with some success. New New Zealand gradually harnessed and transformed Old New Zealand, though it never fully controlled it. The potential power of the state over Maori was not great to 1845 but increased very substantially under Grey. The potential influence of settler society and economy grew quickly, though spasmodically, from 1840, as reflected in the expansion of settler population and sheep farming. The new state and society impacted on Maori in four main ways: conquest, 'swamping' and two types of conversion – 'soft' and 'hard'. The aims of conversion included both Europeanisation and subordination. The soft variant emphasised the former aim, and the hard the latter.

Conquest, the successful application of military force or the threat of it to reduce Maori to subordinacy, was tried at Wairau in 1843, at Wellington in 1846, at Wanganui in 1847 and at the Bay of Islands in 1845–46. We will see that, except at Wellington, the state's success in these conflicts was very limited. 'Swamping' happened when Maori became so geographically interspersed among, economically and socially interlocked with, and demographically outnumbered by Europeans that they lost their capacity to control engagement with them. Engagement could be controlled in various ways, but most were underwritten by the capacity for effective resistance, or for co-operation that was sufficiently important to Pakeha to be valued by them. Once swamped by their Pakeha partners, particular Maori communities lost the power of effective resistance or valued co-operation, and consequently lost independence. Both swamping and conquest made Maori vulnerable to hard-edged conversion: harsh, though non-military, pressure to sell land and to accept Pakeha definitions of land sales, treaties, law and state–Maori relations. When Maori could resist, or when their co-operation was crucial, hard conversion had few teeth. When they had neither option, it often had its way with them. Swamping may have occurred in the immediate vicinity of Wellington town as early as the mid-1840s, and in Auckland in the early 1850s. It came to the South Island in the early 1860s, when the Pakeha towns there burgeoned as a result of gold rushes. But swamping, conquest and hard conversion were not immediate problems for most Maori until the 1860s.

Before the 1860s, this left soft conversion. Irate settlers frequently advocated conquest and hard conversion, and celebrated swamping and fatal impact where they perceived them. But soft conversion was the policy most consistently pursued by the state between 1840 and 1860, in practice as well as rhetoric. It was humane and relatively cheap, and it was believed to be effective. The underlying assumption was that of the 'White Maori': relatively enlightened and civilisable 'better blacks' whose highest aspiration was to become as white-like as possible as quickly as possible, voluntarily subordinating themselves to the state in the process.

As with the plan for French New Zealand, the five horsemen of this peaceful apocalypse of Maori independence were to be God, money, land sale, law and the voluntary cession of sovereignty by treaty.

On 6 February 1840, Maori and Pakeha notables of Northland gathered outside James Busby's house to sign the document known to history as the Treaty of Waitangi. Having debated it the previous day, and having received satisfactory explanations from Hobson, Busby and Henry Williams, 43 Northland chiefs signified their assent to it. Over the next eight months, in various parts of the country, almost 500 more Maori did likewise. Over the next 150 years, Waitangi – day, place and document – became encrusted with myth and meaning, controversy and sanctity. Historian after historian has described the 'scene at Waitangi' to the point where it has become a central tableau in the collective memory, like Christ's Nativity or the landing of the Pilgrim Fathers. The treaty, 'a praiseworthy device to amuse savages', has always had dismissive critics. In 1877, Chief Justice James Prendergast described it as a legal 'nullity', and was echoed in 1992 by Clem Simich, National Party MP for Tamaki. Maori activists have seen it as a fraud and as a binding but unfulfilled contract, sometimes simultaneously. But the treaty is now frequently described as New Zealand's founding document, its Three Commandments or Magna Carta, and 6 February is the national day. The Waitangi Tribunal, established in 1975 to give effect to the treaty, is of great current importance. Some recent writers come very close to telling us that there is only one Treaty, and that the Tribunal is its Prophet.[45] Dismissing the treaty, or accepting it as unquestionable, are not options open to historians.

Regrettably, there was not one treaty, or set of treaties, but at least five. The first was the English-language versions of the Waitangi document, which did not vary significantly among themselves. This gave Maori the 'rights and privileges', and implicitly the duties, of British subjects; guaranteed their possession of all their land and property; and specified that if they wished to sell land, they had to sell to the Crown. The British got full sovereignty – the Maori ceded 'absolutely and without reservation all the rights and powers of Sovereignty' – and there was no mention of continued chiefly power. The immediate practical impact of this idealised conception of British rule was roughly nil. What it did do was entrench the illusion that Britain acquired control of New Zealand in 1840. Pakeha saw the English version as *the* treaty for 130 years, but the notion that 500 Maori chiefs woke up one morning brimful of loyalty to Queen Victoria and blithely gave away their authority is, and should always have been, ludicrous.

The second version of the Treaty of Waitangi, written in the Maori language, had a closer relationship with reality but contained its own contradictions. The key difference between it and the English version was that it split the powers with which it dealt into two: 'kawanatanga', or governorship, which went to the British; and 'rangatiratanga', or chieftainship, which was retained by the Maori. Chieftainship was not mentioned in the English version, in which all sovereign or governmental rights and powers went to the British, though Maori property rights were guaranteed unless voluntarily alienated. It is possible that 'rangatiratanga' was an honest attempt to translate 'ownership'. But it is more probable that it was a deliberate or semi-deliberate act of deceit by those who translated the treaty into Maori, notably Busby, Henry Williams and his son Edward. We should understand their motives. They knew Maori would not give away their chieftainship, yet they honestly believed that the treaty was now the only way that the Maori could be saved from physical or spiritual extinction at the hands of the agents of vice.

The English version was not easily compatible with the Maori written version, but there was also a tension *within* the latter. The British received 'te kawanatanga katoa', or complete government, perhaps better translated as full governorship. The Maori received 'te tino rangatiratanga', the unqualified exercise of their chieftainship – not easily compatible with complete government on the face of it.[46] One way around this is to believe that most Maori signatories saw governorship as the loose and vague suzerainty of a nominal head, with Pontius Pilate and James Busby as precedents, and this may have been true of some. But hundreds of Maori had visited Sydney before 1840, and they are likely to have made their kin fully aware that the governors of New South Wales exercised real power in their province. After all, chiefs had been seeking gift-exchange relations with Australian governors since the 1800s on precisely the basis that they were powerful and important European chiefs. Especially in Northland, Maori are likely to have realised that signing the treaty implied agreement to a big increase in settlement and in the power of the British state in New Zealand.

Difficulties such as these with the English and Maori written versions of the treaty have recently led to valiant attempts to construct what is in effect a third version: the 'spirit' or 'intent' of the treaty. There may be some present or future merit in this. It is not clear to everyone that a few paragraphs fudged up by a bunch of mediocre, biased and possibly deceitful British Maori-language scholars in 1840 is a suitable bible for Maori–Pakeha relations in the twenty-first century, infallible and omnipotent. Reshaping the treaty into what enlightened Maori and Pakeha today would have liked it to have been has its attractions. But it is hard to see the historical merit, because the intents of the two parties were clearly in conflict. The British wished to convert Maori into Brown Britishness and subordinacy, whereas the one thing we can be sure of about Maori motives for signing is that they did not want this.

English-language and 'intent' versions are not the historical treaty. Unfortunately, this is also true of the written Maori-language version. Fewer than fifteen per cent of Maori signatories actually signed their own names, as against making a mark or a moko. Some of these signatures were laboured and probably reflect nominacy – the capacity to write your name but little else – rather than literacy.[47] This does not indicate the level of Maori literacy in 1840: the older, higher-ranking men most likely to sign were also the least likely to be literate. But it does indicate that most 'signatories' could not read the Maori version, let alone the English one. They may have had literate Maori secretaries advising them, but there is not much evidence of this. In any case, why should powerful chiefs, self-confident in their oral culture, abandon the traditional practice of making solemn and binding verbal agreements on the basis of formal discussion at major meetings called for the purpose? The signatures, marks and moko were concessions to Pakeha ritual, snapshots of the great event. The historical treaty, perhaps, was the fourth version: a series of oral agreements *among* chiefs, as well as between them and those speaking for the Governor, which must have varied from treaty meeting to treaty meeting. The trouble is, how do we now know what was in them?

We can make some guesses. Hobson's interpreters shifted emphasis between English and Maori written versions in a direction that improved the chances of Maori consent. This suggests they were capable of shifting it further in the same direction in the oral version. French Catholic missionaries summarised the discussions at Waitangi as follows: 'All the chiefs will preserve their power and their possessions'; 'they had not the slightest intention of ceding their territory or their sovereignty'; they 'do not want the governor to extend his authority over the natives, but only over the Europeans.'[48] One modern but traditional Maori account of the treaty signing emphatically denies that sovereignty, let alone chieftainship, was ceded by Maori.[49] Yet, as this account suggests, it does seem likely that Maori saw the treaty meetings as significant ceremonies marking some kind of new deal. To guess what it was, we need to turn to a 'fifth version' – one that broadens the deal considerably beyond the Treaty of Waitangi.

It is absolutely clear that the British move into New Zealand in 1840 was predicated upon Maori consent. How else could Hobson have hoped to establish a colony with £4,000 and a dozen policemen? The imperial government constantly stressed that Maori consent had to be obtained, and the fact that the Treasury stressed this most of all shows that reliable parsimony joined less reliable philanthropy as a motive. Annexation, wrote the Lords of the Treasury in 1839, must 'be strictly contingent upon the indispensable preliminary of the Territorial cession having been obtained by amicable negotiation and with the free concurrence of the native chiefs'.[50] The advent of the state and of mass settlement in the 1840s did receive substantial Maori 'free concurrence', and signing the treaty was only one of three symbols of it.

Another was the acceptance of the agents of the state – governors, magistrates, police and others – inside and, to some extent, outside the main European settlements. British law and the machinery of state often received a surprisingly enthusiastic reception among Maori from 1840 right into the 1860s.[51] Many chiefs accepted state appointments, notably as 'assessors' assisting the resident magistrates. Even more remarkable was the third act of consent: Maori enthusiasm for settler neighbours, and willingness to sell land for them to settle on. Numerous voluntary Maori offers of land and appeals for European settlers in the 1840s can be documented. Maori were the midwives of the new towns, financing them by selling them land cheaply, and ranking with or above the New Zealand Company as promoters of European settlement. Some land was sold by people who did not own it; more was sold by Maori with partial rights, excluding co-owners; other deals were clear acts of European trickery, bullying or wishful thinking. But dodgy deals were difficult to implement, to impose on Maori who had not been swamped or conquered. Grey and McLean came to recognise this, and they sought to obtain the agreement of at least a working majority of owners because, without it, 'sales' had a tendency to be more nominal than real. The ceremonies marking such sales were intriguingly reminiscent of treaty meetings. Both sides clearly saw them as important rituals; one side believed the agreement to have been clearly written out; the other believed it to have been clearly spoken out. Agreeing to the treaty, welcoming agents of the state and selling land were three intersecting acts of Maori consent to the advent of Pakeha state and society. We need to explain all three.

Converting Consent

Over 500 Maori chiefs agreed to the Treaty of Waitangi in 1840. Hundreds more accepted official positions, or otherwise welcomed the state, in the years after it. Thousands agreed to sell land. Some Maori made all three gestures of consent; some made none; but members of most major groups probably made one or another. Contemporary Europeans had little doubt that the explanation for this Maori acceptance of European colonisation was the triumph of conversion. As much owing to judicious management by Pakeha teachers as to their inherent convertibility, Maori had seen the light. Another explanation, more modern but no less Eurocentric, is that naive Maori were duped, deliberately or not, by silver-tongued Pakeha who succeeded in talking them out of their land and independence, if not their cultural autonomy. This is an important part of a 'victim' tradition, which portrays Maori as the pathetic victims of unrelieved tragedy, the objects rather than the subjects of history's sentence. Maori allegedly 'misunderstood' the true implications of their acts of consent. This misses the point that before the 1860s most Maori had the power to make their understanding the real one. It was usually the Pakeha who misunderstood the situation.

Tribal politics and the rivalry for mana were clearly one set of influences behind Maori consent. Signing treaties and land deeds, accepting official positions and establishing gift-exchange relationships and alliances with the state or important Pakeha within it were privileges that tended to be restricted to chiefs. They therefore became a hallmark of chieftainship, and were sought by some for that reason. Sale of disputed or co-owned land by one set of claimants was the ultimate assertion of ownership, or of mana over the other claimants.[52] As usual, rivalry for mana was difficult to distinguish from more practical motives. A leading Wellington land seller, Te Puni of Te Ati Awa, when asked why he had sold other people's land, disarmingly replied, 'How could I help it, when I saw so many muskets and blankets before me?'[53] But he and his associate Te Wharepouri were also seeking to bilk rivals within the Ngati Toa-led alliance that had claims to the land; to gain a valuable and mana-enhancing settlement of Pakeha; and to use it as some sort of buffer against Te Rauparaha's pretensions to overlordship. Towns functioned as buffers not only through their own power but also because enemies were reluctant to attack your Pakeha for fear of scaring away their own. Such factors had special influence in partial vacuums and disputed ground left by the Musket Wars: Auckland, New Plymouth, Wellington, Nelson and Christchurch. Auckland exists at Auckland, and not at Thames as Cook originally suggested, partly because of Hongi Hika.

The Musket Wars are unsung determinants of twenty-first-century Pakeha demography.

Rivalry was most intense within single kin and neighbour zones, and the three acts of consent seem to have moved in spasms in accordance with this, as well as with politics inherited from the Musket Wars. Ngati Kahungunu, for example, were not great treaty signers, but they did co-operate and compete to lease and sell land in the 1840s and 1850s, eventually lapsing into civil war over the matter in 1857. They fought less over selling in principle than over the propensity of one leading chief, Te Hapuku, to sell land of which he and his immediate hapu were not the sole owners. Te Hapuku formed an alliance with McLean and became addicted to land selling to assert and enhance his mana. Rivalry intersected here with the pairing of mediators, each using his status or alleged status in the other society to lever up his status in his own.[54] McLean and Te Hapuku used each other to help establish reputations as 'Maori doctor' and 'tohunga Pakeha'. Rivalry for mana, of course, was the traditional Maori mechanism for rapidly disseminating change. It helped the spread of pa, guns and Bibles, and it helped increase the depth and breadth of engagement with the European economy before and after 1840. Signing treaties, selling land and establishing special relationships with the state became fresh currencies of rivalry. Possession of, or partnership with, Pakeha settlers was also a long-standing currency, and here inflation set in from the 1830s. A couple of Pakeha parked in the tribal garage was no longer enough, and the big players began to deal in whole towns. Maori who had acquired towns early found they posed new problems of control; those who had not, wanted them and sold land cheap to get them.

The instant settlements of 1840–41 were not the first Pakeha towns in New Zealand. On one estimate, Pakeha settlers increased sevenfold over the 1830s, from about 300 to about 2,000, a rate of increase not that much lower than the 1840s.[55] Until the 1830s, Pakeha came as isolated individuals, in sojourning shiploads or in stations. Individuals were incorporated into Maori communities as 'Pakeha Maori'; relations with sojourners were stabilised by mutual need, by the sex industry and by the brevity of their visit; stations were linked by marriage alliance or its mission substitutes. But from about 1830, settlers and sojourners formed clusters, sometimes quite townlike. Kororareka was described as a rough 'town' of 200 huts in 1831. Its population figures are sometimes confused with those for Europeans in the Bay of Islands as a whole, and they fluctuated during the 1830s. In 1839, it had at least a hundred European inhabitants, respectable as well as disreputable, some with comfortable homes and gardens. Northern Nga Puhi had taken over the overlordship of Kororareka from the southern alliance after the Girls' War of 1830, but there were signs of growing internal autonomy and respectability in the 1830s. A temperance society was formed in 1836, an educational institution for mixed-race children in 1839, and an association for the maintenance of law and order in 1838. We should not expect too much from the new-look hellhole. The number of temperance society members was equalled by the number of grogshops. The first Pakeha legal penalty, tarring and feathering with raupo fluff, was imposed upon a visitor from Sydney for the crime of debt collecting.[56] But the community was still beginning to control its own 'crime' rather than leaving it to chiefly overlords.

Greater Kororareka, the Bay of Islands urban area, was much larger in European population than the town itself – at least 530 Europeans in total in 1839.[57] Some lived in clusters approaching or even exceeding that of Kororareka. Mair's trading station at Te Wahapu and Clendon's at Okiato each had about 50 Europeans. The southern Nga Puhi entrepreneur Pomare's pa at Otuihu contained within it a town-like assembly of Pakeha – 131 in 1837, according to one account.[58] Pomare provided them with two pubs, the Sailor's Return and the Eagle Inn, with shutters and a verandah painted green, surely the most unusual structures in the whole archaeology of Maori pa. Pomare ran the grog and sex trades himself, and controlled his Pakeha himself. Clendon and Mair did similarly, functioning as junior Maori chiefs, held responsible for their people. But even Pomare must have found 130 Pakeha quite a handful, and Pakeha autonomy was increasing at Kororareka, where both grog and temperance trades were European-run, and perhaps in the Bay of Islands as a whole.

A similar situation may have been developing on the other coast of Northland, in the Hokianga, where Europeans quadrupled to over 200 between 1831 and 1839. The timber stations of the Coromandel were also said to contain 200 Europeans. Even where they did not form proto-towns, clusters of stations were more able to provide mutual support than their isolated predecessors. Outside Northland, European clustering may have been most important in the South Island, whose estimated 700 European residents in 1840 were a very significant minority in relation to a Maori population of about 3,000. Marlborough contained about 200 Europeans, half of them at Te Awaiti, which was described as a town; Banks Peninsula had about 100 in several hamlets and stations, and there were at least 300 along the Otago and Southland coasts, some in little communities, such as Codfish Island and Johnny Jones's Waikouaiti, which were more townlet than station.[59]

While 'town' might be too strong a term for most settlement clusters outside Kororareka, these concentrations of Europeans were of a new order of size compared with the stations and camps that had preceded them – half to a few hundreds as against dozens. Size was not the only difference. Some were economically more mixed, deriving their living from a package of activities rather than just seals or just souls. Some contained European women – ten per cent of the adult European population of the whole Bay of Islands; twenty per cent of that of Kororareka in 1839.[60] White wives for white husbands meant that marriage alliance became less effective in linking Maori and Pakeha communities. The Bay Europeans also became so numerous that they were no longer the vassals of a single patron chief. Their patrons might all come from the same tribal group, but, as we have seen, this did not necessarily reduce rivalry. More masters means less mastery – divide and avoid being ruled. The same process of pluralising and therefore loosening control had increased missionary autonomy and effectiveness after the death of Hongi.

This new autonomy in the larger European clusters was fragile and embryonic. It did not represent anything like the 'evil empire' posited by the advocates of official British intervention. Autonomy derived from the slight weakening of links of marriage alliance, of economic dependence and of Maori social control; from competing multiple masters, and the growing numbers and value of settlers to Maori – not from European power. Even the 450 European men of the Bay of Islands, however rough and tough, were no great military threat to the heirs of Hongi Hika. Nga Puhi destroyed Kororareka in 1845, despite the efforts of the British army and navy, and they could have done so more easily in the 1830s. But killing the gaggles of geese that laid the largest golden eggs was the last thing they wanted to do.

In Northland, parts of the South Island and perhaps elsewhere, Pakeha in the late 1830s were beginning to present a problem of calibrated control. Some were no longer responsible to a single Pakeha or Maori chief, who could also be held responsible for them. They needed to be tribalised. Some Maori may have agreed to the treaty, or to the local advent of the state if they did not sign, to create Ngati Pakeha. There is quite a strong correlation between the distribution of Pakeha settlers and that of Maori treaty signatures.[61] A governor would free the chiefs from the burden of ruling the large new Pakeha communities, and assist them in policing the Pakeha–Maori interface. He would enable them to avoid the risk of decreasing the flow of Pakeha through heavy-handed forms of control, and help them to increase it. There is a sense in which signing the treaty and accepting the state may have been intended as substitutes for marriage alliance.

The need to establish more sensitive forms of control over Pakeha was restricted to areas neighbouring the new settlement clusters, especially Northland, which contributed around 200 of 500 signatories. Other Maori may have signed treaties, accepted officials and sold land as means of breaking the Nga Puhi monopoly on access to Europe. Another possibility is that the concept of partial sovereignty, over Europeans only, was mentioned in the treaty debates. Right up to January 1840, partial sovereignty over European existing settlements was the option most discussed by the British, and this might have percolated through to New Zealand. Whatever the case with these supplementary possibilities, the suggestion is that Maori saw the new governor's authority as substantial and significant, but restricted to Pakeha.

The Maori neighbours of the European settlement clusters of the later 1830s developed a good idea of their benefits as well as their costs. The settlements employed Maori labour and bought Maori food – initially they had very little agriculture of their own. They provided a regular source of European goods, as against the sporadic one of ship visits, or even the intermittent and limited supplies provided by stations. This was especially important for consumables such as gunpowder, tobacco and sugar. Planting Pakeha instead of potatoes on part of your land made economic sense, as well as boosting mana as the latest currency of rivalry. Planting Pakeha towns in a competitive environment required that substantial areas be sold cheaply, and sometimes acceptance of the state machinery that negotiated the sales and policed the town.

It can be argued that Maori never expected the numbers of settlers they got, and this may have been true in the early 1840s and before. Te Wharepouri, seller of Wellington, complained that he had expected only nine or ten settlers to stem from his sale, one for each hapu, on the pre-1840 Pakeha-Maori model of a tribal trader. As he watched the thirteenth ship and the 1,300th Pakeha sail in, a mere six months after the first, he can be forgiven for feeling, like Dr Frankenstein, that he had created a monster. But it is very difficult to see how such expectations could have survived the early 1840s, which clearly showed that large sales could lead to large towns. Is it really conceivable that Maori were ignorant of Wellington, Auckland, Nelson and New Plymouth years after their establishment? Maori misapprehensions about the possible scale of settlement are likely to have been restricted to the early 1840s and before.

Some sellers, even in the early 1840s, clearly did expect sales to generate substantial numbers of European neighbours, and intended them to do so. Among Ngati Kahungunu, one chief requested, 'Let your payts. be large and let also the Number of white Men be large.'[62] Te Hapuku wrote to Grey 'offering to sell land and asking him for European settlers direct from England for a larger town'. Karaitiana planned a town of 104 European families.[63] It was the Pakeha town, not the official payment, that was to be the main return on the land sale. Another chief declared: 'Should the Pakeha wish to purchase land here, encourage him; no matter how small the amount he may offer, take it without hesitation. It is the Pakeha we want here. The Pakeha himself will be ample payment for our land, because we commonly expect to become prosperous through him.'[64] The guns, cash, blankets and trinkets laid out or promised at the sale ceremonies were merely a bonus, though sometimes a valued one. Beneath this overt price was a tacit one: an ongoing relationship with the cluster of settler neighbours created, and intended to be created, by the sale.

In pre-contact times, a Maori group in the Wairarapa is said to have exchanged all its land in return for canoes with which to emigrate to the South Island. Maori leaving for the Chatham Islands from Wellington in 1835 gifted all the land allocated them by Te Rauparaha to their allies.[65] There are few, if any, cases of similar total abandonment and departure with land sales to Pakeha. This in itself supports the view that sellers expected an ongoing relationship with the settlement their sale was intended to create. Specific provisions for Maori landing places in the deeds of sale for Napier town also seem to indicate that an ongoing trading relationship was considered to be part of the deal, and there were similar oral or written provisions in the sale treaties of other towns, such as Dunedin.[66]

In the oral component of land deals, Pakeha themselves commonly spoke in terms of an additional, ongoing price – over and above cash and trinkets. Their version of this price differed from the Maori, emphasising such things as civilisation, schools and hospitals, but the two intersected on continuing economic benefits and the fact of an additional price. Governor Gore Browne wrote in 1857 that 'from the date of the Treaty of Waitangi, promises of schools, hospitals, roads, constant solicitude for their welfare and general protection on the part of the Imperial Government have been held out to the Natives to induce them to part with their land'.[67] Historians also note that 'government agents laid great stress on the "advantages" to Maori of selling, including the uses of ready cash and the benefits of long-term settlement'.[68] Research on South Island Maori motives for sale also supports the notion of a tacit price. Buyers and sellers had 'radically different views of the nature of the deals which had been concluded. These misunderstandings included not only the details of the sales but also the nature of the relationship which had been established between the Crown and the tribe . . . Ngai Tahu saw the exchange in terms of the establishment of an ongoing and mutually beneficial relationship.'[69] In all, it seems probable that many land sales involved a tacit price as well as an overt one, and that Maori sellers considered the former to be an ongoing partnership between them and their new settler neighbours.

Perhaps these local partnerships, created by land sale and Pakeha settlement, and endorsed by sale ceremonies, treaty signings and acceptance of magistrates and the like, were a fifth, living version of *the* treaty. By no means all Maori entered into them, but the many who did were, voluntarily and in full possession of their faculties, accepting large-scale Pakeha settlement and the substantial advent of the colonial state. The likely Maori view was that neither state nor settlers were to have control over them, though each partner might expect a varying degree of influence over the other. In contrast, the Pakeha expected control over Maori, and in principle rejected Maori influence over them. In practice, they frequently accepted persisting Maori autonomy and acquiesced in Maori influence, such as the release of Maori offenders from gaols in Pakeha towns, or even the application of Maori law to Pakeha. Driven by their myths of empire, they always did so grudgingly, reluctantly and with the intention of reversing the situation as soon as possible. Yet, outside the big towns, acquiesce they did, and a miscellany of local partnerships was the reality of ethnic relations for much of the period 1840–60. Sometimes Pakeha were the senior partner, sometimes Maori were; but the median situation is probably best seen as one of rough parity. It may be the nearest thing we will get to the 'real' treaty, the founding bargain that actually existed on the ground, rather than on paper.

The terms of partnership were constantly renegotiated. The two parties had different definitions of Maori consent; of the tacit price involved in land sales; of the extent and nature of land sales (as we shall see in the next chapter); of the treaty; of the local role of the state; and of who was junior or senior in the local partnership. Such issues turned on who had the power and the need to enforce their definitions. This varied over space and time. In 1844, one Northland chief struggled gallantly with the problem of defining partnership. He tended to the view that he was senior partner to the small settlement cluster of Whangarei, whose leading settler was Gilbert Mair, and there was an iron fist under his velvet glove. But he was willing to be reasonable as he sought to resolve disputes through his lieutenant Eru and through a letter to Gilbert Mair.

> Friend I have heard from Eru that your actions is wrong therefore I urge you to be circumspect. It was us who bestowed the land yet later on in these days you have invited some strange Europeans to go and occupy. This is not right . . . Now concerning a certain block of land which you did not complete payment of . . . This also is improper. And the sacred place where you have been stripping the bark off the trees is wrong. Eru will arrange for you to get the necessary trees on unconsecrated land . . . Our conversation has been good and with a view to bring forth the good and hide the evil away out of sight. Do you therefore act accordingly for the reason that I love you and your children and your wife also for you belong to me.
>
> This is all to you Mr Mair, also to all the Europeans in Wangarei [sic]. This (Document) is like a newspaper to search out wrongs in every portion of the country . . . If the Europeans will not listen, and continue to do wrong, neither will the Maoris take heed, therefore I will place the transgressors in a very small place indeed. But if you the Europeans will do their part, I will do mine and will make amends for any wrong acts of the Maori people.
>
> Cease therefore to invite the European indiscriminately to that place. Allow only a few to settle there. Otherwise I shall be very angry – very wroth indeed – leave me a portion, a half of my Kainga – do not appropriate the whole.[70]

The chief was John William Heke Pokai, better known as Hone Heke. His attempt at persuasion failed, and he did become angry – very wroth indeed. In the mid-1840s, he and other chiefs, north and south, put definitions of partnership, land alienation, the nature of British Empire in New Zealand, and of the limits of Maori consent, to the test of war.

Limiting Consent: The Warring Forties

Before discussing the consequences of Heke's wrath, we need to turn our eyes south, where three local outbreaks of conflict took place between 1843 and 1847. All can be seen as episodes in the same 'Southern War' between the British and Ngati Toa 'empires'. The latter was a fragile and divided entity, consisting of imperfectly conquered enemies and jealous allies of Ngati Toa – a tribe that was less than united itself. Yet it was a remarkable one, the nearest thing New Zealand could boast to an African-style 'conquest state'. It was a very loose and new indigenous empire.

In the 1820s, as we have seen, Te Rauparaha came south in the longest-lasting and farthest-reaching cycle of the Musket Wars, forced out by his Waikato kin and searching for land, guns and greenstone. He picked up allies from at least seven tribal groups from northern and southern Taranaki, Whanganui and southern Waikato, some not linked to him by kinship. His advent in Wellington about 1822 was initially more peaceful than that of Hongi in Waikato or Te Wherowhero in Taranaki, but war soon broke out with the local Rangitane, Ngati Ira and Muaupoko, and with Ngati Apa and Ngati Kahungunu neighbours, north and east of Wellington. Te Rauparaha established himself on Kapiti Island, the key to the Cook Strait region. Kapiti was easy to foray from but hard to attack. The strategic brilliance of the choice is obvious every time you look at the island, now held with almost equal tenacity by the Department of Conservation.

Kapiti, together with the whaling and trading stations and even sheep farms he sponsored on and around it, gave Te Rauparaha a secure base and superior access to Europe, especially its guns. He used these advantages to overcome his rivals, extend his raids and conquests, and acquire more influence and allies. In 1827, he and his associates began a series of expeditions outside the North Island, beginning in Nelson and Marlborough, and ending in Westland, Southland, the Chathams and the Auckland Islands. In the early 1840s, Te Rauparaha's overlordship extended in varying degree over substantial territories on both sides of Cook Strait: Nelson, Marlborough and northern Westland; Wellington, Horowhenua and the Manawatu. At the time, this was a bigger empire than that of the British in New Zealand, and in the new town of Wellington it was not clear who ruled whom. When Te Rauparaha parked his canoe outside the Thistle Tavern and went in for a few rums, no-one asked him to pay.

Rauparaha was a man of many parts, a Maui-like trickster, master politician and New Zealand's most famous poet. He is said to have composed the famous haka that precedes All Black rugby matches. Some of his parts were terrible, even in the context of the Musket Wars, and there is nothing Eurocentric about disliking his brutalities – in the districts of his victims, it is a very Maori thing to do. About 1824, he treacherously killed the great Ngati Ruanui poet Oraukawa

– a lethal literary tiff – and the atrocities he performed on Ngai Tahu during the *Elizabeth* incident in 1830 were not wholly the figment of lurid Pakeha imaginations. But in the end his most remarkable achievement was that he held together Maoridom's first pan-tribal polity, and that in doing so he unintentionally paved the way for the biggest success of British conquest before the 1860s.[71]

Ngati Toa Rangatira was a small tribe. Its loose and insecure hegemony was based on Te Rauparaha himself, the linchpin of a precariously balanced structure, on superior access to things European, and on judicious coercion and conciliation of vassals and allies, in which gift exchange, marriage alliance and the generous reallocation of land featured as much as force. It was like a new, artificial kin zone. The rivalry for mana within it was even more intense than within normal kin zones, but less constrained by blood ties. Te Rauparaha seems to have wished to encourage but at the same time limit European settlement. He co-operated with the New Zealand Company in the founding of Nelson and at least acquiesced in the founding of Wellington, taking a share of overt and tacit prices in each case. But his allies, notably Te Ati Awa, competed with him in selling land and founding towns, so threatening his monopoly over access to Europe.

The settlers themselves wanted to establish their own agricultural town-supply districts, not being satisfied with Maori ones. They encroached on land they believed they had bought, but which elements of the Ngati Toa alliance did not. When Te Rauparaha and his formidable lieutenant Te Rangihaeata stopped one such encroachment at Wairau in 1843, a posse of settler constables set out from Nelson to arrest them under Captain Arthur Wakefield and Police Magistrate Henry Thompson. The settlers and their law were beaten in a confused fight, and 22 were killed (some after surrendering), including Wakefield and Thompson. Between two and six Maori were also killed, including Te Rangihaeata's wife, Te Rongo.[72] To the rage of the settlers, FitzRoy could do little but give Ngati Toa a good telling-off. He did not have the power to enforce his definition of British colonisation. Te Rauparaha did.

This demonstrates the local falsity of the British Empire, but it caused problems in the loose Ngati Toa empire too, stemming not from Pakeha power but from their value. Te Rauparaha could not afford to frighten off Europeans, and some of his Te Ati Awa allies considered the Wakefields to be 'their Pakeha'.[73] When Grey sought to enforce the British definition of Maori consent in Wellington in 1846, Te Ati Awa and others sided with him against Te Rangihaeata and an upper Whanganui ally, Te Mamaku. Fighting broke out in the Hutt Valley and the Kapiti coast, near Wellington town. Te Rauparaha himself, caught in the cleft stick of wanting to restrain Pakeha power without risking their value, remained neutral. Although Grey now had ten times the troops of FitzRoy, he was unable to inflict a decisive military defeat on the resisting faction. But without the full support of the Ngati Toa alliance, indeed with the active opposition of large sections of it, Te Rangihaeata gained no clear victories either. The decisive blow came when Grey boldly and treacherously seized Te Rauparaha. Caught naked and unarmed in his house, the old chief struggled desperately until, according to one version, a sailor grabbed his testicles 'and held on'.[74]

Te Rangihaeata withdrew north of the Manawatu River and kept the British Empire at arm's length from there. Te Mamaku fought again, at Wanganui in 1847, but his lower-river kin supported their town, not him, and the brief campaign ended indecisively.[75] Te Rauparaha was released in 1848, but his mana never fully recovered, and he died the following year. The British Empire gained some substance in the top of the South Island and the bottom of the North. Grey had removed Te Rauparaha and slotted into his place, the sorcerer dethroned by his apprentice.

In a sense, British power on the shores of Cook Strait was inherited from Ngati Toa through the conquest of the conqueror. Such occurrences were not uncommon in the history of European imperialism. An intensification of European contact upsets the delicate balance of a fragile pre-existing empire. Europe then inherits its earth, with the help of its own subjects. This sort of imperialism was more that of the vulture than the eagle, but was no less effective for that.

In 1834, Henry Williams commented on the young Hone Heke's apparent conversion to Christianity and civilisation. 'I certainly have hopes of this man though he has always been a daring impudent fellow, but what cannot divine grace accomplish. Is anything too hard for omnipotence?'[76] In this case, the answer was yes. The tension between Maori rejection of the new state's pretensions to power over them and the desire for valuable settlers, and between differing definitions, was clearly apparent in the Northern War of 1845–46, at the Bay of Islands. One faction of Nga Puhi, under Heke and the older chief Kawiti, stressed the rejection of state pretensions; a second, under Tamati Waka Nene and other chiefs, stressed the value of settlers and trade. This grouping appears to have cut across the long-standing Nga Puhi division into western, northern and southern alliances. The power base of Waka Nene's group was western or Hokianga Nga Puhi, but even here Heke had his sympathisers, though the two local factions appear to have agreed to keep the Hokianga itself neutral. Much of Heke's support came from Hongi's northern Nga Puhi, but Kawiti was a southerner. The disagreement over power and value was a matter of degree, not kind. Both factions rejected state power over them, and valued interaction with settlers. State interference in such forms as the imposition of customs dues and the development of Auckland as a rival to Nga Puhi's

Kororareka had reduced the European trade in the Bay of Islands. In resenting this, Heke fought for more European contact, not less.[77]

Heke and Kawiti hit upon the British flagstaff as a symbol that allowed them to rebut state pretensions to empire without attacking settlers. Kawiti stated that 'if the flag were only for the whites and the land we have sold them, we would not take up arms . . . but this flag takes away the authority of the chiefs and all our lands'.[78] FitzRoy rose to the bait after Heke had amputated the flagstaff three times, and garrisoned Kororareka with his few troops and his only warship. Heke cut down the flag a fourth time, despite the garrison. New Zealand's first town and £50,000 worth of settler property went up in flames as an unintended consequence. Auckland panicked, but Britain's Nga Puhi allies kept Heke occupied in a low-intensity kin war, in which prisoners were returned at the end of each day's fighting, while FitzRoy called in reinforcements from Australia. These fresh troops mounted two expeditions in May and June–July 1845. The first seized the neutral or semi-neutral chief Pomare and destroyed his coastal pa, presumably including the two pubs. It then proceeded inland against Heke's pa at Puketutu. The British did quite well tactically in the ensuing engagement, but they were prevented from attacking the unfinished pa by the intervention of Kawiti and forced to withdraw. The second expedition, under Colonel Henry Despard, following up a sharp defeat inflicted by Waka Nene on Heke at Te Ahuahu on 12 June, came to grief against Kawiti's pa of Ohaeawai on 1 July – a humiliating blow to both the British and their myth of conquest.[79]

FitzRoy then tried to make peace on the basis of covert recognition of Maori independence, with a face-saving cession of a small piece of land that belonged mainly to his allies and to neutrals. The attempt failed. Grey arrived to replace FitzRoy in November and suspended peace negotiations. Unwisely in retrospect, he wrote that it was 'absolutely necessary to crush either Heke or Kawiti before tranquillity could be restored to the country'.[80] With Despard, 1,300 soldiers and sailors, and a growing number of Maori allies said to have reached 850, he mounted the largest expedition of all, in January and February 1846, against Kawiti's new pa of Ruapekapeka, held by a few hundred warriors. A heavy bombardment eventually breached the outer defences, and the British and Maori rushed in, only to find the pa virtually empty. One interpretation – possibly originating with Heke himself, a propagandist of Grey-like talent – maintains that the garrison were at Sunday prayers. Another is that they had deliberately evacuated the pa, hoping to trap the British in the bush outside.[81] The trap was missprung, and an indecisive engagement took place in the bush outside the pa. The British then destroyed the pa and withdrew.[82]

Grey claimed a great triumph at Ruapekapeka and complete victory in the Northern War as a whole. He convinced most historians and some contemporaries. Ruapekapeka itself is probably best seen as a tactical draw, with strategic benefits arguably favouring the resisters. It is true that Waka Nene had the better of Heke in their war within a war – in which neither Kawiti nor the British were involved. It is also true that the British proved themselves dangerous opponents in clashes outside fortifications at Kororareka and Puketutu, and that the resisters found the war a great economic strain. But the British failed in their aim of crushing or capturing Heke and Kawiti, and the resisters, on balance, had the better of them in battle. The northern attempt to transform false empire into real by conquest had failed, and Heke's prominent independence until his death in 1850 appears to bear this out. He is said to have planned a descent on Auckland in 1847, but was dissuaded by the determination of Waikato and Ngati Whatua to fight him if he attacked their town. Te Wherowhero of Waikato informed Heke that 'between Ngapuhi and the pakeha was his body – it must be disposed of first'.[83]

One did not have to accept the myth of conquest to find the Northern War surprising. For all its faults in leadership and logistics, the British army, unlike the civilian posse at Wairau, was a formidable military organisation. Its proud regiments – warrior guilds disconnected from their home societies and disproportionately Catholic Irish – combined discipline, ferocity and esprit de corps. Moreover, they consistently outnumbered Maori and were full-timers fighting part-timers. The British had a larger and more mobile socio-economic surplus, and full-time troops. War with them was a more continuous and economically demanding affair than fighting tribal enemies.

The older Nga Puhi warriors were very experienced, but they were still part of their hapu's labour force. They had periodically to return home from the battlefront to participate in the economic round. So Kawiti found himself defending Ohaeawai with 100 against 600. Added to this, the British had artillery: mortars, rockets and howitzers, as well as conventional cannon. These weapons threw anti-personnel ammunition, intended to pulverise the garrison, as well as barrier-piercing projectiles. Although Maori pa had been adapted to cope with musket-armed enemies, incorporating rifle trenches, salients for crossfire and musket-proof flax matting, their wooden construction, high firing platforms and coastal or hilltop location made them vulnerable to artillery. The *Alligator* expedition of 1834 had destroyed pa with both sea- and land-based cannon, and the British did the same to Pomare's Otuihu in 1845. Inland pa had no problem with warships, but they did with land-based cannon, and they could often be surrounded. They could outlast the supplies of a besieging tribal force, but not those of the British. The citadel or fortified-village function of pa, protecting the sinews of war and economics, meant that their loss would be crippling. Maori might still overcome armed settlers, make successful raids and ambushes, and occasionally come close to matching regular troops in open engagements. Maori even had some cannon of their own – one did some damage with a single shot at Ohaeawai.[84] But these guns were old and very poorly supplied with ammunition – the Ohaeawai round consisted of bullock chain. The Maori could not outgun the British; they could not expect to defeat them often in formal battles outside fortifications; and they could not defend traditional or musket pa against them. European military prophets exaggerated when they claimed, before 1845, that any one Maori group could be conquered by a hundred soldiers and a couple of howitzers. But they did not exaggerate by much.

One key to Maori success in overcoming these problems was simply that they had not suffered fatal impact, crippling impact or anything like them. While modern historians accepted Grey's victory claims, they have long recognised that Heke and Kawiti mounted a very vigorous resistance, that another large section of Nga Puhi vigorously 'collaborated', and that a third section remained neutral. They also recognise that Nga Puhi were the prime Maori mediators of European contact – chief victims of fatal impact, if it existed. Why, then, did historians not ask themselves how a demoralised, dislocated and severely damaged group was able to mount such a diverse and dynamic military response to Europe? Indirect residues of the myth of fatal impact may help explain this strange failure to confront the obvious.

Apart from simple survival, another key to the effectiveness of Maori resistance was a refusal to be intimidated by frightening new technology. This is apparent in their response to the gunfire of the early explorers, and it was apparent at Puketutu when Maori faced Congreve rockets for the first time – the same weapons that had lit Washington with 'red glare' when the British destroyed it in the War of 1812. These giant skyrockets were not very effective, but they were terrifying, as the American national anthem commemorates. One flew around inside Puketutu pa as though it would 'twist and turn in pursuit of the people until it had killed them every one', like some early heat-seeking missile. Heke calmed his people by leaning on the gatepost of his pa and asking sarcastically, 'What prize can be won by such a gun?' One member of the garrison did flee in terror from the pa and encountered Kawiti's taua, hidden in the bush outside waiting to attack the British in the rear. His account of the 'frightful gun' began to unsettle the tense warriors. Kawiti's response was more prosaic than Heke's but no less effective. 'I know all about all sorts of guns; all guns will kill, and all guns will also miss. This is in the nature (*ahua*) of guns; but if you say one word more I will split your head with my tomahawk.'[85] The ingenious British are also said to have used poison gas at Ohaeawai, in the form of 'stench balls'. They 'contained some poisonous substance, the effect of which was expected to deprive the rebels of all animation', but had no recorded effect.[86]

This refusal to be intimidated by the new pervades the whole Maori response to Europe, and it is not easy to explain. It was suggested in Chapter Four that, though Maori understood nature in terms of supernature, their attitude to neither was unquestioningly fatalistic. Magic was contestable, evil spirits could be frightened off, nature could be harnessed, as symbolised by Maui. Such attitudes were quickly applied to the things and thoughts of Europe. Maori had no precedents for dealing with this order of difference, and this may have been an advantage to them. Other tribal societies, with more experience of strangers, took longer to recognise that Europe constituted a new order of difference, and were more inclined to attempt traditional solutions to the problems it brought. Maori had less opportunity to doubt that new solutions were required; some borrowed from Europe and adapted, some wholly new, designed as antidotes to it. We have seen signs of this in early contact; we will see more below in looking at Maori attempts to transcend the tribe. It was also apparent in the Maori technological response to attempts at conquest: the development of the modern pa system, an early type of trench warfare.

This new system of war had three basic elements. The first was the anti-artillery bunker. From Ohaeawai in 1845 throughout the New Zealand Wars, these regularly sheltered Maori garrisons from heavy bombardments. Bunkers varied in design, but all used earth, not wood, to counteract shot and shell. The garrison sat out the bombardment in these, and then proceeded through trenches or tunnels to a separate set of firing trenches – a trench-and-bunker system. The British found it very hard to accept that the latest in military hardware – culminating in an Armstrong gun that threw 110-pound shells at the Gate Pa in 1864 – could be rendered ineffective by mere holes in the ground. The simple survival of the garrison therefore had an important shock effect on attacking troops, who expected them to have been 'blown to the devil'.[87]

This augmented the second element of the system: a diverse bag of tricks, some from the Musket Wars, some new, designed to stop ferocious British assaults, which were pressed home with far less regard for casualties than any tribal chief could contemplate. Techniques included the careful siting of firing trenches to enfilade attackers; the use of a light outer palisade to slow them up while they were shot down – substituting for barbed wire; the tight organisation of Maori musket fire on the 'platoon fire' principle, which ensured that a commander always had some loaded barrels at his disposal; the use of bastions and other firing positions whose strength or even existence was camouflaged; and false targets that attracted storming parties and exposed them to hidden firing positions on their flanks. Such tricks, traps and surprises did the same job as the rapid-fire rifles and machine guns of later trench warfare. They compensated for the fact that Maori were usually armed with slow-loading and short-range muskets and shotguns.

The third element of the system involved changes in the location, function and costs of construction of pa. Traditional pa were economically vital and valuable, though they, too, might be abandoned for reasons of tapu. Modern pa normally had little economic or direct strategic value. They used more earth than wood, and earth was cheaper. They tended to be built on lower ground than traditional pa, and had easier access on at least one face to invite assault, yet always had an escape route on the other. More tailored battle sites than forts, they were cheap, expendable and escapable. If the British massed so many troops and guns that they had a chance of taking them, the garrison simply left, knowing that the massing had cost more than the pa. These virtues made the modern pa strategically flexible, adjustable to the strategic requirements of each particular campaign, but most ingredients of the system were discernible in the pa of the Northern War. At Ruapekapeka, you can still see Kawiti's anti-artillery bunkers.

Some characteristics of modern pa were apparent in Musket War pa; some were apparent in European sieges and field fortifications; but in few, if any, cases were all these characteristics present before 1845, and nowhere did they form so integrated a system. Europeans were very reluctant to recognise its implications and simply could not believe that Kawiti could have invented it without European help. As late as 1987, a historian wrote that 'it is difficult to believe they could have sprung, unfledged as it were, straight from Kawiti's inventive mind'.[88] But there was nowhere for him to have plagiarised from. Someone had to invent modern trench warfare. Why not Kawiti? Two models of his pa were made. One went north to Britain. It aroused considerable interest at the time, but ultimately its underlying lessons were ignored, to be expensively rediscovered in 1914, and it languished in a museum. The other went south, to other Maori tribes.[89] Among them, its lessons were learned.

CHAPTER NINE

Converting Conversion

The period 1847–60 was one of peace between Maori and Pakeha. The wars of the 1840s taught each a modicum of caution in dealing with the other and forced some concessions to each other's definitions of land sale and partnership. There were no more Wairau Affrays. Grey's dubious but effective version of conquest established Pakeha dominance in and around Wellington and Nelson towns, and this was further entrenched by swamping. Growing numbers and the establishment of embryonic Pakeha economic hinterlands around these towns were key aspects of swamping. They tended both to mesh local Maori into the Pakeha economy and to marginalise them through sheer bulk: the town became more important to them than they were to it. Maori chiefs still carried some weight as allies, and Maori communities in and near the town retained elements of independence, but the curve in their relative power was clearly downward, and there was increasingly little doubt about who was the senior partner. In Auckland, a similar process occurred, but with swamping leading conquest. Te Kawau, the Ngati Whatua co-founder of Auckland, expected to exercise a certain amount of authority inside his town, and was able to do so in 1844, when he forced the civil authorities to release an imprisoned tribesman. In 1851, however, when Ngati Paoa, another tribe with an interest in Auckland, attempted to do the same thing, the state had enough military force to induce them to back down.[1] Between 1844 and 1851, the Pakeha of Auckland made the shift from junior to senior partnership with their immediate Maori neighbours.

By this time real empire clearly existed in and around Auckland and Wellington, and perhaps in other major settlements too. Swamping and conquest had done the job here, and at the end of his governorship, Grey claimed that conversion had succeeded in transforming and subordinating the rest of the country. In 1852, he wrote that

> Both races already form one harmonious community, connected together by commercial and agricultural pursuits, professing the same faith, resorting to the same Courts of Justice, joining in the same public sports, standing mutually

> and indifferently to each other in the relation of landlord and tenant, and thus insensibly forming one people.[2]

This was not as unconvincing as it now seems, and it was endorsed by missionaries such as Robert Maunsell, who celebrated the 'rising tide' of civilisation among the Maori, and ethnographers like Arthur Thomson, who published lengthy tables on 'The Progress of the New Zealanders in Civilization'.[3] 'One harmonious community' was an obvious exaggeration, but the wars of the 1840s could be dismissed as teething troubles – the birth pains of empire. And it was a fact that Maori were engaging very eagerly, not only with treaties, but with all four other agencies of conversion: God, money, land and law. Most Maori had not been subordinated by guns or numbers, but had they been transformed into Brown Britons with the help of the Wizard's wand?

God and Money

The growth of the Pakeha economy and society, combined with state assistance in such forms as subsidies to mission schools, lent much more muscle to the old unofficial or semi-official agencies of conversion: economics and religion. We have seen in Chapter Six that Maori engagement with European trade and technology up to the 1830s did not convert them, though it did change them. But the advent of mass European settlement intensified economic interaction. There was a prospect of economic conversion: of addiction to European ends as well as means, commercial values as well as the goods themselves; of uncontrolled land selling; of trade with, and employment by, Europeans corroding tribal structures. If economic interaction with settlers became an addiction, and land sales were the only route to it, Maori might gradually sell off their whole patrimony. Maori entrepreneurs might have emerged, using their profits to make more money for themselves, rather than for their kin group. Maori working for Pakeha faced the danger of becoming 'proletarianised': cut out from their kin groups and transformed into wage-working individuals, taking second place to Pakeha in the job queues but dependent on wages all the same – a 'reserve army' of labour at the disposal of the Pakeha economy.

Even where a Maori community retained its cohesion, where its entrepreneurs and labourers worked for it rather than for themselves, there was a danger of economic interaction becoming 'gridlock'. In a Maori community bordering or contained within a large town, the level of direct interaction could become so great, and come from so close, that it was impossible to conceive of doing without it, or even of limiting it. In such situations, the Maori community needed the Pakeha economy much more than it needed them, and the prospect of effective resistance or valued co-operation was lost. Were Maori converted by capitalism? Did they succumb to its three temptations and dangers: addiction to capitalist ends as well as means; the corrosion of kin groups by capitalist individualism; and economic gridlock, with a large, close, neighbour town? The scale of economic interaction suggests that these risks were real enough.

Maori consumption of European goods is impossible to calculate accurately, but it was great and growing. In 1856, it was officially estimated that Maori paid £51,000, or nearly 60 per cent, of the North Island's annual £87,000 of customs dues.[4] A common rate of duty was ten per cent. Rates were higher on some items, but many British and Australian goods were admitted free of duty,[5] and if we take ten per cent as an average, this suggests a Maori consumption of £500,000 worth of imported goods per year – about £10 per capita. It has been suggested that addiction to European goods was a powerful motive for land sales, the easiest source of cash.[6] But the proceeds of land selling, at the measly prices doled out by Grey and McLean and accepted by enthusiastic Maori town-planners, can have met only a fraction of such a bill. Grey and McLean paid out only £61,847 for the 32 million acres they bought between 1846 and 1853.[7] The figures for Maori consumption are very unreliable, but the impression of a massive Maori economic engagement with Pakeha is not.

Maori engaged quite widely in extractive industries. Kauri gum, mainly supplied by Maori diggers at this time, averaged £20,000 per year in export value in the 1850s, with the vestiges of the flax industry adding another two or three thousand.[8] More flax was used within New Zealand by Pakeha ropemakers. Shore whaling, involving Maori crews and even Maori owners, continued strongly in the 1840s, beginning a long decline in the 1850s. Maori were also involved in goldmining. At the early goldfield of Aorere, Nelson, in 1856, Maori family groups made up 600 of 1,900 diggers.[9] 'The speed with which Maori learnt the trade of the goldminer was as disconcerting to the old settler as was the spirit of Maori independence to the new immigrant.' Two Maori took 25 pounds of gold, worth about £1,600 (about 25 years' wages for a manual labourer), in one day early in the Otago gold rush in 1862.[10]

Services were another source of income. From the moment Horeta Te Taniwha welcomed Cook and supplied random geological samples to his scientists, Maori participated in European travel, science, exploration and tourism. Vaunted European overland explorers of the 1840s and 1850s were guided by Maori who had usually been there before and were paid for their services.[11] European travellers had Maori guides. They were sometimes wrongly advised that the next tract of country was extremely dangerous, absolutely necessitating well-paid guides. A whare Pakeha, an accommodation house for European travellers, was built at Manawapou in the early 1850s, and there are other cases of these early Maori tourist hotels.[12] Mail contracts, ferry tolls and stock droving were also sources of cash outside the towns, as was the sale of moa bones or alleged moa bones. The sex industry continued, much diminished, but still sometimes tribally rather than individually organised.[13] Maori labour was important in public works, and, from the 1850s, in sheep shearing, and Maori agricultural production for Pakeha markets was massive.

In 1848, an Auckland newspaper remarked that the Maori 'are our largest purveyors of foodstuffs; so large indeed as nearly to monopolize the market and to exclude the Europeans from competition'. 'It is likely that but for the Maori trade Auckland business would have collapsed during these hard years.' Maori were described as the 'very life blood' of the Auckland economy.[14] In 1853, 2,000 Maori trading canoes landed at Auckland and Onehunga – many more than once, of course. Their cargo included large quantities of potatoes, maize, onions, cabbages and peaches; moderate quantities of kumara, pumpkins and grapes; and small quantities of melons, apples and quinces. The actual weight is difficult to calculate because this produce was measured in variable 'kits'. Some 2,500 bushels of wheat and 132 tons of Maori-milled flour were also brought in, along with 67 tons of fish, 10 kits of pipis, and 60 of oysters; 1,366 pigs, about 800 chickens, ducks, geese, and turkeys, and 16 goats. The number of pigs, poultry and goats was down sharply from 1852, and stayed down in 1854 and 1855, suggesting Pakeha were beginning to produce their own. In addition to food, Maori supplied fuel and building materials, in the form of 2,320 tons of wood and a little raupo reed; stock feed – 5,300 bundles of grass, plus a little straw; and extractive products, including 249 tons of kauri gum and some flax, for use in Auckland or export overseas. These products had an estimated market value of £12, 879.[15] They did not include goods grown for Maori consumption, those sold in the small settlements outside Auckland, those brought by land to Auckland itself or those brought by Maori-owned coastal ships, as against canoes. As many as 111 Maori-owned ships were registered in 1867, and their numbers may have been greater in the 1850s. They voyaged to the South Island and Australia, as well as along the North Island coasts.[16]

Economic interaction on this scale did have some corrosive effect on tribal organisation, and some merging effect on Maori communities close to large towns. A few individualist Maori entrepreneurs and detribalised workers did appear. It has even been suggested that, by 1860, Maori chiefs were forming an embryonic class of capitalists. One South Island community experimented with individual tenure and production, the 'new custom of making every one equal', because chiefs were using tribal land for personal profit.[17] But broadly speaking, socio-economic conversion does not seem to have been very great. Work on the gold and gum fields was sporadic and tribally organised, as was labour for Pakeha and agricultural production. Hawke's Bay Maori shearers organised for higher rates, using tribal organisation to impose solidarity. The rate set by runanga edict – 45 shillings per hundred sheep – was much higher than that achieved by the market or by early Pakeha unions.[18] Profits were put to individual use, but also to tribal uses. As early as the mid-1830s, the flax trade had declined from its frenetic peak in 1831, partly because of declining prices, but also because Maori had acquired the guns they needed, and stopped producing. This was a Maori pattern of production and consumption, not a capitalist European one. The same pattern can be discerned in the building of flour mills in the 1840s and 1850s. Far more were built than were needed to process the available wheat, because mills had become a currency of group rivalry. Other currencies also emerged; as usual, mixing mana and pragmatism. The year 1848 saw 'a great rage for buying horses' in South Taranaki,[19] and one gets a clear impression of successive fashions or minor currencies of rivalry. The tribes were commercialised, but commerce was also tribalised.

The desire for neighbouring settlers with whom to interact economically was a key incentive for land selling, but there were two ways of getting the one without the other. One was to lease. Theoretically, leasing was only permissible from the Crown, but illegal leasing direct from Maori was quite common. There were even cases of simultaneous payment to both owners. Grey and McLean quickly realised that the Hawke's Bay Maori preference for leasing was a major threat to land sales. If Maori could get economic interaction without sale, the flow of offers would diminish. They could not easily stop Maori from insisting on payment from those they saw as their tenants, but they could stop the tenants from accepting leases from Maori, and they went to considerable trouble to do so.[20]

With local exceptions, leasing failed to break the equation whereby intense economic interaction demanded land sale. What did break it for some regions was the development of arm's-length interaction – large-scale trade with big towns by tribes living at some distance. The Waikato relationship with Auckland was a case in point – it was they who sent most of the 2,000 canoes to Auckland. Waikato kept their market town at arm's length, and combined this with access to Old New Zealand-style shanty ports at Raglan and Kawhia, and a small, scattered and therefore controllable number of European neighbours to whom small pieces of land had been sold. Waikato chiefs expressed their preference for small private sales – whether recognised by Pakeha law or not – as early as 1843. The Crown 'only wants large tracts; but the common Europeans are content with small places to sit down upon'.[21]

The capacity to separate economic interaction from land sale is also illustrated by an unpublished study of South Taranaki. The Taranaki, Ngati Ruanui and Nga Rauru tribes parted with little or no land, but from the 1840s they deepened and broadened their engagement with European products and economics. They began erecting flour mills from 1847, paying European builders 400 pigs per mill. Flour was sold in New Plymouth, as well as used by Maori themselves – a mix of boiled flour, milk and sugar was a favourite children's treat. Among the Taranaki, bullocks and carts were plentiful, and there were four Maori-owned stores. Ngati Ruanui grew their own tobacco and milled their own gunpowder under the guidance of a Nga Puhi ex-whaler, but trade with New Plymouth and Wanganui was substantial.[22] From about 1850, in contrast to some other regions, Waikato and Taranaki did not have to sell land to generate intense economic contact.

Mass Maori engagement with Christianity began about 1830, as we have seen, released from Northland by the death of mission master Hongi Hika and carried by freed Maori slaves, along with its adjunct, literacy. Peace brought Christianity, and Christianity brought European missionaries. From 1835, mission stations, churches and chapels proliferated. European missionaries were culturally and economically useful because they brought books, greatly supplemented the teaching of literacy by Maori agents of contact, and traded or could be forced to trade. But chapels and churches were not materially useful, and both missionaries and churches spread fast partly because they became currencies of rivalry, like mills and muskets. In 1845, Ngai Tahu of Banks Peninsula sent two of their coastal ships to Wellington for a missionary, explaining that 'their pride is hurt, that at Otago there should be a Minister, whilst at Banks Peninsula, which they now consider the Head Quarters of their tribe, there is none'.[23] A North Island missionary remarked in 1842 that 'it is a point of honour among the N. Zealanders to have a foreigner among them and especially a priest. It is also a temporal resource for them.'[24]

Something of a church rush took place in the 1840s. By 1850, the Tauranga/Whakatane region had eleven Catholic chapels and the Rotorua region fourteen, serving an average constituency of fewer than a hundred Catholics each. An average of only thirteen people regularly attended each expensive chapel – their purpose was more mana than meeting a demand for pews. The Ngati Ruanui tribe, which was not large, had 30 churches in 1848.[25] The 745 Maori in Wellington town had eleven churches and chapels of all denominations – one for every 68 men, women and children.[26] Christianity and literacy themselves, which were in fact distinct from missions and churches, may also have become currencies of rivalry. 'When Christianity became recognised as a taonga, something of value in Maori terms, no group could afford to get left behind in the rush.'[27]

By the early 1840s, missionaries claimed 42,700 Anglican converts, plus 16,000 Maori Methodists.[28] Bishop Pompallier had two priests who had each notched up more than a thousand converts, and as early as 1841 he claimed 45,000 Maori in the process of conversion to Catholicism.[29] There were still many thousands of unconverted Maori as well – people who had not gone 'mihinare'. When asked if he were Christian, one replied, 'No, I am a devil.'[30] If the Maori population in 1840 was anything like our guess of 70,000, then something quite remarkable was happening here. Saving 103,700 souls out of much fewer than 70,000 was miraculous indeed. But the soul counts were rather like American body counts in the Vietnam War, not to be taken very seriously, and may have stimulated high estimates of the Maori population to make room for mission scores. Maori were also very versatile Christians, prone to double- or even triple-dipping. Te Heuheu Iwikau of Ngati Tuwharetoa bluntly informed a 'Church' (Anglican) missionary that 'when you are in Taupo I am a Churchman. When the Wesleyan missionary is here, I belong to his church. When the R.C. priest calls, I am a Papist, and when no European is here, I am a Heathen.'[31] Swapping easily between denominations, and even adhering to two or more simultaneously, was quite common. Maori showed a persistent reluctance to accept the Christian doctrine of denominational exclusivity. Why should people have only one form of worship?

The initial pleasure of Henry Williams and other missionaries at finding that thousands of Maori had been miraculously converted without the benefit of white converters was soon marred by the realisation that there was something not quite kosher about this instant Christianity.

> Heard much of the baptism which had been introduced by this man Neira which I condemned in toto. His ceremony appears to be the washing of the head which has always been considered sacred by the New Zealanders in warm water out of an iron pot the person at the same time confessing his sins vainly imagining that thereby his sins will be pardoned, a washing away of sin and a release from *Tapu* very much according to native custom. A perfect cheat of Satan and what an abominable perversion of baptism![32]

Like iron made into patu, Christianity made by Maori into Maori religion was changed in the process. The equivalent visual symbol to the iron patu is the Maori Madonna, carved at Maketu in 1845 by Patoromu, in which both Mary and Jesus have full facial moko. European missionaries rejected such things as 'impious caricature', but Maori did not always care very much about that.[33]

Some Maori were bribed to convert with tools and blankets, as well as by less direct benefits. Their Christianity could be seen as a mere means to an end – literacy for example, or access to books for themselves. Early on, books were sometimes considered to be useful held upside down – magic talismans. In 1842, a Taranaki man offered a pig for a Bible; in 1849, a Wairau woman offered sex for one.[34] Such things, combined with God as currency and tattooed Madonnas, can give the impression that Maori engagement with Christianity was mercenary or superficial, and several European observers harboured such suspicions. 'Though Christianity has been embraced very extensively yet many are under the bondage of fear with regard to maori gods and maori witchcraft and maori tapu. Perhaps of many it might truly be said . . . They served the Lord and feared their own gods.'[35] But as a settler observed in 1857, too tight a definition of Christianity would leave few 'real' European Christians either.[36]

Mercenary and superficial conversion did occur, especially in the 1830s, but on balance the evidence suggests that, by the 1840s, Maori engagement with Christianity was real, deep and broad. By the 1850s, over 60 per cent of Maori counted themselves as Christians,[37] and I do not dispute their claim. Whether their Christianity was what the European missionaries hoped is another matter.

A Maori conversion *of* Christianity was apparent from the first. Not only was it used as a means for obtaining literacy and mana, but it was also adjusted by its Maori missionaries. European missionaries like Williams sometimes expressed horror at this, but more often the differences were glossed over. In 1830, as we have seen, evangelism in New Zealand was taking too long to bear fruit in the eyes of the British organisations funding it. There was talk of abandoning the attempt to convert an 'incorrigible and irreclaimable race'.[38] European missionaries in New Zealand needed successes, and there was an incentive not to inquire too closely into their nature. Thereafter, the soul race between the three missions gathered force, and missionaries were not inclined to be excessively rigorous about their own scores, though they constantly criticised the laxity of their rivals.

This European rivalry intersected with the height of the Maori one. Maori Christians were more willing to present their faith in a form European missionaries would accept to attract mission stations and their associated benefits, including a reputation for welcoming Pakeha and their trade. Both sides bent their definitions towards each other sufficiently for a European-style conversion to appear to have taken place. In the 1850s, at times varying from region to region, Maori enthusiasm for missions declined. This was partly because, as with any other currency of rivalry, saturation point had been reached. Missionaries, like muskets, ceased to be as useful for asserting superior mana when everybody had them. But another factor may have been a growing Maori desire to distinguish themselves from Europe, in religion as in other things.

Catholicism and Methodism had long been used by Maori as 'denominations of dissent' – ideologies that helped distinguish one group from another. There are many cases of a Maori group adopting one of the secondary denominations to help mark itself off from Anglican rivals, and sometimes also to emphasise autonomy from Pakeha state and society.[39] Catholicism enjoyed a spasm of popularity in the early 1840s, partly for this reason and partly because it was somewhat more willing to incorporate Maori tradition than its rivals. When one Methodist missionary asked a Maori why he had opted for Catholicism in 1841, the reply was: 'Why . . . their religion is good *because they are not afraid of sin*.' The emphasis is Anglican.[40] Pompallier even made an attempt to co-opt Maui, allegedly telling some Ngai Tahu that 'Hine, the wife of the Maori god Maui, was the Virgin Mary'.[41] This put Maui in direct competition with God the Father for the paternity of Christ, and whether

Catholicism incorporated Mauism in Maori minds, or the other way around, is a moot point.

Catholicism and Methodism were not the only denominations of dissent available. There were also a surprising number of home-grown ones. The most important of these 'prophetic' movements emerged from 1862, when Taranaki's Te Ua Haumene began developing his remarkable Pai Marire, or 'Good and Peaceful', religion, also known as Hauhau. Important subsequent movements included those of Te Whiti and Tohu of Parihaka; of the great prophet-generals Titokowaru and Te Kooti; the Tariao and Pao Miere movements in and around Waikato; and Te Maiharoa's movement in the South Island in the 1870s. But prophetic movements actually pre-dated the 1860s, in considerable bulk.

The best-known early movement was that of Papahurihia, or Te Atua Wera, a young tohunga attached to both northern and western sections of Nga Puhi. His influential cult emerged in 1833, but there is some evidence of a widespread movement evangelising a new god, Wheawheau, as early as 1822. Apart from Papahurihia, several other prophets and movements appeared in Northland and elsewhere in the 1830s and 1840s, including the so-called 'Warea Delusion', or Tikanga Hou (New Doctrine), in Taranaki in 1845. The most widespread movement, or group of movements, appears to have been that known variously as Kai Ngarara (Eat Lizard), Wahi Tapu (Sacred Places) or Whakanoa (Deconsecrate), whose most obvious feature was the removal of tapu through deconsecrating rituals, such as eating demonic lizards. There may be analogies with African 'witchcraft eradication' movements. Kai Ngarara emerged in Taranaki in the early 1850s under the leadership of Tamati Te Ito, who believed that the accidental breaching of tapu was a cause of disease. His answer was to remove tapu, not to enforce it; his religion offered much more than good physical health; and it seems to have spread far and wide. In all, over 50 nineteenth-century Maori prophetic movements can be documented, and the actual number was probably greater. A substantial minority of these pre-dated the 1860s.[42]

Modern historians have tended to interpret the prophetic movements as desperate 'revivalist' responses to crippling impact and conquest, and as syncretic cults that merged Christianity with traditional Maori beliefs. There is something in each view – Kai Ngarara, for example, was partly a response to disease – but both underestimate the bulk and duration of these religious developments. They often preceded conquest and crippling impact, even in the particular times and places that such things did occur. They were numerous and enduring enough to suggest a general relationship with both Christianity and tradition, but the myths of fatal impact and conversion are not it. Until recently, historians have also underestimated the biblicalism of prophetic movements such as Pai Marire, which some scholars now describe as an 'orthodox' Christian church similar to Pentecostalism.[43] This is, I think, going too far.

Traditional features persisted even in Pai Marire; there were novel elements outside both Maori and European Christian traditions; written Maori was literally a biblical language, learned from the Bible, and the use of biblical forms in it may exaggerate the biblical content. Describing Pai Marire and other movements as 'Christian churches' is legitimate in a sense, but it reflects a broadening late twentieth-century European definition of Christianity, bringing it more into line with nineteenth-century Maori definitions. It should not be allowed to obscure the extent to which nineteenth-century Maori and European Christianities differed. But it remains true that even the most traditionalist prophetic movements had Christian elements. Hakopa Nikau, the prophet of Tikanga Hou in 1845, sent the missionaries and their books away and believed that there was 'no Bible, no sin, no Sabbath, no hell, no devil', but still maintained that his religion was Christian.[44] Titokowaru, who revived ritual cannibalism and the worship of the ancient god Uenuku, had his twelve apostles and ended his letters: 'Arise, that you may be baptised, that your sins may be washed away, and call upon the name of the Lord.'[45]

There was also a sense in which the prophetic movements were biblical but not Christian. At least half the movements aligned themselves with Judaism; for example, by calling themselves 'Hurai', or Jews, and by shifting the Sabbath to Saturday.[46] Again, this point can be overstated and over-Europeanised. Monogenist European missionaries quite often suggested that Maori were degenerate descendants of one of the lost tribes of Israel – Marsden's evidence for 'Semitic Maori' included the fact that they were avid traders.[47] Maori Judaism has been attributed to this missionary hint. But such plagiarism was unnecessary. Judaism is the Bible's obvious alternative religion, its obvious denomination of dissent, and Maori were quite capable of deducing this for themselves. Substantial chunks of the Old Testament did not become available in Maori until 1840. But snippets were translated and published before this; oral transmission of Old Testament stories must have occurred; and Jews are not absent from the New Testament. Maori biblicalism was shifted from Christ and towards Jehovah. This did not mean straight conversion to Judaism any more than to Christianity, but it did distance the new Maori religion from its European cousin.

The content of the prophetic movements was new, though it drew heavily on the Bible, but newness is not so clear of the prophetic mechanism itself. There were prophets – matakite, or seers – before contact, and it was argued in Chapter Four that pre-contact religion must have undergone many changes. It may be that the normal mechanism for making these changes was a 'prophet'. For the post-contact prophets, prophecy itself was often less important than a role as the 'mouthpiece' or medium of a new god, or a fresh aspect of God. The term 'prophet' is conventional and convenient, but it may be something of a misnomer. Perhaps the key function of prophets, both before and after contact, was to adjust the supernatural to match changes in the social and natural worlds. How far this differed from the role of normal tohunga, or priests, is an interesting question, to which the answer may be: not very far.

Another intriguing feature of the prophetic movements was the links and similarities among them, which were quite strong despite many variations. Papahurihia had some influence outside Northland, had successor prophets in the 1880s and 1890s, and has followers to this day.[48] Before the 1860s, missionaries used 'Papahurihianism' as a general name for Maori heresies, as they saw them. Their denigration was misplaced, but their sense that the movements had much in common was not. Taranaki appears to have been the Maori Palestine, perhaps because it was a kind of mixing place for Maori and European influences – strongly independent yet interacting heavily with Europe. Te Ua's Pai Marire, the archetypal prophetic movement, had roots in Kai Ngarara. 'The truth may be that the Hauhau faith absorbed Kaingarara.'[49]

Pai Marire in turn merged into subsequent movements, converting the Maori King in 1864 and influencing his own religion, Tariao, which was formally established in the 1870s and is often seen as a development of Pai Marire. Te Whiti, Tohu and Titokowaru also saw themselves as successors of Te Ua, and there were many variants of Pai Marire in both the North and South Islands. 'The mode of worship common to both movements suggests that the movement led by Te Maiharoa was a southern manifestation of the Hauhau faith.'[50] Each prophet struck his own balance between old and new, and I do not wish to understate their differences – it was the differences that enabled them to function as denominations of dissent, distinguishing one Maori group from another. Yet, at the broadest level of analysis, they seem to have been variations on a similar theme – different manifestations of a single new Maori religion. This religion may have extended beyond the prophetic movements.

Some prophets had links with biblical denominations of dissent. It is difficult to cut through missionary rhetoric on this issue – Anglicans, Methodists and Catholics regularly blamed each other for Maori heresy. But a whole host of Taranaki prophets had Wesleyan backgrounds – Tamati Te Ito, Te Ua, Titokowaru and Te Whiti all did time as Methodist preachers, possibly together. Papahurihia and Kingite religion had Catholic links. Papahurihia welcomed Bishop Pompallier as his 'younger brother' and declared himself both Catholic and Papahurihian.[51] Te Kooti's Ringatu Church considered itself to be very closely related to Anglicanism, distinguishing itself from other movements by dissenting from dissent. Judaic elements are apparent in the teachings of a great many prophets, and sometimes appeared without prophets. Ultimately, one has to wonder whether there was much difference between Maori Christianity, as practised out of sight of European missionaries, and the prophetic movements. There is something very similar about the early Maori Christian missionaries and the prophets. The former usually stayed just below the threshold at which European missionaries cried 'heretic'; the latter just above.

In sum, what we may have here is a new Maori religion of many variants, which converted European Christianity as much as it was converted by it. There were elements of syncretism, the merging of old and new, but this can be exaggerated. The conversion of Christianity by Maori was not solely a matter of retaining elements of tradition, but of developing non-European interpretations of Christianity, non-Christian interpretations of the Bible, and new elements that were neither traditional, nor Christian nor biblical. Europeans were separated from their God as they had been from their technology, and literacy was especially important here. Literate Maori, and groups that had literate members, did not need European missionaries to interpret the Bible for them.

This conversion of conversion can be seen as having five key components: European missionary Christianity; Maori Christianity, which fluctuated in both its content and the degree to which its difference was obvious to Europeans; Maori biblicalism, with a non-Christian emphasis on the Old Testament and Judaism; the numerous 'prophetic' movements; and a tendency to float between or simultaneously adhere to two or more of these positions. In 1877, an Anglican missionary observed that Tariao and Ringatu in the Bay of Plenty 'appear to be on the best of terms and do not show any feelings or bitterness towards those who adopt the rival form, nor even to those who still adhere to us. Te Kooti's people do not object to joining our service, and will allow us to preach to them.'[52]

All five components appear to have been present from the 1830s; they were not sequential developments. But the cohesion of their Maori content, and the extent to which their form was prominent in European eyes, changed over time. In the 1830s and 1840s, the rush phase of conversion, Maori and missionary definitions of Christianity bent towards each other, and Maori were acclaimed as instant converts. Between the 1850s and the 1880s, the definitions diverged, and Maori appeared to apostatise. Most European missionary activity was abandoned during the wars of the 1860s, but when the missionaries returned they found that Maori Christianity had survived well, but differently, without them. At one level, the shift was more in European perception than Maori content. But at another, there was an increasing merging of Maori religion from the 1850s into something quite close to a distinguishing and unifying ideology. Denominations of dissent, biblical or prophetic, were used less to distinguish one Maori group from another, and more to distinguish Maori as a whole from Pakeha. The development of a shared collective identity was very far from universal among Maori. But it was potentially revolutionary, and it had important political and military as well as religious manifestations.

Land and Law

Grey and his state backed the push to Christianise and commercialise Maori, and supplemented it with a modest welfare programme. Many Maori took advantage of the hospitals, schools and gifts of seed, tools and equipment that he provided or subsidised. Literacy spread with Christianity, to the point where it has been suggested that Maori literacy rates were higher than Pakeha.[53] While this may be an exaggeration, it is certain that thousands of Maori could read and write very well in their own language by the 1850s. European officials and magistrates were often accepted and welcomed, even in some inland districts distant from clusters of Pakeha settlement. 'The coming of "the law" was hailed as enthusiastically as the coming of the gospel.'[54] But these officials were welcomed as mediators, ambassadors and settlers, valuable in themselves, not as rulers.

Outside the major settlements, to which police were mainly restricted, Pakeha law lacked coercive power and worked only when Maori let it. They did so quite often – where it intersected with Maori law; where it dealt with new problems in a way that satisfied Maori; where it proved convenient in settling Maori–European disputes; and sometimes perhaps even for its own sake. But, even in the late 1860s, when the power balance had shifted considerably in favour of the Pakeha, a great many Maori did not consider themselves obliged to obey Pakeha law when it did not suit. A pro-government chief, of Kauae in South Taranaki, told proudly in 1867 of allowing Pakeha law to try an adultery case and fine the offender £5. 'He declined to pay, of course, but British law was welcome at Kauae.'[55] In 1869, an Auckland journal waxed sarcastic about Maori immunity to the law.

> I would I were a Maori
> To be above the law;
> To row, and fight, and yell, and shout,
> and give the policeman jaw! . . .
> Then I would I were a Maori
> To do whate'er I choose
> Without the dread of magistrates
> Or those detested 'blues'.[56]

The law's grip on Maori was even more limited before the 1860s. Even in large towns, there was some reluctance to arrest them, for fear of retaliation or rescue parties. There were many cases of Maori being released from gaol through some form of chiefly pressure, even in large Pakeha towns, and even as late as 1868.[57] Outside such towns, Maori acceptance of European law was purely voluntary. A Maori seeking compensation from a Pakeha for an offence remarked, 'I want no European law, I am tired of that; I will take the Maori law for it.'[58] Maori law was sometimes applied to Pakeha, especially where small numbers of settlers lived among Maori majorities – swamping in reverse. It was noted in 1860 that 'at various places the Natives have seized vessels belonging to Europeans, for real or imaginary offences, and extorted money from the parties, without the slightest reference to the properly constituted authorities of the Colony'.[59] Settlers complained bitterly and frequently about such incidents and about Maori immunity to British law. Crime statistics seem to bear out the substance, though not the justice, of their complaints. In 1858, the Maori rate of assault and drunkenness convictions in Pakeha courts ran at 4.2 and 2.7 per cent of the Pakeha rate.[60] 'The Natives generally consider themselves an independent nation, and not amenable to British law.'[61]

The Maori system of social control, like Maori religion, may have been changing as a result of contact. While there were still killings for witchcraft and adultery, together with lethal tribal feuds, into the 1860s and beyond, the number may have been diminishing, and adapted versions of European ideas might be grafted on to customary law. A 33-article code of laws was circulating among Waikato Maori by 1864. It forbade murder, feuding and some other customary practices, just as British law would have liked. But it was rather unBritish in that almost half its articles dealt with sexual conduct. They licensed sex between unmarried women and men, and decried, but specified no punishment for, sex between unmarried men. 'If an unmarried man sins with another unmarried man they must cling to the faith and the provision of the Law.'[62] Maori legal systems may have been in flux, but the flux clearly did not amount to the imposition of British law on most Maori.

On the other hand, outside regions that had achieved arm's-length interaction, land selling proceeded apace. Between 1846 and 1853, the golden age of Pakeha land buying, Grey and his master land buyer Donald McLean purchased no less than 32.6 million acres – just under half the whole country. The price paid averaged less than a halfpenny per acre.[63] This seemed conclusive evidence that conversion was working like a charm. Maori were falling over themselves to sell land cheaply, contributing to a spread of settlement that gave more and more Pakeha exemplars and neighbours, and forced and tempted Maori into ever-closer engagement with the Pakeha economy. Land selling had become a currency of rivalry – indeed, almost an addiction in some cases. But several factors meant that this vast alienation was not what it seemed.

First, the tacit price discussed in the last chapter meant that land sale made more sense, and disadvantaged Maori less, than low overt prices suggest. Few Maori intended to sell the whole of their land, but only to sow a part of it in settlers. While partnership with these settlers remained at rough parity, they did receive a substantial tacit price for their land in the form of economic interaction with their new neighbours. Second, definitions of the extent and timing of the sales were contestable, and, as with the price, Maori were often able to impose their definitions rather than accept Pakeha ones. This factor interlocked with a third – some forms of Maori and Pakeha land use were not incompatible. Fourth, there was a major distortion embedded in the gross figures for land sold compared with land retained, and for Pakeha numbers compared with Maori.

There are many cases in which Maori and Pakeha differed over the extent of land sales and on the residual rights of the sellers. At the places and times at which Maori had the power, it was their definition that prevailed. When the balance of local power shifted in favour of the Pakeha, through conquest or the threat of it, or through swamping, they were able to impose their definitions. This happened in the 1840s in and around some large settlements. The troops, or their swamping substitute, arrived much later elsewhere. Until they did, the Maori definition of the extent and nature of land sales – of areas that had been reserved, for example, for continued Maori use – held considerable sway. The vast tracts of land sold did not turn wholly white instantly. Like empire itself, land sales could be myths on maps. Nominal alienation took place the day the deed was signed; *substantive* alienation took place the day Maori customary use ceased, and the gap between the two could be decades long.

The early sheep stations of the 1840s and 1850s joined whaling, trading, timber and mission stations, and there were more similarities than mere name. Sheep stations, too, often relied on the co-operation of local Maori. The early Wairarapa pastoralists could not have run flocks if Ngati Kahungunu had not wanted them to – 'we wish for some white people to feed sheep' – and had not supplied food, labour, building materials and, above all, free land. 'On most stations trade with the Maoris . . . would have brought in additional cash income.' Some pastoralists contracted informal marriage alliances with their Maori neighbours, like whaling station masters before them.[64] Ngati Kahungunu were also the midwives of pastoralism in Hawke's Bay. Even in Canterbury and Otago, where the Maori population was thinner and the Crown the main landlord, Maori food supplies and labour were important on some stations.[65] There was an Old New Zealand dimension to what was territorially the main form of the spread of New New Zealand settlement: extensive pastoralism.

As with whaling and timber, the basis of this collaboration was that Maori and Pakeha land use was compatible in the short term. Early pastoralism was so very extensive, a few thousand sheep to a hundred thousand acres, that meeting a sheep must have been quite an event. Grazing sheep, spread very thin, did not preclude hunting and gathering on the same land. Burning-off might reduce weka populations, but introductions of new game – pigs and wild cattle – might help compensate for this. Herbert Guthrie-Smith did not particularly like his Ngati Kahungunu landlords pig hunting on 'his' Hawke's Bay sheep station as late as the 1880s, but he could not do much about it, and graciously accepted the inevitable.[66] South Island runholders were less gracious about continued Maori use, but it persisted until late in the nineteenth century. Seasonal weka hunting in the Mackenzie Country, for example, long co-existed with pastoralism and only ceased in 1895 'because rabbit poison had devastated the weka population'.[67] The spread of sheep did not automatically imply the demise of traditional land use, any more than the vast land 'sales' did. It was only when the runholders began to fence and freehold that Maori ceased to seek plants, birds, eels and pigs in and around the sheep runs. It was only then that nominal alienation became substantive. We will see in Chapter Fourteen that the end of a sheep-rush phase of rapidly expanding but very extensive pastoralism can be dated to the late 1860s. Thereafter, pastoralists progressively began to convert nature, to intensify their land use: freeholding, fencing, sowing introduced grasses to replace native ones, and running more and more stock per hectare. This ratcheting-up of the intensity of pastoralism progressively reduced the compatibility of Maori and Pakeha land use, but the process was not completed until about 1900.

These factors applied with special force to South Island Maori. Between 1844 and 1860, virtually the whole of their vast island was sold off.[68] Shady deals and competitive selling by Ngai Tahu chiefs were important factors, but contested definitions were also significant. Some historians still interpret Ngai Tahu history in terms of victim ideology, and it may be correct that the South Island is the place where the myths of fatal impact and conversion came most nearly and quickly true. But Ngai Tahu coped well with their Old New Zealand neighbours up to 1848, and even after the foundations of the Otago and Canterbury settlements in 1848 and 1850, partnerships with some degree of parity was maintained.[69] Trade with the new settlements compensated for the loss of the land that settlers actually occupied, and Maori continued to use nominally sold land that settlers did not occupy (or used only for very extensive pastoralism), for hunting and gathering.

In the 1860s, however, two developments gave Pakeha both the power and the need to shift definitions. The gold rushes quickly boosted the Pakeha population to swamping levels, and the very extensive phase of pastoralism was succeeded by the pasture-conversion phase. It was at this stage that sheep farming clashed with Maori seasonal use. Had this happened earlier, when the Otago and Canterbury settlers were still below the swamping threshold, Ngai Tahu would still have had the power to do something about it. In the 1850s, they had disputed the exclusive Pakeha use of 'alienated' land and definitions of the extent of sales with some success, and forced some runholders to pay Maori rental as well as Crown rental.[70] But gold-boosted Pakeha numbers were so relatively huge that Ngai Tahu lost the power of effective resistance or valued collaboration, and the power to very successfully contest definitions. The declining curve of Ngai Tahu relative power and the rising curve of Pakeha power and need intersected in the late 1860s, finally making the vast sales substantive and turning false empire in the interior of the South Island into real.

Apart from the immediate vicinity of Auckland and Wellington townships, the South Island is the best case for the thesis that Pakeha achieved dominance over Maori before the 1860s. Even here, the thesis may be false. But even if it is not, we have to take account of a subtle reshaping that is part of the myth of conversion. Auckland and Wellington towns and the South Island made up over 60 per cent of the country in terms of acres, but only ten per cent in terms of Maori. The two-thirds of New Zealand nominally alienated by 1861 was mainly in the South Island. Less than a quarter of the North Island had been sold by 1861. The same sleight of mind is still regularly applied to population figures. One day in 1859, the total Pakeha population overtook the Maori. By 1861, 100,000 Pakeha heavily outnumbered 60,000 Maori. But three-quarters of these Pakeha were in Auckland, Wellington and the South Island, together with something like a sixth of Maori. Elsewhere, in main Maoridom, 50,000 Maori interacted with 25,000 Pakeha. Here, Maori had the power to impose their definition of consent, or at least to force Pakeha to negotiate with it, and to indicate clearly to posterity what it was.

At the broadest level, it was a partnership between two autonomous spheres, one ruled by governors and governments, the other by chiefs and tribes, jointly policing the interface. At the local level, the nature of particular partnerships varied, from very close to very distant, and from Pakeha seniority in the relationship to Maori seniority. In the archetypal middle was rough parity, a twinning but not merging of town and tribe. Until the 1860s, as far as most Maori were concerned, the British empire over them was false. Contact – ongoing interaction – was real and substantial, but empire was not.

CHAPTER TEN

Conquest?

The wars of the 1840s firmed up the boundaries between Maori and Pakeha spheres, and set limits on their interference with each other. With varying degrees of recognition, rage and reluctance, governors and settlers tacitly, and sometimes explicitly, conceded that Queen Victoria's writ did not run outside the European settlements. 'They respect our laws and customs,' wrote the new Governor, Colonel Thomas Gore Browne, in 1856, 'but do not consider the former to extend beyond the lands alienated to us.' He expressed polite surprise at the discrepancy between this situation and 'the reports generally circulated in England'. 'Sir George Grey was perhaps led to view their condition in too favourable a light, and often spoke of a future rather than an actual state.'[1] Four years later, Browne noted that the situation remained the same. 'English law has always prevailed in the English settlements, but remains a dead letter beyond them' – namely, in about 80 per cent of the North Island.[2] As a perceptive contemporary noted, these were 'strange words for the Governor of New Zealand to have to use twenty years after the Treaty of Waitangi'.[3] Some settlers were more blunt. 'It is absurd to talk any longer about such shams as the nominal supremacy of the Crown.'[4] But despite sporadic tensions and frictions at the interface, New Zealand's two spheres – the British colony and independent Aotearoa – got along surprisingly well. Between 1847 and 1860, there was not only peace but also a degree of co-operation between Maori and Pakeha spheres, in economics in particular. Yet, thereafter, co-operation collapsed into conflict: the long and bitter wars of the 1860s.

The outbreak of these wars was triggered by the sale of some Waitara land in Taranaki to the Crown by a junior Ati Awa chief, Teira, against the wishes of the senior chief, Wiremu Kingi Te Rangitake. War ravaged Taranaki in 1860–61, and erupted anew in 1863 when George Grey, who returned for his second spell as governor in 1861, invaded the Waikato heartland of the Maori King Movement. Warfare continued to 1872, developing into a bewildering series of intersecting conflicts spread over much of the North Island and involving most Maori. Broadly, however, the wars of the 1860s can be grouped into two: mass conflict in Taranaki and Waikato, 1860–61 and 1863–64, in which the principal combatants were the Maori King Movement and the British Empire; and the numerous and diverse campaigns of 1864–72, which pitted Maori resisters, often the followers of prophets, against colonial soldiers and 'kupapa' – Maori fighting on the government side.

The causes of this catastrophe in ethnic relations have been the subject of historical debate.[5] One view, that the wars were about sovereignty, is true enough but does not really explain their outbreak. Why did the British suddenly become unwilling to share sovereignty in 1860, when they had done so, however much they begrudged and papered over the fact, for the previous twenty years? Another view, dating from 1860 and still influential, is that these were 'Land Wars': Pakeha desire to obtain Maori land plus Maori desire to retain it equals war. There are at least two problems with this. First, there was no overall shortage of land available to Pakeha, who had much more land than they could use. Millions of acres sold by Maori to the Crown had yet to be sold to settlers. Pakeha owned about twenty times as much land per capita in 1860 as they do now. Most of it was in the South Island, it was very unevenly distributed and much of it was only nominally alienated. But even in relatively crowded New Plymouth and Auckland, the hot seats of settler pressure for land, there were many thousands of Crown acres available for settlement. These towns did want particular key pieces of Maori land – not only for the land itself but because the Maori hold on it was thought to block the manifest destiny of each settlement. New Plymouth settlers could have gone to the South Island for land in 1860, as many had to do afterwards, but doing so would have ended hopes of a 'Great Future' for New Plymouth. We will see in Chapter Twelve that Great Futures were key myths of Pakeha settlement, individual as well as collective aspirations. More importantly, it was not New Plymouth and Auckland that fought the Taranaki and Waikato Wars, or made the crucial decision to fight them. Local settlers had the motives, but they did not have the means. The second problem with the 'Land Wars' view is that many of the groups that supported the war – the South Island settlers, most missionaries, the governors, the Australian colonies and, above all, the imperial government – were clearly not motivated primarily by the desire for Maori land.

The imperial government was to some extent manipulated into war – not so much by Browne or his alleged settler puppet-masters in the Taranaki War, as by Grey in the Waikato War. But successful manipulation owed less to land greed or clever conspiracy than to the myths of empire, which motivated Browne, Grey and other pro-war groups, and inclined the imperial government to succumb to their pressure for troops. Like that in 1840, the final stage of British intervention in 1863 was a matter of the tail wagging the dog by using the ganglion of shared mythology, which also stimulated the wag reflex in the tail. The precedents and prophecies of empire and settlement, the self-images of governors and settlers, the ethos of a colonising and progressive race, demanded that the British rule the whole of New Zealand in fact as well as name. To people subject to the myths of empire, and to hardening racial ideologies, there was something unnatural, unEuropean, about white communities living in equal partnership with blacks. If New Zealand had contained no land at all, and Pakeha and Maori had both been societies of boat people, these ideologies might still have pressured the former to assert their sway over the latter.

Those distant from the ethnic interface, in London or the South Island towns, could believe that real empire over Maori existed in 1860, and that Maori resistance was a reactionary and aggressive rebellion that had to be suppressed. Between 1861 and 1863, Grey pumped reports into London alleging a widespread Maori conspiracy to attack Auckland. Like Busby's fatal impact reports in 1837–38, these sometimes stretched credulity, or should have. Among Grey's evidence of aggressive Maori intent, enclosed in a despatch of 7 December 1861, was a story told to Henry Monro by a Maori who wished to be known as Whare ('House'), earlier in the year, after he had 'freely helped himself' to hard liquor. Whare claimed that 'almost every chief of note' among the Kingites, including Wiremu Tamihana, had 'entered into a plot to attack Auckland', and had already cut a road through the bush for the purpose. All the French missionaries were involved too, he added, settling to his bottle. 'Bishop Pompallier and Father Garavel not only approved of it, but had instigated it.' The Franco-Maori plan was to 'clear off all the English' and invite the French to take possession. Perhaps in response to a query, Whare noted that the French in Auckland were to secretly mark their houses and so be spared. Nga Puhi were to strike Auckland simultaneously in support of their hereditary enemies, Waikato. The conversation lasted from 11 p.m. to 3 a.m., and a good time was had by all.[6]

Other evidence of Kingite conspiracy was more convincing, though still false. Grey was able to portray his invasion of Waikato in 1863 as a pre-emptive strike, aimed at a last-ditch stand against the march of progress by savages whose convertibility had unfortunately been overestimated. There were a few dissenting voices, notably that of Archdeacon Octavius Hadfield, who borrowed lines from a British periodical to describe Grey's justification for invasion. 'Nothing is more revolting than to have the oppressor attributing, with sanctimonious self-complacency, the evil consequences of oppression to the natural depravity of the oppressed.'[7] But the myths and precedents of empire predisposed London to believe Grey.

The façade of empire was harder to accept for those on the spot, governors and North Island settlers, on whose doorsteps independent Maori still fought tribal wars and laughed at or flirted with the law as it suited them. Until the later 1850s, however, swamping, apparent conversion, and land selling made it seem as though real empire was gradually and peacefully replacing false. New land sales occurred; old land sales shifted from nominal towards substantive;

the Maori neighbours of large settlements were swamped by scarcely perceptible degrees. The Pakeha sphere grew; the Maori sphere shrank; and Maori independence could be seen as an irritating but passing feature of a period of transition. False empire, the illusion and prospect of control, acted as a placebo for the reality of Maori independence. But in the later 1850s, developments punctured the illusion and seemed to give Maori autonomy prospects of permanence. This was unacceptable to the myths of empire.

The Rise of Pan-Tribalism

The 1850s saw the emergence of three pan-tribal movements. Two – the Kai Ngarara religious movement and an 'anti-land selling', or landholding, movement – originated in Taranaki around 1850. The nature of these movements is shadowy and disputed, and their connection is unclear, but the time and place of their origin suggests some link. Landholding was probably not a tight and formal alliance or 'league'. It was so described by the settlers to smear it by association with such discreditable things as Chartism and trade unions.[8] But an alliance of Taranaki tribes against land selling, and a loosely linked landholding sentiment embracing other tribes, did grow and broaden in the 1850s. Among the most interesting things about it was that it originated with tribes who had sold virtually no land, who objected not only to prospective local sales but to other tribes selling their land. Kai Ngarara, whatever its religious character, also had pan-tribal elements. Its leader, Tamati Te Ito, stated that 'we wanted to combine all the Maori people from Mokau to Patea in one body'.[9] Kai Ngarara helped lay the groundwork for Pai Marire in the 1860s, which was also emphatically pan-tribal, and landholding sentiment performed a similar service for the third 1850s development: the King Movement.[10]

A series of large intertribal meetings from 1854 culminated in the inauguration of the great Waikato chief and Musket Wars general Potatau Te Wherowhero as Maori King in 1858. Wiremu Tamihana, 'the Kingmaker', of the Ngati Haua tribe of Waikato was also a leading figure. The prominence of Waikato or Tainui tribes in the leadership, and in the great war between King and British Empire in 1863–64, has combined with subsequent developments to give the impression that the movement was largely a Waikato phenomenon. But from the outset, tribes from elsewhere supported the King Movement. During the Waikato War, a minimum of fifteen of 26 major North Island tribal groups are estimated to have sent contingents to fight for the King, and several others provided some kind of support. It was clearly not kinship, traditional alliances or immediate self-interest that drew in most of these tribes. 'I and my people,' said a Tuhoe chief before leaving for distant Waikato, 'will march to show sympathy for the island in trouble.'[11] Pan-tribalism on this scale was unprecedented in Maoridom; its emergence requires explanation.

Aotearoa in 1769 was a monolingual world. There was no person in it who did not share language with all others. To Maori, Europeans must instantly have constituted a newer order of strangeness than was the case with peoples who had no previous experience of linguistic difference, analogous to the arrival of alien beings who communicated by sign language or telepathy. Collective names for the new Them came into use: 'strange people', 'white people', 'ship people'. Despite the heavy Pakeha emphasis on Englishness and Britishness, 'European' was often their local self-designation, and still is, and this could conceivably reflect Maori influence. Europe, 'Uropi', was easier to transliterate than England, 'Ingarangi'. 'Pakeha' was in use by 1814. The origins of the word are disputed. One historian, possibly tongue in cheek, has suggested that it was a transliteration of 'bugger you' – 'a term of endearment amongst sailors'.[12] But 'Pakepakeha', or 'pale-skinned fairies', is a more likely source. 'Pakepakeha' were 'imaginary beings resembling men, with fair skins'.[13] Pakeha who find such origins offensive can comfort themselves with two considerations. First, Maori visiting Australia in 1815 were greeted by Aboriginals with the words 'Bougerree you, bougerree you!', optimistically translated as 'Very good you'.[14] This may mean that, from an Aboriginal viewpoint, Maori were Pakeha too. Second, words are allowed to change their meaning, and they did. Maori in the 1850s used Pakeha to mean all Europeans, for Viennese as well as Aucklanders, but it was increasingly and legitimately co-opted to mean New Zealand European. The term 'New Zealander', in European mouths, shifted from Maori to settler, though we will see in Part Three that the settlers could remain 'British' as well. But they were a local variant of Briton. A Pakeha proto-people began to form and cohere in the mid-nineteenth century, partly by contrasting itself to Maori, and perhaps the reverse was also the case.

The first known use of the term 'Maori' in its modern sense was in 1801, within ten years of the beginning of regular contact, and by the 1830s it was common in Maori mouths.[15] It was also quite common in European mouths, but here it competed with 'New Zealanders' until mid-century. Maori names for the whole country, which may not have existed at all before contact, also came into use. As we have seen when looking at the spread of disease, Maori neighbour zones may have been merging into one by the mid-nineteenth century. Networks of interaction, involving first warfare, then gift giving, visiting and wandering for work, were intersecting across the whole country. The process was still very incomplete in the 1850s, but it was being reinforced by Maori use of Pakeha communications and transport networks, shipping and postal services. Maori were also beginning to share increasingly similar forms of religion, as we have seen, and they also shared a common problem: Pakeha.

Although Maori had quite successfully resisted conquest and converted conversion, there were limits to what they could do about swamping. The direction of change in partnerships in and around Auckland and Wellington towns, pessimistic prototypes, obviously favoured Pakeha. Many Maori from out-regions had visited these towns by the 1850s. Most Maori could still impose their own definitions of price and sale, but there was a tendency for this to become less true over time. Pakeha were gradually eroding Maori definitions of sale and price where they could, which meant that land sale was gradually eroding Maori independence. Some chiefs and groups, still confident in their capacity to impose their definitions, locked in to rivalry through sale or keen to establish close economic interaction by selling to attract settlers, continued to sell. Others, especially where arm's-length economic interaction had been established, and perhaps influenced by a vague but growing sense of Maoriness, turned against land selling. They formed the pan-tribal landholding and King Movements. These organisations were not pan-Maori in the sense that they embraced the whole of Maoridom – this was far from the truth. But they were pan-Maori in the sense that they knew no zonal boundaries. All Maori could theoretically become members. This very embryonic and incomplete sense of collective identity also stemmed from contrasting Us to Them – a vague sense of shared unEuropeanness.

Tribalism remained immensely important, sometimes compatible with pan-tribalism, sometimes competing with it. Yet pan-tribalism did rise from the 1850s, and it has been downplayed in retrospect, partly because of the myths of empire and their historiographical residues. There is also some tendency among Maori to rank the tribe above all else, and to see Maori unity as a Pakeha invention. That, too, seems to be a retrospective gloss on history. Te Ua Haumene, prophet of Pai Marire, instructed his lieutenants: 'Do not be concerned for your own village. No, be concerned for the whole land.'[16] Wiremu Tamihana sought 'some plan by which the Maori tribes should become united; that they should assemble together and become one, like the Pakehas'.[17] The adherents of Kai Ngarara in the 1850s saw it as a movement that would 'combine all the race together, and become strong to have their own way with the white people'.[18] A 'gradually strengthening feeling of nationality' among Maori was apparent to Donald McLean as early as 1856.[19]

The pan-tribal movements were not necessarily hostile to the Pakeha; they were not declarations of Maori independence – this already existed. 'I do not desire to cast the Queen from this island,' wrote Tamihana, 'but from my piece. I am the person to overlook my piece.'[20] But they, especially the King Movement, did harden Maori independence and raise its profile to a point the myths of empire could not tolerate. They made it too obvious that British empire over Maori was false and necessitated war to make it real. Conversion had failed; time to try conquest.

The Wars of the 1860s

At first, the British hoped that war could be localised in Taranaki, with Maori in general taught subordinacy by particular example: 'condign punishment' for Wiremu Kingi and his few initial supporters. 'By refusing to buy [Waitara],' wrote a colonial politician, 'the evil might have been postponed, but it was sure to break out at some time & in some form & and I do not think a better case or a more timely opportunity could have been selected.'[21] Maori also saw the issue as much broader than Waitara; outside tribes, including the King Movement, swiftly came to Wiremu Kingi's support; and quick, cheap British victory in Taranaki failed to eventuate. Consequently, first Browne in 1861, then Grey in 1863, decided to crush the King Movement directly through the invasion of Waikato.

Military operations in Taranaki lasted from 18 March 1860 to 17 March 1861.[22] To some extent, they were an extension of an Ati Awa civil war of 1854–58, when land-selling and landholding sections of the tribe, the latter helped by the South Taranaki landholding alliance, had fought several engagements. But the military role of the land-selling Ati Awa was insignificant in the Taranaki War; a British army that grew rapidly from 900 to 3,500 troops, mainly imperial, were their proxies. From March, Ati Awa were joined by the landholding South Taranaki tribes; from May, they received limited Kingite support; and from July, large-scale Kingite support, not just from Waikato but also from Tauranga and Taupo. The total number of Maori to serve in the Taranaki War may have exceeded 2,000, but not all were ever available at the same time. Parties constantly came and went for economic reasons. As in the Northern War, the Maori compensated for inferior resources with modern pa, mass producing them by the dozen. These pa acted as bases for Maori raiders, who thoroughly devastated the Pakeha farms outside New Plymouth. The cordon of pa also absorbed British thrusts from New Plymouth until the end of 1860. One pa, Puketakauere, repulsed an attack on 27 June with heavy British loss; another, incomplete, pa at Mahoetahi was taken on 7 November, with heavy Maori loss. Most pa were simply abandoned to expensive British expeditions, and official victory claims over such incidents rang hollow, even at the time.

Sing a song of sixpence
A tale about the war
Four and twenty niggers
Cooped up in a Pa
When the Pa was opened
Not a nigger there was seen
Is not that a jolly tale
To tell before the Queen.[23]

In the new year, a fresh British general, Thomas Pratt, adopted the more promising strategy of countering trench warfare with trench warfare, digging through the pa cordon along the Waitara River, holding the ground gained with strong redoubts, and so threatening the Ati Awa economic base area. A Maori attack on one of the redoubts was bloodily repulsed in February 1861, but in general the Maori merely dug new pa as Pratt dug up the old. Both General Pratt and Governor Browne were forced to conclude that victory in Taranaki was not possible. They were both sacked for this fact and replaced by Grey and Duncan Cameron, an able Scots general with a reputation built in the Crimean War and the reform of army education. Grey and Cameron, whose relationship oscillated between efficient co-operation and bitter feud, made careful preparations for an invasion of Waikato. Armed and armoured steamers were acquired for the Waikato River, the Great South Road and protective forts were built, a supply organisation was established, a military telegraph linked Auckland to 'the Front', and three extra regiments and other reinforcements were prised out of the imperial government. Cameron's revelation to London that Grey's allegedly imminent 'Maori rebellion' had not persuaded the settlers to spend any money on their own defence came too late to stop the flow of imperial resources.[24]

The figures for the British forces in this, the largest of the New Zealand Wars, easily become confusing. The number of imperial troops in New Zealand as a whole rose rapidly from about 8,000 in July 1863 to about 12,000 in May 1864 (counting naval forces serving on land), of whom about three-quarters were available for the Waikato. The colonial government contributed a few hundred colonial regulars – the Forest Rangers and the Colonial Defence Force cavalry – and, briefly, a substantial number of militia and volunteers from Auckland. After October 1863, the latter were progressively replaced by Military Settlers, also known as the Waikato Militia, recruited largely from the Australian and Otago goldfields on the promise of confiscated Maori land. Their numbers eventually reached about 5,000 (including units later recruited for Taranaki and Hawke's Bay), but little more than half of these were useful in the Waikato War. Counting replacements for the ten British infantry regiments, and a few hundred pro-British Waikato and Arawa, the total British mobilisation or turnover in New Zealand as a whole was well over 20,000; the Waikato mobilisation about 18,000, and the Waikato peak strength about 14,000. We simply do not know the resisting Maori strength, but a mobilisation of around 5,000 and a peak of 2,000 or 3,000 is a reasonable guess. The Maori high command, in which Tamihana and two Ngati Maniapoto chiefs, Rewi Maniapoto and Tawhana Tikaokao, were prominent, was shadowy and informal, but effective, especially given Maori traditions of competitive disunity. In the context of colonial wars generally, these forces were quite large; in the New Zealand context they were enormous.

The invasion commenced, promisingly for the British, with a small victory at Koheroa in July 1863. But their advance was held up for three months by a group of modern pa centred on Meremere, and by a Maori campaign against Cameron's line of communications. These pa were not contiguous, but they were a defensive 'line' in the sense that they supported each other in blocking the British advance. When Cameron finally assembled enough men both to protect his communications and take Meremere, the Maori simply abandoned it, eliciting a crescendo of frustration from the settler press. But it was now that the new British advantage, a large and constant inflow of resources, began to make itself felt.

In the Northern and Taranaki Wars, the British had made sporadic expeditions from a base, leaving the Maori some time to disperse, recoup themselves and reassemble in between. Cameron, however, was able to mount a continuous offensive, and he caught the Maori army only half reassembled at Rangiriri, the second Waikato defensive 'line', on 20 November. Cameron's army was able to storm a lightly held part of the extensive Rangiriri fortifications, but seven assaults against the rest failed, with 130 casualties. The Maori partly evacuated the pa, which was never surrounded, in the night. A rearguard, playing for time in the hope of reinforcements, or genuinely attempting to negotiate, raised a white flag of truce – something Maori had done previously in the Taranaki War. Cameron chose to interpret the flag as one of surrender. After some confusion, 180 warriors were made prisoner and incarcerated on Grey's Kawau Island off the Northland coast, from which they escaped in 1864. Cameron pushed on south up the Waikato and occupied the King's capital of Ngaruawahia in December. Grey hoped the Maori would submit, but Ngaruawahia had no great military or economic significance, and they did not. Instead, they fortified the third and greatest 'Waikato Line', an awesome constellation of modern pa centred on Paterangi.

This defensive system would have done well on the Western Front in World War One, and Cameron – whose insight into the modern pa system exceeded that of his contemporaries – had no illusions about his inability to storm it. But chance in the form of a Maori guide, coupled with a capacity for boldness with which Cameron was not generally credited, enabled him to outflank it in February 1864 – marching 1,200 British regulars through the bush at night, unseen and unheard by nearby Maori scouts. This force sacked the important Maori town of Rangiaowhia, killing some non-combatants in the process, and withdrew to await the Maori response, which Cameron hoped would be a battle on open ground. With daylight reinforcements bringing his strength to 2,500, Cameron thought he could win. Tamihana agreed with him. Just as Cameron, tacitly and reluctantly, conceded the superiority of Maori in modern pa, so Maori, tacitly and reluctantly, conceded the superiority of British regulars in encounter battles, if only because they were more numerous. The Kingite army withdrew from the Paterangi Line, fighting only a rearguard action at Hairini to cover their evacuation.

The Paterangi operations gave the British one of the three main agricultural heartlands of the Waikato tribes. In retrospect, they were even more decisive – the first permanently damaging defeat suffered by Maori in the New Zealand Wars. A subsequent battle was fought at Orakau between 31 March and 2 April, at which Maori displayed exceptional blundering as well as exceptional heroism. Although beloved of legend, this encounter was much less important than Paterangi in reality. Rewi Maniapoto, an able general who had never wanted to fight from a position that breached the most basic principles of the modern pa system, became the unwilling hero of 'Rewi's Last Stand'.

The Waikato War had no satisfying climax, so two were invented. One was Orakau, which was said to have crushed the King Movement. In fact, further modern pa defended the remaining economic heartlands of Waikato. They were never taken but became the new 'aukati', or boundary, between what became known as the 'King Country' and the Pakeha sphere. The second occurred at Tauranga, to which the Waikato fighting spilled over in 1864. Since late 1863, Cameron had been very much aware that the Kingite forces in Waikato had been receiving ammunition and reinforcements from the south. In November and December, he sent substantial expeditions to Raglan and Thames to cut the flow. But supplies and warriors continued to come to Waikato through Tauranga, and in January 1864 Cameron despatched an expedition to cut that conduit too.

The Tauranga Kingites returned home and, being too few to attack the fortified British camp at Tauranga, sought to provoke an attack on them – by raids, challenges and, eventually, by building a pa right under its nose: the Gate Pa. In late April, despairing of decisive victory in the Waikato, Cameron seized the opportunity to strike a clear-cut blow and led his strategic reserve to Tauranga. The Gate Pa was so close to a port that the British were able to bring an exceptional array of artillery against it – seventeen mortars and cannon, including a modern Armstrong gun throwing shells weighing 110 pounds. These guns opened up on 28 April, and the next day excelled themselves by throwing about a hundred rounds each into and around the Gate Pa. Confident that the garrison had been pounded into ineffectiveness, a storming party of 300 men, with 500 more in close support and 900 more further back, moved in to assault the garrison of 230 men and one woman. Within ten minutes, the stormers were streaming back in utter rout, leaving 100 killed and wounded behind them. The garrison, deafened but safe in anti-artillery bunkers 'like ratholes everywhere, with covered ways and underground chambers', had survived the bombardment, lured the stormers into the pa and shot them down.[25] The Maori collected up the British rifles and left in the night.

British frontal assaults were not as unwise as they seemed to armchair strategists. Because modern pa had escape routes and could not be properly besieged, assaults were virtually the only way of destroying the garrison. But the Gate Pa was enough to convince Cameron that assaults would fail, however careful the preparation and however great the bombardment. The 'decisive blow' that would give the British full and clear-cut victory in the Waikato War was not possible against completed modern pa, 'and if her Majesty's troops are to be detained until one is struck, I confess I see no prospect of their leaving New Zealand'.[26] Although the British at Tauranga won a subsequent battle at Te Ranga in June, rushing an incomplete pa, this was only partial compensation for the disaster at Gate Pa, and there were no further battles in the Waikato War. There was widespread dissatisfaction among contemporary Europeans with the results of the war, and it is tempting to reverse the legend and suggest that Maori secured a limited victory as they had in the Northern War. The only hitch with this is that it would not be true. The thousands of imperial troops and millions of imperial money did succeed in conquering and confiscating around a million acres of Waikato land, in taking Ngaruawahia and Rangiaowhia, and in permanently weakening the power of the King Movement. The British victory was limited but real, and it was a turning point in New Zealand history.[27]

The last imperial campaigns were fought in Wanganui and South Taranaki in 1864–66. The most successful occurred in 1865, when Cameron pushed empire north from Wanganui in a methodical operation, avoiding the modern pa of Weraroa and profiting from a decline in the cohesion and strategy of Maori resistance. South Taranaki Maori, with limited help from the King Movement, fought brave but unwise open battles at Nukumaru and Te Ngaio, and were beaten. A new kind of war emerged in the midst of the old, fought by the adherents of new Maori prophets on the one side, and colonists and kupapa on the other, without much imperial help. Followers of Te Ua and his Pai Marire Church launched three attacks in Taranaki and Wanganui, only one of them successful – an ambush of a detachment of imperial and colonial troops on 6 April 1864. A Pai Marire attack on Sentry Hill redoubt failed the same month, and a descent on Wanganui town was repelled by Lower Whanganui kupapa in May at Moutoa Island. The grateful settlers of Wanganui erected a monument of this event in honour of their Maori protectors. The conflict was becoming rather like a civil war.

Pai Marire missionaries travelled to the East Coast in 1865. Although their intentions may have been peaceful, they were involved in the killing of a missionary, C. S. Volkner, and were seen as a threat by some local chiefs. These chiefs combined with the government to attack the local supporters of Pai Marire. Civil wars among both Ngati Porou and Ngati Kahungunu were superimposed on this, with colonist arms and money giving the kupapa factions the upper hand. By 1867, the complex of conflicts on both east and west coasts had died down. All but one of the imperial regiments were withdrawn. The settlers began to hope that the wars were over, and credited this to superiority of colonial over imperial troops – despite their objections to the departure of the latter. They sometimes forgot to mention their 'native auxiliaries', but kupapa like Ropata Wahawaha of Ngati Porou, Kepa Te Rangihiwinui of Whanganui, and Henare Tomoana of Ngati Kahungunu were key figures in government successes.

In mid-1868, however, Pakeha hopes were dashed by the outbreak of fresh fighting, which flared up on both east coast and west in the smoking ruins of the old. In South Taranaki, the prophet Titokowaru, hitherto a peacemaker, took to arms and swept south in a staggering series of campaigns, reconquering the lands painstakingly won by Cameron in 1865 and threatening Wanganui town. On the east coast, Te Kooti, a kupapa imprisoned on dubious evidence of secretly helping the enemy, escaped from exile in the Chatham Islands with 300 fellow prisoners. He formulated his own religion, Ringatu, and hoped to be left alone by the government. He was not, and responded by defeating pursuing forces and making a terrible raid on Poverty Bay on 10 November 1868. He killed 34 of his Pakeha enemies and at least 20 of his Maori ones, including harmless children and old people in both cases. The victories of Titokowaru and Te Kooti threw the colony into its worst military crisis before the threat of Japanese invasion in 1942. Pakeha talked of returning all confiscated land, and abandoning self-government in exchange for the return of imperial troops. The King Movement thought seriously of rejoining resistance, and Maori defeat in the Waikato War verged on being overturned.

But 1869 was a better year for the colonists. Their most able commander, Colonel George Whitmore, forged his colonial soldiers into a formidable force and managed to retain the support of key kupapa leaders, despite his possession of one of history's least charming personalities. Suddenly switching his main striking force from west coast to east, Whitmore discovered that, for all Te Kooti's brilliance as a guerilla leader, he was no master of the modern pa. Whitmore and Ropata inflicted a severe defeat on Te Kooti at Ngatapa in January 1869. Some 120 male prisoners were massacred after this engagement, in retaliation for Poverty Bay – mainly by kupapa, but with the endorsement of Whitmore and a government minister. Colonists and kupapa then hunted Te Kooti and his diminishing band across half the North Island for the next three years. He mounted further successful raids and miraculously evaded pursuit, but also suffered repeated defeats before finding sanctuary in the King Country in 1872.

After Ngatapa, Whitmore returned to deal with Titokowaru. In early February, he was about to be dealt with by him at the superb modern pa of

Tauranga Ika, near Wanganui, when the great Ngati Ruanui general suddenly lost his support, owing to an internal dispute. Most of his warriors left him over the next two months. This appears to have aborted renewed Kingite involvement, foreshadowed by a bloody raid on Pukearuhe, North Taranaki, on 13 February 1869. A combination of enemies that the colonists themselves doubted they could overcome had been very narrowly avoided, and Pakehadom drew back from the brink of unimaginable defeat. The colonists' good fortune did not extend to the capture of Titokowaru, who first checked and then evaded pursuit, taking refuge, like Te Kooti, in independent Maoridom – in his case, central Taranaki.[28] Although it seemed far from certain at the time, the New Zealand Wars were over.

The significance of the New Zealand Wars is camouflaged by the fact that they were small, especially in comparison with the great world conflicts of the first half of the twentieth century. More New Zealanders died at Gallipoli than in Anglo–Maori conflict. But we need to repatriate our yardsticks of comparison. In the local context, the 18,000-man British army massed during the Waikato War was huge, and the 5,000 soldiers assembled to oppose them represented a staggering feat of social efficiency by a traditionally fragmented tribal people. Low casualties did not indicate low intensity. High casualties in battles usually result from the rout of one side, the follow-up of victory, when the victors cut down fleeing enemies. Routs were rare in the New Zealand Wars. The Maori developed a military system that gave them the opportunities to rout their enemies, but they lacked the numbers to follow up. The British, imperial and colonial, had the numbers but not the opportunities. The wars were spared great blood baths. But the historical importance of human conflict is not measured solely in blood.

Until the 1980s, New Zealanders were not very interested in their great civil war, at both the top and bottom of historical memory. Books on it were few, non-scholarly and far between; research on children's games has found that few played Maori and Colonists. They played other peoples' history, Cowboys and Indians, instead.[29] Liberal academics, scholarly ostriches, avoided the subject from contempt for military history, often well deserved, and in the less forgivable belief that if you ignored war it would go away. Wider neglect stemmed partly from the notion, which grew from the 1880s, that history was something that happened overseas, and partly from the centrality of the legend of good race relations in New Zealand ideology. New Zealandness consisted significantly in the belief that Pakeha had the best blacks, and treated them best – a key way of telling the difference between New Zealanders and Australians. Forgetting or downplaying the wars was important here, as was massaging them into the least disagreeable shape possible: a good clean fight, dotted with incidents of courage and chivalry, after which the two peoples shook hands and made up. Remarkable instances of reconciliation, courage and chivalry did take place, but the two peoples killed each other's children as often as they shook hands on the battlefield.

The wars of the 1860s had their impact on Pakeha political, economic and cultural history. They saw the rise of the central state and its alter ego, the national debt. By virtue of the workings of compound interest, we are still paying for the wars. Maori proved too formidable a foe for the provincial governments; the colonial government handled the Pakeha war effort as its first major project. This contributed to a centralising process that resulted in the fall of the provinces in 1876. Imperial troops and their hangers-on, plus military expenditure, could and did double the population and economic activity of particular settlements in an instant. The boost was temporary, but we will see in Chapter Fourteen that they sometimes had permanent after-effects. Julius Vogel, architect of a great public works drive in the 1870s, claimed repeatedly that his policy was aimed at speeding up the swamping of the Maori hinterland – an implicit acknowledgement of the limits of military victory.[30]

Pakeha collective identity also received a boost from the wars – low-key, ambiguous and played down in retrospect, but not insignificant. Pakeha regions differed in their enthusiasm for war, and dependence on kupapa led the colonial government to seek to restrain general anti-Maori, as against anti-resister, feeling. When soldier, newspaper editor and future Premier John Ballance made denigratory blanket statements about Maori, kupapa chiefs complained bitterly and the government stripped Ballance of his officer's commission.[31] Yet to some extent, conflict must have reinforced the Pakeha sense of Us through confrontation with a Maori Them. It also contrasted New Zealand Britons to metropolitan ones. The alleged superiority of colonial to imperial troops was a constant theme of settler writing on the wars from 1860.[32] Bold settler frontiersmen, selected for initiative by migration and inured to hardship and self-reliance by an idealised outdoor life, were thought to be much more of a match for Maori than the hidebound marionettes of the imperial army and their pompous and unimaginative generals. Antagonism to the imperial government was very strong indeed during the withdrawal of the imperial legions, 1867–69. But the embryonic military sense of a Pakeha Us was not anti-British. It implied that self-reliant yeomen settlers manifested Britishness better than imperial regulars. This myth of martial New Zealandness, later known as the 'Anzac legend', became central in Pakeha collective identity. It actually dates from the New Zealand Wars, though it was partially aborted by the embarrassment of frequent defeats by Maori. The New Zealand Custer, Thomas McDonnell, known for a time as 'Fighting Mac', was the heroic embodiment of the settler-soldier, the master Maori fighter. He was a competent leader and a dangerous personal enemy, a master of taiaha combat who also carried two revolvers, presumably slung low.[33] But he failed to die at his Little Big Horn, a humiliating defeat by Titokowaru in 1868, and history never forgave him.

The tension between imperial and colonial soldiers was not the only cleavage among Europeans during the wars. A few deserters from the imperial forces fought on the Maori side. British attempts to credit Maori successes to the advice of such renegades were nonsense, and their numbers were insignificant, but they did have disturbing potential. While the best-known renegade was Kimble Bent, an American, most were Catholic Irish. The Irish nationalism known as Fenianism was strong internationally in the 1860s. Fenians raided Canada from the United States in 1866, and a Fenian wounded Queen Victoria's son, the Duke of Edinburgh, in an assassination attempt while he was visiting Sydney en route to New Zealand in 1868. This event exacerbated conflict in Westland that was taking place at the same time, known as the 'Hokitika Riots' or 'Fenian Riots'.

The minimalist interpretation of these, and of subsequent riots in the 1870s, is that they were sectarian scuffles between Catholic and Protestant Irish – of no great significance. This may be true, but it is clear that the New Zealand government took them very seriously and that the factions involved had access to arms. One historian has described the situation in Westland in 1868 as 'close to civil war'.[34] There are one or two signs that Fenian Irishmen supplied ammunition to resisting Maori at around this time, and that the 'renegades' fighting with Maori had Fenian sympathies.[35] The possibility of Irish-Maori alliance may not have seemed entirely far-fetched at the time, but its main historical significance, perhaps, is in highlighting its opposite. A very high proportion of imperial troops in New Zealand, perhaps over 40 per cent, were Catholic Irish, and Irish were prominent in the colonial forces as well. The great majority fought against Maori with vigour. The Irishmen involved had been forced from their own communities by poverty and had adopted new communities in the form of their regiments. They fought less for 'Queen and Country' than for the regiment and each other. But this does not affect the fact that they made an important contribution to Maori defeat, and that Maori were not the only people in the wars to supply the British with kupapa. A key aspect of British imperialism was persuading its victims to conquer each other.

The wars also produced cleavages within Maoridom. In most conflicts, there was a third side: the Maori kupapa, also known as 'friendly natives', 'Queenites', 'Government' or 'Kawanatanga Maori' and 'Native Contingents'. The motivation, degree of commitment and importance to the military outcome of Maori fighting on the British side varied greatly. In the wars of the 1840s, pro-British Maori were important in determining the results of conflict; they were influential in securing some British success in the south and in limiting failure in the north. But the Maori allies of the British tended to fight a war within a war, at different levels of intensity and with different – usually more moderate – war aims. Both resisters and 'collaborators' were organised tribally or subtribally. In the clash between King and Empire, 1860–64, kupapa were neither numerous nor very influential. The breadth of support for the King Movement did not unite Maoridom, but it came surprisingly close, and this restricted the numbers of kupapa in this period. It was in the last group of conflicts, 1864–72, that the motives and commitment of kupapa ranged most widely and that their importance was greatest.

Commitment ranged along a spectrum from very weak to quite strong, but was seldom total. At the weak end, groups took the field to collect wages or appease a suspicious government, and did little damage to the enemy. There were instances of a bet each way. When war came to the territories of groups that did not want it, they deliberately split into collaborating and resisting factions – and perhaps neutral as well – to cover all contingencies and be certain of being represented on the winning side. Even at the more highly committed end of the spectrum, kupapa war aims very often diverged from government ones, to the great frustration of Pakeha commanders. An Arawa unit of the regular colonial forces, which the government had gone to some trouble to 'detribalise' – separate from its chiefs and indoctrinate as European-like soldiers – disobeyed orders without hesitation when tribal interests seemed to demand it. Whanganui kupapa allowed Titokowaru to escape from a trap in 1869 to return a similar favour rendered them by his father in an earlier tribal war.[36] On the other hand, kupapa sometimes campaigned with more ruthlessness and determination than the Pakeha. Government pay, supplies and equipment often meant that kupapa shared the economic advantage of Pakeha troops. The pay replaced them in the tribal economy, enabling them to campaign for longer, and to field a higher proportion of their manpower than was possible for resisting groups. But for all this diversity, there were still patterns in Maori military collaboration. Unlike the Irish in the British army, they were very seldom resocialised – 'retribalised' into communities whose first loyalty was to their unit. The first loyalty of virtually all kupapa was to the tribe.

The sudden and massive increase in Maori willingness to fight for the government from 1864 is one of the most intriguing features of the wars. The progressive withdrawal of both the King Movement and the British Empire from active operations were factors. The disengagement of imperial troops, completed by 1866, left the colonial government more dependent on local allies, and more willing to conclude bargains favourable to them – including the four Maori seats in Parliament in 1867. The diminishing embrace of the King Movement after 1864 was also important. Maori support for the movement during the Waikato War was very great. Large sections of what later became the four leading kupapa tribal groups – Whanganui, Te Arawa, Ngati Kahungunu and Ngati Porou – fought actively for the King in 1863–64. A small minority of Waikato supported the British, and a majority of Arawa fought in the Tauranga theatre for particular tribal reasons that happened to coincide with those of the British. But apart from this, the greatest British effort of the New Zealand Wars attracted very little Maori support. From 1864, however, increasing numbers of Maori backed the government against other Maori. They did so despite the fact that other pan-tribal movements, notably Pai Marire, were taking the lead in resistance. One type of pan-tribalism united Maori; the other appears to have fragmented them.

We need, I think, to distinguish between two kinds of pan-tribalism: 'intertribalism', which builds itself from tribal bricks without threatening them, *federating* tribes; and 'supra-tribalism', which to some extent *transcends*, even subverts, tribes, positing higher loyalties and threatening elements of the established order. One can seldom fix the Maori pan-tribal movements of the 1850s and after firmly in these categories, but most did tend more in one direction than the other. The landholding and King movements were intertribal, though the latter may have had supra-tribal elements. Pai Marire and the subsequent prophetic movements of Te Kooti, Titokowaru, and Te Whiti of Parihaka were more supra-tribal. They were not wholly incompatible with tribalism by any means, but they do appear to have been somewhat subversive of it. The propensity of prophets to lead social as well as ethnic resistance in this kind of context is well known internationally, and the Maori prophets may have been no exception. It could have been the social aims of the prophetic movements, a threat to tribalism and chiefly authority, that led to the upsurge in the kupapa response from 1864.

My impression is that the prophetic movements regularly compromised with tribalism, which remained the stuff of Maori life, but that there was also some real tension with it, and with some traditions. The pan-tribal movements sometimes preached explicitly against tapu, 'witchcraft', muru and parochialism.[37] As Titokowaru marched south towards Wanganui in 1868, he was joined by the mass of some tribal groups but not their traditional chiefs.[38] The mutual antagonism of Te Kooti and his own tribal establishment is well known. He did greet a senior chief of his own tribe with the words 'Salutations, my father!' at Poverty Bay, but only as a sarcastic preliminary to killing him.[39] To carry this speculation a stage further, the wars of 1864–72 may have doubled as something of a failed and forgotten revolution within Maoridom, as well as a struggle between it and the Pakeha. Both Maori and Pakeha establishments won out, helping each other to do so. As with the Maori challenge to Pakeha, the full extent of the supra-tribal challenge to tribalism was subsequently written out of history.

Because the wars contravened powerful myths of racial harmony, Pakeha subsequently tried to distance themselves from them, as well as downplay them, and at least the former tendency persisted. 'The Maori,' wrote a leading historian in 1991, 'were fighting an imperial war, against the British army, and not against the settlers . . . There were few instances of fighting between settlers and Maori . . . Many books give the quite wrong impression that the fighting was between settlers and Maori.'[40] In a survey of university students in 1994, Maori respondents preferred the term 'Pakeha' in describing the European side in these conflicts. But the great majority of Pakeha respondents 'distanced themselves from historical injustices . . . by choosing the terms "British" and "European" over "Pakeha" in describing the colonial period and Land Wars'.[41] This is largely correct for the wars of the 1840s, and of 1860–64, when imperial troops were indeed the main combatants on the European side. But it is very clearly untrue of the wars of 1864–72, when resisting Maori had two main enemies: several thousand each of colonial troops and kupapa.

In a kind of mirror image of Pakeha evasions, the role of kupapa is also downplayed in Maori memories. Might-have-been history is a dangerous game, but it is very hard to see how the later wars could have been won without kupapa help. A sense that the tribe or subtribe was the largest unit of collective identity clearly influenced kupapa. They cannot be seen as quislings or traitors, because they acknowledged no entity higher than their tribal group. From their viewpoint, the British were fighting for them rather than vice versa. This was especially so in the 1840s, when there was little in the way of a competing pan-Maori identity. It remained important in the 1860s, but by this time it was not the whole story. The wars of the 1860s may conceal a lost history of Maori nationalism, pan-tribalism clashing with tribalism as well as Maori with Pakeha. In each pair of rivals, it was the latter that triumphed. But each did so only narrowly, securing victory as much in the collective memory as on the field of battle.

It can be argued that the Maori military system proved itself to be qualitatively superior to the British in the New Zealand Wars. If the sides had been equal in numbers and resources, yet still fought in the same ways, the Maori would have won. The main key to this was the modern pa system, which was reinvented in Europe in World War One as a response to the same problem of overwhelming firepower. The superior per capita efficiency of the Maori war effort is a useful corrective to blithe assumptions about European superiority, and to notions that peoples like the Maori could not innovate and adapt. In war as in politics, the new forms of organisation drew on, but also transcended, both European and Maori tradition. But we must remember that the remarkable political and military innovations of Maori resisters did not bring them victory. Maori successes placed important limits on defeat, and for a time Pakeha had to share their limited victory with the kupapa. But government victory on points pierced the hard shell of Maori independence, and allowed coercion, non-military subversion, the seductions of conversion, and sheer demographic and economic swamping to slowly empty out the contents. In the decades after the wars, real empire finally marched, flooded or crept into even the innermost sanctums of independent Aotearoa.

CHAPTER ELEVEN

Swamps, Sticks and Carrots

In 1882, the respected Pakeha medical scholar Dr A. K. Newman regaled the New Zealand Institute, founded in 1869, with a clear analysis of the Maori past, present and future entitled 'The Causes Leading to the Extinction of the Maori'. Newman argued that Maori were dying out even before contact, which had merely hastened a natural process. Pre-contact Maori, asserted Newman, died from an impressive range of diseases including rheumatism, scrofula, epilepsy, dropsy, leprosy, consumption and 'a malarious fever'. Maori also killed themselves and each other in thousands through war, murder, infanticide and other lethal customs. Newman's unique access to pre-contact suicide notes, presumably telepathic, enabled him to deduce that 'suicide was exceedingly common'. 'Under the painful operation of tattooing some died.' Others 'died through sheer fright' after being bewitched, through nostalgia, or through being killed by their kin in times of scarcity. 'Sometimes great Maori chiefs dropped dead from excessive excitement.' In the smorgasbord of death that was New Zealand prehistory, poison berries and the dreaded katipo spider also took their toll.

New dishes were added after contact, including alcoholism, tuberculosis and influenza (though not syphilis). Before and after contact, 'mental depression' and the common cold were big killers. Maori 'throw up the sponge' easily in face of minor ailments – 'they seem to have no pluck'. High death rates were joined by low birth rates, caused by early promiscuity, 'excessive sexual indulgence' and fatness 'which, as in all lower animals, leads to a lessened fertility'. The katipo was joined by another killer animal: the horse. Horses facilitated the dissemination of infectious diseases, killed Maori who fell off them and caused abortions among women riders. Mixing blood did no good. 'The off-spring of half-castes . . . are a very feeble race and rapidly tend to extinction . . . the two races will never mingle.' 'I hope I have made it clear,' concluded Dr Newman, 'that the Maoris were a disappearing race before we came here . . . Taking all things into consideration, the disappearance of the race is scarcely a subject for much regret. They are dying out in a quick, easy way, and are being supplanted by a superior race.'[1]

Newman's was a minority position among Pakeha prophets of Maori doom, but only in so far as he attributed imminent Maori demise to a natural life-cycle of races rather than the fatal impact of Europe. Between the 1870s and the 1900s, especially in the first half of the period, fatal impact mounted its last stand. Most Pakeha believed that Maori were dying out fast. From 1906, when census evidence that the Maori population was recovering became difficult to ignore, fatal impact gave way to a somewhat kinder prophecy, total biological and cultural assimilation, whereby Maori would survive only as a 'slight golden tinge' on the skins – and in the cultural symbols – of the Pakeha.[2] Theoretically, this meant that Pakeha policy towards Maori need amount to nothing more than humanely 'smoothing the pillow', in Isaac Featherston's famous phrase, of a dying race or culture.[3] In practice, it sometimes seemed as if Pakeha were smoothing the pillow over the mouth of a patient who was not dying fast enough.

Between 1870 and 1916, Pakeha launched a climactic assault on Maori independence, identity and importance. Maori sought to prevent their subordination, assimilation and marginalisation. The Pakeha push took three forms: demographic swamping, coercive sticks and tempting carrots. These were adapted versions of the old dynamics of empire: fatal impact, conquest and conversion. But swamping – simply drowning Maori in a growing sea of Pakeha, like some White Peril – was a particularly unflattering form of fatal impact to European racial egos, and contemporary accounts did not emphasise it much. Maori responded along two main lines, different means towards the same end. One was disengagement – avoiding interaction with Pakeha state and society, while continuing to interact economically and technologically. The other was engagement – accepting the Pakeha embrace but seeking to soften it, even subvert it towards Maori interests. In the 1870s and 1880s, disengagement tended to be associated with pan-tribal organisations and areas that had resisted during the wars of the 1860s. Neutral and kupapa regions leaned towards engagement. But Maori in Northland and the South Island used both strategies throughout, and elsewhere this distinction began to blur from about 1890. A continued emphasis on marriage alliance, in which South Island Maori specialised, was in a sense a third strategy.

The remarkable effectiveness of Maori resistance in the New Zealand Wars placed strict limits on the government victory. This combined with the participation of kupapa in that victory to provide some protection for Maori independence in the decades after the wars. But the fact of government victory, however narrow, immediately gave Pakeha the whip hand in some conquered regions, such as South Taranaki and central Waikato, and enhanced their sticks and carrots in other resisting and collaborating regions. Ultimately, government victory turned the tide against Maori independence, in its fullest sense of states-within-states, though its limits meant that the tide ran out slowly. Resistance and collaboration declined together, because the value of the latter was a function of the effectiveness of the former. Once the government was convinced that Titokowaru and Te Kooti were no longer military threats, it needed Kepa and Ropata much less.

The rise of control by the Pakeha state can be traced through three stages on the spectrum of empire: 'false', 'loose' and 'tight'. False empire has been defined above as large-scale interaction, and even mutual dependence, of two parties on the basis of rough parity. It generates the illusion but not the substance of empire. Loose empire was real but incomplete and indirect; a partial, arm's-length control that did not normally dominate the internal lives of Maori groups, but which enabled the state to enforce its vital interests. Tight empire was more comprehensive and direct, though even under it control was not total. There was some room for cultural and social autonomy, and distinct identity, in tight empire, but the state was able to do such things as impose direct taxes and define and punish Maori crime. The decline of resistance and its alter ego, collaboration, were keys to movement along the spectrum. Yet Maori groups that fought quite successfully in the 1840s but not in the 1860s, and that did not fight at all, were also subordinated. How did this come about? The short answer is swamping and its allies.

Swamps and Marriage

Swamping was simply the massive outnumbering of a shrinking or static Maori population by a growing Pakeha one. Maori population statistics after 1857 are much more reliable than the earlier wild guesses, but they are still not very reliable. There was no Maori census between 1857 and 1874, and census counts for resisting areas were based partly on guesswork and second-hand information until the twentieth century. It is hard to see how estimates for the Urewera, for example, could have been at all accurate until the late 1890s. A feature of persistent Maori independence was that you did not let the government count you. These factors may have led to an exaggeration of population decline, but decline there probably was. Recent research asserts firmly that birth rates were growing from about 1850, as we have seen. Yet infant mortality remained high; life expectancy for adults was low; and there appears to have been a substantial drop in population associated with the wars, owing less to direct casualties than to disease, food shortages, land loss and disrupted fertility patterns arising from conflict. As we have seen, the Maori population declined from about 60,000 in 1858 to about 48,000 in 1874, and then to a nadir of about 42,000 in 1896, after which a steady rise began – a rise that marked the final failure of fatal impact, though not necessarily assimilation. The growth of Pakeha population was more important for swamping than Maori population decline.

The Pakeha population doubled in the 1870s, as it had in the 1860s, and continued to grow rapidly in the North Island to 1886. Rates of growth were much lower thereafter, but were still quite substantial in the 1890s and 1900s. By 1881, Maori were only 8.6 per cent of New Zealand's population, by 1901, 5.5 per cent, and by 1921, 4.5 per cent – a small minority. As with pre-1860 land-sale and population statistics, the raw figures reshape deceptively. The number of Pakeha neighbours mattered more to particular Maori groups than the total. Maori were much more demographically significant in the North Island, where most of them lived, than in the South, making up 17.5 per cent of the North Island's population in 1881 and about 10 per cent in 1901. The figures need to be broken down further. Between 1874 and 1901, on official statistics, Maori declined from a majority or near-majority to around 30 per cent in Northland, the Waikato-King Country and the East Coast; from substantial minorities of between 20 and 32 per cent to 10 per cent or less in Taranaki, Wanganui and Hawke's Bay; from 4 or 5 per cent to 1 or 2 in Wellington-Manawatu and the Auckland region; and from about 1 per cent to about 0.5 in the South Island. Only in the Bay of Plenty region did Maori remain a majority in 1901.[4]

Even this regional breakdown does not tell the whole story. Maori concentrated differently from Pakeha; there was a subregional tendency for a high Maori population and the land retention it implied to mean a low Pakeha one; and Maori remained majorities in important subdivisions of statistical regions, such as Hokianga, central Taranaki, the King Country and the Urewera.[5] But many Maori groups were well and truly swamped by 1901 – outnumbered more than ten to one by local Pakeha. In such circumstances, violent or non-violent resistance seemed less viable, and economic, political and military collaboration carried less weight. There were also economic and social dimensions to swamping.

In the 1850s, European settlements gradually grew their own hinterlands at varying speeds, ceasing to rely on Maori town-supply districts. Three factors boosted the process in the 1860s: the wars disrupted trade; more reliable steam-driven coastal shipping developed, enabling Pakeha regions to help feed each other; and the sheer growth of the Pakeha population stimulated European farming. Economically, Maori became less important to Pakeha, but the reverse was not necessarily true. Some Maori groups, especially those neighbouring large towns, became more tightly dependent on the Pakeha economy than ever. This did not necessarily lead to conversion by capitalism – the dissolution of Maori communities into individualised entrepreneurs and proletarians – but it did inextricably enmesh Maori with their neighbours. Economic interaction became economic gridlock, and in these circumstances resistance was almost impossible.

From the 1890s, export dairy farming, which had commenced with refrigeration in the previous decade, began to take off, first in Taranaki, then in

Waikato, Northland and other regions that had been strongholds of independent Maoridom. Pakeha dairy farming displaced Maori agriculture not only geographically but also as a core business of towns such as New Plymouth and Tauranga, whose Maori trade was important right up to the 1880s. Farming sheep for meat, a much more intensive exercise than farming for wool, burgeoned at the same time. This new stage in the intensification of sheep farming put an end to the complementary use of land by Maori seasonal hunter-gatherers and pastoralists, completing the process of tightening land alienation that the freeholding and pasture-converting phase of pastoralism had begun in the late 1860s. Where Maori retained their powers of effective resistance or valued collaboration, they could combat the pressures to sell land for the new forms of farming, and dispute Pakeha definitions of alienation. But as these powers faded, agricultural displacement grew.

The social dimension of swamping was more complicated. It consisted of two related but conceptually distinct phenomena, intermarriage and gene mixing. Initially, half-caste children were possibly less the fruit of intermarriage than of the sex industry, as some mildly sarcastic Maori names for them suggest – 'utu pihikete' (paid for with biscuits) and 'o te parara' (out of the whaler's barrel).[6] 'Half-castes' were offspring of a parent of each race, while 'mixed bloods' had any percentage of the other – they were the offspring of half-castes. Censuses registered half-castes, not mixed bloods. The nineteenth-century heyday of interracial sex, and therefore presumably of half-caste births, must have corresponded with the great days of the sex industry; say, 1820–50. 'There is no evidence that contraception was practised', and large-scale abortion or infanticide now seems unlikely.[7] European commentators occasionally recorded surprise at the low number of children these fleeting liaisons produced, but they wrongly believed that Maori children as a whole were exceptionally few, and half-Maori were not necessarily visually distinguishable from full Maori. Moreover, this was also the heyday of marriage alliance: the period in which marriage linked the highest proportion of Pakeha to Maori communities. Research on early South Island mixed marriages shows that while they themselves may not have been very prolific, those of their half-caste offspring were.[8] In short, it seems likely that Maori took on a large percentage of the European genes they acquired to 1945 before 1850. 'Mixed blood' acquired in this period naturally tended to proliferate over the generations as Maori with European blood intermarried with those without, whether or not there was continuing intermarriage with Europeans. An indicator of the discrepancy between half-castes and mixed bloods may be seen in about 1916, when studies of the Maori Battalion in World War One and of 4,000 Maori pupils in Native schools suggest that about half of all Maori were of mixed blood, while according to the 1916 census only 12.6 per cent of Maori were half-castes.[9]

The natural diffusion of European genes from the early half-castes, combined with intermarriage, rapidly reduced the number of 'pure-blooded' Maori. This was, and still is, mistaken for evidence of fatal impact or its successor, biological assimilation, symbolised by the frequent assertion that pure-blooded Maori have almost died out. This is true in a technical and historically unimportant sense, but the implications associated with it are not. There are few 'pure-blooded' English either – it took one Frenchman only a couple of centuries to taint a whole country. Are 'real English' therefore extinct? Except in cases of total isolation, like New Zealand before 1769, racial purity is a myth, as is the notion that genetic admixture has necessary cultural implications. It is hard to see how a great-great-grandfather from Nantucket, who spent two weeks in New Zealand, reduces your Maoriness, any more than a dash of French, Dutch or Irish blood reduces your Englishness.

The number of Maori wives living with European husbands registered in censuses between 1881 and 1906 was small, fluctuating around 200.[10] This surely cannot have reflected the whole story of intermarriage, but the great binding institution was certainly in trouble in the later half of the nineteenth century. One historian has concluded that intermarriage was in decline from the 1860s to the early twentieth century.[11] Marriage alliance continued to be important in bonding its Maori and Pakeha partners in the residues of Old New Zealand throughout the later nineteenth century. But the capacity of marriage alliance to link Maori with New New Zealand, the centres of mass settlement, was less great. Value-laden stereotypes are a danger in analysing this issue. It has sometimes been argued that, in places such as British India, dusky maidens and their pillow talk acculturated sahibs and softened their imperialism. The arrival of white women, memsahibs, then spoiled the fun and hardened imperialism. Such theories may owe as much to the port-enhanced retrospective lubricity of ex-sahibs as to fact. Yet it is true that a single sex of strangers can be easier to incorporate, through marriage, than two sexes of them. The arrival of alternative, white, wives, hardening senses of propriety and racial exclusivity, and the sheer mass of settlement combined to reduce the effectiveness of marriage alliance in binding the two peoples. In the mid-1860s, a Polish gentleman, Sygurd Wisniowski, lived in New Zealand, and subsequently published his view of it in a novel, *Children of the Queen of Oceania*.[12]

> If you stay here for any length of time, you'll find that if we insisted on closing our homes to everyone who had a liaison with the delightful dusky daughters of the tribes, our ladies would be quite deprived of masculine company . . . Besides, our own (colonial) ladies are such prudes that we have occasionally to embrace the half-castes just to keep in practice . . . Our society has no interest at all in the relationship between respectable men and Maori women. We are too circumspect even to consider such a question. Society ignores Maori mistresses. Anyone who mentions their existence outrages propriety.

Even discounting for sensationalism, there is probably some truth in this, though just how much is difficult to gauge. Maori mistresses of Pakeha leaders of New New Zealand to some extent succeeded the Maori wives of Pakeha leaders in the Old. Rumours of uncovenanted 'Maori wives', as they were still sometimes called, were attached to the names of a number of important Pakeha throughout the nineteenth century, and even into the twentieth. They included Resident Magistrate Major Isaac Cooper, merchant W. H. Wright, the provincial politician Charles Brown, the military leader Gustavus von Tempsky, businessman Alma Baker, pastoralist Edward Riddiford, colonial ministers Walter Mantell, F. D. Bell and John Sheehan, George Grey himself, and the important 1920s Prime Minister J. G. Coates. Some of these men did spasmodically display a more enlightened attitude to Maori issues than their contemporaries. The Maori women concerned do not appear to have lost status within their own society. The remarkable scout, spy and mediator Lucy Takiora seems to have had successive affairs with several Pakeha leaders in Taranaki in the 1860s and 1870s, but retained considerable influence with both resisting and collaborating Maori, as well as with the government. Her favours were less a fringe benefit of status on the racial interface than a cause of it.[13] But, as Wisniowski alleged, Maori mistresses were officially unmentionable in Pakeha society, which diminished their effectiveness as mediators.

The effectiveness of marriage alliance was also reduced by it being a one-way street. Maori women married Pakeha men, but Maori men seldom married Pakeha women, with a handful of exceptions up to the 1880s. Maori noted and resented the double standard. At Bristol in 1863, a member of a troupe of Maori entertainers and lecturers, Horomona Te Atua, spoke to an English audience on the subject.

> He had not seen that the laws had had the effect of making the English and Maori nations one nation. In his opinion, the best plan to unite them would be that the two races should marry together (laughter and applause). They might laugh at his suggestion but those were his thoughts. That would be the best way to make them keep the laws. It would greatly improve them in every respect (laughter and hear, hear). Some of the New Zealand women had married English settlers, but the British ladies had not married with the Maories (laughter). They were taught in the Word of God that they should do unto each other as they would be done by . . . New Zealanders were anxious to give their females to Europeans, but their example had not been followed by the English (cheers and laughter).[14]

The demotion of Maori partners from wives to mistresses of important men, and the one-way street, were compounded by the effects of swamping. While the proportion of the static or shrinking Maori population tied to Pakeha communities by intermarriage may have increased a little in the 1870s and 1880s, the proportion of Pakeha tied to Maori obviously decreased greatly.

There was not enough intermarriage in some Maori regions, and too much in others. When war broke out in Waikato in 1863, marriage-alliance families in that region underwent traumatic divorce. Maori wives and most children stayed in the Waikato, Pakeha husbands and some children went to Auckland, and the split was painful for all concerned. Where levels of intermarriage were greater, as in the South Island, the split was virtually impossible. There were simply too many shared children. Marriage alliance had worked so well that divorce, and therefore resistance, had ceased to be an option – a social 'gridlock' equivalent to the economic one discussed above. Reducing risks of warfare was a traditional purpose of marriage alliance, and it cut both ways: a Pakeha community that shared numerous offspring with a Maori one was less likely to attack it. But where Pakeha held the whip hand in other spheres, close marriage alliance could work to disadvantage Maori. Maori communities that could not do without very direct and close social and economic partnerships with Pakeha were not in a position to resist, or to threaten resistance. In most regions, whatever the absolute situation, intermarriage diminished relatively, binding a smaller proportion of Pakeha to Maori. By 1900, marriage alliance had worked too well in a few regions, and was in need of revival in most.

All dimensions of swamping hit hardest in the South Island. One recent study of southern Maori paints their history from 1850 to the 1920s in terms of almost unrelieved victim ideology, implying that their socio-economy was repeatedly crippled or destroyed. We are told that land selling and the expansion of pastoralism reduced Ngai Tahu to poor outcasts as early as 1850. By the 1880s, it is difficult to find fresh adjectives for their new 'depths of poverty and despair'.[15] We discover that the small community at Moeraki in Otago had 2,000 sheep, 40 horses and 50 cattle only in reference to their being destroyed by bad weather in 1886.[16] Such interpretations leave the existence of a rather dynamic Ngai Tahu polity in the present as something of a mystery. We have to ask what went right as well as what went wrong, yet do so without merely reversing the victim–agent pendulum.

On official statistics, the South Island Maori population declined steadily from 1857, and did not begin to recover until the 1920s.[17] There is no doubt that Ngai Tahu's economic circumstances were very poor by 1890, when it was reported that 46 per cent of them had insufficient good land to support themselves and that 44 per cent had no land at all.[18] But oppressive loose and tight empire cut in later than victim ideology suggests, and the delay in ending independence helped the persistence of identity. False empire was roughly analogous to what one historian has called a 'honeymoon period' in South Island ethnic relations. He dates its end to about 1865 in Canterbury, and a little later in Otago, Southland and Westland.[19] As we saw in Chapter Nine, other evidence supports this. Loose empire came with the swamping gold rushes and the intensification of pastoralism. Tight empire may date from about 1879, when the prophet Te Maiharoa's community of Omarama was broken up by the Armed Constabulary, with a gunfight narrowly averted through Te Maiharoa's decision. Te Maiharoa had links with Kai Ngarara and Pai Marire. Omarama was established on a Pakeha sheep run in North Otago in 1877. It represented the strategy of disengagement and passive resistance, similar to that being practised at Parihaka in Taranaki at the same time.[20] Tight empire enabled Pakeha to define land alienation; more effective restrictions were placed on the taking of eels, weka, ducks and pigs. Ngai Tahu had fewer alternatives to farming their remaining lands, if they had them, and to labouring for Pakeha if they did not.

From the 1870s, Ngai Tahu shifted emphasis from disengagement to engagement, notably in politics. H. K. Taiaroa, elected to Parliament in 1871, at first emphasised the co-operative variant of engagement, assisting the government against Te Maiharoa while trying to soften its approach.[21] Taiaroa put his weight behind what was to become a century-long Ngai Tahu political campaign against the Pakeha definition of land sales. Complaints about the government's failure to keep its side of these bargains commenced as early as 1850, but gathered force from the 1870s, with £3,000 being collected in 1877 alone for legal battles. The campaign met many disheartening defeats, but it also had some successes around 1880, in the 1900s, in 1920, 1945 and 1991. As important as these was the way in which Te Kerema (The Claim), acted as a focus for persistent identity. The precise nature of this identity was contested vigorously by South Island Maori themselves. The Taiaroa and Karetai families competed for leadership of southern Ngai Tahu; northern and southern sections competed for leadership of both claim and tribe, which now tended to go together. Ngai Tahu used the claim to continue their drive, dating from the eighteenth century, to impose their mana over other groups, such as Ngati Mamoe. The other groups responded by spasmodically reasserting, reinventing and perhaps even inventing their own identities. The use of the claim as a currency of rivalry sometimes helped and sometimes hindered its role as a strategy for obtaining redress, as it does in the present. In either case, it proved that South Island Maori were not dead.[22]

That identity and even a degree of economic and social autonomy survived the demise of southern Maori independence is also indicated by the muttonbirding industry. Well into the twentieth century, children left school for three months for annual visits to the Titi, or Muttonbird, Islands in Foveaux Strait, coming from as far north as Kaiapoi. Women gave their occupation as 'muttonbirding' in the 1926 census; and the industry was going strong in 1940.[23]

> Muttonbirding is the only [sic] modern survival of native enterprise ... which has withstood the destructive competition of the scientific and progressive undertakings introduced by the white man. But it has not only persisted ... it has also expanded ... There is, moreover, a definite though imponderable value in this annual gathering of clans ... The hands of friendship and the unity of related groups are renewed and strengthened, so that there exists among these descendants of Ngaitahu and Ngatimamoe a cohesion and communal sympathy such as are rarely found among similar groups of Europeans.[24]

There was a degree of biological and cultural assimilation in the South Island, but this had advantages as well as disadvantages. Owing to the establishment of prolific mixed-race families in 1820–50, coupled with what was apparently a persistent preference for Pakeha husbands among Ngai Tahu women, the majority of Ngai Tahu were of mixed race by 1878, and the last 'pureblood' was said to have died in 1910.[25] As in the country as a whole, the European genes of Maori differed somewhat from those of Pakeha. Ironically, the Maori of Otago and Southland may have been more English than the local Pakeha, whose leading ethnic group was Scots. The preference for Pakeha husbands may reflect an acceptance of European perceptions of racial status, but it seems more likely to stem from the perceived material advantages of such spouses, and perhaps to a folk belief that European genes helped immunise children against European disease – white husbands as the equivalent of a polio injection. Deliberate policy may also have been a factor – a persistent marriage-alliance strategy. In the 1900s, there was apparently some reversal of this policy, to preserve chiefly blood lines and cement land claims, which suggests group leaders still had the power to direct marriages.[26]

It seems that something of a split emerged between the descendants of the early Maori-Pakeha families and the main stream of Ngai Tahu, who were also increasingly of mixed blood.[27] The early mixed families in the Deep South were patrilocal – living with Dad's community – whereas those in the north were more often matrilocal. Wives and children are said to have adopted the husband's culture, whereas among Old New Zealand Pakeha Maori families generally it was usually the other way around. But the European culture of the old sealing, trading and farming settlements that survived on the shores of Foveaux Strait until the 1860s was not that of mass-settlement Otago and Southland. There is some evidence that, in the late nineteenth century, their European-Maori descendants were linked to, yet separate from, both mainstream Pakeha and mainstream Ngai Tahu. They saw themselves, and were seen as, a little different from either; they were even more landless than Ngai Tahu proper; and they were more prone to urbanising and the acquisition of European skills. Many 'lived as Europeans' according to the census definition, and were excluded from Maori population statistics. Including them would flatten the graph of Ngai Tahu population decline.

This group is the closest New Zealand came to developing a bi-culture like the Métis of Canada or the Griqua of South Africa. That it came no closer is evidence of the persistent strength of Maori identity. Some southern 'Métis' simply disappeared into the Pakeha population in the twentieth century. But the heavily swamped Ngai Tahu found some of their more Europeanised kin a useful mediator group, or a potentially useful fifth column in Pakeha society, ready to return to their Maori allegiance when the time was ripe. This supplemented the strategy of persistent marriage alliance. One almost gets the impression of Ngai Tahu riding both European and Maori horses, shifting balance from one to the other as circumstances required. Demographic, economic and social swamping, with just a touch of threatened conquest at Omarama, had eliminated Maori independence in the South Island by 1880. It had subordinated Maori, and largely marginalised them. But, even in its South Island stronghold, it had not assimilated them, or destroyed them as a distinct group.

Sticks and Carrots

Loose empire arrived in the Lower Waikato, South Taranaki, parts of the Bay of Plenty and the East Coast, and perhaps Taupo, between 1864 and 1870, in the train of government troops, and tightened thereafter. In these regions, direct conquest did the job swamping had done in the South Island and in the environs of Wellington and Auckland. But in the 1870s these swamped and conquered regions still represented only a minority of Maori, though a growing one. Outside them, and outside the effective authority of the Pakeha state, many Maori still lived in areas that continued to be protected by collaboration and resistance – non-violent, violent and threatened. The government feared renewed warfare not only for the possibility of military defeat but also for the expense and the bad publicity. It was busily engaged in tempting out migrants and money in the 1870s, and war and massacre tended to stem the flow. On the other hand, the sticks and carrots available to the state were improving. Swamping added muscle to both.

The most obvious stick was the Pakeha regular army, the Armed Constabulary. Established in 1867 out of the pre-existing miscellany of colonial military units – against the wishes of the British War Office – the Constabulary became somewhat more like a police force in 1869, with the replacement of Colonel Whitmore by Commissioner St John Brannigan. Demilitarisation was more nominal than real, and a shrinking but still formidable constabulary continued to man the frontiers of Pakehadom until its abolition in 1886. Its abolition was an important marker – a practical and therefore convincing government recognition that the Maori threat had faded. But all police continued to be issued with firearms to 1905, and the Constabulary was succeeded by a small regular force, called the 'Permanent Militia' or 'Permanent Force', which marched against Maori on several occasions in the 1890s, sometimes with machine guns and cannon.

While the regular army shrank from 1869, it could still be supplemented by volunteers and kupapa, and various developments increased the power of the state at the same time. For various reasons, a mid-nineteenth-century Maori community was more formidable militarily than a Pakeha community of the same size, or even two or three times the size. It was only when Pakeha pooled their economic surplus or access to credit, and expressed their power through the central state and its full-time armies, that they gained an advantage. The state's capacity to persuade its citizens to pool resources was limited in the 1860s. Thereafter, however, its power grew, helped by telegraph, telephones and rail, which enabled it to respond more rapidly and effectively to the various outbreaks of Maori resistance between 1881 and 1916. New types of firearms, including the machine gun, became available, to Pakeha but not Maori, though they would not necessarily have been much use against modern pa. Technology was only part of a massive tightening of the state's power over all its citizens, Maori and Pakeha. From the 1880s, Maori prospects of effective resistance declined, and the government need for collaborators fell with it.

Another state instrument, combining the characteristics of both stick and carrot, was the Native Land Court. Established in 1865 after a dry run in 1862, this notorious institution was designed to destroy Maori communal land tenure and so both facilitate Pakeha land buying and 'detribalise' Maori. It was quite successful, especially in achieving its first aim. Between 1865 and 1873, the court granted tenure to a small number of the owners, usually ten, who sometimes acted as individuals rather than trustees for their hapu. Thereafter, all Maori with rights to a particular piece of land were eligible to be registered as individual shareholders in it by the court. But they had to be there to be registered. If a few of many owners decided to take their land before the court, this pressured the others into doing so too, to protect their rights – otherwise the land might be sold from under them. Individual shareholders succumbed to pressures to sell more readily than did groups. They could be committed to selling by a preliminary payment, 'takoha' or 'tamana'. When prospective buyers had acquired a number of these promises to sell, they could 'apply to the court to partition out their total interest. This placed non-sellers in a difficult position; they were often left with small, fragmented and uneconomic segments, which they could choose to retain, or they could capitulate and sell, too.'[28]

The Land Court process also prised Maori out of independence and into the state's embrace. Maori disengagers who owned land on the Pakeha side of the frontier lost it to engager co-owners by boycotting the court. The temptation to 'go inside' by attending the court and accepting its adjudication was great. Compensation Courts in the late 1860s, returning 'Native Reserves' of confiscated land to those who accepted state authority, acted to lever out resisters in much the same way. Land Court proceedings were expensive, surveys were charged to the Maori owners, and the costs combined with declining income, and perhaps rising consumer expectations, to tempt many Maori into debt. With economic opportunities limited by swamping, the way out of debt was increasingly to sell land.[29]

The debt cycle and the Land Court created a vortex into which much Maori land was sucked in the 1870s and 1880s. Especially where ruthless Pakeha co-operated with selfish Maori, land was lost through moral if not legal fraud. 'Very often, when the land was sold, the majority of the owners knew nothing about it.'[30] Between 1861 and 1891, Maori land in the North Island halved from 22 million to 11 million acres, or from about 80 to 40 per cent. Less than a sixth of this land was lost to confiscation, the rest to sale. From the late 1860s, government and private land buyers followed the expansion of loose empire into more and more Maori districts, unconcerned about whether empire was present through conquest, conversion or swamping, and helping to tighten it. Pakeha power to define land alienation increased greatly. Compensations such as town-tribe partnerships and the hiatus between nominal and actual alienation still existed, but they were smaller, fewer and briefer, less effectively underwritten by Maori power. Much of the remaining Maori land in 1890 was not suitable for agriculture, and 2.5 million acres of it was leased to Pakeha. In the 1890s, the new Liberal government undertook a fresh spasm of land buying, which netted 2.3 million acres for £562,000, in addition to 400,000 acres acquired by private buyers. Land buying slowed greatly in the 1900s, but by 1911 Maori held only 7 million acres, a quarter of the North Island. By 1920, they held 5 million acres, most of it leased to Pakeha, and only a fifth usable for Maori agriculture.[31]

But, even with the Land Court, the picture of naive Maori victims succumbing to legal chicanery and the blandishments of cunning Pakeha land buyers and storekeepers can be overdrawn. Old reasons for selling persisted. Rivalry for mana continued, with the court itself as an arena. Old currencies included impressive hui and tangi, and the building of meeting houses – which seems to have boomed in the late nineteenth century.[32] Fresh currencies, at least among Ngati Kahungunu, included such things as tombstones, bridal dresses, and buggies for chiefly transport. 'A buggy became the status symbol of a rangatira.' Karaitiana Takamoana had a 'Maori Club', a substantial hostelry, built in Napier to accommodate his hapu when they visited town.[33] Such things cost money, of which land selling was increasingly the easiest source, but they were also symbols of group mana, cohesion and dynamism. Money from land sales was also still used by Maori for capital investment. Maori, too, went in for dairying and sheep farming when they could. A Nga Puhi chief, Rawiri Taiwhanga, had been New Zealand's first commercial dairy farmer in the

1830s.[34] But Maori participation in the farming revolution of the 1880s and after was severely limited.

The central problem was that participating required capital-intensive re-equipping. Pakeha, even quite poor ones, were able to do this because banks and, later, the state were willing to supply them with credit. Dairying in Taranaki was not very successful in the 1880s, when banks would not supply credit, but took off in the 1890s, when they did.[35] Maori had access to *consumer* credit, a slate at the store, and it was this that caught them up in the cycle of debt and land sale. But they did not have access to *capital* credit – loans for capital investment. Land owned under traditional tenure, and even shares owned under Land Court tenure, was not considered good security for capital loans. Further, Maori were not party to the subtle systems that established creditworthiness in Pakeha eyes. This greatly hampered their capacity to exploit agricultural developments, and reinforced the pressure to sell land. The choice, as Ngati Porou agricultural reformers recognised early, was between selling some land and using the proceeds to develop the rest, or leaving the lot undeveloped. Arguably, this was more realism in harsh circumstances than naivety. The problem in agriculture paralleled that in military and transport technology. While the pace of change was slow, Maori were able to accumulate enough ships, guns and iron tools over long periods of time to maintain parity with Pakeha, and to use superior techniques – teamwork and the modern pa system – to give themselves a qualitative edge. When the pace of change quickened, inferior access to credit and the new technology – factors beyond Maori control – led to their falling behind. These factors cut in hard in the late nineteenth century.

Engagement with the state, in national and local politics, administration and law, was another carrot. Maori continued to be tempted into this for mana, the desire to participate in the framing of laws affecting them, and the hope that they could subvert or at least soften the weight of the state. Civil law enforcement by Pakeha courts and police also functioned as a stick. But it could only strike where loose empire was already established, though it did help tighten it. Where Maori independence was intact, the law was not very effective, and Pakeha still noted and resented it. There was widespread Maori resistance to the dog tax , introduced in 1881, because this was the first direct tax that the state seriously attempted to impose on Maori. It was a symptom of the long-delayed advent of empire.

From the end of the Waikato War in 1864 until 1916, this package of sticks and carrots, helping and helped by swamping, was applied to Aotearoa – autonomous Maoridom. The general picture can be traced to some extent through the Maori rate of convictions for assault. In 1858–67, the Maori rate per capita was less than a seventh that of Pakeha. In 1868–77, it was about a quarter; in 1878–87 it rose sharply to a half, and in 1888–97 to three-quarters.

In 1898–1907, it was over 80 per cent of the Pakeha rate; climbed well above it in the next decade, 1908–17; was two and a half times as high in 1918–27; and remained much higher to the present. A large decrease in the Pakeha rate from the 1870s, and a large increase in the Maori rate from the 1910s, contributed very considerably to this pattern, but so did the increasing grip of Pakeha law over Maori.[36]

Different balances of swamping, coercion and seduction struck different Maori regions and groups at different times. There was a broad division between areas that had resisted during the wars of the 1860s and those which had collaborated. Outside this were two regions, the north and south of the North Island, that had done their resisting and collaborating in the 1840s and thereafter pursued a mix of both strategies. Moderate, non-military resistance and collaboration was another variation, and we can adapt the contemporary terms 'outsiders' and 'insiders' to describe it. Insiders did not actually fight for the state in the 1860s, and were not potential military allies thereafter, but did engage and co-operate with it quite actively. Partly swamped groups near big cities, Te Ati Awa of Wellington and Ngati Whatua of Auckland, were examples of insiders, as were resister groups that had submitted in some degree during the wars, such as the section of Ngati Ruanui under Hone Pihama. Outsiders kept themselves at arm's length from Pakeha state and society as far as possible, without actually offering resistance.

Major centres of resistance included central Taranaki, the Urewera Mountains and the King Country. Each of these areas was an independent Maori state in the 1870s. They were not strictly tribal entities but had elements of pan-tribalism. Central Taranaki was centred on Parihaka and led by its prophets Te Whiti O Rongomai, Tohu Kakahi and, from the early 1870s, Titokowaru. Parihaka was a substantial township, its population swelled by adherents of Te Whiti's movement from other regions. It engaged with Pakeha economics, technology and even culture. But it did not engage with the state or accept its writ. An example of this was its successful protection of Wiremu Hiroki, who killed a surveyor in 1878 in South Taranaki and then took refuge at Parihaka. The prophets of Parihaka had an ideology of non-violence, but the state was not certain of this. Until 1881, the confiscation of central Taranaki's broad acres, effected on paper in 1865, remained a figment of the bureaucratic imagination – a classic example of both nominal land alienation and false empire, a myth on a map.

From 1877, the government tried to prise open Parihaka with carrots in the form of £54,000 worth of bribes, without success. From 1879, it used a small stick – surveying some of the land under armed guard in preparation for sale and settlement. Adherents of the prophets responded with non-violent but well-organised resistance, notably the ploughing up of survey lines. This resistance was temporarily effective, but in 1881 the government pulled out its biggest stick in the form of 2,500 troops, 1,600 of whom marched on peaceful Parihaka in November. The prophets were imprisoned, the town dismantled, and that was probably the end of Parihaka as an independent state, though not as the centre of an autonomous movement. Te Whiti and Tohu were still ploughing up disputed land and harbouring fugitives from Pakeha justice in the 1890s; 'defying Pakeha sovereignty' in 1905; and their deaths in 1907 were seen as key blows to 'the fast-dying idea of Maori nationhood'.[37] Loose empire, it appears, came to central Taranaki in 1881; tight in 1907. But the capacity of the Parihaka movement and the town itself to act as a focus for Maori identity and cultural and social autonomy did not die with its independence or its founding leaders. 'The influence of Te Whiti and Tohu lives on. On 5 November 1981, several thousand people gathered on the marae at Parihaka to celebrate their identity as a people and to acclaim the mana of their chiefs.'[38]

Although some land bordering the Urewera had been confiscated in 1866, and the interior penetrated by colonists and kupapa between 1869 and 1872 in the hunt for Te Kooti, the chiefs of Tuhoe were able to impose and maintain an aukati (boundary) around their mountains from the 1870s to the 1890s. In 1895, the threat of violent resistance to surveys triggered an expedition by colonial troops, armed with machine guns. According to James Cowan, the chronicler of the New Zealand Wars, who had gone along for the ride, war was quite close.[39] But a compromise agreement was reached with the help of neo-kupapa mediators, balking Cowan of first-hand experience of his subject, which to some extent formalised the independence of the region. Its legislative shape was the Urewera Native Reserve Act of 1896. The Act was ostensibly intended by the government to allow Tuhoe to 'govern themselves in accordance with their own traditions', and was therefore exceptionally enlightened in principle.[40] In practice, it appears to mark the beginning of the encroachment of loose empire in the Urewera. Elsdon Best raced its effects in his effort to record the 'traditional lifestyle' of Tuhoe.[41] By the 1900s, schools established in the late 1890s were 'taking on the appearance of a Pakeha trojan horse'.[42] By 1920, much land had been sold or leased, and Tuhoe had experienced two decades of poverty.[43]

Empire in the Urewera was not tight in the 1900s and early 1910s, nor complete even in loose form. Hare Matenga, 'the Maori Bushranger', took refuge in 'the vast, almost unknown territory' on the northern fringes of the Urewera, and 'the majesty of the law was set at defiance' for four years before he was captured in 1907. 'Matenga had highlighted that at least one region remained out of reach of the authorities.'[44] In the 1900s, a new prophet emerged in the region, the remarkable Rua Kenana, a successor to Te Kooti in the leadership of the Ringatu Church.[45] By 1907, he had established a community of 600 people at Maungapohatu, the sacred Stone Mountain of Tuhoe. Like Te Whiti's, Rua's policies were peaceful and progressive. He strove to modernise trade and agriculture, and experimented with banking and mining. But they were also independent, rejecting Pakeha laws and taxes.

In 1916, in the midst of World War One, a state increasingly intolerant of dissent ordered another invasion of the Urewera, resulting in what historians have called 'the last shooting in the Anglo–Maori Wars'.[46] While this affair should not be sensationalised, it should not be minimised either. The expedition was 'conducted like a military operation', with some of the police themselves believing their commander was 'determined to have a shoot-out'. Three columns of police, some armed with rifles, were involved, the main column 57 strong and accompanied by a medical officer for casualties. The Maori did not intend violent resistance – their shotguns were loaded with birdshot – but Rua was seized and a substantial gunfight broke out in confused circumstances. Two Maori were killed and at least two wounded. Four police were wounded – one in the genitals, which 'looked like a plum pudding' from the effects of the birdshot. Rua was gaoled after a trial so suspect that it aroused a Pakeha outcry.[47] Released in 1918, he struggled to maintain his movement until his death in 1937; his Ringatu Church lives on.

In 1882, a British visitor to New Zealand, J. Kerry-Nicholls, decided to explore the northern heart of the North Island. He expected to find it 'part of the British empire'.

> I soon, however, learned that the extensive region ruled over by the Maori king was, to all intents and purposes, an *imperium et imperio* situated in the heart of an important British colony, a *terra incognita*, inhabited exclusively by a warlike race of savages, ruled over by an absolute monarch, who defied our laws, ignored our institutions, and in whose territory the rebel, the murderer, and the outcast took refuge with impunity.[48]

Value judgements aside, this was precisely accurate. The King Country, a regional name that persists to the present, was the clearest example of the states-within-states that survived the wars. Its core was Ngati Maniapoto territory, hosting many hundreds of refugees from Waikato proper after 1864. Kawhia, Waikato territory that had survived conquest, was an Old New Zealand port throughout the 1870s, like Kororareka in 1830. In 1874, the population of the King Country was estimated at 7,000; in 1882–83 its territory was estimated at between 7,000 and 10,000 square miles, or up to 22 per cent of the North Island. Both population and territory fluctuated with changes in adherence to the King Movement.[49] Long portrayed as an isolated dying place for the irrelevant vestiges of Maori independence, left alone only through Pakeha disinterest or benevolence, the King Country was in fact a more enduring and successful polity than some Pakeha provinces – its economic viability compared favourably with that of Southland. Like the Urewera, the King Country was said to be exempt from population decline, although the evidence on this is mixed.[50]

Economic and even diplomatic relations with Pakeha did not stop at the King's aukati, but the colonial state's authority certainly did. Pakeha guests were allowed, but only if they had the equivalent of a visa. In addition to nine Pakeha killed in the 1869 raid on Pukearuhe in North Taranaki, Pakeha trespassers were killed in separate incidents in 1870, 1873 and 1880, and several others were imprisoned. No effort was made to avenge or punish any of these incidents by the King Country's nominal sovereigns, the Pakeha government. Criminals from Pakeha justice, including the arch-rebel Te Kooti, found safe refuge there. In no case did the government take a stick to the King Movement; instead, it sought to use carrots, making a series of seductive offers including recognition of Kingite autonomy, if not full independence. One large but not immediately successful carrot was an amnesty for 'war criminals' in 1883, including Te Kooti himself. Far from looking upon the King Country with disinterest, the government was almost desperate in its desire to open it up.

Carrots did eventually succeed in opening the King Country to loose empire, but the moment is difficult to date precisely. King Tawhiao's visit to Te Awamutu in 1881, the conventional marker, has been shown to be too early – the visit was to make peace with the government, not to submit to it.[51] The entry of the Main Trunk railway, a police station and the Native Land Court, and the arrest of the prophet Te Mahuki, between 1884 and 1890, are more likely markers. The Kingites were still opposing dog taxes and surveys in the 1890s; but these harbingers of empire were now there to oppose. The growing weight of the Pakeha state and economy were factors in the demise of Kingite independence, as were internal disputes. Slices of Kingite support were prised off by land selling and leasing on its fringes from the late 1860s, notably among Ngati Haua. But some of these sales were only nominal for a time, and some groups returned to their Kingite allegiance. The decisive dissension appears to have been between Ngati Maniapoto and Waikato in the 1880s, combined with the death of Tawhaio, the great prophet-king, in 1894. Ngati Maniapoto chiefs felt that engagement with Pakeha could be better controlled if allowed in voluntarily. They and Ngati Haua may also have felt that the supra-tribal element of Kingism was subverting their mana.

From the 1890s, the King Movement turned from disengagement to protest, combined with a degree of engagement with the Pakeha state. A Kingite MHR, Henare Kaihau, entered the Pakeha Parliament in 1896, and Tawhaio's successor, King Mahuta, served briefly on the Legislative Council from 1903. Loose empire, then, arrived in the King Country about 1890. Tight empire may have had to wait until World War One, when the King Movement passively resisted conscription. They were successful in that none of their people was forced into the army in time to fight in the Pakeha war, but not in avoiding mass arrest and repression.

Official Pakeha statistics in 1891 registered twenty 'principal tribes' in the North Island, and apportioned all but 500 of the Maori population to them. The five leading government allies (Ngati Porou, Arawa, Ngati Kahungunu, Whanganui and Nga Puhi) accounted for four of the top five placings in tribal numbers, and for 20,663, or 53 per cent, of all North Island Maori.[52] It may be that the five would not have done so well in 1860, and that their extra embrace was not solely due to Pakeha statistical favouritism. The mana, power and influence resulting from their success in the wars may have enhanced the capacity of these groups to impose their names on their neighbours. In the immediate aftermath of the wars, there does appear to have been something almost amounting to subimperialism among some kupapa tribes. There were Maori Military Settlers. Whanganui received confiscated Ngati Ruanui land just south of the Waingongoro River in 1866, and a party of their warriors was in occupation until early 1868, when they decided they were too homesick. Nga Rauru, supporters of Titokowaru, were taken under the Whanganui wing in 1869, were protected by them from government revenge, and may have been counted with them in censuses. Lower Whanganui may have gained influence with their upriver kin in a similar way. Both Nga Rauru and Upper Whanganui marched with Kepa against Te Kooti from 1869, kupapa of the kupapa.[53] A similar story could probably be told for the pro-government sections of Ngati Porou and Arawa. The Rongowhakaata resisters of Poverty Bay complained unavailingly in 1874 that Ngati Porou kupapa chiefs were still being used by the government to 'administer their affairs'.[54] Accurate before-and-after political maps dated 1864 and 1872 might show that the pro-government sections of these groups expanded their 'empires', just like the government. There *were* Maori winners of the New Zealand Wars.

Another fruit of collaboration was the four Maori seats in Parliament. The relevant Bill was passed in 1867, and the first election was held in 1868.[55] Humanitarian principles may have been a factor in some Pakeha support, but the need to keep the kupapa on side was probably more important – the Bill was introduced by arch-pragmatist Donald McLean. Certainly it was to kupapa chiefs – Te Moananui of Ngati Kahungunu, Mete Kingi of Whanganui, and a Nga Puhi descendant of Waka Nene, Frederick Nene Russell – that the first seats went. In 1872, two more leading government allies, Wi Tako Ngatata of the Wellington Te Ati Awa and Mokena Kohere of Ngati Porou, were appointed to the Legislative Council. Kupapa and insiders dominated the four seats for the rest of the century. This engagement with Pakeha politics reached Pakeha levels of political vituperation. A circular letter in an 1876 election campaign described one sitting Maori member as 'an ignorant bastard' and his tribe as 'Ngati Falsehood'.[56] But political engagement did not amount to assimilation – voting 'was almost entirely tribal'.[57] Parliament became yet another arena of rivalry, though the fact that there were only four seats also stimulated intertribal negotiation and bargaining. Only four seats out of 70, combined with language barriers in the House, meant that the parliamentary representation was not of much use to Maori until the 1890s. But the seats persist to the present, and they have had spasms of utility.

The fruits of collaboration were not insignificant, but they did turn sour quite quickly. Kupapa and insiders tended by definition to engage more with Pakeha state, society and economics at the local level. Their military power, including modern government guns, and their status with the government meant they were less vulnerable to sticks in the immediate postwar period. But, with their policy of engagement, they were more vulnerable to swamping and carrots. The debt cycle and the vortex effect of the Native Land Court appears to have had most impact in kupapa regions. Land sales burgeoned in Hawke's Bay from 1870, and in Lower Whanganui and Arawa country from 1879, though there was still some delay between nominal sale and full alienation. On official statistics, fertility was higher in collaborating than resisting districts in 1874, dropped thereafter with land loss, and then recovered towards the end of the century.[58] But this could reflect the difficulties of counting in no-go resistance regions. Schools and the law also extended some sway over collaborators earlier than resisters. In short, after a postwar 'honeymoon period' lasting for most of the 1870s, swamps and carrots began to corrode kupapa independence and material conditions faster than was the case in the King Country and the Urewera. Local treaties were breached as local Pakeha gained the demographic, economic and legal muscle to get away with it. To this extent, the government's friendship proved to be more dangerous than its hostility.

Once they noted the corrosive effects of engagement, some kupapa leaders sought to call a halt to it, or at least exert tighter control over the process. They, too, turned towards strategies such as protest, pan-tribalism and even resistance itself. Ngati Kahungunu, whose kupapa chiefs were particularly self-confident and competitive land sellers, found loose empire starting to bite in their region in the 1870s. They responded with the 'Repudiation Movement', which sought, without much success, to have land sales overturned through political pressure and legal action.[59] Empire arrived in Arawa country between 1878 and 1891. In 1878, 'an armed party of Arawa occupied the Native Land Court, repelled the police, and forced the Court to adjourn to hear a disputed claim'.[60] But in 1891, 'five Arawa chiefs were arrested for nonpayment of the dog tax and put to work with shovels and wheelbarrows outside the Tauranga jail, conspicuous examples of the force of the law'.[61] This would simply not have been possible in the 1870s at the same place; and it would still have been dangerous in the

King Country at the same time. Lower Whanganui also came close to turning their government guns against the government, in 1880. Kepa objected to the survey of some land, occupied it with an armed force and closed the Whanganui River to Pakeha. Kepa's 'battle-hardened' and well-armed warriors, with at least two government rifles each, and 'the tribal cohesion and power built up in war', were 'a powerful inducement to caution' on the part of the government.[62] It enabled him to protect Whanganui independence for about as long as resistance did the job for the King Movement. But in 1890s, with Kepa's ageing and death, Whanganui attempts to disrupt steamer traffic on their river came to nothing once the police were called in.[63]

Nga Puhi of Northland, the largest official tribal group of all, were a special case. They had done most of their resisting and collaborating in the 1840s, but they did foray into both in the 1860s. In 1864, they gave help, arms and refuge to Kingite prisoners who had escaped from Kawau Island, and from 1869 they supplied some troops to the government for the last stages of the war against Titokowaru.[64] They appear to have swapped horses between resistance and collaboration with some skill, although it may be that the two strategies were associated with different sections of the tribe, heirs of Heke and Waka Nene respectively. Between them, the two strategies proved to be quite effective in slowing the advent of real empire in the north. In 1864, twenty years after Grey's 'decisive victory' at Ruapekapeka, a disgruntled Frederick Maning wrote: 'Here in the north there is no more hope of establishing the supremacy of the law than there is of flying in the air.'[65] Thirty-four years later, in 1898, the complaints of the Hokianga County Council were little different. 'As a matter of fact they are neither now or have been for several years prepared to submit to the law.'[66]

The persistence of Maori autonomy, and even independence, in the north was helped by the relatively slow growth of the local Pakeha population, and the situation varied subregionally. The imposition of Pakeha law and land purchasing increased from abou. 1870 in some subregions, and this may have influenced Northland Maori towards a policy of political protest and pan-tribalism from about 1880. They were the mainstays of the great Kotahitanga, or unity movement, which held large Maori 'parliaments' in the 1890s and linked itself back to the tribes that had signed the Declaration of Independence in 1835.[67] Although it developed links with a parallel Kingite parliament, Kauhanganui, established in 1891, Kotahitanga was supported mainly by kupapa groups. In 1893, they reminded the government that but for kupapa help, Pakeha 'authority and sovereignty of and over New Zealand would have ceased long ago, and the white people would have abandoned these islands there and then'.[68]

A useful definition of substantive sovereignty or real empire is that the sovereign power removes the capacity of its subjects to make war among themselves. An indicator of the persistence of Maori independence was therefore the persistence of tribal feuding, and Nga Puhi featured quite prominently here. There were several lethal feuds in the 1860s – ten people were shot in skirmishes in the Hokianga in 1867–68 alone. In 1879, four people were killed and three wounded in intra-tribal fighting. In 1888, near Whangarei, two hapu fought possibly the last tribal battle in Maoridom. 'Pa were built, a day was fixed for fighting, arms were prepared, a vigil kept with the sentries of either side singing the ancient chants . . . four were killed and four wounded, before the dispute was settled, in traditional fashion through the mediation of ranking men connected with both sides.'[69] Pakeha land buying may have sparked off the dispute, but the Pakeha state had nothing to do with stopping it. In 1903, however, when a Rarawa–Nga Puhi dispute almost flared into war, 50 government troops intervened and seized the guns of the combatants. Empire, it seems, had finally arrived in the Far North.[70]

The decisive event may have been the 'Dog Tax War' of 1898. From the 1880s, prophetic movements burgeoned afresh in the north, including those of the Jewish-Maori storekeeper Hone Toia and the women prophets Maria Pangari, Ani Karo and Remana Hi. These had links with each other, with the earlier Northland prophet Papahurihia, with Pai Marire and with Parihaka. The movements involved a local rejection of government authority, expressed in dog taxes and local body rates. 'Hone Toia prophesied that if dogs were to be taxed, men would be next.'[71] In 1887, 23 of Remana Hi's followers were arrested after the 'Battle of Waihou', in which five had been wounded by police gunfire. From about 1895, resistance centred on Hone Toia's supporters, based at Waima near Kaikohe, who 'in effect, established their own "state within a state"'. In 1898, the government sent in 120 troops, two cannon and two machine guns, supported by a gunboat and 60 naval volunteers, to suppress it. Violence appears to have come close. State victory, initially at least, was no foregone conclusion. Hone Toia and 70 men lay in ambush, and, according to one Pakeha observer, 'they would have slaughtered our men without being seen'. But Hone Heke, a Maori member of Parliament and great-nephew of the 1840s resister, was able to mediate and prevent bloodshed after only two shots had been fired. Hone Toia and his chief supporters were imprisoned. 'Substantive sovereignty had finally been imposed on the Far North.'[72]

Economic swamping and at least partial conversion intensified with the demise of political independence and the loss of land – a chicken-and-egg relationship. Collaborators may have suffered first, but in the end both resisters and collaborators were damaged by this process, genuine victims at last. As early as 1872, the kupapa minority of Waikato living at Raglan had sold off so much of their land that they are said to have ceased agricultural production entirely.[73]

By 1904–05, famine, flood, land loss and isolation had reduced Tuhoe to dire economic straits.[74] It was very difficult to maintain tribal cohesion and lifestyles once an economic base in the form of land had been lost, as was the case with 44 per cent of Ngai Tahu by 1890. 'Detribalisation' set in, creating a section of Maori who had no kin-based operational group. Its size is unknown in the North Island, but it probably grew quite rapidly from the 1890s. It was not entirely impossible to maintain cohesion despite land loss, as we have seen in the Ngai Tahu case, and even in this 'nadir' period the success of sticks, swamps and carrots was qualified, delayed and contested.

Dire as it was, Maori economic decline can be exaggerated. In 1891, Maori per capita had less than a quarter the sheep and half the cattle of North Island Pakeha, but about six times the pigs and over 40 per cent more acres in crops.[75] Even in 1921, they had much more land per capita than North Island Pakeha, though some of it was useless. Added to this, some Maori acquired land under European title. 'Maori land' does not equal, and is less than, land owned by Maori.[76] Court tenure, giving blocks to scores of individual shareholders, sometimes hampered economic farming, but it is not clear that individual *ownership* ever precluded communal *farming*, even before the consolidation schemes pioneered by Ngati Porou from the 1880s, whereby owners pooled their land to form an economic farming unit.[77] The court's detribalising aim was less successful than its land-selling one. The converting processes of land alienation and the Europeanising of Maori farming were never completed. Enough land and tribal cohesion remained to enable Maori to mount what has been called a 'rural renaissance' from the 1920s, though the truth is that rural Maoridom never died. Even before this 'renaissance', some Maori, notably Ngati Porou but also a number of other groups, managed to climb aboard the technological escalator of the new farming.

There were also alternatives to both the old farming and the new available to Maori. These included tourism, an important Arawa industry from the 1870s; fishing – most of 52 commercial fishing boats operating from Tauranga in 1908 were Maori-owned and -run;[78] and certain extractive industries that required little capital for entry. The gathering of edible fungus for sale to China, rabbiting for food, skins and bounties, and various other minor activities such as the sale of huia feather at £1 each could be counted among these. The most important was probably kauri-gum digging. In 1893, 3,110 Maori were gumdigging in Northland – a third of all diggers.[79]

Like team employment in shearing and contract harvesting or labouring on public and private works, participation in these Pakeha industries did not mean the corrosion of the tribe. As long as the work was done seasonally or temporarily, by tribally organised groups, and with the proceeds used to some extent for tribal ends such as hui and tangi, it did not indicate detribalisation or assimilation. 'The Pa', as kainga came increasingly to be called in the twentieth century, seemed a marginal fringe community only in the eyes of its Pakeha neighbours. Competition, co-operation and the key institutions of hui, tangihanga and the display of group mana and identity through symbols such as meeting houses, went on as before. Maori religion moved back along the spectrum to a point Pakeha accepted as their kind of Christianity, and there was some revival of missionary activity. It featured new denominations of dissent, such as Mormonism and Seventh-Day Adventism, and Maori still went and got their missionaries from overseas when they did not come fast enough themselves.[80] Prophetic religions and other pan-tribal organisations fluctuated in their support but kept a Maori collective identity alive, in both competition and co-operation with immensely tough and resilient tribalism. The decline of resistance and collaboration, to the point where Maori were no longer feared or valued by Pakeha, meant they desperately needed some sort of fresh leverage – to prise concessions from the state, and soften and subvert its weight. The sequel to this book will show that even this challenge was not beyond them.

In the end, contact did become empire. Maori cultural autonomy and identity survived the impact of Europe; Maori political independence did not. By the 1890s, the state could seduce or coerce most Maori if it wanted to, and by 1916 virtually all were subject to its sway. The myths of empire eventually came nearly true – they proved to be dynamics of real history, as well as myths. Empire did arrive in the end; why then should we make such a fuss of its mythical dimension? One of at least three reasons is that the myths obscured the actual story of Maori resilience and created a history that was not fair to them. They were not tricked by treaty, suborned by tools and cash, duped in land sales, awestruck by European Christianity, swept away by European disease or conquered by European military superiority. Instead, they converted conversion, limited conquest and defied fatal impact. Maori society and culture was damaged – severely in some times and places – and it did change massively. The population halved in the century or so after 1769. Political independence was ultimately ground down. Maori bent under the weight of Europe, eventually to the point where the Pakeha state was able to pass a rope over the Maori tree and kept it bent and politically subordinate. But Maori did not break. Given the real odds, given the myths and given the precedents, which is the more remarkable, the more worthy of featuring largest in our history books: the bending or the absence of the breaking?

The second reason for emphasising myth is that it proved to be self-actualising. The myths of empire and the illusion of a pre-existing, unofficial and evil false empire were key influences on British intervention in 1840. False empire predominated between 1840 and 1860, and it worked surprisingly well. It camouflaged the fact that interaction between Maori and Pakeha spheres was based on rough parity, and that this had some prospect of permanence. When the camouflage was removed by the rise of pan-tribalism, the myths of empire and associated dreams of 'great futures' for Pakeha were a key cause of the wars of the 1860s. The myth of conquest then exaggerated British and Pakeha successes, but it also helped ensure that they did secure some sort of victory. It made ultimate defeat almost unimaginable, and here as elsewhere encouraged Europe to try, try and try again, like Robert Bruce's spider. After the wars, myth created the illusion that Maori independence had quickly and completely disappeared. Large chunks of Aotearoa were still independent in 1880, but not all historians noticed them. European dominance over most Maori was achieved a full half-century later than some people still think it was, and half a century is a very substantial proportion of New Zealand's post-contact history. When empire celebrated its centenary in 1940, it overestimated itself by a hundred per cent. The myths of empire helped both exaggerate and cause empire over Maori. Because the myths were not peculiar to New Zealand, the same may be true of European empire elsewhere.

Third, the fact that empire came late had important implications for the future. In East Britain in the fifth and sixth centuries, the Anglo-Saxon invaders quite quickly overcame, displaced and submerged the natives, and a distinct Romano-Celtic culture did not survive, though it left more legacies than was once thought. In West Britain, though empire came to Wales in the end, it came slowly enough for the native culture and language to survive. Similarly, in New Zealand, slowing empire was not wholly a heroic but ultimately fruitless act of swimming against the swamping tides. The survival of a distinct, though never frozen, Maori culture owes something to British humanitarianism, and to the fact that the 'White Savage' stereotype was more prominent in New Zealand than in some other colonies, and this should be acknowledged. But it clearly owes even more to Maori resilience – a resilience that consisted partly of staunch resistance, but also of eager, adaptive and innovative engagement with the things and thoughts of Europe. Survival was obviously significant for itself, and it provided a base for a gradual and subtle reassertion of Maori importance in the first half of the twentieth century, and a less subtle reassertion in the second half.

Maori independence faced formidable enemies in its long contest with Europe. Dutch, French and Australians killed Maori, and Maori killed them. Maori themselves were important agents of both contact and empire. They magnified and sharpened the various agencies of conquest, conversion and fatal impact, as well as resisting, subverting and converting them. To pretend that this was not so is to merely invert the myths of empire without transcending them. The metropolitan British were also formidable enemies of Maori independence. The Pakeha legend of Old British military incompetence underestimates them, as does a Maori legend of a benign if sometimes misguided

British Crown – contrasted to greedy and ruthless settlers. It is true that London was more tolerant than Wellington of Maori independence, but it, too, was subject to the myths of empire, and to the manipulation of agents who were even more subject. After all, it was thousands of imperial troops and millions of imperial money that turned the tide against Maori independence in the Waikato War. Yet, in the end, Maori found that the most persistent and formidable enemies of all were the 'swamping tides', the new British of New Zealand: the Pakeha.

PART

3

Making Pakeha

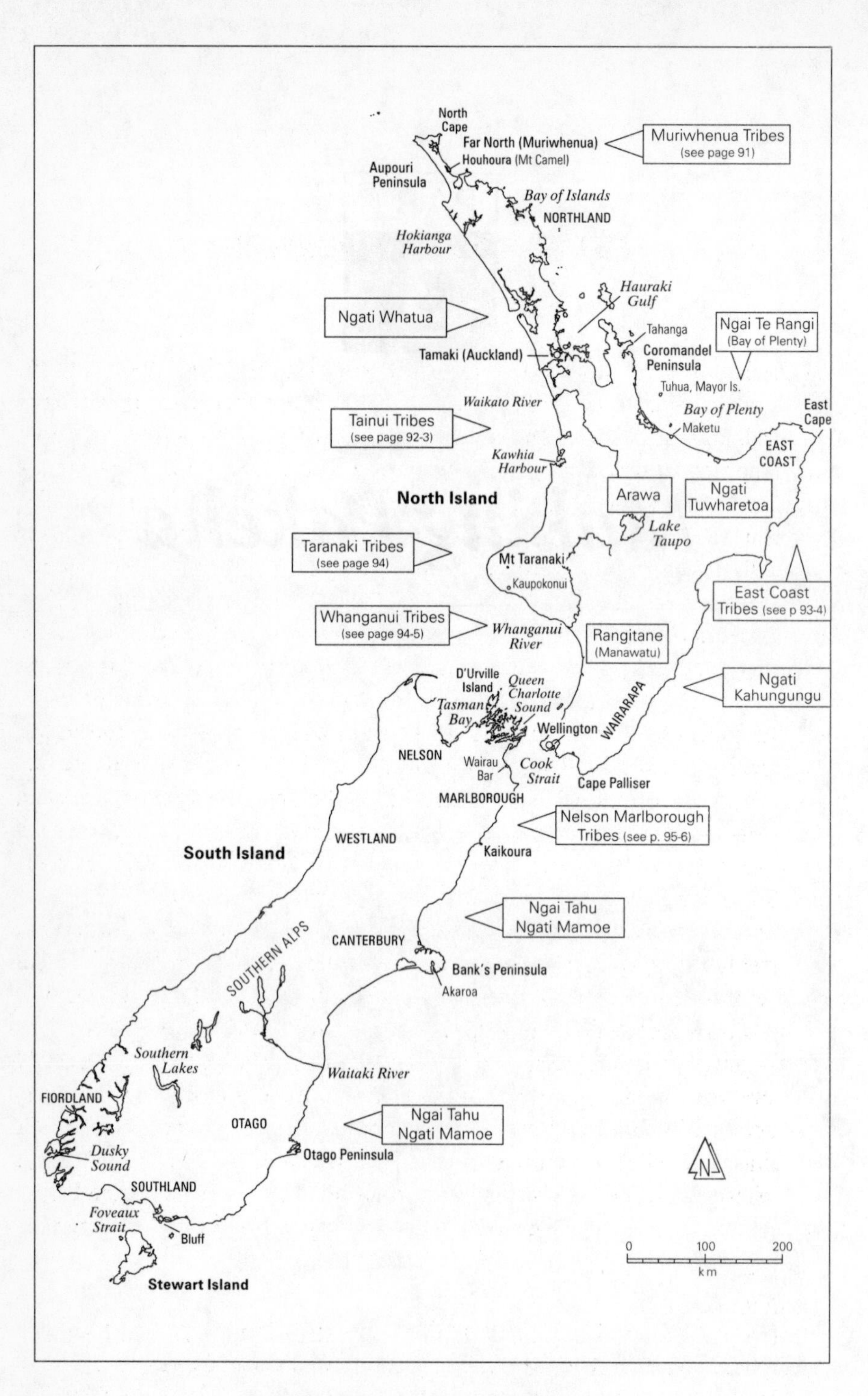

Pre-History and Early Contact

New Zealand's first European community was established in 1795 at Facile Harbour, Dusky Sound, Fiordland. The earliest capital of contact, the scene of New Zealand's first reflections on the wonders of progress and civilisation, and of the first brewing of beer, the first Pakeha settlement was subsequently abandoned and forgotten. There are no pilgrimages to the site of Pakeha nativity. Perhaps it was because the first community arrived by accident, had absolutely nothing to do with Maori and was dominated by the desire to get out, not on.

In September 1795, the 800-ton ship *Endeavour*, under Captain William Bampton, sailed from Sydney for India. The poor state of the ship and 'stress of weather' forced the *Endeavour* to put in to Facile Harbour, where it promptly sank (later leading to the legend that it was Cook's *Endeavour*, come home to die). The community thus founded consisted of 244 people – easily the largest cluster of Europeans in New Zealand until the 1830s. Some of these people lived at Facile Harbour for 21 months, eventually being rescued by the American whaler *Mercury* in 1797. Forty-five men and one woman were escaped convicts, stowed away at Sydney with the connivance of some of the crew. There were also a few officers and gentlemen, but they were not the same people.

It was not a happy community. The chief mate argued with the captain soon after landing, and resigned; stores were stolen and thieves flogged within a couple of weeks. The economy consisted in living off capital in the form of the ship's provisions, slaughtering seals and fitting out boats with which to escape – getting out was the shared driving dream. The boats in progress could not fit everyone, and Captain Bampton sought to maintain order by changing the selection of those to be marooned. Tempers frayed. The new chief mate, Mr Waine, quarrelled with a passenger, Mr Alms, calling him a 'S—n Puppy'. The mysterious epithet was 'so foul an execration' that Alms challenged Waine to a duel with pistols. The fourth mate, Mr Murry, recorded the exchange.

> MR A: You must fight me.
> MR W: I cannot.
> MR A: Then, Sir, You are a COWARD, a DASTARDLY COWARD! Mr Murry, you hear what I say. I call Mr Waine a Coward, who would dare to affront a gentlemen and refuse him satisfaction. Mr W. you are a Coward, I shall publish this in India.

MR W: Well, if you call me a Coward I shall act accordingly.
(He then left the Cabin).[1]

Over the next century, this tiny, squabbling, temporary European community was succeeded by a proto-people half a million strong: the Pakeha of New Zealand. The bare bones of their history has been recounted in Part Two, as a backdrop to their relations with Maori. The following chapters flesh out the story of the making of the Pakeha, 1840s–80s. Subsequent history is reserved for a sequel, as are dimensions such as sport and childhood, whose key shifts cross the great divide between the colonial era and the era of 'recolonisation', 1880s–1960s, when links with Britain tightened, against the grain of our expectations, and Pakeha society was transformed. There are seldom clear cuts in history. The transition between colonial and 'recolonial' eras did not happen in a day, but took place unevenly between the 1880s and the 1900s, with prologues and postscripts outside even those years. Part Three therefore reaches forward and back to accommodate the inconvenient way in which history shifts, but the main focus is on the foundation of Pakeha society, 1840s–80s.

Pakeha colonisation is no heroic tale of virtuous pioneer-farmers slowly and steadily overcoming adversity, or of supine loyalty and subordinacy to Britain, as it often used to be told; nor a nasty morality parable of boring, grey but greedy settlers leaching all the life, morals and colour out of our past, as it is sometimes told today. The proto-Pakeha were ruthless, even merciless, towards both nature and natives, but they were also dynamic, sometimes hysterically so. The drama has been largely written out, a strange act of retrospective taming, and so has the wider significance. Like Maori settlement, this is the story of the colonial reproduction of a people, in this case the formation of a neo-Britain. The story happened differently here to anywhere else, but its fundamentals are shared. Anyone who believes that this makes the story less important needs to think again.

Between the sixteenth and the nineteenth centuries, exploding Europe populated the Americas, Australasia and the extreme ends of Africa with colonial or creole peoples and their associated plants, animals and diseases. The first leading mother country was Spain; Portugal, the Netherlands and France were important; and the Irish, Germans, Italians and others contributed their millions to other people's neo-Europes. But the late leader was Britain. The total number of neo-Britains that survive today, discounting for French, Spanish and Dutch contributions, is something less than the sum of the states of the USA and Australia, the provinces of Canada and South Africa, and New Zealand. Most of these emerged from separate colonisations – primary, from the British Isles themselves, or secondary, from those neo-Britains that had matured enough to reproduce.

For some time, the history of these entities, or clusters of them, has largely been written in post-colonial or nationalist mode. This stresses the uniqueness of each state or cluster, enhancing present identity by asserting past difference, or at least by underplaying similarity. General histories of Canada, the United States, Australia and New Zealand read like so many biographies of the Apostles, each pretending that its subject was the only one. Most neo-Britains have the same list of 'unique' national characteristics: egalitarianism, pragmatism, anti-intellectualism, 'colonial ingenuity' and the like. This stems in part from a very common human fallacy: the tendency to confuse separate identity with uniqueness. In the case of neo-Britains, too strident a hunt for uniqueness pursues a chimaera, a Holy Grail. There are scores of them, and to claim that features of a given settler society were 'unique' can set you up for a fall. New Zealand shares the general story of the reproductive expansion of Europe. But it also has as much right to that story as anywhere else, and as much responsibility to contribute to the analysis of it.

Post-colonial history, of course, plunged into the parochialism trap in reaction to colonial history: the study of New Zealand or Canada as a subordinate expression of British history, a practice quite rightly rejected in the more recent past. But healthy individualism does not require one to deny that parents and siblings exist. To over-react to the 'colonial cringe' is to still be dominated by it. Yet there is one respect in which New Zealand is unique, and has been since Newfoundland joined Canada in 1949. It is the only stand-alone neo-Britain. The others could not take the pace on their own, and clustered together in the federal nations of the United States, Canada and Australia. The task of the historians of these clusters was to forge federal identities; of New Zealand, to forge a separate one. Part Three of this book seeks to tell the tale of the making of Pakeha in itself and for itself as the founding act of the majority of today's New Zealanders. All histories have to stop somewhere, and the reader must look elsewhere for sustained comparisons between neo-Europes.[2] But this book does acknowledge that much of New Zealand's story is shared, and suggests that the country's size, isolation, recency and stand-alone status may enhance it as a case study in a wider saga: the formation of neo-Europes through the interaction of fragment, frontier and the ethos of expansion. In New Zealand, as in some other nineteenth-century neo-Britains, the most remarkable feature of the story was its speed. If there is a general explanation for this, New Zealand history suggests that it lies at the intersection of mythology and economics: the dream-driven mass migration of people and money.

CHAPTER TWELVE

The Pakeha Prospectus

In the half-century 1831–81, the European population of New Zealand increased by 50,000 per cent – from fewer than a thousand people to half a million. Although birth rates were very high, the ship beat the womb as a route of entry. Over 400,000 came, of whom almost 300,000 stayed, while the number of births was around 250,000.[3] Subsequent growth rates pale into insignificance against these swamping tides of people, which laid the demographic foundation of Pakeha New Zealand. After 1880, the womb took the lead and continually extended it. The migrants of the 1830s–80s are the ancestors of most New Zealanders. Who were these people? Why did they come? What in heaven did they hope to find at the other end of the earth?

The founding population of Pakeha New Zealand was part of a massive nineteenth-century European diaspora involving around 50 million people.[4] The motives of these emigrants are a problem that daunts experts. Most children and some married women did not have much choice. Some people made a rational economic decision, based on objective information, to move to a place where they would gain more money. Some were drawn out by the process known as chain migration, anchored by an early migrant who then brings out friends and family. More general traditions of migration to particular destinations drew out others. Others again were partly bribed by assisted passages or free land. Many, especially from Ireland after the terrible potato famine of 1846–48, and from southern and eastern Europe, were pushed out by sheer want.

All these factors contributed to the peopling of New Zealand, but they do not finally explain it. New Zealand did not want the people with the strongest push, and inherently it had the weakest pull. It wanted people from Britain, then one of the richest countries in the world. The United States and the colonies of Canada and Australia were also in the market for Britons, and they were far larger, closer and more established destinations. Between 1815 and 1930, they imported about 40 million people between them, of whom a quarter were Britons.[5] They could have absorbed the ancestors of the Pakeha without even noticing them. This chapter tries to explain how Pakeha New Zealand was peopled, against the odds, by migrants drawn mainly from the British Isles – directly or indirectly. It argues that they were not so much pushed out of Britain by actual and immediate costs, or pulled in to New Zealand by actual and immediate benefits, as prised out of their British contexts by powerful myths and prophecies. These Pakeha myths of settlement were the New Zealand variant of a wider British or neo-British ethos of expansion, a sort of momentum between push and pull. The myths began as bait for migrants; they became the prospectus New Zealand was considered obligated to fulfil, a history written in advance.

The Colonising Crusade

In the old Pakeha myth of origin, Edward Gibbon Wakefield, the New Zealand Company and its affiliates, and the decade of the 1840s take precedence as of right. Pakeha New Zealand was peopled in a single process by a 'better stock', by which was meant, at minimum, better than the convict Australians. This is obviously false: the European pioneers came before the 1840s, many *were* convict Australians, and the companies contributed only 15,600 – about four per cent – of the founding population.[6] E. G. Wakefield himself did not come down to us until 1852, although He did send His Son. Historians have long debunked the myth of 'better stock', and are beginning to discount Wakefield, the 1840s and even the 1850s, and to focus on 1860–80, when most of the founding population arrived. In terms of pure numbers, of demographic history alone, this is absolutely correct. But myths do not become unimportant merely because they are false, and the myth was not entirely false: there *was* a single process of foundation.

The peopling of Pakeha New Zealand and its cultural construction, the growth of a New Zealand image in people's minds, were two interlocked processes. The same individuals organised both, in a continuous line from Wakefield in the 1830s and 1840s to Julius Vogel, the colonial politician who was chief architect of the peopling and imaging of the 1870s and 1880s. Peopling and imaging by the companies in the 1840s, by the provincial governments in the 1850s and 1860s, and by the colonial government in the 1870s were phases of the same process. They had the same basic purpose, very often the same administrators, similar motives and similar tools, and they were aimed at the same market. The purpose was to swiftly and thickly seed New Zealand with British people and money, meeting the 'one great overriding want of *getting peopled*'.[7] The administrators were company leaders and officials, provincial and colonial politicians, and formal or informal publicists and emigration and loan agents in Britain. The intersection between these roles was so great that New Zealand coloniser, politician and publicist were almost synonyms. Many men served formally in two or more of these roles. Some, like William Fox, served in all. However bitterly they feuded among themselves, however much they disagreed on the details and variants of the policy, all were committed to it, and their efforts need to be considered as a whole, 1830s to 1880s. All were prophets of the same god: organised, progressive and British colonisation.

The arch-prophets Wakefield and Vogel were strange heroes for a rather prim Pakeha culture. One was a convicted kidnapper, who hypnotised people into frothing fits as a party trick, and taught his son Jerningham to do the same. The other was a brilliant and ebullient Jew in a mildly anti-Semitic age, and a journalist to boot. Neither they nor most of the lesser prophets were above feathering their own nests. Money, as well as people, was persuaded to migrate. The Holy Ghost of the leading trinity was Thomas Russell, the shadowy financier who led in almost as many private millions of money as Vogel did public. We will see in Chapter Fourteen that New Zealand colonisation was a self-contained economic system from which many hoped to profit. There is no doubt that the propaganda was often as short on truth as it was long on cunning and energy. There was an element of the 'New Zealand Bubble', of grand fraud. But there was also a genuine crusading zeal, which converted numerous enthusiastic disciples, some with no possible self-interest, and brought hundreds of thousands to the Holy Land. While the New Zealand colonisers claimed that they were hampered rather than helped by an imperial government that did not know its true British duty, officials were part-time prophets. The Colonial Office was sometimes supportive of the New Zealand Company, and Grey gave the Canterbury Association a great deal of help in buying land.[8] The process paralleled and sometimes merged with the First New Zealand Crusade: the drive to convert the Maori. In this Second Crusade, prophet/profit was both an obvious pun and a providential convergence. The prophets were caught up in their own con, the 'godlike art of colonisation' as a later Edward Wakefield was to call it,[9] and so, like it or not, was New Zealand history.

The colonising crusaders made occasional use of free land grants (especially for military migrants), extensive use of assisted passages (120,000 from the colonial government alone between 1863 and 1880) and a sort of state-boosted chain migration known as the nominee system, which supplied between a fifth and a quarter of the assisted immigrants. But we will see that an assisted passage was not normally enough in itself to induce migrants to choose New Zealand, and the majority were at least partly persuaded by propaganda. This took many forms.

In the 1840s and 1870s, company and colony set up large organisations in Britain that mounted public meetings and lecture tours, advertised extensively and set up networks of hundreds of part-time agents, largely clergy and schoolteachers, who persuaded people personally and were paid on commission.[10] In the 1840s, the New Zealand Company had fifteen staff at its London headquarters in Broad Street; the Colonial Office in Downing Street had only

25 to run the British Empire. In the 1870s, the New Zealand government had 73 immigration agents in Scotland alone, and advertised in 288 Scottish newspapers.[11] Numerous other agents operated in Britain in the years in between, paid or sent by provincial governments, working as private consultants for fees from prospective emigrants, or promoting New Zealand for free as an act of philanthropy or enlightened self-interest. Several major pictorial displays in London were backed by the crusaders: a 'New Zealand Panorama' in Leicester Square in the late 1830s, which it was claimed 'everybody has seen' by 1840;[12] paintings by G. F. Angas at Piccadilly in 1846; another Leicester Square panorama from 1849 to 1851; and Nicholas Chevalier's 150 sketches of New Zealand scenes at the Crystal Palace in 1871. Many other painters of appropriate images were sponsored by prophets such as Wakefield and Grey.[13] New Zealand displays at British exhibitions, precursors of the modern 'Expo', fulfilled the same crusading function. Exhibitions in New Zealand and overseas became symbolic festivals of progressive colonisation, as well as advertisements, an enduring exhibitionism, often celebrating achievements that did not yet exist. But the main medium was print.

The earliest New Zealand Company literature described the precipitous hills of Wellington as undulating plains, perfect for grapevines, wheat and olives – 'the rain but seldom falls during the day'.[14] The Hutt River was said to be as broad as the Thames, and navigable for 80 miles into the interior instead of the actual six. 'The Banana and a few other tropical fruits form immense orchards in New Zealand.'[15] Such gross fictions tempt us to dismiss crusader propaganda as ludicrous oversell, and to assume that the Victorians did so too – they also were familiar with deceptive advertising, which they called 'puffery'. The newspaper advertisements, placards in pubs and rail carriages, hoardings, handbills, 'flaming posters' and even 'sandwich men' used by the crusaders reinforce this impression.[16] Is it reasonable to attribute the genesis of Pakeha New Zealand to so crass and transparent an advertising campaign? The answer is yes, for several reasons.

Sheer mass was one. The crusaders published at least 40 books and 100 pamphlets in Britain, 1837–80. They sponsored, encouraged or indirectly generated hundreds of articles in British newspapers and periodicals, and ran their own newspapers in Britain.[17] Cynical contemporaries and migration scholars today share a tendency to dismiss emigration propaganda, and it is probably true that when it was blatant it was read sceptically. As with modern advertising, the market might discount lurid individual tracts and snigger at the banana orchards. But repetition crept under their guard, then as now. The market could also forget the source of its information – forget that the author of the well-written account of New Zealand you read or were told about last year was a paid publicist or a colonial politician. Although there were always some counter-currents, crusader propaganda came close to monopolising information about New Zealand through the simple volume of volumes. If you wanted information about New Zealand, it was very hard to avoid. It still is. Propaganda became subliminal when it merged imperceptibly with what appeared to be objective geography, ethnography or history. Government statistics, the New Zealand *Handbooks* and *Yearbooks*, and New Zealand history itself – all have their roots in crusader propaganda.

Wakefield and the New Zealand Company did not directly launch the main avalanche of people, but they did launch the avalanche of print – at least 20 books and 50 pamphlets, 1837–50. The themes in these were then taken up by non-company authors, with a second peak in publications as well as people in the 1870s. This literature formed the idea of New Zealand in British minds, and it was ultimately this, as well as assisted passages and chain migration, that brought out the ancestors of most Pakeha. Wakefield knew exactly what he was doing. 'It is most desirable,' he wrote to one of his New Zealand authors, 'that your labours should produce, not a mere mass of facts, but a well selected collection.'[18] As Premier, Vogel himself edited the first *New Zealand Official Handbook* in 1875, explicitly to attract emigrants and investment.

'Letters back' from pioneers were an important influence on emigrants, generating some paper-chain migration, and probably preventing more by debunking the excesses of emigration literature. Most of the New Zealand letters back we know about were managed by the crusaders – prompted, selected and published by them, and of course supporting their views. 'I shall try and persuade our emigrants to write,' wrote one company official. 'I know a great many of them have written in the warmest praise of our favoured district, and all the complaints that I have heard arise only from the . . . fellows who would do no good no where.' 'Gentlemen,' wrote an obliging John Perry to the directors of the New Zealand Company, 'I cannot express to you my gratitude for having conveyed me from the British shores to rest with my family in New Zealand.'[19]

Unmanaged letters back were probably an important counter-current, but perhaps not as much as one might think. A reluctance to admit mistakes, and an inclination to persuade other people to share them to reduce the sense of error, appears to be human nature. 'Come on in,' one cries through chattering teeth, 'the water's fine.' This was certainly the case with Gujarati Indian migration to New Zealand. An exhaustive study concludes that 'The frequent letters and visits home would have exaggerated the wealth and opportunities in New Zealand. To have depicted a less than rosy picture would have deemed the migrant a failure. Informants have vividly described how returning relatives to Gujarat depicted New Zealand as "a land of promise".'[20] The British were human too; the 'boosterism' of their settlers, proclaiming each frontier town the pinnacle of progress to any passer-by, was notorious,[21] and may well have found its way into letters back. The colonising crusade had a tendency to convert its victims, like a vampire's bite.

The convergence between private and public interests in the New Zealand colonising crusade becomes clear when we consider four authors, linchpin prophets, who wrote in the 1850s hiatus between the company and central government spasms of settlement and propaganda. They were Thomas Cholmondeley (*Ultima Thule, or Thoughts Suggested By a Residence in New Zealand*, 1854), Richard Taylor (*Te Ika a Maui, or New Zealand and Its Inhabitants*, 1855), Charles Hursthouse (*New Zealand, or Zealandia, The Britain of the South*, 1857) and Arthur Saunders Thomson (*The Story of New Zealand: Past and Present – Savage and Civilized*, 1859). All four books included history as well as geography, ethnography and 'Hints for Emigrants'. Their 2,200 well-written pages were all published in London between 1854 and 1859, and they arguably make the 1850s, not the 1950s, the high point of New Zealand general historiography.

Hursthouse was a professional propagandist, speckling his 1857 book with plugs for particular suppliers of emigration equipment, such as cork swimming belts, and concluding a previous one with a plug for himself, at half a guinea per emigration consultation. He freely admitted his self-interest but noted: 'The dentist advises a tooth out – are we to turn away in agony because he will be paid for drawing it?'[22] On the other hand, Richard Taylor was a respected and influential Anglican missionary; Thomson was an able medic and scientist, and New Zealand's best general historian before William Pember Reeves; and Cholmondeley was a remarkable social philosopher who foreshadowed Charles Darwin, Henry George and almost everyone else. All, even Hursthouse, were sometimes heavily critical of the New Zealand Company and the colonial and provincial governments. These were no mercenaries, and their books could not be dismissed as mere puffery, then or now. Yet all, like every other crusading writer, advocated British emigration to New Zealand with the enthusiasm of the evangelist.

In the late 1830s, when New Zealand first entered the mass-migrant market, most British had never heard of the place, and most of those who had knew only two things: that it was vaguely associated with Australia, an arid waste populated by convicts, and that it itself was populated by cannibals. New Zealand jokes were cannibal jokes. Emigrants as late as 1855 were advised to draw comfort from the hope that they might disagree with Maori digestions.[23] Australia and the Maori were persistent problems for the colonising crusaders, and there were others. For more than two centuries, North America had been the customary destination for British emigrants. This natural 'westward tendency'[24] of migration had been checked by Anglo–American warfare between 1776 and 1815, but by the 1830s it had well and truly restarted. Emigration meant North America, and the various established colonies of

Australia and South Africa squabbled vigorously for the scraps. By the 1840s, Sydney and Cape Town, let alone New York, were already cities, destinations in themselves and solid bases for emigrants who planned to push further inland. Kororareka was not in the running.

Added to this, agricultural land was usually costlier in New Zealand than in the other destinations. If acquiring one's own farm was the major motive for emigration, as is very widely assumed, then New Zealand was on the face of it the worst place to choose. Its fields were distant as well as dear. Long voyages were notoriously uncomfortable and dangerous, especially for children, and the voyage out to New Zealand was the longest of all. It was also the most expensive. Assisted passages, which the New Zealand crusaders shelled out in thousands, were only a partial solution to this, for two reasons. The colonising crusaders wanted money as well as people; assisted passages reduced the former as it increased the latter. Emigrants were also influenced by the 'psychological cost' of migration, the traumatic wrench of uprooting yourself from everything you know and love. This is diminished by the possibility, real or imagined, of returning home. The crusaders could not risk offering *return* tickets, and at £20 even a steerage passage back from New Zealand was beyond most wage earners' means. A codfishing boat could take you from Cork to Newfoundland – or back – for as little as ten shillings.[25] On top of all this, various developments to the 1850s lowered the tone of emigration: the transportation of convicts to Australia, the state-backed export of paupers masterminded by Robert Wilmot Horton,[26] and the massive outflow of impoverished Irish. Emigration came to be seen as a form of social excretion, and however good this might be for Britain's domestic health, few volunteered to be labelled excrement for the sake of the public good. The New Zealand crusaders had to guide potential emigrants through a veritable maze of choices: to shift or not to shift; out-migration rather than urban migration; British possessions rather than the United States; Australasia rather than South Africa or Canada; New Zealand rather than Australia. At every step, there was every chance of losing customers.

The crusaders addressed some obstacles directly. The Cannibal Maori was whitened into a Brown Briton and settlers' helpmeet, who, in case one did not quite buy this, was dying out anyway. Apart from mere paradox, there was one little problem: the New Zealand Wars. Discounting the gold rushes, peaks in Anglo–Maori conflict correspond closely with troughs in immigration, except in 1863–64, when military settlers were brought in *for* conflict. The Wairau and Poverty Bay 'massacres' in particular were unmitigated public relations disasters. Apart from portraying the wars as minor, the crusaders applied two techniques, both of which were also used in other contexts. The first, heavily stressed by the linchpin prophets of the 1850s, was to paint the 1840s and its wars as a brief Dark Age, a character-building temporary travail, arising from mismanagement by autocratic governors and ended by the advent of self-government in 1853–56. In the 1850s, crusading literature repeatedly pronounced Anglo–Maori conflict dead as a doornail. This made the wars of the 1860s all the more difficult to handle, and brought the second technique into play: seeking to conceptually stretch out New Zealand in British minds, splitting it into distinct provincial identities, only one or two of which had Maori problems, or even any Maori at all. Such stretching or regionalising of the New Zealand image was a stock technique, also used for other purposes, 'various settlements for various tastes'.[27] The New Zealand model had different makes, catering for all preferences, and with teething problems such as the massacre of customers restricted to a few only.

Australia was another problem that refused to go away. Initially it was an unwanted associate, tarring New Zealand with its brush. Stretching served here, too, to split New Zealand off from Australia and its convict population, imbibing vice with their mothers' milk. New Zealand's own thousands of weaned, second-hand convicts were swept under the carpet, where they have remained. But the parallel stretching of Australia, which taught Britain that Victoria and South Australia did not have first-hand convicts either, the end of convict transportation to New South Wales in 1840 and, above all, the discovery of gold in Victoria in 1851 meant that stretching the Tasman boomeranged. The crusaders quickly contracted it again, to allow New Zealand the rich markets of the diggings – but not too much, because they wanted diggings without diggers. 'Gold has changed the Australian character,' declared Richard Taylor, into 'a sordid selfish spirit.' 'We don't go to *New Zealand*,' emphasised Hursthouse in 1857, 'with pick and pan, to snatch dear won nuggets, gulp gallons of rum, and then, rich or ragged, hurry home . . . I, for one, would regard New Zealand diggings as a public nuisance and a national misfortune . . . I sincerely trust that Ballarat and Bendigo will remain exactly where they are, and never approach New Zealand nearer by a mile.'[28] When Bendigo and Ballarat did arrive, with the discovery of gold in Otago four years later, this required another agile somersault.

Direct denigration of competitors was a common feature of New Zealand crusading literature. South Africa was too hot and Dutch, Canada was too cold and French, the United States was too hot and cold, and had too much democracy and slavery, while Australia had all sorts of problems. The hitch with this game was that the competition, especially Australia, struck back. Australia specialised in exploiting earthquakes, notably those at Wellington in 1848 and 1855. A Sydney publisher's *Account of the Earthquakes in New Zealand* showed an interest in this country seldom matched since by the Australian book trade. An Australian by-name for New Zealand, 'The Shaky Isles', survives to this day, and the New Zealand–earthquake connection was also noted in Canada and South Africa. Hursthouse retaliated. 'I for one would rather encounter two New Zealand earthquakes than one African puff-adder or half a Canadian winter.'[29] But, for all this, Australian competition in particular remained powerful. Throughout the peopling period, there were times when destinations like Marvellous Melbourne threatened to beat New Zealand from the field.

Three, four or even six months in a leaky boat was another persistent obstacle. Crusader literature sought to make a virtue of necessity by turning the voyage into a long holiday – a gluttonous one. Long lists of provisions were a feature of crusading publications to the point where some resemble giant menus. Cabin passengers breakfasted at nine o'clock on rolls, toast, cold meat and hot chops; lunched lightly at noon on ham, tongue, beef, pickles, bread and cheese in preparation for dining at four on preserved salmon, soup, goose, saddle of mutton, fowls, curry, a ham, plum pudding, apple tarts, cheese, fruit and nuts, washed down with stout, champagne, sherry and port. They then hungrily awaited tea at seven o'clock and supper at ten. This, along with 'many a merry game on deck', such as 'all fours' races – 'which were much complained of this morning by those who had already gone to bed' – dancing, snaring albatrosses and shooting dolphins, accentuated the positive. Some negatives such as seasickness were diminished, to two or three days despite the cuisine; others, such as giant cockroaches whose own cuisine consisted of the toenails of sleeping passengers, were eliminated entirely.[30]

The deadliest negative was shipboard disease, to which children were especially prone. This was a major disincentive to emigration, and, to be fair, the colonising crusaders tried to deal with it in reality as well as rhetoric. The conditions on company emigrant ships in the 1840s, and still more on colonial ships in the 1870s, were usually relatively good, even in steerage and despite the prevalence of sailing ships over steamers to the end of the peopling period. But, in the travel industry, 'usually' is not good enough. On 15 February 1842, the men of the New Zealand Company's preliminary expedition eagerly awaiting the *Lloyds*, which had brought out their families, found that 65 of their children had died en route.[31] The *Brother's Pride* in 1863 lost 46 people to disease, including 31 children.[32] The *Scimitar* in 1874 lost 25 children, and most ships lost at least a few. An aspect of children's culture almost too horrible to contemplate is that voyaging children learned they were prone to die. Children aboard the *Mongol* disliked the grizzled quartermaster whose duty it was to lower their corpses overboard. One, eight-year-old Mary Jane Johnson, saw through to his kind heart, called him 'uncle' and made him promise not to do to her what he had done to her two sisters. He drew what comfort he could from the fact that she did not die until after landing, and was buried ashore.[33] Worst of all, in 1874, the *Cospatrick* took fire and sank in the South Atlantic with the loss of all 430 emigrants – the ancestors of thousands of New Zealanders who might have been.

Overall, direct measures never quite succeeded in laying to rest problems like Maori, Australia and the dangerous voyage out. Even in the 1870s, there was a strong chance that a family with six children, en route to New Zealand to give them a better future, would lose one of them. This was true of all emigration destinations, but it must have seemed most true of the furthest. To persuade people to take this risk, to play New Zealand roulette with their children, required more than petty puffery, the denigration of competitors and the minimising of Maori, earthquake and voyage dangers. It required a subtle assault on the complex British market, centred on three motifs: 'progress', 'paradise' and 'Britishness'. It is to this people market, Victorian Britain 1830s–80s, the Pakeha Hawaiki, that we now turn.

The New Zealand of the North

An intriguing feature of mid-nineteenth-century Britain is the sense in which it did not exist. Welsh, Scots, English and, of course, Irish were still distinct peoples, with different economies and societies as well as cultures. Each was also highly regionalised to the point where, within each country, let alone between them, language or dialect made some people incomprehensible to others. Only 43 per cent of North Welsh spoke fluent English in 1858; 54 per cent of all Welsh still spoke their native tongue in 1891.[34] The British were linguistically more diverse than the Polynesians as a whole, let alone the Maori. As with the Maori, religion sometimes blurred tribal differences and sometimes reinforced them. Irish tended to be Catholic, Scots Presbyterian, and English Anglican. In the first half of the nineteenth century, Dissent took over Wales, with 80 per cent of Welsh turning from church to chapel by 1851.[35] But all four countries had large and important religious minorities. As well as region, ethnicity and religion, the Pakeha Hawaiki was also fragmented by class, a concept slightly more useful than it is problematic.

Class can be conceived in at least three ways: as category, as culture and as community. Broad class 'communities' are not local clusters of workers or nobles living together, but collective identities that stretch across whole nations, including some and excluding others on grounds of class, and giving their members some sense of community with each other. Class communities do not necessarily embrace the whole of their 'natural constituencies'. A working-class community might not include all workers, but only those who place some weight on being workers – such that a Cornish worker feels more loyalty to a Kentish worker than to a Cornish farmer. This kind of class, whose members are at least vaguely conscious of their community, gets most attention from historians, for quite good reasons. So large a lump, which transcends local and vertical loyalties, has considerable capacity for acquiring political and economic power, and for generating historical change. So when modern scholars say 'class', they often mean class community, or *tight* class. Yet tight classes are arguably rare and recent. Scholars debate whether nationwide class communities emerged in Britain before, during or after our peopling period, 1830s–80s. There are, however, two other forms of class – looser and more abstract, but also older and more pervasive.

One is the class 'category', which can be defined as the intersection of two variables: labour, or paid work, and capital, or productive property. There are actually four such intersections: the upper class, which owns but does not work; the middle class, which both works and owns; the lower or working class, which works but does not own; and the neglected lowest class, which neither works (at least not regularly or legally) nor owns. These categories can seem abstract in themselves, but they can be very roughly associated with four class 'cultures', or subcultures, which have substance in daily life. Each has its own variations of lifestyle, tradition and ways of thinking, although they share a lot as well. We will call these class cultures 'genteel' (the upper class), 'respectable' (the middle class), 'decent' (the lower or working class), and 'disreputable' (the lowest class or underclass). Each class culture contained several groups, some central and well established, some newer, more insecure and more marginal. In practice, class cultures tend to blur at their margins but can be distinguished at their cores.

In Britain, the core of the upper or genteel class were the nobility and the old landed gentry, respectively a titled and untitled aristocracy. The existence of untitled aristocrats gave this British class unusual flexibility and can camouflage the fact that some emigrated to places like New Zealand because few of the titled did so. In most European countries, the old landed gentry would have had titles too. The notion that the titled British aristocracy were particularly 'open', willing to incorporate newcomers by marriage or otherwise, has been questioned,[36] but this did not matter much because the untitled aristocracy, or old gentry, supplied the capacity to incorporate. The core of the middle or respectable class were the owners and managers of industrial, commercial and financial enterprises, large and small. Archetypally urban, but allied to substantial commercial farmers, they were a major driving force behind the Industrial Revolution, and are sometimes known as the 'bourgeoisie', haute and petite, high and little.

The core of the decent or lower class were 'skilled' and 'semi-skilled' workers. Skilled workers were formally specialised tradesmen or artisans, who had served an apprenticeship. Semi-skilled workers were informally specialised, as with machine operators in factories. The core of the lowest or disreputable class, variously known as the 'residuum', the 'sunken tenth' or the 'lumpen proletariat', were professional criminals, 'public' prostitutes, who did not conceal their trade, beggars and other urban street folk, and rural tramps and vagrants. Some of these earned money, of course, but their work was either very irregular or not considered legitimate or decent. The irredeemably disreputable were the basic social antitype, defining what not to be, just as unsalvageable savages were the basic racial antitype. Contemporary descriptions of the two are often interchangeable. Other groups oscillated around these cores, sometimes uncomfortably torn between two classes, sometimes comfortable in a hinge-like role.

Victorian Britain would be complicated enough if it had stayed put during the New Zealand peopling period, but it was changing: shrinking, growing, shifting, mixing, merging, separating and reshuffling. A fluid as well as fragmented fragment is just our luck. The shrinking was geographical and conceptual, stemming from changes in transport and communications. Navigation canals, turnpike roads and railways contracted England by a factor of about ten in terms of travelling time in the century before 1880. The population read a dozen times more books and wrote a dozen times more letters to each other in 1900 than in 1800.[37] This broadened the zone in which community could be imagined. At the same time, population and production were growing massively, though unevenly. The population of the British Isles doubled in the 50 years before 1831, to 24 million, and came quite close to doubling again in the subsequent half-century, despite the depopulation of Ireland. On one optimistic calculation, production overall grew fourteen-fold.[38] More recent studies emphasise the slow-burning and uneven character of growth, its older agricultural origins and the fact that much of it occurred outside factories. But growth there was. Its engines were the commercialisation of agriculture – farming on a large scale for the market rather than on a small scale for yourself, which intensified in the 1830s; steam-powered industrialisation, which concentrated industry much more than water, horse or hand power; and urbanisation.

Some areas and some occupations commercialised, industrialised and urbanised more than others, and the British therefore shifted more as well as bred more. They shifted occupations as well as homes, and both were known as 'places'. One type of shift was into a neighbouring place, town or county. Another was to move to a more distant, different and prosperous place, often in the old metropolis of London or newly huge metropolises like Liverpool, Glasgow, Manchester and Birmingham. Another shift was to emigrate, and the great British cities and colonies were products of the same demographic explosion, though shifting to one was not necessarily a prerequisite stage for shifting to the next.[39] All these shifts involved greater mixing of people from different regional and ethnic groups, forcing them to a more intense confrontation with their differences and similarities. There was a massive English migration into South Wales, similar in scale to that into New South Wales, and an even larger Irish migration into England.

The Act of Union with Ireland in 1800 completed the political unification of the British Isles, and various factors were also separating the British Isles from continental Europe. One was war. We tend to look forward from 1815 to

1914 in considering the nineteenth century, and so sometimes forget that the British of the 1820s and 1830s were a postwar generation, for whom the world war of 1793–1815 loomed large. This long conflict with Revolutionary and Napoleonic France put a stop to grand tours and turned genteel tourism inward. It also helped sever political links with Europe. Since the Middle Ages, Britain had often had continental possessions or associated states – bits of France as late as the seventeenth century, the Netherlands from 1688 to 1701, and, from 1715, Hanover, which made Britain a part-German power. The link with Hanover was suspended during the wars, and finally cut in 1837, though its after-effects lasted long enough to bias early German migrants to New Zealand towards Hanover. Except Gibraltar, there were no more continental commitments, ending a complication for British 'nationalism'.

Yet another process of change was social reshuffling. Its most overt form was increasing social mobility. It has been suggested that this, combined with meritocracy, the ideal of equality before the law and the power of cash to dissolve old strata, moved Britain towards an 'effectively classless' situation by the beginning of the nineteenth century.[40] There are abstract and actual problems with this. Abstractly, there is a sense in which it is as hard to have social mobility without class as it is to climb a ladder without rungs. One has to have something to be promoted to and from. The actual gulf between higher- and lower-class lives in Victorian Britain should also be remembered. Highest and lowest had different conceptions of space and time; the former moved on four legs and used pocket watches; the latter moved on two and used the sun. Dress and manners made the two instantly distinguishable; accent meant this remained true even for the blind. The rich drank wine in private houses; the poor drank gin or beer in public houses, and died on average about fourteen years earlier than the rich. The Earl of Yarborough's stock of cigars was worth more than one of his labourers might earn in a lifetime.[41] By mid-century, the urban rich had water supplies and sewerage systems; the poor had only water supplies, which to add injury to insult sometimes doubled as the sewerage systems of the rich.[42] The death of class in nineteenth-century Britain can be exaggerated.

But something curious *was* happening: a fluidity that went beyond social mobility; a blurring of class lines, a mixing of class characteristics. The New Zealand evidence discussed in later chapters suggests that we need a concept of 'class-cultural mobility' to understand this. Social mobility seeks permanent *promotion* across class boundaries; class-cultural mobility seeks the *adoption* of selected elements of other class lifestyles without leaving your own. We still tend to accept the nineteenth-century assumption that most people below the securely genteel aspired to social promotion, and a great many certainly did. But cultural mobility involves people who adopt aspects of the lifestyles of other classes without accepting either their ideology or their mix of labour and capital. The lower middle class and the upper working class had similar incomes, houses and relationships with work and property, but the latter drank in pubs and joined unions, whereas the former did not. Many middle-class respectables adopted elements of genteel culture without making, or wanting to make, the full shift. Highest and lowest classes sometimes adopted each other's recreations, such as gambling, prostitution and blood sports. Class-cultural mobility involves bits of class culture that split off from their class and float along the social spectrum, sometimes in adapted form, and 'down' as well as 'up' the status hierarchy. Eating oysters and drinking gin were working-class habits that became genteel. Eating cheddar cheese and drinking tea went the other way. This fluidity can be mistaken for evidence of classlessness.

In Victorian Britain, gentility, respectability, decency and disrepute had all slipped their moorings and begun to float, sometimes with hands at the helm and sometimes without. The two great Victorian examples of hands-on or semi-managed social reshuffling were the broadening of gentility and the attempt to split off the decent from the disreputable. The former tendency is sometimes known as the 'cult of gentility', or even the 'mania for gentility'. It involved a merging and clashing with the ethics of respectability, as well as an expansion of gentility to incorporate new groups such as medical doctors. It is discussed in the New Zealand context in the next chapter.

The second reshuffle can be called 'moral evangelism'. In the first half of the nineteenth century, there was still a strong cultural alliance between decent and disreputable. Both were prone to riot, revel and drunkenness; to crimes acceptable within their own class such as poaching, fighting and gambling; to unauthorised holidays such as 'Saint Monday'; and to blood sports like bear and badger baiting, cockfights and barefist boxing.[43] In the second half of the century, however, a major movement or series of movements were mounted to split decent from disreputable. This attempted to control popular culture and convert or marginalise the disreputable savage within.

Since the late eighteenth century, observers had been staggered by the growth in British production and population. This process of broadly continuous upward development was attributed to God, Nature, free trade, racial character or rational but long-term historical laws, and it came to be called 'progress'. It came fully of age with the great Crystal Palace exhibition in London in 1851, which included a few New Zealand items. One glance at the Crystal Palace 'was quite sufficient to account for the greatness of the nation to which it belonged'. Six million came and glanced.[44] In the 1830s, however, progress was not yet an unambiguous concept. One, older, variant assumed progress towards some end, good or bad. This was sometimes linked to religious millennialism, in which the world must end, or to the belief that societies, even empires, aged like individuals through infancy, prime, decay and death, as Edward Gibbon

Wakefield had shown even Rome had done. Between 1815 and 1848, it seemed as if the end of progress in Britain, too, might be bad, and that it might be nigh.

The period was one of want amidst progress for much of the population, and was punctuated by protest, riot and rebellion, by Irish, Luddites, Chartists and the amorphous rural protest movement known as 'Captain Swing'. Government forces killed more Britons at 'Peterloo', Manchester, in 1819 and Newport, Wales, in 1839 than Maori did between these years on the 'violent frontier'. British historians seem to have returned to the view that the threat of revolution was quite serious, and one study suggests that fear of bitter divisions and social collapse was a motive in migration to the United States up to 1848.[45] A deep fear of economic insecurity and of social disharmony endured beyond this into the late nineteenth century. Migrants took it to New Zealand, where it lasted even longer.

England survived these crises, however, and tended to attribute its survival to its strong, ancient but flexible legal and political institutions, which T. B. Macaulay and others came very close to worshipping.[46] The remarkable institutional capacity for non-violent defensive revolution, or pre-emptive reform, and for co-opting leading troublemakers into the political nation (notably in the broadening of the electorate in 1832) was thought to have put progress back on course, or revealed its true, infinite nature. This institutionalism merged with older ideas of Protestant liberties and English destiny, and with developing notions such as free trade and individualist enterprise, both bottomless wells of economic and social advance. This new concept of endless progress can be seen as a secular religion that abolished the need for an end to the world.[47] It also helped introduce a new conception of historical time, in which history could happen fast. The 1840s may have been the point when ideas of infinite progress overtook finite. In 1840, Macaulay could write of an overseas tourist sketching the ruins of a dead London from London Bridge. Within a few years, in his *History of England*, he could look back, patronisingly but benignly, at an inferior past from a superior present, comfortable with the conviction that the future would do the same to him. Fears of the end of progress in Britain were joined by the hope that it would never end.

In a sense, these collective hopes and fears were duplicated at an individual level. During the early nineteenth century, it became clear that Britain's population was increasing at a rate that some feared, with Malthus, the economy could not sustain. The idea emerged, with Edward Gibbon Wakefield as a major midwife, that some people and some capital had been rendered redundant, fated to diminishing opportunities for profitable employment and investment. Which is it to be, migrationists preached, the colonies or the scrapheap? On the other hand, the lurching but generally upward course of progress increased aspirations for social and cultural mobility. More people knew how the other half lived; more people were known to have hurdled the barriers of class.

'Bettering oneself' or 'getting on', to use the contemporary colloquialisms, were becoming ever more widely shared aspirations, though they might involve adoption as much as promotion. One key for the colonising crusaders was hitching 'getting on' to 'getting out'. You did not get on or out solely for yourself. Individualism was important, but the conventional emphasis on it tends to obscure the way in which families broadened and deepened aspirations. 'Think of the children' was a compelling invitation to extend the range of one's hopes and fears. Provident or insecure parents looked ahead 20 or 30 years, not five or ten; and sought six opportunities for work, marriage or property, not one. Personal progress was underwritten by collective progress, which expanded the stock of opportunities for individuals and families. In sum, progress involved both hopes and fears, individual and collective. Some hoped to rise, some feared to fall, for themselves, their offspring and their society.

Progress contributed to social stability by expanding opportunity and improving living standards. But finite, stuttering or uneven progress also bred insecurity. Even infinite progress had its price: the displacement of the familiar, a very uneven distribution of benefits, and, especially, the vices of urban industrialism. Giant cities were both symbols and prices of progress, homes to Mills Dark and Satanic as well as James and John Stuart, wens as well as wonders. Some people imagined paradises in which progress was guaranteed, where it had no price or had been rolled back to the point before its costs appeared. There are various ways of categorising these secular paradises or utopias. Apart from El Dorado, a 'paradise' of moveable valuables to be raided and raped, two basic types were Utopia proper and Arcadia. Utopia emphasised collective action, civilised refinement and the godly city or benign state. In élitist versions, its ideal inhabitants were virtuous community leaders, Platonic Guardians; in more egalitarian versions they were public-spirited good citizens. Arcadia emphasised natural abundance, individual virtue and the rural life. Its ideal inhabitant was the sturdy yeoman, living self-sufficiently and independently with his family on his own farm.

Some looked up to heaven for paradise; some looked back to an idealised past; some looked forward to the benign end result of progress, if finite, or a wonderful waystation, if infinite. Others looked out. The link between colonialism and utopianism dates back to the origins of both. Thomas More's original *Utopia*, published in 1516, was a fictional island alone in the ocean. Francis Bacon wrote of a utopian South Sea island, a scientists' paradise, 'with deep caves for experiments on refrigeration'.[48] In the seventeenth century, the British searched the Americas for an 'earthly paradise, similar to if not the veritable site of the Scriptural Eden'. When they thought they had found it, they sometimes called it 'New Britain'.[49] The British utopian socialists Robert Owen and William Morris had some direct influence on New Zealand, and may in turn have been influenced by it. Owen's associate Robert Pemberton and the famous inverse-utopian Samuel Butler certainly were.[50] English populist utopianism, often couched retrospectively as 'the world we have lost', spoke of Merrie Olde England, the sturdy self-sufficient yeoman and rural virtue in general, and of harmony between classes, the mutual respect of master and man.

The prices of progress were also serpents in paradise. The giant cities were sometimes seen as a writhing mass of them, a place where dangerous disreputables bred like maggots, and decent folk were prone to join them. Industrial and human wastes were thought to create miasmic vapours conveying disease, which had the temerity to strike at high and low alike. Ironically, this led urban-based respectables to look outwards for antidotes – to the redemptive power of the healthy country life. Decent working people, crowded into newly industrialised areas, looked backwards to an idealised past. The arcadian anti-city element in this 'rural myth' can be exaggerated. The affluent suburbs developing in the Victorian era, 'a marriage between town and country', have been described as 'bourgeois utopias'.[51] It was industrial urban elephantiasis, megalopolis not polis, that was the problem. Retrospective folk utopias were often urban with country qualities, or part agricultural, part cottage industry.[52] Bustling seaports, healthy sea breezes wafting away the vapours of their few smithies and tanneries, and market towns were seen as benign, a complement not a contradiction to the villages and farms around them.

Class community was another potential serpent in paradise. We need not agree with the various British historians who argue that working-class community began to emerge in the troubles of 1790s or 1815–20 to accept that the threat of something like it was widely perceived – and deeply feared by the genteel and respectable.[53] Disreputable folk devils, or decent folk suborned by them, were bad enough alone; collected into a crowd, mass, mob or rabble, they were a nightmare. There also seems to have been a certain tightening in the higher classes, a turning away from vertical to horizontal perspectives involving an increasing interest in each other and a decreasing interest in their social 'inferiors' as individuals. Thomas Carlyle, the great prophet of progress who saw it as a war against nature led by captains of industry, described this as an 'abdication on the part of the governors'.[54] Changes in genteel architecture and manners, for example, reflect an increasing distance from servants and labourers. In extreme cases, servants were supposed to face the wall when a proper person passed.[55] Decent folk resented this. Tenant farmers whose fathers had worked beside their labourers, or at least known their names, now ignored them and wore kid gloves and hunted foxes.[56] Both higher and lower disliked different aspects of the tightening of class, and disliked the implication that class would be set against class. The serpents here were not class itself but class community, and the distance and disharmony it was thought to imply. This shared dislike of tight class and its trappings became a central and enduring feature of Pakeha ideology.

The Victorians naturally believed that they were best at progress; that they had the best chance of building Jerusalem in their green and pleasant land, and this boosted collective pride. At the same time, as we have seen, actual and symbolic encounters with non-European 'Thems' were on the increase, reinforcing conceptions of 'Us', often with the help of racial thought. Old ideas of nationalism merged with new in this context, firmed up and extended their scope, abetted by the shrinking, mixing and separating processes noted above. One English development was the widening of populism, an amorphous folk nationalism that emphasised the 'English people' or the 'common folk'. It was made compatible with regionalism and class through an important sleight of mind we will call the 'backbone concept'. The people of Lancashire or Kent, or even working or farming people in general, were the 'true English', the salt of the earth and the backbone of the country, unlike sly Londoners. Populism's enemy was not the upper classes as such, but either some vague conspiracy of evil oligarchs or else gentry who had forgotten their responsibility to treat decent people decently. Here, populism converged with the folk utopianism in which mutual respect between master and man was restored.[57]

A second important development in collective identity was the rise of 'Anglo-Saxonism' – the belief that the descendants of Hengist and Horsa formed a distinct race, superior to others and uniquely addicted to liberty and justice. There were moderate and purely romantic variants, but Anglo-Saxonism tended to merge nationalism and racialism, and to fuse both with ideas of progress and paradise. Progress worked best in England for racial reasons. Free institutions, which enabled progress to survive the tremors of 1815–48, were a prerequisite of any English paradise, the Anglo-Saxons' natural birthright. John Bull, the quintessential Englishman, was a sturdy yeoman directly descended from the 'primitive but Arcadian communities' of ancient Saxony.[58] Even the early forms of Anglo-Saxonism had considerable powers of inclusion, easily embracing Americans and Germans, and it was to develop a still wider reach in the late nineteenth century. But it was also linked to harder, more exclusive racialisms that emphasised the permanence of racial type, the need for racial purity and the inevitability of racial antagonism. Anglo-Saxons were often thought to thrive only in the right physical environment, or at least the right latitudes.

These and other developments reinforced English nationalism before and during the New Zealand peopling period. They did not reinforce British pan-nationalism. 'Britain' was very often merely a euphemism for Greater England. It was used as such even in Ireland in the nineteenth century and in New Zealand into the twentieth, and we must continue to be aware of this narrower usage. But another, broader, usage was developing, contesting other collective identities. Welsh, Scots and Irish nationalisms were also being invented or reinvented in the nineteenth century, partly for similar reasons to English nationalism, partly in reaction to it.[59] Catholic Irish nationalism was conventional in that it opposed alien rule through politics, protest or resistance. Scots and Welsh nationalism in the Victorian era was unconventional in that it did not. It might advocate tartans, haggis and Robbie Burns, collective identity and distinctiveness, cultural and to some extent institutional autonomy. It rarely advocated independence. In this sense it was a 'colonial nationalism' of a type later developed further in New Zealand. Welshness and Scottishness clearly fitted more easily into some pan-nationalist idea of Britain than into English nationalism, or Britain as mere code for Greater England. If one wished to accommodate, say, Scots, then a broader idea of Britain came in handy.

Anglo-Saxonism could incorporate the non-English peoples by simply adding 'and Celts', and it sometimes did so. But Anglo-Saxonism was greatly reinforced by antagonism to the Irish. This appears to have increased in response to the migration of Irish to England, and to have gained strength from merging racial and social antitypes. It reached its apotheosis with the English historian Edward Freeman's comment on the United States in 1881: 'This would be a grand land if only every Irishman would kill a negro and be hanged for it. I find this sentiment generally approved – sometimes with the qualification that they want Irish and negroes for servants, not being able to get any other.' This, of course, was an extreme position, but it indicates how far one could go while remaining Regius Professor of Modern History at Oxford rather than the inmate of a prison or lunatic asylum.[60] Moderate versions allowed the Irish sentimentality, vivacity and impetuousness – 'feminine' qualities that still contrasted unfavourably to the manly, rational and progressive Anglo-Saxon. Comparisons between the Irish and the Maori were not necessarily intended as a compliment to either. Relative to the Irish, Scots and Welsh were not so bad, especially if one emphasised Anglo-Saxon penetration of both countries, and perhaps split north from south and highlands from lowlands, dumping the dross into a 'Celtic Fringe'. It may be that Irish and British, like Maori and Pakeha, by their contrast with each other helped to invent their substantive collective identities, and that the two processes were not very far apart in time.

English or British nationalist pride often claimed a peculiar genius for war and empire, which was also cause, proof, and product of progress. Decisive battles were portrayed as the steps in Britain's rise, with the great heroes Nelson and Wellington as the banisters. The intersection between British military history and New Zealand place-names is no coincidence: Wellington, Nelson, Collingwood, Hawke, Marlborough, Blenheim, Picton, Napier, Hastings and two Havelocks. The sepoy (or kupapa) tradition of European imperialism, whereby subordinate peoples were persuaded to conquer each other, worked best if camouflaged by some form of higher unity. Anglo-Irish and Scots generals had been very prominent in the triumph over the French, and Napoleon was a useful unifying ogre. Much of the British army was non-English, especially Irish. This goes some way towards explaining the paradoxical Victorian admiration and contempt for their army. Wider ideas of Britain were convenient here – and were not too unsafe, because war and empire happened abroad.

Urban migration may have foreshadowed the tendency to be more British away than at home by reducing ethnic and regional differences – in dialect, for example. London may be the place where popular Britain was invented. Scots in London might stick together, but they had also to make themselves understood to Southrons. The British subgroups mixed when they went to London, and they mixed even more when they went abroad. Pakeha and Maori living in Sydney, and New Zealanders and Australians living in London, frequently note that they have less in common home than away, and they cannot help but be influenced by the tendency of the natives to merge them. Something similar may have happened to English, Scots, Welsh and Protestant Irish when they went to the colonies – mixing more than they did at home and forming a new 'Us' through confronting a shared 'Them'. Hints of the intensification of Britishness outside Britain, in war, the empire and the colonies, remain in language. 'British gentleman', 'British pub' and 'British yeoman' sound wrong; 'English' is the adjective that slips more easily off the tongue. But 'British soldier', 'British Empire' and 'British colonies' sound right. Britishness was still a tender young plant in our period, but it was growing, and it was growing faster for migrants to the colonies than for stay-at-homes. Like the racial identities to which it was closely related, it was a cloak you put on when you went out.

The Pakeha Myths of Settlement

Wakefield was not named Edward Gibbon for nothing. The New Zealand colonising crusaders set about exploiting these hopes and fears, and the changing ideas of progress, paradise and Britishness. This was difficult in a vacuum of attitudes to New Zealand, and like good modern publicists the crusaders sought to adapt some existing preconception, some thin end of the wedge. They found it on London Bridge, for Macaulay's ruin-sketching overseas tourist happened to be a New Zealander. Macaulay's New Zealander appeared in 1840, a throw-away line in an extended warning that popery was still dangerous, camouflaged as a review of Ranke's *History of the Popes.*[61] It had absolutely nothing to do with New Zealand, which was mentioned as one might cite Timbuktu, or Furthest Tartary or the Back of Beyond. Edward Gibbon himself had used it before in the same way in the eighteenth century, Anthony Trollope and Keith Sinclair's grandmother did so in the nineteenth, and Aldous Huxley and Bertrand Russell in the twentieth.[62] This Antipodean New Zealand, a minor convention in British culture, symbolised the last survivor of some apocalypse or the most distant perspective imaginable from which to comment on one's own society. It was related to the Green and Noble Savage and, to the extent they thought of them at all, Gibbon and Macaulay thought of their New Zealanders as Maori.

Such trifles did not bother the colonising crusaders, whose literature often made reference to the New Zealander (now white) on London Bridge. The motif came to displace the cannibal as a common-usage symbol of New Zealand. After an 1855 earthquake, the Australian press cruelly inverted it into a London cockney gazing at the ruins of Wellington – from a ship because the Hutt River Bridge had fallen down.[63] But neither nineteenth-century Australian sarcasm nor our own affects the fact that this slender wisp of ideology was interwoven with others to become 'the Britain of the South', the organising principle of the New Zealand myths of settlement and, therefore, to some extent, of New Zealand settlement itself.

Comparisons of aspects of New Zealand to aspects of Britain began with Cook, and they did not necessarily mean much. People normally describe the new by analogy with the known. Cook simply said that New Zealand quails were like English quails, hardly a phrase from which nations are built.[64] It was not obvious to everyone that New Zealand was potentially a progressive British paradise. Some American whalers considered it a 'hoal', 'a most horrid place as ever I was in'.[65] It many respects it is not easy to imagine two places more dissimilar than nineteenth-century New Zealand and Britain. Most settlers found the predominant New Zealand forest, for example, unfamiliar, alien, even hostile. The term 'bush', which took hold early, itself reflects this. 'Bush' hints at an obstacle to be cleared; the more benign alternatives, 'woods' or 'forest', were much less common.[66] But New Zealand, like the British Isles, consisted of two main islands; it was very roughly the same size as Britain and was very, very roughly in the antipodal latitudes. For the crusaders, this was enough. The Britain of the South motif and its variants, along with paradise and progress metaphors, pervaded crusader literature. Most other settler colonies also used parental imagery, but the New Zealand addiction was extreme.

In 1836, E. G. Wakefield lectured a House of Commons committee on the merits of New Zealand as the ultimate colony. 'Very near to Australia there is a country which all testimony concurs in describing as the fittest in the world for colonization, as the most beautiful country with the finest climate, and the most productive soil; I mean New Zealand.'[67] The special link with Britain was quickly entrenched in Wakefield's 422-page *British Colonization of New Zealand*, volume one of the crusader prospectus and 'the basic source of information for the first emigrants'.[68] Company literature portrayed New Zealand from the outset as a 'LAND of PROMISE', specially suited to the English or British, and a future 'great seat of wealth and naval power – in short, to be in the Southern Ocean what the British Isles were to the Northern'.[69] Critics of the New Zealand Company had no doubt as to which preconceptions it was exploiting. In 1838, the London *Times* warned its readers against the 'Arcadian visions of the New Zealand Association'.

> In the gorgeous fancy of Mr Edward Gibbon Wakefield and the minor magicians by whose wand it has sprung into existence, [New Zealand is to be] a moral and political paradise . . . We are to have a Radical Utopia in the Great Pacific, wherein . . . the doctrines of Jeremy Bentham and Robert Owen are to realize such unheard of triumphs as shall utterly shame and outstrip the laggard progress of more antiquated nations.[70]

But the crusaders outpublished their critics, and comparisons of New Zealand with both Paradise and Britain became common and uncontroversial. Arcadia, Utopia, 'the Eden of the world', an 'earthly paradise' and 'the land of milk and honey' appeared even more often in later crusader literature than in company tracts.[71] The titles of books on New Zealand published between the 1850s and the 1880s included *The Land of Promise, The Wonderland of the Antipodes, The Wonderland of the World, An Earthly Paradise, The Future England of the Southern Hemisphere, The England of the Pacific, The Britain of the South* and *Brighter Britain!* By the 1860s, London newspapers had forgotten the sarcasm of the *Times* in 1838 and absorbed the idea that New Zealand 'is destined to become the Great Britain of the southern hemisphere' or 'the Great Britain of the Pacific'.[72] In 1851, *Chambers' Papers for the People* asserted that New Zealand 'would literally become, as many orators, writers, and economists have prophesied, another Great Britain in the Austral Ocean'.[73]

Emigrants themselves imbibed this mythology, at least until they arrived. Alfred Fell fell asleep on the first night of his voyage out 'and dreamed of New Zealand being a *perfect fairy land*', and later referred to it as 'our fancied Eldorado'. Alexander Marjoribanks wrote of emigrants crowding the decks as the mountains of real New Zealand loomed, 'all full of hope and anxiety to see what had been represented to us as a sort of earthly paradise'.[74] The linchpin prophets claimed that these images survived the landing. 'Sentimental settlers,' wrote Thomson, 'often designate New Zealand the Britain of the southern hemisphere.' 'New Zealand is popularly styled the antipodes of England,' asserted Hursthouse, 'Queen of the Pacific and future Britain of the South.'[75]

There were many variations on the theme of New Zealand as a progressive British paradise. Some were general, broad-brush portrayals; others were specific – aimed at particular categories of potential British migrants. One broad-brush technique was to present New Zealand as having the perfect environment for Anglo-Saxons, especially in terms of climate. Dr Arthur Thomson was a particularly convincing publicist of 'this remarkable salubrity of the climate of New Zealand for Anglo-Saxons'. In Australia, he wrote, 'it is already apparent that Anglo-Saxons and Celts in a few generations must deteriorate both mentally and physically.'[76] 'Where there is perpetual sunshine and serenity,' agreed Hursthouse, 'man degenerates into an emasculated idler.' This climatic paradise offered Anglo-Saxons more children and more life itself. In New Zealand, continued Thomson, 'Anglo-Saxon settlers multiply fast from births and die slowly from disease'. Climate gave more time for progress. 'It is the opinion of persons who have sojourned in different parts of the world that the Anglo-Saxon race can work and expose themselves to the climate of New Zealand for more days of the year and for more hours in the day than in any other country.'[77]

It is not easy for us to grasp how seriously people took this climatic determinism in the mid-nineteenth century. They were not mad, or merely pioneering the genre of trans-Tasman jokes. Thomson, a well-qualified medical doctor who had written his thesis at Edinburgh University on the racial effects of climate, was a very respectable scientist in contemporary terms. He backed his claims with official statistics showing low settler mortality. These were dubious because the settler population was disproportionately young, but Thomson 'forgot' to make this point, and few did it for him. Climatic determinism was also a point where hard and soft racialisms converged, and it was strengthened by the intersection. For monogenists, who believed human diversity arose from the rapid adaptation of a common stock, cold could turn Adam white, and heat turn Australians black, in a century or two. For polygenists and Anglo-Saxonists, who emphasised the permanent difference of various racial stocks, temperate latitudes were the only proper homes for Anglo-Saxons; either they or their testicles died in the tropics. People suspected the sun of causing immorality and racial degeneration, just as we suspect it of causing melanomas. The only clime with any chance of being intrinsically as good as New Zealand for the English/British was Britain itself, except that there one found the unhealthy miasmas of industrial urbanisation.

In crusader literature, New Zealand's remarkable climate combined with staggering natural fertility. Yet it was not New Zealand nature itself that was abundant. It was no more than a latent paradise, waiting to be fulfilled. Hursthouse dismissed the native fruits of New Zealand nature with contempt. The kiwi was 'a grotesque looking creature . . . like a hedge hog on stilts'. As for the favoured Maori fruits, tawa 'eats like sloe steeped in tar', kiekie like 'artichoke flavoured with turpentine', and karaka was flavourless except for 'a slight taste of wizened quince'.[78] All were small and negligible in value. Imported British plants and animals, on the other hand, burgeoned in New Zealand to abnormal crops and sizes. Early settlers at the Hutt grew a turnip 80 centimetres around the waist; New Plymouth turnips were smaller, but yielded 150 tons to the acre. Christchurch had a four-kilogram carrot; Dunedin a 9.5-kilogram beetroot and a 25-kilogram cabbage. There was a half-ton pig, and sheep nurtured in New Zealand were 50 per cent fatter than 'the thin short-pastured dried-up animals of Australia'. 'The sheep, like every other domestic animal introduced from Australia into New Zealand, becomes larger in the new land.'[79] When E. G. Wakefield himself arrived in New Zealand, he, too, found it a vegetable paradise. 'Every thing was ultra *couleur de rose.* Such land – such Country – such crops – such vegetables . . . The carrots were not like ordinary carrots, they out carroted carrots.'[80]

Crusader fervour and Wakefield's impressive capacity for self-deception explain his carrot-tinted spectacles, but one hesitates to argue with a 25-kilogram cabbage. It is true that New Zealand's climate was quite good for British vegetables, and that the ash and other nutrients in newly cleared soil provided a virgin bonus: a few seasons of unusually good crops. But, as we saw in Chapter Two, most New Zealand soils were not especially fertile. The crusaders' fertility chants and worship of giant vegetables had a function more important than the mere reflection of reality. Like their plants and animals, Britons would do better in New Zealand – and New Zealand would be the better for it. It was a potential paradise, not an actual one, and there was no doubt in crusader minds about who was best placed to unleash the potential. 'Without a British emigrant population, New Zealand can rise to be no more than Tahiti, the Sandwich Islands, the Fejees, or any other semi-savage island group of the South Pacific.'[81]

Many European observers managed to look past the Maori and be struck by a certain *emptiness* about New Zealand. The plains of the South Island, which were thinly peopled, and the alien bush, which was sometimes grave and silent, provided kernels of truth for this powerful myth. Some disliked the emptiness. Sarah Mathew found the site of Auckland in 1840 'a gloomy country, without flowers, or fruits, or birds, or insects. I cannot but fancy it accursed.'[82] It infused many with a strong sense of latency, an urge to fill. Some felt the need to fill it with a past, a tendency we have noted with the early explorers and their eye for ruin-like rock formations, and with the Smithing of Maori history. Others felt the need to fill it with a future, to *fulfil* this latent paradise. A major subtheme was the remarkable absence of dangerous, noxious and troublesome animals. 'In New Zealand,' wrote Hursthouse with intent, 'farmers never have their fields ravaged by the blundering elephant, or by marauding monkey or raccoon', failing to note the danger of being crushed by a falling cabbage.[83] William Yate, who did fall victim to the beast within, found none without: 'no lurking tiger . . . no savage beast to hide himself during the day and make his predatory excursions in the darkness of the night . . . New Zealand seems to be reserved by Providence for the use of man.'[84] The notions that the English/British had a unique genius for colonisation and that New Zealand was a climatic paradise especially for them made it easy for the crusaders to specify which type of man Providence had in mind.

Here was a concept of a new Britain-in-waiting, which had to be brought to fruition by Old Britons. It found expression in crusader poetry.

A land there lies
Now void; it fits thy people; thither bend
Thy course; there shalt thou find a lasting seat;
There to thy sons shall many Englands rise;
And states be born of thee.[85]

New Zealand was to be a form of South British Insurance against an unfavourable outcome to finite progress up north – to play Carthage when Britain Tyred.

Fifty years hence – look forward and see it,
Realm of New Zealand, what then shalt thou be?
(If the world lives, at the Father's So Be It.)
All shall be greatness and glory with thee!
Even should Britain's decay be down-written
In the dread doom-book that no man may search,
Still shall an Oxford, a London, a Britain,
Gladden the South with a Home and a Church![86]

The latent New Zealand paradise, once wedded to select and progressive Old Britons, could be expected to produce an impressive offspring: the Britain of the South. Britain of the South prophecies were pervasive but varied in emphasis. Two variants were 'Better Britain' and 'Greater Britain'. These labels are intended to indicate two clusters of ideas that diverged from a common base – the reproduction of Britain – and are important themes of both this book and its sequel.

Better Britain ranked paradise over progress; Arcadia over Utopia; and quality over quantity. Greater Britain inverted these rankings. Better Britain saw New Zealand as permanently subordinate to Old Britain, though the child was to be an evolutionary improvement on the parent. Greater Britain envisaged a bigger, bolder and less subordinate future, and was prepared to take more risks with select stock to obtain it. In practice, the difference between the two variants was often less clear-cut than bald definition implies; the same people often held to elements of both. But the differences were significant.

There were obvious senses in which New Zealand was to be Better Britain. Clearly, it was to be better for individual Britons than remaining at home. No-one migrated to be worse off. Equally clearly, it was more British than the United States, traditionally the main migrant destination. The USA had been at war with Britain as recently as 1815; there were further serious war scares until the 1860s; and Americans, if nobody else, remembered what had happened to Washington in the rockets' red glare. 'Will you like to hear,' asked Richard Taylor rhetorically, 'the honoured institutions of your country ridiculed and that "Britisher" is a constant butt for them to pass their jokes on?' Even in the 1870s, Americans did not 'think much of John Bulls'.[87]

New Zealand was also to be more British than Britain in the sense that English, Scots and Welsh were to mix more. The linchpin prophets heavily criticised the attempt to keep Otago exclusively Scottish, and applauded its partial failure as much as Otago pioneers bemoaned it. They saw the mingling of the British peoples as desirable.[88] Scots were welcome if they mixed. Irish and other non-British groups were less welcome. Hursthouse claimed that 'New Zealand bears little more resemblance to Ireland than to Crim Tartary or Lilliput', and that 'the "Lads of the Shamrock" are seldom heard in New Zealand'.[89] But he added, rather half-heartedly, that he regretted this, and the crusader bias against Catholic Irish was more evident from their practice than their preaching. New Zealand emigration networks in Ireland leaned heavily towards Ulster, where half the population was Protestant.[90] This clashed with other crusader imperatives, such as the need for brides. It therefore crumbled to some extent in the 1870s, but the crusaders were not keen on advertising the fact. Dislike of second-hand migration from Australia, and of non-British and non-European migrants, was strong in some circles, less so in others.

There were ambiguities in the use of 'Britain'. Better Britain's stock was to be racially homogenous, as well as select in other respects, yet to blend Scots, Welsh and English. New Zealand was to be better than Britain, but subordinate to it, as well as smaller than it. 'Britain' was used in both broad and narrow senses, with 'England' as a common synonym for the latter. New Zealand was very English but better, as visiting novelist Anthony Trollope discovered in 1873.

> The New Zealander among John Bulls is the most John Bullish. He admits the supremacy of England to every place in the world, only he is more English than any Englishman at home. He tells you he has the same climate, – only somewhat improved; that he grows the same produce, – only with somewhat heavier crops, – that he has the same beautiful scenery . . . only somewhat grander in scale and more diversified . . . that he follows the same pursuits and after the same fashion, – but with less of misery, less of want, and a more general participation in the gifts which God has given to the country.[91]

The Greater Britain variant was less interested in ethnic or religious exclusivity. Wakefield himself was not too fussy about the denomination of his Elect. Critics joked that he planned to follow Presbyterian Otago and Anglican Canterbury with Catholic and Muslim settlements. Vogel 'did not wish to restrict assisted passages to British settlers'.[92] A Greater rather than Better British immigration policy allowed in Irish, non-British and even non-European minorities in the 1860s and 1870s. In extreme form, the Greater Britain prophecy claimed that New Zealand's future was so brilliant that it would ultimately not simply replicate but transcend Britain, down-written doom or not.

'New Zealand is a larger and by nature a much richer country by far than

Great Britain,' wrote Hursthouse, inflating it from a real 66 million acres to 78 million, and then rounding it up to 80 million for good measure.[93] Progress worked faster. 'Five years in a young growing colony like New Zealand, is a period of time equal to twenty years in an old grown country.'[94] Between 1846 and 1852, asserted Thomson, 'the child had become a man proud of his increasing strength and confident of a splendid future . . . New Zealand, England's most distant colony, will in a few generations cast a lustre over Queen Victoria's reign which men absorbed in the turmoil of European politics cannot fully comprehend.'[95] Cholmondeley referred to New Zealand as 'a nation that is to be, a giant yet in his cradle'; the 'Infant Hercules' was sometimes his nickname. 'The commerce of New Zealand is only in its infancy,' wrote another prophet, 'but this infancy is that of a Hercules from which, when it has reached manhood, we are warranted to expect a giant's strength.'[96]

Young Hercules was often associated with the strangling of local serpents in paradise: the unconverted Maori and the autocratic governors who kept the settlers from the free institutions that were their birthright and a key to progress. His rise, once untrammelled and combined with the expected vast maritime commerce, produced Greater Britain. 'It is not enough to call New Zealand the Britain of the South . . . New Zealand is much superior to Britain . . . in predicting for it the most brilliant future we know . . . that we are far, very far, below the inevitable truth.' Gazing at the future site of Hamilton in 1863, a journalist was tempted to 'draw pictures of the future when this plain shall be the seat of a great central town . . . a town of iron and coal . . . and Old England may then be a dependency of the Britain of the South – who knows?'[97]

Both Better and Greater Britain motifs implied a reproduction of Britain. The former suggested that the new would be qualitatively superior to the old, yet mirror it more than other neo-Britains – in terms of ethnicity, for example. Greater Britain, on the other hand, was a more expansive and less exclusive vision of the future, emphasising quantity as much as quality, and eventual parity with, or even superiority to, Britain. The Greater British expectation was of ultimate independence, though not of the elimination of British links – free membership of a family of Greater Britains, unlike the enduring subordinacy implied by Better Britain. Such ideas foreshadowed notions of imperial federation and of free and equal associations of the 'English-speaking peoples'. Julius Vogel, who cherished direct British links more than some of his peers, argued in 1865 that 'the colonies would become great nations, affluent trading partners for Great Britain, and forever allies'.[98] In the mid-nineteenth century, 'it had gradually become a common assumption that they [the white colonies] would eventually obtain complete independence from the mother country'.[99] Difficult though it may be for New Zealanders of today to believe, Greater Britain offered an American model of New Zealand's future, in contrast to Better Britain's Scottish one.

The author of the original *Greater Britain* was Englishman Charles Dilke. He visited New Zealand in 1866, and found that Greater Britain was somewhere between puffing rhetoric and a local act of faith.

> Closely resembling Great Britain in situation, size, and climate, New Zealand is often styled by the colonists 'the Britain of the South', and many affect to believe that her future is destined to be as brilliant as has been the past of her mother-country. With the exaggeration of phrase to which the English New Zealanders are prone, they prophesy a marvellous here-after for the whole Pacific, in which New Zealand, as the carrying and manufacturing country, is to play the foremost part, the Australias following obediently in her train.[100]

The Better–Greater distinction was to some extent echoed in the colonising crusade's versions of Arcadia and Utopia. Arcadianism was a major element of crusader propaganda, and it struck responsive chords in Britain. Wakefield and company offered escape from the great wen and industrial unrest, the urban price of progress. The linchpin prophets emphasised the desire for a freehold farm, the domain of the yeoman, as a major motive for emigration. Crusaders, early and late, aimed at country capitalists, countrymen and countrywomen. All waxed lyrical about the abundance of New Zealand nature and the regenerative effect of rural life. These themes were very important, but four factors suggest that arcadianism alone cannot describe the types of paradise New Zealand was said to represent.

First, as we have seen, New Zealand nature was not in itself abundant. It required British progress to flower into paradise. There might be omelettes growing on trees and pigs begging to be killed, but they had to be imported 12,000 miles. Conventional Arcadias were not Bring Your Own. Second, if New Zealand was an arcadia, then it was to be achieved by very utopian means: collective action by state-like organisations (the companies) and by actual governments, provincial and colonial. Most crusaders worshipped at the altar of free enterprise, but believed it had to be kick-started by collective action, heavily boosted by it, and restarted if necessary. They drew much less of a distinction between public and private than did their heirs. Collective action did not stop at the beach, in either prospect or reality. Much inland settlement followed, both literally and figuratively, paths laid out by the state.

Third, there was always some emphasis on cities, which as we have seen were not considered inherently evil. Cities and civilisation were linked in semantics, history and perceived contemporary reality. Instant civilisation, with cathedrals and libraries planned in Britain or on the voyage out, was an integral part of the Wakefield prospectus. There were always to be towns, conceived from the outset as 'future cities',[101] albeit with town belts of open land girding their loins against urban industrial vice. Hursthouse prophesied 'flocks and herds and golden crops, surrounding the busy city, teeming with "civilised life"'. Vogel's vision of progress included 'flourishing towns' as well as 'smiling agricultural districts'.[102]

Fourth, the crusader prospectus incorporated an instant collective identity that was not merely arcadian and rural but also British and progressive. 'Arcadianism' does not easily accommodate the heavy emphasis on progress. Arcadianism, involving native natural abundance and steady, natural, farm-led growth powered by virtuous individuals, contested with utopianism: abundance stemming from the British insemination of raw New Zealand nature, and fast, artificial, town-led growth powered by progressive collectivities. In the colonising era, 1840s–80s, it was utopianism that predominated; only to be retrospectively replaced with arcadianism as a new present rewrote history to suit itself. But, characteristically, the crusaders wanted to have their cake and eat it: both Better Britain and Arcadia, and Greater Britain and Utopia. That the latter pair outpaced the former in the colonising era, and that the reverse happened thereafter, was not planned by them.

Better or Greater, New Zealand was to be the Britain of the South, and was also to be an impressive list of specialist paradises – for brides, governesses, carpenters, gentry, invalids and investors. English wood pigeons 'would find New Zealand a paradise', and so too would balding humans. After two years in Auckland, wrote one woman settler, 'My hair, from being thin and weak, is now so thick that I can scarcely bear its weight.'[103] More important crusader paradises were aimed unerringly at weak links in the Victorian social and cultural system.

One was the brides' paradise. In the nineteenth century, male Europeans had at least two disproportionate habits: dying in infancy and migrating in youth. In Victorian Britain, this led to an imbalance of sexes, a 'surplus' of unmarried adult women estimated at over 500,000 in 1861 and 700,000 in 1871.[104] The corresponding 'surplus' of single men in the colonies, including New Zealand, was a major hitch in crusader plans, which prescribed a balance of sexes for social health and instant civilisation – decent wives kept decent husbands from falling into disrepute. But it was a hitch that Wakefield for one had long predicted, and the crusaders believed they had the solution: the mass importation of brides. A brides' paradise therefore joined the glittering array. 'Fancy,' wrote Mary Swainson in 1854, 'the mother of a [servant] woman I had for a month had a wooden leg, a son of 22, and six [other] children, yet has just been married again!! No-one need despair after that I think.'[105] Lower-class women were expected to serve a term as servants before marriage, and from the 1860s assisted passages were offered to thousands of single women. The improved marriage prospects of migrants' daughters were emphasised too. Managed letters back asserted to prospective immigrants that 'the prospects of your daughters would be increased a hundred-fold'.[106]

There was also the investors' paradise. The original New Zealand Company plan was founded upon a proportion of its shareholders being absentees, investing their spare cash rather than themselves in New Zealand's certain progress.[107] That land values would double every three years was 'a natural law almost as certain as gravitation'.[108] The certain, safe and secure progress and Britishness of New Zealand was promulgated to large and small British investors; and the resulting reputation was nurtured carefully by the crusaders, notably Thomas Russell. An important part of the duties of New Zealand's representatives in London was 'a constant nursing of British public opinion on the state of the New Zealand economy'.[109] Like what later became its most famous baking powder, Greater Britain was '*Sure* to rise'.

Other specialised paradise images were aimed at particular British classes, or sections of them. One gets the impression that the secure cores of the Victorian classes were happy where they were, and that they did not tend to emigrate. But around the cores were two insecure groups: those who hoped to rise and those who feared to fall. These were the prime targets of the New Zealand crusaders. The crusaders themselves were genteel and respectable; they wanted more of their own ilk – to justify their own migration, sustain notions of 'better stock' and of England replicated, provide leading citizens for the new society, and attract the money such folk were supposed to bring with them. 'A little capital will go a long way in New Zealand,' wrote Hursthouse, 'but *some* capital is absolutely necessary.'[110] 'Any young man with £1,000, or, if married, £2,000 will do capitally,' wrote Canterbury founder John Robert Godley to the genteel. 'But discourage anyone who has not some capital . . . There is no opening for a *poor* gentleman.'[111]

There were allegedly some openings for poor gentlewomen, however – in the form of governesses. Maria Rye, an enthusiast for women's migration, portrayed New Zealand and other colonies as a governesses' paradise. Impoverished English gentlewomen without marriage prospects were encouraged to come to New Zealand and civilise it by training genteel children and then marrying their uncles.[112] Persuading wealthy gentry and respectables to abandon the fleshpots of London and the solid dinner tables of Manchester was quite a challenge, but the crusaders tried to rise to it. The paradises they offered to the genteel, and to those respectables content with their class, were complex in theory and renegotiated in practice. They are discussed in later chapters, with the questions of whether gentry did indeed get in, get on, get on top and stay on top.

A problem with secure gentry and with other sections of the migrant market was that those whom the crusaders wanted most were least inclined to come. The point where push and pull, as well as myth and reality, intersected best was probably the artisan. New Zealand was presented as a paradise for craftsmen, the ideal escape route for 'competition-crushed tradesmen' – mainly carpenters and the like, but extending as far as hairdressers.[113] In Britain, the shift from wood to iron and coal as raw material and fuel made many carpenters redundant – Henry Mayhew estimated almost 6,000 in London alone in 1839.[114] In New Zealand, wood dominated and carpenters were in great demand. Their wages were two to three times as high as those of an unskilled labourer, and they and other artisans with skills appropriate to New Zealand had the best chance of any decent folk of achieving of acquiring property and climbing up a class if they chose to. But even the attraction for artisans cannot wholly be explained by rational economics. A maker of dolls' eyes slipped into New Plymouth in 1842, along with many other inappropriate craftsmen.[115]

The disreputable were not invited to New Zealand, but they were the crucial stick with which the decent were threatened if they did not come. Perhaps influenced by moral evangelism from above, perhaps by other factors, decent people's dread of disrepute was on the increase in our peopling period, for their children as much as themselves. In Britain, their mid-century voluntary investment in education, which took most of their children to some sort of school well before the state took much of a hand, is one sign of this.[116] Another is the almost universal fear of the poorhouse, a dreaded badge of disrepute. A third is the equally widespread dread of a pauper's burial, which boosted friendly societies, trade unions and insurance companies, and shows that the fear of disrepute extended beyond death. Decent young single men and women, and an emerging subcategory known as the 'deserving poor', victims of sudden misfortune, were considered particularly vulnerable to disrepute, and they were targets of the colonising crusaders, especially in the 1860s and 1870s.

The crusader prophets were all agreed on the need to keep out the disreputable, but to get enough decent folk they had to buy into this emerging distinction between deserving and undeserving poor. 'The scum and scrapings . . . beggars, vagabonds, and rogues . . . are fit for nothing whether at home or abroad,' wrote even the relatively liberal Thomas Cholmondeley, who had read Mayhew's work on London. 'They are almost universally vile, diseased, and weakly; or if strong, utterly depraved . . . An emigration of the poor certainly, *but not of the worthless poor*.'[117] 'Above all,' stated Vogel's 1875 *Handbook*, 'let those be warned away who think the Colony a suitable place to repent of evil habits.'[118] Two indicators are enough to show that the antipathy to disreputable serpents in the New Zealand garden was widely shared. When, in 1842–43, two parties of boys from the Parkhurst penitentiary were sent out by the imperial government, 'their arrival was greeted with dismay'.[119] 'They have sent the seeds of crime and immorality,' declaimed the infant local press, 'to be scattered over the length and breadth of New Zealand.'[120] Arthur Thomson sarcastically noted that the British government had sent out a judge and Supreme Court apparatus along with the boys to keep them in business. Second, even in the worst troughs of immigration, such as 1843–47, offers of convicts were refused, and New

Zealand sent 98 of its own locally fallen to Tasmania instead.[121] That the locally fallen, home-grown disreputables would be few was another basic crusader axiom. 'In New Zealand those only are poor who from sickness cannot, or from idleness and intemperance will not work.'[122]

'England,' wrote Thomson in 1859, 'has no future for most of the present generation . . . the working man from the cradle to the grave lives little above starvation, and has nothing to hope for, whereas in New Zealand there is a great future for him within thirty years, room for enterprise, and many chances of success.'[123] The stick with which the decent were threatened was the class below; the carrot they were offered was 'success' – the class above. Strictly speaking, the crusaders never offered a labourers' or a servants' paradise, though these and similar terms were common in the literature. High wages and good living conditions were promised, but were presented as merely paving decent people's path to respectability or 'independence'. Even Wakefield, often thought to have intended to keep workers in their place with his 'sufficient price', never saw this as a permanent obstacle to their social promotion. The idea was that the high price of land would compel decent migrants to serve a substantial term as hewers of wood and drawers of water before moving on to their own land, with fresh migrants slotting in below them.

Such constant expansion, of course, was one of the ways in which crusader plans were locked in to progress. The archetypal example of a self-made independency, the respectable little paradise offered to decent folk, was the owner-operated farm. Coupled with assisted passages, these incentives did attract decent people in their thousands, but seldom in enough thousands to allow the crusaders to be as selective as they wished to be. The proportion of trained servants and agricultural labourers was never as high as they would have liked.

The hunt for agricultural skills led to an extraordinary intervention in British domestic affairs by the New Zealand state in the 1870s: an open alliance with the National Union of Agricultural Labourers.[124] Led by Joseph Arch, the union was behind the rural protest movement known as the 'Revolt of the Field', beginning in 1872. It supported the migration of union members to New Zealand, especially in periods when its efforts to improve farm wages were having little success, through farmer intransigence and the oversupply of labour. Conversely, farmers referred to New Zealand earthquakes, massacres and the loss of the *Cospatrick*, and tried to prevent both union officials and New Zealand emigration agents from obtaining venues for public meetings. The colonial government brought union officials to New Zealand on fact-finding missions, treated them royally and took care that they found the right facts. The officials in turn published crusader tracts and brought out groups of their members as migrants. A comparison with Judas sheep is perhaps too harsh. The guided tours of other 'big wigs' became an increasingly important part of crusader propaganda, and of the somewhat more modest boosterism that succeeded it.

> They really are the most dangerous guides . . . they paint all *couleur de rose.* They merely pass through the country as birds of passage – and that under the most enjoyable circumstances – they are feted and banqueted . . . see all the bright side of life, and have no idea of what a *struggle* it is . . . These people return, and naturally crack up the country where they have been so pleasantly entertained . . . and people are more and more confirmed in their view that New Zealand is an El Dorado – poor things![125]

An unlikely panoply of paradises, puffing poetry and slogans, grandiose prophecies and giant vegetables may seem a slender foundation for proposing that these images were taken seriously or widely shared. It is quite true that one should make a discount for rhetoric, and doubt that settlers cared much whether their great-grandchildren would live in Better Britain or Greater Britain, Arcadia or Utopia. These formal myths of settlement were not accepted as gospel but unofficially renegotiated by the migrant fragment, subverted by the practical realities of the New Zealand frontier and changed over time to match changes in real history. One change, noted above, was the shift in favour of Better Britain over Greater Britain from the 1880s, reversing the earlier rank order. This shift was associated with the many-faced phenomenon of 'recolonisation', which dominated New Zealand history between the 1880s and the 1960s, and is a central theme of the sequel to this book.

Another process of change was the ongoing ricochet between Britain's idea of New Zealand and New Zealand's idea of itself, reflections bouncing between two distorting mirrors like the broader contact ricochet between European Us and non-European Them. More changes stemmed from the interaction of formal and informal myths of settlement. The formal mythology was the official Pakeha prospectus, what the colonising crusaders hoped settlers *would* hope. The informal myths were what settlers *did* hope; they strengthened the authorised version where they converged with it, and weakened and subverted it where they diverged – an important tension. Yet for all the puffery, change and renegotiation, there is, I think, good reason to believe that the formal myths of settlement, the progressive British paradise, really did bite deep into the minds of the founding Pakeha.

One example is the success of the climatic paradise, which allegedly restored the health of invalids, especially Anglo-Saxon ones. Many settlers are known to have migrated at least partly in the hope of improving their health. New Zealand was successfully marketed as a miracle cure. Another example is the staggering borrowing propensities of the settlers, outlined in Chapter Fourteen. They may not have bought the idea of Greater British progress lock, stock and barrel, but they certainly borrowed as though they did.

Despite some contradictions, the deeper functions and mutual support of the various myths are also likely to have increased their bite. Like Maori myths of settlement, they prescribed individual as well as collective behaviour in new situations, and soothed the pains of change. Diminishing the psychological costs of emigration was important. The crusaders came very close to telling emigrants that they were not emigrating at all but exchanging one familiar Britain for a new improved one, with virtues enhanced and vices eliminated. Unfertilised but safely serpentless nature – 'There are no wild animals and the natives are very well behaved'[126] – presented migration as a *safe* adventure. New Zealand was secure as well as safe. Promotion for decent folk insured against social upheaval, which the mid-century British still feared. Chartists should know, wrote Hursthouse, who thought of everything, 'that the steady labourer inevitably becomes the yeoman freeholder'.[127] And promotion was certain for all those with a modicum of virtue; individual progress was guaranteed by collective progress. Premier Julius Vogel officially informed prospective decent migrants that 'every industrious immigrant who is blessed with good health may rely upon success in the colony'.[128] Various prophets of colonisation offered migrants different New Zealand lotteries, but a common quality was that everyone would win. 'In old-world lotteries of life, there is one gigantic prize to innumerable blanks; in new-world lotteries of life there may be no gigantic prize, but there are innumerable goodly prizes and scarcely any blanks.'[129]

This was seductive if paradoxical imaging: exotic familiarity, dynamic security, sure gambles, safe adventure. There are echoes in New Zealand's portrayal of itself in the present, and this may be further evidence of the myths' deep bite. In the 1990s, 225 years after Joseph Banks first pressed New Zealand plants between the pages of Milton's *Paradise Lost*, an indignant citizen's letter to a newspaper concluded: 'What is this country coming to? It was once a paradise.' A 138.5-kilogram pumpkin reached maturity in Helensville, and New Zealand was still being advertised in Britain as 'a paradise for immigrants' where 'health and education are free and a 16 oz. steak and a litre of wine cost £2.70'.[130] The colonising crusaders offered a complex of paradises, and they bequeathed a paradise complex.

In the colonising era, 1830s–80s, the Britainising of New Zealand was practised as well as preached, by ordinary settlers as well as crusader prophets. It was the former who grew the giant vegetables. There were many references to parts of New Zealand as paradise-like or Britain-like that were not intended as advertising.[131] Most actually refer to converted, not unconverted, nature, and the process of conversion, of making the wilderness flower, was a process of Britainising. Like some early explorers, the settlers were prone to what has been described as a 'mania for acclimatisation', especially, though not exclusively, of British plants and animals. Many, such as flowers, songbirds and ornamental trees, as well as game fish and animals, were desirable rather than essential.[132] The early effort put into these introductions when more basic needs urgently demanded attention suggests a widespread urge to make New Zealand Britain-like. Many settlers eagerly engaged with the myth of New Zealand as the progressive British paradise, writing it in their houses, plants and animals as well as on paper. They succeeded well enough that a visitor to New Zealand in 1894 could exclaim, 'In England again, by Jove!'[133]

By no means all migrants, of course, swallowed the Pakeha prospectus whole, or even most of it. But it was imbibed by many, and at least tasted by most. The migrants it hooked were very varied, but they did have one thing in common: the long voyage out. Like a funnel into which disparate ingredients were poured, the voyage concentrated and homogenised expectations of New Zealand. The crusaders provided a library for each migrant ship, dominated by multiple copies of their own tracts. Early and late, crusader dignitaries made speeches of farewell; surgeons, chaplains and captains lectured and preached en route. Shipboard newspapers, debates in the cabin and discussions in the hold disseminated and reinforced key myths. Scots migrant Jane Finlayson and her shipmates were given classes by a crusader agent on their voyage out in 1876. 'He was saying today we will soon know as much about New Zealand as if we had been living there for years.'[134]

Migrants swore their vows to Greater Britain in three stages, like the rites of the Catholic Church. The decision to migrate to New Zealand was baptism; the indoctrinating voyage out was catechism; and the decision to stay in New Zealand, to settle not sojourn, was confirmation. After all, though the crusaders mounted the greatest campaign in New Zealand advertising history, people did not buy Greater Britain like some brand of soap. They staked their children's lives on it. But Greater Britain – progress without the price, paradise without the serpent, and Britain without the Irish – was a hard act for history to follow.

CHAPTER THIRTEEN

Getting In

The crusaders wanted genteel, respectable and decent English, Scots and Protestant Irish; moneyed, or else young, healthy and rural; with a balance of men and women. They wanted the decent working people among these migrants to desire social promotion to respectability above all, but to be willing to serve a substantial apprenticeship as labourers and servants. What did they get? Like the origins of the Maori, this is an area where the myths are stronger than the published evidence. Some myths were contemporary: what people hoped or believed would happen, or was happening at the time. Others were retrospective: what historians hoped or believed had happened. To make matters more complicated, the contemporary formal myths of settlement were often contested and subverted by informal myths. Both were real historical forces, not mere fictions to be debunked, bringing out migrants and structuring their expectations of, and actions in, their new land.

The Pakeha 'Great Fleet', one up on Maori, contained eight 'canoes', or distinct streams of migrants. Each had a different balance of settling and sojourning, class, gender and ethnicity, a different fit into crusader plans, and different fates. Their names – Tasman, Gold, Company, Independent, Military, Colonial, Provincial and Special Settlements – were less resonant than *Tainui* and *Arawa*, but they were no less important for that.

The oldest, Tasman, 'canoe' had been eddying people across that sea since the 1790s, and continues to do so to the present. In the nineteenth century, it favoured males and Irish, and it was prone to sojourn rather than settle. Its contribution to the founding fragment was quite large, and it was seen as largely disreputable. The colonising crusaders did not like it much, nor did they like the larger, later, Gold stream, which brought in something like 100,000 people in the 1860s. This stream also favoured males, Irish and Australians, but its catchment was broader – it included substantial minorities of Americans and Germans, for example. It, too, was seen as disreputable, but was actually quite mixed and ambiguous in terms of class. Independent migrants – those who organised and paid for their own migration, and did not come for gold rushes or from Australia, were a third stream. They trickled in fairly steadily throughout the peopling period and were more moneyed, genteel, respectable Scots and English than most.

Theoretically, the crusaders had more control over the other five canoes. Two of the smallest were the Company stream of the 1840s, and an underestimated Military stream. This was formed mainly from military pensioner migrants to Auckland in the 1840s, Waikato military settlers in the 1860s and the many hundreds of regulars from the imperial regiments who took their discharges in New Zealand. The 58th Regiment contributed 1,110 settlers before departing in 1858.[1] The Military stream, too, was prone to be Irish, who did much of Britain's fighting, but it was assumed that service in the Queen's army converted Catholic Irish into something better. Retired officers, very much less Catholic than their men, were important contributors to the desired social tone. The Military and Company streams were probably similar in size at 10,000 to 15,000, which puts the latter in perspective. But the Company stream was mainly English and Scots, and it appears to have had an exceptionally large genteel minority, though some promptly went away again. The Colonial stream, largest of all at about 120,000 people, consisted of the migrants assisted out by the colonial government, especially in the 1870s. Provincial governments, notably Otago and Canterbury, also assisted out substantial numbers in the period 1853–71.

Both colonial and provincial authorities also indirectly assisted private entrepreneurs to organise the Special Settlement stream. These echoed the company settlements, or tried to, though on a smaller scale. Some sought ethnic exclusivity, like Scots Otago. Successes included the Germans of Puhoi, who arrived between 1863 and 1876, whose Wakefield was Martin Krippner; the Highlanders of Waipu, who arrived, via Nova Scotia, in 1853–60 under their prophet Norman McLeod; and the Protestant Irish of Katikati, brought out between 1875 and 1885 by George Vesey Stewart, a crusading projector and publicist equal to any. He is said to have brought 4,000 Ulster folk to New Zealand, some of them genteel.

Failures included an abortive partly Italian settlement at Jackson Bay, South Westland, in and around 1878, and an attempt by a Hamburg company in the early 1840s to colonise and annex the Chatham Islands. The latter project was abetted by the New Zealand Company (whose artist Charles Heaphy portrayed the peaty islands as 'a lush and fertile landscape'), but not the imperial government, and it never got off the ground.[2] France Australe did get off the ground, at Akaroa as we have seen, but not very far. The Special Settlements stream was diverse and interesting, though quite small. We should register these different types of entry, but, with the exception of the Colonial stream, the evidence does not allow us to analyse them separately in any depth. We need to look at the net effect of the great colonising crusade, the overall shapes of the Pakeha founding fragment and its fit with crusader plans.

Getting Britons

Crusader publicists had an incentive to exaggerate their success in getting Britons: making New Zealand seem more Britain-like to the next echelon. During the recolonial era of New Zealand history, 1880s–1960s, this tendency was reinforced by a much stronger retrospective myth of racial homogeneity, symbolised by the slogan '98.5 per cent British'. Various statistical and semantic sleights were employed to achieve such figures. In extreme form, this mythology asserted that New Zealand was not just British but English. It still surprises some people to learn that English, or Anglo-New Zealanders, are not and never have been a majority of the population of New Zealand. The English and Welsh share of the Pakeha population peaked at about 62 per cent in the 1850s, but at that time over half the population was Maori. The English/Welsh share of Pakeha never again exceeded about 53 per cent, while Maori never fell below 4 per cent of the total population.[3] Ethnically, New Zealand is not, and never has been, mainly English. But it remains true that, after overtaking Maori in the 1860s, the English were always the country's largest ethnic minority. Welsh are difficult to pick out because most statistics conflated them with English. A book on the Welsh in New Zealand can do little more than list Welsh surnames and place-names.[4] Although boosted by assisted immigration in the 1870s, their share of the Pakeha founding fragment was less than 2 per cent – much less than their share of the home population.

The most striking ethnic distinction between the populations of the British Isles and Pakeha New Zealand is the great over-representation of Scots in the latter. Scots made up about 10 per cent of the population of the British Isles in the mid-nineteenth century, but up to 24 per cent of Pakeha.[5] That Scots were to New Zealand what the Irish were to Australia – the chief lieutenants of settlement – is an axiom of folk history, but the implications have not yet been fully explored. In peak years, as many as one-third of all Scots emigrants came to New Zealand.[6] They clustered in Otago and its offshoot, Southland. It is often implied that the Scottish 'Old Identity' was swamped by the gold-rushing 'New Iniquity' in the 1860s, but this does not appear to be true, though there was some dilution. Using Presbyterianism as a proxy for Scottishness, Otago and Southland were still about half Scottish in 1871.[7]

In the south, Scots filled the role that English filled elsewhere. Scots were both concentrated and widespread. In 1871, Presbyterians were between 17 and 20 per cent of the Pakeha population of all other provinces except unusually English Taranaki and Nelson.[8] The stereotypical Scot is a reinvented Highlander, kilt, dirk and sporran.[9] Romanticised Highlanders were being incorporated into the majority culture in nineteenth-century Britain just as the Maori were later to be in New Zealand, and for much the same reasons. But most Scots (over 80 per cent) in both Scotland and New Zealand were Lowlanders. In the

Lowlands, too, a process of Anglicisation or Britainisation was taking place, but was only beginning to bite in mid-century. Scots were overwhelmingly Presbyterian, and, as with Irish Catholicism, their church shored up their cultural distinctiveness. New Zealand was twice as Scottish as the British Isles, and this was to have its effects on Pakeha culture.

Thus far, the colonising crusaders were doing quite well in achieving their ethnic aims. Until 1860, they managed to keep the proportion of Irish quite low: around 12 per cent of Pakeha, heavily concentrated in Auckland province, which was the main beneficiary of military settlement and at that time had the closest links with Australia. But from 1860, the gold rushes, improving access from Australia to the South Island and the overriding need for brides and servants meant that the crusaders temporarily abandoned control of Pakeha ethnicity. The proportion of Irish rose to nearly 19 per cent in 1881.[10] Tasman, Gold, Military and Colonial were the key Irish streams. Two percentage breakdowns of the overall ethnicity of the 100,000 1870s Colonial assisted immigrants give differing results – English and Welsh 47.6/50.8, Scots 19.5/16.6, Irish 29.5/25. But the high proportion of Irish is clear enough.[11] It was only Catholic Irish who were considered undesirable, and the crusaders concentrated their efforts on the Protestant north, with some success – 46 per cent of Canterbury's Irish were from Ulster, which had only 22 per cent of the population of Ireland in 1861, and Ulster provided 48.5 per cent of the Irish males and 62 per cent of the Irish females assisted out by all provinces between 1858 and 1871.[12] Yet only a fifth or a quarter of New Zealand Irish were Protestants, despite the boost from G. V. Stewart's Ulstermen in 1875–85 and the strong bias of the crusader recruitment drive towards Protestants. This suggests that Catholics, especially in Ulster, exploited systems intended for their Protestant neighbours, so subverting crusader plans. The special role of Irish single women is discussed later in this chapter.

Australian influence, the Gold and Tasman migrations, was much greater than the number of Australian-born (less than 5 per cent) and much less than the total number who came through Australia (perhaps 50 per cent). British migrants bound for New Zealand very often came via Australia, and their stay there might be short or long. Only 4.8 per cent of the New Zealand population in 1871 were Australian-born, and this declined to around 3 per cent in 1881, but this was the mere tip of an Ausberg. Most Australians (especially adult males, who were the most common crossers of the Tasman) were not native-born in this period; those who were native-born were disproportionately inclined to stay in Australia,[13] and until the 1900s they were only a fraction of the people with significant Australian experience living in New Zealand. It is also possible that the number of Australian arrivals has been substantially underestimated.[14] Another somewhat deceptive statistic is *nett* migration – those who came minus those who left. In the 1870s, for example, when gold had ceased to be the main magnet and when most immigration from Britain came direct, nett immigration from Australia to New Zealand was only 7,000 – a pale reflection of the 50,000 who went one way and the 43,000 who went the other.[15] Sojourners can be as important as settlers, and in any case the people who came from Australia to New Zealand were not always those who went the other way.

How long it takes to make an 'Australian' or a 'New Zealander' is a vexed question; and the possibility of an Australasian collective identity – vague and loose, but real – complicates the picture further. Some people, in contrast to the colonising crusaders, did not see the two shores of the Tasman world as significantly different places. Their movements were more akin to internal than external migration. To hazard a guess, it may be that that 20 per cent of the founding Pakeha population was born or bred in, or substantially influenced by, Australia. This influence was especially strong in the gold provinces of Otago, Westland and Nelson, and also in Auckland and Southland.[16] The reverse was equally true, and equally forgotten. 'New Zealanders' may have made up as much as 17 per cent of 1880s immigration to Victoria.[17] Very occasionally, the crusaders deliberately sought migrants in Australia, but on the whole the high proportion of Australians was not good news from their perspective. 'To draw people from the extremely undesirable pool of eastern Australia was desperation indeed.'[18] Australians were too Irish, too convict and too digger. Australia was an uncontrolled gateway into the progressive British paradise, through which disreputable serpents could slither unchecked. Australians worried about 'Kiwi bludgers' in the later twentieth century inverted these concerns.

Australians came by themselves, despite the colonising crusaders; Catholic Irish hijacked systems created by the crusaders for Protestant Irish, or were intentionally resorted to when other cupboards were bare. Germans and Scandinavians seem to have been preferred to Catholic Irish, largely for racial reasons, though in the 1840s Britain's Hanoverian connection may have been a factor too. Definitions of 'Anglo-Saxon' could be broadened to include these groups. Germans first settled in 1836, but did not begin arriving in any numbers before 1843. Scandinavians came later. Bishop Ditlev Monrad, one-time Prime Minister of Denmark, and a group of followers fled to New Zealand from Bismarck's Prussians after the Schleswig-Holstein War of 1864, only to flee back again in 1869 from Titokowaru. Over 4,000 Scandinavians, Pakeha racial ideology's favourite foreigners, were assisted out in the 1870s. The German-born share of the population peaked in 1867 at 1.3 per cent, and was about 1 per cent in 1881, but if we allow the Germans their children, their proportion was over 2 per cent. The number of Scandinavians was similar.

The Chinese entered from the early 1860s, aiming for the Otago goldfields. They came mostly from the 'Four Counties' outside Canton, initially via the open Australian gateway. There was some early antagonism to their entry, but it was less strong than it later became, and between 1871 and 1881, Chinese displaced Germans as the leading non-British immigrant minority in terms of birthplace. However, they were not allowed to breed. Cultural practices – wife at home, husband sojourning abroad – and immigration restrictions combined to keep out Chinese women. Restricting women more than men was an important and enduring way of acquiring useful labour without long-term risk to ethnic homogeneity. There were only fourteen Chinese women in 1896 among 3,700 men; and Pakeha women would not marry Chinese men either. This genetic control, and its own sojourning habits, meant that the Chinese minority – over 5,000 at peak – did not grow as it might have done.[19]

The Chinese experience illustrates that the ethnicity of immigrants and of the subsequent population does not necessarily correlate very closely. Different groups have different sojourning habits and gender balances, different propensities to procreate or assimilate – 'ethnic' difference can be merely nominal. A few groups, most notably Gujaratis and Dalmatians, sneaked in after the great peopling period of the 1840s–80s. Broadly speaking, however, it was this period that established New Zealand's ethnic pattern to the 1950s. To risk rough estimates, English were the largest ethnic minority, at about 45 per cent of the Maori and Pakeha population. There were three other major ethnic groups: Scots, at around 20 per cent; Irish, at about 18 per cent (roughly a quarter of whom were Protestants); and Maori, at 9 per cent. If Australians were treated as a separate 'ethnic' group, they too would be in this category of size, and English, Scots and especially Irish would diminish. There were four smaller but still significant groups – Germans, Scandinavians, Chinese and Welsh – at 1 or 2 per cent each, and dozens of tiny ones. The largest of the very small ethnic minorities in the period 1860–90 was Americans, of whom there were 1,732 in 1881.[20] As with Australians, they represented the tip of an iceberg of influence. America contributed few settlers but a great many sojourners, notably ocean whalers and gold-rushers.

All this represented a qualified success for the drive to acquire Britons. In sheer bulk, given New Zealand's disadvantages such as youth and distance, success was staggering. At its peak, in the 1870s, the New Zealand colonising crusade captured around 10 per cent of British emigrants (and at least 6 per cent of Irish) to all destinations, and almost half of all British and Irish emigration to Australasia.[21] But Greater Britain was more ethnically diverse than the crusaders would have liked, and much more diverse than subsequent myths of homogeneity allow. Camouflaged by these myths, and reduced by real homogenising forces, subtle ethnic differences nevertheless persisted into the twentieth century, a matter discussed in the sequel to this book.

Willingness to migrate to New Zealand from the British Isles was not evenly distributed, even within the key regions of northern Ireland, Lowland Scotland

and southern England. Why were people from some counties more prone to migrate to New Zealand than others? To what extent was the New Zealand colonising crusade, with its assisted passages, recruitment networks, direct advertising and carefully nurtured image of New Zealand responsible for the differences? We do not know, but by marrying research into the birth places of nineteenth-century Canterbury migrants (by Keith Pickens) to a general statistical study of English and Welsh migration (by Dudley Baines) we can make some guesses.[22]

New Zealand-prone (or at least Canterbury-prone) English counties can be divided into three main groups: the West Country counties of Cornwall, Devon and Somerset; the South Midland counties of Oxford and Gloucester; and the London hinterland counties of Surrey, Essex and Kent. Other research tends to confirm that these counties were important sources of people for the whole of New Zealand, not just Canterbury.[23] Two further Canterbury-prone counties, Cumberland and Huntingdon, fall outside these groups. All these counties contributed 33.5 per cent of the English population of Canterbury but only 18.5 per cent of the population of England.[24] Each county had at least 50 per cent more migrants in Canterbury than its share of the English population would lead us to expect; and each group included one county that was more than 100 per cent over-represented: Cornwall, Oxfordshire and Surrey. These counties appear to have had no common pattern of internal urbanisation, agricultural collapse, low wage rates or high literacy that might explain their special link with New Zealand.

On the face of it, West Country migration to New Zealand is easily accounted for. That region – especially Cornwall – had a high rate of emigration to most destinations. New Zealand simply got its share of a Cornish diaspora. High general emigration would also explain the high Canterbury migration of the two English counties outside the three main groups (Huntingdon and Cumberland), and of the Irish county of Kerry. But some counties with high general emigration rates were *not* attracted to New Zealand, and some with low rates *were* attracted. Crusader effort or chain migration, or both, may explain the variation. Crusader effort was probably a factor in the London hinterland's liking for New Zealand. London was the chief centre of this effort; if you were looking for agricultural workers and rural artisans from a London base, then Surrey was an obvious place to go. Being near but not in major urban centres was also a feature of the New Zealand-prone counties of Scotland and Ireland.[25] Many Scots came from around but not in Glasgow and Edinburgh. Antrim and County Down – the most New Zealand-prone county of all – were close to Belfast, a primary centre of crusader effort. Carlow was fairly close to Dublin, a secondary centre, and quite attracted to New Zealand; Wicklow was even closer and was very attracted. Substituting migration to New Zealand for internal migration to the local big city might also be a factor, though Baines discounts this as a general explanation for emigration.

The South Midlands New Zealand-prone counties, Oxfordshire and Gloucestershire, were neither suburban nor given to general emigration. The latter was also true of the London hinterland counties. Surrey, the most New Zealand-prone of all English counties except Cornwall, had a particularly low rate of general emigration. In five of the ten New Zealand-prone English counties, then, New Zealand was overcoming a double difficulty: attracting above-average numbers of emigrants from populations that had a below-average tendency to emigrate. It was a destination to which you emigrated when you did not like emigrating, and it is very tempting to link this with the Britain of the South image.

More specific and local factors were no doubt influential too. Rollo Arnold argues that subregional variations within counties were important, and the current trend of English regional history is to emphasise subregion rather than county. The recent enclosure of commons, an unusual number of small freehold farms, and Dissenting religion – all could be factors in making a subregion New Zealand-prone. Wychwood in Oxfordshire was one such district. '"New Zealand" must have been a household name in the Wychwood villages.'[26] But not all such subregions became New Zealand-prone. The availability of information through return migrants, letters back and crusader advertising and literature must also have been part of the equation.

Baines found that the variable with which county emigration rates correlated best was the previous decade's emigration rate. The thesis that emigration causes emigration is somewhat circular, but it does suggest that chain migration may have been more important in Britain than is generally thought – chain migration is normally associated more with Ireland and other non-British migrant sources. This does not necessarily imply chain migration in the narrow sense of relative bringing out relatives in a steadily thickening stream over a substantial period of time. We should probably add the concepts of 'clump' and 'bridge' migration to that of 'chain'. Two-thirds of all emigrants from Oxfordshire to New Zealand in the 1870s left in one year – more clump than chain. Kent had a relationship with New Zealand dating from the 1840s – perhaps a prerequisite for a boom in Kentish migration in the 1870s.[27] It could be that migratory counties, or subregions within them, developed emigration traditions, where emigration was a more prominent part of local ideology, a more commonly considered option, than elsewhere. New Zealand history suggests that such local traditions in the source society could be linked to specific destinations, or even that they could derive from such links.

This was certainly the case with non-British migrants. Most Chinese – and, later, Greek, Dalmatian and Indian – immigrants came from the same small subregion of their homeland. Amidst vast seas of people who had never heard of New Zealand were tiny islands of knowledge, often highly idealised, where

New Zealand was a name to conjure with. 'Queen Street', Auckland, was a by-name for the New Worlds in at least one Dalmatian village. The New Zealand-prone counties of England, or parts of them, may have had the same sort of special link. Where there was a low general inclination towards emigration, as in Surrey or Gloucester, these links were conceptual bridges between a particular and unusual source and a particular and unusual destination – 'bridge' migration. The bridges could be crossed by chain or clump migrants, assisted or unassisted, pushed or pulled. In Wychwood and a sprinkling of tiny districts like it, the name sighed by the ghosts of departed migrants was 'New Zealand'.

Getting Gentry

In 1841, a young English gentleman, Alfred Fell, sailed to Nelson with a little capital. On the voyage out, the crusader code stressed the gentility of cabin passengers. All was done 'in a gentlemanly way', and cabin passengers were expected not to get vomiting drunk – 'we are all supposed to be too much the gentlemen for that'.[28] On landing, however, things changed very suddenly.

> We are all friendly and happy together. There are but two classes here – ourselves and the labouring class . . . Distinctions of rank I never hear of, or false notions of pride. We go into each others' houses, and are hail fellows well met. There are no gentlemen (though some can boast of gentlemanly blood), but all are workers.[29]

Yet Fell quickly became a member of a small and genteel Nelson élite. He 'held so many pursestrings that he possessed great influence and people were warned not to offend him'.[30] He returned to Britain in 1859 a wealthy man. His son became a knight and member of Parliament. Colonial life blurred class boundaries and 'mixed together . . . all elements of society'. Jack considered himself in many respects as good as his master. But there were still boundaries to blur and elements to mix. Master was still Master, and Jack was still Jack.

The top end of the Pakeha fragment is obscured by such ambiguities. Some historians believe that New Zealand was classless, or that it had no gentry. Some would concede that gentility came out on the ships but feel that it was corroded by various egalitarian forces in the new land – fragment transformed by frontier. Class *was* looser in New Zealand than in Old Britain; forces hostile to it, or subversive of it, were strong; class categories blurred even more than they were doing in Britain. As in other neo-Britains, egalitarianism was powerful. Yet much egalitarian rhetoric, examined closely, did not deny the existence of class. It emphasised equality before the law, the proud birthright of (adult male) Britons; it disliked *tight* class or class community, and very overt or oppressive class distinctions; it demanded abundant, though not equal, opportunity for promotion and adoption across class lines; it rejected class antagonism and insisted on harmony between classes. But the existence of class cultures, a ranked set of differing lifeways, merging at their margins but distinct at their cores, was taken for granted.

Much 'egalitarianism' was shared by high and low alike. It may be better defined as 'populism', a vague but powerful ideology that accommodated loose class and reinforced and subverted different aspects of the formal myths of settlement. We will see later that it forced compromises on gentility. But it did not keep it out. The notion that gentry did not come to New Zealand in significant numbers is partly an understandable reaction to excessive claims of comprehensive neo-feudal genteel dominance until 1890. Ironically, it may also draw on the belief of some Marxist historians that the British aristocracy and old gentry were subsumed by the middle class in the seventeenth century, which is not so. There is also a hint of the colonial cringe in the view that New Zealand had no upper class: can you have a middle without a top? But the main problem is too narrow a definition of gentility, which fails to take account of the existence of an untitled British aristocracy, the old landed gentry; of the nineteenth-century expansion of gentility well beyond this; and of the fact that class cultures can survive large numbers of new entrants, as long as those entrants take on its mores. The crusaders sought gentry, and they got them, though not the kinds they would have preferred.

Wakefield wanted 'real lords' to give tone to his settlements. He got only one or two, but he did get quite a few lordlings: baronets and younger sons of old landed families. Of an 1866 sample of 314 South Island large landowners, 17 per cent were sons of nobles, baronets, prominent old land gentry, bishops, admirals and generals. Most of the 60 per cent in the sample's 'upper middle class' category, which included 'squires', or lesser landed gentry, and rich Scots lairds, would also have defined themselves as genteel, and been accepted as such.[31] Wakefield and his successors acquired many more new, marginal and aspirant gentry, together with a category of people who were trying to reconcile gentility and respectability. Cabin passages, which gave you private accommodation, the right to dine with the ship's captain and other privileges, probably correlate quite well with at least aspirant gentility. They required both money and manners; four months in the cabin would have been an agony of embarrassment if you did not know the difference between a soup spoon and a dessert spoon, or which way to pass the port. You would at least have learned very quickly.

Between 4 and 22 per cent of migrants on each company ship came in cabins.[32] Higher percentages were more common early; lower late. There were also small percentages of cabin passengers on most subsequent migrant ships – in Independent, Military, Special Settlement and even Tasman streams, though seldom Gold, Provincial and Colonial. Some gentry left again, but those who arrived early and remained had their influence enhanced by a 'first-in' factor: the tendency of frontier opportunities to favour the early bird. Although their social and economic dominance can easily be exaggerated, people recognisable as gentry were very prominent in colonial politics to 1890, with a strong bias towards those who had arrived before 1860.[33] New Zealand gentility was broader than in Britain, where it was broadening anyway; it was even more open to newcomers who met its conditions; it worked more than its ancient archetype – sometimes even manually. But genteel migrants did come. Why?

In Britain, there had long been exceptions to the rule that the upper class did not work: the higher ranks of the church, army, navy and government were well-established genteel professions. These occupations often simulated ownership and leisure. Army officers bought and sold their commissions for several thousand pounds. Anthony Trollope, a senior bureaucrat in the burgeoning Post Office, found time to hunt twice a week and write one and a half novels a year.[34] Other professions were also struggling for gentility in our peopling period: doctors, lawyers, bankers and others. They used techniques such as keeping the cashbox well away from the desk, keeping 'gentlemanly hours' and sending their children to the burgeoning second rank of public schools, stamp machines of gentility. The old professions feature very frequently indeed in the 'father's occupation' slot of the biographies of prominent settlers. Not all these professionals wanted gentility; not all gained it. But many did claim it, and in New Zealand there were fewer people who would argue with them. Some did argue. A visiting naval officer in 1851 complained: 'I'm afraid our party was a little "mixed" for we afterwards discovered that Mrs Webster before her marriage was *servant* to Mrs Hobbs . . . It does not do to ask impertinent questions of "who or what people are" in this part of the world for they spring up in the Colonies like mushrooms and very often like those fungi are anything but *pure* earth.'[35] The officer himself was a surgeon, a profession that had ranked with barbers a century before.

The genteel paradise offered by the crusaders had some propensity to make itself true. If enough gentry came expecting to find their ilk, then find them they would. Whatever its other faults, wrote Hursthouse, Wakefield's systematic colonisation 'drew to New Zealand a much higher class of emigrants than had ever left the Mother Country since the Cavalier settlements of Delaware and Virginia'.[36] True or false, the notion of New Zealand as 'the Gentleman's Colony' was quite widespread.[37] A British ally of the crusaders, Sir Charles Buller, MP, wrote in 1843 that 'more men of good family have settled in New Zealand in . . . three years' than in Canada in 30.[38] The idea percolated as far the imperial adventure novels of G. A. Henty in the late nineteenth century.[39]

New Zealand may have seemed to offer better opportunities of promotion to those respectables who aspired to gentility. Less rigorous definitions and a lower, cheaper standard of keeping up appearances were important here. Mary Ann Martin, an author and wife of humanitarian jurist William Martin, noted that there was less need to 'cut a dash on Tompkins', the contemporary equivalent of 'keeping up with the Joneses'. This was not *freedom* from status anxiety but the amelioration of it. Lady Martin was pleased that the servant accompanying her when she travelled could be less well dressed, less well mounted and less white than in Britain, but she still had to have one. Another early gentlewoman was trapped at home by shabby gloves.[40] New Zealand gentility was cheaper and easier, not cheap and easy.

New Zealand also offered fresh routes to gentility. Cabin passage itself conferred a degree of instant promotion. Both sheep farmers and merchants could be genteel if they met certain conditions, and some marginally genteel professions were upwardly revalued in the new land. In a context where credit was crucial, as we shall see in the next chapter, bankers had enhanced status. Money did not in itself confer gentility, but money to lend came close. Surveying was another profession whose status increased. Ten surveyor's apprentices, employed by the New Zealand Company in 1841, were contractually guaranteed to be given cabin passage and treated as gentlemen.[41]

The hopes of those who wished to rise were coupled with a fear of the fall – the miseries of 'genteel poverty and precarious independence'.[42] If you were unqualified for the still-restricted range of genteel professions, or found them overfilled, you could not work and remain genteel, and consequently you could neither recoup losses or take advantage of new economic opportunities. Genteel culture became a trap, and the crusaders played cunningly on this. Officially, the escape hatch was to be New Zealand's sure progress, which would reverse the decline in genteelly inherited capital and make it grow again. This merged with the prospect of status inflation – small ponds made relatively bigger fish. Hursthouse used the fictional example of Mr Brown, a struggling gentleman in England with a capital of £2,000 invested at a miserable 3.5 per cent. In contrast to England, Brown finds that working manually himself and 'putting Mrs Brown in the kitchen for an hour or two' costs him no caste and does not result in his being 'sent to Coventry'. Insignificant in England, despised by the wealthy and noble, Brown emigrates to New Zealand, puts out his money at 25 per cent and joins the élite. 'Virtually, emigration has knighted Brown.'[43]

There are hints of a real attractiveness to insecure gentility in an intriguing divergence between the regional origins of élite and non-élite migrants. Decent folk from the north of England (including Yorkshire and Lancashire) were disinclined to migrate to New Zealand, and the crusaders were not too keen on Satanic mill country either. Northerners made up 32 per cent of the population of England but only 16 per cent of the English-born population of Canterbury. Among a sample of the élite (namely provincial councillors), on the other hand, northerners comprised nearly 35 per cent – by far the largest regional group.[44] Membership of early colonial and provincial legislatures usually implied broadly genteel status, and there is no obvious reason why middle- or working-class northerners should be two or three times as successful at gentrifying themselves than other groups. It may therefore be that they were genteel when they came out. One possible explanation is that Anglican northern gentry had missed the bus of local industrialisation, which here more than elsewhere was led by urban respectables of Dissenting religion. This led the northern gentry to a somewhat desperate emphasis on exclusive schools and sports, such as Rugby School and rugby union.[45] They saw the vices of industrialism near at hand, and the élitist Canterbury settlement may have seemed another solution to their problems.

Similar factors might have applied to Scotland, where respectables also contested leadership with the gentry more than they did in southern England. Presbyterianism, like northern English Dissent, ranked respectable virtues high. Scots were not over-represented among the Canterbury élite, but in that province they were more prone to be Highlanders than elsewhere, and perhaps less prone to be genteel. Scots *were* over-represented among Wellington provincial councillors and members of Parliament, however, making up about 26 and 30 per cent of each group, well above their proportion of the provincial population.[46] They were also over-represented among large landholders throughout the colony.[47] Impressionistic evidence suggests that a mercantile 'Scotch clique' formed something of an élite in Auckland too. Some members, such as John Logan Campbell, a leading merchant later known as the 'Father of Auckland', had unambiguously genteel backgrounds. Australian gentry – a contradiction in terms only in New Zealand folklore – may also have been attracted to New Zealand. Only 1.6 per cent of Canterbury's general population were born in Australia, and only 7.6 per cent departed for New Zealand from there. Yet the corresponding figures for provincial councillors are 7 and 25.3 per cent.[48] Over one-third of a sample of 1850s Otago large landholders had Australian experience.[49] Although one historian has dismissed the notion that rich Australian pastoralists (also known as 'shagroons' or 'squatters') were numerous, the evidence is against him. The confusion may arise from the distinction between Australian birth and Australian experience.[50] The likes of William 'Ready Money' Robinson were induced to cross the Tasman by such factors as drought in Australia and the opportunities of a newly opened frontier. But they may also have bought the crusader prospectus, despite the Sydney literature on Wellington earthquakes. The image of New Zealand as an unusually genteel destination was not universally accepted, but it was more than obvious crusader puffery or retrospective myth. It was also a contemporary myth, one with an obvious power to become self-realising.

Some evidence suggests that it was not just northern England and Scotland genteel migrants who had missed buses. Quite a number of New Zealand-bound gentlemen had missed out on hoped-for careers or emigrated because their health had broken down. It may be that southern England was increasingly becoming the heartland of British gentility in the nineteenth century – the region where the shift into new professions and new investments without loss of status was easiest, and where genteel class culture and class community were most easily maintained or acquired. Northern Britain was more marginal for gentry, and it was in these regions that New Zealand recruited a disproportionate number of its genteel migrants. New Zealand also seems to have been attractive to, and relatively tolerant of, other marginally genteel groups, such as wealthy and well-educated English Catholics and Jews. There are references to New Zealand being a favoured destination for 'remittance men' too: the place where the black sheep of 'good' families were not thrown entirely to the proletarian wolves. An illegitimate daughter of Benjamin Disraeli is said to have been 'shipped off to colonial obscurity in New Zealand'.[51] It was also very attractive to professionals struggling for new gentility. Medical doctors are a major example. Infant Wellington had thirteen doctors in 1843; by 1881 there were 317 in the colony.[52] Many did not practise but became merchants, pastoralists and politicians. Four provincial superintendents and the Speaker of the House of Representatives in the 1860s were non-practising doctors. Gentility and the doctors' grip on the medical professions were later used to lever each other up, subordinating or marginalising competitors like homoeopaths, midwives and chemists. Gentility was a prerequisite for the most lucrative practices – even relatively relaxed colonial gentility drew the line at personal examinations by the lower orders.

The expansion of gentility in eighteenth- and nineteenth-century Britain involved some merging with middle-class respectability, but also a clash with it. Gentility was traditionally characterised by leisure, which was both symbolised and made possible by the employment of servants. What might be called the genteel 'leisure ethic' did not consist simply in the absence of paid work, or in professions simulating this, but in traditions of unpaid social and political leadership, *noblesse oblige* and public service. Respectability, on the other hand, was characterised by work. The Protestant work ethic preached that those who did not work were useless to others and unfulfilled in themselves. In eighteenth- and nineteenth-century Britain, the leisure ethic percolated down into the upper ranks of the respectable as part of the cult of gentility. But the work ethic remained strong in the respectable, and perhaps even percolated up with moral and religious evangelism and ideas such as 'muscular Christianity'. Unstoppable force met immovable object, and people looked for ways of reconciling the grand clash. Broadening the definition of genteel work was one means, and this converged with the desire of more and more professions to gentrify themselves, and of declining gentry to restore their fortunes. Perhaps migration to New Zealand was another way of reconciling genteel leisure and respectable work.

Although the evidence can only be qualitative rather than quantitative, one cannot help but be struck by the way in which some genteel settlers took pleasure in productive, even manual, work. They noted that this was more permissible in New Zealand than in Britain, and some formed this impression before they left. Work was associated with moral regeneration and the 'simple life', with being useful and fulfilled, and with the great mission of converting New Zealand nature and natives. Enthusiastic settlers like Harry Atkinson celebrated 'the great work that is set us, of subduing and replenishing the earth', and they were eager to take a hands-on approach to it.[53] Neither the crusaders nor a section of their genteel clients were entirely happy about this. They acknowledged that a passing period of *déclassé* work might be required, and sought to make a virtue of necessity by portraying it as a 'pic-nic'. Weld wrote that intending sheep farmers should initially set an example to, and share the privations of, their labourers – 'the eye of the master has a great and magical power'. When the breaking-in was done, however, 'he will find it more profitable to confine himself to superintendence alone'.[54] For many, it was a long picnic, and some did not like it. The shortage of cheap and deferential labour, especially domestic labour, was widely bemoaned, and this drove some gentry back to Britain. But some clearly did like it.

The belief that migration could reconcile work and gentility may have been especially important for gentlewomen. The languid, leisured gentlewoman, prone to fainting, the vapours and the dreaded 'ennui', was a stock Victorian stereotype, identified and debunked by A. James Hammerton.[55] That gentlewomen were grossly over-represented in mental asylums may suggest that it was a real and stifling straitjacket from which some were keen to emerge, as well as a stereotype. Hammerton concentrates his debunking on the unmarried impoverished gentlewomen whom the New Zealand crusaders and others were trying to persuade to migrate as governesses and higher-class brides-to-be. He shows that these migrant women were much more interested in work, as against marriage and languid leisure, than they were supposed to be. It could be that this applied to gentlewomen in general, not just poor and unmarried ones. Genteel women as well as men were subject to the clash of work and leisure ethics. The growing gender imbalance was also beginning to hint that wife and mother was not the only possible destiny. One response to these factors may have been the emergence of feminism in Britain. Another may have been the re-energising and revaluation of traditional household, family and philanthropic work. A third may have been gentlewomen's interest in migrating to places like New Zealand.

'You are a coward and a traitor,' the remarkable Mary Taylor told her friend Charlotte Brontë in 1850. 'A woman who works is by that alone better than one who does not.' Taylor lived in Wellington between 1845 and 1859 as a single woman, buying and selling cattle and establishing and running a drapery business before returning to England and writing a novel designed to 'inculcate the duty of earning money' into all women.[56] Taylor, of course, was far from typical; she clearly transcended conventional constraints to an unusual degree. But she was not wholly disconnected from her time and place. A number of migrant gentlewomen's memoirs reveal a certain satisfaction in the work involved in pioneering, in being 'of value'. This work – in home, family, farm and garden – was usually unpaid and appeared to be conventional, but it was very different from the languid leisure of the old genteel archetype. These activities were sometimes presented as temporary drolleries of the 'pic-nic' variety; there was a certain wryness in some gentlewomen's reflections on such things as their own pride in a full pantry, but there was clearly a real satisfaction behind this. 'The letters and diaries of women in New Zealand,' writes Raewyn Dalziel, 'show that in the colonial context, this role provided demands and challenges that held a high degree of personal reward and satisfaction . . . the break-through was accomplished in the migration process.'[57]

As with gentlemen, none of this implied the abandonment of the desire for servants and the leisure and ritual hospitality they permitted. For reasons discussed below, colonial gentlewomen found domestic servants inadequate, hard to get and harder to keep, and the Flight of the Servants was their great *cri de coeur*. Yet servants were considered essential, as the desperate hunt for them indicates. Gentlewomen wanted to retain 'leisure' as well as adopt work. They wanted to bake their cake and have it served to them, and this may have encouraged their support for migration.

New Zealand may have been an attractive destination to various categories of gentry – threatened, disgraced, new, marginal, aspiring, and those who wished to reconcile work and leisure ethics. Its attractiveness may have been especially strong in the period 1840–60. Élite and non-élite were therefore somewhat different fragments, with gentry somewhat biased towards the north and 1840–60, and non-gentry towards the south and 1860–80. Because of the first-in factor and the role of the 1840s settlements as centres of secondary colonisation, the bias to earliness increased the importance of the gentry. This did not necessarily mean that they were dominant, or that they fully maintained their class culture in the colony, or instantly formed a nationwide class community. These issues are discussed below. But it does mean that gentility was significant in colonial New Zealand. There is a sense in which the gentry were a potential ruling class, who then had to import someone to rule.

Subverting the Prospectus: The Populist Compact

Amidst the confusing welter of migrant motives, one stands out as almost universal: the desire to 'better oneself', to 'get on'. This applied especially to people at the bottom of the heap, who had furthest to get. Formal and informal myths of settlement were agreed on its pre-eminent importance. How far New Zealand delivered on this, how people did indeed get on, is discussed in the following chapters. But here the apparently simple and cohesive concept of 'getting on' needs to be reconstructed into five variants.

One was *enhancement*, the mere qualitative improvement of the lifestyle a migrant had enjoyed in Britain – more bread, more beer and a larger hovel or tenement. The second was *promotion*, or its inverse, the avoidance of demotion. This was conventionally the major definition of 'getting on', and the major definition of its modern equivalent: 'social mobility'. As noted in the last chapter, it required class categories and cultures – rungs to climb up, symbols to prove that one had climbed. Together, enhancement, promotion and the avoidance of demotion comprised a central element of the crusader prospectus, the formal myths of settlement. For workers, the classic form of promotion was the acquisition of an 'independency' – archetypally a small farm, but also including small businesses of various kinds, such as pubs, stores and workshops. Enhancement involved higher wages for the decent and higher incomes for the respectable. It increased the chances of promotion, decreased the chances of demotion and made life more pleasant in the interim. Where formal and informal myths diverged was on the speed of promotion. The crusaders hoped that the decent would serve a long term as labourers and servants. Decent folk themselves hoped for a short term. The drive for promotion was indeed a crucial force behind the migration of Pakeha, but it was not the only one. There was another side to 'getting on', which fitted even less well into crusader plans.

A third variant of getting on, a concept introduced in the last chapter, was *adoption* – the annexation and adaptation of aspects of other class lifeways, without actually leaving your own. This can be discerned between the lines of the letters back of labouring migrants. Most, as usual, were selected or prompted by the crusaders, and they paint a rosy picture. But, in a deeper sense, they were quite subversive of crusader ideals. They note that labourers in New Zealand get high wages and that jobs are plentiful, as planned, but they also emphasise that they eat large quantities of prime roasts of meat, have leisure, own their own houses, ride and own horses, and hunt. These were not decent or working-class activities; they were not even primarily respectable, or middle class. Even wealthy urban respectables and prosperous farmers did not normally own their own houses in Britain, and middle- and lower-ranking respectables did little riding and hunting. These activities were genteel.

The letter writers were struck, and knew that their readers would be struck, by the possibility of living as gentry without being gentry, without the money or the manners and without necessarily aspiring to social promotion at all. ''Tis better to be living here like a gentleman than to be in England starving.' 'A working man is thought of much here as a gentleman is in England.'[58] The hunting, housing, riding, leisure and meat eating was not done in genteel form, and the genteel content was only partial, but it was highly valued. The 'working man's paradise', as an end in itself, was a subversion of the crusader ideal, a creature of the informal, not the formal, myths of settlement. The adoption of attractive elements of the lifestyles of other classes, while remaining content in one's own, proved an enduring lure for migrants. In 1993, an immigrant wrote: 'When I left Europe in 1940, I chose New Zealand because I had seen a photo with cars outside a workingman's club. New Zealand was then truly God's Own Country.'[59] It was not simply that even workers could have cars, horses or houses, but that they could do so while remaining workers.

Not everyone wanted promotion to a higher class. On the positive side, some were content with the community and security of their own class, especially when their lifeways were enriched by enhancement and adoption. On the negative, they feared the peer sneer – the contempt of old peers and new for those who struggled to 'get above themselves', the embarrassment of mastering unfamiliar manners and customs. The danger for the crusaders – and their heirs in running New Zealand – was that workers content with their own class became what might be called 'social settlers', permanent denizens of the working class aware of their permanence. 'Social settlers' had the potential for tight working-class community, for class politics and class conflict. Decent folk who did not desire promotion were not actual serpents in the garden, but collectively they were potential ones. Hence the crusader preference for 'social sojourners' – people who saw their working-class status as temporary and were locked into the system by their aspirations for promotion. Every student politician knows how hard it is to organise or motivate a constituency that changes very three years. The New Zealand crusaders were well aware that 'social sojourning' underwrote harmony and security, and pre-empted dissent and rebellion.[60] Adoption meant that not all workers wanted promotion to the respectable middle classes.

The fourth variant of getting on was equally subversive of the official prospectus, although crusader literature sometimes hinted dangerously at it. It might be called 'custom shedding'. Customs sometimes seem to have a life of their own, growing, tightening and outliving their functions. Major contextual changes are an opportunity to slough them off. Maori seemed strangely willing to shed some customs, such as cannibalism, as though they had been looking for an excuse. Similarly, for European settlers migration was a chance to select cultural baggage – to discard as well as take. Highly overt class differences in dress as well as diet, excessive deference towards the upper classes and customs that publicly implied subordinacy were leading candidates for the discard pile. In 1873, Anthony Trollope noted a marked New Zealand reluctance to accept gratuities. 'The offer of money was considered to be offensive', even among recent working-class migrants. Trollope accidentally knocked down the drying clothes of a young migrant woman, who 'though she was in tears at the nuisance of having to wash them again, refused the money that I offered her, saying that though she was only a poor Irish girl without a friend in the world, she was not so mean as that'. 'It is odd,' he observed of the abandonment of tipping, 'that so excellent a lesson should be learned so quickly.'[61]

There was an element of custom shedding, as well as other forms of getting on, in many working people's prompt and unceremonious dumping of domestic service as an acceptable long-term career. Perhaps changes in the British fragment help explain the New Zealand antipathy to domestic service. Servants in early modern Britain were treated in some respects as members of the employing family – eating with them, for example. More rigid divisions began to develop in the great houses of the high nobility as early as the seventeenth century, culminating in the complete separation of servants' quarters and the even the pretence that servants did not exist, noted in the last chapter. But the family model of service persisted in smaller genteel and respectable households, and persisted even longer in working-class folklore. In the nineteenth century, a 'professional' model of service began to spread, categorising skills, offering advancement within a servants' hierarchy, improving conditions with such things as servants' sitting rooms and making possible some pride in the job – personal maid as 'lady's lady', for example. The television series *Upstairs, Downstairs* was set in this context. Potential New Zealand servants may have come from the time and space between these two models: after servants had been kicked out of the family sitting room, but before they had their own. An additional factor in New Zealand may have been the Maori reluctance to become servants. Pakeha were even less likely to like an occupation rejected by those they saw as racially inferior.

In any case, language hints at the deep roots of antipathy to domestic service in New Zealand, and a strong need to reduce the stigma of subservience in those who did serve. Thomas Cholmondeley used the term 'friend' for master in 1854. This was probably an antiquated usage even then, yet it also appears in the 1884 *Official Handbook of New Zealand*. Some wealthy Wellington gentry in the late nineteenth and early twentieth century were careful to avoid the word 'servant' in speaking to their servants.[62] Well into the twentieth century, the New Zealand propensity for the mistress to work alongside her servants was used as bait in advertising for servant migrants.[63] 'Domestic' or 'house' servants were terms used in Britain to distinguish them from 'farm servants'. Farm labourers were described this way in English statistics until the 1870s, and occasionally in New Zealand to the 1850s. But the term 'farm servant' was quickly discarded in New Zealand, and the 'domestic' in 'domestic servant' became a redundant survival. For whatever reasons, domestic service was a custom most decent migrants to New Zealand hoped quickly to shed – much more quickly than the crusader prospectus had envisaged.

The fifth and final form of getting on might loosely be called 'restoration'. For the decent, this meant implementing a populist paradise or folk Utopia. New Zealand was to be England as it should be, and allegedly had been – steady jobs and good living conditions, together with mutual respect between master and man, were to be restored. For the respectable and genteel, restoration consisted in the moral regeneration of the 'simple life'. The slogan was '*back* to the land'. These were concepts of New Zealand as England with the clock turned back, the lost world found, and both higher and lower classes were agreed that tight and conflicting classes had no place in it. There may have been something comparable among Irish migrants to Australia and New Zealand. Migration allowed Irish working men, in particular, to 'step back again into their past, or rather, an idealised version of it'. In a sense, they were 'possessed of the belief that all could be aristocrats'.[64] At the very least, the act of migration made them superior to stay-at-homes who had accepted their lot. It made them Better Irish of Greater Ireland, and the same applied to their co-migrants from across the Irish Sea. This sense of superiority, of a populist paradise restored to bold migrants, did not have a lot to do with crusader paradises or their myths of Better Stock.

These unauthorised motives for migration to New Zealand were semi-tangible but strong, and they helped create a powerful and enduring colonial populism. This consisted not only in egalitarianism, or a dislike of overt class distinctions, but also in a dislike of sectionalism of all kinds. As in other countries, populism's normal enemies were not whole classes or large sections of society but small and shadowy conspiracies. If a class culture tightened and broadened into a nationwide class community, however, it could become an arch-enemy. It was not classlessness but class harmony that was the imperative.

Colonial populism derived to some extent from its source fragments: the folk utopias of Old Britain and Old Ireland. It was reinforced by the reality of the frontier: the shortage of labour, which drove wages up, made jobs plentiful and forced the genteel and respectable to sometimes indulge in manual work, encouraging them to acquiesce in a social revaluation of such work. An Australian observer of the colonial shift in manners claimed in 1859 that 'the revolution set in when gentlemen began to dress sheep for scab'.[65] But egalitarianism and populism also drew on the space between fragment and frontier. As Fell and Trollope found, deferential customs were shed too fast to be wholly explicable by gradually developing or local factors. Colonial populism existed outside Britain, yet was not peculiar to any particular neo-Britain. It was a feature of the ethos of expansion, drawing people out and changing them as it did so, such that migrants going from different fragments to different frontiers developed similar characteristics.

Renegotiated in these ways, the Pakeha myths of settlement sometimes facilitated crusader peopling plans, and sometimes upset them. Two examples were rural and female migrants, both key crusader targets. During the 1870s, in particular, when the policies of Julius Vogel were in full swing, there were many complaints that the Colonial stream of assisted immigrants was too urban and too disreputable, as well as too Irish. Subsequently, 'it became an historical tradition to bad-mouth the Vogel immigrants'.[66] Yet modern historians may have swung the pendulum back too far in suggesting that assisted immigrants were predominantly rural with just a 'sprinkling' of townsfolk.[67] About two-thirds of English and Welsh migrants to all destinations came from cities.[68] New Zealand could have been different, of course, and the crusaders certainly tried to make it so. But their success can be overestimated by the assumption that many assisted migrants who gave their occupation as 'general labourer' were in fact agricultural labourers. The reverse is in fact more likely, because the New Zealand immigration agents' preference for agricultural workers was well known, and applicants for assisted passages were notoriously reluctant to let a few facts stand in their way – many lied about their ages, for one thing.

Second, the crusader focus on farm workers can be exaggerated too; over time they allowed pragmatic realities to compromise their ideals. We will see in the next chapter that there were industries more important to colonial New Zealand than farming. Artisans and semi-skilled non-farm workers exceeded farm workers among the English assisted migrants of 1876, and it is not clear that the crusaders would have seen this as very undesirable. Third, a vast category of migrants, many of them unassisted and from the Australian streams, were not farm workers. These soldiers, sailors, miners, navvies, timber workers and the like are discussed in Chapter Sixteen as 'crews'. They were recruited or, rather, recruited themselves, indiscriminately from different countries and classes, townsfolk and countryfolk, but they were less agricultural, and less interested in being agricultural, than crusader ideals and arcadian retrospects allowed. Relative to some destinations, the colonising crusaders did quite well in getting countryfolk. But it seems unlikely that most English migrants to New Zealand were farmers or farm workers.

It remains true that the crusaders tried hard to get farm workers in the 1870s. Over one-third of male English migrants assisted to New Zealand in 1876 came from agricultural occupations.[69] Whether this was high or low depends on perspective. It was twice the agricultural proportion of all British migrants at the time, but lower than the colonising crusaders hoped. As the 1870s wore on and the Revolt of the Field subsided, the availability of English farm-worker migrants declined. The crusader prospectus was subverted by conflicting aims: English *and* countryfolk. Irish received around 15 per cent of assisted passages to New Zealand early in the decade; 42 per cent late.[70] Over three-quarters of Irish emigrants assisted out in 1876 designated themselves farm workers – as we would expect from a migration pushed by the collapse of Irish agriculture. About 45 per cent of Scots migrants in the same year came from agricultural occupations. Irish and Scots migrants, then, were more rural than English. The desire for countryfolk was strong enough to push the migrant hunt away from England and towards Ireland.

The problem of conflicting aims also applied to single women. The crusaders could not get enough single women. There were only six females to every ten males in 1860s New Zealand,[71] and because children were evenly split, this greatly understates the shortage of adult women. There were about two and a half times as many men as women between the ages of 20 and 39 years in 1861, twice as many until 1871, and above 50 per cent more until 1881. The crusaders wanted servants, and they wanted brides-to-be, to sop up, civilise and anchor chaotic surplus males. Young single women served both purposes, and not enough could be found in the English countryside. The crusaders had to resort to London and Ireland. Of the 4,000 young single women assisted out to Canterbury between 1858 and 1871, 25 per cent were from London, as compared with only 11 per cent of assisted single and married men.[72] Like the hunt for farm workers, the hunt for brides and servants also drove the crusaders to Ireland, where young single women, especially Catholics, were unusually willing to emigrate. The Irish were by far the closest to gender balance among the assisted migrants of the colonial stream, women even exceeding men in some years, and this also applied to the provincial stream. No fewer than 32 per cent of the single women imported into Canterbury by the provincial government were Irish – much higher than the Irish proportion of both single and married men.[73]

There are signs that New Zealand's Irish girls may have been an unusual group – ironically enough, a kernel of truth in the myth of Better Stock. The imbalance between their literacy rate and that of their male compatriots was far less than in any other ethnic group. Fewer Irish women than men signed their names by mark on marriage registers in 1881, whereas the reverse was markedly the case in every other denomination.[74] New Zealand was an esoteric destination for young Irish women, assisted passages or not, and it may have helped to be able to read about it. These women subverted the crusader prospectus in several ways.

First, they were part of the flight of the servants – many did serve a term as servants, but from the viewpoint of genteel crusaders it was too short. Second, like Irish men, they reduced the Britishness of New Zealand. Third, they helped to ensure that ethnic difference persisted – to a greater degree perhaps than Irish men. The notion that Irish, in New Zealand and elsewhere, had large families in the later nineteenth century is more folklore than fact. But Irish women maintained Catholicism – and therefore Irishness – in other ways. The crusaders presumably hoped that Irish women would marry non-Irishmen, and that Irishness might therefore peter out. Historians have noted that some Irish women did marry non-Catholic husbands, but in Canterbury at least, more than half stuck to fellow Catholics, who were only about fourteen per cent of potential husbands. That is, Catholic Irish men had a much better chance of procreating in New Zealand than other single men, because a significant section of potential brides were biased in their favour. Church attendance and associated social activities were also important sources of spouse meeting. Furthermore, women were, for various reasons, more attached to their churches than men – among other things, they were more inclined to insist that the offspring of religiously mixed marriages were brought up in their maternal church. An English father may therefore had been less damaging to Irishness than an English mother. All this meant that, when the immigration gates increasingly closed against the Irish from about 1890, New Zealand Irishness was better able to hold its ground – thanks to its foremothers having bent the crusader prospectus.

Women in colonial New Zealand, especially lower-class single women, were more prone to be Londoners and Irish than were men. The founding fragment differed along lines of gender as well as class, region and ethnicity. Motives for migration also differed according to gender. It was officially assumed that male heads of families made the decision to migrate. Crusader literature sometimes recommended that men break the news gently to their wives. At the same time, it recommended very strongly that there *be* wives – the importation of single women was only a backstop measure. Hursthouse advised intending male migrants that a wife was 'something far prettier and more fruitful than patent plough, thrashing-mill, or thorough-bred'.[75] But for many married women, marriage and migration were merged decisions. A great many migrants married just before they left home; spouses said yes to New Zealand as well as each other. Like recent brides, single women tended to make their own decision to emigrate. Some travelled with kin, but most did not.[76] Nor can we assume that single women travelling with kin, or women who married before the decision to migrate, were simply doing what they were told.

Genteel and respectable women may have seen migration as a chance to reconcile conflicting work and leisure ethics. Both they and lower-class women might have been interested in greater freedom as well as greater value – in a degree of custom shedding. For most of the nineteenth century, genteel and respectable Victorian women lived under a host of petty restrictions, of which corsets, many made from New Zealand whalebone, serve as a symbol. After early childhood, girls could run, play, fight, and bathe less freely than their brothers.[77] Women's travel was also restricted by custom, flimsy footwear, the need for an escort and hesitations about ladies riding horses. The experience of genteel and respectable missionary wives shows there was some effort to maintain such restrictive customs in New Zealand,[78] where circumstances meant they became more onerous. Mud roads and thinly scattered settlement doubled the anti-social effect of travel restrictions, for example – 'solitary confinement in paradise'.[79] Lower levels of peer-group pressure, sheer necessity and the eagerness of some women to grasp the opportunities these changes provided seem to have combined to relax these restrictions. Horse riding was much more common among women in New Zealand than in England. An important distinction between the genteel Bay of Plenty settler and author Adela Stewart, who ultimately did not like New Zealand, and her women acquaintances, who did, was that the latter rode whereas the former did not.[80]

We should be careful not to overstate this liberty of distance. It applied only to some women; a high price in work was often paid for it, especially below the servant-keeping classes; and it was usually more a matter of degree than of kind. But hints of somewhat greater freedoms do poke through the record. Customs were sometimes shed before actual arrival in New Zealand; either custom shedding was a female motive for migration, or it was part of the migration process itself. Aboard the migrant ship *Red Jacket* in 1860, 'bear fighting', a type of wrestling, became 'very popular with both sexes'. Two enthusiastic, genteel and female exponents of the art once burst through a cabin wall, locked in combat. We should not read too much from one incident, but when mid-Victorian lady wrestlers crash through walls, surprising the gentlemen at their port, is it unreasonable to suggest that something a little strange was happening?[81]

In 1864, Thomas Todd wrote from Dunedin to his wife in Britain, urging her not to forget 'to tell me the name of our dear little daughter'.[82] Statistics and cold analysis can never tell the whole story of migration to the other end of the world, which for individuals is the end of an old life as well as the beginning of a new. European migrants to most destinations in the nineteenth and twentieth centuries shared hopes, public or secret, of the triumphal return of the native. Prospective migrant Dennis Cochran hoped to

> get amazingly rich in a remarkably short space of time and return home . . . possibly punch the heads of one or two obnoxious persons, make them open their eyes . . . at my riding up on horseback or in a beautiful carriage . . . Then I marry a beautiful lady, settle down in some delightful country seat and beget lots of angelic little Cochrans.[83]

Many migrants from Europe to other destinations did make it back: something like a quarter participated in return migration.[84] Few non-genteel migrants made it back from New Zealand. Michael O'Farrell wrote from New Zealand to his brother in Ireland: 'There is one thing I can tell you . . . roaming beyond the seas isn't as nice as some people think.' He noted that 'a lot of fellows go mad after coming out', and listed a few suicides. 'You scarcely ever see the "Old Dart" again once you leave it.' Since he was actually trying to persuade his brother to come out, one shudders to think what a really negative letter back would have been like.[85]

This great uprooting, little death and little birth, is one of the few things shared by all New Zealand families. From the tropical Pacific lagoon in the eleventh century, when the stay-at-homes wailed as the first settlers pulled out; through the mother dragged screaming up the dry Dalmatian hills as the boat took away the eleven-year-old son she would never see again; to the cultured English who left London for Putaruru in the 1960s, migration to New Zealand left its scars. What recompense did it have to offer?

CHAPTER FOURTEEN

Taken In?

As the first crusader ships sailed into Port Nicholson, or Wellington as it was soon to be known, in 1840, 'the passengers were all on deck straining their eyes to catch a glimpse of civilization. Little was said, though disappointment was visible on the countenance of everyone.' Where were the fields for wheat, vines and olives, let alone the banana orchards? There appeared to be nowhere to live as well as nothing to live on. Ramshackle shelters were soon built, but this did little to mollify the next echelon. 'You cannot conceive of the disappointment of being turned into this wretched set of hovels,' wrote one disgruntled settler. 'Did those mud hovels scattered along the beach,' wondered another, 'represent the City of Wellington?'[1]

Even so, with its fine harbour and relatively large number of moneyed gentry, Wellington was the good news. Early settlers compared portless New Plymouth to 'a solitary rock in the ocean', and the 'Garden of New Zealand' did not harvest its first wheat until 1844. Decent settlers, without money, lived on New Zealand Company rations and work schemes while company funds lasted. They threatened to blow the whistle on the colonising crusade before it had properly begun, 'that the Poor may not be entrapped into the eviles of approaching ruin and present oppression in this strange land'.[2] At both New Plymouth and Nelson, a sort of Corporal Swing appeared in the early 1840s, with stock theft, wilful damage, strikes, riots and even rumours of armed uprising. When Nelson working men referred to 'this Splendid country', it was with the most bitter sarcasm. Both labourers and capitalists had been

> cast on a miserable and barren soil inhabited for ages by only canabals . . . Poor unfortunate victims they have fell a sacrafice [to] the tongue of flattery about this Splendid country . . . for instead of finding Elysian fields and Groves adorned with every beauty of Nature, they have found unsightly and barren Hills and Mountains . . . Instead of the bread fruit tree ther is the flax tree in a Swampy piece of ground.[3]

The company's agent at New Plymouth feared violence from the 'good for nothing loafers, who besiege the office door with God knows how many brats, squalling in the genuine style of English beggars'. When New Plymouth settler Sarah Harris wrote, 'the forest is behind me and the sea in front', we can tell which way she was facing.[4]

The above replays the first part of a tune traditional in the historiography of early settlement. But the downbeat of initial disappointment is normally quickly followed by adaptation and development. Nobody likes their collective birth to be too much of a disappointment. The upbeat did occur, but not quickly, not for everyone and not in the ways the crusaders had hoped. The inconvenient literature of disappointment, the 'taken in' genre, was a weak but steady counter-current to crusader propaganda. If it were not for crusader wiles and some bias in the record towards those who stayed, it would have been stronger. It seems that only 85 of the original 436 Wellington 'capitalists' – land-buying migrants, mainly genteel – remained in 1848, though some replacements had trickled in. That is, Wellington had a maximum approval rating of 20 per cent among those who had the money to vote with their feet. Nelson kept 40 of its 60 capitalists, perhaps because they were poorer.[5]

Five-year-old Auckland, a joint venture between the British government, Sydney commerce and Ngati Whatua enterprise, was 'a beggarly collection of poverty stricken huts and wooden houses', 'a horrid place always raining . . . everything dirty and shabby, the people all Jews or people from N. S. [New South] Wales'.[6] Ten years after its foundation in 1848, Dunedin was still a squabbling village of a thousand people. Local crusaders like the Reverend Thomas Burns found the climate bracing; others thought it 'detestable', 'four seasons in one day', and drank to keep warm. The eccentric activist J. G. S. Grant lectured on 'Grog – the element in which Dunedin lives, moves and has its being', despite its Presbyterianism.[7] Ten-year-old Christchurch society was believed by some to be already in decay. 'We teem with beastly Australians,' wrote a genteel settler in 1861. 'All the old Canterbury spirit and style and tone has been swamped by these Australians and heap of half breeds.'[8] In 1850, infant Wanganui town was a hamlet of 200 with a reputation for debauchery and a staggering death rate from drunken drowning.[9] Realistic re-enactments of First Settlement in the 2040 Bicentenary will be impossible because of the risk of alcohol poisoning, even for actors.

Right through the nineteenth century, the crusader prospectus 'took in' its thousands. In 1887, a disappointed gentlewoman-sojourner published the original *Taken In* under the pseudonym 'Hopeful'. Like many others, 'I also believed in "the sunny south as the land of promise, the land of plenty, and the land of hope;" but how different were the real facts!'[10] The novelist William Satchell wrote of a 'Land of the Lost' in the 1900s. His Northland kauri gumfields were the backwater of a backwater, 'where all the wrecks of the world are thrown up to rot . . . Every inch of this north country is poisoned with dead hopes.'[11] The crusaders took themselves in too. Edward Gibbon Wakefield had likened emigration to 'stepping into a grave';[12] so it proved for him. After a brief and high-handed foray into colonial politics, his acolytes lost confidence in their prophet, though not in his creed, and he fell into 'a deep depression'. He spent the last seven years of his life secluded in one room of his Wellington home, unvisited except for a niece and two bulldogs. 'Day after day he sat brooding on his remoteness from his London friends and the squalor of frontier Wellington, his creation and now his prison.'[13]

Wakefield died in 1862. His son Jerningham returned to Britain in 1844 and lived the life of a genteel rake, a frequenter of the better brothels of London and Dublin. Like Samuel Pepys, he disguised the disreputable bits of his diary in a foreign language, in his case Maori. Typically, Jerningham spoiled the effect by drawing an erect penis in the margin.[14] Emigration can make both one's homes inadequate, and he went back to New Zealand in 1850, where a political career – and every other – proved abortive. Three months before his death in 1879, he told George Grey that he was ill and destitute. His clothes had been seized; he had been turned out of a barracks for the old and indigent for sleeping in a shed, and arrested and fined for stealing flowers – probably big ones – from the government domain.[15] Another prominent crusader, politician and poet, Alfred Domett, wrote an equally pathetic letter to Grey in the same year, begging for a knighthood. The notion of Domett as the great colonial failure has recently been revised upwards, but he himself agreed with it. 'My life has been, God knows, at best but a failure – but it would not be so manifestly so to the world and my friends – if I succeeded in what I am now proposing.'[16] In the 1840s, the playbill at J. H. Marriott's gaslit Royal Victoria Theatre in Wellington included *A Dead Shot, or Who's the Dupe?* Played to the crusader élite, it was an insensitive selection.[17] Instant civilisation was not instant enough for Domett and the Wakefields. Was the whole colonising crusade a gigantic fraud, its own prophets among the victims? Were the hundreds of thousands brought by it to New Zealand simply 'taken in'?

Taking Out: Sheep and Gold

The basic problem behind the 1840s complaints about the organised settlements was that the crusaders had forgotten one tiny thing: an economy. To the extent that it existed at all, early economic planning vaguely envisaged mixed farming on the English model, supplying the local, Australian and British markets, mainly with grain, and supplemented by commerce based on the Maori trade and the Old New Zealand extractive industries, such as flax and whaling. As we have seen, the Maori trade did deliver – too well for some settlers' liking – and Old New Zealand also helped. But the hoped-for expansion of whaling and flax did not happen, and the development of Pakeha agriculture was awesomely slow. Ten years after their foundation, Auckland and Wellington had about a quarter-acre in crops, a half-acre in grass, a cow and half a horse's leg per Pakeha person.[18] A dozen Devonshire tenant farmers could still out-produce New Plymouth. The cows and acres were quite productive, but the Pakeha settlements could not feed themselves, let alone earn much money from agricultural exports. This was no basis for Greater Britain. Legend has it that it was sheep that saved the day, and legend is partly right.

On 15 March 1773, Dr Johann Forster found himself flanked by livestock, owing to a reshuffle of Cook's *Resolution*'s hold. They included goats, two ewes and a ram, which it was hoped would 'make an agreable present to the New Zealanders'. They did not make agreeable neighbours for Forster. 'I was sore beset with cattle & stench on both sides.' The sheep 'shit & pissed on one side whilst the five goats did the same afore on the other side'. Forster's ovine shipmates failed to acclimatise. They were poisoned by unfamiliar vegetation (perhaps tutu) at Queen Charlotte Sound. The goats survived, only to be eaten by the chief 'Goubiah'. 'Thus,' wrote Cook, ' all my fine hopes of stocking this Country with a breed of Sheep were blasted in a moment.'[19] But the appetite of the Yorkshire woollen industry and the pastoral potential of Australasia were too strong for tutu and Goubiah.

Sheep farming is said to have commenced in the region of Iraq about 9,000 years ago – roughly the same time that proto-Polynesian pig farming began in New Guinea. Archaeology suggests that Syrian troops in the Roman army of occupation may have helped develop the British taste for mutton.[20] By 1300, England had about fifteen million sheep and wool was the leading export industry. At this time, wool was shipped to the industrially more advanced economy of what is now Belgium for processing into yarn and cloth – an economic relationship foreshadowing that of England and New Zealand. Around 1400, however, factors such as wartime disruption on the Continent allowed the English to start adding their own value, through the textile industry of Yorkshire.[21] In the eighteenth century, wool became one 'leading edge' of Britain's Industrial Revolution, and soon Britain was clothing and blanketing a good part of the world. In the early nineteenth century, powered mills and factory-production techniques borrowed from the Lancashire cotton industry boosted capacity; finer wools, like that of the Spanish merino, were increasingly desired (for worsted fabrics); and Yorkshire's traditional sources of wool (Britain itself, Spain and Germany) shifted emphasis to meat to feed growing populations. The owners of the wool-hungry mills of Bradford looked further afield – to Bombay, to the Cape of Good Hope and to New South Wales.

Merinos developed in Spain by the fourteenth century from the crossing of local and North African sheep.[22] They were somewhat stubborn and contrary animals, with a powerful homing instinct – orphaned lambs are said to have stuck by their mothers' graves to the death.[23] But they were hardy and produced good-quality fleeces. The first merinos were brought to Sydney from Cape Town in 1797, after fat-tailed Cape sheep and a Bengali breed had failed to thrive. The founding Australasian flock, derived from England, was established by Elizabeth Macarthur between 1801 and 1819 – her husband John got the credit. Meat was initially more important than wool; the latter boomed in the 1830s. Wool prices declined in the 1840s, when four million Australian sheep were boiled down into tallow for soap, but by 1850 Australia had permanently displaced Germany as Yorkshire's main source of wool.[24]

The role of Australian sheepmen and sheep money in New Zealand pastoralism is disputed, but there is no doubt that many of the sheep themselves are of Australian descent. Ovine migration across the Tasman began in 1833, and began to boom ten years later. Sheep were cheaper to breed than to ship, and natural increase within New Zealand soon became the main source of expansion in sheep numbers. The best New Zealand terrain for sheep was open, flat or rolling hill country, clothed in native grasses. Tracts of this existed in the south-eastern North Island, interspersed with bush and scrub, and in the eastern South Island, where bush and scrub were less common. Such terrain was one prerequisite of early pastoralism; others were money, skills and virtually free land. All intersected in the Wairarapa region of Wellington province. Wairarapa sheep farming began in 1843 and migrated north to Hawke's Bay and south into Marlborough in the late 1840s, when total numbers passed 100,000. Southward expansion continued in the 1850s, with the Wairarapa strains merging with those from secondary centres of sheep settlement at Banks and Otago Peninsulas and with fresh immigrants from Australia. By 1858, there were 1.5 million sheep, with Canterbury and Hawke's Bay the leading areas, followed by the Wairarapa, Marlborough and Otago.[25] Numbers increased almost sixfold in the next decade, to 8.5 million in 1867, mainly in the South Island. Although the pace of expansion slowed thereafter, New Zealand seems to have overtaken Britain's flock size in the 1920s, becoming Greater Britain in sheep at least within the statutory hundred years.[26]

There is no doubt that wool was central to the New Zealand economy from the late 1850s, when it briefly became the leading export.[27] It was not insignificant to Yorkshire either. As early as 1861, 8.6 per cent of British wool imports came from New Zealand, and the Bradford Chamber of Commerce took an interest in New Zealand farming and packing techniques.[28] But the role of sheep farming is somewhat overstated, misunderstood and perhaps too rigidly distinguished from other industries. For one thing, in the earliest phase of sheep farming, there was a surprising degree of association with the whaling industry, a shift of capital from whales to sheep involving the same people and the same places – something that also took place in Australia. John Howell in Southland, Johnny Jones in Otago, the Rhodes brothers in Canterbury, and

John Bell and George Ross in Wellington were all whalers turned sheep farmers before the advent of organised settlement in their regions. The relationship was reflected in colonial lending legislation, such as the Wool and Oil Securities Act of 1858.[29] Bell and Ross, and the Northland master trader J. R. Clendon made the first exports of wool (to Australia, like coals to Newcastle) in 1834, ten years before the Wairarapa pioneers C. R. Bidwill, Charles Clifford and Frederick Weld.[30]

As we saw in Chapter Nine, Maori were midwives of some early pastoralism, and another link between it and the Old New Zealand industries was its 'extractive', or at least finite, character. Native pasture was regularly burned off so sheep could feed on the succulent young regrowth. Early runholders found that their most useful tool was a box of matches, and some became addicted to arson.[31] But repeated burning eventually led to erosion and a decrease in soil fertility. Sowing English grasses was the solution, but this was expensive and difficult, and usually implied freeholding to make the investment worthwhile. As long as vast acreages were cheaply and securely available, leasing and exploiting native pasture while the going was good, with your sheep spread thin, made more sense. Indeed, the essence of profitable sheep farming in the early phase in each region was to pay next to nothing for the land. Clifford and Weld leased 30,000 acres in the Wairarapa from Ngati Kahungunu for precisely nothing, and 200,000 acres in Marlborough from Ngati Toa for £12 a year.[32] Runholder and landowner were initially more antonyms than synonyms, and the rents paid to tribal and provincial governments were very low until the later 1860s.

Huge tracts of cheaply leased land, however, were clearly a finite resource. The runholders' major early market was also finite. We tend to assume that wool for overseas export was the significant product of sheep farming from the outset, but live sheep to sell to other would-be runholders must initially have been more important. The price of sheep was set by the high cost of importation from Australia, at twenty shillings or more per ewe, whereas the price of wool was set by the competitive British market – say, eight shillings for the average fleece in the 1850s. Even at the low lambing rates of around 50 per cent that prevailed on some early runs, the lambs were worth more than the wool, and of course the one did not preclude the other. There was a boom period, a 'sheep rush', from 1843 to about 1867, during which runs spread and were stocked to the full carrying capacity of unimproved pasture. This is evident from the rate of increase in sheep numbers. Until 1867, sheep multiplied at least 70 per cent every three years. From 1867, the rate of increase suddenly dropped sharply to around 15 per cent and remained there throughout the 1870s.[33] To 1867, sheep farming boomed largely through its own growth.

During the boom period, free land, free grass and a large local market could mean staggering profits for those first in. 'Sheep farming,' observed the *Otago Witness* in the 1850s, 'presents visions of quite dazzling wealth.'[34] Samuel

Butler doubled his £4,000 capital in four years (1860–64) in a Canterbury sheep run, which helped make up for the paltry £69 3s 10d he received in royalties from his famous book *Erewhon.* Others did even better. Alfred Barker invested his £7,000 in a Canterbury sheep station in 1850, and died in 1873 worth £80,000.[35] Local crusaders promptly dismissed Wakefield's equation of 'squatting and barbarism', at least as a temporary measure, and plunged into the sheep rush themselves. In 1850, J. R. Godley wrote: 'All agree that there is no field of investment now open in the world at once so safe and so profitable as pastoral husbandry in New Zealand.'[36]

High profits were not guaranteed, however. Even the Otago hill country was normally cooler than Australia and warmer than Britain, and this relative 'climatic paradise' was a key to the success of New Zealand farming in that it reduced drought and the expensive need to feed and shelter stock over winter. But snowstorm, drought and flood still cost early runholders thousands of sheep, and put some out of business. One run lost half its ewes and almost all its lambs to the snows of 1867, which were said to have killed half a million sheep in Canterbury alone.[37] The native kea may not have been guilty of the mayhem it was said to cause by sitting on sheep's backs and pecking their kidneys out. But native tutu, the sheep's first enemy, did take a toll, as did imported animals. Wild dogs ravaged flocks; wild pigs killed and ate newborn lambs.

From the late 1860s, rabbits were the worst enemy. There is no recorded case of their killing sheep directly, but they did kill pasture by the county. The acclimatisation of ferrets, badgers and even mountain lions was advocated to deal with them, like the old lady who swallowed a fly. Rabbit control became a significant industry, with large stations employing up to 140 rabbiters, and with exports of 100 million rabbit skins in the 1880s.[38] Some runholders ranked their employees, especially shearers, with rabbits as the arch-enemies of profit, and it is true that skilled labour was sometimes scarce and transient. The notorious sheep diseases scab and footrot also did great damage. On some terrain, creating pasture was a constant struggle against the resilience of native fern and scrub.

The travails of the runholders can therefore make poignant reading. Jeanie Collier, in her sixties when she became the first woman runholder in 1854, had difficulty in rising in the morning on her South Canterbury run because her nightcap froze to her pillow.[39] Inexperienced sheepmen nearly poisoned themselves by mistaking strychnine for soda, took the wooden shears for the world's lowest rate of sheep shearing, and had trouble making bread. 'Willie trying to make bread,' reads one station logbook, repeated three days later. 'And later this entry, almost with the ring of tears in it, "Willie wasting good flour and yeast." '[40] Herbert Guthrie-Smith took over Willie's station, Tutira, and 'warred' with its native vegetation for 30 years before it was 'stamped, jammed, hauled, and murdered into grass'. His 'run' was in fact a constellation of 'sheep camps', clearings in the scrub to which the sheep stubbornly restricted their fertilising manure. 'I say, Harry,' he once asked his shepherd, 'wouldn't it be grand if sheep wouldn't always pee in the same place?' 'Ah, Sir', replied Harry, 'Tutira would be heaven then.'[41]

Such problems tend to be associated with the pioneering stage of sheep farming, but some were actually more acute *after* the late 1860s. The best land was taken up, and so the likes of Guthrie-Smith were forced onto more marginal stations. Rabbits and hares were still being introduced and protected to 1867; the great plagues of them began in Southland and Otago about 1868, and spread north in the 1870s and 1880s. But the key shift was the exhaustion of cheap but high-quality leasehold land, of native pasture and of the local market for live sheep. From the late 1860s, sheep farmers had to invest heavily to maintain their returns: fencing, mechanising, laying down pasture, improving breeds, struggling to replace the live sheep market with boiling-down works, meat-preservation plants and eventually refrigeration, and, above all, freeholding. In this post-1867 phase, runholders with good land, low debt and access to capital or credit for the necessary developments continued to make profits; others were vulnerable. This shift – from a 'rush' phase with some of the characteristics of an extractive industry, in which growth was very rapid and opportunity and profit plentiful, to a steadier, more sustainable but less profitable phase – was mirrored in other dimensions of the New Zealand economy.

Wool was important, but it was only one of three major groups of industries, each of which was roughly equal in importance up to 1879. The second was gold. Apart from a small and largely abortive rush to the Coromandel in 1852, New Zealand's first goldfield was at Aorere in Nelson, where £120,000 worth of gold was produced by up to 2,000 diggers between 1857 and 1859. Although small in comparison with the great Otago and West Coast rushes of the 1860s, this field founded the town of Collingwood, boosted the Nelson economy and provided a precedent for subsequent goldfields administration. The Otago gold rush began in mid-1861 and flowed successively through four major fields by 1865: Tuapeka, Dunstan, Wakatipu and Taieri. These fields produced over £6 million in five years, magnified and transformed Otago, and boosted the economic fortunes of the colony as a whole. Gold exports were worth £2,400,000 in 1863, compared with £1,400,000 for all other exports. There was also a smaller rush, about the same size as Aorere, to Wakamarina in Marlborough in 1864–65. The richest rush, on the west coast of the South Island (split between Nelson's Buller district and Canterbury's Westland), began as a trickle in 1864 and yielded over £8 million between 1865 and 1870. From 1862, the North Island got into the act to some extent. The Thames-Coromandel region of Auckland province produced gold in fits and starts, with a £3 million burst in 1868–73. Gold exports totalled £46 million by 1890.[42]

One strand of New Zealand historiography tends to discount the impact of the gold rushes. In reaction, other historians have argued that they explain almost everything. Both have a case. The great rushes, to Otago and Westland in 1861–67, were very concentrated in time and space, and can be seen as a tidal wave that came and went quickly, taking most of its profits with it. It came largely from Australia and was restricted to the South Island, so clashing with the twentieth century's North Island dominance and a desire to forget the Tasman world. The crusader disdain for diggers may also have had some continuing effect.

It is true that nineteenth-century gold rushing was a phenomenon much wider than New Zealand. The peculiar human tsunami that began in California in 1849 was clump migration on a massive scale, unorganised but so culturally, demographically and economically cohesive that it seemed organised. The focus of what was in a sense the same rush leaped the Pacific to Victoria and New South Wales in the 1850s, lurched back to New Zealand in the 1860s, then sped on to Queensland, Western Australia and across the Indian Ocean to South Africa. Chinese and continental Europeans were quite prominent in this modern Golden Horde, but British and Irish and their colonial descendants predominated. The driving dream seems to have been El Dorado – the 'Homeward Bounder' or fabulously rich claim that would enable the miner to retire home in luxury. Few achieved it. Most miners and their accompanying hangers-on lost velocity and fell out along the way like exhausted lemmings, perhaps as many as 100,000 of them in New Zealand. These people and their gold did have a substantial impact on New Zealand history.

Lemming is not entirely fair. One miner did find only two shillings and threepence worth of gold, and kept it as a souvenir.[43] Another lost his pile to a gust of wind while inspecting it in his cupped hand.[44] But, contrary to legend, most miners made money. While the richness of paydirt varied, alluvial gold was often quite widely distributed throughout a field. Westland and Central Otago had thin Maori populations and little surplus food to feed large goldfield populations. Miners could hunt and gather, but even with guns and pigs New Zealand nature could not feed thousands, and you could not mine while you hunted. Food and everything else were therefore brought in from outside, at hugely inflated prices. Because miners had to buy this to keep mining, a wholly unsuccessful miner was a contradiction in terms. The basic cost of living on the Dunstan field was estimated at ten shillings and sixpence per day, double a labourer's normal wage.[45] You needed at least an ounce of gold a week simply to survive as a miner. For miners, the trick was to make a profit *after* high expenses, from especially rich claims. These were rare, and the lottery element emerged at this level. For those supplying the goldfields, however, there was no lottery but a reliable bonanza, raking in the high expenses and the bulk of gold produced.

This crucial goldfields support industry consisted partly in people who travelled from rush to rush like the diggers themselves: publicans, theatre managers, storekeepers, barmaids, dancing girls, prostitutes and bankers – the last were 'almost as quick off the mark as the diggers when a new field was discovered'.[46] But this travelling 'supporting cast' was slightly less transient than the diggers themselves, and was quickly reinforced by locals. No fewer than 64 storekeepers, butchers and bakers had established themselves at Tuapeka in 1861 within weeks of gold being found. Cartage to goldfields could earn £90 or even £120 a ton in the early days of a rush.[47] A small string of packhorses could yield its owner £50 a week.[48] One could even make £25 a week from a goldfield newspaper round.[49] A crucial question about the gold rushes, not very well answered by historians, is what happened to the gold? The ore itself went overseas, mainly to mints in Australia, but, thanks to the goldfields support industry, much of the money paid for it remained in New Zealand, where it helped kick-start other economic activity. Just how much stayed in New Zealand depended on the success of local entrepreneurs and provincial governments in plugging in to nearby goldfields.

Gold, at peak, increased Otago's population fivefold in two years, though many diggers then left again. The Scots 'Old Identity', which had swamped its Maori-Pakeha predecessors, dreaded swamping in its turn by the Australian 'New Iniquity'. There was something of a moral panic, and a large and expensive police force was imported wholesale from Victoria to control the golden hordes. But fears were outweighed by recognition of the stimulus to progress gold would bring. Gold was a dangerous and unanticipated tool, but like wool it could be bent to crusader purposes, especially in districts unlikely to opened up by other means. 'Gold is the talisman that transforms with magic power the bleak and sterile wilderness to a region of luxury and wealth.'[50] Disdain for diggers diminished promptly once they brought wealth to one's neighbours.

The provincial governments offered rewards for gold discoveries from the 1850s, and they and their merchants vied energetically in the goldfields support industry. Under Superintendent James Menzies, Southland sought gold eagerly within its own boundaries and, when this largely failed, became almost piratical in its raids on Otago. Southland sent a gold escort into Otago to siphon off ore, established a police station at Queenstown, on its neighbour's territory, and police of the rival provinces scuffled on the border.[51] Another local Vogel, James Macandrew, long-serving Superintendent of Otago, nearly came to blows with the colonial government over control of the goldfields in 1867.[52]

Several governments competed for shares of the West Coast rush. Nelson officials and merchants were first in. Superintendent John Robinson drowned on a prospecting expedition to the Coast in 1865. His successor, Alfred Saunders, used a knowledge of phrenology – assessing character by head shape – to select Thomas Kynnersley as commissioner of Nelson's own Buller goldfields.[53] It worked, and Kynnersley was so popular that diggers sometimes lied about the provenance of their gold when banking it, to give Nelson rather than Canterbury the duty of two shillings and sixpence per ounce. The Buller fields, combined with exceptionally rapid agricultural development, helped make Nelson an early exporter of capital, a source of investment for the rest of New Zealand. Nelson also captured a share of the Westland goldfields support industry, supplying nearly nine per cent of imports to Hokitika in 1866. Dunedin merchants used their Otago experience to capture fifteen per cent, and at least nine Dunedin firms established branches in Hokitika. The big winner from Westland, however, was Victoria, which supplied about 54 per cent of imports and many diggers and rushers direct. 'The West Coast was an economic dependency of Victoria, Hokitika a trans-Tasman suburb of Melbourne.'[54] This revived and realigned the Tasman world, on the axis South Island–Victoria as well as North Island–New South Wales.

The big loser from Westland was Canterbury, which owned it. The Port Hills, between Christchurch and its harbour, were beaten by the Canterbury crusaders with their remarkable Lyttelton tunnel, but the Southern Alps were too much for them. It was not for want of trying. Canterbury spent £10,000 on a grand trans-alpine gold escort, but it was entrusted with little ore. The provincial government struggled to drive a cart road through the Alps, trying various passes, but had to settle for little better than a stockroute over Arthur's Pass. Even this cost £139,000. The Coast continued to obtain its supplies 'from everywhere but Lyttelton'. Canterbury spent £103,000 on administering the first six months of the Westland rush, and in return received £44,000 in gold duty. Unable to benefit from its own gold rush, Canterbury gave up and acquiesced in the separation of Westland, first in 1868 as a county and then, for three brief years from 1873, as a full province. 'It would be a sad thing after all for Canterbury to find she was on the wrong side of the island,' a Cantabrian remarked in 1865.[55] As far as West Coast gold was concerned, it was.

Geographically, Auckland was much more fortunate with its rush, in that Thames was easily accessible. But Thames gold was guarded by Maori and by quartz reefs, obstacles that took time and money to overcome. From 1868, the Maori obstacle was gradually negotiated open, and the capital was acquired for the stamper batteries and other complex machinery required to mine from quartz. Direct British investment in high-technology New Zealand goldmining was not important until the 1890s. Auckland merchants were the major source of capital, or rather the major conduits of credit, and some made large fortunes. Mines like the Caledonian were 'positively wonderful' for Auckland entrepreneurs, 'turning out gold by the ton'.[56] Smaller businessmen did well from the goldfields support industry. Thames was the second-largest town in

Auckland province in the 1870s, with over 7,000 people, and it is easy to forget that Auckland itself was partly a gold town.

Auckland's experience shows that the rushes of the 1860s were only the first phase of goldmining. As with wool, the early rush was followed by a less dynamic and more capital-intensive phase. This was also true in the south, and again investment was largely local. There were important quartz mines around Reefton and Inangahua on the West Coast, and the hunt for alluvial gold in Otago also became more mechanised. Hydraulic sluicing washed away whole hills and sifted them for gold. This development is traditionally associated with the 'corporatisation' of mining and the increasing dominance of outside investment. But some research suggests that co-operatives of local diggers quickly formed companies and remained important throughout the nineteenth century.[57]

The rush phase of goldmining lasted only a few years in each region – to the mid-1860s in Otago, the late 1860s in Westland and the early 1870s in Thames. In each case, it was succeeded by a longer and more capital-intensive phase of lower activity, in which types of production – dredging, hydraulic sluicing, quartz mining – were diverse and heavy equipment was moved from site to site as yields diminished. From the 1890s, a third phase cut in: still more capital-intensive and industrial, more sedentary, more narrowly oriented towards quartz and much more overseas-owned. In the 1860s and 1870s, goldmining together with its support industry was a vast chunk of all economic activity. Gold exports to 1880 were roughly equal to wool, at over £35 million.

The Progress Industry and Its Allies

The third leg of Greater Britain's economic tripod was a linked group of economic activities we will call the 'progress industry'. It had two prominent components. The first was public works, most notably those that attacked distance: roads, bridges, railways, postal and telegraphic communications, and port facilities. The second was organised immigration itself: the founding of instant townships and the government assistance and encouragement of subsequent immigration. War was an ally of the progress industry. Attacks on Maori 'obstacles to progress' had a similar purpose to attacks on physical obstacles; both were mounted by governments and both had similar demographic and economic effects, suddenly injecting large amounts of people and money into particular regions and leaving a residue after they had served their initial purpose. Gold rushes also had these effects – they, too, were natural allies of the artificial progress industry.

Public enterprise was always important to the progress industry and its allies. From the 1840s, the companies, which were quite state-like organisations, local authorities, imperial, colonial and provincial governments mounted and funded the various military, public works, immigration and propaganda campaigns. From the 1850s, they tried to kick-start various industries by offering bounties to first producers – of colonial-made paper, tableware, woollen cloth, preserved meats and dairy products, and many other things, as well as preserved protein products. A flax boom in the 1870s was stimulated by a government reward of £2,000 for effective processing machinery.[58] There was even government support for goldmining.[59] State ownership of businesses began in the late 1860s, when the State Life Insurance Office and the Post Office Savings Bank were established. From the 1870s, government increasingly ran large chunks of the transport and communications infrastructure, as well as built them. State postal and telegraphic services and railways became large employers; state-run railway workshops were among the largest colonial factories. Clearly, the state was sizeable before its various heydays after 1890. But private companies, such as Union Steam Ship Co., also contributed to the transport infrastructure; the state contribution subsidised business profits and boosted business activity. Public and private providentially converged and were closely allied; twentieth-century tensions between them should not be read back into the nineteenth. Both were run by the same people, and both were locked in to the progress industry.

Private enterprise was locked in through such things as the speculative building of houses in large towns, which was predicated on the assumption that governments would keep immigrants coming. Many other businesses and speculations operated on the same assumption. It was progress that made land values, for example, 'sure to rise'. Public roadmaking, railmaking and military campaigns required private supply and support. Imperial military expenditure and colonial, provincial and local authority loans provided much of a massive inflow of overseas capital. The government-nurtured image of New Zealand as an investors' paradise was important to private overseas borrowing, as were the high interest rates progress made possible. War, gold, roads and rail 'opened up' the interior in more ways then one. They cleared bush and created camps, which had to be fed and might subsequently turn into towns. The progress industry created a temporary but huge domestic market: for food for its crews and fresh immigrants, for horses, bullocks, and food for them, and for fuels and construction materials.

These alliances meant that the key distinction was not between public and private enterprise, but between 'natural' steady growth and 'unnatural' artificially boosted growth. Agriculture lay at the heart of the former, and towns were a useful symbol of the latter. The concept of natural, slow but steady, farm-led growth has deep roots in eighteenth-century European and twentieth-century New Zealand ideology. It echoes the distinction between natural Arcadia and artificial Utopia noted in Chapter Twelve. Arcadia features larger in mythology; Utopia featured larger in colonial history. In farm-first mythology, virtuous pioneer farmers moved individually out into the wilderness and subdued it. Their energy in realising nature's potential produced a surplus, which led to the growth of towns and services. The country bred the towns. 'Most of the towns and cities,' the *Encyclopaedia of New Zealand* tells us, 'have been established to service the rural areas.'[60] This did happen in some places, especially leading wool regions. But it was the progress industry and its allies that created most towns, which then grew farming hinterlands, or died if they did not.

Unlike sheep and gold, something like the progress industry was always an implicit part of crusader plans. Indeed, it was the colonising crusade on the ground – the two can conveniently be merged in the term 'progressive colonisation'. There was always an element of pyramid selling, about which Hursthouse made no bones. 'Emigrants of 1840 sell their surplus to the emigrants of 1842, and both do the same by the emigrants of 1844.'[61] This logic was inherent in the paradises offered working men and serving women, who were to acquire property and so join the middle classes after serving their term, being replaced by infinite fresh cohorts of migrant labourers and servants. Such factors underpinned the ideology that demanded progress; the essence of the game was that the inflow of people and money, and their spread across the land, should not stop, though they might lurch and spasm. Very often, growth came through growth.

Between the 1840s and the 1880s, progressive colonisation mounted a quadruple assault on nature, natives, emptiness and distance, each of which served the others. The best-known campaign was the Vogelian spurt of public spending in the 1870s, for which central government borrowed £10 million between 1871 and 1876. Julius Vogel became Treasurer in William Fox's colonial ministry in 1869, which in 1870 launched a drive to 'recommence the great work of colonizing New Zealand . . . to re-illumine that sacred fire' through massive borrowing for public works and immigration. This was the climax of progressive colonisation. But it was by no means the whole of it. As Edward Stafford, Leader of the Opposition, noted, it was 'no new idea'.[62] Public debt actually expanded more rapidly in the 1860s than in the 1870s – eightfold between 1862 and 1869, compared with threefold in the 1870s. Even in the 1840s, the companies spent perhaps £1 million attacking emptiness through settlement, and the imperial government spent as much attacking natives.[63] The assault on nature was the process of 'opening up' or 'clearing' the country, and then replacing one ecosystem with another, as when native bush was displaced by alien grasses, mostly English. Progressive colonisation physically converted raw New Zealand into Greater Britain. Let us now look a little more closely at the way the progress industry and its allies powered the colonial economy, focusing first on public works, and then on four activities in which the private sector was more prominent.

Railmaking was the centrepiece of Vogelism. In 1870, there were only 46 miles of public railway in the country. By 1879, a further 1,100 miles had been laid. Rail knitted the eastern South Island first. Christchurch and Dunedin were linked in 1879; Wellington and Auckland 30 years later. Wellington was linked up with the Manawatu, New Plymouth and Napier between 1882 and 1891, but Whangarei did not join the Main Trunk line until 1925; Tauranga until 1928; Gisborne and Dargaville until 1942. New Plymouth was not linked by rail to Auckland until 1933.[64] Rail was not necessarily superior to sea or river transport, but it did mean you could put the 'rivers' roughly where you wanted them – Vogel created rivers like Paoa before him.

Ultimately, railways changed the shape of New Zealand and entrenched the dominance of the four main centres, Dunedin and Christchurch first. They helped shrink the country to a fraction of its former size in travelling time – the same process that had occurred a few decades earlier in Britain. Railmaking represented about two-fifths of all public capital formation between 1870 and 1900,[65] with a very heavy bias towards the 1870s. Government spent £10 million on rail between 1871 and 1881.[66] Rail construction was a significant industry in itself; its workers had to be fed, clothed and housed, and raw materials and equipment supplied. Much came from Britain, but some locomotives, wagons and boilers were produced locally from the early 1870s. Government railway 'workshops' – in fact, substantial heavy engineering works – were established at Christchurch in 1872, Dunedin in 1875, Wellington in 1877 and Auckland in the 1880s.[67] Whole forests were felled for railway sleepers.

Most railways were built by public enterprise, and this is also true of roads. Roads boards were the first type of widespread local authority below provincial level. By 1875, there were 314 of them. Roads of various types and qualities, of course, were important from the beginning of settlement. Beaches were the most basic; the main streets of several major towns were initially known as 'The Beach', underlining the dominance of the sea even on land. Roads beyond the beach were at first mere tracks, long dustbowls in summer, quagmires in winter, hopelessly rutted by wheels and hooves. Doing better than this, with raised roads, log-based 'corduroy' roads or 'metalling' with gravel, was an expensive business. The imperial army built the Great South Road from Auckland at about 30 man-years a mile.[68] Many honorary 'roads' remained in service throughout the nineteenth century and beyond, passable for wheeled traffic only if you were lucky. The numerous rivers were a major problem; most were crossed by fords and ferries until the 1870s. But some remarkable roads were built, staggering acts of self-confidence by embryonic communities.

Roads were a metaphor for progress and colonisation itself in the colonial mind; there was an almost religious respect for their powers. Wellington connected itself to the Wairarapa with a road over the daunting Rimutaka Ranges by 1859. Christchurch planned and drove its £200,000 tunnel through the Port

Hills between 1857 and 1867, a staggering enterprise for an infant town, linking itself with its port of Lyttelton to unleash a hitherto-retarded progress.[69] Godly community or not, its cathedral had to wait. Roadmaking, even over rivers, boomed in the 1870s, 'the busiest bridge-building period New Zealand has ever seen'.[70] Central government alone spent £1,100,000 making nearly 2,000 miles of roads and tracks between 1871 and 1881.[71] Road and rail obviously had great importance, both as the basis of a national communications infrastructure and as major industries in themselves. They also had great symbolic significance: paths of civilisation, bringing order and doom to natives and nature; huge, smoking, iron engines leading the charge of progress. The symbolism led to their overshadowing other elements of the progress industry.

Public enterprise, national, provincial and local, dominated the creation of road and rail networks. Private enterprise was more prominent in four supporting elements of the progress industry: shipping, working animals and their feed, timber-based activities, and the supply of capital. The 'romance of rail' may conceal the possibility that shipping remained more important for internal communications during the whole nineteenth century, especially in the North Island and most especially in Auckland province. This is illustrated by the fact that the pioneering rail and telegraph lines served the sea: the original 46 miles of rail built in the 1860s linked Dunedin, Christchurch and Invercargill to their ports, as did the first telegraph lines. The tonnage of all ships on the New Zealand register tripled between 1861 and 1871, then tripled again in the next decade. Sailing ships provided a majority of the registered tonnage to 1890. During the 1870s, their number rose from 323 to 447, and they remained numerically predominant, especially in Auckland.[72] But coastal steamers were disproportionately important because of their greater average speed and regularity. Although a minority of the Auckland fleet in 1881, they provided two-thirds of the total shipping tonnage entering that port, and 77 per cent to 94 per cent of the tonnage entering Wellington, Lyttelton and Dunedin.

Coastal steamers first appeared in the 1850s.[73] By 1870, there were 61, averaging 100 tons, and by 1880 there were 125 slightly larger ships.[74] 'By the time of comprehensive returns in the early 1870s, there was in excess of a million tons of shipping entering and clearing New Zealand ports [annually] in the coastal trade.'[75] Coastal-shipping volumes increased sixfold over the next quarter-century.[76] Rail did not displace sea transport; the two boosted each other, and steam featured large in both. This, of course, boosted coalmining in turn – in Northland (where a mining company at Kawakawa employed 120 people in 1880),[77] Westland, Nelson, Waikato and elsewhere.

Although British-built ships were always important, shipbuilding was another significant local industry, partly because of the high rate of shipwrecks

– about 500 by 1866. The first New Zealand-built ship probably dates to about the twelfth century, when the original Hawaikian canoes wore out. The first European-built ship was begun by sealers at Dusky Sound in 1793, and completed by Captain Bampton and our first European community in 1796. There were already shipyards in Northland in the 1820s, which continued to be a centre of shipbuilding until the 1980s. In 1842, 42 craft averaging twenty tons were built in New Zealand as a whole. Scores of smaller whaleboats, the short-distance lorries of European colonisation, were also built. Steamers were also locally built – 34 by 1869. Auckland shipwright Henry Niccol built 181 ships during his career, including sixteen steamers. The construction, supply, support and crewing of New Zealand shipping must have employed thousands. The 1867 census shows 3,537 'mariners' alone.[78] Virtually all of these ships were privately owned, 85 per cent of them by New Zealanders,[79] but they still relied to some extent on public works. Wharves, breakwaters, silt dredges, deeper channels, customs posts, lighthouses were all necessary to keep the ships sailing and steaming. Harbour boards were big spenders.

Working animals – bullocks and horses – helped power the progress industry. In Britain, rail actually increased the demand for horses. More people and more goods moved about more, and horse transport took them to the trains. The same seems to have happened in New Zealand, where horses increased in number even faster than people. Horses were expensive in the early 1850s; bullocks were cheaper and preferable on poor roads. There were 115 horses per thousand Europeans in 1851, and some of those were actually owned by Maori. But by 1858, there were 254 per thousand, much of the breed stock having been imported from Tasmania. By 1867, despite the large inflow of people, there were 302 horses per thousand, and 333 by 1878. The equine ratio peaked at 400 per thousand in 1911, and declined slowly thereafter with the development of the petrol engine.[80] Comparable figures for bullocks are unavailable, but it required a team of eighteen to move one timber dray, and thousands of these patient animals were pulling goods about to the end of the century and beyond. Both horses and bullocks were used to power winches and mills of various kinds, until steam took over, as well hauling goods and carrying people. There was little point in roads without horses or bullocks. Working animals were as much an industrial and urban phenomenon as rural. Lumbering camps, railmaking camps, army camps and the towns that sometimes sprang from them were full of horses.

One horse for every three people was a vastly higher ratio than in Britain, and, from the 1860s, New Zealand horses were cheaper to buy. Mild winters and more easily available grazing meant they had always been cheaper to keep. Easier access to horse ownership, like house ownership, had interesting social implications, some of which are noted in Chapter Sixteen. But what counts here is that the raising, working and maintenance of horses and bullocks were major activities, employing blacksmiths, farriers, wheelwrights, coachbuilders, carters, 'bullockies', operators of livery stables, saddlers, stockbreeders and the producers of feed crops, especially oats. New Zealand's 162,000 horses in 1881 required over half a million tons of fodder – and produced a similar amount of fertilising dung. Oats, whose output always exceeded wheat even during a wheat-export boom in the 1870s and 1880s, were more a power source than a cereal, functionally more akin to coal production than wheat production. In 1867, there were 101,000 acres in oats, compared with 79,000 in wheat, barley, potatoes and peas combined. Oat production quadrupled in the 1860s, and then quadrupled again in the 1870s.[81] Breeding and feeding horses and bullocks were important industries, though they did not feature in export statistics. Their rise was linked not just to agriculture and pastoralism, but to the progress industry. Horses and bullocks helped make roads and rails, and haul timber. They carted goods and people to the ships and trains, and pulled and carried them along the roads.

Timber was the main construction material of the progress industry, and everything else. It was used for buildings of all kinds – much more than in Britain, where brick and stone featured large. One-room shacks and lean-to shelters, 50-room mansions, and 100-metre-long woolsheds were all built of wood. Wood was much more important for packaging than it is now – almost everything was boxed or barrelled. Wood was also used for ships and boats, carts and carriages, furniture, implements, fences, bridges, railway tracks, telegraph poles and 'corduroy' roading. Especially before the growth of domestic demand for coal late in the century, there was a vast demand for firewood as well – not simply for home heating but for water heating, ironing and cooking, and industrial uses such as boiling down sheep. Modern New Zealanders are used to rating industries on their contribution to exports, but timber exports in nineteenth-century New Zealand were only the tip of the woodberg. Auckland kauri dominated timber exports, and even in that province exports represented only a quarter of total production – valued at £563,000 in 1885 in Auckland and £1,250,000 in the colony as a whole.[82] Elsewhere, timber was felled and processed overwhelmingly for internal consumption. It has been estimated that three million tons of firewood per year was consumed in the mid-1880s.[83] A vast amount of small-scale non-commercial felling and gathering of wood presumably does not appear in any statistics.

It took two men six weeks of backbreaking work to pit-saw enough wood for a small house. Steam-powered mills replaced pit-sawing in the 1860s; there were 150 mills in 1876, 243 in 1891, and 414 in 1905, employing up to 300 people each but averaging fewer than 20.[84] Woodworking factories of various kinds, such as Union Sash and Door and the Auckland Timber Company, and innumerable carpenters, joiners, coopers, cabinet-makers, shipwrights and coachbuilders were always among the largest and most numerous colonial industrial concerns. At least 30,000 wooden houses were built in the 1860s, and 40,000 in the 1870s.[85] What the retrospective export bias of New Zealand economic history may conceal is that the pyramid of industries based on wood was comparable in importance to wool and all its works. Like roads and rail, the wood was worked in the name of progress. 'In 1878 the optimistic belief of the directors of the Auckland timber companies that shops and dwellings must continue to spring up like mushrooms and boom conditions last forever was incorrigible.'[86]

Kauri, totara, rimu and other types of native timber were creamed off like the moa before them, then mopped up as demand required and new technology permitted. The more accessible timber of Marlborough was creamed off by twenty steam mills in the 1870s in about five years, and shipped south to help build Christchurch. The same city had previously creamed off and mopped up the timber of Banks Peninsula, and the small forests of North and South Canterbury. Dunedin drew timber by sea from Auckland and a variety of minor ports, and then from Southland and the Catlins in South Otago as rail permitted.[87] But, like moa, the logs were often moved by water – coasts and rivers. The rivers were sometimes nudged along by giant dams, whose pent waters thundered thousands of logs down to the sea when released. The dams had their heyday between 1890 and 1914, when the industry leaned more heavily towards kauri, exports and Auckland. But timber was also very important prior to this, indirectly as well as directly. Timber milling was the quintessence of the assault on nature – opening up the country, conquering the bush. Removing the enemy was almost the least of it. Logging and milling provided potential farmland and roads to it. It provided markets, cheap building materials and paid work for farmers struggling to establish themselves, as well as cash income for logs. It supplied a vast chunk of the fuel and raw material used by the progress industry.

One of the points where public and private enterprise converged most was the supply of money – to fund sheep farming, war, the later phase of goldmining, as well as progress itself. The money came partly from local sources. The three mainstays of government revenue were the resale of land, co-opting profits foregone by the original Maori sellers; customs dues, paid by Maori and Pakeha alike; and the gold duty. Money made by private individuals in New Zealand was also reinvested in elements of the progress industry, such as shipping and timber, as well as in wool and post-rush goldmining. Old New Zealand entrepreneurs made a contribution. Johnny Jones of Waikouaiti bankrolled many Otago settlers and enterprises in the 1850s and 1860s, and the Rhodes brothers did likewise in Canterbury and Wellington. Nelson capitalists appear to have been prominent reinvestors. Nelson's growth slowed after 1867, partly because its bid for rail failed, but also because prime local opportunities for investment were exhausted. The province made an unusually early shift from extractive, progress-led economics to sustainable, farm-led economics. Nelson money therefore found its way to other provinces and helped fund their progress instead. The goldfields were also an important source of reinvestment, especially in Otago and especially to manufacturing. But most of the money came from overseas – from Victoria, New South Wales, Scotland and, above all, England. It came in various ways.

Immigrant nest eggs may have been significant. Only a minority of immigrants arrived with much cash, but one gets the impression that it was quite a large minority, and funds left in Britain could be used to pay for imports to New Zealand. In 1842, before formal systems for overseas borrowing were well established, the settlers managed to import 90 per cent more by value than they exported.[88] Balance-of-payments deficits, an excess of imports over exports, characterised the New Zealand economy to 1886, when they totalled £44 million.[89] But more important than cash in the migrant suitcase was the capacity of some migrants to pull more money in after them in the form of loans and investments from Britain or Australia – the chain migration of money. Jardine Mathieson of Hong Kong lent (and lost) £76,000 to William Bowler and Company of Wellington in the early 1860s. Wellington merchant Waring Taylor, brother of Mary, borrowed (and lost) large amounts from English relatives – £23,500 in one case. Logan Campbell invested the money of his Scots friends and relatives. Immigrants who returned to Britain had a tendency to leave their money in New Zealand. Some large private investors sent their money but not themselves. Absentee ownership was an integral part of early crusader plans, and independent investors such as the English aristocrat Algernon Tollemache were important sources of finance. Tollemache had New Zealand investments totalling at least £250,000 in the late 1860s. 'Tollemache was just one of a surprisingly large group of aristocratic British rentiers, albeit indisputably the leader of the group.'[90]

Direct investment by large British companies seems to have been more a feature of the 1890s and beyond than of the earlier period. Small investors and lenders tended to operate through intermediaries, such as British lawyers and their New Zealand agents. One such agent, James Sclanders, lent 333 farmers an average of £400 each between 1870 and 1902. Small Scots investors funded the New Zealand Loan and Mortgage Agency (NZLMA) to the tune of £300,000 a year in the 1870s.[91] British and Australian trading banks established themselves in the 1840s, but the banking system only became fully pervasive in the 1860s, when overseas players were joined by the indigenous Bank of New Zealand (BNZ). Exotic or indigenous, all these banks borrowed money in Britain and Australia, and lent it out in New Zealand. They were increasingly important sources of credit from 1861.

The founder of the BNZ, the NZLMA and associated companies, as well as New Zealand Insurance (founded 1859), was Thomas Russell, the private sector's answer to Julius Vogel. His father was an Irish Protestant carpenter, promoted to architect in family tradition. The family migrated to Australia in 1833, when Thomas was three, and shifted to Auckland in 1840. Like his three brothers, Russell founded a law firm – the four firms still employed over 300 lawyers in the 1990s. But Thomas was 'a businessman first and a lawyer second'; from the 1850s he promoted an astonishing range of ventures, becoming member then leader of a tight Auckland business élite, known as the 'Limited Circle'. His ventures included the confiscation of Waikato Maori land, organised during a brief foray into politics in the early 1860s – illustrating the convergence between war and progress in the minds of financial crusaders. Ultimately, Russell's speciality, like Vogel's, was extracting money from Britain and spending it in New Zealand. By 1886, companies associated with him had borrowed at least £5 million.[92]

How large was the total tide of immigrating cash? Double handling and other problems in the statistics mean that it is not easy to tell precisely. But according to one estimate, public and private overseas borrowing or investment amounted to £71 million by 1886. Some £25 million was remitted back in interest over the period, making a nett monetary immigration of £46 million.[93] This figure does not count the imperial government's military expenditure in New Zealand, which may have totalled something like £5 million by 1870. Most of the overseas inflow went to the progress industry and its allies. Taking account of local investment in this complex of industries, and making allowance for the contribution of overseas loans to the sheep industry and other economic areas, it seems reasonable to assume that progress in itself was at least as important as wool and gold in the colonising era, even in direct and purely monetary terms. Another type of calculation supports this. Imports exceeded exports by well over £37 million by 1879 – New Zealand bought that much more from overseas than wool and gold could pay for. Public and private borrowing for progress and immigrant nest eggs made up the balance. Wool, gold and progress each contributed between £35 million and £40 million by 1880.

New Zealand's ability to attract this tide of cash is as remarkable as its success in getting peopled, and has interlocked explanations. Migrants brought money, and money brought migrants. The colonising crusaders portrayed New Zealand as an investors' paradise, safe, secure and British as well as profitable. They were quite right about the profitability – interest rates in New Zealand were around twice those in Britain – but this was a self-actualising myth. The image was marketed before the reality existed, and helped create it. Perhaps more interesting than interest is the cultural-economic phenomenon that progressive colonisation engendered – the fervent and infectious faith in itself, prosaically interpreted as 'the spirit of gambling which, as several historians have remarked, was typical of the colony'.[94] The gambling spirit did exist. Charles Dilke got his first newspaper in Hokitika for free in 1866 because the newspaper boy insisted on tossing his coin, double or quits.[95] But there was more to the creed of progressive colonisation than a mass poker game. It was assumed that the money on the table would continue to grow, and that almost everyone would win.

Those less committed to New Zealand were less prone to be infected by this creed, but it did not help them much. While the New Zealand banks flung themselves wholeheartedly into the progress industry, the English and Australian bankers overseeing the New Zealand business of the Bank of New South Wales were sceptical. In 1865, they noted 'the infatuation which has seized upon everyone by the fact that the whole thing was done upon credit', and sought to rein in their New Zealand managers.[96] For five years they failed. The managers were incorporated into local élites, made local investments on their own account, wined and dined with local crusaders and were converted to progressive colonisation and its 'insatiable demand for credit'. They lent above, around and despite orders from their overseas superiors. For all its caution, the Wales found itself one of two banks to whom the extremely progressive province of Southland, out to 'lick creation' by means of rail, owed £400,000 on assets of £34,000. The bank's Dunedin branch doubled its advances between 1866 and 1869, despite strict orders to reduce them. Eventually, in 1870, the overseas directors recaptured their bank by wholesale sackings. Other banks kept lending. Once moving, even the sceptics found progressive colonisation an escalator difficult to jump off.

There was a curious inversion of formal relationships in this process, reminiscent of the Colonial Office's relationship with George Grey. The British authorities saw through Grey's documentary machinations and produced the shrewd marginalia that have so impressed historians, and they eventually sacked him. But they did not do so until he had spent millions of their money. London bankers and officials had similar ineffectual qualms as Thomas Russell and Julius Vogel strode the London money market. In 1875, the British Secretary of State for the Colonies was 'rather startled . . . at the financial speed at which New Zealand was travelling'.[97] Russell, Vogel and their colleagues overrode such hesitations, whistling south Britain's spare millions like packs of Pied Pipers.

As Colonial Treasurer or Premier from 1869, and Agent-General in London from 1876, Vogel proved more than a match for the doubts of the Bank of England about lending to the New Zealand government. He borrowed or renegotiated £18,450,000 in London in the 1870s.[98] Russell's leading Auckland pack was supported by similar groups in Wellington and Dunedin, all with partners or puppets, allies or offices in London or Scotland. When Russell met his London boards of directors, there was no doubt about who was boss, and it was not London. 'Indeed, the early quarrels between the home and colonial boards suggested that the colonial directors regarded their London counterparts as officials in a branch office of an Auckland concern.'[99] The majority of British companies operating in New Zealand 'owed their foundation to initiatives taken by . . . New Zealand groups . . . Although they were British companies with a head office in England or Scotland, they operated in fact as if they were New Zealand companies domiciled in New Zealand.'[100] Who was exploiting whom in this relationship? In finance at least, the colonial cringe appears to have been preceded by a metropolitan one.

This New Zealand-led New Zealand–British financial system underwrote progressive colonisation, and it was helped by images of the progressive British paradise. 'I am delighted by the way the home population now fairly appreciate this most blessed of colonies,' wrote Logan Campbell in an optimistic moment of the 1870s, 'as is well proved by the way they stake their money on us.'[101] Even a sceptical English banker noted in 1865 that New Zealand 'is regarded here as the Gt Britain of the Southern hemisphere'.[102] Uneasy British officials comforted themselves with the notion that New Zealand was somehow special. 'They are driving the good ship along under terrible pressure of canvas . . . the risks are great . . . But New Zealand is perhaps the one colony that can bear such high pressure.'[103] By the 1880s, writes an economic historian, New Zealand companies 'enjoyed a special (and quite undeserved) reputation with the [British] general public as an exceptionally sound investment, presumably because New Zealand was looked upon as the most British of the colonies'.[104] Campbell, in unkind return, referred to 'ye Milch Cow John Bull'.[105] Once young New Zealand clamped its teeth on a cash-rich teat, it was goodbye nipple.

Making It: Manufacturing and Farming

The progress industry had a number of lesser allies, most extractive, some old, some new, and all pursued with progressive frenzy, a rush mentality. Whaling continued sporadically until the 1960s. Kauri gum became an important export from the 1860s. Flax reappeared as a significant export industry in the 1860s and early 1870s, with over 6,000 tons of processed flax exported from 300 small mills in 1873. Apart from rabbits, hunted as pests and for skins and even canned meat, wild pigs were hunted and processed industrially; edible fungus, named 'jew's ear' or 'Taranaki wool', was gathered by the ton for sale in China – £78,000 worth was exported between 1872 and 1882. Other extractive industries were projected but failed to take, including copper and antimony mining, and smelting from iron sands. The New Zealand Iron and Steel Company predicted progressively that the country would soon be one of the leading iron and steel producers in the world, and lost £300,000 in the early 1880s trying to prove it. The first oil well appeared in Taranaki in 1866; the 1875 *Handbook* lost little time in comparing the province's prospects to Texas, but Dallas failed to eventuate at New Plymouth, for another century at least.[106]

Manufacturing and farming were to some degree independent of the progress industry. They produced either for export or for an ongoing domestic market that was not wholly reliant on booming, boosted progress, and which survived its eventual demise in the 1880s. But they, too, were allied with and stimulated by the progress industry. Various factors encouraged local manufacturing from the outset. Neither the organisation of pre-assembly-line factories nor the holds of sailing ships were conducive to the export of large manufactures, and 12,000 miles from London or even 1,200 miles from Sydney was a long way to send things, especially big ones. It was also a long way to send them back to be fixed. A workshop set up to maintain and repair imported equipment and machinery could find the shift to making it quite easy, especially in an age when most machines were neither very complex nor assembly-line produced.

Manufacturing, processing and repair occurred at home, in workshops, in factories and in mills. The making and repairing of things at home for home use or for sale, including the processing of things grown at home – fruit into jam, pigs into ham – was an important economic activity, though hard to measure. A spin-off was repairing or converting things, as against making them from scratch. This, of course, forms the basis of the tradition of 'Kiwi ingenuity'. Such a tradition also features in other colonial societies, but we have as much right to it as any, and it has roots in fact. Some early issues of the *Auckland Times* were printed on a converted washing mangle. 'We never mince, though we often mangle matters.'[107] Charles Ayton, a Liza-less Henry, once fixed no fewer than 56 holes in his single bucket.[108] A culture of high technical competence and creative expression through craft – art simulating work – can arguably be traced to the need to fix, adapt and make for yourself. Women were important in 'handicrafts' – home-based manufacture for sale, usually involving a single worker or family. At best, the worker bought her own raw materials, owned her own equipment, such as a sewing machine, produced her product herself from start to finish and sold to more than one consumer, wholesaler or retailer, for a reasonable rate. At worst, under the notorious 'piecework' system, she received her raw materials from a middleman, produced only part of the product and worked long hours for a low piece rate, without his even having to meet the overhead of working accommodation. Such practices increased in the 1880s but were present before that.

A second type of manufacturing occurred in workshops, most very small, but the definition of them can be extended to include operations employing as many as ten or twenty people. The key identifiers are that workshops were fairly small, that the owner worked with his employees, and that the production process was craft-like and unified, rather than split into separate jobs. The organisation of the building industry was very workshop-like throughout the nineteenth century – even the largest building outfits consisted of no more than a master builder and a dozen employees. Unlike factories, workshops might engage in repairing and maintaining things as well as in making them. The great majority of statistical 'factories', of which there were 1,093 averaging 10 employees each in 1877–78, were workshops on this definition.[109]

In larger-scale manufacturing, we need to distinguish between large factories proper and mills. The former fabricated finished goods from multiple previously processed materials, as with a biscuit factory. The latter processed a single material from its raw state, as with a flour mill. Factories proper were at the top of the manufacturing hierarchy. They normally required mills, in New Zealand or overseas, to process their 'raw' materials, often of more than one kind: clothing factories needed woollen and cotton mills, as well as thread and buttons; biscuit factories needed flour mills and sugar mills, as well as tins and boxes for packaging; boot factories needed tanneries as well as hobnails, soles and laces; implement factories needed timber mills and iron 'mills' or foundries.

Milling required a less complete economy, and came in two main subtypes: renewable and extractive. Renewable milling processed renewable resources, such as wheat and wool. The dairy 'factories' and freezing works that emerged with refrigeration from 1882, and the tanneries and boiling-down works that preceded them, were in fact this type of 'mill'. Some renewable mills, such as sugar refineries and iron foundries, processed imported raw materials, but they were not very common in the colonial period. Extractive milling processed non-renewable, home-grown raw materials, such as flax and timber. These mills were often connected to extraction itself: timber and flax mills were located close to their source of supply, and sometimes the same operation obtained the raw material as well as processed it. In this sense, post-rush mining of gold and coal was very mill-like. Extractive milling and mining in the colonial era was quite mobile. Flax, timber, gold and coal would be creamed off in a particular place, and then the same owner would move the same staff and equipment to another. Renewable mills, of course, were more sedentary. Their catchment areas continually supplied their wool and wheat, and they did not have to move in pursuit of their raw materials.

These distinctions are not academic but are important tools for understanding industrialisation in New Zealand and other neo-Europes. Large factories were not common in colonial New Zealand, but mills and workshops were. There were 450 flax and timber mills around 1874, employing anything from a dozen to a hundred or more people each. Renewable mills could be quite large and industrial, and they were established early. A bullock-powered woollen mill was established at Nelson in 1845; by the 1870s, stimulated by government bounties, woollen mills near Dunedin and Christchurch employed 400 to 500 people each. The first steam-powered flour mill was established in 1841; there was a large, three-storeyed water-powered mill near Wellington in

1845; by the 1880s, crusader J. C. Firth's Auckland flour mill boasted 100 electric lamps, five storeys and 40 elevators.[110] Despite the rarity of large factories proper, the colonial economy quickly became at least semi-industrial, and to a considerable extent it had the progress industry to thank for it.

Timber mills and coalmines were themselves parts of the progress industry; extractive flax milling and goldmining were obvious allies of it. Moreover, the progress industry generated a high demand for the products of some renewable mills, workshops and factories: processed food, drink, clothing and footwear; rail sleepers, bridging and building components; milling machinery, mining equipment, tools; foundry and kiln components, ironwork, bricks, tiles and pipes; saddles, harnesses, carts, wagons, boats and ships. Even steamships, giant gold dredges, stamper batteries for quartz mining, rail carriages and locomotives were New Zealand-made. Heavy industry peaked in the 1900s, when progressive colonisation made its last stand, and there was some exporting, especially in the 1880s. But New Zealand's 'industrial heritage' dates from the 1840s. It was surprisingly early, varied and substantial in total, though generally very small in its parts. Some was directed towards consumer goods and supplying sustainable, renewable, infinite activities with equipment. Beyond this, it was aimed not at exports but at the market provided by the progress industry and its allies. It, too, was partly locked into progress.

There are many ways of classifying New Zealand farming – by type of product (wool, wheat, oats, cattle, etc.); type of production (intensive/extensive; agricultural/pastoral); destination of product (home consumption, local supply, inter-regional or overseas export); tenure (leasehold/freehold); acreage; and value. None is entirely satisfactory. Farms often mixed their types of products, destinations and even tenures. Acreage was a very poor guide to substantive size: 300 good acres close to town and port were often worth 3,000 acres of poorer, more isolated land. A simple threefold classification, into large, small-to-medium and 'semi-farms', may be as good as any.

Large farms were worth tens of thousands of pounds, and yielded a genteel income of at least £2,000 a year, rising as high as £35,000 in exceptional cases. They required at least a few permanent employees; a few had scores; half a dozen or a dozen was more typical. There were 616 freeholds of over 5,000 acres in 1874, and 1,124 Crown pastoral leaseholds, averaging 12,600 acres each.[111] Robert Campbell, Eton-educated scion of a family of Australian sheep-lords, held almost a million acres. One subtype was the classic sheep station. They began as small camps in the rush phase; some grew to substantial villages centred on the runholder's mansion. One station boasted a three-seater privy – for employees rather than owners, needless to say.[112] Stations might combine several leased runs with a growing freehold; wealthy pastoralist families might own several stations, operated as a unit. The other subtype of large farm was the 'high farming' mixed-product great estate, such as John Grigg's Longbeach. This Canterbury holding, on 32,000 acres of expensively converted but fertile Canterbury swamp, had a permanent staff of up to 150.[113] Such estates produced wool, mutton, beef, wheat, breeding stock and other products. In the 1850s and 1860s, stations came to encompass much of the prime land in the South Island and in Hawke's Bay and the Wairarapa, leasing from Maori and the Crown. Various pressures discussed elsewhere soon led to mass freeholding, and leased stations retreated to the uplands, where they remain today as the only viable form of very extensive farming. On the downlands and lowlands, freehold stations persisted but were increasingly joined by estates and other categories of farm.

Small-to-medium farms produced incomes of £100 to £1,000 a year and were worth thousands. The lower limit is the capacity to sustain a family without outside work. Typically, these farmers worked manually themselves, employed few if any permanent staff and relied on family, seasonal and casual labour. One subcategory was specialist farms, producing one product such as beef, oats or wheat, but I have come across few examples of these before the 1880s. A second subtype was the small sheep run, often leased, a poor relation of the stations. Some sources suggest runs with fewer than 3,000 or 4,000 sheep were scarcely viable before the 1880s, though smaller flocks were an important part of mixed farming. Stud farms and stock breeding were usually associated with other types of farming.

The main subcategories were small town-supply and mixed medium farms. Both engaged in a range of activities, and the main distinctions between them were size and the destination of their produce. Town-supply farms did just that, emphasising fresh food, and they tended to be small but valuable. Improving daily communications extended the town-supply districts, especially from the 1860s, but the local market was limited. The archetypal medium farm was the mixed-production unit of around a thousand acres within 50 miles or so of a port. Its mix of products was similar to the great estates, perhaps with the addition of cured pigmeats. Mixed medium farms ran substantial numbers of sheep, especially in Canterbury. In Britain, they would have been considered large. They were of the size, location and type Wakefield had hoped would sustain gentility, but did not because of limited markets and a lack of soil fertility, transport and labour. They produced partly for the local market (distinguished from town-supply farms by a tendency to sell preserved foods rather than fresh) and for overseas export, but perhaps mainly for inter-regional export within New Zealand. Until the 1870s, they were restricted to the best land of Nelson, to Canterbury and several coastal districts of Otago – these areas shipped food to Wellington and Auckland – and to the hinterlands but not the outskirts of most main towns.

Semi-farms were in a sense not farms at all. They were not 'viable' – they could not sustain a family without outside work. The border between them and farms proper is difficult to fix. The size threshold increased with the distance from ports or markets, and with the natural vegetation, quality and state of development of the land. Either 50 acres and £500 value or 100 acres and £1,000, would be a reasonable guess, and I think that on the whole the evidence favours the latter. Semi-farming was usually mixed rather than specialised before the 1880s, and produced mainly for home consumption and local markets. It subdivides into two ranges rather than types.

The first was part-time farming, a long-term supplement to other activities. At the top of this range were such people as cartage contractors who had 50 acres or so in oats for their teams; storekeepers who ran small dairy herds of a dozen cows; and brewers who grew a few acres of their own hops. In the middle were established worker-farmers who ran a well-developed farmlet in combination with, say, a seasonal but regular local job. A few seamen might be found in this category, and it was apparently quite common among self-employed goldminers after the rush phases. For these people, farming made a package with other work; neither yielded a living alone, and the two normally had to be geographically close together. At the bottom of the part-time range was the five- or ten-acre section in and around small towns. The large 'backyards' inside such towns, with their poultry, potatoes, vegetables and perhaps pigs, and with a cow grazing on the roadside, were almost off the scale. The second range of semi-farms might be called 'proto-farms': blocks in various stages of development that were not yet viable farms but their owners hoped would become so. At the top of this scale were marginal farms, teetering on the brink of viability. At the bottom were blocks of primeval bush, scrub or swamp, producing nothing at all, but whose owners had big plans.

After the rush phase, sheep stations mainly produced wool for export, but the other categories of farming had a close alliance with the progress industry, as well as some tendency to simulate it. The native fertility of soils was finite and was 'mined' to exhaustion. Land itself was finite, and the 'conversion' of land into farmland through fencing, freeholding and the introduction of grasses became something of a mania. Mass Pakeha settlement burned off and logged as much or more forest in its first four decades than early Maori – no mean arsonists themselves – had done in their first four centuries. Hill forests burnt into 'sheepwalks', where even sheep can scarcely walk, are still evident today. 'There is a lot of historical evidence to suggest that the early settlers were to some extent carried away by their own enthusiasm for the process of improvement and farm formation and that they rarely stopped to calculate.'[114] Farming to supply the ongoing local market, food for permanent settlers, developed after a slow start. By the 1860s, as we have seen, the Pakeha settlements were largely feeding themselves and each other, displacing imports and Maori suppliers in most, though not all, basic foodstuffs. There was also spasmodic overseas exporting of provisions, as well as wool. In the 1870s and 1880s, there was a wheat-export boom in Canterbury, with crops grown industrially in large acreages and harvested by big workforces and mechanised equipment. But much farming supplied either its own rush phases, which varied regionally and according to types of farming, or the progress industry and its allies.

Supplying farming rush phases was a matter of producing animals and seed to stock other New Zealand farms. We have seen that this provided a large market for live sheep until about 1867. The rush phase in pasture, which demanded locally produced exotic grass seed, lasted longer. Producing grass seed, notably cocksfoot, was an important farming activity, of which Banks Peninsula was a major centre. Harvesting cocksfoot here employed thousands in season. In Taranaki, Titokowaru and his people entered this industry in the 1870s, reportedly making £3,000 a year growing pasture for Pakeha.[115] Stud farms, favoured by gentry such as George Whitmore as a means of spreading investments further than sheep, produced horses and cattle for other farms, as well as for progress. Spasms of war in the north, gold rushing in the south, and spasms of public works and timber rushing in both, provided temporary but huge markets for work animals and meat animals, fodder and foodstuffs. The sheer size of the progress industry in relation to the rest of the economy, its demand for animal energy, and the associated need for capital stock and seed, meant that the domestic market for farm produce was proportionally far larger than today. Colonial farming, as against runholding, was not an export industry but was still significant. It owed much of its growth to the progress industry and, in many cases, its origins as well.

Despite legends, it is hard to see how subsistence, isolated, archetypally arcadian small farming can have been very viable in colonial New Zealand. Farmers needed to buy and bring in tools, equipment, breeding stock and seed crops, and supplies of flour, sugar and tea. These could be acquired on occasional visits to a distant store, but bringing them in often required dray roads, which local authorities did not build to isolated single farms. Buying stock, equipment and supplies, moreover, required money. Where capital and credit were limited, as was the case with most small farmers in the process of establishing themselves, money could only come from outside work or the sale of farm produce. Outside work might be obtained at a distance, and sometimes was, but nearby was obviously preferable in that it permitted the farmer to continue to break in or run the farm. Nearby work required nearby employers. The sale of farm produce also favoured nearby markets and required the means of getting to them regularly. If farms needed nearby markets for fresh produce, then they cannot have been isolated.

With minor or temporary exceptions, the products of small farms were not exported overseas until the advent of refrigeration, and not in really significant quantities until the 1900s. John Stuart Mill was perhaps the first to recognise that the beauty of Wakefield's plan for instant townships was that they provided an instant market for agricultural products. Wool and wheat, the products of large farms, did not need preservation to be exported overseas; the products that were the staples of New Zealand small farming (meat, cheese, butter, milk, eggs, fruit and vegetables) did. Techniques for preserving such produce did exist before refrigeration – smoking, drying, salting, canning and pickling – and producing provisions by these means was a significant element of colonial agriculture. But export markets for provisions were limited and unreliable, and unlike wool such exports required a local infrastructure – transport by road, rail or water, and often processing facilities larger than small farms could themselves provide. Supplying fresh food was a better prospect, but this was even more dependent on a local infrastructure and a nearby market.

It was the progress industry and its allies that provided local markets, employers and transport. Camps were only temporary markets and employers, but they were large and numerous, they created transport routes, cleared away both nature and natives, and they sometimes turned into towns. As towns, they could process, package and export farm produce, as well as provide transport networks, markets and employment. Aside from wool and wheat, farming achieved take-off with the help of the progress industry and its allies: its camps and its towns. The precedence of farming in the history of Pakeha settlement is largely a myth.

Taking Off: The Camp Town Races

The progress industry had its own internal momentum, growing at least partly through its own growth. It tended towards extractive or finite economic activities, yet to conceal this finity from itself. This pattern of spasmodic booms, illusions and rushes, in particular industries as well as particular regions, gave progressive colonisation a certain hectic underlying unity. It also created a regionally and locally varied history of colonial economics, where different places achieved take-off into long-term economic viability in different ways and at different times.

Not all regions had war or gold, but most had one or the other, and all had progress. Six of the ten provincial regions, including Auckland, had their central towns established as organised settlements: archetypal progressive colonisation. Westland was founded by gold. Only three of the 10 provincial regions – Hawke's Bay, Marlborough and Southland – were established 'naturally' by pastoralism, and the last two received important gold boosts. Natural or unnatural in origin, each region subsequently experienced one or more spurts of growth stemming from gold, war, progress, or all three. When the spasms passed, they struggled to maintain as much as possible of the momentum. Wool produced some underlying incremental growth, and something close to booms in Canterbury, but generally speaking it was war, gold and progress that produced regional take-off.

Auckland boomed between 1861 and 1864 with the concentration of troops and colonial and provincial assisted immigration. Inwards overseas shipping tripled, imports quadrupled and the provincial population increased 75 per cent to 42,000.[116] Activity then dropped with the transfer of troops but remained well above 1860 levels. Thames gold created another boom in 1868–73, again with some residual effect. Auckland progressed in fits and starts during the 1870s, growing more slowly than the rest of the country, but still expanding its population by over 50 per cent, and then boomed for a third time in the first half of the 1880s, when growth in the South Island had ceased.

The Auckland economic experience illustrates two important themes, the first of which is the overestimation of wool in the colonial economy. Auckland provided only two per cent of national wool exports in 1878. Apart from Taranaki and Westland, no provincial region had fewer sheep than the largest.[117] If wool was so important, how did Auckland survive and grow rapidly without it? Second, Auckland shows that the progress industry was much wider than Vogelism, from which the province drew little direct benefit. But it did benefit from public progress before and after Vogel – assisted immigration and military settlement, as well as war itself in the 1860s, and public works in the early 1880s, when local authorities spent £500,000 on and, more importantly, in Auckland town. Moreover, its private crusaders, led by Thomas Russell, stood in for the state – sinking their war money into the attempted conversion of Waikato swamps with a fine fervour; shifting their gold money to timber to attack the forests of Northland and Coromandel; redistributing London goods and London credit to the surrounding regions and even to the country as a whole through the Bank of New Zealand and its affiliates. It was this public and private progress that accounted for the third Auckland boom, in the early 1880s. The Auckland economy differed from the rest of the country; it was lively but in some respects less 'developed' – more dependent on sail and water, for example, and less dependent on rail and steam. This remained true until World War One.

But Auckland's difference can be exaggerated; it was still a beneficiary of the progress industry, and its mercantile élite and sea- and credit-borne links with non-contiguous hinterlands were arguably not that different from Wellington, although here Wairarapa wool was also important. Wellington town had the same number of people as Nelson in 1864, Christchurch was not much bigger, and all three were less than half the size of Auckland and Dunedin, which had 12,000 and 16,000 respectively. Wellington town and province spurted by 50 per cent in population in 1864–47, boosted in part by the shift south of both the war – especially important to the Wanganui region of the province – and the capital. Both town and province spurted again, by over 70 per cent, between 1874 and 1878 with Vogelism and the invasion of the 'Great Bush' of the south-central North Island. Hawke's Bay and Taranaki experienced similar growth at the same time and for the same reasons.

Wellington province suggests that cattle numbers correlate better with local spasms of progress than sheep numbers. The province's cattle population stayed static at 49,000 between 1861 and 1864, then jumped to 75,000 in 1871 on the backs of war and the transfer of the capital, then jumped again to 186,000 by 1886 on the backs of rail and the clearing of the 'Great Bush'. When these activities stopped, cattle numbers dropped, despite the advent of refrigeration in 1882, to 155,000 in 1891.[118]

Progress in one region could also help farming in another; like timber and credit, food was traded inter-regionally through the rail and sea networks created by the progress industry. Auckland and Wellington did not have contiguous hinterlands large enough to feed their towns and progress workers, and imported food from Nelson and Canterbury.[119] Ironically, the railmaking state failed Wellington – by no means the last time the possession of central government was to be a double-edged sword. When government shelved plans for a railway from Wellington northwards, in 1881, the locals built it themselves – a remarkable example of communal enterprise from the heartland of state dependence. The Wellington-Manawatu Railway Company was led by wealthy local businessmen but had many small shareholders; it was a co-operative colonising crusade in miniature, which 'served at least temporarily to unite the people of Wellington', a difficult feat. By 1886, the railway had 'opened up' the Manawatu and plugged it firmly into Wellington town, beating off competition from Wanganui and Napier for one of the richest hinterlands of all.[120] Even this solitary rail triumph of private enterprise was helped by large land grants from the government.[121]

Marlborough and Nelson provinces each doubled in population (in 1861–64 and 1864–67 respectively) through gold booms; the latter boom also created Pakeha Westland. Gold gave an even greater stimulus to Otago in the same period. From 1864 to 1881, Dunedin was New Zealand's largest city, with impressive stone buildings and a university established on its twenty-first birthday, in 1869. Its status as the jewel in progressive colonisation's urban crown was displayed in an international exhibition in 1865. It was a somewhat unsavoury jewel, with high mortality, slums as well as mansions, and a bowel problem. A recent historian notes a contemporary estimate that Dunedin produced 20,000 tons of excrement in 1864 – an impressive eight pounds per day for each man, woman and child, and a mystery the historian will no doubt explain in due course.[122] Even so, Dunedin was a substantial and dynamic city within twenty years of its foundation. Otago's pattern of growth was many quick steps forward with the gold rush, and then a few steps back, then a steadier but still rapid climb to 1881, when it had four times as many people as twenty years previously. Its cultivated acreage, including land in sown grasses, grew 50-fold in the same period.

Goldfields support and public-spending efforts to emulate a gold-rich neighbour could be as much of a boost as gold itself. While the population of Otago grew 80 per cent, 1861–64 (with the census years concealing the swift arrival and departure of some miners), that of Canterbury doubled and that of Southland quadrupled. Christchurch, too, grew into a substantial city, reminding everyone of an English town, 'as civilised as if it were a hundred years old'.[123] It was larger than Auckland for a period around 1880. Otago and Canterbury dominated state rail construction in the 1870s. Other provinces had to fight hard for their futures. Nelson failed to plug itself in to the national network after a long and bitter struggle.[124] Along with the natural deficiencies of its harbour, this explains why Nelson finished out of the major money in the race for urban progress, despite its dexterous exploitation of the goldfields support industry. The Big Five of the 1860s became the Big Four thereafter. In sum, gold or war, supplemented and maintained by progress proper, triggered take-off at varying trajectories in Otago, Nelson, Marlborough, Westland, Wellington and Auckland. Progress itself, supplemented by war or gold, did the job in the rest of the country. The pattern was not dissimilar for smaller districts and localities, and the small towns at their centres.

Wool was not wholly inimical to other types of farming, or to towns. Some runholders feared pressures for closer settlement, especially when they held good land on Crown leases; others favoured it. They appreciated the reliable local labour small-farming neighbours could provide, and the higher land prices closer settlement generated. A study of the Clutha district in Otago shows that in this fertile town-supply region large and small farmers helped establish each other.[125] Here and in other regions, such as South Canterbury in the 1870s, big farmers extended their operations beyond sheep and joined small farmers in the more varied and intensive use of land. A few large farmers were lone crusaders who developed groups of farms and towns themselves as private entrepreneurs. Such 'squire towns' included Morrinsville and Martinborough. Sheep wealth stimulated overseas shipping and the growth of the large towns in which the sheeplords spent their money and sometimes lived. But it did not generate a lot of progress between port-city and station. Wool was a robust and imperishable product compared with butter or meat, and stations were relatively self-sufficient in creating and processing it. Wool did not demand a sophisticated transport or processing infrastructure. Throughout the nineteenth century, and as late as 1952, wool bales were carried over the dunes by bullock dray to the Wairarapa and Hawke's Bay coast, then taken out by surf boats to small coastal steamers without so much as a hint of rail or port facilities.[126] This changed somewhat after the sheep-rush era, when wool scouring, fellmongery, boiling-down and canning works appeared, but it is still not easy to point to many towns outside Canterbury and Hawke's Bay that were created mainly by the wool industry.

Gold, on the other hand, was a prolific breeder of towns, though the infant mortality rate was high. Okarito on the West Coast, now notable only for whitebait and Booker Prize winners, briefly became a bustling metropolis of 4,400 people in 1865–66, hosting 76 ships in two months and with its own newspaper. Brighton sprouted 160 retail businesses in five weeks in 1866, including 53 hotels. In 1864, Hokitika was nothing. In 1865, it had 246 buildings including 67 hotels. In 1866, it had 102 hotels, as well as dance rooms, gambling rooms, skittle alleys and shooting galleries, plus an opera house seating 1,200. By 1867, it had three theatres, a cricket club, a skating rink and a waxworks with models of the Prince and Princess of Wales, the Pope, the Australian bushranger Ben Hall and the Maori killers of Volkner, so catering for all tastes. Its population may have peaked as high as 7,000, and it was the second port in New Zealand, measured by customs revenue.[127] Contemporaries believed they were witnessing the birth of a new Melbourne, perhaps even more marvellous than the old. Locals described it to Charles Dilke in 1866 as 'the "most rising place" on earth'.[128] Most visitors today would confess that Hokitika has fallen a little behind Melbourne, but it remains a locally important town even so. Like Hokitika, the other towns of the West Coast, of Central Otago and of Thames-Coromandel got their start from gold.

Other towns got their start from war. During the war years of the 1860s, it was frequently alleged that particular Pakeha communities were seeking to 'get up' campaigns for the business they would bring. This was unfair in that New Plymouth, Wanganui and even Auckland simply did not have the influence to push the colony, let alone the British Empire, into expensive wars. It was also unfair in that war sometimes came very close: it did not do the Pakeha communities of Kororareka and Poverty Bay much good. But when the fighting was kept at some distance, the fact is that it did boost business greatly, especially when the imperial government was paying. Military campaigns also founded towns, such as Patea and Hamilton, that began as military posts. Military settlement proper established the mass Pakeha colonisation of Waikato, the Bay of Plenty and South Taranaki. War was almost as good as gold.

Like its allies, progress itself made towns. The instant townships of the 1840s – Auckland, Akaroa and Wanganui, as well as Wellington, Nelson, New Plymouth, Dunedin and Christchurch – are the obvious examples. Subsequent special-settlement towns such as Te Puke and Feilding, which brought in immigrants from overseas, and local ventures such as the towns of the

Wairarapa, established as islands of smallholding among the sheep runs in the 1850s by George Grey and the Small Farm Association, were not so different in conception. Rail *made* towns as well as linked and boosted them. Timber milling, small businesses and agriculture followed the railway line.[129] Rail camps like Otorohanga and Winton became towns, while many hamlets such as Palmerston North and Hastings received their vital boost from rail. Local people were well aware that their futures depended on rail links, and politics sometimes seemed to consist in the competition for them. When rail reached Waipukurau on New Year's Day 1875, a large crowd of locals and excursionists from Napier celebrated the event like a battle won, which indeed it was.[130]

Many small towns began as road junctions, ferry stations or merely natural points on the road to break one's journey. Towns like Woodville in the north and Cromwell in the south were originally known as 'The Junction'. A great many towns began as lumbering camps and ports. 'Littledene', or Oxford in North Canterbury, which H. C. D. Somerset has made the archetypal New Zealand farming community, began as a timber town – 'the mills made the township'.[131] So did Helensville, Rangiora, Stratford, Eltham, Tapanui, Waimate South, and many towns of Northland. The list begins to sound like the New Zealand version of the song 'I've Been Everywhere', and timber milling had. Coal made and boosted towns in Northland, Waikato, Otago and Westland, keeping the likes of Huntly, Westport and Greymouth alive after their war and gold starts.

There were as many as 115 New Zealand ports in the nineteenth century; and, as with rail, they competed desperately to attract shipping and so turn themselves into towns with futures.[132] Some ports served extractive, finite industries, and died when they did, unable to make the crucial shift to port plus long-term hinterland. Foxton, or Port Manawatu, boomed and busted with the local flax and timber industries. The 42 timber-exporting wharves of the Kaipara Harbour handled 250 ships annually as late as 1900, before fading into a backwater. Other ports competed for the same hinterland. Oamaru spent £14,000 on a wharf in 1867, which was opened with 'public rejoicing and an elaborate ceremony', but the port was soon locked in a death struggle with Kakanui and Moeraki. Kakanui seemed to be winning in the 1870s, but silted up in the 1880s. Moeraki scored a coup in 1869, when it was visited by Prince Alfred, Duke of Edinburgh, in mistake for Oamaru. But the latter's completion of a breakwater bilked Moeraki, which was left to stagnate with its famous boulders for solace.[133] Oamaru duelled indecisively with Timaru in the 1880s, with the two freely duplicating each other's expensive harbour works in a 'notorious instance' of the costs of small-town rivalry.[134] But whatever the long-term costs, in the short term two sets of port facilities created twice the progress, in jobs and business.

New Plymouth, the classic victim of harbourlessness, put up a heroic struggle against unkind nature, planning extensive harbour works from its foundation. Port mania stimulated its desire for Waitara, but the offspring bought with so much blood became a rival – a characteristic of the great urban races. 'The [harbour] works at Waitara were hurried forward in what was in effect a race with New Plymouth', which the former won. The latter had to watch in chagrin as 276 ships cleared its rival in 1902. The New Plymouth Harbour Board overreached itself in the struggle and defaulted on its repayments of a London loan. An extension of the New Plymouth breakwater in 1917 finally turned the tide in its favour, after 75 years of struggle, two wars and the only loan default by a colonial public institution in the history of the British Empire to 1914.[135]

The storekeepers and hoteliers of the camp towns produced by war, gold and progress would all have asserted that, whatever the case with others, *their* town had good prospects of permanence and continued growth, and the authorities were prepared to support this key delusion. In gold-rush Westland, the hotels of Hokitika began as shacks, tents and shanties, but within three years became three-storey buildings with lifts. The storekeepers of Charleston put plate-glass windows in their shops and planned a hospital. A gaol and a courthouse were built in Brighton in 1866.[136] These are not the acts of people who believed that they were living in ephemeral shanty towns. Gold-rush retailers offered rewards for fresh discoveries in their locality that might keep their shops alive; gold-rush newspapers always denigrated distant new rushes. It was, of course, harder for storekeepers to shift than for the soldiers, navvies and diggers they served. Retailers who did business from substantial premises may have had an advantage while the going was good. They were then stuck with an immovable and unsaleable investment when the railhead, roadhead, rush or war moved on. They were therefore more stationary than the actual staffs of the gold, war and progress industries. They had personal incentives to make their town work, to tout local versions of progressive colonisation.

Infant Feilding's backers in 1875 used 'our experience of the rapid progress made in similar spots' to 'picture this infant town grown into a vigorous and beautiful manhood'. No fewer than 181 newspapers started up in New Zealand between 1860 and 1879, the great majority in camp towns.[137] Each trumpeted its local version of the Pakeha prospectus, featuring their particular infant prodigy as the London of the South. A great many lost these camp-town races. One book lists 240 ghost towns, or losers. The prohibitionist Premier William Fox laid out a 'teetotal township' at Crofton in the Manawatu in 1875, which for some reason failed to sprout. Formal status as towns indicates definite winners. Some nineteen town councils were gazetted in the 1860s – eighteen of them in the South Island; more than two dozen emerged in the 1870s, with more than a third now in the North.[138] Many country districts had tiny nodal points that saw themselves as present or future townships. Very often it was the township, or some neighbouring camp, that had allowed the country district to grow, not vice versa.

The progress of regions, towns and farms – indeed, of colonial Pakeha New Zealand as a whole – seems to have followed this pattern: sudden foundation, then a struggle for viability, then one or two sudden lurches of rapid development. If these lurches brought the region, town or district to the point where sustainable economics became possible, take-off was achieved. If it did not, the place died, became a backwater or was absorbed into somewhere else's hinterland. We need to think of a strange footrace in which some competitors are dropped on to the course by helicopters and hit the ground running at varying speeds. They then struggle uphill, the lead depending on the energy they have brought with them, or can borrow from people holding drinks in paper cups on the sidelines, and on their luck with pole positions. About half the runners are then injected with anabolic steroids once or twice, and sprint forward at almost incredible speed, still uphill. Either the drugs or the momentum stemming from them carry some to the crest of the course before the effect wears off, and they stagger downhill to the finishing line known as long-term viability. Some starters get no steroids and drop out well back; others exhaust the steroid boost before reaching the crest and collapse. A few tortoises finish without drugs, moving slowly and steadily, but it is the drugged hares that take the glittering prizes. Tripping, blocking, elbowing and illegal team racing are not unknown. War, gold, credit, the progress industry and its dynamic myths are the different types of steroids. This Ben Johnson theory of colonial progress suits the history of nineteenth-century New Zealand quite nicely.

In sheer scale, the result was impressive. New Zealand's rate of population growth – say, 500 to 500,000 in the period 1831–81 – was far faster than that of New South Wales in its first half-century – 1,000 to 83,000, 1788–1841; indeed, it was much faster than that of Australia as a whole, whose European population was only 190,000 by 1840.[139] It was faster than the growth of the United States in the seventeenth and eighteenth centuries, faster than Canada to about 1850, and faster than Britain during the Industrial Revolution. But New Zealand was by no means alone; other neo-Britains in the mid to late nineteenth century, such as Victoria, grew as fast, even faster. An ideology of progressive colonisation, I suspect, was a key in all these cases, the dynamic myth and reality behind the neo-British boom.

The progress industry did not simply facilitate the growth of the colonial economy, to a large extent it *was* the colonial economy. Australasia was unusual in its emphasis on the role of governments. Small colonies were inspired by the belief that they should be big, and legislated and borrowed this conviction into reality. Public spending on 'infrastructure' in Australasia was 'almost seven times that spent in an average developed economy' between 1865 and 1914. It was nearly three times the amount spent by South African governments, and twelve times that spent by Canadian. Some obvious necessity to create an infrastructure for infant economies cannot wholly explain this. 'The levels are so very much higher . . . that it appears unlikely that age alone can account for the difference.' State-controlled economies, a series of Five Year Plans before Lenin, are not the answer either. The providential convergence between public and private enterprise was basic. 'While a desire to increase business profits may not have been the reason for their behaviour, it should be clear that the business community benefited . . . The Australasian pattern was unmatched anywhere in the world.'[140]

Only one colony was even more profligate than free-spending Australia, and that was New Zealand. Greater Britain was a world capital of state-boosted progressive colonisation, just as the crusaders had intended it to be. For all the accidental allies, the hitches in their plans, the irritating fits and starts, and the number of local and regional failures, the colonising crusade had matched a demographic miracle with an economic one. It had created growth by preparing for it, with immigrants, ports, roads and rail. It was not only the trains that would one day run along the rails that constituted progressive colonisation, but also the railmaking itself, and the potent prophecies that powered it. As the linchpin prophet Arthur Thomson wrote with reference to Canterbury, it was 'an instance of a great fact being founded on a great fiction'.[141]

CHAPTER FIFTEEN

Getting On

'Getting on' was the great colonial game for individuals and families, as well as for towns, districts and regions. For all classes, success was a matter of mixing three sets of variables: the desired type of getting on – enhancement, adoption or promotion; initial advantages; and local opportunity. Some initial advantages favoured the genteel and moneyed respectables: capital, connections and, especially, access to credit. Others crossed class: skills in high demand, colonial experience and luck or initiative in such things as being first in to a particular region, industry or other outcrop of opportunity. Getting in early, participating in the creaming off rather than the mopping up, improved your chances of getting on. Progressive colonisation ensured that opportunity was quite abundant, but also that it came in spasms in space and time. It was by no means evenly distributed among classes either. As with regions, towns and districts, the trick was to achieve take-off, to achieve long-term viability, by exploiting a particular spasm of progress-boosted opportunity. You might then change horses from extractive, finite, rush-phase activity to sustainable, settled, ongoing activity. People who made this switch became a 'settled core' in particular localities; others had to move with progress; and the distinction between stayers and movers, discussed in the next chapter, was an important one. But even stayers tried to engender further progress in their locality. 'Making it' into ongoing viability could be seen as a resting place, where you awaited the next spasm of progress and opportunity that would allow you to make more.

Access to credit was another key to getting on. Like the cultural history of credit discussed in the last chapter, the social history of credit is important in New Zealand. We need to distinguish two types: capital credit, used to buy houses, land, substantial stock and equipment, or businesses; and consumer credit, used to buy goods for consumption. In an economy where circulating cash and substitutes such as cheques were sparse, most people had access to consumer credit. A storekeeper who did not run a slate would have found it hard to do business. Even the motley crews of progressive colonisation, such as navvies on public works, had access to tied consumer credit through their employer. They were lent food, clothes or money against future wages, which came at long intervals to ensure repayment. But there was a massive amount of litigation over small unpaid debts, and even consumer credit was more accessible to those who looked as though they might be in the same place next week. This was a strong incentive to appear stable and respectable, even if you were not.

Capital credit was still more restricted. Gentry had a clear advantage here. Their class culture demanded automatic credit, and often received it, though they were not always as religious about repayment. Their range of connections was wider, extending across more regions and more countries than those of the classes below. They socialised and intermarried with the wealthy and with bankers, or had shares in banks and other loan agencies themselves. When lenders were prepared to descend further down the social spectrum, they preferred people who already had assets as security for the loan.[1] Capital made credit; money made money. Much of the tide of British credit dragged in by progressive colonisation was available for redistribution to private borrowers in New Zealand through banks and other agencies. It could help gentry and middle-class respectables enhance their lives or adopt expensive bits of other class lifestyles. It could help respectables who wished to, and could meet certain conditions, secure promotion to gentility. It could even help those decent working people who already had some money or assets borrow their way to enhancement, adoption or promotion to respectability. What it could rarely do, however – at least until the state entered the lending market in the 1890s – was help decent people without money to get on.

Getting On Decently

While it fell far short of a 'workers' paradise', colonial New Zealand did provide decent working people with opportunities for enhancement and adoption. Wages were substantially higher than those in Britain, at least until the 1880s. Prices were higher too, but this was particularly true of imported luxuries, and some basics were quite cheap. Servants and labourers might earn between £20 and £60 a year in the 1840s and 1850s, often with bed and board in addition, valued at about £17.[2] This was about twice as high as the prevailing rates in Britain, while prices were only about 50 per cent higher.[3] Wages increased greatly in the 1860s. Eight shillings a day was occasionally achieved by unskilled men, and five or six shillings was common – an annual rate of £75 to £90 a year. It has been claimed that New Zealanders had by far the highest average incomes in the world in 1865 – up to £78 per capita. 'There seems little doubt that the average New Zealand living standard in the mid-1860s was significantly higher than that in Australia, which was in turn significantly higher than that of either the United States or Britain.'[4] This is somewhat deceptive. It may not take sufficient account of high prices, and the year 1865 was a peak both of rush-phase goldmining and of imperial military expenditure. Comparisons with late 1840s California and early 1850s Victoria might be more apposite. But it does seem clear that in terms of real wages, in most if not all years between the 1840s and the 1880s, workers did better than in Britain.

They also did better in some other respects. The demand for servants and wage labourers was high somewhere most of the time, though not everywhere all of the time. Inner-city housing was sometimes very expensive, but small blocks of land were usually quite cheap to rent or buy, as were horses from the 1860s. Meat was cheap, and outside the largest towns it was possible to hunt game for yourself, a striking contrast to Britain's poaching laws. 'There is no-one to say that they are mine; those that get them have them.' Fresh fish, shellfish, duck, wild pork and, later, venison were so abundant in some districts that the social valuation placed on them in New Zealand became much lower than in Britain. These were significant forms of adoption in themselves – adapted, bowdlerised fragments of gentility in working-class lives. The land might be three acres of bush; the houses might be more like huts – one decent migrant wrote proudly home about his eighteen-square-metre 'house', purchased for £46. About half of all houses in the 1860s, and a third in the 1870s, had only one or two rooms.[5] The horses might be nags, but by the 1870s there were plenty of them. 'Nearly all the people have a horse to ride to work.' 'Working men in this country don't believe in much walking.'[6]

Much early, proto-trade unionist protest and strike action by workers appears to have been aimed at the defence of leisure. The famous 'four eights' – eight hours' sleep, eight hours' play, eight hours' work and eight shillings a day – were advocated by Wellington carpenter Samuel Duncan Parnell and others from the 1840s. Even in Presbyterian Otago, where hard work ranked with drink and Jesus Christ, the 'good Old Scotch rule' of ten hours a day is said to have been quickly subverted.[7] The hours were as important as the shillings. Praise of meat diets, prime roasts, free and abundant wood and game, cheap or accessible horses and houses, the absence of 'bitter oppression' and harsh masters (though not oppression or masters) features at least as large in the decent letters back collected by Rollo Arnold as the official motive for decent migration: the desire for social promotion. Some decent folk did get what they wanted, not what the crusaders had wanted them to want.

The various adoptions, such as hunting, were also part of a wider range of ways of supplementing wages, which were especially important to family economies. Few families depended solely on the wages of unskilled fathers, but on a package of activities in which most family members were involved. Apart from caring for, and sometimes educating, younger children, and the endless backbreaking work of operating households without the assistance of servants or machines, mothers in towns took in laundry or boarders, and sometimes engaged in part-time wage work or piecework. Older boys and girls worked for neighbours to 'earn a little and learn a little', and paid their wages into the family coffers. In both town and country, women, children and men worked to substitute for buying in goods and services, selling any surplus. They made and repaired things, grew and processed vegetables and fruit, produced eggs and dairy products. They used not only the land that they owned, leased and rented, but also public land and unoccupied sections – to gather firewood and graze cows and horses, for example. The existence of such informal 'commons' was very important. In towns, children scavenged for rags, bottles and scrap metal, and performed odd-jobs for cash. In the country, they collected firewood for home and sale, hunted rabbits, fished and collected wild berries and shellfish. Hunting and gathering traditions survived into the twentieth century as the family picking of blackberries and the gathering of toheroa – gourmet shellfish that now look like becoming the last of the long line of progressive colonisation's victims. Family-package economics was important in Britain too, but in New Zealand there was more to hunt if not to scavenge, and more usable land around decent houses.

Higher real wages, more numerous jobs, more extensive family package opportunities, cheaper or more accessible land and meat, houses, horses and hunting meant that many, perhaps most, decent migrants did indeed 'get on' in terms of enhancing their living conditions and adopting converted bits of those of other classes. But there were major qualifications to this positive picture. First, better was not great. Translating old money into new is notoriously difficult, partly because consumer expectations and the definitions of luxuries and necessities change over time, but £50 a year in the 1850s may represent the buying power of something like 7,500 1990s New Zealand dollars, or $145 a week. This meant enhancement and adoption for single males, relative to their lives in Britain, but it did not mean paradise even for them. It was only marginally sufficient for large colonial families, even with supplements, and, with a few exceptions, women were paid about half of male rates.

Second, while waged work was quite abundant, it was spasmodic and restricted in availability. It was available mainly to fit men and fit single women – ill health or injury was also economic disaster. Married male wage workers won only part of the family bread, but it was still a large part. Very often, high daily or weekly rates did not mean equally high annual rates. A great deal of manual wage work was seasonal or otherwise sporadic, and many reaped high wages for only a part of the year. Some drew their jobs from spasms of progress, and when these passed, so did the jobs, along with some of the opportunities for family economics. One could move to a fresh region and a fresh spasm of progress, but unencumbered adults were more mobile than families. Moreover, if you owned your own house and land, the demise of local progress reduced its value and saleability. Desertion of families by fathers is said to have been high, though much was intended as temporary. Divorce rates were much lower than today, but the ratio of single-parent families may have been similar, through desertion, job-driven separation, paternal deaths through dangerous jobs, and maternal deaths through childbirth.[8]

All this meant that pockets of poverty were quite common. It was not endemic but patchy, spasming like an inverse mirror image of progress. Examples of severe unemployment and want in particular years, seasons and places extend well beyond the establishment phase of the 1840s. Auckland produced a 'Report on the Increase of Pauperism' in 1866, and distributed 80,000 emergency rations to the needy in six months of 1867. Dunedin had over a thousand men unemployed in the winters of 1861 and 1864.[9] Generally, however, colonial poverty had a nasty bias. It tended to avoid young, healthy men and single women. The latter had marriage opportunities, discussed below, and safe servant slots, undesirable in many respects but useful for weathering recessionary storms and less dependent on progress than male manual labour. Instead, poverty hunted children, mothers, the young and old, as well as the sick, lame and helpless of both sexes and all ages.

Informal aid networks were weaker in a new society. Informal charitable networks can be underestimated, but they were variable, selective, parsimonious and humiliating – both to the recipient and to the society in which there was supposed to be no need for them. Relief was distributed by genteel 'benevolent societies' and by provincial governments and local authorities. In the 1860s, it was 'spartan in the extreme'.[10] The destitute, sick, young or old were concealed in institutions that were no great advance on the English poorhouse. Public hospitals, in which most people preferred not to be seen dead, administered 'outdoor' as well as 'indoor' relief. There were 37 public hospitals by 1882, admitting 5,500 patients a year.[11] Only £50,000 was spent on them in 1880 – about 1.3 per cent of central government spending.[12]

Orphanages and related institutions such as 'Ragged' and 'Industrial' schools were established from 1857. Many more girls than boys were abandoned in the nineteenth century, with an intriguing shift to the reverse in the twentieth.[13] In gold-rush Dunedin, jewel in the colonial crown, 200 children attended Ragged schools. 'Seventy-six very poor but respectable homes, where the fathers were ill, unemployed, or dead, contributed 127 of the pupils while a further 45 children came from 27 families living in degradation and moral squalor.' These were the lucky ones. The chief of police gave the names of 53 unschooled children living in the same conditions, and said he also knew of twenty nameless children, presumably abandoned young vagrants, living in the streets.[14] We need to remind ourselves that unemployment and poverty in colonial New Zealand was patchy, regional, periodic and seasonal. It was not the lot of whole classes. But this was small comfort to those who were crippled by it. Being abandoned nameless in the streets of 1860s Dunedin was not something you recovered from next year.

The third major qualification to the decents' success in getting on was the problem of promotion – of getting up a class. Not everyone wanted this, but many did. Education could enhance lives and facilitate adoption. It was also, in principle, one of two main routes to promotion – for workers' children if not themselves. 'An education was a passport to respectability.'[15] From the introduction of compulsory education in 1877, it was an important means of access to white-collar work – arguably an important form of social promotion. But the picture before 1877 is less clear, and it is also unclear, despite legends, that colonial New Zealand was educationally an improvement on Britain. According to one estimate, about 31 per cent of school-age (six to fifteen years) children attended school in 1858, with a further 20 per cent attending Sunday school only.[16] Sunday school might have been a source of basic literacy, as in Britain, and home tutoring was presumably significant. One boy was taught good Latin in this way. 'Mother used to lift me up to the top of a high barrel from where I could not get down, to say my Latin grammar while she washed the dishes.'[17] Whatever the method, it was estimated that 54 per cent of school-age children could read and write in 1858. The overall literacy rate was 63 per cent, which it seems was lower than in Britain at the same time. 'The present consensus is that educational opportunities expanded during the period 1750–1850, so that by 1840 between 67 per cent and 75 per cent of the British working class had achieved rudimentary literacy.'[18]

From the 1850s, led by Nelson and Otago, provincial governments in New Zealand boosted primary schooling, supplementing community efforts and the private market for decent education. Private and public schools established by the genteel for their own children, discussed below, may also have had spin-off benefits for the decent, such as free places. By 1871, 54 per cent of children were attending primary school, with a further 18 per cent at Sunday school only – a total of 72 per cent. This was probably similar to the percentage of children receiving some schooling in Britain before the introduction of a compulsory education system there, in 1870.[19] Children's literacy in New Zealand increased much less (to 59 per cent), which may say something about the quality of some schools. New Zealand had not done badly in building an education system from scratch, but it had not done enormously well either, and Britain had kept pace. Moreover, white-collar jobs were not numerous in New Zealand before the 1880s, and until then education may not have paved the way to promotion for many.

Before the 1880s, promotion from decency to respectability normally depended on the second main route: the acquisition of an 'independency' – an owner-operated business. This might be small but sufficient to reliably sustain a family. Skilled workers who owned no more than their skills and the immediate tools of their trade were merely decent, or working class, but if their trade was in demand in New Zealand, they were best placed of all workers to achieve respectability. They could do this either by acquiring the means of production within their own trade – such as a butchery, bakery or workshop – or by saving the cash to acquire another type of independency altogether, such as a farm. The differential between skilled and unskilled rates of pay was much higher than in the twentieth century. A carpenter earned at least twice as much as an unskilled labourer. Progress and its allies provided good opportunities for those in the right trades. Even a very brief rush of gold, or military and public works expenditure in a particular locality could propel artisans across the worker–owner line and set them up to survive in quieter times. A few were propelled further, into the upper ranks of respectability, by building their workshops up into mills or factories, where they had the option of bidding for gentility for themselves or their children. We will see below that some chose not to take it.

Carpenters, builders and related wood trades may have been the most numerous and consistent beneficiaries of the progress industry and its allies. Wood was the preferred building material of colonial progress, as we have seen. Tradesmen, rather than large investors, appear to have built and sold most houses, in Auckland at least. Some carpenters arrived from Britain with a little capital, and those who did not found plenty of work from the outset, at high rates. They could soon move on to small farms if they chose, and many did. Of 36 men who established farms in the Clutha district of Otago, no fewer than 20 per cent were carpenters – the first-equal group, along with those who had been farmers before.[20] Not all artisans matched their success. A group of Frenchmen were assisted to the colony as 'mechanics' in the 1870s, but were compelled to become ballet dancers on arrival.[21] But trades such as shipwright and blacksmith also did well. Tradesmen feature disproportionately in the New Zealand *Cyclopedias* of the 1890s and 1900s, the studbooks of those who made it into middle-class respectability, wherein personal pasts were sometimes adjusted to suit the present. Thanks in particular to the progress industry, the artisans' paradise came nearly true.

Semi-skilled or informally specialised workers such as carters, ploughmen and ferrymen had some success in achieving promotion too. They tended towards contract labour, which was better paid than wage work and was believed to carry more status and independence. From labour contractors, selling their skills in small groups while owning little but their basic tools, the semi-skilled were sometimes able to become capital *and* labour contractors, owning substantial capital stock or equipment. As with tradesmen, the key for them was owning their own means of production. A bullock team and dray, plough and team, or ferry and jetties represented substantial investments, extending the list of owner-operators considerably. There were also opportunities in harvesting and threshing machines, specialist stores and other small businesses that required some skill and some capital. Quite often, such businesses were associated with farmlets and used as stepping stones to full farms. People without either recognised skills or capital, however, found gaining an independency more difficult. Their targets were what we will call 'open' independencies – open to people without formal skills or qualifications. These included general stores and pubs, but the archetypal open independency was a small farm.

At the core of the Pakeha prospectus, of the folk history of New Zealand settlement and of colonial arcadianism in general was the yeoman – the sturdy settler of small means who hewed his own farm from the wilderness. The ideal yeoman had several interconnected roles. Morally, he was the guarantor of rural virtue, the hero of Arcadia, the 'backbone' of Better Britain. Practically, he was to be the cutting edge of progress in the hinterland, breaking in difficult country, particularly the bush, and bringing it into production. There was also a military role. The archetypal yeoman was very similar to the archetypal armed Briton, whose military virtue was inherent, not taught. The two intersected very neatly in the military settlers, whose ideological forebears can be traced back to Ulster and Rome. Nature and natives were to be conquered by the very same people. Bush settlers were shock troops of progressive colonisation, armed with sword and plough, gun and match. Finally, there was the crucial political role of disciplining and controlling workers, noted in Chapter Thirteen. Workers seeking to become yeomen had, it was thought, little time or inclination for disreputable behaviour, and were not vulnerable to subversion by unionists or Chartists. The yeoman was the colonising crusade's insurance against class conflict and disrepute.

Yet despite this, and despite the constant inflow of immigrants, the agricultural conquest of the hinterland was slow – a major hitch in the crusader programme. The unplanned emphasis on sheep farming, which was often said to monopolise land that should properly be used for small mixed farming or 'close settlement', was part of the problem in some regions, as was Maori ownership in others. But to some extent, both were scapegoats for a less obvious malaise: the reluctance or inability of decent folk to hew farms from the wilderness even when wilderness was available. In the 1840s, to be sure, there were genteel complaints to the opposite effect, about the unseemly speed with which the decent made their way on to smallholdings, so evading their terms as employees. The New Zealand Company only made such smallholdings available as a last resort, and they were very small indeed. But over the whole period, these complaints were outnumbered by regrets about the tendency to cluster in or near the towns. Many people who were supposed to want farms did not, and many of those who did want farms were not getting them. The shock troops of progressive colonisation were proving a little reluctant to go over the top, and were suffering high casualties when they did.

An obvious but easily forgotten fact is that farm making did not consist in stepping on to some land and scattering a few seeds. Turning raw land into farmland was either a costly or a time-consuming business, and it became more so as one descended the ladder of land types. Leaving aside unusable land, high-country sheep farming, whose high entry cost normally excluded the decent, and swamp land, whose high drainage costs did likewise, there were three broad categories of land with small-farming potential. Flat or rolling-hill native grassland, close to ports and large towns, was the best. Even this cost several pounds per acre to convert to fenced and sown pasture or cropland after its unassisted fertility had been exhausted. It was snapped up quickly by those who were moneyed or first in. It was this rapid creaming off of prime land, a quick closure of opportunity, that increased pressure for closer settlement through political action from the late 1860s. Next came scrub and fernland, which required a long, costly and sometimes bitter struggle to convert. It had to be burned off, ground down by heavy stocking and sometimes sown in transition crops to prevent the regrowth of resilient native plants. Last came bush land. Estimates of the cost of clearing this went as high as £60 per acre and as long as 30 years. Developed farms, even small ones, were beyond the slowly filling purses of unskilled workers, and this was also true of substantial blocks of prime raw land, which usually required some instant cash or credit to snap up. Scrub or bush land could be acquired for as little as five shillings an acre in the 1850s, or even free through military grants, though £1–3 per acre was more common. But the purchase price of such land was merely the deposit on a farm. The major cost was development; and when the land was cheap, raw bush, the cost was very high.

An undeveloped landholding was very far from a viable farm. Especially until the 1870s, there was a tendency to inappropriately apply British conceptions of farm size to New Zealand. In England, 400 acres was a large farm, and 40 acres of fertile, well-developed land, close to services and markets and linked to them by good roads, might be a viable holding. In New Zealand, 400 acres was a small-to-medium farm, and 100 was probably closer than 40 to the lower limit of viability, though this obviously varied according to fertility and access to markets. It was always productivity per farmer, not per acre, that was the key to the success of New Zealand farming. All this means that when historians talk about the large number of freeholds in nineteenth-century New Zealand, they are not talking about viable farms. Most freeholds were homes, not farms, and some were neither homes nor farms.

In 1878, there were a total of 26,000 freehold 'farm holdings', but 16,000 of these were under 100 acres – including 11,500 under 50 acres, and 6,000 under ten acres. Some holdings under 100 acres, exceptionally fertile or close to town, were no doubt viable; but conversely, many proto-farms and undeveloped blocks over 100 acres were not. This leaves roughly 10,000 possibly viable freehold farms, as against farmlets, proto-farms and totally undeveloped landholdings. Ten thousand farmers represented about eight per cent of the Pakeha male population aged over twenty years.[22] More than 1,500 of these holdings exceeded 1,000 acres (including almost 700 exceeding 5,000 acres) and were beyond the reach of the vast majority of self-made farmers. If the aim of decent folk was to acquire a viable freehold farm, as the crusaders hoped and some historians still imply, then most failed.

The yeomen myth survived real history partly through its own momentum and partly through distorting 'farm-first' retrospect, but also through other factors. These included the illusion of widespread farmholding conferred by widespread landholding. Land ownership in nineteenth-century New Zealand *was* extremely widespread – the number of holdings was equivalent to about 50 per cent of the adult male population in 1882.[23] But the great bulk of these holdings were homes, urban or suburban sections, farmlets, proto-farms or blocks of totally undeveloped land. As we have seen, such holdings could represent an improvement on living conditions in Britain. Land ownership may also have helped anchor people, making geographic settlers from sojourners. What it did not in itself represent was the economic guts of respectable independency: productive property sufficient to live on. The conceptual blurring of land ownership and independency, whereby the emasculated symbols of farms had the cachet of the thing itself, was to prove an enduring force in New Zealand history. The yeoman's freehold independency was devalued first into a farmlet or proto-farm, then into a freehold house and section, then into a mortgaged house and section. Unproductive property became the illusion of productive property, conferring middle-class respectability and a 'stake in society', with lawn mowing as its ritual harvest.

We have noted that not everyone wanted promotion to a higher class. Some successful respectables did not seek promotion to gentility, as we shall see; some decent folk were uninterested in respectable independencies. Many of those who were interested were hesitant about suicide missions – unwilling to engage in the gruelling and chancy marathon of converting an outback bush block into a farm. Hence the irritating reluctance of potential yeomen to fling themselves into forlorn assaults on nature. Of those who did try, many failed. Abandoned blocks and small-scale bankruptcies were common. But some people, even unskilled people beginning with little capital, did succeed. There were enough to provide a substantial kernel of truth to the myth of the colonial yeoman, and there were several keys to the success of this important minority.

One key was making the move into farming very early or very late in the colonial era. The 'sufficient price' imposed by the companies in the 1840s and early 1850s (usually £1 or £2 per acre), designed to slow the movement of wage labourers on to the land, was not that high for prime land close to towns.

Some fortunate decent folk, usually those first in, did obtain such land and develop it into productive farms. Land prices dropped dramatically in the 1880s, and struggling proto-farmers who survived that decade were washed to viability by the tide of refrigeration in the next. Another key was leasing. Almost 10,000 people in 1882 leased land from the Crown.[24] Some leased holdings were urban or suburban; some were rural, but below the threshold of viability; ten per cent were large pastoral leases, of little interest to yeomen. Government schemes to lease land to small men, state-boosting the number of renting pseudo-yeomen, expanded after 1882. But viable leased farms may have increased the number of small farmers by as much as a half prior to that. A curious aspect of the freeholders' paradise that was supposed to be colonial New Zealand is the willingness of its denizens to accept leaseholds. Leasing improved the small farmers' chances of achieving viability because purchase capital was reserved for development. Along with reluctant yeomen, this suggests that the freehold imperative, supposedly burning in every colonial breast, has been retrospectively exaggerated.

A third key, covered in the last chapter, was the influence of the progress industry and its allies. Progress cleared new land, rendered it accessible and provided markets and employment. It was especially important to self-made yeomen, who were most in need of outside wage work while they were breaking in their farms. They also needed markets for non-farm products, such as game, timber and jew's ear fungus, and for first-phase farm products: things that bush proto-farms could produce before they were fully cleared and ploughed into pasture or cropland. Early clearings and the natural space between trees were used to pasture a few dairy cattle, pigs and fowls, and to grow vegetables, exploiting the 'virgin bonus', the temporary high fertility of newly cleared soil. Such produce either did not carry well over long distances or required processing into preserved provisions in towns, as with the 'milled' butter blended, salted, barrelled and sold by storekeepers. The local markets for fresh food, camp towns and transport networks provided by progress were therefore important. Like regions and districts, individual yeomen farmers were sometimes established, or boosted to viability, by the progress industry and its allies.

A fourth key to self-made small farming may have been the absence of richer competition. It was not merely that those who started with advantages succeeded better than those without, but that the opportunities of the advantaged sometimes reduced those of the disadvantaged. The fate of Waikato War military settlers illustrates this and confirms that small farming was extremely precarious, even when raw land was free. Around 80 per cent of the soldiers who received land grants in the mid-1860s had left by 1874. The continued insecurity of the Waikato, Tauranga and Opotiki regions, a result of persistent Maori independence, was part of the problem, but so was the fact that the 50-acre grants given to private soldiers were too small for viability. Many men simply walked off their proto-farms, despairing of buyers – this was still causing rating problems to local authorities in the 1920s.

Some privates did succeed in making it to viability and stability, but they tended to be those in districts where higher-class competition was weakest. Officers received much larger grants than their men (up to 500 acres); they generally also received first-choice locations – closer to town, for example; and they were subsequently better placed to buy up the land of failed neighbours. They were therefore more successful and persistent. Over 25 per cent of the officers of the First Waikato Regiment retained their farm grants in 1874, as against 11.5 per cent of the men. Opotiki, however, was a telling exception. Here, officers did not get the best land, and perhaps for this reason they did not remain to dominate subsequent aggregation. Three dozen men in one parish were therefore able to build up viable farms of over a hundred acres, to persist and to get on. In this rare officer-free parish, 68 per cent of military settlers were still there in 1874. In better-officered Te Papa parish, near Tauranga, only 10.4 per cent of the men persisted.[25]

This process of reshuffling many unviable holdings into fewer viable holdings occurred in other regions too. One success was often built on three failures. Those with better access to cash had a better chance both of avoiding failure and of buying up the land of failed neighbours. If no-one local had much access to cash, and outside buyers did not step in, the aggregation chances of the poorly financed improved. Established stations and estates, which were no longer in the market for aggregation, could be helpful to neighbouring small farming, providing work and markets, and encouraging transport – substituting for the progress industry. But the military settler experience suggests that in new frontier regions it was the absence of gentry that was an advantage to yeomen. The presence of wives was also an advantage in persisting and succeeding. The First, Second and Third Regiments of Waikato Militia were recruited largely from single men; the Fourth from married men. Men of this regiment were 50 per cent more likely to have stayed on their grants (for three years at least) than the other regiments. The fifth key to getting up, especially for decent folk starting with nothing, was marriage, which was also a part, though not the whole, of the colonial woman's lot.

Women's Lots

At the end of the colonial era, in 1881, 43 per cent of adult men, but only 15 per cent of adult women, had never been married.[26] Unmarried women remained quite a substantial minority, and some married women spent an important part of their working lives outside the family economy. Small numbers of women worked in many waged occupations, but the leaders were domestic service, the clothing industry and education. There were 9,000 female servants in 1874, and 15,000 in 1881, about three times the number of males and easily the largest female occupation.[27] Domestic service in New Zealand enhanced women's lives in comparison with service in Britain, because it was paid at twice the rate and new jobs were readily available. Anecdotal evidence suggests that servant women were very ready to dump particularly unsatisfactory employers.

But domestic service transgressed unofficial migration motives, reduced the chances of meeting marriage partners and was extremely hard work – more so than in Britain because fewer servants were employed per household. Despite a sellers' market for employment, living conditions were poor. Employers were not prepared to go so far in attracting scarce servants that they endangered status differentials. The fittings of a servant's bedroom in one mansion cost £7, compared with £47 for the bedroom of an employer's child.[28] Hours were long and often lonely, and movements were restricted. For these reasons, servant work in hotels was preferred to private homes; but most servants had to work in the latter, at least for a time. 'Semi-skilled' female cooks, a cross between domestic servants and artisans, may have done unusually well. Cooks were in high demand, and the wage differential between male and female cooks appears to have been exceptionally low.[29]

In the clothing industry, decent women worked as 'tailoresses' in workshops and in the clothing factories that grew up from the 1860s. Such work was often preferred to domestic service because it was less restricted, subservient and lonely. But wages were low. Respectable women, and even genteel women who had fallen on hard times, also made clothes for sale – as 'dressmakers', normally working from home. Dressmaking was considered more respectable than tailoressing, though the pay was apparently even lower. Respectability was retained at a cost in money, an interesting indicator of its importance in people's minds. Conditions for dressmakers may have improved in the 1860s, with the New Zealand advent of the sewing machine, only to deteriorate again in the 1880s. Women working in the clothing industry for wages or at piece rates numbered 2,500 in 1874 and 4,600 in 1881.[30]

Teaching was the leading women's profession. It was available to the genteel, respectable and even, temporarily, to academically gifted decent girls, who could serve a brief term as pupil-teachers. In 1882, women made up one-third of a thousand full teachers in state-assisted primary schools, 40 per cent of 411 assistant teachers, and 80 per cent of 668 pupil-teachers.[31] A 'female bonus' was of enduring importance to the quality of New Zealand education. Teaching drew a higher proportion of female talent than of male because it was one of the few options available to the former, but women had inferior access to the higher and more permanent ranks of the profession. On average, they were therefore both better and cheaper than male teachers. An impressive group of lady principals found satisfying niches schooling genteel and respectable girls, especially after the emergence of girls' secondary schools in the 1870s.[32] For full teachers such as these, gender differentials in pay appear to have been lower than normal.

Governessing, a cross between teaching and domestic service, was a less satisfying niche for gentlewomen. Opportunities were few; small household staffs meant pressure to play up the servant role and play down the teaching; and governessing tended, like dressmaking, to be a genteel job of last resort. Anecdotal evidence suggests migrant governesses were generally disappointed in New Zealand; most women teachers had less able males in authority over them, and the careers of decent pupil-teachers were short. 'My ideal of New Zealand life has been spoiled,' wrote governess Elizabeth Long in 1880, 'and although it is undoubtedly the paradise of servants, I am afraid the paradise for governesses has yet to be discovered.'[33]

It has been claimed that married rural gentlewomen were as much afflicted by the dreaded ennui as their sisters in Britain, and no doubt this was true of some.[34] But others did succeed in a degree of reconciliation of gentility and respectability, work and leisure. The classic example at the genteel end of the compromise was prolific author Lady Mary Anne Barker. She married Frederick Broome in 1865, after the death of her first husband, Sir George Barker, but did not change her name to Broome until 1884, when Frederick was also knighted. No-one was going to take away her title, live knightly husband or not, and no-one would have questioned her gentility. She avoided the dirty work and the dirty woolshed on her sheep station, hunted vigorously for servants and was seldom happy about her prey. But she almost enjoyed occasional forays into fending for herself and became an expert in cooking, or at least the supervising and planning of cooking. She also enjoyed tramping, riding, hunting, eeling, ice-skating, tobogganing and arson – burning off more tussock than needed to be burned, in 'the exceeding joy of "burning" '.[35] At the respectable end of the compromise, the classic examples are the women of the Richmond-Atkinson clan of New Plymouth and Nelson: more genteel working-women than working gentlewomen. Jane Maria Atkinson, née Richmond, wrote: 'I love Taranaki more every day. I suppose I was born to live here . . . the delight of finding everybody of value is very great . . . anyone who will work is sure to get on.' [36]

> Lely [Maria Richmond] seems rather disgusted at seeing me scrub about and look dirty . . . but I consider myself a much more respectable character than when I was a fine lady, did nothing for anybody, and made a great many people do things for me . . . When my pantry shelves . . . [contain] a round of boiled beef, a roast leg of pork, a rhubarb pie, 15 large loaves and 8 pounds of fresh butter . . . I feel as self-satisfied and proud as any mortal can be . . . I don't mean to say that I think there is to be no division of labour or distinction of class . . . but that things in England have gone too far.[37]

This philosophy percolated through to Atkinson's aspirations for her daughters. 'I want my girls to have a boy's education,' she wrote to Mary Taylor in 1870, 'because it is a better education than what is called a girl's since it better exercises the faculties . . . so-called "feminine refinement" is fatal to female usefulness.'[38] The tension between a model of idealised British feminine gentility and this model of colonial genteel respectability, or respectable gentility, is also discernible in a family disagreement of the Logan Campbells. John Logan Campbell was exceptionally snobbish, giving Auckland the dubious distinction of being disliked by its own Father. This attitude was shared by his wife, Emma (née Cracroft Wilson), daughter of an eminent Canterbury gentleman and presumed Mother of Auckland. The town, she wrote, was full of 'low people playing at being fine ladies . . . There is no one I wish ever to see again.' John eventually changed his mind about his urban offspring and endowed it with Cornwall Park, but not before he had exiled his real offspring to Europe to be 'tamed and polished' into gentry, away from local contamination. It was a strange reverse desertion; his daughters begged to be allowed to return home, but John felt their gentility could not be risked. One daughter, Ida, died in exile. The other, Winifred, disliked the life of 'ladylike aimlessness' to which she was condemned. Romanticising work, she wanted to do 'something engrossing which brings brains, imagination & everything into play . . . I wish . . . I was a boy, and wouldn't I work!'[39]

Baking your cake and having it served to you was indeed a goal of genteel and respectable migrant women, and some succeeded. Exactly how many had and achieved such goals is impossible to say. John and Emma Logan Campbell rejected the colonial compromise model in principle, but not so clearly in practice. Both respected and admired Thomas Russell, whose father was a carpenter. Jane Maria Atkinson, who fully espoused the colonial compromise, may also have been exceptional in her preference for respectability over gentility. Again, there may have been some tension between principle and practice. When Premier Edward Stafford stayed with her clan at New Plymouth in 1856, he slept on a feather bed for the first time in ten years – the Richmond-Atkinson colonial compromise did not exclude feather beds.[40] The middle position, represented by Lady Barker, may have been more common among the élite – respectable gentility rather than genteel respectability. It applied to gentlemen as well as gentlewomen but was perhaps stronger in the latter. It is tempting to link the attitudes involved to subsequent developments in New Zealand women's history, such as the early mass entry of higher-class women into secondary and university education, and the early achievement of votes for women in 1893.

Combined with the opportunities of the teaching profession, with the shedding or at least easing of some restrictive customs, and with the various forms of enhancement and adoption that crossed sexes, some women did get on in their own terms. But getting on by reconciling genteel leisure and respectable work was open only to those classes, and the best-paid work opportunities, notably teaching, selected for class as well as gender. Women's waged work increased greatly from the 1880s. In the colonial era, it offered limited enhancement to some decent women, adoption opportunities to a few, and promotion to even fewer. In Charles Kingsley's 1850 novel *Alton Locke*, an English clothing worker bemoans her lot. She longed to go 'out to the colonies' and become 'an honest man's wife . . . It would be like getting into heaven out of hell.' Heaven or hell, marriage was a key to getting on for the majority of decent women.

For most people, nineteenth-century marriage was an economic as well as social decision. This contravenes a myth of romantic marriage, falling in love with a pre-destined soul mate, which dates from the age of chivalry, was renewed in European higher classes in the nineteenth century and spurted among all classes in New Zealand from the 1940s. The nineteenth-century New Zealand reality is hard to gauge but appears to have been much less romantic and more rational. Sometimes it was a slow, cautiously calculated rationality; at others the prompt seizure of opportunity by people in a hurry.

'Well, John, have you found a wife?' 'No,' he said. 'Can you tell me where to find one?' . . . 'Yes, there is one at Mrs Otterson's, if you can get her.' So servant girl Sarah Sharpe recorded the conversation that led to her marriage to John in 1840s Wellington. Her father had disliked her going into service, and she jumped at the opportunity to be her own mistress. She was particularly proud of building her own kitchen, though children had come quickly. 'My husband could not leave his work to do it . . . I got a little maid to mind the children, while I put up a mud kitchen, 20 ft. long and 12 ft. wide.'[41] Mrs Baker was very taken by the attentive James Hewett on her voyage out. 'You are so good to me I cannot think of any better way of rewarding you than by giving you my daughter Ellen.' Much to her surprise, he said quite seriously, 'Thank you, I will take her,' and he did.[42] A widower with nine children came to buy fowls from Adela Stewart. Her servant Agnes so impressed him with her quickness at catching them that he immediately proposed marriage. Agnes refused him, but not before considering it seriously.[43] There are examples of courtships lasting only four or five days, and of aspirant husbands advertising in newspapers as though seeking a business partner.[44] One ungracious husband, when asked in old age why he had married his illiterate Irish wife, replied 'in the early days, 1860–1880, women were scarce and hard to find'.[45]

We should remember that unromantic marriage does not preclude companionate marriage. It envisages that respect and affection develop after marriage rather than before. But these anecdotes suggest a calculating approach to marriage, opportunist rather than cautious, casual or romantic. Both sexes shared this attitude, but the buyers' market for husbands presumably meant that it was more bride- than groom-led – the brides' paradise had a limited amount of substance. Whether it was the bride herself or her family who made the decision is unclear. In Britain, tight communities provided the context of courtship, and families, especially mothers, tended to control it. This was also true of colonial New Zealand, but less often. Single migrant women made their own decisions, and community was looser. Whoever selected the husband, selection was probably designed at least partly to increase the chances of getting up. The argument that the drive for social promotion was stronger in decent working women than in decent men, and that the former used marriage as a means to this end, may smack of dubious stereotypes of male folklore: the Pushful Wife and the Mercenary Bride; ruthless female social climbing, marrying for gain; ambitious wife pushing easygoing husband. It is important to note that marriage was only part of the promotion strategy – another was extremely hard work. But it would have been strange if women had not taken some advantage of colonial circumstances to be more selective than was possible in Britain, and there were good reasons for gender differences in the desire for promotion.

One was that enhancement, adoption and wage-work opportunities, while not entirely closed to lower-class women, were much more open to men – and to higher-class women. Not only were there fewer alternatives to promotion, but the semi-tangible incentives for remaining working class were lower. We will see in the next chapter that women could enjoy something similar to the bonhomie and comradeship of unskilled, devil-may-care 'crew culture' – by becoming prostitutes – but they sacrificed repute in doing so. Added to this, women may have had less 'fear of the peer sneer'. People doubted their capacity to conform to the manners and customs of the class above, and feared mockery if they failed. A much higher proportion of wage-working women than men had done time in domestic service, though seldom as much as their employers wished. This experience may have made them more self-confident about their capacity to handle the cultural demands of social promotion. They knew which spoon to use in supping with respectability, even if their husbands did not.

More importantly, the typical form of social promotion for the 'unskilled', a small independency, gave women far more security against the common perils of male death, disability and desertion than did family economics or reliance on wage work. Women with dead, absent or incapable husbands could run small businesses themselves, and they did. There are many examples of women running pubs, stores, farms and trade workshops after the demise of their husbands. For example, 245 women ran farms on their own in 1874.[46] More importantly still, promotion to respectable independency instantly doubled the cash value of women's work. Women normally received around half male wages. The labour in a pound of butter made for you by a dairywoman in your employ cost half that made by a dairyman; it cost the same bought from a farmer whether the farmer was male or female. Who controlled these increased profits was another matter, of course, but women's chances of doing so were obviously better if the profits existed. It made sense for decent women to try to get up through marriage, and there is some evidence that they did so. It was usually not a matter of instant promotion through marriage by marrying far up the social spectrum, but of marrying those husbands of your own class who had the best chances of getting on, especially with your help: the skilled rather than the unskilled.

A recent study of single-women migrants to Canterbury between 1857 and 1871 suggests to me, though not to its author, that working-class women *did* use marriage in New Zealand as a means of social promotion.[47] By 1879, 90 per cent of these women had married. Over 80 per cent of those brides on whom information was found were from 'unskilled' occupations; over 80 per cent of grooms were from higher occupational categories. Over half of these were working class, but they were *skilled* workers – the decent group with by far the best chance of promotion to respectability. They and respectable men were the preferred husbands of these decent women. Unskilled workers, though more numerous and quite well paid in this period, were avoided like the plague.

Another type of evidence may support this conclusion. New Zealand's overall illiteracy rate in 1858, as estimated by census responses, was 25 per cent – probably not dissimilar to that of Britain at the same time. Other nineteenth-century 'literacy' statistics actually measure nominacy – the ability to sign your name on marriage registers. On this criterion, New Zealand in 1858 was 12 per cent 'innominate', compared with 18–31 per cent in the New Zealand-prone counties of England in the 1860s. The New Zealand rate also varied regionally – from 8 per cent in Otago to 40 per cent in Stewart Island – but the main point is that New Zealand *illiteracy* rates were similar to those in Britain, while *innominacy* rates were clearly substantially lower. In 1881, only 3.2 per cent of New Zealand grooms registered with a mark, compared with rates varying from 8.3 to 29.9 per cent in English counties.[48] In short, marriage in New Zealand seems to have selected for literate husbands. It was not that brides preferred literate husbands, but that they preferred respectable and skilled decent men, who were more likely to be literate, to the unskilled.

The lower marriage chances of unskilled men may be due partly to lower chances of meeting potential brides. Unskilled males had a greater tendency to live in male-only camps, and not in gender-balanced core settlements, than did skilled males. But women's preferences were probably also a factor, and there are signs that they stubbornly preferred no husband at all to an unsuitable one. A significant minority never married – perhaps something like the fifteen per cent of adult women who were unmarried in 1881. In England, only 12 per cent of women never married.[49] Migration may not have yielded more husbands but better ones. The average age of brides was around 23 – three or four years younger than their husbands. In the light of the disproportion of males, the great colonial bride hunt, 'it is surprising that the age at which women married for a first time was not lower'.[50]

Research on social mobility – promotion and demotion – in the recolonial era, from the 1880s, suggests that movement was quite common but slow, proceeding in small steps over more than one generation.[51] While there are examples of large and rapid promotions in a single lifetime, the same was probably true in the preceding colonial era – though perhaps to a lesser degree because the progressive colonisation of fresh regions and industries supplied more opportunity. A classic route of getting on began with the marriage of a decent woman to a skilled man of the same class. The two then proceeded in tandem to build an independency. The woman worked in the business, doubling her remuneration but maintaining the respectable illusion that she did not work. 'My father was an umbrella maker and had his own shop. My mother helped with the sewing of the umbrellas, but she never went out to work.' Another woman's mother 'didn't work for pay after she married, but she worked in the business with my father . . . Women didn't work in those days.'[52]

A woman-led drive for promotion to respectable independency, in which selective marriage was part though not the whole of the strategy, has at least two interesting implications. First, it means that the unskilled majority of working men feature larger in Pakeha history than they do in ancestry, which may have contributed to an underestimation of their role in the former, and of the progress industries they crewed. They had reduced chances of becoming fathers, and it was they, rather than Maori, who ultimately suffered a form of fatal impact. These matters are discussed further in the next chapter. Second, the fortunate section of unskilled men who did manage to marry were best placed, and perhaps best motivated, of all unskilled men to achieve open independencies – notably farms.

The archetypal example of the colonial self-made man was the 'unskilled' labourer who became a small farmer. Such a man might save enough for the deposit on a block of raw bush from his wages but was less well placed than the skilled to save the cash, or obtain the credit, for development costs. 'Outwork', contract or wage labour outside the proto-farm, could be a substitute, but this was not as easily compatible with farming and farm formation as some assume. If you were working out, you were not working in. If you were helping someone else with bush clearing, sewing, harvesting or calving in the optimal season, then you were not doing your own. You needed to bring some land into production quickly to free the wages of outwork for stock, seed, equipment and imported supplies. The concept of outwork can be expanded to include farm formation itself, bush clearing and ploughing-in, as against actual productive farming. In the absence of substantial cash or credit, the best chance of turning land into a farm required that outwork and inwork occur simultaneously through a partnership of two people, usually a marriage. The husband was normally the outworker; the wife the inworker. During the process of farm formation, which in bush country could take up to 30 years, it was the inworker who did most actual farming. It seems to follow that, in the early decades of settlement, the literally *self-made* pioneer small farmer, starting from nothing, was likely to be a woman.

This fits well with what we know of the actual division of labour on small farms. Apart from domestic work and management, motherhood, childcare and child training, and the myriad of import-substitution activities such as dressmaking, candle making, food processing and medical care, the woman's domain included herb and vegetable gardens, dairying and poultry. Often it also included pigs, orchards, potato fields and beehives. Small farms in the process of establishment would not have had much else. They seldom ran substantial herds of sheep or beef cattle, and cropping on any scale had to follow bush felling, stump clearing and ploughing-in. Their produce was mainly fresh food for local markets, or provisions, and it was often produced by women. Even on a larger farm like that of Adela and Hugh Stewart in the Bay of Plenty, Adela made butter, salted and spiced beef, and smoked fish, some of it for sale, and sold lemons, onions, cucumber, tomatoes and honey from hives she herself maintained. She sold up to 10,000 eggs per annum, together with 200 ducks and chickens, made £18 selling cut flowers in one month, and spent at least one 'busy morning plucking godwits'. Hugh ran a small flock of sheep and a few cattle, rather inexpertly. Adela's profits were called 'pin money'; Hugh's were called 'farm income', but at around £100 a year the former may well have exceeded the latter.[53]

Becoming a sturdy yeowoman was an improvement in the decent woman's lot in her own terms. It increased her centrality in the family economy, doubled the value placed on her saleable production and improved her security. We should not, of course, simply reverse the pendulum and understate the role of hardworking, admirable and indispensable farmers' husbands. Their outwork was clearly vital to the process of small-farm formation from a standing start. As valuable to their wives as any patent plough, they were true colonial helpmeets. Myth, history and folklore subsequently inverted the actual relationship between the sturdy colonial yeowoman and her husband. 'The farmer and his wife', used in the above context, was a contemporary myth that subsequently became true. The 'farmer's wife' was portrayed as a hardworking, indispensable, admirable adjunct to a masculine occupation, but an adjunct all the same.

Women's gains were reined in – sometimes as they were being made. The infrequent redistribution of large cash wage packets, like large seals or moa, could yield more status and control within the family than the frequent distribution of small items of produce such as eggs or cabbages. Factors such as this combined with legal disadvantages, especially before the Married Women's Property Act of 1884, to enable men to sometimes appropriate the profits of women's work. In the longer terms, as orcharding, poultry and pig farming, market gardening and – above all – dairying became formalised and profitable industries, men took them over, as they had done aspects of Maori gardening and gathering, and projected their dominance back in time. The incentive to mythologise was strong because male dairy farmers preferred not to be reminded that they were doing what their fathers might have seen as women's work. Technical pioneers like Isabel Button in horse racing, Edith Halcombe in Jersey cattle breeding, and Marion Stewart in poultry farming became marginal in the industries they had helped found. Button competed successfully in training and racing trotting horses until 1896, when new rules in racing clubs forced women out. In the early twentieth century, Stewart published articles on poultry farming under her initials, because she was 'not allowed to reveal that she was a woman.' She noted that men had taken over the industry 'now that it pays well'.[54]

Furthermore, greater independence, security and centrality did not necessarily compensate for drowning in pregnancy and drudgery. An Otago pioneer woman wrote: 'I used to have sixteen hours a day cooking, washing, ironing, sewing, and mending.' She also listed making butter, baking bread, salting meat, gathering wood, clarifying tallow and making candles, omitted cleaning, childcare and much else, and added: 'In my spare time I milked three cows.' Standards of housekeeping might be lower than in higher classes and later times; older children were a major help; and extract of opium might be used to keep younger children quiet. But respectable independency often involved greater pressure for clean clothes and clean doorsteps and, even when it did not, running home, family and farm, with fewer facilities and community support than in older societies, was almost unimaginably hard. Servantless women in colonial New Zealand must have almost disappeared under vast families and staggering volumes of work.

Pregnancy was often permanent. 'Mum's hobby was having babies. She seemed to be always pregnant . . . If she wasn't having a baby one year, she was losing it. She had to go down to the well in the daytime to draw water and she'd have a miscarriage. Where there is two years in between us, she miscarried in between . . . it followed with having all the heavy work to do.'[55] Successful pregnancy may well have seemed an escape from the frying pan into the fire. One group of Canterbury families averaged 9.3 children, and the overall average in 1876 was seven live births each.[56]

These children were brought up by inworking mothers and older sisters more than by outworking fathers, and investing affection in them was risky, though it was still done. A stroll through any old cemetery reveals the interest death took in young children in the nineteenth century. What would now be seen as minor ailments struck fear into parental hearts, and children half expected the death of siblings. When Martha Adam's baby took sick, her nine-year-old son asked, 'Mother, where must I dig the grave for the baby, up the valley?'[57] Fathers suffered here too, of course, and dying infants suffered worst of all, but it is mothers' memoirs and letters that change tone for a few painful pages, losing their cheer. Lady Barker's jolly tome took time out for a chapter on 'Death in Our New Home' – a home 'baptized, as it were, with tears', and similar agony can be read in the child-death diary entries and letters of women missionaries.[58] Infant mortality was an important incentive for the maintenance of religious faith – 'little angels only lent' – and burying their dead, especially their young dead, increased the migrant sense of belonging. Colonial New Zealand women did get on, through waged and unwaged work, marriage, promotion, enhancement, adoption and custom shedding, but personal progress had its price, in drudgery, pregnancy, sadness and loneliness.

Getting On Top

Between the genteel and decent upper and lower classes, there were at least three tiers of middle-class respectability. The highest were wealthy farmers, urban business families and manufacturers who either chose not to take on genteel class culture, or who were not accepted into it because they could not muster the necessary modicum of genteel characteristics. My impression is that the highly respectable were not numerous in the colonial era. The temptation to join the gentry if you could was considerable; there were more routes of entry than in Britain, and the gates were open somewhat wider. The compromise between gentility and respectability may have made the former less objectionable to those of Dissenting religion, who in England would have considered the gentry frivolous or immoral. There were significant exceptions, however.

As in Britain, some wealthy respectables – usually Dissenting or evangelical by religion, and often from northern English manufacturing backgrounds – did not aspire to the effete and ungodly trappings of gentility. In the late 1850s, for example, the woollen-mill owner Joseph Preston took his £50,000 out of Yorkshire and sunk it in the other end of the wool industry – Otago sheep stations. The Prestons and some other respectable Otago runholders allegedly had no aspirations to gentility – no town house, large mansion, governess or public schools.[59] Auckland farmer and speculator John Dilworth and Nelson shipping agent Thomas Cawthron built up fortunes of £150,000 and £230,000 respectively but appear to have had modest lifestyles, few pretensions to gentility and a preference for unspectacular, though massive, philanthropy.[60]

Towards the end of the colonial era, a group of professional managers also began to emerge, emphasising businesslike, expert professionalism rather than genteel professionalism. These private sector bureaucrats were more organisationally efficient than their genteel predecessors, but less bold and entrepreneurial. They were managers of sustainable economics rather than extractive, madly booming and busting progress. James Mill, son of a migrant carpenter, who built the giant shipping company Union Steam Ship Co. from Johnny Jones's merchant flotilla, was transitional between the two types of management. Partly a prototype of the recolonial manager and a pioneer of its credo, which preferred cartelism to competition, he also became an accepted member of the genteel-respectable Dunedin élite.[61] The new managerial category appears to have been rare, subordinate or both before 1890.

Wealthy manufacturers were perhaps another category of exception to the rule of a genteel élite. In northern England, factory owners lent considerable strength to the upper-middle class. Josiah Clifton Firth, of Congregationalist Yorkshire manufacturing background, came of this stock, maintained its type of economic activity in New Zealand and perhaps deliberately maintained its class culture as well. He became extremely wealthy before his fall; crusaded with great energy; founded Pakeha Matamata; had landed estates, a mini-castle and close connections with Russell's Limited Circle and its diverse speculations. Yet he seems to have operated somewhat apart from the Circle; served as a private in the Waikato War; had radical, even pacifist, sympathies; and took special pride in the technology of his giant timber mill, 'reputed to be the most up-to-date in the world'.[62]

In New Zealand, large factories were scarce, and some of those that did exist were owned by entrepreneurial gentlemen, or corporate collections of them. This was most true of industrially organised mines and mills. The self-made large manufacturer was probably a little more common than the Firths and Prestons. Henry Shacklock, a prominent stove manufacturer, began as a tradesman, became a master tradesman, and built up his factory from there. Shacklock 'remained at heart an ironmaster', first among peers as far as his employees were concerned – more like a super-master artisan than a later nineteenth-century Yorkshire mill owner, and certainly not genteel. Other major names in colonial manufacturing, such as Thomas Kempthorne in pharmaceuticals, Robert Hannah in shoes, and James Gear in meat products – each boosted by the gold rushes – also had artisan roots, but it is not clear whether they stuck to them. Gear retired to his estate with his meat fortune and described himself as a 'settler' – in some contexts, this term conveyed considerable substance until well into the twentieth century. But he may be the 'butcher' who was tolerated at some genteel Wellington social functions yet sneered at behind his back.[63] Self-making into gentry was relatively easy from an educated respectable background but not from an uneducated decent one. Promotion from there normally had to wait for the next generation.

At the bottom tier of respectability were the fortunate, married minority of unskilled workers who made it into independency, discussed above. Many small farms were economically marginal until the 1890s. The other traditional component of this 'lower middle class' were white-collar workers, office-working subordinates of genteel officials, merchants and bankers. This group was not very prominent or numerous before the 1880s. Between top and bottom, however, was a more successful group, a middle-middle class: small but secure businessmen, master artisans and medium farmers. Most had either a little money, credit or formal skill to start with, or had received a boost from progress and its allies, or took a long time to build up their substance, or all three. These middle respectables were by definition *local*; they had to stay put, or at least simulate staying put. Occupational mobility could stand in for geographical. After careers as soldier and goldfields publican, who served both Julius Vogel and an elephant in his Victorian pub, James Bodell sunk roots into Tauranga from the 1860s and accumulated assets worth £4,000 by 1878. He 'got on' through occupational versatility, a census taker's nightmare. He was a farmer, auctioneer and commission agent, port official, photographer, gingerbeer wholesaler, gold prospector, grocer, real estate agent, insurance agent, general merchant, cattle buyer, debt collector, timber miller, shipowner, brewer, barber and undertaker. In small towns, 'it was particularly common for hotel keepers and storekeepers to have a wide range of occupations'.[64] Like the self-made yeomen, middle respectables – local worthies – were an archetypal colonial group; unlike them, they were archetypal in reality as well as legend. These Cyclopedians were the epitome of solid colonial citizenry; one could list examples forever, which is just what their *Cyclopedia* did.[65]

A few respectables rose to regional or national prominence before the 1880s. Artisan-teacher-storekeeper John Robinson, who had been involved in radical agitation in 1830s England before migrating in 1843, was Superintendent of Nelson between 1856 and his death by drowning in 1865. He was elected and re-elected in explicit opposition to a genteel clique known as the 'Supper Party'. Charles Carter and John Masters were, with the help of Governor Grey, leaders of the Small Farm Association, which established islands of close settlement among the sheep runs of the Wairarapa between 1853 and 1867. All three of these men, like proto-unionist 'Eight Hours' Parnell, rose to respectability from skilled decency and made their mark on the young colony. Some middle respectables made their way into provincial councils, the colonial Parliament and even Cabinets. Irish Catholic farmer-publican Patrick Dignan, who immigrated to Auckland in 1841, gradually made it to prosperity and to local, provincial, and central politics, though he 'rarely spoke in the House'.[66] Jeweller and newspaper editor John Ballance, goldfields publican and storekeeper Richard John Seddon, and farmer John Bryce became names to conjure with from the 1880s. But the number of regionally or nationally prominent respectables was small before the 1880s, and their influence was greatest at the local level.

Middle respectables were the quintessential small-town élite, leaders of the 'settled core'. In such towns and their surrounding districts, the small businessmen and master artisans of Main Street and the solid medium farmers of the surrounding countryside carried weight. These three groups were prominent in street directories, in public meetings and in local voluntary organisations, notably friendly societies or lodges – Oddfellows, Freemasons and Rechabites. In infant Hastings, they made up almost three-quarters of the town's freeholders. Between 1886 and 1901, only a little outside our period, artisans (seven), shopkeepers (six) and businessmen (six) held nineteen of 27 positions on the borough council, compared with four for sheep farmers, three for professionals and one for working men.[67] A fourth respectable subgroup was the managers of the camps, mills and mines of the progress industry.

The balance of power between these middle-class subgroups shifted over time and space. In the colonial era, medium farmers more often followed the lead of the other groups than they did subsequently. The spokesman for all four groups was often the local newspaper editor: town booster and local crusading propagandist par excellence. Sometimes respectable district elders saw their interests as conflicting with those of the local gentry, if any; sometimes they were thought to converge. In keeping with the rules of colonial populism, the villain of land monopoly and selfish genteel class interest was often someone else's gentleman. Middle respectables were significant in most places, but their ascendancy appears to have been greatest where the gentry were weakest. This may have exaggerated their association with small towns and their districts. It was not that middle respectables were absent in the main towns and their hinterlands – on the contrary, they were numerous – but that the gentry were present, and on top.

Traditionally, the New Zealand gentry have been associated with sheep farming, and it was certainly one of their citadels. Sheep farming had the highest private entry cost of the three great groups of industries – from £2,000 to £5,000 was variously estimated as the minimum to start and stock a viable leasehold run. Among the pre-1860 settlers at least, it was the gentry who were most likely to have this kind of money. Genteel manners and connections also improved one's access to credit and wealthy partners. There was therefore an early marriage between sheep and gentry, though it was not so universal as some historians imply. Apart from the Prestons and their ilk, some decent folk became self-made sheeplords, perhaps the ultimate in 'getting on'. There was a window of opportunity early in the sheep-rush phase for shepherds, many of them Highland Scots. Their skills were scarce, their wages high, promotion to manager was possible, and leasing land was cheap. Sheep were expensive, but urban gentry were sometimes willing to supply capital to highly skilled sheepmen for a share of the profits. Among 37 of the earliest Wairarapa runholders, no fewer than eleven were shepherds, ten of them Scots.[68] The most successful worker-sheeplords of all were the Hebridean brothers Allan and John McLean. Beginning as shepherds and then runholders in Victoria, they boosted their fortunes supplying the Victorian goldfields, moved to Canterbury in 1852, and held 500,000 South Island acres in 1858. Although 'a somewhat eccentric figure', Allan McLean behaved quite genteelly, entertaining lavishly, retiring to a 23,000-square-foot, 53-room wooden mansion in Christchurch and endowing 'a home for women of refinement and education in reduced or straitened circumstances'.[69]

The McLeans were typical in that sheeplords were disproportionately prone to be Scots and to have had Australian experience. But they were not typical in beginning as working class. Generally, a frugal shepherd could save enough money for his own run in a couple of centuries. Seventy per cent of an 1850s sample of Otago runholders were well educated – there was 'undoubtedly a preponderance of well-educated young men from good families'. At least 77 per cent of a large 1866 sample of South Island large landowners had genteel backgrounds, and only one per cent were working class.[70] The humble minority of sheeplords took advantage of early and exceptional windows of opportunity, were boosted by the progress industry and its allies, or rose to the top in a long series of small steps. They may have been more likely than Nonconformist respectables to try to take on genteel lifeways, or ensure that their children did so.

On the whole, the convention that sheep country was gentry country seems to stand up, but sheeplords were never the only New Zealand gentry. Two urban groups could also be genteel, on our definition and their own: merchants, financiers and some other types of big businessmen; and professionals such as lawyers, doctors, clergy, military officers and government officials. Some gentry lived in both town and country, as in England, without it being clear which was the second home. In town, a few lived as 'pure' gentlemen, without direct involvement in the management of their investments. But many blatantly engaged in trade.

John Logan Campbell agonised about just how far into trade he could stoop. Campbell, the grandson of a baronet, cherished his gentility – indeed, his standards were untypically high. He qualified as a medical doctor but did not practise, made his fortune as a merchant, then recouped it partly as a pastoralist but mainly as a brewer. He found the 'keg trade' a 'disgusting business . . . particularly disagreeable and distasteful'. It was not for moral reasons – 'I drink my pint of good burgundy nearly daily', and his wife Emma found a drop of cognac 'like the cut of a whip to a tired horse'. It was because 'it is not gentleman's work . . . We ran the risk of being put in coventry by any spiteful person setting it abroad that we were mere chandlers.' Like Mary Taylor, Campbell was exceptional, but his contemporaries understood his obsession with gentility. His partner William Brown tried to comfort him. 'I don't think [wine merchants] come down from undefined "Merchants" – rather better I fancy, for "wine Merchants" rank next if not equal to "Bankers" or money merchants.'[71] In the country, embryo sheeplords learned to rough it, reading Greek under a blanket on two forked sticks, living on mutton, tea and damper, and actually lending a hand in, as well as supervising, the mustering, dipping and shearing. This helped raise the status of manual labour – not only because manual workers were more respected as people, but because manual work had to be less disdained – and so made its contribution to colonial populism. It did not eliminate genteel culture.

There was never a rigid divide between the rural and urban wings of the New Zealand gentry. The first Wairarapa runs were partly funded by Wellington merchants, who took shares in the flocks of their friends, the pioneer pastoralists. As time went on, the links between urban and rural wings multiplied and strengthened, though the balances between them varied regionally. The Wellington socio-economy continued to be led by a pastoral-mercantile élite, with the latter wing increasingly dominant from about 1870. Mercantile 'control of the rural sector was effectively maintained through scale of personal holdings, through liens and a network of nominee arrangements, and through monopoly of the means of supplying and servicing rural properties'.[72] In Auckland, where pastoralism was unimportant, the mercantile wing was always dominant, but it, too, developed many landed interests. Before self-government took full effect and the capital moved south to Wellington, in the mid-1860s, a genteel official group, centred on the governors, was somewhat distinct from the economic élite, centred on Thomas Russell. Thereafter, economic and official élites tended to merge. In Canterbury, the balance between merchants and pastoralists favoured the latter much more than in Auckland and more than in Wellington. But even in their Canterbury stronghold, many sheeplords had urban investments, town houses and mercantile links.[73]

In Scots and Presbyterian Otago, middle-class virtues such as the work ethic were highly valued. Perhaps partly for this reason, its historians are reluctant to call the provincial élite 'genteel'. Yet, of the business élite estimated to have made up the top 4 per cent of the city's population, 'almost all' were well educated, enrolled their sons at the two public schools, belonged to the two 'gentlemen's clubs' and were interlocked with a rural wing. 'In partnership with the wealthiest estate holders, to whom they were tied by business and kin links, they constituted an informal board of directors for the provincial economy.'[74] It may be true to say that the Otago élite – and the Auckland élite, for different reasons – were subculturally *less* genteel and more respectable than those of Canterbury and Wellington. But, given a time machine, would historians have been willing to tell the Cargills that they were not gentlemen? In other regions, the balances between merchants and pastoralists, genteel and respectable, varied as in the big four. Pastoralism and gentility were strong in Marlborough and Hawke's Bay, weak in Taranaki and very weak in Westland. The two pairs were more evenly balanced in Nelson and Southland.

This urban-rural colonial élite is best described as a gentry, or the upper class, for a variety of reasons. It is not clear, as noted earlier, that you can have a middle without a top, or that the definition of gentility as untitled aristocracy, still often applied by New Zealand historians, is sufficiently broad. The élite saw themselves as genteel; tone-setting elements would have been recognised as such in Britain and had connections with the British gentry. Promotion was easier and definitions were broader than in Britain, where they were easing and broadening anyway, but the gates were kept. To enter, you had to take on a sufficient modicum of genteel culture. This culture, or subculture, was maintained in New Zealand – looser, compromised and colonial, but still marked. The gentry did not simply maintain their lifeways as individuals and families, but interacted, networking from the outset. At first these networks were local, then regional, then national. The gentry did not directly dominate colonial society as individuals, ruling particular fiefs; their direct vertical grip on the rest of society was quite weak, and countervailing populist forces were strong. But the gentry grouped faster than other classes; they had a greater geographical reach; they benefited more from progress and its allies as well as wool; and they benefited from the prevailing populist belief that democracy consisted in choosing your rulers, not in being them. They were therefore able to dominate, though by no means monopolise, some forms of power. The remainder of this chapter explores these issues.

A study of novels written before 1914 and set in New Zealand indicates that the archetypal colonial hero was honest, moral and unpretentious, prepared to carry his own bags at a pinch and scrupulous in his populist denial of the importance of class – of class conflict and excessive distance, that is. But he was still very much the gentleman. Fictional New Zealand gentlewomen were less helpless than their British mothers – heroines rode well, villainesses did not – but they were still ladies.[75] The characteristics of colonial gentility included genteel manners, customs, dress and accent; at least the appearance of genteel education (much genteel correspondence assumes a knowledge of French, and some of Greek and Latin as well); entrée to 'society', genteel connections and creditworthiness; a genteel residence, other property and a genteel occupation, or none at all. Ungenteel people might have some of these things, and one did not have to have them all to be genteel – about three-quarters would do. If you did not possess the necessary modicum, you might be marginalised and mocked, however wealthy.

Genteel customs of interaction and hospitality were maintained. Foes 'cut' each other dead in the street, friends called, acquaintances or properly introduced strangers left their cards. Balls, parties and dinners were held, sometimes with colonial adaptations at which commentators sneered or found droll, such as getting to balls by bullock dray, and packing-case dinners. 'Candles in black bottles barely concealed by ivy, and the entrée, oyster patties, appeared after dessert!'[76] Gentlemen's clubs were established very quickly as homes away from home for the male élite. There were efforts, inconsistent and not uniformly successful, to recruit officers for the colonial militia and regular forces from the gentry. Colonel Whitmore for one insisted on this. Commissions helped confirm gentility. Those who served even a few months as captain in an obscure corps tended to keep the title for life, though we will see that it did not necessarily confer much practical authority. Duelling, a genteel form of population control, was not unknown in the 1840s, when at least two duellists were killed and three wounded. The real figure may be higher, because the custom was illegal and therefore concealed. Leading colonial civil servant, the mild and genteel William Gisborne, considered himself honour-bound to duel after a piece of fruit was thrown at him at a ball – there is confusion as to whether the offending object was an apple or an orange.[77] Visiting opera companies and French wines found a ready market, as did makers of family crests, though respectable 'adopters' may have been among the buyers of all three. Above all, servants, marriage, schooling, wealth and politics served to maintain the colonial versions of genteel class culture, and to convert it to class community.

There is ample evidence of a widespread, large-scale and persistent hunt for domestic servants in colonial New Zealand. As suggested above, this in itself implies a strong desire among the élite to maintain gentility. Servants were useful to respectability but vital to gentility. Young gentry could survive servantless for brief periods but not permanently. Servants provided the necessary leisure for their masters and mistresses to engage in the activities that buttressed genteel culture, such as socialising, charity, genteel sport and politics. They permitted genteel tribal rituals, such as the calling system, and lavish hospitality, with guests often staying overnight. The calling system involved uninvited ritual visits where hosts had the option of declaring themselves nominally absent. But you could not tell callers yourself that you were 'not at home'. As Adela Stewart and other ladies discovered, genteel hospitality was very difficult without servants – not so much in the cooking department, where colonial compromisers could cope, but in serving while others ate, danced and bonded. Holding genteel hui enhanced the mana of the host and allowed the bonding of networks into community. In colonial Canterbury, a 'Flying

Squadron' of young gentry, the Sloane Rangers of Erewhon, attended every social function over a wide spread of stations, mixing fun and class formation.

The very rich had domestic staffs of half a dozen, occasionally even a dozen, mostly female, with grooms, coachmen and gardeners outside the house. Butlers were rare, and female cooks – who were called 'Mrs', married or not – were often the senior servant.[78] Substantial staffs were exceptional. In 1901, only two per cent of servants worked in homes employing three or more. The percentage would have been higher earlier. Under the colonial compromise, however, and given that ritual was as important as the volume of work, one overworked servant was enough, and one or two was the norm. This meant that, though there was a constant struggle with the drive of young single women to keep their domestic service as brief as possible, gentility was able to obtain just enough servants to survive. A maximum of sixteen to eighteen per cent of households had servants between 1874 and 1896, assuming that each census 'servant' represented a servant-keeping household. Because some houses had more than one, and some 'servants' worked in hotels and the like, the real figure is likely to have been closer to eleven to thirteen per cent.[79] Some upper and even middle respectable families had a servant too, but these figures do represent an upper limit on the numbers of the gentry.

Another function of servant-facilitated hospitality was to provide for the closed courtship necessary for in-marriage within a single class. Many a marriage among the small Tauranga élite of the late nineteenth century had its origins at Adela Stewart's parties at her house, Athenree. In 1881, she, Hugh and their current servant, Agnes, hosted 50 people to dinner, quoits, tennis, high tea, dancing, and supper at midnight, followed by soup at two in the morning. The party ended at three, but nineteen guests stayed the night and for breakfast and a picnic the next day. Poor Agnes. This was only one of many functions at which 'flirtations, engagements, weddings were the order of the day, many of the former two taking place at Athenree!'[80] Tennis and parties were important in genteel courtship. Genteel children remembered 'lots of parties' in private homes; ungenteel children did not.[81] The marriage might not be arranged by parents, but the context in which it was made was. Cross-class matches did take place, but scandal tended to exaggerate their number. Of a sample of South Island large landowners, 75 per cent of males married into their own class, despite the shortage of brides, and the genteel Wellington élite was also very endogamous.[82]

Schooling was a crucial means of both genteel gate-keeping and promotion to gentility. A high proportion of migrant gentry were very well educated – 112 of 360 South Island large landowners in 1866 had been to university, mainly Oxford and Cambridge, and Christchurch was named after an Oxford college by a nostalgic old boy. Such parents wanted at least basic genteel educations for their children but for some years relied on a patchwork of measures to achieve this. Governesses, tutors, educational sojourns in Britain and even home teaching by parents may have been initially important, but very small private schools appear to have become the mainstay quite quickly. Private 'academies', like that of the Misses Dodd for Dunedin's young ladies, offered music, French, drawing, embroidery, and presumably reading, writing and reckoning, for substantial fees of up to £80 per annum – a lucky labourer's whole wage. Timaru had nine such schools in 1869, as much for the neighbouring sheeplords as for the 1,400 locals.

'Public' secondary schools for boys emerged quite quickly, endowed with land from the public estate but also charging heavy fees for both day pupils and boarders. Christ's College, Christchurch, was founded in 1855; Nelson College in 1856; Otago Boys' High School in 1863; and Wanganui Collegiate in 1865. From the 1870s, numbers grew, girls were catered for too, universities emerged and the patchwork of genteel education grew into a network.[83] Despite some free places, it was generally restricted to genteel children, and to respectable children whose families had aspirations. It appears to have catered for fewer than three per cent of children of the relevant ages between 1875 and 1900, and a major component of its curricula was gentility.[84] Very private schools that do not feature in the statistics probably supplemented this figure somewhat, but they, too, were often for the genteel. Schooling helped select respectables to enter the gentry, but also helped keep out everybody else, bond the junior élite, and their parents too, through boards of governors and the like.

Money made money, and it made most for the gentry. Although few arrived with vast fortunes, many migrant gentry did have some capital or capital credit. Because their arrival was biased towards the earlier half of the colonial period, they derived more benefit from the first-in factor. They had better access to credit and moneyed partners than any other class, and privileged access to the 'public' companies that burgeoned from 1860. Companies, partnerships and personal contacts increased their reach. Unlike other classes, they could extend financial tentacles to fresh outcrops of progress without shifting themselves. They were an able, entrepreneurial, speculative group, addicted to the progressive colonisation they themselves pushed. They were bolder than the succeeding generation of managers; some were so bold that they overreached themselves, even before the 1880s. There were regional, periodic and personal busts as well as booms, but booms predominated to the late 1870s. There were hundreds of gentry with assets of over £20,000, scores with over £50,000 and dozens with over £100,000 – just how many hundreds, scores and dozens it is at present impossible to say. But the assumption that large personal fortunes were very rare is inaccurate. Such fortunes were greatly culled and reduced in the 1880s. Individual wealth was sometimes shakily based on credit, speculation and inflated prices – thousands attempted their own colonising crusades. Wealth was restricted to an élite of gentry and upper respectables. But wealth there was, and it came from progress and its allies as well as sheep.

While there was sometimes serious competition at regional and local levels, and while neither the respectable nor the decent could ever be dismissed, the gentry appear to have had a firm grip on political power from the advent of the provinces in 1853 until 1890. There were high turnovers in provincial councils and the colonial House of Representatives. Up to 54 per cent of MHRs in a given Parliament might be novices.[85] But a core of colonial politicians changed very slowly and, old or new, the great majority were genteel. Of 62 Wellington City provincial councillors, 79 per cent were 'high white collar', and 73 per cent had arrived before 1853. The 'high white collar' category consisted of merchants, pastoralists and professionals – gentry on our definition, with a few possible exceptions. Of the 40 Wellington MHRs elected by 1896, 87.5 per cent were high white collar, and 23 had arrived before 1860. Not one man from five other occupational categories was elected to Parliament for Wellington before 1884. Genteel dominance of Wellington local government was less marked but still strong.[86] These figures may well be indicative of the whole colony. The genteel grip on politics was somewhat weaker in Nelson and Westland, and possibly in Auckland and Otago. But it may have been even stronger in Canterbury, Marlborough and Hawke's Bay.

Among the dozen colonial premiers between 1856 and 1884, the only person who might not have been recognised as genteel was Sir Julius Vogel, and that would have been partly on grounds of anti-Semitism. Ten of the twelve had arrived before 1853, and eight had been New Zealand Company colonists. At the local level, genteel dominance was less complete. We have seen that in Hastings, middle respectables were a large majority on the borough council – nineteen out of 27, or 70 per cent. But the genteel minority, four sheep farmers and three professionals, tended to serve much longer terms. They contributed only 25 per cent of members but over 50 per cent of years in office. The local mercantile-pastoral gentry, Thomas Tanner, J. N. Williams, and William Russell and other 'Apostles', did not wholly dominate the infant town, but they did exercise grossly disproportionate influence. Apart from the borough council, 'sheepfarmers controlled the Hawke's Bay Education Board as well as the school committee, though their children attended private schools'. William Russell, the local member of Parliament, 'was the acknowledged political and social leader of Hastings'.[87]

The gentry rapidly networked themselves into tight regional élites partly through pre-migration links, shared voyages and settlement experiences, and voluntary organisations. These means of bonding applied to all classes of early settlers but affected gentry more because they stayed put more and regularly interacted more. These élites were regional, not national, to the 1860s – they were still some way short of a national class community. They shared power with respectables to a considerable extent in some regions and localities. But there were more important constraints on their rule than this. One was the weakness of the vertical grip of the gentry on society, noted above. Particular gentry did have informal fiefs of employees, tenants and clients linked to them by loans and patronage. The Hastings example suggests that, even outside such fiefs, local gentry could wield considerable influence on their localities. Vertical slices of allegiance owed to a specific gentleman or genteel family can be underestimated. But they still covered only a minority of the population. Great estates in 1891 averaged only a dozen servants and permanent labourers each.[88] Tenants, clients and semi-dependent or beholden neighbours would have boosted this number, but not very much, and less in large towns than in the country and in small towns. The gentry were indirect, collective rulers, not direct, individual ones. Their rule depended less on the sum of powerful parts than in their power as groups, discussed further in the next chapter.

The gentry were united on fundamental principles, such as maintaining their rule, dominating the Maori and pushing progressive colonisation. Beyond this, there were divisions among genteel politicians, often bitter, and this limited their effectiveness. The label 'Continuous Ministry' was restricted to the governments of 1870–90, and was more a contemporary term of abuse than a historical reality even then – except perhaps in the period 1869–77, when changes in ministry were less important than the continuity of Vogel's progressive colonisation campaign.[89] Individuals and cliques oscillated between poles on particular issues, of which centralism versus provincialism was the most clear-cut. Pork-barrel politics, obtaining the maximum public expenditure for your constituency, and parochial provincialism and localism were common. But it is not true to say that they were universal. The leading colonial premier, Edward Stafford, who led and ran both the government and the civil service for two-thirds of the period 1856–70, was emphatically nationalist from the outset. Feud and faction revolved as much around personalities and power struggles as issues, and they were bitter. Stafford's closest associates, including J. C. Richmond, described him as 'a bragging Irishman and a mountebank', a 'ripping snob'. 'If he was not such a snob – he'd be a capital fellow no doubt – but he is a cad and all his other qualifications are lost in that,' wrote Whitmore from his glasshouse.[90] What Stafford's enemies said can be left to the imagination. Both he and his arch-rival William Fox were flawed but very clever gentlemen, and Stafford at least was also an effective organiser.

There was also some division along liberal–conservative lines. The terms were used loosely, and often as terms of abuse, just as they are today. Pressure for 'closer settlement' – for the replacement of large sheep runs with small farms – was sometimes associated with 'Liberal' politics. It increased from the 1860s, notably in Otago, and sometimes brought conservatism out of the closet in reaction, especially among large leaseholders whose lands were vulnerable to it. But it was supported by many gentry. Some hoped to profit from the increased land values closer settlement brought about; some genuinely believed that the country needed yeomen to make it flower; and some recognised that populist forces had to be propitiated. George Grey emerged from retirement shooting bulls at Kawau to lead a crusade against 'conservative' centralism. His was the first nominally 'Liberal' government, 1877–79. Stafford, the arch-centralist, who helped convert Vogel on this issue, was a Tory, or conservative, but he was a populist one, an admirer of Peel and Disraeli. He actively supported the secret ballot (finally introduced in 1871) and the widening of the franchise, and he appointed Donald Reid, leader of the Otago closer settlement movement, to his short-lived ministry in 1872. But he was no radical democrat. 'The lower class would always trust and elect gentlemen,' he once declared. They were 'too jealous of rising men of their own class' to elect them. Until the 1880s, he was generally quite right. This brings us to the most important constraint on genteel rule of all: the populist compact, or Pakeha treaty, whose roots were discussed in Chapter Thirteen.

Indirect and limited genteel rule never meant that decent and respectable adult men were politically powerless. While claims that the adult male franchise was virtually universal from the outset are exaggerated, the property qualification was very low and quite easily evadable. Miners were even exempted from it in 1866, and transience and apathy towards politics were probably as important in restricting the enrolled electorate, which was equivalent to at least 60 per cent of the adult male population in 1855. The ratio of electors to adult males dipped in the 1860s to under half, then rose to about 57 per cent in 1871, 67 per cent in 1879, and 84 per cent in 1881.[91] The gentry did not keep the decent and respectable out of the political nation, and many would not have wanted to if they could. The prevailing view, across classes, was that democracy consisted in being able to select your rulers from the 'natural' ruling class. This was matter of attitudes as well as money. Colonial parliamentarians received no salary, but they did receive a sitting allowance of £1 a day, which would have yielded £140 in the long session of 1877. Working men simply did not expect to be their own rulers, but increasingly they did expect that their rulers would meet certain conditions prescribed by the populist compact.

Article one of this treaty was that class distinctions, while allowed, should not be too oppressive or overt, and that a superficial but significant egalitarianism be maintained in some contexts, such as forms of dress and address. Gentlemen proved they were real gentlemen by not topping it the nob. Absentee landowner Sir Henry Young, on a rare visit to his estate of Omarama, treated his employees with too much disdain. He was mocked to his face, burned in effigy, and left in a fury.[92] The gentry might be natural rulers, natural incumbents of high political and economic office, arbiters of their own high society, but they were not natural leaders in other contexts. While Whitmore and other strong personalities could establish some sway, genteel but junior colonial officers do not seem to have had the authority over their men that English landowners might have had over their tenants in uniform in a war fought in nineteenth-century England. In the emergencies, routs and mutinies of Titokowaru's war, it tended to be sergeants, not officers, who did the leading. Even Whitmore is alleged to have abused a drunken soldier with the words: 'You are drunk, sir.' The soldier responded: 'Well I am drunk but I'll get over that; but you're a fool and you'll never get over that.' The story may be apocryphal, but it is hard to imagine its even being told about the Duke of Wellington.[93] There was a tension between formal and informal leadership. The gentry might rule as a class; they might rule their own employees, tenants and clients as individuals; but they did not exercise much 'natural authority' over other collections of colonials.

Article two of the populist compact was that classes work in harmony rather than in the selfish pursuit of class interest, and that overt, tight class community be discouraged. While not universal, this view was very pervasive, and it crossed class. It was clear in colonial newspapers. 'The newspaper was argued to be the voice of the community rather than of a section of a community.' 'The office of a journal,' announced the *Nelson Examiner* as early as 1842, 'is to bind together by the ties of a common interest the various elements of society.'[94] Most genteel politicians paid at least lip service to the core populist principle of class harmony. A few claimed to represent the bottom against the top, including George Grey, autocratic proconsul turned tribune of the people. A few claimed to be representing the top against the bottom, though seldom openly. Most claimed to be representing both top and bottom – 'all classes', in the favourite contemporary phrase – and that there was no fundamental conflict of interest between them.

Article three of the compact was simply that the pump of progress should be primed, so that a sufficient supply of real and mythical opportunity was available. The ruling class could rule its head off as long as it ensured some chances for enhancement, adoption and promotion for the ruled, and kept to the other articles of the populist compact. If it failed in this, its days were numbered.

CHAPTER SIXTEEN

Lumped, Split and Bound

In mid-1991, two small children starved to death in a house in an English village after their mother had suddenly collapsed and died. The absent father and husband was an American airman, and the family was so isolated from its neighbours, friends and kin that no-one telephoned persistently or visited over the days this tragedy must have taken. In a sea of potential human support, they had not a drop to drink. In the midst of modern New Zealand cities, there are regular reports of old people dying in their flats in crowded apartment blocks, and lying undiscovered for weeks. This is the downside of extreme individualism, and humans, *Homo socialis*, have long grouped in communities to prevent it.

In a fully integrated society, a person is like a fly caught in many intersecting webs. Potential webs include kin from nuclear and extended families, the friends and neighbours of your residential community, the cronies and clubmates of your leisure communities, and the school- and workmates of your occupational community. These groups expect certain types of behaviour from you, and reward or punish you accordingly with approval or disapproval, warm shoulder to lean on or cold shoulder. People like to be popular with their peer groups, whose power to impose norms is greater than that of states. At various times, drunken driving, marijuana smoking and tax evasion, for example, might land you in prison but would not bring you the disapproval of your peers. Hundreds of thousands of otherwise law-abiding New Zealanders therefore regularly flout the law: these legal crimes are not social crimes; they are subject to official but not unofficial sanctions.

Various formal and informal associations, such as sports clubs and drinking circles, reinforce, extend and link up your individual webs, meshing them with others to form lumps of connected people, held together by invisible links: a community. The most obvious type is the local community, the village or neighbourhood. But there are more nebulous circles of people well known to you, or well known to people well known to you. At some point, these *actual* communities merge imperceptibly into *imagined* communities, consisting of people whom you do not know but with whom you share myths, norms and values, and membership of some mutually imagined entity – a region, a nation, an ethnic or religious group; a large tribe, race, or tight class. Some of these bind insiders by splitting them from outsiders: they both bind and split. These wider webs link the narrower, more local webs, partly by encouraging them to be similar to each other. When they succeed, you are well and truly caught. Lumping groups people into local communities or small networks; binding links the lumps together into wider, imagined communities; other forces split the lumps apart.

With migration to New Zealand and places like it, a vast swarm of flies burst free from their webs, encouraged to do so by the alleged approach of spiders such as social demotion. Once here, they needed community, and turned spiders themselves, busily refurbishing bits of old web and spinning new in which to catch themselves and others. This chapter investigates their success. Perhaps the most fundamental question in *social* history is what makes a society, an entity with some degree of cohesion, from a welter of disparate communities, and what makes the communities from individuals. How were colonial Pakeha lumped, split and bound? What held them together? A possible answer to this question is that they were not held together, or at least not very well.

Old Lumps and New

In the most original reinterpretation of colonial Pakeha social history in recent times, historian Miles Fairburn has argued that the New Zealand colonists failed to rebuild much community in their new land. Apart from the great uprooting of migration itself, people were kept isolated by thinly scattered settlement, and neighbourless even in country towns by the wide, open spaces between houses. Once landed, they were split anew by massive geographical mobility or transience. Except for a small 'settled core', argues Fairburn, nineteenth-century Pakeha were much more split then lumped. They were 'atomised', not bonded – hardly a society at all. Individualism was rampant, qualified only by nuclear families – the atomic model accommodates the nuclear. The good news about atomism was that it went with considerable prosperity, even for unskilled workers, and widespread opportunities to achieve independencies, especially in the form of landed property. It also freed people from masters and an oppressively high need to conform. Thus, argues Fairburn, the arcadian 'ideal society' that migrants had hoped for was to some extent achieved through atomism and its allies. But atomism also produced enemies that ambushed the ideal society, including loneliness and deficient community – a poor capacity for social interaction, which led to disorder and interpersonal conflict. High rates of assault, drunkenness and civil litigation, contradicting legends of orderly and harmonious pioneers, were key symptoms of atomism.[1]

Atomic metaphors were first applied to Pakeha society by the linchpin prophet Thomas Cholmondeley in 1854. 'Emigration,' he wrote, 'is the drifting of atoms. Colonisation is the regular movement of an organised body . . . Colonisation is a system. Colonisation incorporates . . . it takes charge of a man on starting from his home. It is careful to supply its subject with new ties and positive duties, at the same moment that the old ones are snapped asunder.'[2] The colonising crusaders were comfortable with some degree of arcadianism and individualism, but overall they wanted bonding colonisation, not dangerous and uncivilising atomic emigration. Exploring atomism therefore fits neatly with our inquiry into crusader success – into the extent to which Pakehadom was baked to recipe. Atomisation implies that, in this respect and as this book has defined it, the Pakeha prospectus failed. As we saw in the last two chapters, the cake rose; some individual crumbs did too; but, with the exception of genteel regional élites, perhaps all mushroomed atomically into a welter of separate crumbs.

It is not easy for half a chapter of a general history to tackle atomism. Fairburn's argument is tight-packed and wide-ranging. He raises and discounts many potential objections, often successfully. No general historian can hope to match his use of statistics. Yet atomism is an important theory, and this book must engage with it, while struggling to convey some information about colonial life on the side. Earlier chapters have already differed from Fairburn's view of colonial Pakeha. They rate progressive 'Utopia' above his rural 'Arcadia' in colonising ideology; they see the 1840s, which he dismisses, as a crucible of Pakeha myth, if not reality; they argue that widespread land ownership does not indicate the widespread achievement of independencies, as he sometimes implies. The next two sections address the guts of the atomic thesis: the alleged inputs and outputs of bondlessness. The strength of community is hard to measure in itself. Instead, Fairburn offers factors that he argues were likely to *cause* atomism and were very prominent among Pakeha 1850–80: notably high rates of immigration to New Zealand and of transience and isolation within it. These were the inputs, and they are discussed in this section. He also offers factors that were prominent and likely to have been *caused by* atomism: high rates of hitting, suing and bingeing – arrests for drunkenness tended to stem from being very drunk and a little disorderly in public places rather than private tippling. These were the outputs, and they are discussed in the next section.

Atomism has been controversial, but many criticisms fail to bite. Some are too specific to undercut a broad thesis that rests largely on the evidence of national aggregates. A few hundred grandmothers and acts of neighbourly co-operation do not make a bonded society. Some fail to take account of the bias in the historical records towards those who stay, or of the tendency of community history to exaggerate its own lumping power – myths of cohesion in the past encourage actual cohesion in the present. Others point, perhaps rightly, to weaknesses in some of Fairburn's methods, but reach much the same conclusions anyway. Two alternative means of measuring transience come up with results similar to his: between 50 and 76 per cent of households were not there ten or fifteen years later. Indeed, both suggest a late nineteenth-century transiency rate of 73–77 per cent compared with his median of 57.5 per cent.[3] Because Fairburn tries too hard to show that New Zealand was exceptional, he makes himself unnecessarily vulnerable to the criticism that other countries had high transience too. But the contrast between a New Zealand folk history of cohesive local communities and a picture of localities as temporary holding pens for nomads is interesting enough without having to be unique.

High transience appears to have been a reality – one that contemporaries noted – and the same is quite obviously true of immigration. The Pakeha population at least doubled in each of the five decades after 1830. This was 'demographic shock' with a vengeance; industrialising Britain was not in this ballpark of growth, though some other colonial societies were. Moreover, the atomising effect of this population turnover may have been even greater than Fairburn suggests. Colonial New Zealand had high immigration – over 400,000 people arrived. It also had high emigration – over 100,000 people left. If it was the bondless who arrived and the bonded who left, then both immigration and emigration reduce the quotient of social bonds.

The same applies to transience within New Zealand. Leaving aside births and deaths, if a community of 100 is swamped by 200 newcomers over 10 years, a third of its population can have 10-year-old local bonds. If half the original 100 leave in the same decade, the bonded quotient is reduced to twenty per cent. Something like this was close to the reality in many early Pakeha communities. These 'stayers' were the core of the 'settled core'. Although a minority, they were enough to maintain community life-support systems, and if Fairburn is taken to imply that no significant community existed in colonial New Zealand, then he is clearly wrong. But generally he allows for the exception of settled minorities. The question is whether they, or something else, were enough to weave community into most people's lives. Atomism does make a case to answer. People struggled to build communal sandcastles against the repeated ebb and flow of both arrivals and departures, which often washed away their embryonic efforts. But they struggled rather harder, with better buckets and spades and stickier sand, than full atomism allows. Some old lumps may have survived the great reshuffling of migration and transience, and some new lumps may have formed.

Migration was the big break, but some links spanned it, kinship and friendship among them. Obviously and uncontroversially, many families migrated together and formed the tiniest of all lumps in New Zealand. Some groups of wider kin, friends, neighbours, and master plus servants also migrated together. This 'clump' type of migration was probably more common and a more important source of colonial community than the atomic thesis acknowledges. For one thing, migration tended to inflate kinship and acquaintance. When all else was strange and new, a second cousin once removed could become a functional sibling. 'On this side of the globe,' wrote missionary Jane Williams, 'a slight acquaintance is soon converted into intimacy.'[4] But, families aside, it does not seem that clump migration was the majority experience. Even if it was, it seldom constituted the direct transfer of old communities to new lands. Migrant clumps were easily swamped by strangers or scattered by transience.

Groups of people could also dribble out over time, through chain migration. The experience of small ethnic groups such as the Dalmatians and Gujaratis shows that chain migration could be a significant source of colonial community. Neighbours in old villages were neighbours in new suburbs, or moved until they made this true, and brought out more kin to live with them or across the street.[5] But this was partly a product of minority status – uncommon languages and cultures clustered more than common ones – and chain migration did not necessarily breed community. One family of Irish migrants helped each other out, then dispersed across the country and 'hardly ever met again'.[6] Some 28 per cent of assisted migrants in the period 1871–91 were nominated by someone already in New Zealand.[7] Such nominations did not necessarily imply close association, in either Britain or New Zealand, between nominee and nominator. On the other hand, some state-unassisted immigrants were brought out by friends or relatives.

Clump and chain migration from overseas were not insignificant in tying Pakeha society together, but they were not decisive either. Other factors may represent larger chinks in the atomic model. The voyage out, the sole experience shared by all migrants, is one possibility. Bonding intensifies and telescopes in contexts such as long voyages in small ships. People do more socialising in a hundred days than they would normally do in a hundred weeks or even months. Some bonds survive the landing. One settler spoke of her 'ship-mates', well after landing, as a persistent circle of contacts.[8] There are many other examples of marriages, friendships and partnerships forged on board that persisted after disembarkation.

Bridge migration may also have facilitated the translation of old community into new. The Cornish migrant bridge, for example, had one on-ramp – Cornwall – and multiple but similar off-ramps – mining districts in neo-Britains. Cornish moving into such regions often found other Cornish there before them, and, even when they were complete strangers, integration was made easier. When 40 Cornish families migrated to the Westland mining community of Waiuta in 1920, the '"cousin Jacks" as they became known, fitted in immediately'.[9] They did so partly because they found other Cornish there before them, and partly because they had a bonding kit in their cultural baggage, and this was presumably true in the nineteenth century too. 'Cousin Jack' was the international slang for the Cornish – a travelling costume that bonded strangers wearing it, or at least made bonding easier. As the term itself implies, it was designed to do so. At a broader, looser level, differences of ethnicity and religion, discussed elsewhere, performed a similar service. A fellow Irish Catholic or Scots Presbyterian in a sea of Anglicans, or an English Anglican in a sea of Scots, was less a stranger than they were. But, by definition, this applied to minorities, not majorities. On the whole, while old-world lumps surviving the migration process may have reduced atomism more than Fairburn allows, it does not seem likely that they outweighed it.

Fairburn considers and largely dismisses three possible types of new 'lumps', or sources of community: 'vertical' (hierarchical slices owing informal allegiance to a genteel landlord, employer or patron); 'horizontal' (tight class or class community); and what might be called the 'blob' bonding of cohesive residential communities – neighbourhoods and localities. He is probably right to discount such vertical and horizontal forces as major bonding mechanisms. As we saw in the last chapter, the vertical grip of the gentry over others was not very strong. Some decent and even respectable people were tied to the gentry in various ways, and their informal influence over some neighbours was considerable, but those with tight upward ties were a minority. The gentry grouped horizontally among themselves, into tight though factionalised élites, but it seems likely that other class cultures did not. Regional proto-classes of decent working people may have formed in the cities, notably Dunedin, but apart from the gentry the best evidence for this happening on any scale, and for networking into national class communities, dates from the 1880s, not before.

Residential communities – villages, close clusters of small farms, small towns and neighbourhoods in large towns – were the archetypal colonial bonding context. They clearly did exist, and while transience reduced their long-term residents to a minority, such things as voluntary organisations based on them may have tightened and extended their grip, allowing them to quickly incorporate newcomers. Voluntary associations were quite numerous in the colonial era – sports, social, educational and artistic clubs; friendly societies; voluntary fire brigades, charitable and public welfare associations; proto-unionist craft guilds; political, military, educational and religious institutions. But it seems that most of these organisations encompassed only a minority of people, and that this minority correlated strongly with the settled core and with the respectable and genteel.[10] They tightened residential community among those lucky enough to have it, but perhaps did not extend it very greatly. Military organisations, such as the militia and volunteers, may have been a temporary exception in the North Island among adult males for a brief period of the 1860s. Schools and churches may be the best candidates for institutions that involved most of the people.

Schools of some sort affected a narrow majority of children in 1858 and a large majority in 1871, as we saw in the last chapter, and this did have implications for bonding potential, noted below. But many children in both years attended only Sunday school once a week, and anyway schools did not necessarily bond parents. Religion and its power to bind into imagined communities is discussed later, but we can note here that the power of church attendance to lump into actual communities was not huge. Overall church attendance was first measured in 1874, when regular attenders were equivalent to 39.4 per cent of the population aged over fifteen years. It was probably lower earlier, and rose to 42 per cent in 1881 and 48 per cent in 1886 before dropping steadily.[11] These percentages are much larger than a presumed settled core of 20 per cent or so. But children under fifteen were counted among the attenders, and they should therefore be counted in the base for percentages. Indeed, they may have made up a higher proportion of church attenders than of the population as a whole, because they had no choice. On this basis, only about a quarter of the whole Pakeha population attended church in the 1870s.[12] Neither schools nor churches necessarily bonded the majority of people. But, along with several other considerations, attendance at them does suggest that most people lived in circumstances in which bonding was at least possible.

There is a hint of disparity between church attendance and the notion that the settled core of stayers were a small minority. The fully transient and atomised are not very likely to have been 'usually attending' the same church, which was the basis of attendance enumeration. Yet the number of attenders exceeds the presumed number of stayers, and some stayers – perhaps a high proportion – did not attend church regularly for various reasons, including lack of piety, inertia and the unavailability of churches and chapels of appropriate denominations in particular localities. Some 42.5 per cent of Pakeha were nominal Anglicans in 1874, but this lax denomination contributed only 28.8 per cent of regular church attenders. There seems no reason to believe that Anglicans were especially transient, so this implies that many Anglican stayers did not regularly attend.[13]

The proportion of people linked to local communities suggested by church attendance (much higher than 23 per cent); by day-school attendance (31–54 per cent of children, 1858–71) and by day plus Sunday school attendance (51–72 per cent), are all higher than the minimum figure for the settled core – people who stayed in the same place for more than 10 years – guessed above at 20 per cent. The proportion of Pakeha organised into nuclear families – say, married or widowed men and women plus children under 15 – was very roughly 75 per cent in 1874.[14] Families were less prone to transience than single adults, and obviously more prone to be linked to a locality by schooling. None of these figures is conclusive, and some are very soft, but they do suggest that many more than the 20 per cent long-term stayers lived in circumstances with local bonding potential. The pattern of colonial settlement, which I think made for less isolation than Fairburn claims, seems to me to support this impression.

Colonial New Zealand was much less urban than Britain. But it was still quite highly urbanised for an allegedly rural new society – between 1858 and 1881 the 'urban' proportion, according to various definitions, fluctuated between 24 and 36 per cent. 'Urban' in New Zealand did not necessarily mean large cities. Only the big four exceeded 20,000 in 1881 – all but Wellington exceeded 30,000 – totalling about 25 per cent of the Pakeha population between them. The fifth-biggest town was Nelson, with fewer than 7,000 – Thames had shrunk.[15] Vast cities were not a New Zealand vice or virtue. But even the smallest town, camp or close cluster of small farms provided opportunities for community. Some 40 per cent of the Pakeha population in 1881 lived in towns of over 1,000 people, and another 15 per cent lived in smaller nuclei.[16] Fairburn calculates that the total 'clustered segment' of the population was 62 per cent in 1874, dropping to 55 per cent in 1881. He considers this small; it could be considered quite large, and it is not clear that his 'clustered segment' includes sheep stations, large mixed-farming estates, close clusters of small farms or camps of progress workers.

The clustering question converges with a nineteenth-century debate about Australian and New Zealand patterns of settlement and their relative merits: the former was considered 'centralised' around one large city; the latter 'decentralised'. In 1871, between 21 and 28 per cent of the population of the relevant colonies lived in Perth, Adelaide, Sydney and Melbourne, whereas no New Zealand city had much more than 6 per cent. But if we look at New Zealand towns in relation to their provinces, not the colony as a whole, the picture is very different. In 1871, Dunedin and Christchurch had 25 and 26 per cent of their provincial populations; Auckland and Wellington had 32 and 33 per cent. In Westland and Marlborough, where two towns competed for dominance, centralisation was lower. But Nelson and Invercargill had about a quarter of their provincial populations, and in pastoral Hawke's Bay and agricultural Taranaki, Napier and New Plymouth had 36.6 and 40 per cent respectively.[17] In terms of provincial regions, New Zealand settlement was quite centralised. If we extend the picture to incorporate subprovincial regions and the small farms usually clustered around a town, this seems even more marked. A further 10 per cent of the population of Wellington province lived in Wanganui town – almost 50 per cent of the population of the Wanganui region, and making a total of 43 per cent of the provincial population in the two leading towns. About 55 per cent of Auckland province's Pakeha lived within 50 kilometres of Auckland town in 1881, and 12 per cent lived in and around Thames.[18]

A series of maps showing the pattern of settlement in 1874 indicate that settlement was quite concentrated in the colony as a whole. The great majority of the population of Canterbury, for example, lived within a 50-kilometre radius of Christchurch and Timaru, and a similar concentration around main towns is true of the other provinces.[19] This pattern is what we would expect from reluctant yeomen and progress-, camp- and town-led settlement: spasms of quite concentrated settlement rather than numerous, evenly spread, individual pioneers plunging alone into the wilderness.

'Concentration' is a relative term, of course, and there was ample room for individual isolation in 'clusters' a thousand square kilometres in extent. But it seems unlikely to have been all that common. After all, how would numerous isolated small-farming families and lone frontier farmers have survived? They could obtain their tools, tea and sugar in a few visits a year to a distant store, but they could not sell fresh food or get local work to pay for them if other people did not live nearby. That 72 per cent of children attended some sort of school in 1871 supports the impression of a clustered majority. Some did not attend very regularly, and about a quarter attended Sunday school only. As noted above schools were therefore not necessarily a powerful bonding mechanism for children, let alone parents. Rural isolation and other factors did retard schooling for many children, especially early in the colonial period. But this level of schooling, even if irregular, does indicate that by 1871 at least 72 per cent of families lived close enough to a school to get children there at least once a week.

Many hamlets, small towns and even large towns had a country-like quality. Feilding, despite its hopes of a great future, was in 1893 'so scattered that it is rather a collection of small farms than a village'.[20] Town dwellers everywhere kept chickens, horses and pigs, and even sheep and cattle, pasturing them on roadsides, on unsold land or on the owner's own large 'section'. Because so many towns were laid out with great futures in mind, householders were often separated from their neighbours by unsold sections, sometimes numerous and large. This made town fringes appear more subrural than suburban, and may have been significant in mediating between town and country in various ways. It meant that many small-town dwellers did not live cheek by jowl with neighbours, as they would have done in Britain. But it could not have seriously hampered regular association, as Fairburn suggests it did. It does not take very long to walk or ride across even a ten-acre section. Ten miles of trackless bush might make 'neighbour' an abstraction; ten acres of empty paddock did not. Feilding might be less a town than a coterie of small farms, but the farms were very close to each other, as farms go. Further out of town, high access to horses must have increased the power to associate. In 1881, New Zealand had about six times more horses per thousand people than Britain.[21] Roads were often very bad, but roads and tracks impassable to wheeled traffic were sometimes still traversable by riders. Poor roads were more of an obstacle to economic transport than to social transport. 'The attitude to travel and distance of the rider or [coach, trap or buggy] driver was totally different to that of the pedestrian or dray driver.'[22] Riding was several times faster than walking over substantial distances. Even if allowance is made for bad roads, widespread horse ownership must have significantly reduced the social effects of geographical isolation.

Most people in colonial New Zealand, it seems to me, were unlikely to have been so isolated that they had little chance of achieving community. There were also factors that may have reduced the solvent effect of transience. One was the capacity for pre-existing lumps to survive internal, as well as external, migration, or even to be formed out of the migration process. Vertical, horizontal and residential community may not exhaust the list of major bonding possibilities. The formation of patchworks or networks through the internal equivalents of chain, clump and bridge migration may be another important category of community. Patchwork communities are sets of people who do not live as a solid block but associate regularly, with one patchwork overlaying others in the same geographical space. They require a certain amount of geographical propinquity – you have to be close enough to fellow members to interact regularly. But they do not require solid blobs – hamlets, clusters or neighbourhoods consisting solely or largely of co-members.

The peopling of neo-Britains like New Zealand was one of two great British migrations that were occurring simultaneously, the other being internal migration from country to city. Like emigration, urbanisation was once associated with exploding crime rates, which would have permitted the argument that both internal and external migration led to atomism and its symptoms. But the picture of British urbanisation and crime now emerging is less convenient for the atomic model. British cities, it seems, did not always grow much more disorderly as people poured in. Indeed, British rates of violent crime dropped dramatically over the nineteenth century, 'firmly contradicting the adage that industrialisation and urbanisation necessarily leads to higher rates of crime'.[23]

What appears to have blunted the atomising effect of urban migration was lump, chain and bridge versions of internal migration. People moved together from country to city; urban uncles brought in rural nieces and nephews; and invisible bridges developed between particular villages and particular suburbs, facilitating both departure and arrival. The urban immigrant communities thus formed were not necessarily locally cohesive, a street or two of people exclusively from one village. They could be patchwork or network communities – an uncle next door, an old friend across the street, an ex-neighbour round the corner. Several networks could exist in the same geographical 'neighbourhood'; one might be spread across several neighbourhoods; the networks might be based on jobs, churches, pubs or clubs rather then residence. Some shared context such as religious denomination or region of origin could link new networks together, or even knit them into old networks of long-time town dwellers.

It may be the fact that urbanisation, the other great migration, does not necessarily produce atomism that leads Fairburn to emphasise transience and isolation over immigration as causes of New Zealand atomism. But why shouldn't 'transience' – New Zealand internal migration – have displayed characteristics similar to urban migration in Britain? Patchwork communities were easiest in towns, but New Zealand had its share of those, and horses meant they might also exist in relatively thickly settled country. They were a way in which new lumps could be reshuffled out of older lumps, despite external or internal migration – indeed, as part of the process. They also meant that leaving a neighbourhood or locality did not necessarily mean leaving your community, if the shift was not very far. Although further research is obviously required, there are hints of 'bridges' between particular New Zealand sources and destinations of internal migration – New Plymouth and Nelson in the 1860s; Canterbury and Hawke's Bay from the 1870s; towns and their hinterlands throughout the period; and through the process of secondary colonisation noted in Chapter Eight.

Another factor may also have reduced the solvent effect of transience. There were people among the transient who had strong incentives to take on, or at least simulate, the bonds and norms of core stayers. They might be called 'shifters' to distinguish them from other categories of transients – 'drifters' and 'wanderers'. Shifters moved often, and so boosted transience statistics, but they hoped, or at least pretended to hope, that each move would be the last – that this time they would 'get on', and make it to viability and staying put. Unlike drifters and wanderers, they did not intend to keep moving indefinitely. Participating in informal mutual-aid systems may have been an incentive to simulate staying. Help in times of difficulty, exchanging labour at work peaks such as harvests, and the borrowing of carts, ploughs, horses and other expensive items was predicated on the assumption that you would be around to reciprocate. Fairburn has noted that the evidence for such mutual help is sparse and anecdotal, but it was not the type of thing likely to generate statistical aggregates; and to whatever extent it existed, the appearance of staying must have facilitated participation. The evidence for the widespread importance of credit, on the other hand, is strong, and credit must surely have been an important incentive to simulate staying. Access to most types of credit demanded local repute and a place of abode that had at least the appearance of being fixed.

Shifters bought in to the values of their potential community for these and other pragmatic reasons, and also by sharing its less pragmatic hopes. Fairburn acknowledges that a shared wider ideology limited the frontier chaos caused by atomism, but may underestimate its strength and the extent to which it had local versions that converged closely with the aspirations of individuals. This convergence – the meshing of individual and communal aspirations, whereby the sum of individual achievements in getting on was celebrated as collective achievement – must have reduced the solvent effect of individualism. Large families had a similar effect. They broadened individual self-centredness not only to children but to the schooling, friendships, marriages, jobs and futures children would require. The Pakeha prospectus enforced and homogenised values and norms of behaviour – though only through the unholy alliance between formal and informal myths of settlement. It was no loose common stock of concepts but a force that could help determine community and individual behaviour, and the relations between them. Shifters shared local colonising crusades and local boosterism, both to gain acceptance and in their own and their families' interests. Shifters as well as stayers hoped to get on locally through progressive colonisation; to attract public spending and exploit or restart local progress; to access informal networks for mutual aid and credit; to use formal local facilities such as churches and schools; and to appear decent or respectable to co-users. The hope or the pretence of staying may have bound people to local or patchwork communities almost as effectively as actual staying. Both stayers and shifters, perhaps, were less likely than others to display the symptoms of atomism: bingeing, fighting and being sued.

The transience of wanderers was more fundamental than that of shifters, but it was patterned, grouped and anchored to some extent – a semi-nomadism. Wanderers are the subjects of the next section. Drifters were the classic atoms, men alone, drifting from place to place, job to job, without much pattern, by themselves or accompanied by the most casual and temporary acquaintances. Fairburn posits two types: the 'loafer', 'swagger' or 'vagrant', stigmatised as a disreputable social anti-type or 'folk devil' by contemporaries; and striving achievers serving 'rural apprenticeships' and struggling to get on to independency through mobility. These men were only 'technically vagrants', but there were many of them. Contemporaries found it difficult to tell them apart from the disreputable real thing.[24] Both sorts of lone atom were key producers of the symptoms of atomism; bondless, masterless, extreme individualists who did a lot of bingeing, hitting and being sued, if not suing.[25]

There are two tensions here. First, there is considerable evidence, largely anecdotal but cumulatively quite strong, that drifters multiplied in the 1880s, when the symptoms of atomism began to decline. Second, if transients were the norm, accepted as part of the insider's view of the ideal society, why was their extreme version stigmatised as folk devils? Why should people fear the normal? Direct importation from Britain is not enough to explain this, because, as Fairburn shows, the moral panic over vagrancy increased in New Zealand over time, peaking in 1879 with 1,384 arrests for vagrancy.[26] Both shifters and stayers, perhaps, were uncomfortable with transience, and denigrated its personification – the vagrant – as part of a struggle against it.

What we have here, it seems to me, is a hierarchy of mobility – or, rather, immobility. To some extent it cut across other divisions in society, and to some extent it converged with them. At the top were the immobile, actual stayers, the settled core. Although only a minority in themselves, they were bulked out by the next segment, shifters, who sought to share their norms, bonds and dreams. In terms of grouping and conforming, as against actual moving, shifters were largely false transients. These two segments, together a 'core culture', accounted for somewhere between 25 and 75 per cent of the census population, men, women and children, and were probably a majority, though perhaps sometimes a narrow one, for most of the colonial era. Wanderers and drifters, second to bottom and bottom of the hierarchy of mobility, made up the balance. They were reinforced by categories absent from population statistics: overseas sailors, imperial soldiers and gold-diggers and the like who came and went between censuses. Each segment was mixed in terms of familial status, class and gender – at least one vagrant couple drifted with their baby[27] – but there were sharply different balances. Women, children, parents, and the genteel and respectable, tended towards the top of the immobility hierarchy. Men, non-parents, the decent and the disreputable tended towards the bottom.

Just as Fairburn is unable to show that his likely causes of, or prerequisites for, atomism actually produced it, so am I unable to show that likely causes or prerequisites of community actually did the job. Rural isolation was real and substantial, but was ameliorated by widespread horse ownership, and was anyway not so great as to block most people from some access to community. This does not necessarily mean that they used it, but they did have strong incentives to do so – such as obtaining credit, sharing local colonising crusades and simulating staying to gain local repute. They also had means of doing so: carrying community, especially patchwork community, across the chasms of external and internal migration, and transforming it along the way.

Underlying all this, perhaps, was a basic drive to associate. Once split apart by migration or transience, people tended to regroup as quickly as they could manage, like blood clotting after a wound. They used whatever coagulants were to hand – old, new or intermediate. The 'intermediate' category includes the intensified association of the voyage out, the inflation of kinship and acquaintance, and chain, lump and bridge migration. It was part of the space between fragment and frontier, the ethos of expansion. All in all, colonial New Zealand, with its massive rates of internal and external migration, and its substantial isolation, surely must have been much more atomised than Old Britain. But it does not seem likely to have been predominantly atomised. More likely, atomism and community were in dialectical struggle, with the latter prone to win: growing islands of the bonded in a diminishing sea of bondlessness, with the sea usually, perhaps always, smaller than the land.

Crews or Atoms?

Mass immigration to New Zealand, mass transience within it, coupled with isolation and extreme individualism are among Fairburn's causes of bondlessness – the *inputs* into atomism. It has been argued that they were less strong, and that there were more and stronger countervailing factors, than full atomism allows. Yet if this is so, what caused the symptoms, or *outputs*, of atomism: very high rates of violent assault, of arrest for drunkenness and of civil litigation? If it was not 'bondless atoms of population' who hit, binged and sued or were sued in such great numbers, who was it?

Before pursuing the guilty party, we need briefly to consider whether the crime existed. Was colonial disorder as high as Fairburn claims? High conviction rates, as he concedes, can be caused by factors such as changing definitions of crime and changes in the intensity of policing – a 'control wave' can produce as many arrests as a 'crime wave'. There was some tightening of policing in the 1860s, provoked by fears about gold-diggers. But the rate of arrests for drunkenness and assault was even higher in the 1850s than the 1860s. Other factors, such as the close correlation between changes in drunkenness arrests and changes in actual spirits consumption, suggest that there was some fire in the smoke. A more serious problem is how high the fire and smoke clouds rose. High relative to what? High relative to Britain is a reasonable answer. Rates of drunkenness convictions in New Zealand were three times higher than in Britain in the early 1870s.[28]

But two other baselines of comparison are equally important: New Zealand mythology and the subsequent New Zealand reality. Until about 1880, hitting/bingeing *was* high compared with both. The belief that colonial Pakeha had little crime – as a result of 'better stock', the quick swamping of the agents of vice after 1840 and the innate qualities and successful control of the gold-diggers – is clearly false. Fairburn's numerous statistics are convincing. They show a very high level of bingeing, hitting and suing to about 1880, then a steep and fairly steady drop to 1930 and beyond, except for a small resurgence in and around the 1900s. Variations among provinces were short term and limited.[29] Furthermore, there may well have been even more fire than smoke. Many areas were unpoliced or loosely policed, and in some places and times even tight policing was quite tolerant of hitting and bingeing. The number of blows and binges was therefore much greater than the number of arrests.

There was a crime; indeed, many crimes. Who committed them? Bondless atoms is Fairburn's answer. Without communities to buttress norms and enforce informal sanctions against undesirable behaviour, and without close associates to mediate between individuals, quarrels often came to blows or courts of law. Without company, or much need to retain repute in the eyes of non-existent peers, human atoms resorted to drink for solace against loneliness and got drunk with virtual strangers in pubs in a pathetic travesty of comradeship. This is quite a persuasive picture. There may seem something vaguely contradictory in men alone perpetrating crimes of interaction – it takes at least two to fight or sue, or to get arrested for drunkenness. But this tension is more apparent than real. Crimes happened when atoms clashed because bondlessness had damaged their capacity to interact peaceably. But there are some less tractable problems with the case for the atomic prosecution.

For one thing, while rates of hitting, bingeing and suing were high, other possible symptoms of atomism were not prominent, including suicide, mental breakdown, rotting in gaol for small debts because you had no kin or friends to bail you out, and a high per capita expenditure on policing. It is generally assumed, with Emile Durkheim, that social integration reduces suicide rates, yet allegedly unintegrated colonial New Zealand's suicide rate was low, at least in Auckland.[30] The rate was very low in the 1870s and 1880s, then peaked in the period 1895–1904, against the trend of bingeing, hitting and suing. New Zealand's ratio of mental breakdown, which Fairburn himself associates with the loneliness of atomism, was much lower than that of Scotland, Ireland and England, and it rose 40 per cent in 1874–91, again against the bingeing/hitting trend.[31] A study of imprisonment for debt confirms that suits were high, but also suggests that most sued debtors avoided gaol by paying up, perhaps with the help of kin and friends, or were quickly released through kin and friends paying their debts. Of course, kinless and friendless debtors might have absconded and never been caught, but many small debtors, including working people, did have kin and friends prepared to put their money where their bonds were.[32] Finally, it seems that New Zealand's per capita spending on policing was quite low compared with the rest of Australasia.[33] How does this fit with the notion of exceptionally high disorder?

A second problem is that violence was strangely selective for a situation of frontier chaos. Colonial society was quite well armed with guns. Firearms for hunting were very common indeed. 'Most houses had a gun.' Military rifles were widespread too, especially in the North Island, and carrying revolvers appears to have been quite a common practice. Diggers on the way to the goldfields in the early 1860s would buy up all the revolvers in Dunedin on the way through. Men sometimes went bingeing with guns in their pockets. 'Men down for binge; everyone armed.' As late as 1914, a policeman was completely unconcerned by the revolver he saw in the pocket of a drunk sleeping in Albert Park.[34] Levels of gun toting and gun owning did not match those of the American West, but seem to have been surprisingly high. Yet violent atoms, unrestrained by communal bonds, stopped short of using their guns, normally restricting themselves to fisticuffs. Fear of the law among the lawless, even where there was no law? Or the existence of shared norms, even some kind of community, that effectively allowed or even encouraged fistfights but forbade gunfights?

Women's hitting and bingeing constitutes a third problem. The rate of adult female arrest for drunkenness was less than a quarter of that for men. Some historians would explain this in terms of distinct male and female cultures, which respectively encouraged and discouraged drunkenness. But Fairburn points out that changes in male and female rates in New Zealand move very much in step with each other in the short term, and drop rapidly together from about 1880 in the long, strongly suggesting that male and female bingeing has a linked explanation.[35] He sees this as atomism, for both sexes. Most people, he would argue, were atomised in some degree, but many more men than women were extremely atomised. Yet in the early 1870s, the discrepancy in bingeing between New Zealand and British women was apparently even higher than the discrepancy between New Zealand and British men.[36] New Zealand women binged much less than New Zealand men, but they binged very much more than British women.

Fairburn tells us little about women fighting, but another study suggests it was by no means unknown. Over 300 charges of assault were laid against women in the Auckland Police Court between 1845 and 1870. Almost six times as many assault charges were laid against men in this period, but assault made up a higher percentage of all charges against women than of all charges against men. The same was true of drunkenness. Between them, hitting and bingeing made up 72 per cent of alleged female crime in Auckland, but only 54 per cent of male.[37] Why should the (few) extremely atomised women be even more atomised, even more prone to hit and binge, than the (many) extremely atomised men? Perhaps a large part of the answer to these questions, and symbolic of a still larger one, is provided by Bridget Hawkey and Mary Robinson, two disreputable women of Auckland.

Not all disreputable women were prostitutes, but prostitutes were the leading archetype of female disrepute. Pakeha prostitution is known largely through attempts to control it, which began to intensify in the 1860s and peaked early in the twentieth century. 'Moral panic' is difficult to separate from reality, but estimates of the number of full-time prostitutes went as high as 200 in Dunedin in 1864. 'Every city had its "red light" district which by the 1860s was well established and well known.'[38] Even smaller towns like Invercargill had several known brothels.[39] Apart from brothels in towns, prostitution took place in some pubs and in various establishments in camps and shanty towns of progress workers and gold-diggers. Prostitutes seem fairly seldom to have worked alone, but it is not clear that the Pakeha sex industry was male-controlled. An 1891 Christchurch survey suggests one in three prostitutes worked with 'some sort of male associate', but most brothels are said to have been 'run by madams', older women who 'entered into a private understanding with the whores and took a rent or a share of the earnings'.[40] A survey of Christchurch and Dunedin brothels in 1870 shows that, while one-woman establishments were the most common single category of brothel, almost 80 per cent of prostitutes worked with colleagues. In Auckland, 'that many of them were well acquainted with each other is beyond doubt'. This study of Auckland prostitutes concludes that they were 'part of a small but distinctive criminal subculture'.[41] We will call the places where prostitutes clustered, which were mostly urban, 'binge centres', because it was here, I suggest, that most women's bingeing and hitting, and perhaps most men's, occurred.

Apart from prostitutes, a few male controllers or pimps, other male hangers-on and some children, inhabitants of binge centres included other types of disreputable women: madams, the temporary, seasonal or informal wives of disreputable men, and dancers and hostesses, who may or may not have doubled as prostitutes. The Auckland evidence strongly suggests that it was these women who were responsible for the high rates (relative to Britain) of female bingeing and hitting. Soldiers' wives, who tended to be characterised as disreputable, and who sometimes married successive men in the same regiment – formally or informally – were a 'notorious class' of offender. Over 55 per cent of women convicted of prostitution between 1845 and 1870 committed other crimes the same year. About 30 per cent of women charged with prostitution were charged with ten or more offences of all kinds over the period. There was 'a core of highly conspicuous recidivists in Auckland; women who were constantly being brought before the court – predominantly on drunkenness charges'. Such charges were in fact used to control disreputable behaviour, such as soliciting, indecency and having blatant and rowdy fun, but it remains true that disreputable women often were drunk in public. One champion was Bridget Hawkey, who declared 'she had been drunk for four years and would be drunk for four years more', and accumulated 50 charges in six years. Another champion was Mary Robinson, who with 150 appearances was personally responsible for almost four per cent of women's crime in Auckland between 1850 and 1870.[42] Fairburn has rightly chastised his critics for assuming that the particular necessarily indicates the general, but a few more cases like this and the particular *becomes* the general.

The bulk of women's crime was committed by a small group – disreputable women. This group was much more migratory, transient and kinless than English village women, and therefore less bonded or more atomised. But they were not bondless. Most worked with colleagues and lived in tiny, loose, poor, shabby but distinct communities. These communities were powerful enough to enforce some norms, which often diverged from those of 'core culture' – not seeing informal marriage as discreditable and not co-operating with the police, for example.[43] Disreputable women rarely stabbed or shot each other, and they did not rob banks, but they did hit each other and outsiders, and they did get drunk often. They did not hit and drink because they were depraved in their own terms, or atomised in Fairburn's, but because their 'subculture' permitted hitting and drinking. To them, these legal crimes were not social crimes. Their subculture was arguably only a part of a wider whole, from which they drew most of their clients. In a sense, each disreputable woman had many husbands, and the husbands had similar habits.

The traditional economic division between town and farm was also a social division: townies and farmers. In Chapter Fourteen, it was argued that a third economic sector existed – the progress industry and its allies. This, too, had to be staffed, and the people who staffed it could be called 'crews'. Crews were to progressive colonisation what farmers were to farms. As the term suggests, sailors were the leading archetype of crew culture. Ordinary British sailors did not typically spend whole careers in one or two ships. Even in the Royal Navy, and more so in coasters, whalers and the merchant marine, crews were normally paid off at the end of each season or voyage. Crews were constantly reshuffled, a floating pool of floating labour. Many crews were therefore collections of strangers. But each experienced seaman knew his new workplace and his role in it thoroughly, because ships duplicated each other. In a sense, he also 'knew' his new workmates, because they shared the similar experience and the same manners, customs, slang, prejudices, dress, leisure habits, virtues and vices – the same subculture. Raw recruits were quickly indoctrinated, quickly encouraged or pressured into conformity with prevailing mores. Crews were *prefabricated* communities into which new members could easily slot. There is some analogy with shifting to a new school or a new sports team. The place and people are different, but they duplicate your previous experience; teachers and coaches, desks and balls, curricula and game plans, formal positions and rules, informal customs and folklore.

Sailors were important to New Zealand in the most direct sense. Local 'mariners' totalled about 3,500 in the 1860s.[44] Their numbers were dwarfed by overseas sailors, who came in thousands and stayed in hundreds from the 1820s. Including the crews of deep-sea whaling ships, sailors probably constituted a majority of the Europeans to have been to New Zealand as late as 1860. About 1,000 overseas ships entered New Zealand ports in the 1830s, 1,500 in the 1840s, 3,000 in the 1850s, and over 8,000 in each of the 1860s and 1870s.[45] If there was an average of 25 crewmen per ship, allowing for small trans-Tasman vessels, this represents 500,000 sailor visits, 1840–80. The number of ships declined thereafter, as did the size of crews (steamships needed far fewer men per ton). So, too, did the ratio of sailor visits to the colonial population. Unless they settled, overseas sailors do not appear in the population statistics, but their crimes do. Some stayed for several weeks while their ships were loaded and unloaded. Some may only have gone ashore for a few days before sailing away, but these, of course, were the days in which they did their bingeing and hitting – and whoring.

Some did settle. Desertion was a constant problem for ship captains in New Zealand. In part, crew culture flows directly from ship crews, which bequeathed forms of social and work organisation, and elements of a subculture such as the slang 'cleared out', 'toe the line', 'tell that to the marines' and, very possibly, the term 'mate'. Apart from direct influence, many other male working groups were homologous – they shared some of the forms and characteristics of ships' crews. Military units are one example. Soldiers were very commonly associated with sailors by outsiders. Like sailors, soldiers were important in New Zealand both as settlers and sojourners. Their contribution in the former capacity has been noted above. As sojourners, they and their few families constituted more than a quarter of the Pakeha population of the North Island in 1864. The great majority were imperial troops and their camp followers, who do not appear in the colonial population statistics, though, as with sailors, many of their crimes do.

Both imperial and colonial soldiers were allied to the progress industry, attacking natives and sometimes distance and emptiness – through roadmaking and fort building. 'Navvies' – originally 'navigators', those who dug navigation canals – who built New Zealand's roads, rails, tunnels, bridges, port facilities and large buildings, were also crews, directly involved in the progress industry. Navvies often worked not in industrial complexes of hundreds of workers but in teams of around a dozen, each attacking its allocated section of distance, a few metres of road or rail. Sawyers and mill workers also commonly worked in groups – you could not do much with a kauri or totara tree by yourself. A navvy, sawyer or timber-mill worker who left one gang could quickly slot into another – the job, the trees and the crew culture were much the same. A recent study of kauri bushmen shows that they 'saw themselves as a special breed'. Many were ex-soldiers and sailors; most never married. Nicknames were common, and a man's past was private, but there was powerful pressure to conform – to a code of silence as far as police inquiries were concerned, to internally imposed camp customs, and to pride in a rough and tough lifestyle, involving fifteen pounds of meat a week and no bed sheets. 'The odd man used to have his sheets – but he was bloody odd.' They were very orderly on the job and very disorderly off it, spasmodically whoring, bingeing and sometimes hitting in central Auckland.[46]

Other extractive activities, allies or predecessors of the progress industry rather than direct parts of it, were also staffed largely by crews. Sealing gangs and shore-whaling stations were obviously crewlike in organisation, but this is less obvious in the case of kauri-gumdiggers and goldminers. The Northland gumfields, last resort of the down-and-out, are something of a special case. Maori and Dalmatian diggers worked in teams, but other ethnic groups appear to have worked as individuals – there were some lone atoms, outside both crew and core culture. But even on the gumfields, individualist workers often lived and moved together in bands, splitting up for the day's work and lumping together at night.[47] Goldminers did not normally work alone, but in groups of four to six. Solitary miners were stigmatised as 'hatters' by the majority, a pejorative term.[48]

Outside of the progress industry and its allies, many types of agricultural and pastoral workers grouped in crews. Sheep-shearing gangs are the best known. The gang organisation of shearing began replacing individual shearers in the 1850s, and may have been the dominant form of shearing by the 1860s. The harvesters of grain crops like wheat and oats also worked in gangs, and so, sometimes, did contract ploughmen and fencers – though their 'groups' were sometimes as small as two. Musterers usually worked in gangs of about six, with their own horses and dogs;[49] rabbiters in groups of six to ten, for rations and a penny a skin.[50] Mobile mechanical reapers, threshing mills and chaff-cutters had their mobile crews of between four and twelve men.[51] Some of these workers were actually engaged in farm formation rather than actual farming, and the former was more like the progress industry than the latter. Large-scale wheat cropping was often part of the process of converting native pasture to more productive sewn pasture.[52] Mass ploughing was part of the same process, with a number of ploughmen living in 'plough camps' as they gradually chewed through the topsoil of large estates. Harvesting grass seed was also an element of this hybrid of farming and progress: the large-scale, one-off exercise of creating pasture.

Of course, crew or crewlike organisation was not a feature of all types of farming work. Small owner-farmers typically worked in families, but sometimes rented out their males to crews. Medium and large farmers employed permanent 'farm servants' or labourers, owing more vertical deference than civilian crews. Some rural workers drifted alone and were employed alone. But many did work in wandering 'crews', loose or tight. Their numbers varied and are impossible to fix, but they were very high. Almost half of all census-registered male jobs had the potential to be filled by wandering crews,[53] and many overseas sailors and imperial soldiers did not appear in population or occupation statistics.

There were major variations of many kinds between occupational sub-cultures of these activities and in the tightness of crews as communities. But, to a greater or lesser degree, they shared a lot as well, and 'crew culture' can describe these common characteristics. Their work tended to be dangerous. Insurers assessed mining at thirteen times and bushfelling at 26 times the risk of safe city jobs.[54] On the job, the crews lived rough – in tents, bivouacs, huts, shanties, caves or even curious combinations of all five,[55] as well as on ships and in a few big barracks. Colonial New Zealand's numerous small dwellings had only one or two rooms, but they were not necessarily occupied by only one person, or planted alone in the bush. Crewmen ate large quantities of meat, often preserved, and few fresh vegetables. They used similar slang – arguably variants of the same argot. Most were overseas-born, including substantial cosmopolitan and Irish elements, but with a British and neo-British majority – English, Scots, North American, Australian. Most were single; those who were married were seldom accompanied by wives or children; many never married. Their culture valued strength, toughness and informal manual skills. It was orally transmitted, through folksongs, jokes and 'capping yarns', and it was quite old.

Georg Forster's description of English sailors at Dusky Sound in 1773, John Boultbee's of sealers in the 1820s and Edward Wakefield's of shearers and other transient workers in 1889 are strikingly interchangeable, despite the half-century between each observation. Forster admired the 'honest tars' for their untutored wit, '& their stories, though for the greatest part bawdy'.[56] Fifty years later, in the same place (Dusky Sound), the genteel sealer Boultbee sat 'listening to the wonderful stories related by one of our party . . . I joined the gaping audience without betraying any contempt for this harmless and ignorant pastime.'[57] Wakefield's shearers 'spend the whole of their leisure time spinning yarns . . . totally unfit for ears polite, though often exceedingly amusing'. A few New Zealand crew songs survive, such as 'The Tonguer's Lament' of the 1830s and 'Paddy Doyle's Lament' of the 1860s,[58] though probably part of a wider neo-British and Irish pool. Wakefield described his crewmen as 'a distinct branch of the human family, not by any means unlike the gypsies'.[59]

Crew culture had a number of ambiguous, even schizoid, aspects. First, to outsiders, crews were both heroes and villains. This was especially obvious in the case of soldiers and naval sailors, the heroes of Trafalgar, Waterloo and Rangiriri, the embodiment of martial Anglo-Saxonism. Yet no respectable parent would want their daughter to marry one. This ambiguity has been amply documented in studies of the nineteenth-century British army, and it also applied to servicemen in New Zealand, imperial or colonial. To a lesser extent, this two-faced attitude applied to other crews as well. Merchant seamen were widely acknowledged to be the lifeblood of British trade, instantly convertible into 'Hearts of Oak' in time of war. Yet eighteenth-century gentleman explorers described them as 'British savages', and as late as the twentieth century respectable New Zealand tended to agree. There was even a specialist maritime branch of evangelism, seeking to save savage sailor-sinners, in the form of the Mission to Seamen. Drunken sprees were very common among sailors. 'Violence was also a regular part of a seaman's life.'[60] Whether whalers were agents of vice or rough-hewn but honest and effective agents of civilisation was one of New Zealand's earliest historical debates. Progress workers such as sawyers and navvies fitted the same ambiguous bill. They were vital to the campaigns against nature and distance, the muscle power behind progress, and their strength and toughness was admired to some extent. But their advent in settled communities was also feared, and they tended to be written out of local history, even when they began it, as was very often the case. The itinerant timber-mill workers who pioneered the Pakeha settlement of Hawea and Wanaka were 'little remembered' in local tradition.[61] As we have seen, provincial governments scrabbled for goldfields but feared their denizens.

Much of the two-faced attitude of outsiders to crews stemmed from a real contradiction in their behaviour. They were disciplined on the job and undisciplined off it. When on-duty soldiers marched through town, local settlers lined the street and cheered. When off-duty soldiers marched through Wellington, the reaction was rather different. ' "Up with your shutters and put out your light, the 14th are coming down" . . . and come they did, smashing windows and everything else which came in their way.'[62] Contemporaries were in little doubt that it was off-duty crewmen who did most bingeing, hitting and whoring, and again it was soldiers and sailors who led the way. Richard Hill's history of New Zealand policing documents this, including 'the increase in disorder which invariably resulted from the presence of soldiers'. At New Plymouth, the arrival of fewer than 500 in the late 1850s quintupled gaolings.[63] Imperial military records confirm that the troops were crime-prone. On 30 October 1864, of about 8,000 rank and file, 201, or 25 per thousand, were in 'civil or military confinement'.[64] When counted in 1875, only 1.54 per thousand of the general Pakeha population were in prison.[65] The figure would have been higher ten years before; and higher still if only adult males were taken into account. But even if it were as high as ten per thousand, it was still dwarfed by the military figure.

The British army's sterling contribution to New Zealand crime rates diminished from 1867 as the legions departed, but there was some residue and a colonial military inheritance. The *New Zealand Herald* noted in 1866 that departing imperial troops had left a 'legacy of crime and immorality', including 'a large number of dancing saloons attended by large numbers of loose women'.[66] In 1872, the Auckland police chief reflected on his long list of drunkenness and other offences, and noted that 'discharged soldiers, old [military] pensioners, and the dregs of the [Waikato] Militia regiments are the classes which swell these lists most'. Even in the 1870s, 'it was as often as not the AC [Armed Constabulary] personnel themselves who needed policing'.[67] As for sailors, of the 56 people gaoled in Dunedin in 1853–54, 'half were visiting seamen'.[68] Sailors contributed almost half of the drunkenness convictions in the Wellington Police Magistrates Court in 1844–48.[69] In early New Zealand prisons, 'more often than not, the prisoners were sailors'.[70] The clients of women charged with prostitution were 'typically soldiers or sailors'.[71] Whalers were renowned for disorderliness off duty, and in the 1840s and 1850s they tended to shift their bingeing from the Old New Zealand towns to the New. A child in Wellington in the 1840s remembered 'wild, attractive scenes when whalers came ashore . . . to knock down their cheques' and indulge in 'fights in Upper Sydney Street'.[72] The Napier Resident Magistrate in the 1850s – poor Alfred Domet – was in no doubt that whalers and similar characters were 'the vigorous ruffians that create disturbances during their drunken debauches at this port'.[73] Archetypally, the first response of whaler Tommy Chasland to the advent of the law at Bluff in 1856 was to knock him down.[74]

Sawyers, flax millers, navvies, goldminers and crewlike farm workers also had reputations for rowdiness when unleashed from the job. Some of these men were ex-sailors or soldiers. It was claimed that the wandering workers of Canterbury in the 1850s and 1860s were 'mostly run away sailors'.[75] Sailors or not, there were widespread fears of 'hundreds of unruly woodcutters and sawmill labourers', and 'navvies from the railway works and flax mill workers creating disorder'.[76] According to Hill, 'the "large number of men who have been massed together engaged in the public works of the [Auckland] province" created pockets of endemic disorder and occasional riot'. He also notes the 'pub-orientated disorder associated with railway works, flax mills, and other enterprises' in provinces such as Marlborough.[77] Oamaru in North Otago was an agricultural-crew capital, known for its drunkenness and rowdiness in season. Here and elsewhere, the police reaped their annual crop of 'harvest drunks'. A general characteristic of crews was that they were paid in lump sums. Shearers, harvest workers and the like would proceed from their working stint or season to 'knock down', 'burst' or 'melt down' their pay while 'on the bash' in town.[78] The terminology was the same as the whalers before them, and so were the results.

Apart from its hero/villain status, in both folklore and reality, crew culture appears to have had several other ambiguities. It combined considerable power to enforce its norms with a certain looseness – a persistent individualism and a lack of strong, long-term bonds between particular individuals. Crews were also ambiguous in terms of class. They were objectively most akin to decent working men; they were very often seen as disreputable, at least off the job; and there is some evidence that they saw themselves as respectable, conceivably even genteel in a sense, and that their class origins were mixed. Such features appear in a study of co-operative railmaking workers in the 1900s, when progressive colonisation and its crews staged their last stand. There was little collective action in their camps. Men were 'fully alive to their own interests', but 'those interests were perceived as various rather than identical'.[79] Many goldminers seem to have seen themselves as middle-class respectables. They disliked working for wages, and it is apparently true that they were more literate than the general population.[80] John Boultbee's sealers hated 'scholards', 'swells' and gentlemen, but sealers generally, despite having the world's worst working conditions, were said to have seen themselves as middle-class.[81] Crews were not necessarily wedded to the system by the desire for promotion – 'many co-operative workers did not want to become farmers'.[82] They had some potential for encouraging the formation of the tight, self-conscious working class so feared by both populism and the establishment. But they themselves were not it.

I do not wish to understate the substantial convergence between my conception of crew culture and notions of 'male culture', centred on mateship, and a 'floating rural working class'.[83] But they do diverge significantly. Some views of male culture, notably in recolonial novels, retrospectively romanticise it while conceding that it was concealed under a veneer of inarticulateness or casual bonhomie. No doubt, men did fall deeply in mateship with each other, but the essence of prefabricated community was that the parts be interchangeable. The term 'mate' is still useful when men wish to enlist co-operation and a sense of solidarity from those they do not know. Moreover, crews were not solely male; the disreputable women of the binge centres in which crewmen recharged their subcultural as well as personal batteries were arguably a small but important part of their social segment. Relations between crewmen and crew-women may have been less male-dominated than in core culture; the lives of the latter may have compared favourably to some core women; and exploitation was mutual. But crew culture was still predominantly male and misogynist. Indeed, its elders were selected for misogyny by the fact that no women would marry them. Woman-hating jokes and attitudes were nurtured most by men with whom no women would have sex for free. Nor were agricultural and pastoral workers the major or defining component of crews, as they are of 'the rural working class'. The leading archetype, shearers, were in fact crewmen-come-lately; prone to scurvy, sleeping in berths and drinking 'burgoo', like the sailors their subculture echoed. Their prominence arguably reflects the farm bias of New Zealand history. Most crews were not agricultural, and in the sense of class community they were not working-class either.

A further ambiguity was the phenomenon of orderly disorder, the order sometimes self-imposed. There were no police initially on the early Nelson goldfields, so diggers followed traditional practice and agreed to their own rules. There was no great evidence of mayhem, except 'scenes of riot and confusion which took place through intoxication on every Sunday'. Another goldfield of 3,000 diggers was totally unpoliced for three months.[84] One camp of railway workers was 'a somewhat uproarious place . . . yet there was no serious crime'. Police sometimes adjusted to different standards, while at other times trying to suppress them. 'On some matters the police avoided provocation.'[85] On the goldfields, too, 'drinking and fighting in the streets of the . . . shanty towns were, despite considerable criticism by visitors to the diggings, tolerated to an extent inconceivable in Dunedin'. The head of the new Otago police force protested that his men 'cannot be expected to preserve that degree of order at new rushes which ought to be observed at settled Townships'.[86]

There was a ritual element to some fistfights, which were less spasms of interpersonal chaos than socially endorsed and constrained means of resolving disputes, gaining mana, unleashing aggression and frustration, and providing entertainment. On one Westland goldfield, 'almost every half hour a cry of "fight" would be heard, a space would be cleared in the street, and two half-naked and wholly drunken men would proceed to hammer away at one another until they were separated'.[87] The group cleared the space, held the ring and limited as well as legitimated the fist duel. Guns were not used. Bingeing and fighting were also restricted in time and space. It mostly occurred at predictable times – Saturday or Sunday, payday, port call or the end of contracts or work seasons. They took place either in the camps themselves, often unpoliced or tolerated by police, but with spasms of suppression, or in neighbouring small towns and in the binge centres of large towns and ports, where it was less tolerated. Here, drunken members of core culture, especially if they were respectable or genteel, were much less likely to be arrested than crew. Crew and core cultures were the two social wheels of progressive colonisation, normally spinning independently; sparks flew when they clashed.

The suggestion, then, is that wandering crews, not drifting atoms or a highly atomised mainstream population, were responsible for the high rate of colonial hitting and bingeing. This may also be true of litigation. Gold rushers were enthusiastic suers, helped by easy access to the goldfield wardens' courts. 'The amount of litigation in a goldmining community was extraordinary.'[88] Other crew did less suing but a lot of being sued, especially for debt. 'Co-operative workers sometimes repudiated their commercial debts or left a locality without paying . . . Many of these civil suits were brought by shop-keepers against co-operative workers.'[89] As Fairburn himself notes, 'the plaintiffs in civil suits tended disproportionately to be businessmen and the settled (shopkeepers, merchants, tradesmen, hoteliers), while the defendants tended disproportionately to be manual workers (including miners in mining districts) and transients'.[90]

The clash of wheels was relatively rare, and the tolerance of crew culture relatively great, on the goldfields during the rushes, which did not inflate arrest rates as one might expect. But the rise and fall of bingeing and hitting does correlate with the rise and fall of progressive colonisation. Fairburn himself shows that this was true of Wellington, where hitting and bingeing spasmed with progress – doubling in 1865, for example. They did not correlate with imports and exports, but neither did progress.[91] The nationwide drop in the proportion of unmarried adult males from 1874 to 1901 was much lower than the drop in arrests for drunkenness and violence and in litigation. But crews were partly tamed and converted from the 1880s, and they also aged into greater tractability – many while remaining unmarried.

Ironically enough, the voice of the crews was a genteel-respectable Cantabrian woman, Edith Lyttleton. In thirteen novels and many short stories, most written as 'G. B. Lancaster', she not only 'praises and documents the colonial stereotype', but helped romanticise and broaden it from a crew stereotype into a colonial one: romantic maleness, rough diamonds, manly virtue, deep mateship, the high valuation of physical strength and skill, though not gunslinging, the conquest more of nature than natives. This was part retrospective reinvention, part genuine voice – in its internationalism, for example. Lyttleton lived in London from 1909, set her stories in Australia and Canada as well as New Zealand, and sometimes aimed them at American markets. One was made by Hollywood into a silent film, *The Eternal Struggle*.[92]

Crew culture had origins in the eighteenth century or earlier. It dwelt less *in* countries than *between* them, and the Irish Sea may have been its first home. There was already a common stock of English/Scots/Irish folklore, and perhaps slang, by 1788. Similarly, the Australian shearing song 'Click Go the Shears, Boys' was largely filched from America.[93] While crews had echoes elsewhere – in the subculture of Swedish lumbermen, for example[94] – they specialised in neo-Britains, which were the nineteenth century's fastest progressive colonisers. Wandering crews in New Zealand and other neo-Britains followed spasms of war, gold and progress, and flowed into the ports they boosted. It was more a semi-nomadic, cyclical, progress-patterned type of movement than full nomadism. They formed binge centres, red-light and shabby boarding-house quarters in the main towns. These urban base camps anchored them. Crews were more 'atomised', less well bonded, than some old-world social segments – this was probably also true of colonial core culture. But they had bonds enough to operate successfully. There is a sense in which they were *in* New Zealand, but not *of* it, though New Zealand history owns them as much as anywhere else. They were not wholly part of Old Britain either. Irish, Canadians, Americans and Australians featured large, but crews were the social segment in which the partly artificial subdivisions among the neo-Britains mattered least. Their culture was neo-British and Irish, their argot a 'Lingua Britannica'. Like other folk cultures, theirs did not care about patents, plagiarisms and retrospective nationalisms. Its local vestige was an Australasian layer of culture, claimed by each side of the Tasman without full acknowledgement of the other. Crews were the social expression of the ethos of expansion in its particular nineteenth-century neo-British form, and they rose and fell with progressive colonisation.

Ties That Bind

On 1 November 1876, the provinces were abolished by an Act of the colonial Parliament. It is hard today to imagine a federal New Zealand – how many people know or care that they live in what was once New Munster or New Ulster? The first and last study of the rise and fall of the provincial system, by W. P. Morrell, appeared in 1932. Naturally, the textbook of New Zealand's formal regionalism was published in London, where the first edition was 'not sold out but burned out' by the Luftwaffe during the Blitz. Despite Goering's best efforts, the book survived to be republished, and it dominates the field to this day.

Historians' disinterest in revisiting provincialism may stem from a sense that New Zealand's national destiny and the sheer pettiness and financial fragility of the provinces made their demise inevitable. It is true that to call some provincial careers chequered is to be too kind. Marlborough had two competing superintendents in 1862, and two competing capitals in 1865. Southland province, the vanguard or suicide squad of progressive colonisation, went bankrupt in the later 1860s. Creditors seized the government office furniture, something that is supposed to happen only in revolutions. A chastened Southland remarried Otago in 1871. All other provinces except Otago also had financial crises, ranging from spasmodic to endemic. It is easy to agree with Julius Vogel that 'their doom was only a question of time', and to congratulate him for administering euthanasia.[95]

And yet a glance at the provincial government buildings in Christchurch or Dunedin is enough to make one hesitate. These structures, and perhaps the system they symbolised, were built to last. Some provinces had genuinely distinct identities, with some citizens hoping for separate futures. Not all were always impoverished or tiny in their time. On the point of death in 1876, Otago was as big as Scotland, had more people than Tasmania and five times as many as Western Australia, and a revenue of £500,000. Auckland and Canterbury were nearly as big; Wellington, Nelson and Hawke's Bay were probably financially viable; and the Southland solution of remerger was available to Marlborough and Westland. Taranaki had long been a ward of central government, but dairying and the decline of Maori independence would have saved it in the 1880s. The provincial system could have been renovated rather than destroyed. Why wasn't it?

Economic, historical and ethnic differences among regions have been mentioned in previous chapters. Auckland was exceptionally non-pastoral and non-company, for example, and Otago-Southland was exceptionally Scots. Religion was another force with the power to both bind and split. Religious commitment and unity were important in the foundation of several New Zealand settlements. Free Church Presbyterian Otago and High Church Anglican Canterbury were the largest and best-known cases. The first Anglican

Bishop of New Zealand, George Selwyn, accepted the post in 1841, after his elder brother had declined it. Very much a High Churchman, with what was unkindly described as an embryo tonsure, Selwyn was an extremely muscular Christian, energetically establishing his Church of New Zealand, autonomous from 1858, until his departure in 1868.[96] Other founding fathers and mothers made sterling church-building contributions too. But there is also considerable evidence that organised religion was not enormously strong in colonial New Zealand.

In mid-nineteenth-century Britain, the grip of the churches on decent folk was loosening, and churchgoing was becoming an increasingly respectable and genteel affair. Even in these classes, churchgoers were ranged along a spectrum of commitment, from the deeply religious to very nominal adherents, who visited church at birth, death and marriage, with many gradations in between. Virtually all colonial Pakeha were nominally Christian, but we have seen that regular church attendance was not high. It was lower than in Britain and in the Australian sister colonies, though New South Wales came close.[97] The boosted colonisation of new frontiers could corrode surviving religiosity. Shifting, wandering, poor roading and the simple shortage of pews had their effects. Great deference to priest and parson was among the customs shed eagerly by decent migrants. 'You are not cock of the walk out here, Father.'

The crews appear to have been indifferent, even antagonistic to organised religion. In 1859, sawmillers at Banks Peninsula deliberately 'organised dogfights to try to put an end to the first church services there'. Except among the missionaries, traditional denominational antagonisms were sometimes allowed to lapse. A Catholic priest stood in for a sick Presbyterian colleague at a service in Wellington, which is hard to imagine in Ulster.[98] Migrants, wrote Thomas Cholmondeley in 1854, are 'indifferent to religious forms when they arrive in a new country'. 'Church of England?' he had asked his servant, for census purposes. '"Whatever you like, sir," was the reply; "we always used to go to church in the old country, but here we be kind o' weaned of it."'[99] Migration may have selected for less frequent churchgoers – there are hints of a correlation between New Zealand-prone and low churchgoing districts in England. The higher proportion of lax Anglicans in New Zealand helps explain New Zealand's inferiority in churchgoing to that of Victoria and South Australia, though not to New South Wales.[100]

There were attempts to boost colonial religiosity, from within and without the major churches, which gathered force from the 1880s and 1890s. American 'revivalism' – 'you must pray until your nose bleeds, or it will not avail' – just might have had some effect in New Zealand prior to this. The first American-style wavelet of religious revivalism struck in 1864, when William 'California' Taylor was called to Australasia by divine telegraph. In Christchurch, he drew a thousand people; in Wellington 'several distinguished citizens were converted';

but several is not many, and crowds in Auckland were disappointing.[101] Pentecostal evangelists raided for souls from Australia as early as 1863.[102] Another revival in 1881 produced at least one remarkable double salvation. 'Anne Towers . . . yesterday told Blannie that she had been converted *twice* during the week.'[103] The view that revivalism explains the rise in church attendance, 1874–86, is not very convincing, particularly because it was followed by a steep and long-term decline in church attendance, despite an increase in revivalism.[104]

Pakeha were not an unChristian people, but they were not intensely Christian either. That much adherence was not intense does not make it unimportant, for Pakeha any more than Maori. Shared religion, even when the commitment was loose, did help socialise norms and values. Anglicanism was never a state religion in New Zealand, but Irish Catholics sometimes felt that it came close. A vague, shared Protestantism, self-repressive yet 'progressive', helped loosely bind most Pakeha. Commitment, as indicated by church attendance, varied greatly according to denomination. Between 1874 and 1886, Presbyterians and Catholics were almost twice as likely to attend church regularly as Anglicans, and Methodists – about 8.5 per cent of Pakeha – were four times as devout.[105] Where the tighter denominations intersected with region and ethnicity, the three reinforced each other. Religion clearly facilitated the persistence of difference in some special settlements. Methodism is said to have still been over-represented in mining districts in the twentieth century because of their attraction to chapelgoing Cornish and Welsh in the nineteenth.[106] A 'special settlement' of English Dissenters was established at Albertland in Northland in 1862, and, as late as 1880, 'long graces are said before and after meals with the right hand held up to the face'. Difference persisted among the Presbyterian Highlanders of Waipu, and there were also local pockets and networks of Irish Catholicism – very large ones in Westland, where Catholic Irish made up almost a third of the population and helped lay the foundations of that region's permanent distinctiveness, along with mining, socialism and economic stasis.[107] Scots Presbyterian Otago and Southland were the classic cases of ethnic/religious/regional distinctiveness.

To some extent, then, religion did combine with economics, history and other factors to reinforce regionalism. Otago petitioned several times for full separation, sometimes trying to take the rest of the South Island with it to form a new colony. Auckland, distinctive more through history and economics than religion or ethnicity, also attempted full separation, no fewer than five times, and has still not quite given up hope.[108] James Busby, purveyor of declarations of independence, led the Auckland separation movement's London committee in 1865. Separation sentiment was quite strong and persistent in these provinces. One historian has claimed that 1860s South Island separationism 'became the largest mass movement in New Zealand'.[109] This indicates limits to New Zealand collective identity until the 1870s. But it was always in competition with a colony-wide collective identity, seeds of which existed as early as 1840 or even before, and with other homogenising and binding forces.

An important factor in the abolition of the provinces was a growing tension between 'in-regions' and 'out-regions'. As we have seen, the six original instant townships and their immediate hinterlands – the in-regions – initially dominated their provinces, whose out-regions they had helped form through the process of secondary colonisation. There was little hope of out-regions achieving political power within the old provinces. In Wellington, for example, the 1856 provincial council had 22 representatives from town and around, and eight from all the out-regions. In 1865, the out-regions still had only 10 of 32 seats.[110] One route of escape from dominance by the provincial centres was to form out-regions into new provinces, and legislation permitting this passed a sparsely attended Parliament in 1858. Most major out-regions tried to become separate provinces, some several times, but only four succeeded – one (Southland) temporarily, and one (Westland) very late. The alternative route of escape was to abolish the provinces. Small out-regions were not candidates for separation; they had to be part of something bigger. Micro-regionalism begat centralism at the expense of macro-regionalism, on the ancient principle that a distant master was better than one nearby.

The demands and distribution of progress also played their part. In the 1850s and 1860s, the crusaders had tried to diversify the image of New Zealand in British minds to save some provinces from the taint of wars and earthquakes. The need for this diminished in the 1870s, and progressive colonisation had always had a tendency to collectivise imaging. It was hard enough to create a colonial reputation as a migrant destination, let alone provincial ones. Colonial government security for loans was better than provincial security, especially when provinces like Southland were ruining the game for everybody. As before, the New Zealand image in Britain reflected back into New Zealand's image of itself. On the more practical side, some, notably Stafford and Vogel, came to feel that large-scale public progress, in war and rail construction, for example, was better handled at the top, and pointed to various examples of damaging provincial obstructionism. Ironically, the near-monopoly of 1870s railmaking by Otago and Canterbury must have operated as something of a bribe to persuade them to acquiesce in abolition. Centralising suited the colonial crusaders with the highest hopes. From 1859, Thomas Russell sought to make his companies national, or pan-colonial, as well as provincial, and brought Britain into his Limited Circle as well. He was rumoured to be involved in Vogel's 'sudden conversion' to centralism in the early 1870s, as were Stafford and the major South Island pastoralist John Studholme.[111]

Another factor is that formal and informal regions – the former marked out by Grey on a map in his office – did not always correlate. South Taranaki, for example, looked to Wanganui, not New Plymouth, as its centre. Because Maori dominated central and inland Taranaki, Pakeha 'Taranaki' essentially consisted of New Plymouth and its environs until the 1880s. Some large centres increasingly imported crucial resources, such as food and timber, from outside their provinces. The mixed-farming Waimea district of Nelson was in effect part of Wellington's town-supply area. The wars of the 1860s also boosted centralism: Maori were simply too strong for provinces to handle. It was the wars that broke down revenue-sharing arrangements between colony and provinces, and founded the *national* debt.[112] There was a deeper dimension to this, as we have seen. Conflict, and Maori pan-tribalism, created and consolidated a shared enemy for Pakeha, reinforcing a thin but real collective identity that competed with both regionalism and the South Island desire to be rid of expensive Maori troubles. There is a sense in which Pakeha regionalism foundered on the rock of Maori resistance, and a deeper sense in which the two peoples made each other – as *peoples* rather than tribes and provinces.

Such factors strengthened centralism and weakened provincialism, but my feeling is that they were not enough in themselves. The general impression is of evenly balanced binding and splitting forces, with parity favouring the incumbent. It may have been other homogenising forces that tilted the balance. The deepest of these was a great shrinking process in transport and communications, which knitted New Zealand together like Britain before it. There is a tendency to associate this with railmaking. But railways had hardly begun to bite in 1876, even in the South Island, and in the North they were practically nonexistent. The beginnings of the great shrinking should in fact be dated to the 1850s, when coastal steamers were introduced and coaching and postal services began to improve. A bigger boost came in the 1860s, with the emergence of 'Cobb's coaches', regular steamship services and the introduction of the telegraph. 'The revolutionary break came with the swift adoption of the telegraph from the early 1860s.'[113]

'Cobb and Co.' coaches were introduced in 1861 from Victoria. The name was often used without authorisation, but it implied a fast, regular service and coaches using a new type of suspension, better able to handle poor roads. The first such coaches halved transport time from Dunedin to the Tuapeka goldfield, and by 1863 had reduced travelling time from Timaru to Christchurch to one day, providing a regular thrice-weekly service.[114] Steamships were even more important. It was not so much that steam was faster or cheaper, but that it was much more regular and reliable. By the late 1860s, mail, goods and passengers could leave Dunedin for Wellington according to timetables in the reasonably confident expectation of getting there on schedule. Closer places were linked by steamers providing what was virtually a ferry service. The efficiency of these services was far from perfect, and comfort was not their strong point. But they were the basis of a *national* network of transport and communications.

Inland postal services increased in number and efficiency to feed the steamer services. By 1874, there were 286 – only ten by rail, the rest by horse or coach. In 1855, 4.6 letters per capita of Pakeha population were delivered. By 1875, this had increased over sixfold to 30.5 per capita, delivered by a comprehensive network of 647 post offices. In 1845, there had only been eight.[115] The first telegraph was established in Dunedin in 1861; the South Island was linked to Wellington in 1866; Wellington to Napier in 1868; and Auckland was wired up in 1872 – by lines that avoided the King Country. 'By the early 1870s few towns in the colony were without a telegraph station.'[116] A message between Wellington and Auckland took about three weeks by overland mail in the 1840s, if all went well. Twenty-five years later, it was almost instantaneous. The average age of commercial information regarding Auckland and Dunedin published in the *Lyttelton Times* dropped from 36 and 23 days in 1851, to 1.1 and one day in 1878–79. 'The telegraph permitted the greater integration of trade and markets throughout New Zealand.'[117]

Economics became more national, and so, to some extent, did society. Telegraph permitted the introduction of New Zealand Standard Time in 1868 – even time had varied regionally prior to this. People in Auckland knew a great deal more about Dunedin in 1870 than they had in 1850; they even went to bed at the same time. Information facilitated planned wandering and shifting, and transience helped the homogenising and shrinking process. Shifters might simulate stayers, but their previous experience meant that they did so with less local variation. They reduced the homogenising effect of transience less than the solvent effect. Crews, drifters and their crimes were much the same everywhere, and so was progressive colonisation and the formal and informal myths of settlement. People with links to several provinces had an incentive to imagine a community that incorporated them all.

Some New Zealand historians have stressed regions and localities as the building blocks of the country's history, and this position has its merits. The six main settlements, and the Pakeha regions that grew from them, were founded between 1840 and 1850, an era of inferior communications in which New Zealand was, in effect, much larger than in 1875. Each town was its region's own interface with the outside world. Christchurch's communications with Sydney were consistently better than with Auckland in 1856, though neither was good.[118] This was also the period in which ethnic and religious distinctions between the settlements were most marked. After the fall of the provinces, and in the face of increasing centralising, homogenising and shrinking forces, regionalism lost strong formal and official expression, and had to assert itself in more marginal ways, such as sporting competition. Another way of asserting regionalism was through history: reaching back across the less different near-past to the more different further past, so asserting difference in the present. There are intriguing echoes of Maori tribal tradition here. It seems to me that, in fact, the ideological, economic, social and political dimensions of progressive colonisation, combined with technologically driven shrinking from the 1860s, did tend to iron out regional variations. But it is true that it did not eliminate them.

Two qualifications to the picture of a shrinking and homogenising late colonial society, circa 1875, need noting. First, the absence of difference does not equal the absence of separate identity, though it makes the latter more difficult. Just as identical twins remain distinct in their own minds, so colonial Marlborough and Hawke's Bay could retain informal regional collective identities despite the fall of the provinces, and strong economic, ethnic and social similarities. What limits on difference did do was increase the compatibility of collective identities. They could fit within each other, like babushka dolls, without inconvenient bits of difference sticking out. It was perfectly possible to be a staunch Ashburtonian, Cantabrian, New Zealander, Australasian and Briton simultaneously, and this is important in the study of New Zealand collective identity, at any level. But shrinking and some decline in difference from the 1860s did mean that centralists found it somewhat easier to merge Scots Otago and English Canterbury than their predecessors had found Scotland and England. Shrinking and homogenising did not end regionalism but facilitated its telescoping within 'higher' forms of collective identity.

The second crucial qualification is that homogenising varied in its effects. It varied in space – Westland and Northland, for example, were not fully integrated into the transport and communications system until the twentieth century. It varied in time: 1875 was still early days. It may also have varied by class. While many people engaged eagerly with the new transport and communications networks, early access to them was no more evenly distributed than most other things. Many could afford the train fare from Christchurch to Invercargill or the steamer fare to Wellington a couple of times a decade. Few could afford them several times a year. Telegrams were also quite expensive, and access was restricted. 'There were several groups which benefited immediately from the telegraph system. But it may be assumed that the general public was not one of them . . . The main users were rather the press, business, and the government itself.'[119] New Zealand shrank first at the top.

As early as the 1850s, genteel regional élites had begun knitting themselves together across provincial boundaries in a variety of ways, including intermarriage, friendship, business partnerships, interlocking directorates, and politics. The process provides a sort of case study in the formation of colonial community, though not a typical one. Small networks were formed or buttressed by religion: Catholic gentry (Clifford, Weld, Petre, Vavasour, Ward of Marlborough, O'Connor); Jewish genteel respectables (Montefiore, Nathan, Hort, Levin). Clumps formed in the old country persisted in the new, and acquaintance and kinship inflated. Intermarriage entrenched new networks. Taranaki's Richmond-Atkinson clan, which was also linked to Fell, Ronalds, Hursthouse, Gillies and other notable families, is the classic example of these phenomena. Scattered by the New Plymouth settler diaspora stemming from the Taranaki War, it spread across at least three provinces by 1862, helping to link them up, or at least link their élites. Another 'clan' was centred on the Wakefields, who were linked by marriage and kinship to Torlesse, Dillon Bell and Stafford. The two networks were connected by the partnership of F. D. Bell, Edward Stafford and C. W. Richmond in a large Otago sheep station, and by Stafford's close if temporary political partnerships with C. W. and J. C. Richmond. Ormond/McLean and Featherston/Fitzherbert were more permanent political joint ventures, dominating Hawke's Bay and Wellington respectively. Dr Isaac Featherston, who ruled Wellington 1853–70, had his share of enemies, including the Wakefields, but many friends as well. 'Old Feathery' had two sons-in-law and the brother of a son-in-law in Parliament to keep him company. One, Dr James Menzies, was also Superintendent of Southland 1861–65.[120]

Otago, Auckland and Canterbury families were similarly linked by business and political partnerships, friendships and marriage, and here, too, the networks networked from the 1860s. Cargill progeny married Jones progeny; genteel-respectable Otago whakapapa and company directorates tangled like gorse. Mills and Larnach, as well as Cargill and Jones, invested in Union Steam and the Westland coalfields it annexed. 'The objects of the company,' it announced in 1873, 'are thoroughly Colonial, not local.'[121] Thomas Russell and John Logan Campbell, close friends themselves, were linked by marriage to the Griggs and Cracroft Wilsons, eminent Canterbury gentry and pastoralists, though John Grigg hailed from Auckland. Russell was spider to many webs. The early trustees of his Bank of New Zealand included Logan Campbell and James Williamson in Auckland, Weld and Cracroft Wilson in Canterbury, Stafford in Nelson and W. B. Rhodes in Wellington. Russell also had close business connections with Sir Charles Clifford, baronet of Flaxbourne in Marlborough, and the Fergusson family of Britain, which, with three incumbents, 1873–1967, came close to being hereditary governors of New Zealand. Frederick Whitaker, twice premier of the colony, was one of Russell's chief lieutenants, and Julius Vogel was a friend. Russell occasionally helped out the government by arranging overseas loans for it as a sideline to his own business. This led William Rolleston to note in 1873 that 'the vulgar idea . . . is said to exist, that Mr Thomas Russell is not the representative of the Colonial Government, but the Colonial government is the representative of Mr. Thomas Russell'. In terms of corruption, by the standards of the time, this may not have been fair: both Russell and his government believed their financial interests legitimately converged. In terms of influence, however, it was a fair question.[122]

Politics was itself an important binding force among the gentry. With ten provincial legislatures and two houses of the colonial Parliament, all with a high turnover as well as a permanent core, it must have been a rare genteel family who had no-one on the inside of colonial politics. From 1854, the proto-ruling class met regularly, though not quite annually, at parliamentary sessions, which doubled as genteel conventions. The parliamentary session was also a social season, attended by women as well as men. A bored Winifred Logan Campbell was despatched to the parliamentary session in Wellington in 1882 for a bit of fun – something not easy to imagine today.[123] 'The Session' was a highlight of Wellington high society as early as 1865.[124] Premiers are said to have owed their power to, and to have been toppled by, 'the political ladies of Wellington, that most important but, regrettably, shadowy pressure group'.[125] This smacks a little of 'behind every good man . . .' stereotypes, but, as with the Pushful Wife, there may be some truth in it. When gentlewomen took up a cause, such as temperance or suffrage, they did take gentlemen with them, from across conservative–liberal and regional lines. Whatever their political influence, women helped make the session social as well as political, a focus of genteel class formation as well as genteel rule.

As New Zealand shrank from the 1860s, superior access to the shrinking made it easier for genteel regional networks to network in turn into colonial ones. By the early 1870s, perhaps, the first nationwide class community had formed: a genteel ruling class. Regionalism remained very important – *most* important for the large and voluble minority who opposed abolition – but colonial ties were strengthening. Some politicians very bitterly opposed the abolition of the provinces – a few even advocated violent resistance.[126] But in the end, the provinces were executed by a substantial majority, and they were not restored even in 1877, when the strongly provincialist George Grey became premier. Beneath the vehement rhetoric, and despite bitter feuds and factions, more and more gentry felt that their bonds outweighed their splits. Genteel class formation could have been the straw that broke the provincial camel's back.

Some contemporaries did see abolition as a victory for the ruling class, and it may be that they have been discounted too readily. But 'victory' is too strong a term: class formation facilitated abolition because a social construct had emerged that thought colonially as well as regionally. Similarly, 'ruling class' should not be taken to imply an all-powerful oligarchy, perfectly tight and unified. As we have seen, it did not imply that society was divided into the fiefs of individual gentry. The gentry were quite weak and wayward prefects. Populism and its compact were strong, and the new nationwide class had to compromise with it. Southern gentry were said to be 'abolitionists almost to a man',[127] because fellow gentry from other provinces were better insurance against closer settlement pressures than fellow provincials from other classes. But after 1876, they still had to conciliate such pressures, or at least appear to do so. Many gentry believed in sturdy yeomen too, and in 'democracy', in the sense of the right to choose your rulers. The electorate, the political nation, was greatly extended from 1879. It was almost as though the gentry had to apologise for being a ruling class, and there is a sense in which they did. Tight class was in itself a breach of the populist compact. While rulers compromised, kept their class character at least partly below the surface of public consciousness, and upheld the other articles of the Pakeha treaty, all was fairly well. But if progress and the flow of real and perceived opportunity were to stop, it might be a different matter. The compromise between genteel rule and the populist compact, and the incomplete but important binding of New Zealand into a single imagined community, were both aided by a shared dream: Greater Britain.

Greater Britain

In the decades after the 1880s, New Zealand history restructured and reinvented itself, forming a new cultural and economic system from selected shards of the old. This new era of 'recolonisation', 1880s to 1960s, had its own dynamics and fascinations. It achieved staggering feats in social control and social welfare, in security for the many as against the few, and in the achievement of social, moral and racial harmony, or their illusions. It sought to forget the Tasman world, to incorporate Maori and to forge a neo-colonial relationship with Britain whereby the masses at the periphery lived better than those at the metropolis. Its success stretches accepted definitions of subordinate colonialism.

The recolonial era also reforged paradise, with fresh myths and fresh kernels of truth. The myths were as remarkable and instructive as those of hunters and gardeners, or of progressive colonisers. The recolonial truths may have been better places for most people to live in than their colonial predecessors. Such themes are explored in the sequel to this book. Yet the paradises and prophecies of recolonial New Zealand were narrower, tighter and less bold than those of its predecessor, and the new era rewrote the history of the old. The brevity of the country's human past became a vice rather than a virtue; history no longer happened fast; and the grand prophecies of progressive colonisation became an embarrassment. The dramas of Maori settlement, Pakeha settlement and the great clash between them were tamed in retrospect. Dramatic, dynamic and significant history became something that happened overseas.

New Zealand history to the 1880s is not very long, but it is very fast. In less than one thousand years, a drop in the bucket of time, it formed two new peoples. The story of this process is the ultimate whakapapa, the ultimate acknowledgement of parentage, for today's New Zealanders. It may have wider implications too. Both Maori and Pakeha colonisations were driven and structured by myths of settlement, by dynamics and imperatives that were cultural as well as economic. Both replaced mobile and extractive systems with more sedentary and sustainable ones. All this may be true of other neo-Polynesias and other neo-Britains. The encounter between Maori and Pakeha was also driven, as well as obscured, by partly mythical dynamics, and these powerful myths of empire were not restricted to the Long Bright World. That the story is shared makes New Zealand history more significant, not less.

For the founders of Pakeha society, the colonising crusaders and their converts, the driving and binding dream was Greater Britain. The Irish were grudgingly allowed in; the myths of settlement were reshuffled, adapted and renegotiated; but in the 1870s prophecies of progress and paradise still reigned, varying greatly in particular, shared widely in general. Progress had substance; so did paradise for some, but it was mainly seen as a future, not a present. It was a national future as well as a regional one; a New Zealand future as well as a British one. In 1856, Edward Stafford, colonial New Zealand's longest-serving premier, had noted in Parliament that provincial rivalries might rip this future apart. 'From that moment I determined to be a New Zealander.' He wanted 'a great, powerful, and united people', 'a great nation', 'a strong and united nation', 'intended by nature and God to carry twenty-five millions of people'.[128] Stafford was capable of hypocrisy, but this was not an example of it. He was forced to abandon his Nelson pocket borough because he was thought to neglect its local interests. It could have been Edward Gibbon Wakefield or Charles Hursthouse speaking, or many other leading crusaders and politicians.

In 1853, George Grey prophesied that 'hereafter a great nation would occupy these islands', and he did not mean Maori. 'We who stand in this country,' he informed a receptive Auckland audience, 'occupy a historical position of extraordinary interest. Before us lies a future already brilliant with the light of a glorious morn, which we are to usher in to gladden unborn generations.'[129] In 1873, Julius Vogel informed a no-doubt-delighted imperial government that Britain could 'with justice be proud of having reproduced herself in "the Great Britain of the South" as New Zealand has been aptly called'.[130] The great crusader's subsequent science fiction novel *Anno Domini 2000, or Woman's Destiny* (1889) featured Hilda Richmond Fitzherbert, Duchess of New Zealand, as Under-Secretary of State for [British] Home Affairs, and chanted, 'Progression, progression, always progression.'[131] Even provincialists like Featherston sometimes saw their provinces as part of 'a great future nation'.[132] Separation, wrote an Otago settler in 1862, would be 'the grave of long cherished visions of future greatness and nationality'.[133] Citing American precedent, an 1860s New Zealand periodical argued that 'the ultimate destiny of each British colony is a distinct and independent nationality'.[134] John Ballance wrote in 1870, in his

Wanganui newspaper, that 'the interests of the colony point to independence ... Independence will come to us sooner or later. Is the time not opportune?'[135]

In 1869, the colony had responded very bitterly to Britain's decision to withdraw its legions, leaving settlers to the tender mercies of Titokowaru and Te Kooti. There was public talk of unilateral declarations of independence, and of applying to join the United States. Angry memoranda flew between the governments; the colonial press lampooned Britain as an 'unnatural mother'; and Stafford showed far less deference to the imperial government than did his twentieth-century successors.[136] He was seen as 'a Colonial office *bête noir*', and responded by accusing Britain of 'parsimony or constitutional arrogance ... Her colonies have grown great not because of, but in spite of, any care from her.'[137] Stafford's own successor, Fox, followed him in this at least. In 1870, he 'went so far as to ask that Great Britain arrange for its [New Zealand's] neutrality' in any future British war.[138] This was rhetoric, but the rhetoric was a long way from that of Gallipoli in 1915. The colonising crusaders and their ideology had faults, too numerous to list, but the colonial cringe was not among them.

Unfulfilled prophecies dredged up from the past are embarrassing, for peoples as for people. New Zealand historians have not fully confronted the fact that their subject has a great future behind it. New Zealand's aspirations in the Pacific, which were first an ancillary part of, and then a partial substitute for, her aspirations to Greater Britain, have been portrayed almost as a book of jokes, baby playing emperor in the nursery. In 1883, it was declared in Parliament that 'we are here to build up a nation of our own, not be hangers on'. 'The youthful treble of New Zealand nationalism' has been discerned in such statements.[139] They have been viewed as the tiny nineteenth-century embryos of a nationalism that matured steadily in the twentieth. Yet the embryos were in some respects stronger than the real thing. They envisaged a more independent, grander, Greater British future than the less bold Better British aspirations of their successors.

We need to contextualise these views, not cringe from them. They were formed in an age before continental land masses were thought to be a prerequisite of superpower. Portugal, Holland and Britain, all smaller than New Zealand, and with much less of their own gold, were imperial precedents. America was showing that great nations could grow from small beginnings through progressive colonisation, and New Zealand had in fact made a good start on the same road. The New Zealand Exhibition of 1865, held in Dunedin, was a crude caricature of the Crystal Palace Exhibition of 1851, on which it was modelled. Most of its supplementary medals were given for services to the exhibition itself rather than to the arts, sciences and industries it was supposed to exhibit. But this symbolised progressive colonisation's power to make futures by celebrating them, and the exhibition and its 31,000 visitors were an impressive feat for a seventeen-year-old township.[140] If the growth rates of 1860–80 had continued, New Zealand *would* now be more populous than Britain. In 1875, it must have seemed well positioned for the new progressive sprint history.

Independence was quite widely assumed to be the natural corollary of the colonial reproduction of peoples. It was the New Zealand end of various New Zealand–British systems – E. G. Wakefield, George Grey, Thomas Russell and Julius Vogel – that held the strings, especially the purse strings. Such men, born in Britain, had no need to prove their Britishness or kowtow to imperial governments whose directives they were accustomed to contest. The difference in tone between New Zealand–British government communications in the periods 1850s–70s and 1910s–40s is unmistakable – the former were far less deferential and more combative. 'I would rather enter into no controversy,' wrote Lord Kimberley, the British Secretary of State for the Colonies, in 1870, 'as it is undesirable to give the New Zealanders opportunities for showing their disregard of us.'[141]

This is another matter we should not exaggerate. New Zealand's Greater British future was envisaged as British, sometimes very British, but not as subordinate to, or even smaller than, Old Britain. Ideas of Greater Britain contested with those of Better Britain, which were somewhat more modest and subordinate. Some leading crusaders, including Vogel and Russell, returned to Britain, though whether they saw this as an abandonment of New Zealand or retirement to its old people's home is unclear. They retained their New Zealand interests and investments, or what was left of them. Imminent independence was not taken very seriously; ultimate independence was. Such views were by no means universal; they were not directly part of the daily lives of most minds. They differed greatly in degree, and some were grandiose or rhetorical even in their time. But they were not as megalomaniacal as retrospect has made them seem. And they did strengthen a widely shared driving and binding dream, intertwining it with renegotiated myths of paradise and progress, individual and collective.

Grand dreams were matched by quite grand practice. Pakeha culture and socio-economy in the 1870s was not what the colonising crusaders had hoped. Sheep and gold were much more prominent; progress was much more roller-coaster than escalator. Many decent folk preferred to take the stairs, voluntarily or involuntarily avoiding the individual progress, through faithful servitude to sturdy independence, that had been mapped out for them. Prosperity and opportunity, even in terms of mere enhancement, let alone adoption and promotion, were very far from universal, and they selected for gender and class. Religion was weaker and ethnicity stronger than many crusaders would have wished. Community had to struggle with atomism, and there was some tension between cores and crews – the latter essential but unruly. Crews and other decent non-promoters, and their informal myths of settlement, strengthened populism, which constrained the gentry more than most would have liked. The populist compact forced compromises on genteel rule. Resilient Maori persisted in the works, blocking and subverting the great agencies of empire through both collaboration and resistance, and many shades in between. Resilient serpents in paradise, stubborn brakes on progress, they slowed Greater Britain down and were never as incorporated into it as they were into its successor system. Above all, there were shadows on the horizon, portents of a day when progressive colonisation might stop. All these things marred the triumph of the colonising crusade to the point where some failed to recognise it, but triumph there still was: a proto-people half a million strong, woven from Old Britain, Ireland, Australia; sheep and gold; progress, prophecies and dreams.

Five hundred thousand people from a standing start in 50 years, 1,200 miles from anywhere and 12,000 from *the* somewhere. Four cities, dirty and ramshackle, with orphans and derelicts tucked under shabby carpets of deficient charity, but vibrant with the hum of getting on. Camps, towns and stations sprouting like crazy mushrooms, bloating and bursting, desiccating, hanging on or taking off. Whores, housemaids, ladies and yeowomen levering old world against new to prise out some space for themselves. Publicans, gentry, carpenters: aspiring, conspiring, expiring, making good, or at least making better. Exports projected from ostriches and olives, iron and oil; and actually conjured from fungus, flax, tree resin, seals, sheep and trees; rabbits, antimony, copper, coal and thousand-ton gold dredges. More gold than the Inca ever possessed, sifted, washed and crushed from whole hills. Thousand-year-old trees mown like grass, made into heat, shacks, railway sleepers and 'the largest wooden building in the southern hemisphere'. Hundred-year-old whales carved into giant lumps of lard and melted in the pot into lamp oil for London streets and drunken Cossacks. Primeval forests charred into empty plains or bare-hill sheepwalks where sheep could barely stagger. Violence in bulk, from the casual fist, husband to wife, mate to mate, stranger to stranger; through the bloody horrors of the Musket Wars to the most 'modern' conflict people had yet died in. Horses and bullocks, men and women, steam machines and (London) money pushing and pulling the whole amazing edifice onward and upward – and downward and sideways, but always running fast and frenetic like the headless chook in Katherine Mansfield's story. Slaving, fighting, fornicating, lying, striving, changing, transforming, converting – throw the thesaurus at it – and trying spasmodically to maintain a certain refinement, like a prostitute taking tea and cucumber sandwiches between tricks. A booming, burgeoning neo-Britain, growing hysterically, tamed only historically. Love it, loathe it, or both; this was colonial New Zealand, and boring was the one thing it was not.

REFERENCES

Full referencing is impossible in a work of this kind, because most paragraphs are distilled from many sources. The policy followed here has been to reference quotations, most statistics and many particular points, with more general sources acknowledged where this seems especially warranted. Books cited are published in New Zealand unless otherwise specified.

Abbreviations

AEHR Australian Economic History Review
AJHR Appendices to the Journals of the House of Representatives, New Zealand
BPP Irish University Press Series of British Parliamentary Papers, Colonies, New Zealand
DNZB The Dictionary of New Zealand Biography, eds W. H. Oliver and Claudia Orange, 2 vols, 1990–93
ENZ An Encyclopaedia of New Zealand, ed. A. H. McLintock, 3 vols, 1966
Historical Statistics New Zealand: A Handbook of Historical Statistics, ed. G. T. Bloomfield, Boston, 1984
JPS Journal of the Polynesian Society
NZJA New Zealand Journal of Archaeology
NZJH New Zealand Journal of History
OYB Official Yearbook of New Zealand
TPNZI Transactions and Proceedings of the New Zealand Institute

Chapter 1: The Prehistory of New Zealand

1. Peter Drewett et al., *A Regional History of England: The South-East to A.D. 1000*, London, 1988, 246–59.
2. John Blair, 'The Anglo-Saxon Period', in K. Morgan (ed.), *The Oxford History of Britain*, Oxford, 1988, 68.
3. Michael Trotter, 'Settlements, Sites and Structures around Ship Cove', in Glyn Barratt (ed.), *Queen Charlotte Sound: The Traditional and European Records 1820*, 1987, 115.
4. F. M. Cornford, *Thucydides Mythistoricus*, London, 1907.
5. Bede, *Ecclesiastical History of the English People*, ed. Bertram Colgrave and R. A. B. Mynors, Oxford, 1969.
6. T. B. Macaulay, *History of England*, 4 vols, London, 1849–55, i, chapters 1–2.
7. Thor Heyerdahl, *American Indians in the Pacific*, 1952; Robert Langdon, *The Lost Caravel*, Sydney, 1975, and *The Lost Caravel Re-explored*, Canberra, 1988.
8. Quoted in D. R. Simmons, *The Great New Zealand Myth*, 1976, 168.
9. Jim Allen and J. Peter White, 'The Lapita Homeland: Some New Data and an Interpretation', *JPS* 98 (1989), 129–46. On the validity of Melanesian–Polynesian distinctions, see K. Howe, *Where the Waves Fall: A New South Sea Islands History from First Settlement to Colonial Rule*, Sydney, 1984.
10. Patrick V. Kirch, 'Rethinking Polynesian Prehistory', *JPS* 95 (1986), 9–40.
11. Helen Leach, *1000 Years of Gardening in New Zealand*, 1984.
12. Douglas L. Oliver, *Native Cultures of the Pacific Islands*, Honolulu, 1989, 57.
13. Janet Davidson, *The Prehistory of New Zealand*, 1984, 24. Also see 97.
14. *The Journals of Captain James Cook*, ed. J. C. Beaglehole, 3 vols, Cambridge, 1955–67, iii, 73.
15. Cook, *Journals*, i, 538–39.
16. Quoted in J. C. Beaglehole, 'Eighteenth Century Science and the Voyages of Discovery', *NZJH* 3 (1969), 107–23, 120.
17. Simmons, *Great New Zealand Myth*, 39.
18. Jeff Sissons, Wiremu Wi Hongi and Pat Hohepa, *The Puriri Trees Are Laughing: A Political History of Nga Puhi in the Inland Bay of Islands*, 1987, 54.
19. Teone Taare Tikao, *Tikao Talks*, ed. Herries Beattie, 1990 (orig. 1939), 100, 97.
20. *Na To Hoa Aroha/From Your Dear Friend: The Correspondence between Sir Apirana Ngata and Sir Peter Buck, 1925–50*, ed. M. P. K. Sorrenson, 3 vols, 1986–87, iii, 222–23.

21. In J. M. McEwen, *Rangitane: A Tribal History*, 1986, 4–5. Also see *Buck–Ngata Letters*, i, 266, ii, 151–53.
22. Smith, *The Lore of the Whare-Wananga*, 2 vols, 1913–15.
23. Simmons, *Great New Zealand Myth*, 113.
24. Herries Beattie in *Tikao Talks*, 6.
25. Best, *Maori Religion and Mythology*, part 1, 1924, 12. Also see Giselle Byrnes, 'Savages and Scholars: Some Pakeha Perceptions of the Maori 1890s–1920s', Waikato MA thesis, 1990.
26. 1972 (original 1929).
27. Edward Said, 'Representing the Colonized: Anthropology's Interlocutors', *Critical Inquiry* 15 (1989), 205–25.
28. Simmons, *Great New Zealand Myth* and 'A New Zealand Myth: Kupe, Toi and the "Fleet" ', *NZJH* 3 (1969), 14–31.
29. *Buck–Ngata Letters*, iii, 74. Peter Buck shared Ngata's doubts, ibid., 77–78.
30. Orbell, *Hawaiki: A New Approach to Maori Tradition*, 1991 edn; C. Schirren, summarised in F. Von Hochstetter, *New Zealand: Its Physical Geography, Geology and Natural History*, London, 1867 (German orig. 1863), 207–9.
31. A classic 'Smithian' exposition of the legend is Elsdon Best, 'Maori and Maruiwi', *TPNZI* 48 (1915), 435–47. Smith himself initially thought the Moriori were inferior but not Melanesian – *Hawaiki: The Original Home of the Maori*, 219–20. For recent analyses, see M. P. K. Sorrenson, *Maori Origins and Migrations: The Genesis of Some Pakeha Myths and Legends*, 1979; D. G. Sutton, 'The Whence of the Moriori', *NZJH* 19 (1985), 3–13; Michael King, *Moriori: A People Rediscovered*, 1989.
32. Forster, quoted in Lynne Withey, *Voyages of Discovery: Captain Cook and the Exploration of the Pacific*, Berkeley and Los Angeles, 1989, 290–91, and Crozet, quoted in Ann Salmond, *Two Worlds: First Meetings Between Maori and Europeans 1642–1772*, 1991, 376.
33. Thomson, *The Story of New Zealand, Past and Present, Savage and Civilized*, 2 vols, London, 1859, i, 61; Skinner, *The Morioris of the Chatham Islands*, Honolulu, 1923.
34. Duff, *The Moa-hunter Period of Maori Culture*, 1977 (orig. 1950).
35. Sharp, *Ancient Voyagers in the Pacific*, 1957 (orig. 1956). Also see his 'Polynesian Navigation to Distant Islands', *JPS* 70 (1961), 221–26.
36. Michael Trotter and Beverley McCulloch, *Unearthing New Zealand*, 1989, 31; Philip Houghton, *The First New Zealanders*, 1980, 72.
37. D. R. Simmons, 'Economic Change in New Zealand Prehistory', *JPS* 78 (1969), 3–34; L. M. Groube, 'The Origin and Development of Earthwork Fortifications in the Pacific', in R. C. Green and M. Kelly (eds), *Studies in Oceanic Culture History*, vol. 1, Honolulu, 1970.
38. Kirch, 'Rethinking Polynesian Prehistory', *JPS* 95 (1986), 9–40, esp. 23–24.
39. Sutton, 'A Paradigmatic Shift in Polynesian Prehistory: Implications for New Zealand', *NZJA* 9 (1987), 135–55.
40. Patrick J. Grant, 'Interpretation of Evidence for the Early Prehistory of New Zealand: Reply to Sutton', *NZJA* 10 (1988), 129–34.
41. Leach, *1000 Years of Gardening in New Zealand*, 52.
42. Atholl Anderson, 'The Chronology of New Zealand Colonization', *Antiquity* 65 (1991), 767–95.
43. Caughley, 'The Colonisation of New Zealand by the Polynesians', *Journal of the Royal Society of New Zealand* 18 (1988), 245–70.
44. See Leach, *1000 Years of Gardening* and 'The Significance of Early Horticulture in Palliser Bay for New Zealand Prehistory', in B. Foss Leach and Helen M. Leach (eds), *Prehistoric Man at Palliser Bay*, 1979; Davidson, *Prehistory*, 115–27.
45. E.g. Trotter and McCulloch, *Unearthing New Zealand*, 41.
46. Leach, *1000 Years of Gardening.*
47. *OYB*, 1990, 9.
48. John Coster, 'Dates from the Aupouri Dunes: A Sequence for the Aupouri Peninsula, Northland, New Zealand', *NZJA* 11 (1989), 51–75, quotations, 69, 63.
49. Anderson, 'Chronology of Colonisation'.
50. Simmons, *Great New Zealand Myth*, esp. 321; Orbell, *Hawaiki*, 63–65.
51. See, e.g. Ben Finney, 'Re-learning a Vanishing Art', *JPS* 93 (1984), 41–90.
52 Irwin, 'Against, Across, and Down the Wind: A Case for the Systematic Exploration of the Remote Pacific Islands', *JPS* 98 (1989), 167–206. Also see Paul Johnstone, *The Sea-craft of Prehistory*, London and New York, 1988, 204–18.
53. Peter Bellwood, *The Polynesians: Prehistory of an Island People*, London, 1987 edn, 42–43.
54. Trotter and McCulloch, *Unearthing New Zealand*, 31; Davidson, *Prehistory*, 63.

55. *The Endeavour Journal of Joseph Banks 1768–1771*, ed. J. C. Beaglehole, 2 vols, Sydney, 1962, i, 447.
56. Quoted in Oliver, *Native Cultures*, 46.
57. John Hather and P. V. Kirch, 'Prehistoric Sweet Potato from Mangaia Island, Central Polynesia', *Antiquity* 65 (1991), 887–93.
58. Houghton, *First New Zealanders*, 54, passim.
59. Kirch, 'Rethinking Polynesian Prehistory', 34.
60. Bellwood, *The Polynesians*, 97.
61. E.g. Simmons, *Great New Zealand Myth*, 212.
62. Brian Gill and Paul Martinson, *The Extinct Birds of New Zealand*, 1991, 15.
63. Oliver, *Native Cultures*, 47.
64. Fredrick Moss, *A School History of New Zealand*; 1889, 5.
65. Gill and Martinson, *Extinct Birds*, 13.
66. Apirana Ngata, 1931, *Buck–Ngata Letters*, ii, 184.
67. Nic Bishop, *The Natural History of New Zealand*, 1992, 31.
68. Atholl Anderson, *Prodigious Birds: Moas and Moa-hunting in Prehistoric New Zealand*, Cambridge, 1989. 64–65, 189; Anderson (ed.), *Birds of a Feather: Osteological and Archaeological Papers from the South Pacific in Honour of R. J. Scarlett*, 1979; Gill and Martinson, *Extinct Birds*; Bruce McFadgen, 'Impact on the Landscape', in John Wilson (ed.), *From the Beginning: The Archaeology of the Maori*, 1987, 53–54.
69. Ian W. G. Smith, 'Maori Impact on the Marine Megafauna: Pre-European Distribution of Sea Mammals', in D. G. Sutton (ed.), *Saying So Doesn't Make It So*, 1989; Davidson, *Prehistory*, 130–33.
70. Anderson, *Prodigious Birds*, 73.
71. D. G. Sutton, 'Maori Demographic Change, 1769–1840: The Inner Workings of "a Picturesque but Illogical Simile" ', *JPS* 95 (1986) 291–339. Also see Houghton, *First New Zealanders*, 99.
72. Pool, *Te Iwi Maori: A New Zealand Population, Past, Present, and Projected*, 1991, 37–38.
73. Ibid., 41.
74. Caughley, 'Colonisation of New Zealand', 259.

Chapter 2: Hunters and Gardeners

1. For sequential settlement, see Caughley, 'Colonisation of New Zealand'. For unpatterned, see Atholl Anderson and Rick McGovern-Wilson, 'The Pattern of Prehistoric Polynesian Colonisation in New Zealand', *Journal of the Royal Society of New Zealand* 20 (1990), 41–63.
2. M. S. McGlone, 'The Polynesian Settlement of New Zealand in Relation to Environmental and Biotic Changes', *New Zealand Journal of Ecology* 12 (1990), 115–29; C. J. Burrows, 'On New Zealand's Climate Within the Last 1000 Years', *NZJA* 4 (1982), 157–67.
3. McGlone, 'Polynesian Settlement'; Nic Bishop, *Natural History*.
4. Best, *Maori Religion and Mythology*, part 2, 1982, 353; *Tikao Talks*, 20–21; George Grey, *Polynesian Mythology and Ancient Traditional History of the Maori as Told by Their Priests and Chiefs*, 1956 (orig. 1855), 30–32.
5. See Davidson, *Prehistory*, 31–35.
6. Previous writers have used this concept as a metaphor but have not, to my knowledge, applied it systematically (e.g. Apirana Ngata, 1928, *Buck–Ngata Letters*, i, 183; Duff, *Moa-hunter Period*, 250).
7. Rod Wallace, 'A Preliminary Study of Wood Types Used in Pre-European Maori Artefacts', in Sutton (ed.), *Saying So*.
8. Leach, *1000 Years of Gardening*, 56.
9. Davidson, *Prehistory*, 33, 100.
10. R. H. M. Langer, *Pastures: Their Ecology and Management*, 1990, 18.
11. Anderson, *Prodigious Birds*.
12. Ian W. G. Smith, 'Maori Impact on the Marine Megafauna: Pre-European Distribution of Sea Mammals', in Sutton (ed.), *Saying So*.
13. Caughley, 'Colonisation of New Zealand'.
14. Firth, *Economics of the New Zealand Maori*, 404; Best, *Maori Agriculture*, 246.
15. Davidson, *Prehistory*, 196.
16. Anderson, *Prodigious Birds*, 176–78.
17. S. M. Mead, 'The Origins of Maori Art, Polynesian or Chinese?', *Oceania* 45 (1975), 173–211; Ranginui Walker, *Ka Whawhai Tonu Matou / Struggle Without End*, 1990, 47–48, 62; Bruce Biggs, 'In the Beginning', in Keith Sinclair (ed.), *The Oxford Illustrated History of New Zealand*, 1990, 9–10.
18. Davidson, *Prehistory*, 125.
19. E.g. ibid., 63–65, 68, 82; Anderson, 'Chronology of Colonisation', 789; Duff, *Moa-hunter Period*, 250; J. Davidson, 'Archaic Middens of the Coromandel: A Review', in Anderson (ed.), *Birds of a Feather*.
20. B. Foss Leach, 'Excavations in the Washpool Valley, Palliser Bay', in Leach and Leach (eds), *Palliser Bay*, 92.

21. Leach and Leach (eds.), *Palliser Bay.*
22. B. Foss Leach, 'Maximising Minimum Numbers: Avian Remains from the Washpool Midden Site', in Anderson (ed.), *Birds of a Feather*, 107–8.
23. B. Foss Leach and A. J. Anderson, 'Prehistoric Exploitation of Crayfish in New Zealand', in ibid., 158.
24. Houghton, *First New Zealanders*, 117–18.
25. S. B. Best, 'The Maori Adze: An Explanation for Change', *JPS* 86 (1977), 307–37.
26. Houghton, *First New Zealanders*, 119–24.
27. *The Resolution Journals of Johann Reinhold Forster 1772–5*, ed. Michael E. Hoare, 4 vols, London, 1982, i, 274–75.
28. Anderson, *Prodigious Birds*, 113, and 'Food from Forest and Coast', in Wilson (ed.), *From the Beginning*, 77.
29. Smith, 'Maori Impact on the Marine Megafauna'.
30. Anderson, *Prodigious Birds*, 151.
31. Ibid., 153; *Tikao Talks*, 108.
32. Kevin L. Jones, *Nga Tohuwhua Mai Te Rangi: A New Zealand Archaeology in Aerial Photographs*, 1994, 80.
33. Anderson, *Prodigious Birds*, 149–51, 154, 157, 190.
34. Anderson, 'North and Central Otago', in Nigel Prickett (ed.), *The First Thousand Years: Regional Perspectives on New Zealand Archaeology*, 1982, 122–23; Anderson and McGovern-Wilson, 'The Pattern of Colonisation'.
35. Anderson, *Prodigious Birds*, 151.
36. Jan Allo Bay-Petersen, 'The Role of the Dog in the Economy of the New Zealand Maori', in Anderson (ed.), *Birds of a Feather*, 167.
37. Anderson, *Prodigious Birds*, 117, 129, 134–35; 'A Diary Rediscovered: Bayard Booth on the Shag Mouth Moa Hunting Site', in Sutton (ed.), *Saying So*, 70.
38. G. E. Hamel, 'The Breeding Ecology of Moas', in Anderson (ed.), *Birds of a Feather*, 65; Anderson, *Prodigious Birds*, 154.
39. Ibid., 85.
40. Hamel, 'The Breeding Ecology of Moas', 65; Gill and Martinson, *Extinct Birds*, 42; Anderson, *Prodigious Birds*, 84.
41. Anderson, 'Chronology of Colonisation', 792, and *Prodigious Birds*, 131–39.
42. Bay-Petersen, 'Role of the Dog in the Economy of the New Zealand Maori'.
43. Anderson, *Prodigious Birds*, 154, 130.
44. Richard Cassells, cited in ibid., 117.
45. Anderson, *Prodigious Birds*, 163.
46. Ibid., 180–81.
47. Ian W. G. Smith, appendix 2, in Sutton, 'Maori Demographic Change', 337–38.
48. Andrea Seelenfreund and Charles Bullong, 'The Sourcing of New Zealand Archaeological Obsidian Artefacts using Energy Dispersive XRF Spectroscopy', in Sutton (ed.), *Saying So.*
49. Ibid.
50. Trotter and McCulloch, *Unearthing New Zealand*, 42.
51. Anderson, 'Chronology of Colonisation', 789.
52. Helen Leach, 'Archaic Adze Quarries and Working Floors: An Historical Review', *JPS* 99 (1990), 380–82; Anderson, *Prodigious Birds*, 120–22; D. R. Simmons, 'Artefacts and People: Inter-island Trade Through Queen Charlotte Sound', in Barratt (ed.), *Queen Charlotte Sound*, 166–68.
53. Leach, 'Archaic Adze Quarries', 386; Peter Coutts, 'Fiordland', in Prickett (ed.), *First Thousand Years*, 157; R. H. Hooker, *The Archaeology of the South Westland Maori*, 1986, 28, 34, 50.
54. Anderson, *Prodigious Birds*, 164–69.
55. Ibid., 169.
56. Seelenfreund and Bullong, 'Sourcing of Obsidian Artefacts'.
57. 'Archaic Adze Quarries and Working Floors: An Historical Review', *JPS* 99 (1990), 373–94, 389.
58. Davidson, *Prehistory*, 219–24, and 'Maori Prehistory: The State of the Art', *JPS* 92 (1983), 291–307.
59. This analysis draws in particular on Simmons, *Great New Zealand Myth.*
60. E.g. Richard Taylor, *Te Ika a Maui: New Zealand and Its Inhabitants*, London, 1855, 116.
61. Orbell, *Hawaiki*, 60.
62. Salmond, *Two Worlds*, 157; Taylor, *Te Ika a Maui*, 123–24. Also see Jeff Sissons, *Te Waimana / The Spring of Mana: Tuhoe History and the Colonial Encounter*, 1991, 10–64.
63. J. M. McEwen, *Rangitane*, 3–5; Orbell, *Hawaiki*, 8–9, 12, 25–29, 59. Also see Stephen O'Regan, 'Queen Charlotte Sound: Aspects of Maori Traditional Society', in Barratt (ed.), *Queen Charlotte Sound*, 143, on the mythical *Arai-te Uru* canoe, shared by South Island Maori and Rarotonga.
64. Smith, *Hawaiki: The Original Home of the Maori*, 1904, 203–16.
65. Paraphrasing Duff, *Moa-hunter Period*, Intro. to 3rd edn, x.
66. McEwen, *Rangitane*, 10–13.
67. Jennifer Curnow, 'Wiremu Maihi Te Rangikaheke: His Life and Work', *JPS* 94

(1985), 97–147, 141; Simmons, *Great New Zealand Myth*, 103–5, 165–66.
68. Orbell, *Hawaiki*, 39, and *Natural World of the Maori*, 1985, 143–44.
69. O'Regan, 'Queen Charlotte Sound', 143–44.
70. Simmons, *Great New Zealand Myth*, esp. 66–68.
71. Walker, *Ka Whawhai Tonu Matou*, 45.
72. *Buck–Ngata Letters*, ii, 155.
73. Ibid., i, 97.
74. Smith, *Hawaiki*, 195; Orbell, *Hawaiki*, 46; *Tikao Talks*, 51.
75. Grey, *Polynesian Mythology*, 104–5.
76. Ibid., 171.
77. E.g. Simmons, *Great New Zealand Myth*, 122–23.
78. Salmond, *Two Worlds*, 335.
79. Elsdon Best, *Maori Agriculture*, 1976 (orig. 1925), 245.
80. Grey, *Polynesian Mythology*, 110; *Buck–Ngata Letters*, ii, 13. Also see *Tikao Talks*, 107.
81. See Herbert G. M Maschner et al., 'Hunter-Gatherer Complexity on the West Coast of North America', special section, *Antiquity* 65 (1991), 921–76.
82. Bellwood, *The Polynesians*, 59–61.
83. Irwin, 'The Case for Systematic Colonisation', 186. Also see Sutton, 'A Paradigmatic Shift in Polynesian Prehistory', 144, citing C. W. Meredith et al., 1985.
84. Robert McNab, *Historical Records of New Zealand*, 2 vols, 1908–14, i, 107.
85. B. Foss Leach et al., 'The Origin of Prehistoric Obsidian Artefacts from the Chatham and Kermadec Islands', *NZJA* 8 (1988), 143–70; Atholl Anderson and Bruce McFadgen, 'Prehistoric Two-way Voyaging Between New Zealand and East Polynesia: Mayor Island Obsidian on Raoul Island and Possible Raoul Island Obsidian in New Zealand', *Archaeology in Oceania* 25 (1990), 37–42; Anderson, 'The Chronology of New Zealand Colonization', 785–86.
86. Irwin, 'The Case for Systematic Colonisation', 186, citing personal communication from Bruce McFadgen. Also see King, *Moriori*, esp. 216.
87. Te Karaka, c. 1880, via Tikao, *Tikao Talks*, 102.
88. Sutton, 'The Chatham Islands' in Prickett (ed.), *First Thousand Years*, 164, 172.
89. D. G. Sutton, 'Island and Coastal Fishing Strategies of the Prehistoric Moriori', in Anderson (ed.), *Birds of a Feather*, 135, and 'Moriori Fishing: Intensive Exploitation of an Inshore Zone', in Sutton (ed.), *Saying So*, 127; King, *Moriori*, 17–33.
90. Houghton, *First New Zealanders*, 75.

Chapter 3: The Rise of the Tribes

1. Leach, *1000 Years of Gardening*; Sutton, 'Maori Demographic Change', which cites unpublished research on wild plant foods by Helen Leach; *Tikao Talks*; Orbell, *Natural World*; Davidson, *Prehistory*; Firth, *Economics of the New Zealand Maori*; Elsdon Best, *Forest Lore of the Maori*, 1977.
2. *Journal of a Rambler: The Journal of John Boultbee*, ed. June Starke, 1986, 68–69.
3. Orbell, *Natural World*, 43, citing William Colenso.
4. Anderson, *Prodigious Birds*, 85–6.
5. Barry Fankhauser, 'The Nutritive Value and Cooking of *Cordyline Australis* (Ti Kouka),' in Sutton (ed.) *Saying So*, 216. Also see Sutton, 'Maori Demographic Change', 305–8, citing unpublished work by Helen Leach.
6. Quoted in Orbell, *Natural World*, 21.
7. Sissons, *Te Waimana*.
8. Trotter and McCulloch, *Unearthing New Zealand*, 65.
9. Davidson, *Prehistory*, 140; Anderson, *When All the Moa-ovens Grew Cold*, 1983, 13–15, 25–6.
10. Firth, *Economics of the New Zealand Maori*, 225–30, 287.
11. E.g. *Tikao Talks*, 13–14.
12. Firth, *Economics of the New Zealand Maori*, 147, 291, 319.
13. Fox, 'Hawkes Bay' in Prickett (ed.), *First Thousand Years*, 78; Firth, *Economics of the New Zealand Maori*, 171.
14. Gaela Mair, 'Maori Occupation of the Wairarapa in the Protohistoric Period', in Leach and Leach (eds), *Palliser Bay*, 22; Jones, *A New Zealand Archaeology*, 76.
15. Firth, *Economics of the New Zealand Maori*, 171–72.
16. Anderson, *When the Moa-ovens Grew Cold*, 42–44, and 'Maori Settlement of the Interior of Southern New Zealand from the Early 18th to the Late 19th centuries AD', *JPS* 91 (1982), 53–80, esp. 60–61.
17. J. L. Nicholas, *Narrative of a Voyage to New Zealand*, 2 vols, London, 1817, i, 307.
18. E.g. Richard Cruise, *Journal of a Ten Months' Residence in New Zealand*, 2nd edn, London, 1824, 224.
19. See Barry Brailsford, *Greenstone Trails: The Maori Search for Pounamu*, 1984.
20. Trotter and McCulloch, *Unearthing New Zealand*, 57–58.
21. D. G. Sutton (ed.), *The Archaeology of the*

Kainga: A Study of Precontact Maori Undefended Settlements at Pouerua, Northland, New Zealand, 1990, 13.
22. Leach, *1000 Years of Gardening*, 45, citing the research of Agnes Sullivan.
23. Orbell, *Natural World*, 37.
24. Sissons et al., *The Puriri Trees Are Laughing*, 18.
25. Kevin L. Jones, 'Settlement Chronology, Pa and Environment of Tolaga Bay . . . ', in Sutton (ed.), *Saying So*, 239, 251, 255.
26. Leach, 'The Significance of Early Horticulture in Palliser Bay for New Zealand Prehistory', in Leach and Leach (eds), *Palliser Bay*, 247.
27. Kevin L. Jones, '"In Much Greater Affluence": Productivity and Welfare in Maori Gardening at Anauru Bay, October 1769', *JPS* 98 (1989), 49–75, and 'Traditional Maori Horticulture in the Eastern North Island', *New Zealand Agricultural Science* 23 (1989), 36–41.
28. Fankhauser, 'Nutritive Value and Cooking of *Cordyline Australis*', in Sutton (ed.), *Saying So*. For other references to the cultivation of wild plants, see Davidson, *Prehistory*, 116; Orbell, *Natural World*, 38–44.
29. Orbell, *Natural World*, 31; Atholl Anderson, *Te Puoho's Last Raid*, 1986, 19.
30. Leach, *1000 Years of Gardening*, 41.
31. E g. Alan Ward, 'A Report on the Historical Evidence. The Ngai Tahu Claim', Wai 27, Doc T.1, 1989.
32. Firth, *Economics of the New Zealand Maori*, 227.
33. *Tikao Talks*, 68–69.
34. Houghton, *First New Zealanders*, 137–38; Davidson, *Prehistory*, 191; Trotter and McCulloch, *Unearthing New Zealand*, 77–80.
35. King, *Moriori*, 26, but also see 28 and 42–45.
36. See Salmond, *Two Worlds*, 377–427; John Dunmore, *French Explorers in the Pacific*, 2 vols., Oxford, 1965, i, 182–89, and L. G. Kelly, *Marion du Fresne at the Bay of Islands*, 1951.
37. Quoted in Bernard Smith, *European Vision and the South Pacific 1768–1850*, Oxford, 1960, 87.
38. Dumont d'Urville, *New Zealand 1826–1827*, trans. Olive Wright, 1950, 198–99.
39. General sources on pa and warfare include Elsdon Best, *The Pa Maori*, 1975 (orig. 1927); A. P. Vayda, *Maori Warfare*, 1960; Aileen Fox, *Prehistoric Maori Fortifications in the North Island of New Zealand*, 1976; Janet Davidson, 'The Paa Maaori Revisited', *JPS* 96 (1987), 7–26.
40. Grey, *Polynesian Mythology*, 86.
41. Personal communication, Rei Rakatau to author, 1992.
42. Best, *The Pa Maori*, 160.
43. See e.g. Jones, 'Settlement Chronology, Pa and Environment of Tolaga Bay . . . ', in Sutton (ed.), *Saying So*, 253; Davidson, *Prehistory*, 192–93.
44. On mana and leadership, see Raymond Firth, 'The Analysis of Mana: An Empirical Approach', in Thomas G. Harding and Ben. J. Wallace (eds), *Cultures of the Pacific: Selected Readings*, New York, 1970; Maharaia Winiata, 'Leadership in Pre-European Maori Society', *JPS* 55 (1956), 212–31; Bronwen Douglas, 'Rank, Power and Authority: A Reassessment of Traditional Leadership in South Pacific Societies', *Journal of Pacific History* 14 (1979), 2–27; Ross Bowden, '*Tapu* and *Mana*: Ritual Authority and Political Power in Traditional Maori Society', ibid., 50–61.
45. *DNZB*, i.
46. William Yate, *An Account of New Zealand and of the Formation and Progress of the Church Missionary Society's Mission in the Northern Island*, London, 1835, 104.
47. Bowden, '*Tapu* and *Mana*', 58–60.
48. Ann Parsonson, 'The Expansion of a Competitive Society', *NZJH*, 14 (1980), 45–60, and 'The Pursuit of Mana', in *The Oxford History of New Zealand*, (1981 edn); Kwen Fee Lian, 'Settler Colonialism and Tribal Society: Maori-Pakeha Relations in the Nineteenth Century', VUW PhD thesis, 1986, and 'Interpreting Maori History: A Case for a Historical Sociology', *JPS* 96 (1987), 445–71. Lian draws on the work of leading American anthropologist Marshall Sahlins.
49. Grey, *Polynesian Mythology*, 15; Tikao, *Tikao Talks*, 13 and 22, n. 7.
50. S. M. Mead, *Te Toi Whakairo: The Art of Maori Carving*, 1986, 190.
51. Joan Metge, 'Te Rito O Te Harakeke: Conceptions of the Whaanau', *JPS* 99 (1990), 55–92.
52. Cited in Firth, *Economics of the New Zealand Maori*, 111.
53. Ibid., 117–23.
54. Jones, 'In Much Greater Affluence', 64.
55. Fox, 'Hawkes Bay' in Prickett (ed.), *First Thousand Years*, 67.
56. Bruce Biggs, *Maori Marriage: An Essay in Reconstruction*, 1960.

57. Recent discussions of the concept of 'tribe' in general include Patricia Crone, 'The Tribe and the State', in John H. Hall (ed.), *States in History*, Oxford, 1986; and Stephen Cornell, 'The Transformation of the Tribe: Organization and Self-Concept in American Ethnicities', *Ethnic and Racial Studies* 11 (1988), 27–47.
58. *Tikao Talks*, 142.
59. Atholl Anderson, 'Towards an Explanation of Protohistoric Social Organisation and Settlement Patterns Amongst the Southern Ngai Tahu', *NZJA* 2 (1980), 3–23.
60. Cleave, 'Tribal and State-like Political Formations in New Zealand Maori Society, 1750–1900', *JPS* 92 (1983), 51–92.
61. Aileen Fox, 'Pa and People in New Zealand: An Archaeological Estimate of Population', *NZJA* 5 (1983), 5–18.
62. Biggs, *Maori Marriage*, 25.
63. The concept of imagined groups is adapted from Benedict Anderson, *Imagined Communities: Reflections on the Origin and Spread of Nationalism*, London, 1983.
64. *Buck–Ngata Letters*, ii, 221.
65. Garry Law, 'Cultural Processes Limiting Diversity in New Zealand Prehistory', in Anderson (ed.), *Birds of a Feather*, 270, citing the work of R. R. D. Milligan, 1964; Judith Binney, 'Tuki's Universe', in Keith Sinclair (ed.), *Tasman Relations: New Zealand and Australia 1788–1988*, 1988, 16; Nicholas, *Narrative*, ii, 252; Dumont d'Urville, *New Zealand*, 111; Cook, *Journals*, i, 243.
66. David Young, 'The Buried Canoe', unpublished MSS cited by kind permission of the author.
67. *Buck–Ngata Letters*, i, 105–6.
68. Lian, 'Settler Colonialism and Tribal Society'.
69. Banks, *Journal*, ii, 25.
70. Firth, *Economics of the New Zealand Maori*, 285–89.
71. Nigel Prickett, 'Maori Fortifications of the Okato District, Taranaki', *Records of the Auckland Institute and Museum* 20 (1983), 1–39; Geoffrey Irwin, *Land, Pa and Polity: A Study Based on the Maori Fortifications of Pouto*, 1985.
72. Quoted in Orbell, *Natural World*, 60.

Chapter 4: Life Before History

1. David Simmons, biographical essay in Charlotte Macdonald et al., *The Book of New Zealand Women*, 1991, 663–64.
2. D. G. Sutton, 'The Prehistoric People of Palliser Bay', in Leach and Leach (eds), *Palliser Bay*, 195–96.
3. General sources for this survey include Salmond, *Two Worlds*; Simmons, *Great New Zealand Myth* and *Maori Tribal Art*; relevant essays in *DNZB*, i. An interesting early survey is Ernest Dieffenbach, *Travels in New Zealand*, 2 vols, London, 1843, ii, 72–83.
4. Waerete Norman, 'The Muriwhenua Claim', in I. H. Kawharu (ed.), *Waitangi: Maori and Pakeha Perspectives on the Treaty of Waitangi*, 1989.
5. Buck, *Buck–Ngata Letters* , ii, 221.
6. See Sissons et al., *The Puriri Trees Are Laughing*; Jack Lee, *'I Have Named It the Bay of Islands'*, 1983, 31–34, and *Hokianga*, 1987, 19–32.
7. Davidson, 'Auckland', in Prickett (ed.), *First Thousand Years.*
8. Nicholas, *Narrative*, ii, 219–20
9. L. G. Kelly, *Tainui: The Story of Hoturoa and his Descendants*, 1949; Tamati Ngapora, in Edward Shortland, *Traditions and Superstitions of the New Zealanders*, 2nd edn, London, 1856, 3–9; Evelyn Stokes, *Mokau: Maori Cultural and Historical Perspectives*, 1988, 1–63.
10. Cleave, 'Tribal and State-like Political Formations', 51–92.
11. Kelly, *Tainui*, 287–94. An alternative, less convincing date for this battle is 1780. Stokes, *Mokau*, 65.
12. Curnow, 'Te Rangikaheke', 137.
13. D. M. Stafford, *Te Arawa*, Wellington, 1967.
14. *Buck–Ngata Letters*, ii, 185.
15. John Grace, *Tuwharetoa*, Wellington, 1959; personal communications, Ken Gartner; Tuwharetoa essays, *DNZB*, i.
16. Sissons, *Te Waimana*; A. C. Lyall, *The Mataatua Question*, 1970.
17. Ngahuia Te Awekotuku, *Mana Wahine Maori*, 1991, 37.
18. Yate, *Account*, 151 n; evidence of the Tahitian Jem, in Nicholas, *Narrative*, ii, 219–20; Salmond, *Two Worlds*, 176–78.
19. See T. G. Hammond, *The Story of Aotea*, 156–77; S. P. Smith, *History and Traditions of the Maoris of the West Coast, North Island*, 1910, 2–272; Taylor, *Te Ika a Maui*; C. J. Roberts, *Centennial History of Hawera and the Waimate Plains*, 1939, and *Official History of the County of Patea*; T. H. Downes, *Old Whanganui*, 1915; Ian Church, 'Heartland of Aotea', 1984, unpublished MS, Wanganui Museum.

20. Ruka Broughton, 'The Origins of Ngaarauru Kiitahi', VUW MA thesis, 1979.
21. Downes, *Old Whanganui*; Young, 'The Buried Canoe'.
22. O'Regan, 'Queen Charlotte Sound', in Barratt (ed.), *Queen Charlotte Sound*, 139.
23. Angela Ballara, 'The Origins of Ngati Kahungunu', VUW PhD thesis, 1991.
24. McEwen, Rangitane, 25 and passim. Also see ibid.
25. Maori traditional history of the South Island is summarised in Barratt (ed.), *Queen Charlotte Sound*; Brailsford, *Greenstone Trails*; Anderson, *When the Moa-ovens Grew Cold*; Tikao, *Tikao Talks*. I also draw on several conference papers by Tipene O'Regan.
26. Abel Tasman, Journal, in McNab, *Historical Records*, ii, 22–23; Salmond, *Two Worlds*, 78–82. Salmond suggests a total Ngati Tumata population of 400 or 500, but the 22 canoes assembled to attack the Dutch, containing up to 17 men each, implies this is too low.
27. O'Regan, 'Queen Charlotte Sound', in Barrett (ed.), *Queen Charlotte Sound*, 152.
28. An early example is 'The Story of Te Uira, Chief of the Ngatimamoes', in Hochstetter, *New Zealand*, 222–24. A children's radio series, 'The Lost Tribe of Te Anau', was broadcast in the 1960s.
29. *Tikao Talks*, 101.
30. Fox, 'Hawkes Bay' in Prickett (ed.), *First Thousand Years*, 72–75.
31. Anderson, 'Maori Settlement in Southern New Zealand', 59.
32. Ibid., 62–4; Robert McNab, *Murihiku and the Southern Islands*, 1907, 208.
33. Anderson, *When the Moa-ovens Grew Cold*, 41; Boultbee, *Journal*, 47, 70–73 and notes; McNab, *Murihuku*, 113, 350.
34. On greenstone, see Russell J. Beck, *New Zealand Jade: The Story of Greenstone*, 1970; Brailsford, *Greenstone Trails*; Davidson, *Prehistory*, 33, 84–91, 100.
35. R. H. Hooker, *Archaeology of the South Westland Maori*.
36. Beck, *New Zealand Jade*, 64; Trotter and McCulloch, *Unearthing New Zealand*, 84.
37. Barratt (ed.), *Queen Charlotte Sound*.
38. Best, *The Maori*, i, 340; Skinner, 'The Maori', in *The Cambridge History of the British Empire*, vol. 7, part 2, 11.
39. Yate, *Account*.
40. Boultbee, *Journal*, 72–73.
41. Trotter and McCulloch, *Unearthing New Zealand*, 92.
42. Forster, *Journals*, iii, 426, and ii, 258, 292.
43. Banks, *Journal*, ii, 33.
44. Marsden, 'Observations on the Introduction of the Gospel into the South Sea Islands . . .', in McNab, *Historical Records*, i, 396; Nicholas, *Narrative*, ii, 306–7.
45. Cruise, *Journal*, 268, 275.
46. Grey, *Polynesian Mythology*, 46–61; Pool, *Te Iwi Maori*, 47–48.
47. Nicholas, *Narrative*, ii, 21. Also see Ormond Wilson, *From Hongi Hika to Hone Heke*, 1985, 150.
48. Biggs, *Maori Marriage*, 36–39.
49. Judith Binney, 'Some Observations on the Status of Maori Women', *NZJH* 23 (1989), 22–31; Judith Binney and Gillian Chaplin, *Nga Morehu/The Survivors*, 1986; F. Allan Hanson, 'Female Pollution in Polynesia?', *JPS* 91 (1982), 335–82; Anituatua Black, 'Guarding Jealously the Treasures of Life', *Women's Studies Journal*, 8/2 (1992), 1–14.
50. B. Foss Leach and A. J. Anderson, 'Prehistoric Exploitation of Crayfish in New Zealand', in Anderson (ed.), *Birds of a Feather*, 141–42; Salmond, *Two Worlds*, 165.
51. Ballara, 'Origins of Ngati Kahungunu', 306.
52. Simmons, 'Plus Ça Change: The People and Their Culture', in Barratt (ed.), *Queen Charlotte Sound*, 60–63, 67–68.
53. Margaret Ehrenberg, *Women in Prehistory*, British Museum, 1989. Also see Bonnie S. Anderson and Judith P. Zinsser, *A History of Their Own: Women in Europe from Prehistory to the Present*, 2 vols, New York, 1989.
54. Houghton, *First New Zealanders*, 118.
55. S. M. Mead, *Traditional Maori Clothing: A Study of Technological and Functional Change*, 1969.
56. Ehrenberg, *Women in Prehistory*, 119–24.
57. Simmons, 'Artefacts and People', in Barratt (ed.), *Queen Charlotte Sound*, 171–72.
58. Trotter and McCulloch, *Unearthing New Zealand*, 93.
59. Orbell, *Natural World*, 135; Firth, *Economics of the New Zealand Maori*, 207.
60. Ibid., 207–12.
61. Ibid., 121–23, 187.
62. De Blosseville, quoted in McNab, *Murihuku*, 212.
63. Houghton, *First New Zealanders*, 107; Davidson, *Prehistory*, 48–49. Also see Pool, *Te Iwi Maori*, 34–37.
64. Alexandra Brewis, 'Assessing Infant Mortality in Prehistoric New Zealand: A Life Table Approach', *NZJA* 10 (1988), 73–82. Also see Pool, *Te Iwi Maori*, esp. 34–47.
65. Cited in Firth, *Economics of the New Zealand Maori*, 188.

66. Ngata, *Buck–Ngata Letters*, i, 104.
67. It derives largely from Te Matorohanga via Smith via Simmons, *Maori Tribal Art*, 19–21.
68. *Tikao Talks*, 74, 67.
69. Salmond, *Two Worlds*, 169; Yate, *Account*, 153.
70. Davidson, *Prehistory*, 108–9.
71. Grey, *Polynesian Mythology*, 72–73: Boultbee, *Journal*, 203.
72. Wendy Harsant, 'The Beauty of Taonga', in Wilson (ed.), *From the Beginning*, 137; Anderson, *When the Moa-ovens Grew Cold*, 20.
73. Yate, *Account*, 148–49.
74. Quoted in Salmond, *Two Worlds*, 280. Also see S. M. Mead (ed.), *Te Maori: Maori Art from New Zealand Collections*, 1984, and *Te Toi Whakairo*; Agathe Thornton, 'Some Reflections on Traditional Maori Carving', *JPS* 98 (1989), 147–66; Simmons, *Maori Tribal Art*.
75. Ibid.
76. J. Ormond Wilson, *From Hongi Hika to Hone Heke: A Quarter-Century of Upheaval*, 1985, 75, citing the 'Pakeha Maori' George Bruce; *Tikao Talks*, 156.
77. Sutton (ed.), *Archaeology of the Kainga*, esp. 204.
78. Salmond, *Two Worlds*, 173.
79. Firth, *Economics of the New Zealand Maori*, 100.
80. Anderson, '"Makeshift Structures of Little Importance": A Reconsideration of Maori Round Huts', *JPS* 93 (1984), 92–114; Grey, *Polynesian Mythology*, 75.
81. Sutton (ed.), *Archaeology of the Kainga*, 113–16.
82. Sorrenson, *Maori Origins and Migrations*, 77–78. An interesting ethnographic account of Maori religion was that of Thomas Kendall. See Judith Binney, 'The Lost Drawings of Nukutawhiti', *NZJH* (14) 1980, 3–24, and '"At Every Bend a Taniwha": Thomas Kendall and Maori Carving', *NZJH* 20 (1986), 132–46. Also see Best, *Maori Religion and Mythology*; Orbell, *Natural World*; Simmons, *Maori Tribal Art*; Tikao, *Tikao Talks*, chapters 1–3.
83. Ibid., 25; Curnow, 'Te Rangikaheke'; Grey, *Polynesian Mythology*.
84. *Buck–Ngata Letters*, iii, 48.
85. Best, *Maori Religion and Mythology*, i, 42, 45; ii, 328–85; Yate, *Account*, 142–45; Nicholas, *Narrative*, i, 56–57.
86. Grey, *Polynesian Mythology*, 38.
87. Tikao, *Tikao Talks*, 154–55.

Chapter 5: The European Discovery of New Zealand

1. Withey, *Voyages of Discovery*, 45.
2. Dunmore, *French Explorers in the Pacific*, i, 4–7; Evelyn Stokes, 'European Discovery of New Zealand Before 1642: A Review of the Evidence', *NZJH* 4 (1970), 3–19.
3. *OYB*, 1893, 2; Langdon, *Lost Caravel* and *Lost Caravel Re-explored*.
4. Paul Shepard, *English Reaction to the New Zealand Landscape Before 1850*, 1969, 8–9; Nicholas, *Narrative*, ii, 13; A. H. and A. W. Reed, *Captain Cook in New Zealand*, 2nd edn, 1969, 74, n. 93; Letter of Thomas Kendall, 1822, in Binney, 'At Every Bend a Taniwha', 133.
5. Richard Whately, 'On the Origin of Civilisation', in *Miscellaneous Lectures and Reviews*, London, 1861, 35.
6. Ronald Syme, *The Spaniards Came at Dawn*, London, 1959.
7. Van Diemen et al. to Tasman, 13 August 1642, in McNab, *Historical Records*, ii, 4–13.
8. Quotations from Tasman's Journal and other documents, in ibid., 18–34. Also see Salmond, *Two Worlds*, chapter 3; Andrew Sharp, *The Voyages of Abel Janszoon Tasman*, Oxford, 1968.
9. Van Diemen et al., 22 Dec. 1643, in McNab, *Historical Records*, ii, 37
10. *Dominion*, 18 March 1992 (article on research of Ben Slot); Graham Anderson, 'Tasman Revalued', *Stout Centre Review* 1/3 (1991), 15–17; *DNZB*, i.
11. Brian Hooker, 'New Light on the Mapping and Naming of New Zealand', *NZJH* 6 (1972), 158–67.
12. Banks, *Journal*, i, 472.
13. Dumont d'Urville, *New Zealand*, 33, 43, 58.
14. See Withey, *Voyages of Discovery*; Dunmore, *French Explorers*; Peter Tremewan, *French Akaroa: An Attempt to Colonise Southern New Zealand*, 1990; Harry Morton and Carol Morton Johnston, *The Farthest Corner: New Zealand, a Twice-Discovered Land*, 1988; J. C. Beaglehole, *The Discovery of New Zealand*, 2nd edn, London, 1961, and 'Eighteenth-Century Science and the Voyages of Discovery', *NZJH* 3 (1969), 107–23.
15. See J. C. Beaglehole, *The Life of Captain James Cook*, London, 1974.
16. Withey, *Voyages of Discovery*, 407.
17. McNab, *Murihuku*, 66–67.
18. D. Erskine to Earl Bathurst, 22 June 1822, New Zealand Papers, 2 B 158, Mitchell Library, Sydney.

19. Withey, *Voyages of Discovery*, 355.
20. John Dunmore, 'French Navigators in New Zealand 1769–1840', in Dunmore (ed.), *New Zealand and the French: Two Centuries of Contact*, 1990, 19.
21. Cook, *Journals*, iii, 59–69.
22. Paul Carter, *The Road to Botany Bay: An Essay in Spatial History*, London, 1987, 31.
23. Cook, *Journals*, ii, 131.
24. John White, *Ancient History of the Maori*, vol. 5, 1889, 121–28; also see Salmond, *Two Worlds*, 87–88.
25. Cruise, Journal, 143–44.
26. T. M. Hocken, *A Bibliography of Literature Relating to New Zealand*, 1909, 9, 18.
27. Anderson, *Prodigious Birds*, 17–19; Tremewan, *French Akaroa*, chapter 13.
28. Sorrenson, *Maori Origins and Migrations*, 13.
29. Margaret Steven, *Trade, Tactics and Territory: Britain in the Pacific 1783–1823*, Melbourne, 1983, 68.
30. Harry Morton, *The Whale's Wake*, 1982, 52.
31. McNab, *Historical Records*, i, 36–67. Also see ibid., passim; McNab, *Murihiku*; Steven, *Trade, Tactics and Territory*; W. C. Schaniel, 'The Maori and the Economic Frontier: An Economic History of the Maori of New Zealand, 1769–1840', Univ. of Tennessee PhD thesis, 1985; Morton, *Whale's Wake*.
32. See Neil Gunson, *Messengers of Grace: Evangelical Missionaries in the South Seas 1797–1860*, Melbourne, 1978.
33. F. E. Maning, *Old New Zealand: A Tale of the Good Old Times*, 1964 (orig. 1863).
34. Robert Hughes, *The Fatal Shore*, London, 1988, 264–65; Richard Hill, *The History of Policing in New Zealand*, 3 vols, 1986–95, i, 30.
35. Hughes, *Fatal Shore*; J. B. Hirst, *Convict Society and Its Enemies: A History of Early New South Wales*, Sydney, 1983; McNab, *Historical Records*, i, 264–65. For examples of children's deaths, see *Sydney Gazette*, 22 December 1805; 31 March 1810.
36. D. R. Hainsworth, *The Sydney Traders: Simeon Lord and His Contemporaries*, 1788–1821, Melbourne, 1971, 37 and passim; Also see Russell Ward, *The Australian Legend*, rev. edn, Sydney, 1970, and the associated debate on 'mateship'.
37. Hainsworth, *Sydney Traders*, esp. 126–54; McNab, *Murihiku*; Morton, *Whale's Wake*, chapter 7.
38. Hainsworth, *Sydney Traders*, 142.
39. McNab, *Murihiku*, 155–57.
40. Ibid., 81 and passim.
41. Ibid., 253–58.
42. Thomson, *Story of New Zealand*, i, 291. Also see P. J. F. Coutts, 'Merger or Takeover: A Survey of the Effects of Contact Between European and Maori in the Foveaux Strait Region', *JPS*, 78 (1969), 495–516.
43. Boultbee, *Journal*, 16, 50.
44. Portia Robinson, *The Hatch and Brood of Time: A Study of the First Generation of Native-born White Australians 1788–1828*, 2 vols, Melbourne, 1985, i, 241.
45. McNab, *Murihiku*, 57–66.
46. Hainsworth, *Sydney Traders*, 12. For total convict numbers, see Hughes, *Fatal Shore*, 161.
47. Peter Adams, *Fatal Necessity: British Intervention in New Zealand 1830–1847*, 1977, 25, 27.
48. John Savage, *An Account of New Zealand in 1805*, ed. A. D. Mackinlay, 1939, 90; Wilson, *Hongi to Heke*, 72.
49. *DNZB*, i.
50. Ibid. i; Lee, *Bay of Islands*, 41–43; McNab, *Historical Records*, i, 378, 542; Notes kindly supplied by Margot Foster.
51. R. P. Wigglesworth, 'The New Zealand Timber and Flax Trade 1769–1840', Massey PhD thesis, 1981; Schaniel, 'Maori and the Economic Frontier'; Adams, *Fatal Necessity*, chapter 1.
52. Morton, *Whale's Wake*; Robert McNab, *The Old Whaling Days: A History of Southern New Zealand from 1830 to 1840*, 1913; R. W. McLean, 'Dicky Barrett, Trader, Whaler, Interpreter', Auckland MA thesis, 1994.
53. Binney, 'Tuki's Universe'.
54. M. F. Lloyd Prichard, *An Economic History of New Zealand to 1939*, 1970, 16.
55. Barbara Little, 'The Sealing and Whaling Industry in Australia before 1850', *AEHR* 9 (1964), 125. Also see Binney, 'Tuki's Universe'.
56. Keith Sinclair, *A History of New Zealand*, 1961 edn, 24.
57. *The Letters and Journals of Samuel Marsden, 1765–1838*, ed. J. R. Elder, 1932; Nicholas, *Narrative*.
58. Helen Garrett, *Te Manihera: The Life and Times of the Pioneer Missionary Robert Maunsell*, 1991, 25. Also see Frances Porter (ed.), *The Turanga Journals of William and Jane Williams*, 1974, chapter 1.
59. Williams, *Early Journals*; Hugh Carleton, *The Life of Henry Williams*, 2 vols, 1874–47; Lawrence M. Rogers, *Te Wiremu: A Biography of Henry Williams*, 1973; Robin

Fisher, 'Henry Williams' Leadership of the CMS Mission to New Zealand', *NZJH* 9 (1975)' 142–53.
60. J. M. R. Owens, *Prophets in the Wilderness: The Wesleyan Mission to New Zealand, 1819–1927,* 1974.
61. Adams, *Fatal Necessity*, 26.
62. See map in Judith Binney et al., *The People and the Land / Te Tangata me Te Whenua: An Illustrated History of New Zealand 1820–1920,* 1990, 23.
63. *DNZB*, i (Pompallier); Philip Turner, 'The Politics of Neutrality: The Catholic Mission and the Maori 1838–1870', Auckland MA thesis, 1986, chapters 1, 2, 6.
64. A. T. Yarwood, 'The Missionary Marsden: An Australian View', *NZJH* 4 (1970), 20–33, 21.
65. Robinson, *Hatch and Brood*, 246.
66. Quoted in S. J Goldsbury, 'Behind the Picket Fence: The Lives of Missionary Women in Pre-colonial New Zealand', Auckland MA thesis, 1986, 51.
67. Judith Binney, 'At Every Bend a Taniwha', 132–46, and *The Legacy of Guilt: A Life of Thomas Kendall*, 1968; Greg Dening, *Islands and Beaches: Discourse on a Silent Land, Marquesas, 1774–1880*, Melbourne, 1980.
68. Yate, *Account*, 294, 83–84, 98 n.
69. Binney, intro. to 1970 edn of Yate, *Account*, and 'Whatever Happened to Poor Mr Yate? An Exercise in Voyeurism', *NZJH* 9 (1975), 111–25.
70. Marsden letter, 1820, in Allan K. Davidson and Peter J. Lineham (eds), *Transplanted Christianity: Documents Illustrating Aspects of New Zealand Church History*, 1987, 27; Quoted in Goldsbury, 'Behind the Picket Fence', 42.
71. *DNZB*, i.
72. Morton, *Whale's Wake*, 51.
73. Quoted in ibid., 204.
74. J. Ormond Wilson, *Kororareka and Other Essays*, 1990, 18.
75. Morton, *Whale's Wake*; Schaniel, 'Maori and the Economic Frontier', 100, 180–81, 315–16; Hill, *History of Policing*, i, 51; T. M. Gallagher, 'New England Whalers and the Maori Economic Frontier', VUW MA thesis, 1994.
76. Tremewan, *French Akaroa*, 3–6, 164–66.
77. McNab, *Murihuku*, 66. Statistics calculated from Schaniel, 'Maori and the Economic Frontier', 315–16.
78. Morton, *Whale's Wake*, chapter 9.
79. E.g. Cruise, *Journal*, 114; Nicholas, *Narrative*, i, 92–93; ii, 218; Wilson, *Kororareka*, 70–71.
80. E.g. Thomson, *Story of New Zealand*, i, 253; L. J. B. Chapple and H. C. Veitch, *Wanganui*, 1939, 13.
81. McNab, *Murihiku*, 187; *DNZB*, i (Tommy Chasland).
82. Nicholas, *Narrative*, i, 92–96.
83. Cruise, *Journal*, 120, 315.
84. Hainsworth, *Sydney Traders*, 192.
85. Morton, *Whale's Wake*, 294.
86. McNab, *Murihiku*, 220.
87. Ibid., 71–73.

Chapter 6: The Maori Discovery of Europe

1. Wilson, *Hongi to Heke*, 30.
2. All quotes from Savage, *Account*.
3. Nicholas, *Narrative*, i, 428–31, ii, 3–7; Wilson, *Kororeka*, 28–29.
4. Dunmore, *French Explorers*, i, 4–7; Stokes, 'European Discovery of New Zealand', 5.
5. E.g. *Sydney Gazette*, 1 and 22 December 1805.
6. *Australian Dictionary of Biography*, ii (Philip King), ed. Douglas Pike et al., Melbourne.
7. *Sydney Gazette*, 21 April 1810; Lord in McNab, *Historical Records*, i, 323–27. Also see numerous other references to Te Pahi and the *Boyd* in ibid.; Wade Doak, *The Burning of the Boyd: A Saga of Culture Clash*, 1984.
8. Samuel Marsden 'Memoir of Duaterra', in McNab, *Historical Records*, i, 343. Also see Marsden, *Letters and Journals*, 60–123; Nicholas, *Narrative*, passim; *DNZB*, i.
9. Lee, *Bay of Islands*, 62.
10. Nicholas, *Narrative*, i, 14–15.
11. Lee, *Bay of Islands*, 64.
12. Nicholas, *Narrative*, i, 39–43.
13. McNab, *Historical Records*, i, 346–48; Nicholas, *Narrative*, i, 139, 212, 256–58.
14. Wilson, *Kororereka*, 36–44.
15. Brian Mackrell, *Hariru Wikitoria! An Illustrated History of the Maori Tour of England, 1863*, 1985, 11.
16. John Ward, *Information Relative to New Zealand*, 2nd edn, London, 1840, 71–72.
17. Mackrell, *Hariru Wikitoria*.
18. Morton, *Whale's Wake*, 169; Claudia Orange, 'The Maori People and the British Crown', in Sinclair (ed.), *Oxford Illustrated History*, 26; Wilson, *Kororareka*, 39.
19. *DNZB*, i, contains many examples, including Horeta Te Taniwha and three other Ngati Maru chiefs, as well as Te Rauparaha, Te Pehi, Patuone, Pomare.
20. Gallagher, 'New England Whalers', 37.
21. Hocken, *Bibliography*, 489, 49; Morton, *Whale's Wake*, 166–67.

22. Wilson, *Kororareka*, 40.
23. Cook, *Journals*, ii, 287.
24. See Wilson, *Kororareka*, chapter 1; Lee, *Bay of Islands*, 38; Joan Druett, *Exotic Intruders: The Introduction of Plants and Animals into New Zealand*, 1983.
25. Edward Markham, *New Zealand, or Recollections of It*, ed. E. H. McCormick, 1963, 48.
26. Quoted in Salmond, *Two Worlds*, 251.
27. Nicholas, *Narrative*, ii, 101; Cook, *Journals*, ii, 118; Diary of M. de Sainson, in Dumont d'Urville, *New Zealand*, 207.
28. Made by unnamed Maori to Hochstetter, *New Zealand*, 222. Also see Charles Darwin, *The Voyage of the Beagle*, London, 1906 (orig. 1839), 418–19.
29. Cruise, *Journal*, 14. Also see Cook, *Journals*, iii, 59–65.
30. Nicholas, *Narrative*, i, 23–25, ii, 144.
31. Ibid., 104 and passim.
32. Hocken, *Bibliograpy*, 40.
33. Nicholas, *Narrative*, i, 134.
34. Cook, *Journals*, ii, 289–91.
35. Binney, 'Tuki's Universe', 23.
36. Quoted in Schaniel, 'Māori and the Economic Frontier', 159. Also see Binney, *Legacy of Guilt*, 79.
37. E.g. Cruise, *Journal*, 55, 66–67, 244, 286; Williams, *Journal*, 123; Schaniel, 'Maori and the Economic Frontier', 186–88.
38. Cruise, *Journal*, 18.
39. Quoted in Shaniel, 'Maori and the Economic Frontier', 356.
40. Augustus Earle, *A Narrative of Nine Months Residence in New Zealand in 1827*, 1909 edn, 52. Also see Andrew Sharp (ed.), *Duperrey's Visit to New Zealand in 1824*, 1971, 29–30.
41. For Epsom salts and calomel, see Ian Church, 'Heartland of Aotea', unpublished MS, 1984, Wanganui Museum, 149.
42. Garret, *Te Manihera*, 181. Also see Alfred W. Crosby, *Ecological Imperialism: The Biological Expansion of Europe 900–1900*, Cambridge, 1986, 77.
43. R. Jameson, 1842, quoted in M. P. K. Sorrenson, 'How To Civilize Savages: Some "Answers" From Nineteenth-Century New Zealand', *NZJH* 9 (1975), 100.
44. Church, 'Heartland of Aotea', 203; Evidence of C. O. Davis before the Waikato Committee, *AJHR*, 1860, F–3, 21. Also see *The New Zealand Journal of John B. Williams*, ed. Robert W. Kenny, Salem, 1956, 42.
45. Markham, *New Zealand*, 32.
46. Wigglesworth, 'New Zealand Timber and Flax Trade', 386; Gallagher, 'New England Whalers', 47.
47. Morton, *Whale's Wake*, 203; Blosseville, in McNab, *Murihiku*, 203–4.
48. Calculated from D. U. Urlich, 'The Introduction and Diffusion of Firearms in New Zealand, 1800–1840', *JPS* 79 (1970), 399–410.
49. Markham, *New Zealand*, 68 and passim.
50. E.g. Cruise, *Journal*, 70, 259; Sharp, *Duperrey's Visit*, 48; Gallagher, 'New England Whalers', 32–36.
51. Nicholas, *Narrative*, i, 201–3.
52. Ibid., 210, ii, 172–3; Williams, *Journal*, 53–54, 177; Wilson, *Kororareka*, 49–50, and *Hongi to Heke*, 65–66.
53. Dr Fairfowl, evidence to Commissioner Bigge's inquiry, in McNab, *Historical Records*, i, 554.
54. Quoted in Biggs, *Maori Marriage*, 16.
55. Quoted in Wilson, *Kororareka*, 50. Also see Sharp (ed.), *Duperrey's Visit*, 51–84; Williams, *Journal*, 42; Cruise, *Journal*, 138–39, 162–67.
56. Forster, *Journals*, ii, 292, 302–3.
57. Fairfowl, evidence in McNab, *Historical Records*, i, 554.

Chapter 7: Fatal Impact?

1. Williams, *Journal*, 1826, 32.
2. Quoted in Garrett, *Te Manihera*, 220.
3. McNab, *Historical Records*, i, 401.
4. Patricia Bawden, *The Years Before Waitangi: A Story of Early Maori/European Contact in New Zealand*, 1987, 55.
5. Hill, *History of Policing*, i, 37–38.
6. Dumont d'Urville, *The New Zealanders: A Story of Austral Lands*, trans. Carol Legge, 1992.
7. Nicholas, *Narrative*, i, 420–25.
8. Marsden, *Letters and Journals*, 205.
9. Sissons et al., *The Puriri Trees Are Laughing*, 45.
10. Cruise, *Journal*, 282; Urlich, 'Introduction and Diffusion of Firearms', 399–410.
11. Sources for this discussion of the Musket Wars include S. Percy Smith, *Maori Wars of the Nineteenth Century* . . . 2nd edn, 1910, and *History and Traditions of the Maoris of the West Coast* . . ., 1910; Williams, *Journals*: McNab, *Historical Records*; Marsden, *Letters and Journals*; Sissons et al., *The Puriri Trees Are Laughing*; John Koning, 'Firearms and "Fatal Impact" in New Zealand: An Historiographical Reconnaissance', VUW Hons research essay, 1988; Schaniel, 'Maori

and the Economic Frontier', 219–45; Wilson, *Hongi to Heke*; A. P. Vayda, 'Maoris and Muskets in New Zealand: Disruption of a War System', *Political Science Quarterly* 85 (1970), 560–584; Angela Ballara, 'The Role of Warfare in Maori Society in the Early Contact Period', *JPS* 85 (1976), 487–506. Relevant essays in *DNZB*, i, many by Angela Ballara, are an important new source of information.

12. This notion draws on and adapts Schaniel, 'Maori and the Economic Frontier', 216–30.
13. See Binney, *Legacy of Guilt*, chapter 4.
14. *DNZB*, i; Sissons et al., *The Puriri Trees Are Laughing*; Wilson, *Hongi to Heke*.
15. Philippa Wyatt, 'The Old Land Claims and the Concept of Sale: A Case Study', Auckland MA thesis, 1991.
16. Williams, *Early Journals*, 194.
17. Cruise, *Journal*, 281–82.
18. Evidence of Thomas Kendall and John Hunter to Comissioner Bigge, in McNab, *Historical Records*, i, 443, 503.
19. Nicholas, *Narrative*, i, 331–32, 343, 351–52.
20. Quoted in Harrison M. Wright, *New Zealand 1769–1840: Early Years of Western Contact*, Cambridge, Mass., 1959, 92.
21. 'Return of the Native Population . . . in the Districts Near Wellington', *New Munster Government Gazette*, 1850, in A. S. Thomson, 'On the Progress of Civilization Among the New Zealanders', *BPP*, x, 416.
22. Patricia Burns, *Te Rauparaha: A New Perspective*, 1980; Smith, *History and Traditions*; *DNZB*, i.
23. Harry C. Evison, *Te Wai Pounamu / The Greenstone Island: A History of the Southern Maori during the European Colonization of New Zealand*, 1993; Buddy Mikaere, *Te Maiharoa and the Promised Land*, 1988, chapter 1; Anderson, *Te Puoho's Last Raid*; King, *Moriori*.
24. E.g. Williams, *Journal*, 81, 105, 116, 435–39; Schaniel, 'Maori and the Economic Frontier', 341–42.
25. Urlich, 'Introduction and Diffusion of Firearms', 408.
26. Wright, *New Zealand*; Judith Binney, 'Christianity and the Maoris to 1840: A Comment', *NZJH* 3 (1969), 143–65; Bronwyn Elsmore, *Like Them That Dream: The Maori and the Old Testament*, 1985.
27. Fisher, 'Henry Williams', 142–53.
28. J. M. R. Owens, 'Christianity and the Maoris to 1840', *NZJH* 2 (1968), 18–40. Also see Lian, 'Settler Colonialism and Tribal Society' and 'Interpreting Maori History, A Case for a Historical Sociology', *JPS* 96; Bronwyn Elsmore, *Mana from Heaven: A Century of Maori Prophets in New Zealand*, Tauranga, 1989.
29. See D. F. McKenzie, *Oral Culture, Literacy and Print in Early New Zealand: The Treaty of Waitangi*, 1985.
30. Salmond, *Two Worlds*, 175; Wilson, *Hongi to Heke*, 171.
31. Elsmore, *Like Them That Dream.*
32. Wilson, *Hongi to Heke*, 132–33.
33. Williams, *Journals*, 141, 144.
34. Owens, 'Christianity and the Maori', 23.
35. George Clark, quoted in Wright, *New Zealand*, 137.
36. Williams, *Journal*, 40.
37. Ibid., 143; Schaniel, 'Maori and the Economic Frontier', 353.
38. Saxe Bannister, 'An Account of the Changes and Present Condition of the Population of New Zealand', *Royal Statistical Society Journal* 1 (1838), 362–76, 375.
39. E.g. *DNZB*, i (Te Ngahuru), and see Angela Ballara, 'Te Whanganui-a-Tara: Phases of Maori Occupation of Wellington Harbour c. 1800–1840', in David Hamer and Roberta Nicholls (eds), *The Making of Wellington: 1800–1914*, 1990, 33.
40. Williams, *Journal*, 25 (intro).
41. *DNZB*, i (Patuone).
42. Turner, 'Politics of Neutrality', 59–60.
43. Yate, *Account*, 239–41.
44. Elsmore, *Mana from Heaven*, 65.
45. Philip Turner, 'The Politics of Neutrality: The Catholic Mission and the Maori 1838–1870, Auckland MA thesis, 1986, 145. Also see p. 83 and the numerous DNZB, i, articles on Maori and European missionaries.
46. John Skevington, quoted in Church, 'Heartland of Aotea', 35–36.
47. Williams, *Journals*, 464.
48. Quoted in J. S. Stronge, 'The "Harriet" Story', unpublished MS, Taranaki Museum, 1973, 6. Also see W. B. Marshall, *A Personal Narrative of Two Visits to New Zealand*, London, 1836; Reports in *BPP*, iii, 10–15; Smith, *History and Traditions*, 524–31; Hill, *History of Policing*, i, 66–67; *DNZB*, i (Elizabeth Guard).
49. Markham, *New Zealand*, 78.
50. Quoted in Stronge, 'The "Harriet" Story', 34.
51. Thomson, *Story of New Zealand*, i, 254.
52. Quoted in McNab, *Murihiku*, 182–84.
53. Thomson, *Story of New Zealand*, i, 230–66; Hill, *History of Policing*, i, chapter 1; McNab, *Historical Records* and *Murihiku*.

54. Boultbee, *Journal*, 43–44 n.
55. *DNZB*, i; Boultbee, *Journal*, 80–81.
56. Ibid., 57; Markham, *New Zealand*, 40; Morton, *Whale's Wake*, chapter 17.
57. *DNZB*, i, which notes many other cases of marriage alliance; Markham, *New Zealand*, 40.
58. Savage, *Account*, 88–89.
59. Angela Ballara, *Proud to Be White? A Survey of Pakeha Prejudice in New Zealand*, 1986, 86.
60. Pool, *Te Iwi Maori*, 44.
61. Garrett, *Te Manihera*, 157; Goldsbury, 'Behind the Picket Fence', 183.
62. Adams, *Fatal Necessity*, 41.
63. Earle, *Narrative*, 110.
64. Eliza White, quoted in Goldsbury, 137; Bannister, 'An Account', 366.
65. Fairfowl, evidence in McNab, *Historical Records*, i, 555; A. S. Thomson, 'On the Peculiarities in Figure, the Disfigurations, and the Customs of the New Zealanders; With Remarks on Their Diseases, and on Their Modes of Treatment'. This series of three articles was published in a British medical journal and is summarised in Malcolm Nicolson, 'Medicine and Racial Politics: Changing Images of the New Zealand Maori in the Nineteenth Century', unpublished paper, 1986; A. K. Newman, 'A Study of the Causes Leading to the Extinction of the Maori', *TPNZI* 14 (1882), 468–69; John Owens, 'Missionary Medicine and Maori Health: The Record of the Wesleyan Mission to New Zealand Before 1840', *JPS* 81 (1972), 418–36.
66. Quoted in Morton, *Whale's Wake*, 175.
67. General sources used for this section include Ralph M. Garruto, 'Disease Patterns of Isolated Groups', in Henry Rothschild (ed.), *Biocultural Aspects of Disease*, New York, 1981: Terence Ranger and Paul Slack, *Epidemics and Ideas: Essays on the Historical Perception of Pestilence*, Cambridge, 1992; Judith S. Mausner and Shira Kramer, *Epidemiology: An Introductory Text*, Philadelphia, 1985; William McNeill, *Plagues and Peoples*, New York, 1976; Alfred W. Crosby, *Ecological Imperialism: The Biological Expansion of Europe, 900–1900*, Cambridge, 1986; Pool, *Maori Population* and *Te Iwi Maori*; Adams, *Fatal Necessity* (inc. appendix).
68. See table in Pool, *Maori Population*, 120–21.
69. *DNZB*, i (Te Whakataupuka and Tuhuwaiki).
70. John Goldsmid, *The Deadly Legacy: Australian History and Transmissible Disease*, Sydney, 1988, 29.
71. Adams, *Fatal Necessity*, 42–43.
72. McLean, 'Dicky Barrett', 84–85, citing Dieffenbach.
73. Sutton, 'Maori Demographic Change', 318.
74. Quoted in Adams, *Fatal Necessity*, 45.
75. E.g. Cruise, *Journal*, 293.
76. Philip Ross May, *The West Coast Gold Rushes*, 1962, 291.
77. F. D. Fenton, *Observations on the Aboriginal Inhabitants of New Zealand*, 1859; N. G. Pearce, 'The Size and Location of the Maori Population 1857–96', VUW MA thesis, 1952.
78. Cited in Pool, *Te Iwi Maori*, 35.
79. Dumont d'Urville, *The New Zealanders*, 263; K. B. Cumberland, cited in Pool, *Te Iwi Maori*, 42.
80. Pool, *Maori Population*, esp. 48–55, 234–35.
81. Pool, *Te Iwi Maori*, 56.
82. Including half-castes living as Europeans, and rounded up to accommodate a small amount of likely underestimation (*Historical Statistics*, 81). Pearce's estimate for 1874 is a little higher: 'Size and Location of the Maori Population', 204–7.

Chapter 8: Empire?

1. All quotes in this paragraph and the next are from Tremewan, *French Akaroa*.
2. Hocken, *Bibliography*, 9; McNab, *Historical Records*, i, 323–27.
3. Ibid., i, 598–614, 661–66 ; Patricia Burns, *Fatal Success: A History of the New Zealand Company*, 1989, chapter 1.
4. Adams, *Fatal Necessity*; Ian Wards, *The Shadow of the Land: A Study of British Policy and Racial Conflict in New Zealand 1832–1852*, 1968; Claudia Orange, *The Treaty of Waitangi*, 1987.
5. Hobson, 1839. New Zealand Papers 1820–90, A 1994, Mitchell Library, Sydney.
6. J. O'C. Ross, 'Busby and the Declaration of Independence', *NZJH* 14 (1980), 83–89.
7. D. K. Fieldhouse, *Economics and Empire 1830–1814*, London, 1984 edn, 81.
8. See Burns, *Fatal Success*; J. S. Marais, *The Colonisation of New Zealand*, Oxford, 1927; Michael Turnbull, *The New Zealand Bubble*, 1959; Adams, *Fatal Necessity*.
9. Lance E. Davis and Robert A Huttenback, *Mammon and the Pursuit of Empire: The Economics of British Imperialism*, Cambridge, 1988.
10. King, *Moriori*, chapter 4.

11. Morton, *Whale's Wake*, 231.
12. J. D. Raeside, *Sovereign Chief*, 1977.
13. Quoted in Tremewan, *French Akaroa*, 74.
14. Ibid., chapters 2–3; Adams, *Fatal Necessity*, chapters 2–4.
15. Eliza White, quoted in Goldsbury, 'Behind the Picket Fence', 154.
16. Robert FitzRoy, quoted in Wyatt, 'Old Land Claims', 97.
17. Williams, *Journals*, 22; *DNZB*, i, (George Clark); Garrett, *Te Manihera*, 75, 71.
18. *DNZB*, i; Wyatt, 'Old Land Claims', 157–59.
19. Quoted in Evelyn Stokes, *A History of Tauranga County*, 1980, 55.
20. Markham, *New Zealand*, 83; Maning, *Old New Zealand*, and Maning Papers, Alexander Turnbull Library.
21. J. S. Polack, *New Zealand*, 2 vols, London, 1838, and *Manners and Customs of the New Zealanders*, 2 vols, London, 1840; Wilson, *Kororareka*, 78.
22. Quoted in Erik Olssen, *A History of Otago*, 1984, 20–21.
23. Adams, *Fatal Necessity*, esp. 66, 87–88, 106–9.
24. Montefiore and FitzRoy, quoted in Wyatt, 'Old Land Claims', 181–84.
25. Quoted in Wilson, *Hongi to Heke*, 227.
26. Burns, *Fatal Success*, 81.
27. Quoted in Adams, *Fatal Necessity*, 87.
28. John Ward, *Information Relative to New Zealand*, 2nd edn, London, 1840, 73.
29. Quoted in Morton, *Whale's Wake*, 273.
30. Hill, *History of Policing*, i, 717; personal observation. Pakeha illiteracy in Stewart Island was 60% in 1858, five times the national rate of 12%. Dulcie Gillespie-Needham, 'The Colonial and His Books: A Study of Reading in Nineteenth Century New Zealand', VUW PhD thesis, 1971, 76.
31. R. C. J. Stone, *The Making of Russell McVeagh*, 1991, 47.
32. See A. H. McLintock, *Crown Colony Government in New Zealand*, 1958.
33. *DNZB*, i.
34. On Hobson, FitzRoy and Browne, see Orange, *Treaty of Waitangi*; B. J. Dalton, *War and Politics in New Zealand 1855–1870*, Sydney, 1967; Dean Cowie, '"To Do All the Good I Can": Robert FitzRoy; Governor of New Zealand 1843–5', Auckland MA thesis, 1994; relevant essays in *DNZB*, i.
35. Quoted in George W. Stocking, *Victorian Anthropology*, New York, 1987, 84.
36. John Gorst, *New Zealand Revisited*, London, 1908, 26.
37. Bishop, *Natural History*, 168.
38. B. J. Dalton, 'Sir George Grey and the Keppel affair', *Historical Studies* 16 (1974), 192–215.
39. *ENZ*, i, 835; Hill, *History of Policing*, i, 123.
40. Cowie, 'FitzRoy', 114.
41. Alan Ward, *A Show of Justice: Racial Amalgamation in Nineteenth-Century New Zealand*, 1978.
42. Richard Hill, 'Maori Policing in Nineteenth-Century New Zealand', *Archifacts* 2, 1985, 54–60.
43. Tania Thompson, 'British Government Policy and New Zealand Ethnic Relations: Sir George Grey's First Governorship, 1845–1853', VUW MA thesis, 1994.
44. Curnow, 'Te Rangikaheke', 97–147; George Grey, *Polynesian Mythology and Ancient Traditional History of the Maori*, ed. W. W. Bird, 1956 (Maori orig. 1854).
45. See James Belich, 'Hobson's Choice' (review article), *NZJH* 24 (1990), 200–7. Apart from those cited below, important works on the treaty include William Colenso, *The Authentic and Genuine History of the Treaty of Waitangi*, 1890; Ruth Ross, 'Te Tiriti o Waitangi: Texts and Translations', *NZJH* 6 (1972), 129–57; Orange, *Treaty of Waitangi*; Judith Binney, 'The Maori and the Signing of the Treaty of Waitangi', in *Towards 1990*, 1989; Paul McHugh, *The Maori Magna Carta: New Zealand Law and the Treaty of Waitangi*, 1991.
46. Literal translation of the Maori version of the treaty by I. H. Kawharu, in Kawharu (ed.), *Waitangi*, 321.
47. McKenzie, *Oral Culture, Literacy and Print*, 34.
48. Quoted in Turner, 'Politics of Neutrality', 88, 100.
49. Sir James Henare, quoted in Jane Kelsey, *A Question of Honour? Labour and the Treaty 1984–1989*, 1990, 8–11.
50. New Zealand Papers, 1820–1890, A 1280, Mitchell Library, Sydney.
51. Ward, *Show of Justice*.
52. Ann Parsonson, 'The Pursuit of Mana', in *Oxford History of New Zealand* (1981 edn).
53. Quoted in Burns, *Fatal Success*, 161. Also see Rosemarie Tonk, '"A Difficult and Complicated Question": The New Zealand Company's Wellington, Port Nicholson Claim', in Hamer and Nicholls (eds), *Making of Wellington*.
54. Alexandra McKirdy, 'Maori–Pakeha Land Transactions in Hawke's Bay 1848–1864', VUW MA thesis, 1994; Ballara, 'Origins of Ngati Kahungunu', 502 and passim.

55. Adams, *Fatal Necessity*, chapter 1.
56. Wilson, *Kororareka*; Thomson, *Story of New Zealand.*
57. Busby's estimate, quoted in Wilson, *Kororareka*, 114.
58. Lee, *Bay of Islands*, 185–86.
59. See Adams, *Fatal Necessity*, 26–28.
60. Wilson, *Kororareka*, 114.
61. See Orange, *Treaty of Waitangi*, 62–63.
62. Quoted in McKirdy, 'Maori–Pakeha Land Transactions', 26. On land sales in general, see M. P. K. Sorrenson, 'The Purchase of Maori Land, 1865–1892', Auckland MA thesis, 1955, 'The Politics of Land' in J. G. A. Pocock (ed.), *The Maori and New Zealand Politics*, 1965, and 'Land Purchase Methods and Their Effect on the Maori Population', *JPS* 65 (1956), 183–99; Ann Parsonson, 'The Pursuit of Mana' in *Oxford History of New Zealand* (1981 edn), and 'The Challenge to Mana Maori' in *Oxford History of New Zealand* (1992 edn); Ward, *Show of Justice*, 212–17; Angela Ballara, 'The Pursuit of Mana? A Re-evaluation of the Process of Land Alienation by Maoris 1840–90', *JPS* 91 (1982), 519–41.
63. Mary Boyd, *City of the Plains: A History of Hastings*, 1984, 5.
64. Quoted in ibid., 5–6.
65. McEwen, *Rangitane*, 76; McLean, 'Dicky Barrett', 95–97.
66. McKirdy, 'Maori–Pakeha Land Transactions', 42, 61; Evison, *Te Wai Pounamu*, 354.
67. Alan Ward, 'A Report on the Historical Evidence. The Ngai Tahu Claim', Wai 27, Doc T.1, 1989, 332.
68. M. P. K. Sorrenson, 'Maori and Pakeha' in *Oxford History of New Zealand* (1992 edn), 147.
69. Ward, 'The Ngai Tahu Claim', 332.
70. Hone Wiremu Heke Pokaia to Gilbert Mair (senior), 16 October 1845, New Zealand MS 724, Auckland Public Library.
71. On Te Rauparaha and the rise of the Ngati Toa hegemony to 1846, see Burns, *Te Rauparaha*; relevant *DNZB*, i, entries; Ray Grover, *Cork of War: Ngati Toa and the British Mission, an Historical Narrative*, 1982.
72. On Wairau, see Grover, *Cork of War*, chapters 23–24; Burns, *Te Rauparaha*, chapter 36; Ruth M. Allan, *Nelson: A History of Early Settlement*, 1965, chapter 8.
73. See *DNZB*, i (Te Wharepouri).
74. Grover, *Cork of War*, 281. Also see H. F. McKillop, *Reminiscences of Twelve Months Service in New Zealand*, London, 1849, 201; James Cowan, *The New Zealand Wars and the Pioneering Period*, 2 vols, 1922–23, i, chapter 12; Burns, *Te Rauparaha*, chapter 44.
75. On the fighting at Wellington and Wanganui, see Cowan, *New Zealand Wars*, i, 88–144; Ian Wards, *Shadow of the Land*, 215–351; Rutherford, *Grey*, 99–117.
76. Williams, *Journal*, 376.
77. On the causes of the Northern War, see J. Rutherford, *Hone Heke's Rebellion 1844–46: An Episode in the Establishment of British Rule in New Zealand*, 1947; Wards, *Shadow of the Land*, 95–118; James Belich, *The New Zealand Wars and the Victorian Interpretation of Racial Conflict*, 1986, 30–36; Wilson, *Hongi to Heke*, 251–68; Wyatt 'Old Land Claims'.
78. Quoted in Wilson, *Hongi to Heke*, 276.
79. On the course of the Northern War, see Belich, *New Zealand Wars*, chapters 1–3. For partly compatible interpretations, see *History of the War in the North of New Zealand . . . Told by an Old Ngapuhi Chief*, 1862 (compiled by F. E. Maning and later reprinted with his *Old New Zealand*), and Wards, *Shadow of the Land*. For differing interpretations, see T. L. Buick, *New Zealand's First War*, 1926, and Cowan, *New Zealand Wars*, i, chapters 2–9.
80. Quoted in Belich, *New Zealand Wars*, 65.
81. Heke told the Sunday prayers story to J. Merrett, a journalist, in February 1846. Wilson, *Hongi to Heke*, 276.
82. Belich, *New Zealand Wars*, chapter 3.
83. George Graham, 'Heke's Intended Attack on the Waitemata in 1847: Copy of Notes Thereof Obtained from Whatarangi of Aki-tai-ui; 1891', MSS, Auckland Public Library.
84. Cowan, *New Zealand Wars*, i, 54, 66.
85. *History of the War in the North*, 16.
86. Robert Hattaway, *Reminiscences of the Northern War*, 1889, 6.
87. See Belich, *New Zealand Wars*, esp. 178–88.
88. Wilson, *Hongi to Heke*, 276.
89. Taylor, *Te Ika a Maui*, 350 n.

Chapter 9: Converting Conversion

1. Hill, *History of Policing*, i, 225; Cowan, *New Zealand Wars*, i, 449–50.
2. Quoted in Keith Sinclair, *The Origins of the Maori Wars*, 1957, 42.
3. Garrett, *Te Manihera*, 173; Thomson, *Story of New Zealand*, i, 292–306.

4. Sinclair, *Origins of the Maori Wars*, 91.
5. *ENZ*, iii, 361; Lloyd Prichard, *Economic History of New Zealand*, 139–40.
6. Ballara, 'The Pursuit of Mana?'
7. Rutherford, *Grey*, 187.
8. *Historical Statistics*, 275.
9. Evison, *Te Wai Pounamu*, 382.
10. Salmon, *History of Goldmining*, 37, 82.
11. Brailsford, *Greenstone Trails:* Nancy M. Taylor, *Early Travellers in New Zealand*, 1959.
12. Church, 'Heartland of Aotea', 167; McLean, 'Dicky Barrett'.
13. Church, 'Heartland of Aotea', 185; Stevan Eldred-Grigg, *Pleasures of the Flesh: Sex and Drugs in Colonial New Zealand 1840–1915*, 1984, 30.
14. *The New Zealander*, 14 September 1848; R. C. J. Stone, *Makers of Fortune: A Colonial Business Community and Its Fall*, 1973, 6. Also see Keith Sinclair, 'Maori Nationalism and the European Economy', *Historical Studies, Australia and New Zealand* 18 (1952), 119–34.
15. Thomson, 'On the Progress of Civilization', 417.
16. Simon Ville, 'The Coastal Trade of New Zealand Prior to World War One', *NZJH* 27 (1993), 85.
17. Lian, 'Settler Colonialism and Tribal Society'; Ward, 'The Ngai Tahu Claim', 345.
18. J. E. Martin, *The Forgotten Worker: The Rural Wage-Earner in Nineteenth-Century New Zealand*, 1990, 173–74.
19. Church, 'Heartland of Aotea', quoting missionary William Woon, 163.
20. See McKirdy, 'Maori–Pakeha Land Transactions'.
21. Quoted in Cowie, 'FitzRoy', 79.
22. Church, 'Heartland of Aotea'.
23. Tremewan, *French Akaroa*, 255.
24. Turner, 'Politics of Neutrality', 149 and passim.
25. Church, 'Heartland of Aotea', 136.
26. Turner, 'Politics of Neutrality', 154–55, 146; 'Return of the Native Population . . . in the Districts Near Wellington', *New Munster Government Gazette*, 1850, in Thomson, 'On the Progress of Civilization', 416.
27. Turner, 'Politics of Neutrality', 149.
28. Clarke, cited in Wright, *New Zealand*, 141.
29. Turner, 'Politics of Neutrality'; 25. Pezant and Lampila, *DNZB*, i.
30. Wilson, *Hongi to Heke*, 90.
31. Quoted in Elsmore, *Like Them That Dream*, 23.
32. Williams, *Journals*, 464.
33. Turner, 'Politics of Neutrality', 202–5.
34. Church, 'Heartland of Aotea', 68; Gillespie-Needham, 'The Colonial and His Books', 212.
35. 1857 WMS report, quoted in Elsmore, *Mana from Heaven*, 138.
36. Charles Hursthouse, *New Zealand or Zealandia, The Britain of the South*, 2 vols, London, 1857, i, 164.
37. Elsmore, *Mana from Heaven*, 163; Thomson, 'On the Progress of Civilization'.
38. Owens, 'Christianity and the Maoris to 1840', 23.
39. E.g. Alison Begg, 'The Conversion to Christianity of the South Island Maori in the 1840s and 1850s', *Historical and Polictical Studies* 3 (1972), 15–16; Turner, 'Politics of Neutrality', chapters 3 and 6.
40. Quoted in Turner, 'Politics of Neutrality', 45. Also see 43–54.
41. Begg, 'Conversion to Christianity', 16.
42. On the prophetic movements, see Elsmore, *Mana from Heaven*; C. J. Parr, 'Before the Pai Marire', *JPS* 76 (1966), 35–46; Mikaere, *Te Maiharoa*; Church, 'Heartland of Aotea'; Binney, 'Maori Prophet Leaders', in Sinclair (ed.), *Oxford Illustrated History*; Daniel P. Lyons, 'An Analysis of Three Maori Prophetic Movements', in Kawharu (ed.), *Conflict and Compromise*; Wilson, *Hongi to Heke*, 192–97; William Greenwood, *The Upraised Hand, or the Spiritual Significance of the Ringatu Faith*, 1942; Paul Clark, *Hauhau: The Pai Marire Search for Maori Identity*, 1975; Robin Winks, 'The Doctrine of Hauhauism', *JPS* 62/3 (1953); L. F. Head, 'Te Ua and the Hauhau Faith in the Light of the Ua Gospel Notebook', Canterbury MA thesis, 1983. Two studies that put Pai Marire in an international comparative context are Michael Adas, *Prophets of Rebellion: Millenarian Protest Movements Against the European Colonial Order*, Chapel Hill, 1979; and John S. Galbraith, 'Appeals to the Supernatural: African and New Zealand Comparisons to the Ghost Dance', *Pacific Historical Review* 51/2, 1982.
43. Head, 'Te Ua', 130 and passim; Binney, 'Maori Prophetic Movements', 162.
44. Church, 'Heartland of Aotea', 119 ff; Elsmore, *Mana from Heaven*, chapter 11.
45. Titokowaru to Whitmore, 4 December 1868, *AJHR* 1869, A-10, No. 29, encl. Also see James Belich, *'I Shall Not Die': Titokowaru's War*, 1989, 4–6, 9.
46. Elsmore, *Mana from Heaven*, 188 and passim, and *Like Them That Dream*.

47. Marsden, *Letters and Journals*, 219.
48. Wilson, *Hongi to Heke*, 197–98; *DNZB*, i.
49. Mikaere, *Te Maiharoa*, 59. Also see Head, chapter 5.
50. Mikaere, *Te Maiharoa*, 60.
51. Turner, 'Politics of Neutrality', 66 and passim.
52. Davidson and Lineham, *Transplanted Christianity*, 163–64.
53. Bruce Biggs, 'The Maori Language Past and Present', in Erik Schwimmer (ed.), *The Maori People in the Nineteen Sixties*, 1968, 73. Also see Michael Jackson, 'Literacy, Communication and Social Change', in Kawharu (ed.), *Conflict and Compromise*; McKenzie, *Oral Culture, Literacy and Print.*
54. Ward, *Show of Justice*, 136.
55. Belich, *Titokowaru's War*, 41.
56. *Punch, or the Auckland Charivari*, 1869, 132.
57. Hill, *History of Policing*, ii, 202.
58. 'Papers Concerning the Abduction of the Wife and Child of James Holden', *AJHR*, 1862, D-16.
59. Evidence of C. O. Davis, *AJHR*, 1860, F–3.
60. Calculated from statistics kindly provided by Miles Fairburn.
61. Evidence of C. O. Davis.
62. In Head, 'Te Ua', 181–85.
63. Rutherford, *Grey*, 187.
64. R. D. Hill, 'Pastoralism in the Wairarapa 1844–53', in R. F. Watters (ed.), *Land and Society in New Zealand: Essays in Historical Geography*, 1965. Also see Jeanine Graham, *Frederick Weld*, 1983, chapter 2; *DNZB*, i (F. D. Bell); *DNZB*, ii, (E. J. Riddiford).
65. E.g. Marilyn J. Campbell, 'Runholding in Otago and Southland 1848 to 1876', Otago MA thesis, 1981, 130; P. G. Holland and R. P. Hargreaves, 'The Trivial Round, the Common Task: Work and Leisure on a Canterbury Hill Country Run in the 1860s and 1870s', *New Zealand Geographer* 47 (1991), 21; Evison, *Te Wai Pounamu*, 334.
66. H. Guthrie-Smith, *Tutira: The Story of a New Zealand Sheep Station*, Edinburgh and London, 1926, 135–36.
67. Anderson, 'Maori Settlement of the Interior of Southern New Zealand', 61.
68. Evison, *Te Wai Pounamu*, 404 and passim.
69. Ward, 'The Ngai Tahu Claim', 333–34; Mikaere, *Te Maiharoa* , chapter 2.
70. Evison, *Te Wai Pounamu*, 330, 351–53.

Chapter 10: Conquest?

1. Browne to Colonial Office, 15 April 1856, *BPP*, 194.
2. Quoted in Belich, *New Zealand Wars*, 78.
3. John Gorst, *The Maori King*, ed. Keith Sinclair, 1959 (orig. 1864), 28–29.
4. Henry Sewell, Journal, 21 May 1860, 1859–65, Canterbury Museum.
5. Sinclair, *Origins of the Maori Wars* and *Kinds of Peace: Maori People After the Wars 1870–85*, 1991, 15–18; Alan Ward, 'The Origins of the Anglo–Maori Wars: A Reconsideration', *NZJH* 1 (1967), 148–70; B. J. Dalton, *War and Politics in New Zealand*, Sydney, 1967; M. P. K. Sorrenson, 'Maori and Pakeha', in *Oxford History of New Zealand* (1992 edn), 148–54; Belich, *New Zealand Wars*, 76–80.
6. Henry Monro to Native Secretary, in Grey to Newcastle, 7 December 1861, Colonial Office Inwards Correspondence, Public Record Office, London, 209/165, 391–97.
7. Hadfield to CMS, 7 April 1864 (quoting *Edinburgh Review*, January 1864, 270), Hadfield Letters, 1838–69, CMS Archives, London.
8. Keith Sinclair, *The Maori Land League: An Examination into the Source of a New Zealand Myth*, 1950; Edward Hill, *There Was a Maori Land League in Taranaki*, 1969; Church, 'Heartland of Aotea'.
9. Quoted in Elsmore, *Mana from Heaven*, 129.
10. See Gorst, *The Maori King*; M. Winiata, *History of the King Movement* and *The King Movement*, 1958; M. P. K. Sorrenson, 'The Maori King Movement, 1858–85', in Robert Chapman and Keith Sinclair (eds), *Studies of a Small Democracy*, 1963; Lindsay Cox, *Kotahitanga: The Search for Maori Political Unity*, 1993.
11. Belich, *New Zealand Wars*, 128 and passim; account of Paitini in Elsdon Best, *Tuhoe: Children of the Mist*, 1925, 567.
12. Wilson, *Hongi to Heke*, 86–88.
13. H. W. Williams, *A Dictionary of the Maori Language*, 1971 edn, 252.
14. Nicholas, *Narrative*, ii, 222.
15. Wilson, *Hongi to Heke*, 89–90.
16. 'Te Ua Gospel', translated in Head, 'Te Ua', 63.
17. Tamehana to Gore Browne, 7 June 1861, *AJHR*, 1861, E-1B, 19.
18. Quoted in Elsmore, *Mana from Heaven*. 135, and see 129.
19. McLean to Gore Browne, 14 April 1856, *BPP*, x, 197.
20. Tamehana to Gore Browne, 7 June 1861, *AJHR*, 1861, E–1B, 19.
21. Henry Sewell, Journal, 23 April 1860.

22. See W. I. Grayling, *The War in Taranaki*, 1862; Robert Carey, *Narrative of the Late War in New Zealand*, London, 1863; J. E. Alexander, *Incidents of the Maori War*, London, 1863; Cowan, *New Zealand Wars*, i, chapters 17–24; Belich, *New Zealand Wars*, chapters 4–6.
23. *Taranaki Punch*, 7 November 1860.
24. Belich, *New Zealand Wars*, 124–25.
25. Ibid., 187.
26. Quoted in ibid., 199.
27. On the Waikato War, see J. E. Alexander, *Bushfighting: Illustrated by Remarkable Actions and Incidents of the Maori War in New Zealand*, London, 1873; John Featon, *The Waikato War, 1863–64*, revised edn, 1923; William Fox, *The War in New Zealand*, London, 1866; Cowan, *New Zealand Wars*, i, chapters 26–42; Belich, *New Zealand Wars*, chapters 7–10.
28. On the campaigns of 1864–72, see T. W. Gudgeon, *Reminscences of the War in New Zealand*, London, 1879; G. S. Whitmore, *The Last Maori War in New Zealand*, London, 1902; Cowan, *New Zealand Wars*, ii; Belich, *New Zealand Wars*, chapters 11–13, and *Titokowaru's War*.
29. Brian Sutton-Smith, *A History of Children's Play in New Zealand 1840–1950*, Philadelphia, 1981, 68–69.
30. Raewyn Dalziel, *Julius Vogel: Business Politician*, 1986, e.g. 106.
31. Belich, *Titokowaru's War*, 208–9.
32. E.g. numerous references in Fox, *The War in New Zealand*; G. H. Scholefield (ed.), *The Richmond-Atkinson Papers*, 2 vols, 1960; *The Southern Monthly Magazine*, 1864.
33. *DNZB*, i.
34. Hill, *History of Policing*, ii, 125. Also see ibid., 158–60, 250; R. P. Davis, *Irish Issues in New Zealand Politics*, 1974; *DNZB*, i (William John Larkin and John Manning); *Taranaki Herald* (supplement), 18 April 1868; various references in Army Department correspondence and telegrams, April–May 1868, National Archives, Wellington.
35. James Cowan Papers, 41B, Alexander Turnbull Library, Wellington; Account of Wiremu Kingi, *AJHR*, 1870, A–8B, 28–29; Belich, *Titokowaru's War*, 37–38, 83.
36. Ibid., 272–73.
37. See, e.g. 'Te Ua Gospel', translated in Head, 'Te Ua', chapter 3 and 181–85.
38. Belich, *Titokowaru's War*, 141, 180, 345.
39. Quoted in Parsonson, 'The Pursuit of Mana', in *Oxford History of New Zealand*, (1981 edn) 158.
40. Sinclair, *Kinds of Peace*, 14–15.
41. James Liu et al., 'Social Identity and the Perception of History: Cultural Narratives of Aotearoa/New Zealand', paper in publication, VUW, 1995, 2, 17.

Chapter 11: Swamps, Sticks and Carrots

1. Newman, 'Causes Leading to the Extinction of the Maori', 459–77.
2. O. N. Gillespie, 1930, quoted in W. H. Pearson, 'Attitudes to the Maori in Some Pakeha Fiction', *JPS* 67 (1958), 216.
3. Quoted in Walter Buller, 'The Decrease of the Maori Race', *New Zealand Journal of Science* 2 (1884), 54.
4. From Pool, *Te Iwi Maori*, appendix 1.
5. E.g. Lee, *Hokianga*, 174, 228; Evelyn Stokes, *Mokau: Maori Cultural and Historical Perspectives*, 1988, 177.
6. Atholl Anderson, *Race Against Time: The Early Maori-Pakeha Families and the Development of the Mixed Race Population in Southern New Zealand*, 1991, 2.
7. Biggs, *Maori Marriage*, 21; Pool, *Te Iwi Maori*, 47–49.
8. Anderson, *Race Against Time*, 9–14.
9. Peter Buck (Te Rangi Hiroa), 'The Passing of the Maori', *TPNZI* 55 (1924), 362–75.
10. *Historical Statistics*, 86.
11. Graham Butterworth, *Maori/Pakeha Intermarriage: Five Talks on the Concert Programme*, 1988.
12. Quoted in L. R. Murrihy, 'The Myths and the Portrayal of New Zealand National Character in Nineteenth-Century Pioneer Novels', VUW MA thesis,1984, 30–32.
13. Belich, *Titokowaru's War*, 62–64, 280; *DNZB*, i.
14. *Australian and New Zealand Gazette*, 3 October 1863, quoted in Mackrell, *Hariru Wikitoria*, 72.
15. Evison, *Te Wai Pounamu*, 467, 337–97 and passim.
16. Simbo Ojinmah, 'The Maori Women of the Otago District, 1874–1936', Otago MA thesis, 1989, 63 and passim.
17. *Historical Statistics*, 86.
18. *DNZB*, ii (H. K. Taiaroa).
19. Ward, 'The Ngai Tahu Claim', 33–34. Also see Mikaere, *Te Maiharoa*, 24; P. J. F. Coutts, 'Merger or Takeover: A Survey of the Effects of Contact Between European and Maori in the Foveaux Strait Region', *JPS* 78 (1969), 495–516.
20. Mikaere, *Te Maiharoa*.

21. Ibid., 106; *DNZB*, ii.
22. See Evison, *Te Wai Pounamu*; Ward, 'The Ngai Tahu Claim'; Ojinmah, 'Maori Women of Otago', 107–15. This paragraph also draws on various papers given at the New Zealand Historical Association Conference at Canterbury University in 1990, at which the history of Ngai Tahu and their claim was a major theme.
23. Ojinmah, 'Maori Women of Otago', 85.
24. Basil Howard, *Rakiura*, 1940, 210–13.
25. Anderson, *Race Against Time*, 20.
26. Ojinmah, 'Maori Women of Otago', 15.
27. Anderson, *Race Against Time*; Ojinmah, 'Maori Women of Otago'.
28. Brian D. Gilling, 'Engine of Destruction? An Introduction to the History of the Maori Land Court', *Victoria University Law Review* 25 (1994), 115–39, 131.
29. See references in Chapter 8, note 62.
30. Sinclair, *Kinds of Peace*, 118.
31. Sorrenson 'Maori and Pakeha', in *Oxford History of New Zealand* (1992 edn), 160; Report of the Native Department, *AJHR*, 1920, G–9; Tom Brooking, '"Busting Up" the Greatest Estate of All: Liberal Maori Land Policy 1891–1911', *NZJH* 26 (1992), 78–98.
32. E.g. Stokes, *Tauranga*, 304–5, 418–19.
33. Boyd, *Hastings*, 10; Guthrie-Smith, *Tutira*, 240; Ward, *Show of Justice*, 213.
34. Wilson, *Hongi to Heke*, 109–14; *DNZB*, i.
35. Keith Sinclair and W. S. Mandle, *Open Account: A History of the Bank of New South Wales in New Zealand 1861–1961*, 1961, 115, 145.
36. Calculated from statistics kindly provided by Miles Fairburn.
37. Hill, *History of Policing*, iii, chapter 10. Also see Dick Scott, *Ask That Mountain: The Story of Parihaka*, 1975; Hazel Riseborough, *Days of Darkness: Taranaki 1878–1884*, 1989; Sinclair, *Kinds of Peace*, chapter 6.
38. Riseborough, *Days of Darkness*, 212.
39. Cowan, *New Zealand Wars*, ii, 496–98.
40. Premier R. J. Seddon, quoted in Williams, *Politics of the New Zealand Maori*, 95.
41. Best, *Tuhoe*.
42. Sissons, *Te Waimana*, 187.
43. Williams, *Politics of the New Zealand Maori*, 147; Peter Webster, *Rua and the Maori Millenium*, 1979, chapter 5; Judith Binney, 'Maungapohatu Revisited: Or, How the Government Underdeveloped a Maori Community', *JPS* 93 (1984), 353–92.
44. Hill, *History of Policing*, iii, chapter 10.
45. See Webster, *Rua*; Binney, 'Maungapohatu Revisited'; J. Binney, G. Chaplin and C. Wallace, *Mihaia: The Prophet Rua Kenana and His Community of Maungapohatu*, 1979; *ENZ*, iii, 131–32.
46. Ward 'Origins of the Anglo–Maori Wars', 167.
47. Webster, *Rua*, chapter 9; Hill, *History of Policing*, iii, chapter 25.
48. J. Kerry-Nicholls, *The King Country*, London, 1884, 13–14.
49. Sinclair, *Kinds of Peace*, 39; Kerry-Nicholls, 1; *ENZ*, ii, 223–24.
50. Sissons, *Te Waimana*, 158; Sorrenson, 'The Maori King Movement, 1858–85', in Chapman and Sinclair (eds), *Studies of a Small Democracy*; Sally MacLean, 'Nga Tamariki o te Rohe Waikato: Maori Children's Lives in the Waikato Region 1850–1900, a Case Study', Waikato MA thesis, 1990.
51. Ann Parsonson, 'King Tawhiao and the New Maori Monarchy', paper presented to the conference of New Zealand historians, Wellington, 1972, 21–22. Also see Hill, *History of Policing*, iii, chapter 4.
52. *OYB*, 1893, 361.
53. Belich, *Titokowaru's War*, 43, 276–77.
54. Quoted in Sinclair, *Kinds of Peace*, 86.
55. See W. R. Jackson and G. A. Wood, 'The New Zealand Parliament and Maori Representation', *Historical Studies* 11 (1964), 383–96; Sinclair, *Kinds of Peace*, chapter 7.
56. Quoted in ibid., 95.
57. Ibid., 91.
58. Pool, *Te Iwi Maori*, 96 and passim.
59. Sinclair, *Kinds of Peace*, chapter 9.
60. Ward, *Show of Justice*, 278.
61. Williams, *Politics of the New Zealand Maori*, 76.
62. *DNZB*, i, 492–93.
63. Evidence of David Christopher Young to the Planning Tribunal, Electricity Corporation versus Whanganui River Maori Trust Board, 1988; Ward, *Show of Justice*, 291.
64. Belich, *New Zealand Wars*, 197–98, and *Titokowaru's War*, 273, 276.
65. Maning to Hugh Lusk, 6 July 1864, Maning Papers, Alexander Turnbull Library.
66. Quoted in Lee, *Hokianga*, 240–41.
67. Lindsay Cox, *Kotahitanga: The Search for Maori Political Unity*, 1993, 43.
68. Quoted in Williams, *Politics of the New Zealand Maori*, 62.
69. Ward, *Show of Justice*, 300. Also see Lee, *Hokianga*, 188, 194.
70. Hill, *History of Policing*, iii, chapter 17.
71. *DNZB*, ii. Also see Hill, *History of Policing*, iii, chapter 4.

72. Hill, *History of Policing*, iii, chapter 10; *DNZB*, ii; Cowan, *New Zealand Wars*, ii, 499–502; Lee, *Hokianga*, 240–44; Elsmore, *Mana from Heaven*, chapter 37.
73. McLean, 'Maori Children's Lives', 47.
74. Sissons, *Te Waimana*, 186–88.
75. Calculated roughly from *Historical Statistics*, 54, 184, 186, and *OYB*, 1893, 121, 127, 359. Crops exclude sown grasses.
76. Gary Hawke, *The Making of New Zealand: An Economic History*, Cambridge, 1985, 23–24.
77. See e.g. Stokes, *Tauranga*, 307–11.
78. Ibid., 267.
79. *OYB*, 1990, 501.
80. *DNZB*, ii (Hirini Te Rito Whaanga).

Chapter 12: The Pakeha Prospectus

1. McNab, *Historical Records*, i, 203–5, ii, 518–34, and *Muruhiku*, 57–66, 329–49. McNab reproduces letters from Bampton and Governor King of Norfolk Island reporting the affair, together with Murry's log.
2. E.g. Donald Denoon, *Settler Capitalism: The Dynamics of Dependent Development in the Southern Hemisphere*, Oxford, 1983.
3. These figures are obviously very rough indeed. They are calculated mainly from *Historical Statistics*, esp. 73; Donald Harman Akenson, *Half the World from Home: Perspectives on the Irish in New Zealand 1860–1950*, 1990, chapter 1; 'Immigration', in *ENZ*; and W. D. Borrie, 'The Peopling of Australasia 1788–1988: The Common Heritage', in Sinclair (ed.), *Tasman Relations*, and *Immigration to New Zealand 1854–1938*, Canberra, 1991. Some gaps, especially before 1860, have been filled by guesswork. Some allowance has been made for the tendency of official statistics to understate migration, especially to and from Australia. See John M. Gandar, 'New Zealand Migration in the Later Part of the Nineteenth Century', *AEHR* 19 (1979), 151–68.
4. J. D. Gould, 'European Inter-continental Emigration 1815–1914: Patterns and Causes', *Journal of European Economic History* 8 (1979), 593–679; Dudley Baines, *Emigration from Europe 1815–1930*, London, 1991.
5. Ibid., 9–10.
6. Keith Sinclair, 'Life in the Provinces', in Sinclair (ed.), *Distance Looks Our Way*, Auckland, 1961, 30.
7. Hursthouse, *New Zealand*, i, 265.
8. Burns, *Fatal Success*; McKirdy, 'Maori–Pakeha Land Transactions', 18.
9. Edward Wakefield, *New Zealand after Fifty Years*, London, 1889, 25.
10. Burns, *Fatal Success*; Raewyn Dalziel, *The Origins of New Zealand Diplomacy*, 1975.
11. Burns, *Fatal Success*, 197, 32–33; Tom Brooking, '"Tam McCanny and Kitty Clydeside": The Scots in New Zealand', in R. A. Cage (ed.), *The Scots Abroad: Labour, Capital, Enterprise*, London, 1985, 161.
12. *Journal of Ensign Best, 1837–43*, ed. Nancy M. Taylor, 1966, 216.
13. Judith A. Johnston, 'Information and Emigration: The Image Making Process', *New Zealand Geographer* 33 (1977), 60–67; Leonard Bell, *Colonial Constructs: European Images of Maori 1840–1914*, 1991, 10–34, 139, 66.
14. Charles Heaphy, quoted in Burns, *Fatal Success*, 187.
15. *Chambers' Papers for the People*, quoted in Hursthouse, *New Zealand*, ii, 363. Also see Thomson, *Story of New Zealand*, ii, 12.
16. Johnston, 'Information and Immigration', 63; Rollo Arnold, *The Farthest Promised Land: English Villagers, New Zealand Immigrants of the 1870s*, 1981, 72. Also see Burns, *Fatal Success*; Turnbull, *New Zealand Bubble*.
17. Hocken, *Bibliography*. A hasty search of Poole's *Index to Periodical Literature 1802–1881* in the British Museum revealed 122 articles on New Zealand. This excludes newspapers. Crusader newspapers in Britain included the *Colonial Gazette* in the 1830s, the *New Zealand Journal* in the 1840s, and the *New Zealand Examiner* in the 1860s.
18. Wakefield to Dr G. S. Evans, n.d., New Zealand Papers 1836–87, Mitchell Library, Sydney, C 184.
19. *Letters from New Plymouth 1843*, London, 1843, 11, 37.
20. J. Leckie, '"They Sleep Standing Up": Gujaratis in New Zealand to 1945', Otago PhD thesis, 1981, i, 217.
21. David Hamer, *New Towns in the New World: Images and Perceptions of the Nineteenth-Century Frontier*, New York, 1990, esp. chapter 2.
22. Hursthouse, *New Zealand*, i, 4, and see his *Emigration: Emigration Fields Contrasted*, London, 1853.
23. Rev. Sydney Smith, quoted in Thomson, *Story of New Zealand*, ii, 69.
24. Cholmondeley, *Ultima Thule*, 11.
25. Gould, 'European Inter-continental Migration', 612.
26. Edward Brynn, 'The Emigration Theories of

Robert Wilmot Horton, 1820–1841', *Canadian Journal of History* 4 (1969), 45–65.
27. Cholmondeley, *Ultima Thule*, 13.
28. Taylor, *Te Ika a Maui*, 262; Hursthouse, *New Zealand*, i, 130, 148–49.
29. Hursthouse, *New Zealand*, i, 86.
30. E.g. Arnold Pickmere, *In Thy Toil Rejoice: The Story of J. J. Patterson – Taranaki Pioneer*, 1991, 28; Hursthouse, *New Zealand*, ii, 479–501; Alfred Fell, *A Colonist's Voyage to New Zealand*, 1973 edn, 29–32; John Gorst, *New Zealand Revisited*, London, 1908, 5–22.
31. Allan, *Nelson*, 87–89.
32. Charlotte Macdonald, *A Woman of Good Character: Single Women as Immigrant Settlers in Nineteenth-Century New Zealand*, 1990, 95.
33. Arnold, *Farthest Promised Land*, 59–61.
34. Keith Robbins, *Nineteenth-Century Britain: Integration and Diversity*, Oxford, 1988, 30–33.
35. Ibid., 33; Christopher Harvie, 'Revolution and the Rule of Law', in Morgan (ed.), *Oxford History of Britain*, 484–85.
36. Lawrence Stone and J. C. Fawtier Stone, *An Open Elite? England 1540–1880*, Oxford, 1984.
37. Robbins, *Nineteenth-Century Britain*, 156. Also see Harvey J. Graff (ed.), *Literacy and Social Development in the West: A Reader*, Cambridge, 1981.
38. G. R. Porter, *The Progress of the Nation*, 1912, quoted in Harold Perkin, *The Origins of Modern English Society 1780–1880*, London, 1969, 3.
39. Dudley Baines, *Migration in a Mature Economy: Emigration and Internal Migration in England and Wales 1861–1900*, Cambridge, 1985.
40. Paul Langford, 'The Eighteenth Century', in Morgan (ed.), *Oxford History of Britain*, 447.
41. Arnold, *Farthest Promised Land*, 141.
42. Harvie, 'Revolution and the Rule of Law', 500.
43. J. M. Golby and A. W. Purdue, *The Civilisation of the Crowd: Popular Culture in England 1750–1900*, London, 1984.
44. Henry Mayhew, quoted in Stocking, *Victorian Anthropology*, 4; Colin Mathew, 'The Liberal Age', in Morgan (ed.), *Oxford History of Britain*, 518.
45. Charlotte Erickson, *Invisible Immigrants*, 25–26; Malcolm I. Thomis and Peter Holt, *Threats of Revolution in Britain 1789–1848*, London, 1977; F. M. L. Thompson, *The Rise of Respectable Society: A Social History of Victorian Britain*, London, 1988, 24.
46. Macaulay, *History of England* and *Critical and Historical Essays*, London, 1883.
47. Christopher Lasch, *The True and Only Heaven: Progress and Its Critics*, New York, 1991.
48. Cited in Salmond, *Two Worlds*, 97.
49. Louis B. Wright, *The Colonial Search for a Southern Eden*, New York, 1973, 41.
50. On the neglected utopist Pemberton, see E. H. McCormick, 'The Happy Colony', *Landfall* 9 (1955), 300–34, and John Rockey, 'An Australasian Utopist', *NZJH* 15 (1981), 157–78.
51. Lionel Frost, *The New Urban Frontier: Urbanisation and City-Building in Australasia and the American West*, Kensington, 1991, 8–9.
52. E.g. in the folk ballad 'Our Merry Town', in Patrick Joyce, *Visions of the People: Industrial England and the Question of Class, 1848–1914*, Cambridge, 1991, 366.
53. E. P. Thompson, *The Making of the English Working Class*, London, 1963; Harold Perkin, *The Origins of Modern English Society 1780–1880*, London, 1969.
54. Quoted in ibid., 182.
55. Thompson, *Rise of Respectable Society*, 156.
56. Arnold, *Farthest Promised Land*, 23–27.
57. My conceptions of populism and folk utopianism draw in particular on Joyce, *Visions of the People*.
58. L. P. Curtis, *Anglo-Saxons and Celts: A Study of Anti-Irish Prejudice in Victorian England*, Bridgeport, 1968, 9.
59. See Robbins, *Nineteenth-Century Britain*, and Linda Colley, *Forging the Nation 1707–1837*, 1992.
60. Quoted in Curtis, *Anglo-Saxons and Celts*, 81.
61. Macaulay, 'Von Ranke', in *Historical and Critical Essays*, 542.
62. Gibbon, *The History of the Decline and Fall of the Roman Empire*, ed. J. B. Bury, 7 vols, London, 1897, iii, 44; Aldous Huxley, *Ape and Essence*, New York, 1948; Anthony Trollope, *The New Zealander*, ed. N. John Hall, Oxford, 1972; Bertrand Russell, 'Zahatopolk', in *The Collected Stories*, London, 1972. Also see William Colenso, 'On Macaulay's New Zealander', in *Three Literary Papers*, 1883, and McCormick, 'The Happy Colony'. The convention also penetrated East Anglian folklore, if Keith Sinclair's grandmother is to be believed. See Sinclair, 'Life in the Provinces', 27.
63. Thomson, Story of *New Zealand*, ii, 233.

64. Cook, *Journals*, i, 276–67.
65. Morton, *Whale's Wake*, 154.
66. Judith A. Johnston, 'The New Zealand Bush: Early Assessments of Vegetation', *New Zealand Geographer* 37 (1981), 19–24.
67. Quoted in Harrop, *England and New Zealand*, 39.
68. [Wakefield and John Ward], *The British Colonization of New Zealand*, London, 1837; Burns, *Fatal Success*, 105.
69. Company advertisement reproduced in ibid., 108–9; speech by Lord Ashburton, quoted in E. J. Wakefield, *The Hand-book for New Zealand*, London, 1848, 29.
70. Quoted in A. J. Harrop, *England and New Zealand*, London, 1926, 59, 52–53.
71. For other examples, see Miles Fairburn, *The Ideal Society and Its Enemies: The Foundations of Modern New Zealand Society 1850–1900*, 1989, esp. 21–4. 'The Eden of the World' is from the letter of a Canterbury settler quoted by Hursthouse, *New Zealand*, i, 99 n.
72. *London Illustrated News*, 18 July 1863; *Daily Telegraph*, 16 June 1863, Quoted in Mackrell, *Hariru Wikitoria!*, 59, 40.
73. Quoted in Angus Ross, *New Zealand's Aspirations in the Pacific in the Nineteenth Century*, Oxford, 1964, 53–54. Also see 3–55.
74. Fell, *Colonist's Voyage*, 3,107; Alexander Marjoribanks, *Travels in New Zealand*, London, 1846, 11.
75. Thomson, *Story of New Zealand*, i, 5; Hursthouse, *New Zealand*, i, 83–84.
76. Thomson, *Story of New Zealand*, i, 36–49, ii, 309.
77. Ibid., i, 45, 37.
78. Hursthouse, *New Zealand*, i, 120, 136–37.
79. Ibid., i, 315–16, ii, 344, 377, 411; Leach, *1000 Years of Gardening*, 115–16.
80. *The Journal of Henry Sewell 1853–7*, ed. W. David McIntyre, 2 vols, 1980, i, 146.
81. Hursthouse, *New Zealand*, ii, 525.
82. Quoted in Paul Shepard, *English Reactions to the New Zealand Landscape Before 1850*, 1969, 24.
83. Hursthouse, *New Zealand*, ii, 355.
84. Yate, *Account*, 19.
85. Canterbury Papers, quoted in Thomson, *Story of New Zealand*, ii, 184.
86. Martin Tupper in Canterbury Papers, 1852; quoted in McCormick, 'The Happy Colony', 312–13.
87. Taylor, *Te Ika a Maui*, 459; Emigrant to the USA quoted in Erickson, *Invisible Immigrants*, 67.
88. Thomson, *Story of New Zealand*, ii, 169–70; Hursthouse, *New Zealand*, i, 239–41; Cholmondeley, *Ultima Thule*, 270.
89. Hursthouse, *New Zealand*, i, 191.
90. Akenson, *Half the World*, esp. chapter 3; R. P. Davis, *Irish Issues in New Zealand Politics 1868–1922*, 1974.
91. Anthony Trollope, *Australia and New Zealand*, Melbourne, 1873, 632.
92. Dalziel, *Vogel*, 91–92.
93. Hursthouse, *New Zealand*, ii, 613, and see 557.
94. Ibid., i, 271–72 n.
95. Thomson, *Story of New Zealand*, ii, 238, 280.
96. Cholmondeley, *Ultima Thule*, 224; J. Walton, *Twelve Months Residence in New Zealand*, London, 1839, 20.
97. *New Zealand Examiner*, 19 March 1861; *New Zealand Herald*, 18 December 1863.
98. Dalziel, *Vogel*, 180 (referring to Vogel's *Great Britain and Her Colonies*, London, 1865).
99. Michael Burgess, 'Imperial Federation: Continuity and Change in British Imperial Ideas 1869–91', *NZJH* 17 (1983), 60–80, 63.
100. Charles Dilke, *Greater Britain: A Record of Travel in English-Speaking Countries during 1866 and 1867*, London, 1868, 2 vols, i, 398.
101. E.g. New Zealand Company town planning, quoted in McCormick, 'The Happy Colony', 308.
102. Hursthouse, *New Zealand*, ii, 587; Dalziel, *Julius Vogel*, 80.
103. Hursthouse, *New Zealand*, i, 129, 199–200.
104. A. James Hammerton, *Emigrant Gentlewomen: Genteel Poverty and Female Emigration 1830–1914*, London, 1979, 28–29.
105. Quoted in John Miller, *Early Victorian New Zealand: A Study of Racial Tension and Social Attitudes 1839–1852*, 1958, 165.
106. 1875 *New Zealand Handbook*, quoted in *OYB*, 1990, 380.
107. Turnbull, *New Zealand Bubble*.
108. Hursthouse, *New Zealand*, ii, 359.
109. Dalziel, *Origins of New Zealand Diplomacy*, 53, 65.
110. Hursthouse, *New Zealand*, ii, 622.
111. Cited in Stevan Eldred-Grigg, *A Southern Gentry: New Zealanders Who Inherited the Earth*, 1980, 79.
112. Hammerton, *Emigrant Gentlewomen*; Patricia Clarke, *The Governesses: Letters from the Colonies 1862–1882*, Melbourne, 1985.
113. Hursthouse, *New Zealand*, ii, 657–58; S. Gillingham to Robert Gillingham, 1 October 1842, *Letters From New Plymouth*, 1843, 63.

114. Robinson, *Hatch and Brood*, 212.
115. Burns, *Fatal Success*, 191.
116. Thompson, *Rise of Respectable Society*, 82–83. Also see Gertrude Himmelfarb, *The Idea of Poverty: England in the Early Industrial Age*, New York, 1985.
117. Cholmondeley, *Ultima Thule*, 32–33. His italics.
118. Cited in *OYB*, 1990, 186.
119. Gillian Wagner, *Children of Empire*, London, 1982, 20–21.
120. *Southern Cross*, quoted in ibid.
121. Hill, *History of Policing*, i, 155; Thomson, *Story of New Zealand*, ii, 65, 172.
122. Ibid., ii, 315.
123. Ibid., ii, 313–14.
124. Arnold, *Farthest Promised Land*, 32 and passim; Joseph Arch, *From Plough to Parliament: An Autobiography*, London, 1986.
125. 'Hopeful', *Taken In: Being a Sketch of New Zealand Life*, London, 1974 (orig. 1887).
126. Cholmondeley, *Ultima Thule*, 59.
127. Hursthouse, *New Zealand*, ii, 595.
128. Quoted in Dalziel, *Vogel*, 166.
129. Hursthouse, *New Zealand*, ii, 609. Also see Turnbull, *New Zealand Bubble*.
130. Salmond, *Two Worlds*, 101; *Evening Post*, 22 February 1995; *Sunday Star*, 8 March 1992; *Evening Post*, 6 July 1992.
131. For some examples, see Shepard, *English Reaction*, esp. 18–22.
132. See Druett, *Exotic Intruders*.
133. Quoted in Paul Hamer, 'Nature and Natives: Transforming and Saving the Indigenous in New Zealand', VUW MA thesis, 1992, 39.
134. In Sarah Ell (ed.), *The Adventures of Pioneer Women in New Zealand*, 1992, 38.

Chapter 13: Getting In

1. Thomson, *Story of New Zealand*, ii, 150.
2. Marion Minson, 'Trends in German Immigration to New Zealand' in James N. Bade (ed.), *The German Connection: New Zealand and German-Speaking Europe in the Nineteenth Century*, 1993, 42. Also see Judith Williams, 'Puhoi, the Bohemian Settlement', in ibid.; R. P Hargreaves and T. J. Hearn, 'Special Settlements of the South Island, New Zealand', *New Zealand Geographer*, October, 1981, 67–72; G. L. Pearce, *The Scots of New Zealand*, 1976, chapter 5; Akenson, *Half the World*, chapter 5; Tremewan, *French Akaroa*.
3. See Akenson, *Half the World*, chapter 1, esp. 63, 59–61, 219–33. I have made supplementary calculations from *Historical Statistics*, but note that ethnicity statistics are very approximate.
4. Edwin T. Ashton, *The Welsh in New Zealand*, nd.
5. Christopher Harvie, 'Revolution and the Rule of Law', in Morgan (ed.), *Oxford History of Britain*, 477; Akenson, *Half the World*, 63; *Historical Statistics*, 79. Also see Pearce, *Scots of New Zealand*; Cage (ed.), *The Scots Abroad*; Malcolm D. Prentis, *The Scottish in Australia*, Melbourne, 1987.
6. Rosalind McLean, Review of Cage (ed.), *Scots Abroad*, *NZJH* 22 (1988), 79.
7. Brooking, 'Scots in New Zealand', in Cage (ed.), *Scots Abroad*, 162; *ENZ*, ii, 727.
8. Calculated from Pearce, *Scots of New Zealand*, 141–42, and *Historical Statistics*, 54.
9. Hugh Trevor-Roper, 'The Invention of Tradition: The Highland Tradition of Scotland', in Eric Hobsbawm and Terence Ranger (eds), *The Invention of Tradition*, Cambridge, 1983; Murray Pittock, *The Invention of Scotland: The Stuart Myth and Scottish Identity 1638 to the Present*, London, 1991.
10. Akenson, *Half the World*, 63.
11. Brooking, 'Scots in New Zealand', 161; Akenson, *Half the World*, 206.
12. K. A. Pickens, 'The Origins of the Population of Nineteenth-Century Canterbury', *New Zealand Geographer*, October 1977, 71; Macdonald, *Woman of Good Character*, 63.
13. Robinson, *Hatch and Brood of Time*.
14. John M. Gandar, 'New Zealand Migration in the Later Part of the Nineteenth Century', *AEHR* 19 (1979), 151–68.
15. Calculated from Akenson, *Half the World*, 18, and Borrie, 'The Peopling of Australasia', in Sinclair (ed.), *Trans-Tasman Relations*, 206.
16. Akenson, *Half the World*, 54.
17. Rollo Arnold, 'The Dynamics and Quality of Trans-Tasman Migration, 1885–1910', *AEHR* 26 (1986), 1–20, and 'The Australasian Peoples and their World 1888–1915', in Sinclair (ed.), *Tasman Relations*.
18. Macdonald, *Woman of Good Character*, 3.
19. See *Historical Statistics*, 80; Borrie, *Immigration*; Bade (ed.), *The German Connection*; G. C. Petersen, *D. G. Monrad: Scholar, Statesman, Priest, and New Zealand Pioneer*, 1965; 'Scandinavian Immigration'

and associated articles in *Hovding: The Magazine of the New Zealand-Norway Society* 13 (1983); M. Taker, 'The Asians', in K. W. Thomson and A. W. Trlin (eds), *Immigrants in New Zealand*, 1970; S. W. Greif, *The Overseas Chinese in New Zealand*, 1974; James Ng, *Windows on a Chinese Past*, 2 vols, 1993; Peter O'Connor, 'Keeping New Zealand White', *NZJH* 2 (1968), 41–65; Robert A. Huttenback, *Racism and Empire: White Settlers and Colored Immigrants in British Self-Governing Colonies 1830–1910*, Ithaca, 1976; David Pearson, *A Dream Deferred: The Origins of Ethnic Conflict in New Zealand*, 1990.

20. Calculated mainly from *Historical Statistics*, 79–80, and Akenson, *Half the World*, 63. Note that these percentages are not only very approximate but also beg questions about self-identification, mixed descent, varying rates of reproduction and the persistence of different lifeways. These issues are discussed further in the successor volume.
21. Akenson, *Half the World*, 12–13; Baines, *Migration*, 63–64.
22. Pickens, 'Population of Canterbury'; Baines, *Migration.*
23. Arnold, *Farthest Promised Land*; Macdonald, *Woman of Good Character.*
24. Calculated from Pickens, 'Population of Canterbury', 72.
25. See ibid., 71–72.
26. Arnold, *Farthest Promised Land*, 104–33.
27. Ibid., 128–29, 192–93.
28. Fell, *Voyage*, 8.
29. Ibid., 110.
30. Miller, *Early Victorian New Zealand*, 193.
31. Eldred-Grigg, *Southern Gentry*, chapter 6.
32. Burns, *Fatal Success*, 110, 144; John Mansfield Thomson, *The Oxford History of New Zealand Music*, 1990, 39; W. B. Sutch, *The Quest For Security in New Zealand 1840 to 1966*, 1966, 15, 23.
33. Diana Beaglehole, 'The Structure and Course of Politics in Nineteenth-Century Wellington', VUW MA thesis, 1987.
34. Harvie, 'Revolution and the Rule of Law', 501.
35. Quoted in Lee, *Hokianga*, 169.
36. Hursthouse, *New Zealand*, ii, 640.
37. The phrase was used by Governor Sir James Fergusson in the 1870s. Dalziel, *Vogel*, 160.
38. Quoted in Burns, *Fatal Success*, 247–48.
39. Henty, *Maori and Settler*, Glasgow, nd, 26–27. It was also present in New Zealand's first novel: Major B. Stoney, *Taranaki: A Tale of the Taranaki War*, 1861, 30.
40. Mary-Ann Martin to Mrs Owen, [8?] August 1862, Owen Correspondence, Sherbourne Autographs, British Museum, London; *DNZB*, ii (Emily Harris).
41. Burns, *Fatal Success*, 182.
42. Hursthouse, *New Zealand*, ii, 646–47.
43. Ibid., ii, 612–17.
44. Pickens, 'Population of Canterbury', esp. 71.
45. Eric Dunning and Kenneth Sheard, *Barbarians, Gentlemen and Players: A Sociological Study of the Development of Rugby Football*, Oxford, 1979.
46. Pickens, 'Population of Canterbury', 70; Beaglehole, 'Politics in Wellington', 140–41, 171.
47. Brooking, 'Scots in New Zealand', 173–75; R. D. Hill, 'Pastoralism in the Wairarapa 1844–1853', in Watters (ed.), *Land and Society*, 34–35.
48. Pickens, 'Population of Canterbury', 73.
49. Campbell, 'Runholding in Otago and Southland, 83.
50. Eldred-Grigg, *Southern Gentry*, 76; Erik Olssen, 'Lands of Sheep and Gold: The Australian Dimension to the New Zealand Past', in Sinclair (ed.), *Tasman Relations*, 39.
51. Richard Shannon, 'The Cult of the Prophet' (reviewing Stanley Weintraub's *Disraeli*), *Times Literary Supplement*, 26 November 1993. Also see Dilke, *Greater Britain*, i, 338–39.
52. Michael Belgrave, '"Medical Men" and "Lady Doctors": The Making of a New Zealand Profession, 1867–1941', VUW PhD thesis, 1985, 136, 140–41 and ff.
53. Quoted in Judith Bassett, *Sir Harry Atkinson*, 1975, 8.
54. Quoted in Graham, *Weld*, 32–33.
55. Hammerton, *Emigrant Gentlewomen.*
56. Ibid., chapter 3; *DNZB*, i.
57. Raewyn Dalziel, 'The Colonial Helpmeet: Women's Role and the Vote in Nineteenth-Century New Zealand', in Barbara Brookes et al., *Women in History: Essays on European Women in New Zealand*, 1986. Also see Jane Maria Richmond, quoted in Bassett, *Atkinson*, 6; Scholefield (ed.), *The Richmond-Atkinson Papers*; Frances Porter, *Born to New Zealand: A Biography of Jane Maria Atkinson*, 1989.
58. Letter back quoted in Arnold, *Farthest Promised Land*, 11. See Arnold, passim, for numerous other examples.
59. C. Durning, letter to editor, *Metro*, April 1993, 12.
60. E.g. Hursthouse, *New Zealand*, ii, 595.

61. Trollope, *Australia and New Zealand*, 561.
62. Cholmondeley, *Ultima Thule*. 77; *OYB*, 1990, 187–88; Roberta Nicholls, 'Elite Society', in Hamer and Nicholls (eds.), *Making of Wellington*, 218.
63. Stephen Constantine, 'Immigration and the Making of New Zealand 1918–1939', in Constantine (ed.), *Emigrants and Empire: British Settlement in the Dominions between the Wars*, Manchester, 1990.
64. Patrick O'Farrell, *Vanished Kingdoms: The Irish in Australia and New Zealand*, Sydney, 1990, chapters 1, 8 and passim.
65. Archibald Michie, quoted in John Hirst, 'Egalitarianism', *Australian Cultural History* 5 (1986), 14.
66. Akenson, *Half the World*, 43.
67. Rollo Arnold, 'The Village and the Globe: Aspects of the Social Origins of Schooling in Victorian New Zealand', *Australia and New Zealand History of Education Society Journal* 5 (1976), 1–12, 2. Also see Arnold, *Farthest Promised Land*.
68. Baines, *Migration*, 78.
69. Akenson, *Half the World*, 48, 50.
70. Ibid., 206.
71. *Historical Statistics*, 29.
72. Macdonald, *Woman of Good Character*, 47.
73. Akenson, *Half the World*, 222; Macdonald, *Woman of Good Character*, 41–44.
74. *Historical Statistics*, 94.
75. Hursthouse, *New Zealand*, ii, 621.
76. Macdonald, *Woman of Good Character*, 67.
77. Sutton-Smith, *History of Children's Play*, 129.
78. S. J. Goldsbury, 'Behind the Picket Fence: The Lives of Missionary Wives in Pre-Colonial New Zealand', Auckland MA thesis, 1986.
79. Sarah Courage, *Lights and Shadows of Colonial Life*, 1976 (orig. 1896), 115.
80. Adela Stewart, *My Simple Life in New Zealand*, London, 1906, e.g. 76.
81. Gorst, *New Zealand Revisited*, 16.
82. Macdonald, *Woman of Good Character*, 65.
83. Quoted in Miller, *Early Victorian New Zealand*, 34.
84. Baines, *Emigration from Europe*, chapter 5.
85. O'Farrell, *Vanished Kingdoms*, 27, 30.

Chapter 14: Taken In?

1. Quoted in Miller, *Early Victorian New Zealand*, 42, 115–16; *DNZB*, i (Isaac Featherston).
2. Raewyn Dalziel, 'Popular Protest in Early New Plymouth: Why Did It Occur?', *NZJH* 20 (1986), 3–26.
3. Allan, *Nelson*, 186–87. Also see Miller, *Early Victorian New Zealand*, chapter 9.
4. Quoted in Dalziel, 'Popular Protest', 23.
5. Turnbull, New Zeal*and Bubble*.
6. W. Tyrone Power, *Sketches in New Zealand In Pen and Pencil*, London, 1849, 4; Constantine Dillon in C. A. Sharp (ed.), *The Letters of the Hon. Constantine Dillon 1842–53*, 1954, 69.
7. Tom Brooking, *And Captain of Their Souls: An Interpretative Essay on the Life and Times of Captain William Cargill*, 1984, 75, 91–92.
8. Quoted in Stevan Eldred-Grigg, *A New History of Canterbury*, 1982, 20–21.
9. Belich, *Titokowaru's War*, 23–25.
10. *Taken In*, ix.
11. *The Land of the Lost: A Tale of the New Zealand Gum Country*, 1908, 18.
12. Quoted in Peter Stuart, *Edward Gibbon Wakefield in New Zealand*, 1971,16.
13. *DNZB*, i.
14. *The London Journal of E. J. Wakefield 1845–46*, ed. Joan Stevens, 1972.
15. Wakefield to Grey, 23 December 1878, Grey Autograph Letters, Auckland Public Library.
16. Domett to Grey, 5 July 1878, ibid.
17. Miller, *Early Victorian New Zealand*, 169.
18. Calculated from Lloyd Prichard, *Economic History*, 36, 44–47. A better and more recent economic history, Hawke, *Making of New Zealand*, is an important background source for the rest of this chapter.
19. Forster, *Journals*, ii, 233, 235, and iii, 418; Cook, *Journals*, ii, 167.
20. C. Anne Wilson, *A History of Food and Drink in Britain*, Chicago, 1991 edn, 63, 70.
21. Ralph A. Griffiths, 'The Later Middle Ages', in Morgan (ed.), *Oxford History of Britain*, 208, 217.
22. Fernand Braudel, *The Mediterranean and the Mediterranean World in the Age of Philip II*, 2 vols, London (French orig. 1949), 1975, i, 93.
23. Guthrie-Smith, *Tutira*, 225, 383 n.
24. Blainey, *A Land Half Won*, 49–52.
25. Lloyd Prichard, *Economic History*, 400; *Historical Statistics*, 186–87.
26. Britain had 24 million sheep in 1935 (*Whitakers Almanac*, London, 1939, 1095) New Zealand permanently exceeded this figure in 1927 (*Historical Statistics*, 181).
27. *Historical Statistics*, 275–86.
28. Campbell, 'Runholding in Otago and Southland', 266–67.
29. Ibid., 263.

30. Geoffrey G. Thornton, *New Zealand's Industrial Heritage*, 1982, 41.
31. Lady Barker, *Station Life in New Zealand*, 1973 (orig. 1883), 194–99.
32. Graham, *Weld*, 6, 19.
33. *Historical Statistics*, 181.
34. Cited in Olssen, *History of Otago*, 51.
35. Eldred-Grigg, *Southern Gentry*, 46–47.
36. Cited in Miller, *Early Victorian New Zealand*, 143.
37. Barker, *Station Life*, 173.
38. Martin, *Forgotten Worker*, 58; *Historical Statistics*, 284.
39. *DNZB*, i.
40. Cited in Guthrie-Smith, *Tutira*, 145.
41. Ibid., 163–64, 167 n. On early runholding, also see L. G. Acland, *Early Canterbury Runs*, 1975 edn; R. Pinney, *Early South Canterbury Runs*, 1971.
42. Goldfield statistics are mainly from *Historical Statistics*, 197–99, and Hawke, *Making of New Zealand*, 39–40. The main works on the gold rushes are still J. H. M. Salmon, *A History of Goldmining in New Zealand*, 1963, and May, *West Coast Gold Rushes*. Also see Mike Johnston, *Gold in a Tin Dish: The History of the Wakamarina Goldfield, Nelson*, 1992.
43. Salmon, *History of Goldmining*, 34–35.
44. *DNZB*, i (Thomas McDonnell).
45. Hill, *History of Policing*, i, 584.
46. Sinclair and Mandle, *Open Account*, 18.
47. Salmon, *History of Goldmining*, 65, 57, 83.
48. May, *West Coast Gold Rushes*, 156.
49. Gillespie-Needham, 'The Colonial and His Books', 116–17.
50. Reuben Waite, cited in Salmond, *History of Goldmining*, 143.
51. Hill, *History of Policing*, i, 699–703.
52. Ibid., i, 630–31; Salmond, *History of Goldmining*, 105–7.
53. May, *West Coast Gold Rushes*, 270.
54. Ibid., 480.
55. Cited in ibid., 90.
56. Stone, *The Father and His Gift*, 92.
57. T. J. Hearn, 'Structural Change in the Otago Gold Mining Industry 1861–1923: The Matakanui Example', *New Zealand Geographer* 46 (1990), 86–91.
58. Thornton, *Industrial Heritage*, 14.
59. Ibid.; Salmon, *History of Goldmining*.
60. *ENZ*, iii, 415.
61. Hursthouse, *New Zealand*, i, 314.
62. Fox, quoted in W. David McIntyre and W. J. Gardner (eds), *Speeches and Documents on New Zealand History*, 1971, 42; Stafford, quoted in Dalziel, *Vogel*, 107.
63. *Historical Statistics*, 329, 340. See ibid., 330, for imperial military and naval expenditure (£1,001,000 between 1840 and 1850). The figure for the companies is a guess, but see Burns, *Fatal Success*, and take into account the spending of the Otago and Canterbury Associations, and the Nanto-Bordelaise Company.
64. *ENZ*, iii, 32–35; *Historical Statistics*, 227.
65. Hawke, *Making of New Zealand*, 69.
66. *Historical Statistics*, 343.
67. Thornton, *Industrial Heritage*, 87–88.
68. Calculated roughly from War Office Inwards Correspondence, 33/16, 1862, Public Record Office, London.
69. *ENZ*, iii, 460.
70. Ibid., i, 'Bridges'.
71. *Historical Statistics*, 343; *OYB*, 1990, 645.
72. *Historical Statistics*, 231.
73. Simon Ville, 'The Coastal Trade of New Zealand Prior to World War One', *NZJH* 27 (1993), 75–89.
74. *Historical Statistics*, 231.
75. Ville, 'Coastal Trade', 76.
76. *OYB*, 1990, 528.
77. Thornton, *Industrial Heritage*, 99.
78. *Historical Statistics*, 130; Thornton, *Industrial Heritage*, 6–11. Ville, 'Coastal trade', 82, emphasises the British-built component, especially of steamships, noting that 'only' 34 steamers were built in New Zealand by 1869. But this was over half the total steamer fleet of 1870. In terms of tonnage, dominance of British-built ships increased greatly from the 1880s.
79. Ville, 'Coastal Trade', 85.
80. *Historical Statistics*, 181–82. Also see Malcolm M. Kennedy, *Hauling the Loads: A History of Australia's Working Horses and Bullocks*, Melbourne, 1992.
81. *Historical Statistics*, 174.
82. Stone, *Makers of Fortune*, chapter 6.
83. Rollo Arnold, *New Zealand's Burning: The Settlers' World in the Mid-1880s*, 1992, 154.
84. Duncan Mackay, *Working the Kauri: A Social and Photographic History of New Zealand's Pioneer Kauri Bushmen*, 1991, 27, 24; Thornton, *Industrial Heritage*, 23.
85. *Historical Statistics*, 105.
86. Stone, *Makers of Fortune*, 28.
87. Ville, 'Coastal Trade'; Thornton, *Industrial Heritage*, 18–25.
88. Forrest Capie and K. A. Tucker, 'British and New Zealand Trading Relationships 1841–53', *Economic History Review*, 2nd series, 25 (1972), 293–302.

89. W. Rosenberg, 'Capital Imports and Growth: The Case of New Zealand-Foreign Investment in New Zealand, 1840–1958', *Economic Journal* 71 (1961), 93–113.
90. B. R. Patterson, 'Whatever Happened to Poor Waring Taylor? Insights from the Business Manuscripts', *Turnbull Library Record* 24 (1991), 113–131, (quote 125); Stone, *Makers of Fortune*, 44; Eldred-Grigg, *Southern Gentry*, 77.
91. Margaret Galt, 'Doing Well for Bella: Foreign Mortgages in the New Zealand Financial System 1885–1901', *NZJH* 18 (1984), 50–65; Stone, *Makers of Fortune*, 23.
92. Stone, *The Making of Russell McVeagh*, *Makers of Fortune* and *The Father and his Gift*; *DNZB* i; H. J. Hanham, 'New Zealand Promoters and British Investors 1860–1895', in Chapman and Sinclair (eds), *Studies of a Small Democracy*.
93. Rosenberg, 'Capital Imports and Growth', 71.
94. Sinclair and Mandle, *Open Account*, 64.
95. Dilke, *Greater Britain*, i, 331–32.
96. Sinclair and Mandle, *Open Account*, 31 and passim.
97. Cited in Davis and Huttenback, *Mammon and the Pursuit of Empire*, 43.
98. Dalziel, *Origins of New Zealand Diplomacy*, 53–71.
99. Stone, *Makers of Fortune*, 24.
100. Hanham, 'Promoters and Investors', 58–59.
101. Quoted in Stone, *The Father and his Gift*, 113.
102. Quoted in Sinclair and Mandle, *Open Account*, 40.
103. Quoted in Dalziel, *Vogel*, 169.
104. Hanham, 'Promoters and Investors', 76.
105. Quoted in Stone, *The Father and his Gift*, 112.
106. Thornton, *Industrial Heritage*, 14–15; Stone, *Makers of Fortune*, 82–83; *OYB*, 1990, 493.
107. G. J. R. Linge, 'Manfacturing in New Zealand: Four Years in a Century of Growth', in Watters (ed.), *Land and Society*, 140–41.
108. *DNZB*, ii.
109. *Historical Statistics*, 210.
110. Thornton, *Industrial Heritage*, 26–28.
111. *Historical Statistics*, 168; J. D. Gould, 'The Occupation of Farmland in New Zealand 1874–1911: A Preliminary Survey', *Business Archives and History* 5 (1965), 139.
112. Thornton, *Industrial Heritage*, 46–48.
113. P. G. Stevens, *John Grigg of Longbeach*, 1952.
114. J. D. Gould, *The Grass Roots of New Zealand History*, 1974, 13.
115. Martin, *Forgotten Worker*, 121–22; Belich, *Titokowaru's War*, 283.
116. Stone, *Makers of Fortune*, 8–9; Simon P. Ville, 'The Growth of Foreign Trade and Shipping at New Zealand's Major Seaports During the Nineteenth Century', *AEHR*, 32 (1992), 60–89.
117. Stone, *Makers of Fortune*, 15; *Historical Statistics*, 186–87.
118. ibid., 183–84.
119. Ville, 'Coastal Trade', 81–82.
120. David Hamer, 'Wellington on the Urban Frontier', in Hamer and Nicholls (eds), *Making of Wellington*, 249–54.
121. *OYB*, 1990, 542.
122. Olssen, *History of Otago*, 82, citing an estimate by Dr James Hector.
123. Quoted in Eldred-Grigg, *Southern Gentry*, 97.
124. Lois Voller, *Rails to Nowhere: The History of the Nelson Railway*, 1991.
125. Anthony Lynch, 'The Garden of Otago: A History of Small-Scale Farming in the Clutha Area 1848–70', Otago MA thesis, 1989.
126. J. O'C. Ross, *Pride in Their Ports: The Story of the Minor Ports*, 1977, 89.
127. May, *West Coast Gold Rushes*, 340–51.
128. Dilke, *Greater Britain*, i, 334.
129. For a description of this process, albeit from a slightly later period, see P. J. Gibbons, 'Some New Zealand Navvies: Co-operative Workers 1891–1912', *NZJH* 11 (1977), 54–75.
130. Boyd, *Hastings*, 17.
131. Somerset, *Littledene: A New Zealand Rural Community*, 1938, 2.
132. This is the number listed by Ross, *Pride in Their Ports*, 209–10. Other sources give a total of 112 ports, 59 of them 'well established'. Ville, 'Coastal Trade', 81.
133. Ross, *Pride in Their Ports*, chapter 9.
134. Hamer, *New Towns in the New World*, 147.
135. Ross, *Pride in Their Ports*, chapter 6; Davis and Huttenback, *Mammon and the Pursuit of Empire*, 143.
136. May, *West Coast Gold Rushes*, 219–29.
137. *OYB*, 1990, 413, 342. Also see Patrick Day, *The Making of the New Zealand Press 1840–1880*, 1990.
138. David McGill, *Ghost Towns of New Zealand*, 1980; *OYB*, 1990, 566, 85.
139. N. G. Butlin, 'Contours of the Australian Economy 1788–1860', *AEHR* 26 (1986), 101, 107.
140. Davis and Huttenback, *Mammon and the Pursuit of Empire*, chapter 4 and passim.

141. Thomson, *Story of New Zealand*, ii, 188.

Chapter 15: Getting On

1. Galt, 'Doing Well for Bella'.
2. Lloyd Prichard, *Economic History*, 62–63.
3. Median male wage rates in Britain 1861–1900 were around 12 to 17 shillings a week (Baines, *Migration*, 332–33) – about half the New Zealand norm.
4. J. A. Dowie, 'A Century-Old Estimate of the National Income of New Zealand', *Business and Archives History* 21 (1966), 117–31.
5. *Historical Statistics*, 107–8; Arnold, *Farthest Promised Land*, 246–47.
6. Letters back quoted in Arnold, *Farthest Promised Land*, 118, 246–47.
7. Herbert Roth, *Trade Unions in New Zealand*, 1973, chapter 1.
8. See Roderick Phillips, *Divorce in New Zealand: A Social History*, 1981.
9. Sutch, *Quest for Security*, 50; Olssen, *History of Otago*, 88. Also see R. J. Campbell, '"The Black Eighties": Unemployment in New Zealand in the 1880s', *AEHR* 16 (1976), 67–82.
10. Margaret Tennant, *Paupers and Providers: Charitable Aid in New Zealand*, 1989, 17 and passim.
11. Derek A. Dow, 'Springs of Charity?: The Development of the New Zealand Hospital System 1876–1910', in Linda Bryder (ed.), *A Healthy Country: Essays on the Social History of Medicine in New Zealand*, 1991.
12. *Historicial Statistics*, 97, 333.
13. *OYB*, 1990, 217; Ann Else, *A Question of Adoption: Closed Stranger Adoption in New Zealand 1944–1974*, 1991, 71–72.
14. Olssen, *History of Otago*, 87.
15. Thomson, *Rise of Respectable Society*, 137.
16. *New Zealand Handbook*, 1875, quoted in *OYB*, 1990, 269.
17. Quoted in Sarah Ell (ed.), *The Lives of Pioneer Women in New Zealand*, 1993, 44.
18. R. S. Schofield, 'Dimensions of Illiteracy in England 1750–1850', in Graff (ed.), *Literacy and Social Development*, 201. Also see *New Zealand Handbook*, 1875, quoted in *OYB*, 1990, 269; Gillespie-Needham, 'The Colonial and His Books', 76; A. G. Butchers, *Education in New Zealand*, 1930; Ian Cumming, *History of State Education in New Zealand*, 1978; *Historical Statistics*, 111.
19. Thompson, *Rise of Respectable Society*, 138–39.
20. Stone, *Makers of Fortune*, esp. 27; Lynch, 'The Garden of Otago', 70, also see 164–65.
21. Dalziel, *Origins of Diplomacy*, 42.
22. Calculated from *Historicial Statistics*, 167–68.
23. Claire Toynbee, 'Class and Social Structure in Nineteenth-Century New Zealand', *NZJH* 13 (1979), 75; Fairburn, *Ideal Society*, 96.
24. *AJHR*, 1882, C–1, 9. Also see Gould, 'The Occupation of Farmland in New Zealand', 123–41.
25. P. J. Spyve, 'The First Waikato Regiment and the Settlement Process of the Bay of Plenty 1864–74', Waikato MA thesis, 1981. Also see Ross Hamilton, 'Military Vision and Economic Reality: The Failure of the Military Settlements Scheme in the Waikato 1863–80', Auckland MA thesis, 1968; I. M Bremer, 'The Early Development of the Patea-Waverley District: A Study of the Problems of Settling Confiscated Land', VUW MA thesis, 1962; H. C. M. Norris, *Armed Settlers: The Story of the Founding of Hamilton, New Zealand, 1864–1874*, 1963.
26. Shelley Griffiths, 'Feminism and the Ideology of Motherhood in New Zealand 1896–1930', Otago MA thesis, 1984, 311.
27. *Historical Statistics*, 131–12. These figures include females working in restaurants and hotels.
28. Macdonald, *Woman of Good Character*, 119 and passim. For a rare account of servant life from a servant rather than an employer, see Charlotte Macdonald, 'Maggie Fraser: A Servant in the 1890s', *Women's Studies Association Conference Papers*, 1988, 126–30. Also see Judith Elphick, 'What's Wrong With Emma? The Feminist Debate in Colonial Auckland', in Barbara Brookes et al. (eds), *Women in History: Essays on European Women in New Zealand*, 1986.
29. Macdonald, *Woman of Good Character*, 117.
30. L. C. Duncan, '"A New Song of the Shirt"? A History of Women in the Clothing Industry in Auckland 1890–1939', Auckland MA thesis, 1989; Jane Malthus, 'Dressmakers in Nineteenth-Century New Zealand', in Brookes et al. (eds), *Women in History*, 2, 1992.
31. *New Zealand Handbook*, 1883–84, cited in *OYB*, 1990, 276.
32. See *DNZB*, ii.
33. In Patricia Clarke, *The Governesses: Letters from the Colonies 1862–1882*, Melbourne, 1985, 172.
34. Eldred-Grigg, *Southern Gentry*, 89–92.
35. Barker, *Station Life*, 194. Also see ibid., passim, *DNZB*, i, and *Station Amusements in New Zealand*, London, 1873.
36. Quoted in Bassett, *Atkinson*, 6, and *DNZB*, i.

37. Ell (ed.), *Lives of Pioneer Women*, 174.
38. Ell (ed.), *Adventures of Pioneer Women*, 51–52.
39. R. C. J. Stone, *The Young Logan Campbell*, 1982; *The Father and His Gift*.
40. Edmund Bohan, *Edward Stafford: New Zealand's First Statesman*, 1994, 104.
41. Ell (ed.), *Lives of Pioneer Women*, 21.
42. Ibid., 88.
43. Stewart, *My Simple Life*, 152.
44. Ell (ed.), *Lives of Pioneer Women*, 141; Macdonald, *Woman of Good Character*, 143; Phillips, *Divorce*, chapter 3; Dalziel, 'Colonial Helpmeet', 59.
45. Quoted in Margaret J. Stuart, 'A Space of One's Own: Roles and Images of Women in Historical Society Serial Publications', Waikato MA thesis, 1986, 29.
46. Dalziel, 'Colonial Helpmeet', 59.
47. Macdonald, *Woman of Good Character*, chapters 5–6.
48. *New Zealand Handbook*, 1875, quoted in *OYB*, 1990, 269; Baines, *Migration*, 328–31; Gillespie-Needham, 'The Colonial and his Books', 76; *Historical Statistics*, 94, 111.
49. Thompson, *Rise of Respectable Society*, 52.
50. Macdonald, *Woman of Good Character*, 138.
51. David Pearson, *Johnsonville: Continuity and Change in a New Zealand Township*, Sydney, 1980, 'Marriage and Mobility in Wellington 1881–1980', *NZJH* 22 (1988), 135–51, and 'Mobility and Change in Wellington 1881–1980', *New Zealand Sociology* 7 (1992), 167–87.
52. Quoted in Society for Research on Women, *In Those Days: A Study of Older Women in Wellington*, 1982, chapter 1.
53. Stewart, *My Simple Life*.
54. Quoted in Stuart, 'A Space of One's Own', 82–83; *DNZB*, ii (Halcombe and Button).
55. Quoted in Claire Toynbee, *Family, Kin and Community in New Zealand 1900–1930*, 1995, 48.
56. Macdonald, *Woman of Good Character*, 159; Ian Pool and Fred Tiong, 'Sub-National Differentials in the Pakeha Fertility Decline, 1876–1901', *New Zealand Population Review* 17 (1991), 46–64.
57. Ell (ed.), *Lives of Pioneer Women*, 43.
58. Barker, *Station Life*, 56–58.
59. E. Yvonne Spiers, 'Preston Runholding in the Maniatoto and the Mackenzie 1858–1917', Otago MA thesis, 1987, esp. 15, 176–78.
60. *DNZB*, ii; *ENZ*.
61. Gavin McLean, *The Southern Octopus: The Rise of a Shipping Empire*, 1990.
62. Thornton, *Industrial Heritage*, 28. Also see *DNZB*, i; Stone, *Makers of Fortune*, 139–51; J. C. Firth, *Nation Making: A Story of New Zealand Savagism v. Civilization*, 1890.
63. *DNZB*, i, ii; Thornton, *Industrial Heritage*, 141–42; Nicholls, 'Elite Society', 197.
64. Keith Sinclair (ed.), *A Soldier's View of Empire: The Reminiscences of James Bodell*, London, 1982.
65. *Cyclopedia of New Zealand*, 6 vols, 1897–1908.
66. *DNZB*, ii.
67. Boyd, *Hastings*, 71.
68. R. D. Hill, 'Pastoralism in the Wairarapa, 1844–1853', in Watters (ed.), *Land and Society*, 34–35.
69. *DNZB*, i.
70. Campbell, 'Runholding in Otago and Southland', 40, 83; Eldred-Grigg, *Southern Gentry*, 76.
71. Stone, *The Father and His Gift*.
72. Patterson, 'Whatever Happened to Poor Waring Taylor?', 120.
73. Eldred-Grigg, *New History of Canterbury*, 52–53, and *Southern Gentry*, 55.
74. Olssen, *History of Otago*, 127–28.
75. Murrihy, 'New Zealand National Character'.
76. Stewart, *My Simple Life*, 14. Also see Thomson, *Oxford History of New Zealand Music*.
77. *ENZ*, i, 500; Bohan, in *DNZB*, ii, and *Stafford*, 143.
78. Nicholls, 'Elite Society', 213, 218.
79. Fairburn, *Ideal Society*, 86–87.
80. Stewart, *My Simple Life*, 116, 56 and passim.
81. Sutton-Smith, *History of Children's Play*, 143–45.
82. Eldred-Grigg, *Southern Gentry*, 90; Nicholls, 'Elite Society', 210–11.
83. Eldred-Grigg, *Southern Gentry*, 83–84; Cumming, *History of State Education*, 28–37; Gardner, *Colonial Cap and Gown*.
84. Calculated roughly from *Historical Statistics*, 112–13, 49.
85. Raewyn Dalziel, 'The "Continuous Ministry" Revisited', *NZJH* 21 (1987), 53.
86. Beaglehole, 'Politics in Wellington'.
87. Boyd, *Hastings*, 5–71.
88. Fairburn, *Ideal Society*, 86–87.
89. Dalziel, 'Continuous Ministry', 46–61.
90. Bohan, *Stafford*, 214; Whitmore to Mantell, 17 April 1866, W. B. D. Mantell Papers, Alexander Turnbull Library, Wellington.
91. Calculated from *OYB*, 1990, 67.
92. Robert Pinney, *Early North Otago Runs*, 1981, 159.
93. Belich, *Titokowaru's War*, 143, 146, 155, and note the role of James Livingston in the retreat from Te Ngutu o te Manu, chapter 7.

94. Day, *Making of the New Zealand Press*, 62–67.

Chapter 16: Lumped, Split and Bound

1. Fairburn, *Ideal Society*, 'Local Community or Atomised Society?' *NZJH* 16 (1982), and 'Vagrants, "Folk Devils", and Nineteenth-Century New Zealand as a Bondless Society', *Historical Studies* 21 (1985).
2. Cholmondeley, *Ultima Thule*, 43.
3. Paul Husbands, 'The People of Freemans Bay 1880–1914', Auckland MA thesis, 1992, chapter 5; Caroline Daley, 'Taradale Meets the Ideal Society and Its Enemies', *NZJH* 25 (1991), 136, 142.
4. Quoted in Goldsbury, 'Behind the Picket Fence', 93–94.
5. See Thomson and Trlin (eds), *Immigrants in New Zealand*; Andrew D. Trlin, *Now Respected, Once Despised: Yugoslavs in New Zealand*, 1979; Leckie, 'They Sleep Standing Up'.
6. O'Farrell, *Vanished Kingdoms*, 31.
7. Fairburn, *Ideal Society*, 167.
8. Ell (ed.), *Lives of Pioneer Women*, 21.
9. A. G. Nightingale, 'Waiuta: A History of a Quartz Goldmining Community on the West Coast', Canterbury MA thesis, 1985, 119. Also see Philip Payton, *The Making of Modern Cornwall: Historical Experience and the Persistence of 'Difference'*, Redruth, 1992.
10. Fairburn, *Ideal Society*, chapter 6.
11. Hugh Jackson, 'Churchgoing in Nineteenth-Century New Zealand', *NZJH* 17 (1983), 51.
12. Fairburn, *Ideal Society*, 177–78; Daley, 'Taradale', 143.
13. Jackson, 'Churchgoing', 50; Davidson and Lineham, *Transplanted Christianity*, 183.
14. Calculated from *Historical Statistics*, 49, 72.
15. *Historical Statistics*, 56–60.
16. *OYB*, 1990, 133; Fairburn, *Ideal Society*, 172–75.
17. *Historical Statistics*, 54–57. Also see Hamer, *New Towns in the New World*, 39.
18. Stone, *Makers of Fortune*, 31.
19. See entries on provincial regions in *ENZ*.
20. Quoted in Arnold, *New Zealand's Burning*, 278.
21. See ibid., 244; *Historical Statistics*, 181–82.
22. Kennedy, *Hauling the Loads*, 41.
23. Colin Mathew, 'The Liberal Age', in Morgan (ed.), *Oxford History of Britain*, 549–50.
24. Fairburn, *Ideal Society*, 245–50. Also see Fairburn, 'Vagrants'.
25. Fairburn, *Ideal Society*, 224–25.
26. Ibid., 248.
27. Stewart, *My Simple Life*, 132.
28. Fairburn, 'A Discourse on the Critical Method', *NZJH* 25 (1991), 171.
29. Fairburn, *Ideal Society*, chapter 7; Miles Fairburn and Stephen Haslett, 'Violent Crime in Old and New Societies: A Case Study based on New Zealand 1853–1940', *Journal of Social History*, Fall 1987, 89–126.
30. Peter Luke, 'Suicide in Auckland 1848–1939', Auckland MA thesis, 1982, 19, 47.
31. *OYB*, 1894, cited in *OYB*, 1990, 247.
32. Peter J. Coleman, 'Imprisonment of Debt in New Zealand 1840–1908', unpublished paper, copy kindly provided by the author.
33. Hill, *History of Policing*, iii, chapter 5, and personal communication.
34. Sutton-Smith, *History of Children's Play*, 108; Hill, *History of Policing*, ii, 544, 618; Luke, 'Suicide in Auckland', 190–91.
35. Fairburn, 'Discourse', 171–76.
36. Ibid., 171. The women's rate was 'three times greater', and the men's 'almost three times greater'.
37. Calculated from tables in Robyn Anderson, '"The Hardened Frail Ones": Women and Crime in Auckland 1845–70', Auckland MA thesis, 1981, 41, 43.
38. Eldred-Grigg, *Pleasures of the Flesh*, 37.
39. Hill, *History of Policing*, ii, 714.
40. Eldred-Grigg, *Pleasures of the Flesh*, 38.
41. Anderson, 'Hardened Frail Ones', 61, 110, 114.
42. Ibid., 41, 53, 61, 77–79, 104, 115.
43. Ibid., esp 108, 112.
44. *Historical Statistics*, 130.
45. Calculated from ibid., 234–35.
46. Mackay, *Working the Kauri*.
47. A. H. Reed, *The Gumdiggers*, 1972, 124–25.
48. May, *West Coast Gold Rushes*, 535.
49. Martin, *Forgotten Worker*, 59 and passim.
50. Campbell, 'Runholding in Otago and Southland', 186; Martin, *Forgotten Worker*, 59.
51. Ibid., 6, 14, 122–34.
52. Gould, *Grass Roots of New Zealand History*.
53. Fairburn, *Ideal Society*, 136. Also see Martin, *Forgotten Worker*, 14.
54. *OYB*, 1990, 250.
55. Gibbons, 'New Zealand Navvies', 54–75.
56. Forster, Journals, ii, 270–71.
57. Boultbee, *Journal*, 52.
58. Morton, *Whale's Wake*, 241; Filde's Collection, 631, VUW.
59. Wakefield, *New Zealand After Fifty Years*, London, 1889, 153–54.
60. Neil Atkinson, 'Auckland Seamen and their Union 1880–1922', Auckland MA thesis, 1990, 37.

61. John H. Angus, *Aspiring Settlers: European Settlement in the Hawea and Wanaka Region to 1914*, 1981, 40–41.
62. Reminiscences of early Wellington, quoted in Sutton-Smith, *History of Children's Play*, 7.
63. Hill, *History of Policing*, i, 443, 456.
64. Deputy Quartermaster-General, Original Journals, 'Strength and Distribution of the Forces – New Zealand', War Office Inwards Correspondence 107/7, Public Record Office, London.
65. *Historical Statistics*, 364.
66. Cited in Anderson, 'Hardened Frail Ones', 94.
67. Hill, *History of Policing*, ii, 251, 216.
68. Ibid., i, 492.
69. Sutch, *Quest for Security*, 28.
70. John Pratt, *Punishment in a Perfect Society: The New Zealand Penal System 1840–1939*, 1992, 83.
71. Anderson, 'Hardened Frail Ones', 106.
72. Sutton-Smith, *History of Children's Play*, 7.
73. Hill, *History of Policing*, i, part 2, 442.
74. *DNZB*, i.
75. Martin, *Forgotten Worker*, 17.
76. Hill, *History of Policing*, ii, 262.
77. Ibid., ii, 260, 175.
78. Martin, *Forgotten Worker*, 23, 36.
79. Gibbons, 'New Zealand Navvies', 68.
80. May, *West Coast Gold Rushes*, 109, 285.
81. Boultbee, *Journal*, 16, 50; Robinson, *Hatch and Brood*, 110.
82. Gibbons, 'New Zealand Navvies', 69.
83. See Martin, *Forgotten Worker*; Jock Phillips, *A Man's Country? The Image of the Pakeha Male: A History*, 1987.
84. Hill, *History of Policing*, i, 508–10, 594.
85. Gibbons, 'New Zealand Navvies', 65.
86. Hill, *History of Policing*, i, 571, 603.
87. May, *West Coast Gold Rushes*, 154.
88. Ibid., 253.
89. Gibbons, 'New Zealand Navvies', 65.
90. Fairburn, *Ideal Society*, 229.
91. Fairburn, 'Was there a Distinctive Social Pattern?', in Hamer and Nicholls (eds), *Making of Wellington*, 273–76.
92. Lydia Wevers, 'The Short Story', and Terry Sturm, 'Popular Fiction', in Sturm (ed.) *The Oxford History of New Zealand Literature*, 1991, 211–13 and 501–4. Also see G. B. Lancaster, *Sons o' Men*, London, 1904.
93. 'Folk Songs', in G. B. Davey and Graham Seal (eds), *The Oxford Companion to Australian Folklore*, Melbourne, 1993.
94. Ella Johansson, 'Free Sons of the Forest: Storytelling and the Construction of Identity Among Swedish Lumberjacks', in Raphael Samuel and Paul Thompson (eds), *The Myths We Live By*, London and New York, 1990.
95. W. P. Morrell, *The Provincial System in New Zealand*, 1964 edn, quotes [7], 270–71.
96. Miller, *Early Victorian New Zealand*, 186; *DNZB*, i; H. W. Tucker, *Memoir of the Life and Episcopate of George Augustus Selwyn*, 2 vols, London, 1879; Warren E. Limbrick (ed.), *Bishop Selwyn in New Zealand 1841–68*, 1983.
97. Jackson, 'Churchgoing', 50–57.
98. H. R. Jackson, *Churches and People in Australia and New Zealand 1860–1930*, 1987, 14–15, 39–40, 25, 36.
99. Cholmondeley, *Ultima Thule*, 271–72.
100. Jackson, 'Churchgoing', 47, 55, and *Churches and People*, 6.
101. Brian Gilling, 'Retelling the Old, Old, Story: A Study of Six Mass Evangelistic Missions in Twentieth-Century New Zealand', Waikato PhD thesis, 1990, 65–74.
102. James E. Worsfold, *A History of the Charismatic Movements in New Zealand*, Bradford, 1974, 64.
103. Vicesimus Lush, cited in Davidson and Lineham (eds), *Transplanted Christianity*, 200.
104. Gilling, 'Old, Old, Story', 83–87; Jackson, 'Churchgoing', 51.
105. Ibid., 50.
106. Hans Mol, 'Religion and Churches', in Sinclair (ed.), *Tasman Relations*, 269.
107. *ENZ*, iii, 634; J. C. Crawford, *Recollections of Travel in Australia and New Zealand*, London, 1880, 211–13; Jackson, *Churches and People*, 17–18, 34; Akenson, *Half the World*.
108. Morrell, *Provincial System*, 127–28, 154, 231–2; Eldred-Grigg, *Southern Gentry*.
109. Ibid., 69–74.
110. Beaglehole, 'Politics in Wellington', 105.
111. Morrell, *Provincial System*, 247.
112. Ibid., 161.
113. Eric Pawson and Neil C. Quigley, 'The Circulation of Information and Frontier Development: Canterbury 1850–1890', *New Zealand Geographer*, October 1982, 65–76, 74.
114. 'Coaches', *ENZ*; M. J. G. Smart and A. P. Bates, *The Wanganui Story*, 1972, 133.
115. Calculated from *Historical Statistics*, 259, using the estimated population at the end of 1874. Independent figures for Canterbury are compatible. See Pawson and Quigley, 'Circulation of Information', 68. Also see 'Post Offices', *ENZ*, and Howard Robinson, *A History of the Post Office in New Zealand*, 1964.

116. *OYB*, 1990, 559.
117. Pawson and Quigley, 'Circulation of Information', 70–73.
118. Ibid., 70
119. Ibid., 72. Also see *OYB*, 1990, 560.
120. Beaglehole, 'Politics in Wellington', 181; *DNZB*, i.
121. McLean, *Southern Octopus*, 24 and passim.
122. See *DNZB*, i, ii; Stone, *Makers of Fortune*, and *The Father and His Gift*; Hanham, 'New Zealand Promoters and British Investors'.
123. Stone, *The Father and his Gift*, 184.
124. Nicholls, 'Elite Society', 208.
125. Bohan, *Stafford*, 337.
126. Eldred-Grigg, *Southern Gentry*, 69–74; Morrell, *Provincial System*, 267–68; *DNZB*, ii (John Bathgate).
127. Morrell, *Provincial System*, 279.
128. Bohan, *Stafford*, 99, 201, 296.
129. Quoted in Keith Sinclair, *A Destiny Apart: New Zealand's Search for National Identity*, 1986, 16; Quoted in Chomondeley, *Ultima Thule*, 338.
130. Quoted in Ross, *Aspirations in the Pacific*, 113.
131. Vogel, *Anno Domini 2000*, London, 1889, 28.
132. *DNZB*, i.
133. Quoted in Morrell, *Provincial System*, 175.
134. *Southern Monthly Magazine*, quoted in Sinclair, *Destiny Apart*, 17–18.
135. Quoted in Tim McIvor, *The Rainmaker: A Biography of John Ballance*, 1989, 39–40.
136. See Gerald C. Hensley, 'The Crisis Over the Withdrawal of the British Troops from New Zealand 1864–1870', University of New Zealand (Canterbury) MA thesis, 1957; Belich, *Titokowaru's War*, 219.
137. Bohan, *Stafford*, 282, 125.
138. Dalziel, *Vogel*, 183.
139. Keith Sinclair, *Imperial Federation: A Study of New Zealand Policy and Opinion 1880–1914*, London, 1955, 20.
140. *New Zealand Exhibition, 1865: Reports and Awards of the Jurors*, 1866; Dalziel, *Vogel*, 41–42.
141. Quoted in Dalziel, *Vogel*, 133.

INDEX